CRITICAL DISCOURSE: A SURVEY OF LITERARY THEORISTS

Robert de Beaugrande

Institute for the Psychological Study of the Arts
University of Florida, Gainesville

and

Crump Institute for Medical Engineering
University of California, Los Angeles

ABLEX PUBLISHING CORPORATION
NORWOOD, NEW JERSEY

Library of Congress Cataloging-in-Publication Data

De Beaugrande, Robert.
  Critical discourse.

  Bibliography: p.
  Includes indexes.
  1. Criticism—History—20th century. I. Title.
PN94.D3   1987   801'.95'0904   87-19462
ISBN 0-89391-441-X
ISBN 0-89391-453-3 (pbk.)

Ablex Publishing Corporation
355 Chestnut Street
Norwood, New Jersey 07648

TABLE OF CONTENTS

ACKNOWLEDGEMENTS

This project was made possible by the generous funding of the John Simon Guggenheim Memorial Foundation, which released me for research during the academic year 1984-85. I would like to express my gratitude again here.

I am also indebted to the institutions where I had the opportunity to present and discuss the ideas developed in this book: Stanford and Carnegie-Mellon Universities; the Universities of Maryland (College Park), Minnesota (Minneapolis), Vienna, London, and Amsterdam, as well as Bielefeld and Siegen (Germany); the Summer Institute of Semiotics at Indiana University (Bloomington); the Hebrew University of Jerusalem; the Hungarian Academy of Sciences (Budapest); the Technical University of Berlin; the Federal University of Pernambuco (Brazil); and the State Universities of New York and New Mexico. Most recently, I have profited from lively interchange here with the members of the Crump Institute for Medical Engineering at the University of California, Los Angeles.

I wish to thank the indulgent critics for responding to my sketches: René Wellek, Northrop Frye, Leslie Fiedler, Don Hirsch, Wolfgang Iser, Norm Holland, David Bleich, Bernie Paris, Jonathan Culler, Harold Bloom, H.R. Jauss, and Fredric Jameson. Jauss, Holland, and Paris wrote especially detailed reactions. I was also stimulated by discussions of various ideas with Siegfried J. Schmidt, Teun van Dijk, Hillis Miller, Stanley Fish, Michael Halliday, Luiz Antonio Marcuschi, Jerome Harste, Roland Posner, Alastair Duckworth, Barbara Herrnstein-Smith, Michel Grimaud, Paul Garvin, and my understanding and capable directors at University of Florida and UCLA, Mel New and Gene Yates. Finally, I am inestimably indebted to Walter J. Johnson for his continuing support of my unconventional books.

GRAPHIC CONVENTIONS

To conserve space in the text, references to works by the sample critics are made with abbreviations; Note 1 to each chapter provides a key, and the general key is on page x. References to other works are done with author and date; where relevant, the original publication date follows in square brackets. A reference is not shown when it is identical with the one just before it, and may thus be shared by a whole series of quotes. References with "p." or "pp." are to this book. To avoid brackets or spaced periods, I set each part of a quote in its own quotation marks. I have also allowed myself minor changes of word-forms, mostly in the person and tense of verbs or the endings of nouns, but none I felt would change the meaning or intention of the quote. "Emphasis added" and "emphasis deleted" are given as "e.a." and "e.d." Otherwise, all italics are those of the original source.

Variations in spelling, ("aesthetic"/"esthetic," "hypostasize"/"hypostatize," etc.) were unified unless special distinctions were involved. Russian names were transcribed according to Library of Congress conventions (e.g. "Šklovskij," not "Shklovsky").

References to authors, readers, and so on by masculine pronouns, which we now regard as sexist, are too prevalent in my sources to eliminate altogether, though I reduced them considerably.

FOREWORD

Like many people preoccupied with literature, I often ponder what is at stake: why I would write or read literary texts, what I stand to gain by doing so, and how I could convey all this to anyone else, especially to my colleagues and students. These questions grow acute when our culture tends to relegate literature to the margins of social activity, or to preserve it mainly for unengaging schoolroom exercises in "trivia" —knowledge compiled from isolated facts without regard for usefulness or relevance.

Having been fortunate enough to earn my doctorate at the University of California, Irvine, when the School of Critical Theory was based there, I had the opportunity to hear numerous prominent scholars endeavoring to expound the fundamental issues of literature. However, listening to their lectures and reading their occasional papers often proved insufficient to grasp their ideas. Since I have often declared that the surest (though not always the easiest) way to comprehend complex issues is to write about them, I have now taken my own advice.

During the two years of writing, I felt impelled not merely to expound and synthesize, but also to suggest reservations and counter-positions respecting the critical proceedings I encountered. Moreover, the intent to situate the theorists in a common context had to be balanced with the need to respond to each in accordance with his or her individual method, and to reflect that method back upon itself by pursuing its consequences. Though this dialectic requires some intervention, I have striven to get myself out of the way and let the critics tell their own stories. Even so, I could not escape many difficult decisions in selecting, organizing, and grouping their ideas systematically.

My choice of critics is arbitrary, since no one could hope to cover all those who merit close scrutiny. Due to the space and effort needed to deal with a critic in proper detail, I had to omit or at least postpone encounters with many I would have wanted to include: Meyer Abrams, Roland Barthes, Wayne Booth, Kenneth Burke, Stanley Cavell, Umberto Eco, Stanley Fish, Michel Foucault, Lucien Goldmann, Barbara Herrnstein-Smith, Roman Ingarden, Barbara Johnson, Murray Krieger, Julia Kristeva, Jurij Lotman, Hillis Miller, Walter S.J. Ong, Georges Poulet, John Reichert, Paul Ricoeur, Michael Riffaterre, Louise Rosenblatt, I.A. Richards, Edward Said, Siegfried J. Schmidt, Jean Starobinski, Tzvetan Todorov, Hayden White, and numerous others.

For the same reason, I could not deal directly with forerunners, however important for current criticism: programmatic schools like the Russian Formalists, the French Structuralists, the New Critics, or the Frankfurt School; philosophers like Kant, Vico, Hegel, Schlegel, Nietzsche, Husserl, Heidegger, Cassirer, or Merleau-Ponty; aestheticians like Arnheim, Gombrich, Ingarden, Mukařovský, or Vivas; many-sided thinkers like Marx, Freud, William James, Dewey, Lacan, Sartre, Derrida, or Irigaray; and so forth. However, these figures do appear within the perspectives of the critics I present. Whether those perspectives are faithful to the originals is a question that would require a book far longer than this one. Nonetheless, I remain keenly aware of how much I have omitted or abridged for the sake of concentrating my focus.

Since my project was to integrate the discourse of these critics within my own technique of reading, I could not undertake to consult or summarize what others have written about them. That step would have added one more elaborate layer to an already complex vision of critical discourse, and again the project would have grown unmanageable.

A further omission was necessary regarding the public appearances of the sample critics, who are all charismatic figures, spirited orators, and formidable arguers. I have at least tried to stage a common context for their major published works, so as to emphasize the dialogical or dialectical quality of their discourse. Sometimes I address a single book of powerful impact, as for Wellek and Warren, Frye, and Millett. More often, I summarize a group of works the critic recommended as representative.

To find out how such conspicuous, self-conscious figures might react to models of themselves, I sent a draft of each chapter to the critic with a request for commentary. Worrying about negative reactions became almost obsessive. (Is Culler turning purple? Is Bleich turning pale? Is Hartman disheartened? Is Bloom wilting? Is Frye sizzling? Is Holland flooded with indignation? Is Paris burning?) By and large, though, the responses were positive. Nearly all declared it very unusual to be analyzed and summarized in such detail. Many points were raised and clarified, and the book should be more balanced as a result.

The current burst of activity in critical theory presents an important opportunity that must not be neglected because the discourse may seem too obscure, diffuse, or incompatible. No doubt my search for clarity of presentation has smoothed over important disparities and tensions; but I hope that the result will be useful to observers of the critical scene, including those not professionally concerned with literature. In my view at least, the issues of literary communication are central for assessing many aspects of human mind and culture. Perhaps this conviction is shared by those for whom this book may serve as an interchange.

Robert de Beaugrande
University of California, Los Angeles
May 1986

ABBREVIATIONS

AC: Anatomy of Criticism (Frye)
AIM: Aims in Interpretation (Hirsch)
AL: Aesthetic Experience and Literary Hermeneutics (Jauss)
ALG: Allegories of Reading (de Man)
ANX: The Anxiety of Influence (Bloom)
AR: The Act of Reading (Iser)
BF: The Breaking of Form (Bloom)
BI: Blindness and Insight (de Man)
BRF: The Brain of Robert Frost (Holland)
CCP: Criticism, Canon Formation, and Prophecy:The Sorrows of
         Facticity (Bloom)
CRAP: Carlos Reads a Poem (Holland and Kintgen)
CW: Criticism in the Wilderness (Hartman)
DC: Deconstruction and Criticism preface (Hartman)
DGF: Driving in Gainesville, Florida (Holland)
DY: The Dynamics of Literary Response (Holland)
EH: Ästhetische Erfahrung und literarische Hermeneutik (Jauss)
EI: An End to Innocence (Fiedler)
HAR: The Experience of Thomas Hardy (Paris)
HEA: A Psychological Approach to Heathcliff (Paris)
IE: Innocence and Experience (Hirsch)
IR: The Implied Reader (Iser)
IT: The Ideology of the Text (Jameson)
JA: Character and Conflict in Jane Austen's Novels (Paris)
LD: Love and Death in the American Novel (Fiedler)
LEE: Literary Evaluation and the Epistemology of Symbolic Objects
         (Bleich)
LL: Lesen auf dem Lande (Hömberg and Rossbacher)
MAP: A Map of Misreading (Bloom)
MF: Marxism and Form (Jameson)
NT: No! in Thunder (Fiedler)
OD: On Deconstruction (Culler)

PAF: A Psychological Approach to Fiction (Paris)
PC: Privileged Criteria in Literature (Hirsch)
PIP: Poems in Persons (Holland)
PL: The Prisonhouse of Language (Jameson)
PO: Structuralist Poetics (Culler)
PS: The Pursuit of Signs (Culler)
PU: The Political Unconscious (Jameson)
RF: Readings and Feelings (Bleich)
RT: The Rhetoric of Temporality (de Man)
SAV: Saving the Text:Literature, Derrida, Philosophy (Hartman)
SC: Subjective Criticism (Bleich)
SD: Shelley Disfigured (de Man)
SX: Sexual Politics (Millett)
TAR: Toward an Aesthetic of Reception (Jauss)
TL: Theory of Literature (Wellek and Warren)
UITS: Unity, Identity, Text, Self (Holland)
VAL: Validity in Interpretation (Hirsch)
WL: What Was Literature? (Fiedler)
WOR: Words, Wish, Worth:Worthworth (Hartman)
3FL: Third Force Psychology and the Study of Literature (Paris)
5RR: 5 Readers Reading (Holland)

1

What can texts be?[1]

Texts, whether spoken or written, are among the most common things in our world. We use them so easily that we hardly think about how we can do it. Within our own social group, the activities of our minds are finely attuned by shared language and culture to perform reasonably similar actions on the same text. Normally, we find it easiest to communicate if we ignore the complex problems and personal differences that may be implied in meanings, experiences, expectations, and responses. Instead of struggling for some definitive representation or comprehension of other people or the world, we are content with usable "models." Or, we "objectify" texts by acting as if they by themselves say just what they mean.

However, the convenience of not paying attention to the ways texts function turns out to have major disadvantages. As our objectified and objectifying technology advances, the understanding of understanding is found to be the only solid basis for defining and resituating our own intelligence in a changing environment. The understanding of texts is the decisive instance, the "paradigm case," for all the rest, and cannot be lightly dismissed as a nostalgic involvement with an obsolescent medium in a "post-Gutenberg" age.

Among the general population, the skills of literacy are not well secured. Our lack of insight about those skills leaves us poorly prepared to impart them. When literacy must be explained, provided, and motivated for groups who do not already share its presuppositions, the superficial and simplistic character of our ordinary conceptions of text and discourse becomes painfully evident. We know how to make and use a text, but not how to ensure that other people will know. We dispense bits of advice, hints and cautions, but the effects are frequently disappointing.

All too often, people come to regard writing and reading as unengaging chores without reliable means to ensure good performance. We face the prospect that the use of anything but immediately functional or diversional texts (newspapers, magazines, instructions, and the like) may lose currency in our society. The

---

[1] This outline is merely intended for the general purposes of my survey of critics. For discussions with considerable detail and sources, see my volumes *Text, Discourse, and Process* (1980) and *Text Production* (1984a); and the surveys in Beaugrande 1980-81, 1982a, 1982b, and 1986.

solution cannot be to demand that our institutions and schools merely intensify the traditional language training which has after all done little resolve the situation so far. Instead, a more dynamic training is needed to reveal the text as a meeting-place where people engage and negotiate—not a self-sufficient authority and arbiter of meanings, nor a vehicle for parading stilted usage. This project requires a clearer and more convincing account of how literacy in the broadest sense works or should work.

Various language models have been proposed according to the dominant ideologies of the times. In the early part of the nineteenth century, organic models were in vogue, and language was thought to function the way a plant lives; Darwinian evolutionism added a congenial genetic perspective. By the end of that century, mechanical models were popular, inspired by the rising waves of industrial technology and conceived in terms of force, energy, inertia, and the like. In our own century, behavioristic and depth-psychological models were extracted from research in animal biology or psychotherapy, and the power of drives, rewards, and repetitions was emphasized. Gradually, this trend yielded to cognitive models drawing on research in thought, learning, and memory. The latest trend, as yet still emerging, favors performative models for all human acts, including externalized behavior and internalized cognition.

This history roughly marks the gradual recognition of the higher capacities specific to the human being. Formerly, the strongly determined functions of plants, machines, and animals encouraged the view that the human has essentially slight control over the world, knowing just what is "out there" and reacting episodically to "stimuli," "drives," or "instincts," as each occasion requires. Higher-level conceptual knowledge and planning were acknowledged as pervasive controlling factors only recently. In the long run, research has firmly established a more complex vision of the human being in rich, realistic contexts.

So far, linguistic theories lag behind, preferring to treat language as an independent object composed of sounds, words, or sentences. The reason is clear. When you take hold of a text or discourse (group of texts) to study it, you may feel you have picked up a curious item in the surf only to find it tied with a net to the whole floor of the ocean. Threads spin out in every direction, and the proper places to cut them off are anything but obvious. So every investigation remains implicitly incomplete, work perpetually in progress, leading merely to provisional conclusions.

Another traditional problem is the enlistment of language in the time-honored performance known as "objectivity." The moves are too familiar: pretending that our discourse is a transparent window onto true reality, rather than a complex imposition of our own mental set; disavowing any personal interest in the information; treating the version we approve as enforced by the text itself; and so on. Once the role of discourse has been thus reduced, we can study it in a nicely corresponding form: as a set of artifacts not essentially different from the reassuring world of "real objects" that hold steady while we talk about them. Our

reading of the text is advertised to be the "truth" or "fact" it contains. So expedient a scheme is attractive. A small effort buys a lot of authority —except that, in
another sense, we are impoverished. An objectified text offers sparse opportunities for introspecting or intervening in our own modes of thinking, or for
negotiating those modes with other people. The comforting "objectivity" supposed to guarantee universal certainty suppresses alternative viewpoints, some of
which are probably better than the one we now have. "Reality" is never more
political than when it is asserted to be self-explanatory; and this relation holds
especially for the reality of a text or discourse.

The opposite extreme, however, of total subjectivity, has had an equally
ominous career. Reality gets situated entirely inside the subject's mind. Disen-
gaged from the outer world, the mind can revolve in endless spirals of solipsism
and cease to learn; or can consign reality to some all-knowing spirit or substan-
tialized idea, whose workings are as predetermined, self-sufficient, and uncontrollable as those of "objective reality." So the freedom of subjectivity frequently
becomes another trap, still clouding our view of how the mind works.

Some interaction in between these extremes must be managed, some sharable
space for reality and the mind, for object and subject, that does not leave us
transfixed or isolated. The most obvious testing-ground seems to be discourse,
properly recognized as neither a mere reflection of the world nor a mere vehicle
of personal imaginings. Discourse is our prime chance to mediate between
outside and inside, between what we get from the world and what we give back.
The interchange of texts is the clearest demonstration that many versions of the
world await to be negotiated by subjects. In this sense, "textuality" opens out onto
"intertextuality" and "intersubjectivity" in the same moment.

Thinking about thinking may lead us to postulate a small number of classes
for the basic actions of the human mind. For example, it creates order by
contemplating similarities and differences, or by arranging entities in temporal
sequences, spatial contiguities, or causal contingencies. But even everyday
thinking deals with human experience and activity in a detail and complexity
belied by facile reduction to these abstract classes. The understanding process
continually generates its own elaborate frameworks which, through repeated use,
eventually become habituated and self-evident. Otherwise, we could not move
on to new and more complex things. As long as this progression proceeds
smoothly, the consolidation of knowledge from one level of complexity to the
next appears reliable. But ideal progress is unlikely to last indefinitely. The
necessary strategic information may not be provided in the expedient order or in
the appropriate contexts. Provisional decisions need reconsidering. New motives
and goals bring things into unexpected focuses.

Finally, we sense the pressure not merely to register new varieties of the
familiar, but to revise our thinking. Though this revision might conceivably be
done without discourse, it seldom is in practice. Language allows us to discuss
and organize our actual experiences, as well as to mediate among those we have

not encountered. Alternatives can be formulated and compared; problems and solutions can be negotiated; that which is can be re-estimated in respect to that which is not; and so on. Whether a text or discourse really serves these functions in a specific case remains an open question. Apparently, many needed revisions do not occur. Either we drift into the premature complacency that urges the present state of awareness to be the best; or we fall into premature despair that pictures the mind reaching its final limits. Menaced by these blockages on either side, we try to navigate some average rate that feeds the mind's craving for both stability and change without incurring stagnation or disorientation.

This process too depends vitally upon our abilities to use texts advantageously. Communication regulates the rate and range of our intake of the world and our responses to it. The extremes of boredom and confusion can be skirted with techniques for upgrading what seems trivial and downgrading what seems unaccountable. Viewed in this way, discourse operates not by a principle of least effort, but by a principle of proportionality between effort and result. However, many people have little idea of how to invest effort in discourse, as compared to a more obviously performative event such as a sport. The tendency to perform below one's potential is accordingly widespread in discourse, and skills flatten out at a basic level. Having objectified the texts, the subject resigns itself to being driven by them, even at the risk of alienation, helplessness, or loss of creative initiative.

Recovering some awareness of the performative, event-like character of the text is therefore urgent, particularly of the written text that seems so like a real object. The appropriate perspective deserves to be called "utopian," provided the sense of this term is clarified at once. I do not mean the debilitating utopia that handily excuses partial or imperfect acts on the grounds that completeness and perfection are forever beyond human scope. Nor do I mean the complacent utopia that sees the perfect world hovering almost within reach, to be grasped easily by adopting some political, moral, or religious panacea. Nor do I mean the grim utopia of the totally automated and administrated world where the individual no longer needs to think or worry at all. Instead, I mean the projective utopia wherein the unbounded possibility of further development is construed as an imperative to push each effort as far as we can, and never to rule out later revisions. Rather than abandoning hope in view of the infinite dimensions, we steadily work to expand and progress, knowing those dimensions will never confine us. For this utopia, the true dangers are not error or incompletion, but the premature affirmation or resignation that lead people to hypostasize the status quo into some fixed and ultimate instance.

In this sense, the utopian character of human activities is their most valuable aspect. Some of them, such as olympic sports and performing arts, are easy to regard as utopian foreshadowings. But in a far less spectacular and self-conscious way, communication implies this function too, by projecting the prospect of mutual understanding among human beings with highly diverse personalities and stores of knowledge and experience. Writing and reading present a special challenge, because the persistence of the artifact allows continual reconsideration. Hence, a strong and strategic investment in writing and reading can both engage and revise the mind just where the stakes are highest.

The actual practice of writing and reading is crucial here, but evidently not enough. If the mind is to reflect upon itself, discourse must be made to do the same. The most extensive and accredited reflection upon discourse, at least in our culture, takes place in literature and literary criticism. Among the various functions of literature, the one of greatest interest here is its potential to open a space for diverse, individualistic performances of meaning (Ch. 2). This function renders literature the most complex textual domain in wide distribution. Criticism is one customary activity for mastering this complexity, and comprises the largest available source of documented textual responses, waiting to be made systematic and generally usable. Critical theory in turn proposes to integrate this wealth of documentation and to define its status.

My project in this book is to embark on the next step: subsuming critical theories into a discourse precariously positioned upon an already elaborate tower of complexity. Each level adds its particular utopian tendencies we should regard in the sense I expounded: as imperatives to encompass what may be ultimately impossible, but what can certainly be done better than it has been so far. By necessity, my approach has been emphatically integrative—compacting, rearranging, and comparing the theories so as to bring out their main contours, despite corresponding losses of individuality, personal flair, and subtle detail. Perhaps my search for a comprehensive context of literary communication is especially utopian, but, I would hope, in my preferred sense; and the goal of understanding understanding is undeniably worth the effort of expounding the recurrent themes and preoccupations that a devotion to literature and criticism entails.

2

What can literature be?[1]

This form of the question may be more productive than the usual "what is literature?" Like all texts, literary ones are mere artifacts with an indeterminate communicative status until someone does something with them by applying more or less appropriate and relevant conventions. Despite the prevalence of literature in so many cultures, the nature and force of those conventions have not been well explained. The very term "literature" is rather indiscriminately applied—a collection of works (e.g. "great books"), a school subject that assigns those works, a topic of criticism, a facet of human culture, and so on. How far all these informal definitions coincide is hard to tell. Little is achieved by defining "literature" as the set of texts society agrees to designate as such. We merely restate the fact of literature, without explaining why some texts are admitted over others, why the set changes, and so forth. Evidently, literature *can* fulfill some functions societies consider worthwhile, though obviously, not all of it can do so for everybody all the time. The question is: what criteria and activities can be involved in those functions?

In the past, scholars influenced by linguistics and stylistics would define literature as having "distinctive features" of language that "deviate" from "ordinary language." But this definition involves serious problems. It presupposes an objectified text with independently given "features." Prose is less adequately handled than poetry. No provision is made for treating texts from other types as literature, such as "found" poems; or for using ostensibly literary features in other types, such as advertising and political oratory. Anyway, since most texts could be found to deviate in at least a few features from most others, not much is left on the side of the "norm," which seems highly illogical. Ultimately, the "distinctive features" of a text are more a result of the critic's projections and predispositions, rather than an original cause. Far from solving our problem, "deviation" merely proposes one more factor to be explained.

A second possible definition, less fashionable among modern critics, is that "literature" has a special content. It conveys certain ideas or topics, such as we

---

[1] To avoid prejudicing the contact with the critical theorists later on, I proceed here without citation of numerous relevant sources. Compare Beaugrande (1983, 1986) and the citations there.

might find in cavalier, pastoral, and sacred poetry. But we encounter much the same problems here. We are objectifying the phenomenon, this time to siphon off its "ideas" instead of its "features." We are implicitly favoring poetry over prose. And we find the ideas, whatever we decide they are, changing over time or being involved in plenty of texts we wouldn't want to call "literary." Unless we ask why certain ideas might be assigned to particular types of texts, we continue to pursue peripheral effects more than central causes.

A third definition, in favor among philosophers, is that literature is "fictional," conveying statements that are not "true" or don't "refer" to anything. But plainly, not all fictional texts qualify as literary; the ordinary "lie" displaces the "truth" but gives no rewards. Nor are all literary texts considered fictional, as we see from documentary art. Moreover, the decision about what is true and in what way is anything but a straightforward yes-or-no matter. "Fictions" refer to entities that must "exist" in some sense, or else we couldn't understand the text. Conversely, "facts" are partly created through our acts of perspective, selection, organization, narration, evaluation, and so on, or else we couldn't talk about them. A novel can be "true to life" although all its characters and events were created by the author's imagination. And a historiographic text has to continually reinvent history by interpreting in hindsight and imposing representational, narrative, or dramatic criteria, often carried over from literature. So historical facts cannot be the opposite pole for literary fictions.

A fourth definition could be that literature is "rhetorical," composed with special "figural" techniques of substitution ("tropes") and arrangement ("schemes"), whereas other texts are "logical," composed with a "literal" dedication to truth and consistency. But, like "fiction" versus "fact," this distinction, presupposing "rhetoric" to be optional ornamentation or persuasion, turns out on closer inspection to be another complex gradation. All language is used rhetorically or figurally at least when we substitute words for things, and the arrangement of discourse for the arrangement of the world. All language is also used logically or literally when we give things coherence, identity, and category. At most, these two aspects attain different degrees of prominence and deliberateness in specific cases. Yet even a high degree of rhetoricity doesn't necessarily make a text "literary."

All these attempts to isolate something specific "in" literature remain unsatisfactory. My general conclusion would be that literature can only be defined with a functional description of what happens when people produce or respond to it. The principle I consider most plausible might be called "alternativity." Participants in literary communication should be willing to use the text for constituting and contemplating other "worlds" (i.e., configurations of objects and events) besides the accepted "real world." The text need not appear "fictional" by directly colliding with everyday reality. It may fall anywhere between the extremes of the fantastic and the documentary. Yet the possibility must be left open that whatever world the text is thought to elicit should be related in some interesting and informative way to reality and should show us the latter in perspectives we might otherwise not consider.

This account would explain a society's concern for literature with a more compelling motive than "linguistic deviation" or "fictionality" alone. Since, as psychologists and phenomenologists have found, every society's approved version of reality has to omit or deny certain potential aspects or perspectives, an institutionalized forum for presenting and developing excluded alternatives ought to be necessary and useful. The limitations imposed by common sense or official consensus about how the world "really" is can be transcended there without causing widespread disorientation and conflict. Literary authors are not normally reproached for reporting things they never saw happen, or for transforming things they did. Readers are more inclined to tolerate these actions as a means for sampling diverse visions.

"Poetic" texts would be those during whose use the principle of alternativity is extended to discourse itself. Here too, obvious deviation from ordinary discourse is not required, though often employed to offset the seeming transparency of language. Texts not classified as "poems" can readily be given a poetic function if the organization of their language is regarded as one among several alternatives. Ideally, just as literature as a whole sharpens our sense of the world, poetry sharpens our sense of language. Moreover, the more complex medium of poetry, renegotiating both reality and discourse, can have an especially powerful impact that enables poems to be esteemed as highly significant and enduring expressions.

The consideration of literature and poetry in numerous forms of human education over the centuries signals some hope that using texts this way could bring far-ranging benefits for the general capacities of the human mind. The danger of unduly stabilizing the appropriation of language and the world might be counteracted. Experiences could be attained that would normally be difficult, hazardous, or impossible. The human range of understanding could be expanded and refined far beyond the exigencies of individual behavior. However, we know such results face serious impediments. The prestige of the literary text makes it particularly prone to being objectified, so that the reader's role is hardly noticed. The writer becomes a conspicuous public figure with a cultural mission of regulating meanings. As professional readers, critics intervene with circumstantial materials and proposed interpretations unavailable to most people. Teachers at all levels of schooling control and restrict literary meanings or distract away from textual experiences by overstressing technicalities of history, biography, genre, or trope. Eventually, the ordinary reader may consider his or her own creative use of the text marginal if not unauthorized.

In such a complicated situation, I could hardly claim to address what literature "is," because it "is" what people do with it, and those activities are quite diversified. Instead, I might try to sketch what it *can be* if the principle of alternativity is allowed a dominant function. Most of the critics examined in Part ll would agree that this allowance should be made if literature is to attain its proper valence. But they do not all acknowledge the extent to which aesthetic or critical theories imply a utopian imperative to conceive and experience literature in ways we cannot take for granted in our culture. This factor reflects the comparable imperative, implied by literature itself, to understand our understanding of ourselves and of our reality: the more persuasively and urgently implied, the "greater" a work will seem.

Scholars have long concurred that literature can elicit a change in how we experience. Aristotle described a renewal of perception, and this notion has returned in various guises in most aesthetic theories ever since. The contention of the Russian Formalists and the Prague Structuralists—that literature "estranges" or "de-automatizes" the processing of a text—sounds plausible in view of recent research on perception and comprehension.[2] Everyday reading seems easy, if not automatic, because so many sectors of the complex process are done without attention and thus do not consume much resources or compete with other operations. In return, a high correlation is required between what is expected or predicted and what is perceived or understood. The "alternativity" of literary experiences modifies that correlation. Even if we know in a general manner what the text "is about," because it is famous or already read or fits a genre we know, and so on, the actual experience differs both in quality and quantity from an encounter with comparable materials in nonliterary communication. The ostensibly "same" words, things, ideas, and so on, are endowed with distinctive and intensified functions. Aspects we consider special, such as "deviant" features or "fictional" statements, may act as cues and reminders in this process, but they are not indispensable. We could read any text in a literary and aesthetic fashion; we usually don't when we feel no imperative.

Potentially at least, the literary experience rewards the rise in effort and complexity by expanding and diversifying possible meanings. The reader's response is governed by the intent to control what ensues and to attain some worthwhile result. While there may be no laws or strict rules for processing a text as literary, we certainly don't proceed at random. As with all texts, the decisive principle is the motive to attain a systematic experience in which particular perceptions, hypotheses, significances, and so on, are assigned a current relevance and value. Failure to do so leads toward disintegration, an unpleasant and disorienting state for the mind, especially if occurring on a large scale or over a long time.

This tendency to operate systematically and to resist disintegration helps people to have comparable experiences with the same literary text, though diver-

---

[2] For surveys of this research, see the sources cited in Note 1. On implications for relating psychology and literature, see Beaugrande (1986); Groeben (1980a, 1980b, 1982); Meutsch (1986); Schmidt (1982).

gence is typically greater than for nonliterary communication. The proclivity for the systematic is carried over from our dealings with "reality," but with a major difference. In everyday experience, the advantages of a consistent, reliable environment seem great enough to be worth ignoring or explaining away whatever disrupts coherence. For the world of a literary work, we are willing to be more active in creating such an environment. The main channel of experience passes through the work itself, so that a writer or reader can justly feel that here the coherence of the world is partly his or her own achievement—a sensation much harder to entertain regarding everyday reality. Whereas orientation and management in the real world may be provisionally aided by objectifying it and disclaiming our own role in creating it, no such directive is strategic for a literary world. Thus, our accomplishment there can be a "super-coherent" experience of reinvesting our conventional organizing of reality into a more creative project. The intensity of the engagement is its own greatest reward.

With that goal in view, an author can anticipate the kinds of organization that should encourage such an experience, for instance, by invoking or combining frameworks of conventions or by posing problems to which the author's hoped-for resolutions are among the more satisfying. Yet total control is impracticable and, no matter what the author might think, undesirable as well, because it would limit the work's potential for continued use. A work that tries to give exclusive, pat answers to its own questions impinges on the reader's role and response. As we will see later, critics can use this ratio between closure and openness as a measure of a work's value.

It should follow from the argument so far that literature both stabilizes and modifies not only our communicative potential, but also itself. As a system, it elaborates its own peculiar methods of "systemizing" and eventually must transcend its own standards in order to maintain its functionality. Conventions such as generic forms become stabilized as integrative frames for managing the complexity of individual acts of writing or reading. In exchange, authors and readers feel impelled to innovate against these frames, at least over longer periods of time. Ideally, an author never creates the same work twice; and a reader has a new experience with each reading, even of the same text. In practice, innovation must conform to personal dispositions and skills; under favorable conditions, much more could be done, I suspect, than usually is.

Traditionally, the "aesthetic" aspect of art has been defined as some interaction between "diversity" and "unity."[3] In the usual logic of experience, things are either related and hence significant for each other, or they are not. The "aesthetic" experience tends to subvert this either/or logic with an imperative to consider

---

[3] Compare the formulations in Leibnitz (1720); Hegel (1835); Fechner (1876); Gunzenhäuser (1962); Schmidt (1971). On the derivation of frameworks for organizing perception, see especially Gombrich (1960).

further modes of potential relations and significances. Hence, the aesthetic mode is particularly utopian in the sense of Chapter 1: anything may point away to everything.

The conception of aesthetics as a unifying of diversity has been recently challenged to be a view fit for "classicism," but not for "modernism." However, the question is a matter of degree. A work appears "classical" when its unity is considered a necessary entailment of its organization; and "modernist" when that unity seems powerfully resistant. Hence, classicism emphasizes "harmony," that is, a deliberate equalizing of parts and features and an adhering to some "canon" of prescribed qualities, typically conceived as "imitations" of nature if the latter is deemed the epitome of order. "Modernism" strives for a disequilibrium of parts and a defiance of canons. Yet both tendencies are equally "aesthetic" as projects for regulating the interaction between a "diversity" and a "unity" not "in" the work, but in the context a person produces for the work. "Classical" standards are intended to make the applicable contexts immediately available to an initiated public, so that the harmony seems to be inside the work. "Modernist" standards are intended to evade or disrupt available contexts for a largely uninitiated public. No doubt most periods in the history of the arts had both tendencies; but the nature of the process conveys the impression that the only "modernist" art is whatever appears so right now.

Both sets of standards entail sufficient disadvantages to prevent either one from becoming an absolute. For its detractors committed to earlier canons, "modern art" is simply not "art" at all. Yet "classic art" is, if anything, so readily accepted that few people can experience it with its original impact, and its functions dissipate. The "classic" work seems monumental, inevitable, and the response to it overly rehearsed. The "modernist" work seems calculatedly abrasive, and the response overly opportunistic. Each innovation, if it succeeds in winning an audience, is channeled through the same process whereby "modernism" is relentlessly "classicalized."

How to save art theories from this same rigidifying success has become a major issue in criticism. Just as artists may vie in their endless search for some technique that can never seem natural, harmonious, beautiful, and so on, critics may cast about for some theory that dispenses once and for all with such aesthetic fundamentals as "diversity" and "unity." Yet the "aesthetic" is well-equipped to absorb its own contraries. Each new critical project highlights new perspectives and shifts the perceived ratios of familiar ones, yet without canceling the latter. So we can't depend on the standards of any one period to tell us what art "is." We can only explore what contexts (canons, conventions, archetypes, aspirations, and so on) people bring to it; and what institutions claim authority to describe or control this process.

History undeniably reveals an enormous range among the texts accepted as literature and poetry. This diffusion is to be predicted if alternativity operates both against everyday reality and against any one alternative frame whose total predominance would dissolve the main function of the literary experience. Every trend eventually undermines itself. Romanticism was followed by Realism; Realism by Surrealism; Surrealism by Documentary Art; and so on. Hence, the fit between a work and some class of "genre," "style," "movement," and so on to which it may be assigned is inherently tenuous, making the class itself far more problematic than literary studies has traditionally admitted (Ch. 3). In a functional definition, distinctions between literary subtypes are just as much gradations as those between literature and other text types.

Though a functional definition does not decide which texts must be the literary ones, it suggests that literature stands apart from neighboring communicative domains in terms of its uses. History, philosophy, and theology can all overlap with literature, but in each case, the dominant function is distinctive. I shall briefly sketch some lines for describing those distinctions.

Historical texts are mainly rated for their accuracy respecting specific "facts," whereas literature is rated for its insights into what is in principle revealing about the human situation. (Few critics would insist that *Hamlet* and *Lear* are bad plays because their historical foundations are distorted or doubtful.) The use or discovery of quasiliterary representational and narrative techniques in historiography enables some history texts to survive long after their status as factual accounts has been undermined. Their "past" becomes another alternative world to the present, no longer purporting to be the latter's ancestor or cause.

Philosophy differs from literature by emphasizing explanation over representation. Any represented aspects of reality illustrate explicitly presented conceptions, usually within a single schematic. Literary authors who follow this trend seem to be "philosophizing," and as readers we may feel free to believe their realities mean something quite different (cf. Ch. 6, 8, 11, 13, 16-18). The philosophizing profuse in literary works of the eighteenth and early nineteenth centuries became unreliable, ironic, and finally vestigial, without impairing the literariness of the domain at all. Today, we can esteem works like *Candide* or *La nouvelle Héloïse* as literature without valuing, or even taking very seriously, the authors' philosophical ambitions. And we can prize authors like Shakespeare, whose philosophical outlook we might well despair of reconstructing. A functional differentiation between the literary and the philosophical is therefore feasible, though often evasive.

The situation appears similar in theology. Here, the representation of reality is still more predominantly illustrative, though its explanation proceeds less by logical argument than by assertion of dogma. And that dogma has to be accepted as a matter of orthodox belief. A refusal to do so is a dangerous heresy, which is why wars are much more likely to be fought over religion than over literature or philosophy. To read a sacred text like *The Bible* as literature is to situate its otherworldly reality within a spectrum of alternatives, a heretical move for the true believer. Reciprocally, literary works whose theological groundings were conceived as alternatives to orthodox faith, such as created by Milton, Blake, or

Yeats, get higher literary ratings than a work of the conventional piety we expect from a church hymnal; but they seldom become central texts for an institutionalized religion.

A functional approach might also help to clarify the traditional demarcation between "good" and "bad" literature, or "high" and "low." To create a literary work is to promise an insightful experience. This promise by itself is ambitious in a medium replete with "classics," and the possibilities of failure are manifold. The reader may feel the experience wasn't rewarding, or that the author didn't manage to convey what was proposed. If, as stressed by critics like Iser or Bloom, the reader re-creates the work, then such lapses are readily imagined ("that's not what I would have done").

Also, the engagement of the reader's personality and ideology may deter the enterprise. Proposing alternative realities and questioning the prevailing one can offend those whose investment in that reality is heavy yet inadequately reasoned. Conversely, conventions may be put in question that the reader barely subscribes to anyhow, for example, after the liberalization of Western society passed beyond the ideologizing initiatives of nineteenth-century "reformist" novelists. The original function no longer seems vital, though others may be found, such as a sharpening of social awareness in unfamiliar contexts.

Specific values, even very widespread ones, can undergo radical changes. For instance, "sentimentality" was highly esteemed in eighteenth-century literature, especially in the novel, as the disquisitions of Fiedler and Jauss reveal. Current critics routinely denounce it with equal emphasis. If we adopt a modified version of Schiller's concept of "sentimental" art reverting to earlier forms, sentimentality could be defined as a regressive, usually emotive contemplation dissociated from convincing motivations. To be sentimental is to regress toward childhood or adolescence, when emotions were less stable and integrated; and to displace emotions from occasions when they were genuinely felt over to those where they are artificially or gratuitously indulged. The once-revolutionary gesture that uplifted emotion for bringing insight by challenging the supremacy of reason (e.g., in Rousseau) becomes a reactionary blurring of insight by refusing to reason beyond sensation.

This example suggests that values might be restated in terms of how readers feel encouraged to respond. Yet every inquiry into values runs up against the fundamental ambivalence in the potential uses of literature. An audience may prefer to seek a diversion not to sharpen their sense of the world, but to dull it with escapist entertainments. Artists may know well enough which of these ends they are serving, though the public's response can be unpredictable. Writers and readers who attempt the harder, more constructive task understandably misprize those who prefer the easier, less consequential one. The latter task tends to reduce the functionality of art by stripping the response process of any reflection on the principles of constituting worlds. Complexity is not integrated, but traded for simplicity. And the utopian imperative is undercut by suggesting that utopia is either already here or else too purely imaginary as to be worth attempting. Such uses make literature act as a regressive or conservative force substituting contemplation for action.[4]

On the other side, literature can make life appear more meaningful or coherent than does everyday experience, especially in societies with sharply rising complexity and fragmentation. After experiencing one's world as an arbitrary heap of incidents and accidents, we might turn with relief to building super-coherent literary worlds. The turn might resemble escapism, an alibi for leaving the world as it is. However, the very fact that a literary world seems to reconcile the contradictions of our reality encourages us to formulate them and to see that they can, in principle, be reconciled. Of course, this response, like any other, cannot be compelled. But if we do not respond this way, the fault is not that of literature as a whole, but only of specific works and forces that shape response, or of our own fixity or helplessness as readers. Literature, as Ernst Bloch says, preserves the hope for utopia but doesn't undertake to deliver it. We alone can attempt to do that, and then only as a open-ended project with no final victory or happy ending. In an actual utopia, the intensified and free investment of the subject in constituting its object-world might, as Hegel surmised, overcome the alienation between subject and object enforced by the versions of reality in previous societies like our own (p. 393).

My brief outline in this chapter of a functional approach and some of the aspects of literature it might address will be filled in during the surveys of later on. I hope that until then, it might not be rejected out of hand, though several challenges are frequently voiced. One objection is that its does not fit people's common sense impressions of what they do with literature. Readers feel they are experiencing not their own understanding, but the world of the work, identifying with its characters and their goals, undergoing powerful emotions, experiencing sensations of pleasure and pain, beauty and repulsion, tranquility and terror, and so forth. The higher-level framework I propose seems to abstract away from all those activities, which are undeniably factors of the total process, by viewing them all as constitutive realizations of significance. Still, higher-level descriptions of cognition and performance need not appear intuitively obvious to people who function contextually most of the time. Recursion irritates the practical mind; and self-reference has always been the stumbling block for logic, as logicians from the sophists all the way to Gödel and Hofstadter well know. Hence, whatever it means to think about thinking, to understand understanding, to write about writing, to read about reading, and so on, will probably not be found to fit commonsensical intuitions.

At this stage, high-level abstractions deserve a fair chance, now that descriptions of literature have so long tended in the opposite direction by hypostasizing specific projects and demands: that literature be "beautiful" and "harmonious,"

---

[4] Christian Enzensberger (1977) pursues this thesis, but somewhat one-sidedly.

"instructing and delighting" us, "purging the passions," illustrating "the ideal in nature," and so on. In the long run, such hypostases have proven unhelpfully restrictive, the more so if construed as binding values for authors and critics. We might now work from the other end by seeking a sufficiently high-level framework to encompass the central aspects of literature, and then fitting available projects into appropriate sectors.

For this purpose, my outline might, on the contrary, be attacked for not being abstract enough, for downplaying its own historical and ideological context and thereby hypostasizing an aesthetics peculiar to classical or modernist art in the West. That art is admittedly my primary contact with art in general and supplies most of the illustrations for our sample critics; in Asian art, for example, the philosophical and theological functions were apparently less clearly distinguished from literary ones.[5] Yet here again I would uphold the thesis that seen from a sufficiently high level, some mental processes are fundamental for humans across all cultures. Which level we would need is of course still to be decided.

In any case, my outline is offered not to define literature itself, but to provide a heuristic for engaging contemporary literary theorists. Headway on such a project seems worthwhile enough that judgment of the outline itself should reflect its usefulness in that context. Moving up and down among levels of abstraction is surely a necessary dialectic for pursuing the understanding of understanding. I would simply assert that the nature of literature, however it be defined, renders critical discourse a useful domain for that pursuit.

---

[5] On Chinese theories of literature, see Liu (1975).

3

What can literary theory be?[1]

Though hardly a recent invention, "literary theory" has attained a noteworthy prominence in recent decades. The speculations of Aristotle or Plato had dominated centuries of aesthetic policy. Some "theorizing" was performed by figures engaged more centrally in the production of literature, such as Dante, Sidney, or Coleridge. The "pure theorist" seldom rivaled their renown. Today, in contrast, theory is the center of power and impetus in literary studies, as far as I can judge. A top-ranking theorist is likely to surpass in rank and salary an author-in-residence. The typical critics of past times, the historians, classifiers, evaluators, and interpreters of literature, are receding into relative obscurity.

To some degree, the recent upsurge of interest in literary theory among academic institutions reflects a growing awareness of the urgency for justifying literature and its study to society. So far, however, many theoreticians do not make this factor very explicit or emphatic. They may consider the literary profession adequately insulated by its institutional status, as attested by their own eminent standing. Some of them simply vow to give a theoretical rationale for what literary studies has already been doing in its conventional formats. But the immense preoccupation with describing and explaining literary and critical transactions signals a premonition that the literary profession might otherwise be considered an expendable institution of undefined utility. The marginalizing of literature (Chs. 1 and 2) reflects on criticism as well.

In the past, literature periodically had to be defended against unfairly narrow conceptions of functionality. The result was some such tract as Aristotle's or Sidney's, explaining how literature did (or could) serve desirable functions. Nowadays, only repressive splinter groups like the ludicrously misnamed "Moral Majority" vilify literature as useless and dangerous. The disquieting factor is the *real* majority withdrawing into indifference and refusing to genuinely participate in the arts they may still be willing to patronize.

For a time, literary studies felt content to accept the patronage and construe the increasing marginality of their concerns as proof of an elite awareness or a

---

[1] For a detailed analysis of the critic's activities, compare Beaugrande (1983). I profited considerably from the exposition in Schmidt (1982).

cultural mission in a darkening age. But eventually the possibility had to be raised that the way the professionals were dispensing literature to society may be among the causes of its marginalization. Thus, the latter-day theoretician's "defence of poesie" is just as much a defence of the critic's role—more often as it might be than as it is in daily practice.

The upswing in "literary theory" is thus a belated and mediated response to a broad, complex shift in the social functions of literacy—an indication that a major effort must now be made to comprehend and expound the activities associated with literary texts. Although by no means openly acknowledged by all theoreticians, this goal may help explain their rise to power and their migration into theory from more conventional domains. The sudden concern for "the reader" is in part a homage to the role the critics hope more people will adopt if it can be made to seem more engaging and stimulating.

Anyone seriously reflecting upon the traditional activities of criticism should realize why its credentials might be questioned. Sticking close to the works themselves, the critic is forced to objectify them from various angles in order to extract from them a frame of reference wherein they can be handled. The critic is constantly involved in producing the effects or criteria pretended to belong to the works; and every campaign to make the results stand alone only generates another form of involvement, more devious perhaps, but never innocent of prior intent.

The historical critic would seem to have a straightforward job describing works, authors, and schools in chronological order. But the relevance of this seemingly reliable framework has been increasingly questioned. Authors' biographies may be unenlightening. Influences, techniques, and question-answer chains migrate in odd patterns, skipping across epochs or national boundaries and suggesting quite different currents from those of official or political history. History itself readily becomes a text whose stories are gradually recognized to be literary, and hence more naive enactments of the same problematics they were supposed to organize. The reassurance of temporal order and documentary evidence fades before the prospect of having to rewrite history itself in a new mode before we can use it to make sense of literary history.

The classifying critic is also beset with problems, thanks to the harrowing intransigence of a creative medium. No matter what categories are devised, individual works, including many of the most famous, keep falling out or in between. This elusiveness, a major part of their appeal and a natural product of their richness of alternative perspectives, is maddening to the classifier, especially to one with a nostalgia for the tidy taxonomies of the sciences. Conventional if not mediocre works seem to provide the best fit, but are also of the least interest. The solutions to this dilemma are uniformly unattractive: basing a class on a single great work, as Aristotle did with *Oedipus Tyrannus* for tragedy; keeping strict classes but tolerating as many exceptions as regularities; creating complicated mixed classes like "neoromantic sentimental-ironic tragicomedy"; and so on. At best, the classifier can help reconstruct the ambience wherein a given work appeared, without hoping to capture the work's individual quality.

The evaluating critic is caught in a comparable contradiction. In this pursuit, one derives standards from certain literary works and turns around to pass judgment on other works that don't measure up. Faced with a rejoinder that the standards were illegitimately derived in the first place, so of course the works don't fit, the critic's only rebuttal is to claim superior taste and discernment, better than not only the public's, but the literary author's, by virtue of having experienced large quantities of works. Yet the merit of a single work may inhere in precisely those nonstandard qualities that make it unlike any other. So even if the critic's standards are indeed representative, the failure of a single work to meet them is a problematic, maybe even inverted, measure of its value.

The interpreting critic is even worse off to the extent that reducing the alternative meanings of the literary work to just one runs counter to the major function of literature. The chosen one is often advanced with an exclusive, rather than inclusive, claim to acceptance—as correct, central, authorized, and so on. Here, the interpreter objectifies not only the work, but the interpretation as well, and makes the process into a product lacking the prestige and permanence that abet the objectification of the original work. The critic's distasteful reward is to be left defending embattled ground which a genuine respect for the work should prefer to see displaced.

Such problems might suggest why, when criticism undergoes theoretical scrutiny, the customary proceedings of historicizing, classifying, evaluating, and interpreting become profoundly unsettled. Theorists must now consider whether such activities should be redefined and continued on a more rational basis, if such can be found; or whether they should be abandoned as illusory or inappropriate. Usually, a compromise position is adopted. Even theorists who contemplate abandonment —as Frye does with evaluating and Culler and Iser do with interpreting —still perform those activities to some degree. And whatever new tasks are proposed are partly transformations of these old ones, as in the masterfully agile reformulation of classifying in Frye or of historicizing in Jameson.

Redefining their own role forces critics to devote concentrated attention to the act of reading and responding. They become fairly immune to the old objectifying fictions of the meaning just being there "in" the text, or of the text itself telling us what it means (Ch. 1). Scarcely anyone professes a principled belief in a single "correct" meaning for a given text. However, the facile accusation that reader-based criticism tolerates any old response is inappropriate in every case. Though all our critics acknowledge the "openness" of the literary text, each of them advances a distinctive proposal about whether, how, and how far it can or should be "closed" during response.

The traditional emphasis on the literary author is correspondingly unpopular. Perhaps a reaction has set in against the longstanding bias toward authors.

Perhaps current critics suspect their enterprise will have to get its foremost support from readers, not from authors, who form a marginal group on the contemporary scene. In any event, modern theorists, unlike the classicists, do not issue guidelines to authors. Nor is much weight placed on the role and intention of the author as theoretical entities, except insofar as they relate to readers' responses. At most, the author's intention is permitted to return in transmogrified forms: as a ponderous scholarly apparatus for Hirsch; an inner personality conflict for Paris; an infantile bodily fantasy for Holland; a patriarchal sexual politics for Millett; a desperate, defiant egotism for Bloom; a mythopoetical signature for Fiedler; and so on. Even these constructs are chiefly reasoned backward from reading, and their historical anchoring is usually quite sketchy compared to that of older biographical criticism.

The claim of the critic to attain and present a model response may be indispensable to all criticism, and persists even now in literary theory. The new theoretical emphasis implies a far stronger claim than older traditions did: that the critic's acts are generally valid not just for a given work, but for all reading of literature. However, such claims are expressed in drastically varying forms. Iser and early Holland purport to be describing what the general reader does anyway. Fiedler started out to plead the cause of an elite reader and later decided to favor the general one. Hirsch, Bleich, Millett, Jauss, and Jameson each advocate a specialized way of reading demanding a major initiative before it can be established in common practice. De Man and Hartman assert their way of reading to be enforced by the problematics of language itself. Bloom portrays his as a struggle for personal mastery over a source. And so forth.

The utopian quality of the literary experience makes it unavoidable that any interesting model of reading and response is also an imperative, the more so when general validity is implied. Critics who really considered their response the same as every other reader's would have scant motivation to communicate it. The theoretical exposition is needed precisely because such a response may well not occur. In fact, the main impetus of literary theory arises from this possibility. The theorist can't legitimately offer a model of how all people read a work, but only of how some people might read it. We have a right to ask how plausible, feasible, and worthwhile the model may be. The famous "reader" we keep hearing about seems to hover in a permanent identity crisis.

To say the least, the skill and training of these critics makes their reading atypically intense, thorough, and elaborate. They assign numerous functions to the elements they find. They upgrade seemingly insignificant elements and downgrade seemingly incompatible or incomprehensible ones. They reread the text, bringing altered perspectives to bear. And, most importantly, they try to formulate their results in exemplary ways we may reconstruct and utilize. The fact that the critical text is always a response to a response, and the theoretical text a response to a set of such second-order responses, must not be underestimated, because this setup puts the literary text at several removes (each of them quite problematic) from the theory.

Our theorists are usually confident that their way of reading is the one demanded by the very essence of literature. Their characteristic move is to attune their definition of literature in precisely this way. For most, however, that way of reading is more immediately demanded by a special project: more rigorous scholarship for Wellek and Hirsch, continuity of myth and archetype for Frye and Fiedler, a return to the sacred for Hartman and Bloom, insights into one's personality for Holland, Bleich, and Paris, a displacement of Western metaphysics for de Man, revolutionary awareness for Jameson and Millett, and so on. Thus, their advocacies must always be appreciated in light of their projects.

Not too surprisingly, the combative urge to defend values or interpretations has been transferred to defending theoretical models and projects. In their zeal to move their several theories into prominence, if not predominance, many literary theorists treat each other more as antagonists than collaborators. The benefits of such egotism and partisanship are surely outweighed by the damaging spectacle the profession offers to public view. The total impression is paradoxical: a leading group of exquisitely skilled readers don't seem to understand reading well enough to agree on its barest essentials.

The alternative to such personal partisanship is to pursue the prospect that each one theory may capture some relevant aspect of literary experience and yet falsify the latter at the moment when it denies all the others. My work here is intended to develop that prospect in unusual detail. I have always believed we should learn from as many people as possible, however ardently they may collide with each other. Admittedly, the projects of many scholars may not be well designed for such integration. And the complexity of the literary experience is inherited by critical discourse. But the project is all the more urgent for being so intractable.

As long as it is granted space to operate, criticism will be a self-perpetuating enterprise. Each assault it makes on literary problems leaves fresh problems in its wake. The closure of a work, genre, style, and so on is followed by an opening at some other point of the system. A genuinely useful critique of literature leaves it looking not simple, but more challenging than before. In such a context, critical theory needs no extraneous clash of egos and careers to deflect its progress and postpone its consolidation. The striking plurality of theories we now see is not to be resolved by gladiatorial elimination of participants. The main loser would be literature itself, locked into the eventually triumphant theory and much reduced in the dynamics whereby it had called forth the plurality in the first place. Instead, we should seek to integrate competing theories in a framework that respects their individual valences without hypostasizing them beyond the limits of their insights.

This book retraces my own attempt to navigate a set of literary theories proposed by prominent critics; and to survey what each theory, in my view, performs or projects. To promote fidelity, I have tried to distill out the main points in the actual words of each critic, suitably rearranged and condensed, even at the risk of choppy quotation. I raise some problems that their theories seem to imply but not solve: divergences between theory and application, or between one part of the model and another; disturbing implications of particular arguments; disproportionate emphases at the expense of other factors; conflicts with the results of empirical research on text processing; and so on. Yet like the great literary work, the major critical work is not vitiated but vitalized by its problems. The critical theorist's best achievement is to return us to literature with a new sense, paradoxically reassuring, that literariness will never be totally explained.

4

René Wellek and Austin Warren[1]

When it was first published in 1949,[2] Wellek and Warren's *Theory of Literature* was destined to become a highly unusual and influential attempt, the first in English, to enumerate the main issues that literary theory might address. The two scholars offered a broad survey of past trends as well as a program of future tasks. Making this program seem urgent without offending the prior upholders of the discipline called for some diplomacy. On one side, the profession was defended: "literary scholarship has its own valid" "intellectual methods"; "the true study of literature" is "at once 'literary' and 'systematic'" (TL 16). On the other side, it was asserted that "literary theory, an organon of methods, is the great need of literary scholarship today" (TL 19). In those days, "the only methods in which American graduate schools provided any systematic training" was the "ordering and establishing of evidence," mainly with regard to "authorship, authenticity, and date," all of which, in Wellek and Warren's view, should be merely "preliminary to the ultimate task of scholarship" (TL 68f, 57). Thus, the "valid" and "systematic" state of the discipline was a promise and projection of a future Wellek and Warren sought to shape in particular ways.

Their central thesis was that "literary studies should be specifically literary," that is, "ergocentric" (TL 8, 74). "The natural and sensible starting point for work in literary scholarship is the interpretation and analysis of the works of literature themselves" (TL 139). Homage was paid to the "healthy reaction" of criticism against an "over-emphasisis" upon the "'external circumstances—political, social, economic—in which literature is produced'" (TL 139) (cf. Lee, 1913). A new "concentration on the actual works of art themselves" was being "especially"

---

[1] The key for Wellek and Warren citations is: TL: *Theory of Literature*. Obviously, limiting this chapter to their single joint volume is unfair to the respective oeuvres of the two critics, who have produced many works since then, and who —despite their avowal of "shared agreement" (TL 8)— may not hold the same views (cf. Note 19). But I found it helpful to highlight the impact of the one book as a strategic starting point for my discussion of literary theory in the Anglo-American world.

[2] Some passages of the book were published as early as 1940 (TL 8f) and may have helped to set the stage.

achieved by "the brilliant movement of the Russian formalists and their Czech and Polish followers," as well as by practitioners of "explication de textes" and of "close reading": the "New Critics" such as Cleanth Brooks, Robert Penn Warren, William K. Wimsatt, and Monroe Beardsley, along with R.P. Blackmur, Ronald S. Crane, William Empson, I.A. Richards, F.R. Leavis, Leo Spitzer, Earl Wasserman, and, yes, Harold Bloom and Geoffrey Hartman in their early incarnations (TL 139f, 338f).[3] Though Wellek and Warren don't label themselves "formalists" —"commonly" a designation for "modern critics limiting themselves to aesthetic criticism" (TL 241) —they clearly sympathize with this direction, as we shall see. For instance, they prefer their "conceptions" like "genre" to be "formalistic" ones rather than "subject-matter classifications" (TL 232f).

The book proceeds by parceling "literary theory" into four sections. First come the "definitions and distinctions" concerning the "nature" and "function of literature" (TL 5). Next, traditional procedures for "the assembling and preparing of a text" ("cataloging," "editing," etc.) are pointedly treated as "preliminary operations" (TL 57, 59, 5). The rest of the book is divided between "extrinsic" versus "intrinsic" approaches; befitting the resolve to place literature at the theoretical center, the section on "intrinsic study" is longer than the other three sections combined. Reasonably enough, "psychology," "society," and "the other arts" were made "extrinsic," whereas "metre," "style," and "metaphor" were "intrinsic" (TL 5f). More subtlety is required to see why "ideas" are "extrinsic" (the "history of ideas" is at stake, not literary content); or why "biography" is "extrinsic" when "literary history" is "intrinsic." Perhaps the whole division, however it may be delineated in practice, is fundamentally problematic.

Wellek and Warren are ambivalent about modeling their project after science—an attitude we will keep encountering in American literary theory. They caution against the "scientific invasion into literary study" whereby "the methods developed by the natural sciences" get "transferred to the study of literature" (TL 16). Scholars try to "emulate the general scientific ideals of objectivity, impersonality, and certainty," for example, by "collecting neutral facts" or "studying causal antecedents and origins." In such work, "scientific causality is used to explain literary phenomena by the assignment of determining causes to economic, social, and political conditions." Or, an "attempt" is made "to use biological concepts in the tracing of the evolution of literature." Or, such "quantitative methods" as "statistics, charts, and graphs" are appropriated (TL 16; cf. TL 24, 171, 280, 309).

In Wellek and Warren's estimate, the outcome was typically "limited" success

---

[3] The cited works are Hartman's (1954) *Unmediated Vision*, and Bloom's (1961) *Visionary Company* (TL 338f). Wellek was Hartman's dissertation director.

if not "failure" (TL 16).[4] For example, "professional linguists," except maybe those in "lexicology" and "etymology," "slighted" the "pursuits" of "language study" relevant for "the modern student of literature"; and "the 'behavioristic' school of linguistics" "very consciously" "ignored" the "expressive value" of the "utterance" (TL 176, 178). It was not realized that "linguistic study becomes literary only" "when it aims at investigating the aesthetic effects of language" (TL 176f). Similarly, "we must reject the biological analogy between the development of literature and the closed evolutionary process from birth to death," since biology makes no provision for "variable schemes of values" (TL 256f; cf. TL 27, 236).[5]

Nonetheless, "science" and "literary study" are said to "contact or even overlap," notably in the "fundamental methods" of "induction and deduction, analysis, synthesis, and comparison" (TL 16). These shared "methods" are typically applied by science to general phenomena, and by literary studies to specific works. Wellek and Warren opine that "attempts to find general laws in literature have always failed" (TL 18). "No general law can be assumed to achieve the purpose of literary study: the more general, the more abstract and hence empty it will seem; the more the concrete work of art will elude our grasp." This insistence on addressing the "concrete work" (TL 39, 118, 121, 128f, 132, 147, 262) foregrounds "the necessity of theory growing out of a concrete engagement with texts" (letter from Wellek). If so, the domain of theory may be hard to keep separate from the interpretation of works, as critics like Iser and Culler argue it should be (pp. 129f, 240ff).

One solution could be to "describe as 'literary theory' the study of the principles of literature," its "categories" and "criteria," and to "differentiate studies of concrete works" as "'literary criticism'" or "'literary history'" (TL 39).[6] Yet Wellek and Warren aver that "literary theory" would be "inconceivable" "without criticism or history," and "impossible except on the basis of a study of concrete literary works." Hence, a characteristic striving in *Theory of Literature* is to tailor the contours of each domain of theory very closely to the consideration of works or groups of works. A parallel move is to relate literary theory to

---

[4] "Success" is however allowed for Birkhoff's (1933) use of mathematics in aesthetics, and for the application of "morphology" to "folklore" (TL 261, 130f) (cf. Propp, 1928, whose work is oddly passed over).

[5] "The early genre histories of Brunetière [1890] and Symonds [1890]" are deemed "vitiated by an excessive reliance on the biological parallel" (TL 261; cf. TL 236, 256). For a different use of "evolution," see p. 186f.

[6] Hence, theory as such would not need to "distinguish between 'contemporary' and past literature," as Wellek and Warren indeed "refuse" to do, deploring the "scholarly attitude" that demands "the exclusion of recent literature from serious study" (TL 8, 44). But the distinction does come up at times, for example, regarding fluctuations in emotionality, rationalism, and the separateness of prose from poetry (TL 117, 206, 165). Compare Note 9.

neighboring disciplines so as to maintain the center of gravity firmly on the literary side.

The centrality of the actual work is underscored: "there will never be a proper history of an art" "unless we concentrate on an analysis of the works themselves and relegate to the background studies in the psychology of the reader" or "the author" as well as "studies in the cultural and social background" (TL 130). This move may have been strategic in making the enterprise palatable for more traditional critics. But ironically, many of the trends Wellek and Warren wanted to restrict have flourished rather than diminished in the intervening years.

The two critics had been doubtless made wary by the tendency of early theorists to advance vulnerable generalizations, mainly in the search for tidy classificatory schemes for sorting works according to period, nationality, century, genre, style, size, and so on. As Wellek and Warren suggest, the quasiscientific "analogy to the natural world" favors "the supposition that every work belongs to a kind" (TL 226f). In categorizing, a small number of classes was considered an advantage, two or three[7] if possible. Pairs of contraries were endlessly devised for philosophical, historical, or stylistic schemes, such as "macrocosmos" versus "microcosmos," "Classicism" versus "Romanticism," "simple" versus "decorated," and so on (TL 120, 133, 179; cf. TL 122, 193, 204, 210). Or, tripartite schemes were proposed, such as "the thesis 'rationalism,' the antithesis 'irrationalism,' and the synthesis 'Romanticism'"; or "positivism" ("explains the spiritual by the physical world"), "objective idealism" ("sees reality as the expression of an internal reality"), and "dualistic idealism" ("assumes the independence of spirit against nature") (TL 120, 117).[8] However, such schemes of twos and threes can't "cope with the highly diversified pattern" and the "complex process of literature"; and "the concrete individuality of poets and their works is ignored or minimized" (TL 133, 118). Besides, literature is replete with "transitional forms" and the "contamination" of "genres" (TL 25, 261).[9]

We might see here a variant of the ancient "quarrel between the 'universal' and 'particular' in literature," "going on since Aristotle" (TL 18). Wellek and Warren adopt an intermediary position: "each work of literature is both general and particular" (TL 19). "No work of art can be wholly unique, since it would then be completely incomprehensible" (TL 18, 151) (an argument also advanced by Hirsch, p. 114). "Moreover, all words in every literary work are, by their very nature, 'generals' and not particulars" (TL 18). "We can thus generalize concerning works of art" and still "attempt to characterize the individuality of a work, of an author, of a period, or of a national literature" (TL 19). For this task,

---

[7] "A sober view" "will doubt the sacredness of the number three" (TL 118). We find some extravagant groupings by threes in Chs. 5 (Frye) and 14 (Bloom).

[8] The sources here are Korff (1923-53) and Dilthey (1898, 1907, 1911), respectively.

[9] "Literary history between 1500 and 1800" was a "mingling and contamination of genres," whereas the "contemporary tendency" runs "against the confusion of genres" (TL 261, 25).

some "literary theory" is indispensable, or ideally, "a dialectical interpenetration of theory and practice" (TL 19, 40). The question remains whether this "theory" can make use of traditional classifications enough to incorporate the results of past research. The "traditional genres of the lyric, the epic, and the drama," for instance, are taken not merely as "obviously" "the centre of literary art" but as "formalistic" or possibly "psychological" classes (TL 233, 84).

Presumably, the valence of such old conceptions will have to be re-established by exploring how they function when literary works are produced and received. At times, Wellek and Warren seem to agree: "the nature and function of literature must" be "correlative": "the use of poetry[10] follows from its nature," and its "nature" "follows from its use" (TL 29). "Its nature is in potence what in act is its function; it is what it can do" (TL 238). Yet the "intrinsic" focus draws more attention to the nature of literature than to its function.

A basic definition of literature is urgently needed, but hard to formulate. Powerfully reductive, objectifying proposals are speedily dismissed. The "nominalist" view, advanced by Croce (1909) among others, that "literature" is "a collection of individual" works that "share a common name," says little about "the aesthetic convention in which a work participates" (TL 226). The definition "everything in print" also fails, since literature can be "oral,"[11] and "the 'real' poem" is neither "the writing on the paper" nor the "sequence of sounds" (TL 20, 22, 143, 146). At most, "writing and printing" "have done much to increase the unity and integrity of works of art," and some "print devices" may be used as "integral parts" of "particular works" (TL 143).

The elitist definition of "literature" as "'great books'" goes to a different extreme (TL 21f). It "introduces an excessively 'aesthetic' point of view" and "makes incomprehensible the continuity of literary tradition" (TL 21f)—a point made in various ways by Fiedler, Jauss, and Jameson as well. Greatness cannot exist without some background or comparison; nor indeed can literariness. Besides, the elitist definition tends to dilute Wellek and Warren's major project, evaluation (see p. 32f), by requiring a value judgment at the initial moment of identifying the literary work.

Wellek and Warren prefer to base their definition on "the particular use made of language in literature" (TL 22) —a typical formalist move. "The main distinctions to be drawn are between the literary, the everyday, and the scientific." "The ideal scientific language" should be "purely 'denotative,'" "aiming at a one-to-

---

[10] As in much literary theorizing, poetry comes to stand for all literature. It is suggested that "modern literary theory" might "scrap the prose-poetry distinction"; and that "the distinction between a novel" "and a poem" may be "only quantitative and fail to justify the setting up of two contrasting kinds of literature" (TL 227, 158). To be sure, as we shall see in a moment, poetry was favored also because its theoretical description was the most advanced (TL 212).

[11] Though Wellek and Warren "would sharply distinguish oral epic from literary epic" and might include the *Iliad* among the oral, they refer to "the poem Homer wrote," "Homer's reason for writing the *Iliad*," or "contemporary readers of Homer" (TL 227, 30, 42).

one correspondence between sign and referent"; the "sign is completely arbitrary" ("can be replaced by equivalent signs") and "transparent" ("directs us unequivocally to its referent") (TL 22f). "Literary language," in contrast, "abounds in ambiguities," "homonyms, arbitrary or irrational categories," "historical accidents, memories, and associations" (TL 23). It is "highly 'connotative'" and "contextual," "carrying with it" "an aura of synonyms and homonyms" and maximizing the "expressive" "side" that "scientific language" "wants" "to minimize" (TL 23, 175). "The word is not primarily a sign, a transparent counter, but a 'symbol' valuable for itself as well as in its capacity of representative" (TL 88). Stated this way, the opposition rests on an idealization of both types. The frequent opaqueness and imprecision of scientific discourse is ignored. And literary language is so defined that the poem appears more relevant than the prose work (cf. Ch. 2). Wellek and Warren propose to "call" a "literary work of art" a "poem" "for brevity's sake"; but a more cogent motive, conceded later, is that "the theory and criticism of poetry" were in those days far superior "in both quantity and quality," to that for prose, e.g., for "the novel" (TL 142, 212).

Probably because few definitions or idealizations have been proposed for "everyday" "language," it is "more difficult" to distinguish from the "literary" than the scientific had been (TL 23). "Everyday language" shares the "expressive function" and is also "full" of "irrationalities and contextual changes" (TL 23f). A "quantitative difference" is suggested, wherein "literary language" "exploits" "the resources of language" "much more deliberately and systematically" (TL 24). Here again, "poems" provide the best evidence with their "complex, close-knit organization"; but "every work of art imposes an order" and "unity on its materials." A qualitative difference is also indicated in "the distinction between common speech and artistic deviation" in terms of "distortions from normal usage" and "organized violence committed on everyday language" (TL 177, 180, 171). Such a conception accords with Spitzer's (1930b) idea that a "deviation" in "mental life" should "have a coordinate linguistic deviation" (TL 183). But whereas the special mind-set is essential to literary communication, deviant language is not (Ch. 2). Quite aside from works whose language appears to us ordinary, we can appreciate literature from times and cultures whose everyday language we hardly know, as Wellek and Warren admit (TL 155, 177). To participate in literature, we must be able to make "new" and "strange" (in Šklovskij's words) whatever language we encounter (cf. TL 242).

Another criterion of difference is offered as a corollary of Kant's notion that "practicality" as well as "habit" can be an "enemy" of "aesthetic experience" (TL 240f). Hence, "literature is, by modern definition, 'pure'" of "practical intent (propaganda, incitation to direct, immediate action) and scientific intent (provision of information, facts, 'additions to knowledge')" (TL 239). It is "false" to "locate the seriousness of a great poem or novel" in its "historical information" or "helpful moral lesson" (TL 31). "We reject as poetry or label as mere rhetoric everything which persuades us to a definite outward action" (TL 24). Though this intent does figure in the production and reception of many works, it is not dominant enough to replace all literary intents. As our two critics remark in regard to "ideas," we expect that "practical" "materials" and "information" be "literarily used" as "integral parts of the work" (TL 239).

This "integral" quality is brought out in Wellek and Warren's definition of "the work of art" as "a whole system of signs, or structure of signs, serving an aesthetic purpose" (TL 141). As such, "the work of art" is "an object of knowledge" with a "special ontological status"; "neither real (physical)" "nor mental (psychological)" "nor ideal (like a triangle)"; "it is a system of norms of ideal concepts which are intersubjective" (TL 156). A parallel is proposed: the total "system of language (langue)" is related to "the individual speech act" ("parole") in much the same way as the "literary work of art" is related to any one "individual realization" (TL 152). Both the "system" and the "work" represent "a collection of conventions and norms whose workings and relations we can observe and describe as having a fundamental coherence and identity in spite of very different, imperfect, and incomplete" realizations by individual users. We might also "contrast" the "language system of a literary work of art with the general usage of the time" (TL 177).

This proposal suggests a useful view of the openness of the text. Instead of simply postulating that there must be right and wrong readings (as Wellek and Warren do, p. 34f), we could stipulate that there will be a systemic relationship among the various readings that people who know the language and conventions will be likely to derive from the text. Readings which appear more functional in accounting for the experience among such people and for the relatedness of their results should be given preference. This systemic core would be the operational correlate for the aspect that, in a "Platonist" or "phenomenologist" view, might be the objectified abstraction called the "essence" (cf. TL 153, 156).

Within the system of the work, the "old dichotomy of 'content versus form'" should be abandoned, as the "formalists" suggested (TL 140). We can "rechristen all the aesthetically indifferent elements 'materials,' while the manner in which they acquire efficacy may be called 'structure'" (TL 140f). These "raw materials" would subsume "on one level, words, on another level, human behavior" and "experience" (including "the author's experience"), and on yet "another, human ideas and attitudes" (TL 241, 218). In a "successful" work, "all of these" "are pulled into polyphonic relations by the dynamics of aesthetic purpose" (TL 241). Accordingly, "structure is a concept including both content and form, so far as they are organized for an aesthetic purpose" (TL 141). This "structure" could be modeled within the "polyphonic" "system" of "several strata" propounded by Ingarden (1931): "sound," "syntagmas" or "sentence patterns," the "'world'" ("objects," "plot, characters, setting)'" "viewpoint," and "metaphysical qualities" ("the sublime, the tragic, the terrible, the holy") (TL 151f, 225).

Some problems arise here, for instance, whether all five strata are "indispensable," and whether "stylistics," including rhetorical schemes and "imagery," belongs to the "syntactical" "stratum" (TL 152, 211).[12] If "every work of literary art is first of all, a series of sounds out of which arises the meaning," and if "we can write the grammar of a literary work of art," "beginning with phonology" and "rising to syntax" (TL 158, 176), a spatial or temporal ordering of the strata seems implied, both for reading and for analysis. The surface text retains tight control over its processing. But we need to inquire how a reader or analyst moves up from the "lower" levels to the "higher" ones during the "mental experiences based on the sound structure" of "sentences" (TL 156). Like many critics (and linguists) Wellek and Warren tend to bracket the question by treating linguistic units as independent agents, for example, "sentences and sentence structures refer to objects" and "construct imaginative realities such as landscapes, interiors, characters, actions or ideas" (TL 153). (Iser's model offers the most detailed picture of how this may happen, Ch. 8).

The relationship between literature and reality is conceived here as we might predict for an "ergocentric" method. "The work of art" is "never" a "mere copy of life" or "simply the embodiment of experience" (TL 78). "Literature must not be conceived as being merely a passive reflection or copy of the political, social, or even intellectual development of mankind" (TL 264). "Studies" of "social pictures" from "novels" have "little value" if "they take it for granted that literature is simply a mirror of life, a reproduction" (TL 103). Also, "sincerity" is a "false" "criterion" "if it judges literature in terms of biographical truthfulness" (TL 80) (a criterion applied by critics like Fiedler and Millett, pp. 88, 350f). Still, some "studies" use "literature as social documents, as assumed pictures of social reality," or as a source for "the history of civilization" (TL 102, 20; cf. TL 252). To explore certain "older periods," we may be "forced to use literary material for want of evidence" from "writers on politics, economics, and general public questions" (TL 104).

Wellek and Warren stress that "art imposes some kind of a framework which takes the statement of the work out of the world of reality" (TL 25). We should expect to find "not so much objective facts as complex attitudes" "illustrated in fiction," reflecting for example the "artistic method of the novelist" and the position of the work as "the latest in a series of such works" (TL 104, 78). "The correspondence between a novel and experience can never be measured by any simple pairing off of items"; we must "compare the total world" of the author "with our total experience" (TL 246). "The analogies between life and literature become most palpable when the art is highly stylized": the "writers" "superimpose their signed world on our experience." "The great novelists all have such a world—recognizable as overlapping the empirical world but distinct in its self-coherent intelligibility" (TL 214).

Following these views, the two critics undertake to sort out different kinds of

---

[12] Even the number is uncertain. The fifth stratum in one listing ("metaphysical qualities") is the "fourth and last" in another (TL 151f, 225).

"truth." To accuse literature of lacking "truth" in the sense of "systematic and publicly verifiable knowledge" is a "positivist reduction" (TL 33f). They propose the "alternative" of a composite, "pluri-modal truth": "factual truth" ("specific detail of time and place"); "philosophical truth" ("conceptual, propositional, general"): "psychological truth" ("conscious and systematic theory of the mind"); and literary "truth" ("the view of life" which "every artistically coherent work possesses") (TL 35, 212f, 92, 34). "The reality of a work of fiction" is "its effect on the reader as a convincing reading of life," rather than "a reality of circumstance or detail" (TL 213). The "fictional world" is "commonly" more "integrated" than our own "experienced and imagined world," as well as "less strange and more representative than truth" (TL 213f). When borrowing from other modes of "truth," literature changes their status. It can "apply, illustrate, or embody" a "philosophy which exists in systematic conceptual form outside of literature" (TL 34). Or, it can use "psychology" to "sharpen" its "powers of observation," or to reveal "hitherto undiscovered patterns" (TL 93). But such literature is not actually participating in philosophy or psychology, or much less competing with them (cf. TL 19, 92, 123f).

In respect to "truth," "myth" is a problematic concept. Generally, "myth" is "any anonymously composed story telling of origins and destinies: the explanations a society offers its young of why the world is" (TL 191). But history shows variations in this conception. In the Aristotelian tradition, "myth" was "the irrational or intuitive as against the systematically philosophical" (TL 190). For the "Enlightenment," "myth was a fiction," but for "Vico," "the German Romanticists, Coleridge, Emerson, and Nietzsche" it was "a kind of truth" (TL 190). In "modern" times, "myth" designates "an area of meaning" that concerns "religion, folklore, anthropology, sociology, psychoanalysis, and the fine arts" (TL 190). In particular, "myth is the common denominator between poetry and religion" "for many writers"; "religious myth is the large-scale authorization of poetic metaphor" (TL 192) (cf. Frye, p. 65).

However, "modern man" may "lack myth" "destroyed" by "'intellectuals'" and "the Enlightenment," as Nietzsche claimed (TL 192). Or, we might have "shallow, inadequate," or "'false' myths," such as "'progress,'" "'equality,'" or "universal education." Wellek and Warren consider it a "probably true" "judgment" that "when old, long-felt, self-coherent ways of life (rituals with all their accompanying myths) are disrupted by 'modernism' most men (or all) are impoverished." [13]

Plainly, "myth" is a distinctly positive concept for "our own view" "seeing the meaning and function of literature as centrally present" in "myth," which can "bridge and bind together" "'form' and 'matter'" and enable "a higher level of integration" (TL 122, 193). "'Myth'" is "a favorite term of modern criticism,"

---

[13] Whereas Fiedler would concur, Millett would welcome the "disruption," since for her, myths act as "propaganda" for justifying "racial sexual beliefs" and "misogyny" (SX 404, 71).

subsuming such "motifs" as "the image or picture, the social, the supernatural," "the narrative," "the archetypal or universal, the symbolic representation as events in time of our timeless ideals, the programmatic or eschatological, the mystic," and the "social, anonymous, communal" (TL 190f) (compare Frye and Fiedler). "If the mythic has as its contrary either science or philosophy, it opposes the picturable concrete to the rational abstract" (TL 191). Anticipating Fiedler (in EI and LD) is the remark that "the real" and "successful" "plot" of *Huckleberry Finn* is the "mythic plot" of a "journey down a great river of four" who "have escaped from conventional society"; the "last third" of the book trying to provide "some 'plot'" is "obviously inferior" to the rest (TL 217).

These attempts to define literature and its relationship to reality exhibit a typical trend in *Theory of Literature*: the undisguised reference to value-laden criteria at every level of description. Unlike many theorists, Wellek and Warren do so quite consciously, proclaiming "evaluation" "the central problem of all criticism" (TL 157). "We cannot comprehend and analyze any work of art without reference to value" (TL 156). Merely to "recognize a certain structure as a 'work of art'" or "to spend time and attention" on it "is already a judgment of value" (TL 156, 250). "Structure, sign, and value form three aspects of the very same problem and cannot be artificially isolated" (TL 156). If "structure" is defined as a means for "aesthetic efficacy," then "there is no structure outside norms and values" (TL 140f, 156). Consequently, "the separation between the exegesis of meaning" and "the judgment of value" is "rarely, in 'literary criticism,' either practised or practicable" (TL 250).

Wellek and Warren know that this outlook is by no means universally shared. As Hirsch does much later (p. 119), they complain how "the modern view is inclined to excessive unnecessary relativism," and how "anti-academics within and without the universities" "affirm the tyranny of flux" (TL 247). Although "values" are not likely to be "objective" in the sense of being "publicly verifiable,"[14] a "critic" may "affirm that the value" is "really, potentially present in the art object —not 'read into' it or associatively attached to it, but with the advantage of a special incentive to insight, seen in it" (TL 249f). To be sure, "the values" are not "there for *anyone*," but "realized, actually valued," only by "readers who meet the requisite conditions" (TL 249). "The 'classicists' who appeal to the suffrage of all men of all times and lands tacitly restrict their 'all' to 'all competent judges.'" The mental processes of experiencing values are not at issue here, since for Wellek and Warren, any "theory" for "the psychology of the reader" must engender "a complete confusion of values" (TL 147).

Modern "relativism" is contrasted starkly with the "Classical" or "Neo-Classi-

---

[14] Though conceding that "there is no completely objective method of establishing classifications," Wellek and Warren disavow "complete" or "mere subjectivity" or "mere subjectivism," and insist that their broad conception of "the total meaning of the work of art" is not "a plea for arbitrary subjective misreadings" (TL 59f, 18, 162, 173, 42).

cal" standard, which took "works of ancient origin" as the best models and remained "intolerant" or "unwitting of other aesthetic systems" (TL 230, 234). Criteria included "a rigid unity of tone," "stylized purity and 'simplicity,'" plus "a concentration on a single emotion" (TL 234). Literature was exhorted to present "the typical, the universal," and to "heighten or idealize life" (TL 213). The "Aristotelian" viewpoint appealed to an "educated hedonism," whereby literature, such as the tragedy, "'ought to produce, not any chance pleasure, but the pleasure that is proper to it'" (TL 230). Classicist theory was "a mixture of authoritarianism and rationalism" and tried to be "regulative and prescriptive" (TL 230, 233). Conversely, "modern" "theory" is "clearly descriptive" and "doesn't prescribe rules to authors" (TL 235). This change may have encouraged that decline of evaluation lamented here. Related causes might be the "modern" use of "'private symbolism'" rather than "the widely intelligible symbolism of past poets"; plus "the vast widening of the audience" and the "more rapid transitions" in recent times (TL 189, 232). The diversification of functions naturally emphasizes the problematic character of stable value systems.

Still, on the highest level of generality, "most men seriously concerned with the arts agree" that "literature has a unique" "value" (TL 240). "The aesthetic experience" is "a perception of quality intrinsically pleasant and interesting, offering a terminal value and a sample and foretaste of other terminal values" (TL 241). "What" "art" "articulates is superior" to the "self-induced reverie or reflection" of its "users"; "it gives them pleasure by the skill with which it articulates what they take to be something like their own reverie or reflection and by the release they experience through this articulation" (TL 31). Literature gives "pleasure in a higher kind of activity, i.e., non-acquisitive contemplation" accompanied by a "pleasurable seriousness" of "perception" (TL 31).

Accordingly, "the aesthetic experience" "is connected with feeling (pleasure-pain, hedonistic response) and the senses; but it objectifies and articulates feeling—the feeling finds, in the work of art, an 'objective correlative,' and it is distanced from sensation and conation by its object's frame of fictionality" (TL 241). This account is compatible with the "formalist" conception of "the poem" as "a specific, highly organized control of the reader's experience," under the condition that "the tighter the organization, the higher the value" (TL 249, 243). Indeed, the "criteria of greatness in any realm of theory or practice" appear to be "'a grasp of the complex, with a sense of proportion and relevance'" (TL 244) (cf. Reid, 1931).

Thus, the hedonistic account is merged with the formalist one, so that the enjoyment and value of a work are made commensurate with its "complexity" and "coherence" (TL 36, 93, 104, 109, 123, 130, 212, 239, 243, 246). Following Bosanquet (1915), Eliot (1933), and Pepper (1945), Wellek and Warren approve the "criterion" of "inclusiveness: 'imaginative integration' and 'amount (and diversity) of material integrated'" (TL 243). "Provided a real 'amalgamation' takes place, the value of the poem rises in direct ratio to the diversity of its materials."

Similarly, "the maturity of a work of art is its inclusiveness, its awareness of complexity," including "ironies," "tensions," and "purposed ambiguity" (TL 246, 194). "We are content to call a novelist great when his world, though not patterned or scaled like our own, is comprehensive of all the elements we find necessary to catholic scope" (TL 214). "The literary work" that "continues to be admired must possess" "a 'multivalence': its aesthetic value must be so rich and comprehensive as to include among its structures one or more which gives high satisfaction to each later period"; only "a community" rather than "a single individual can realize all its strata and systems" (TL 243) (cf. Boas, 1932). The notion that "each generation leaves elements in the great work of art unappropri-ated" allows for a "desire to affirm" the "objectivity of literary values" without a "commitment to some static canon" (TL 247). Hence, values need not entail the "subjectivity" of literary studies that makes Wellek and Warren uneasy (cf. TL 18, 42, 44, 152, 156, 162, 168, 173, 249).

Multiple structuring gives "great" works a lasting potential for innovative experiences, for making things "new" and "strange" in the conceptions of "Ro-mantics" and "formalists" (cf. TL 242). "Each more recent 'movement' in poetry has had the same design: to clear away all automatic response, to promote a renewal of language." The "pleasure in a literary work is compounded of the sense of novelty and the sense of recognition" (TL 235). "The criterion" is "novelty" "for the sake of the disinterested perception of quality" (TL 242; cf. TL 25). "It is the essence of the aesthetic norm to be broken" (TL 242) (cf. Mukařov-ský, 1964 [1932], 1970 [1936]). Hence, "when we return again and again to a work," we find "new levels of meaning, new patterns of association" (TL 242f). Yet here is another plausible impediment to evaluation: the recognition of an innovative work requires critics to perpetually call in question their own current values that are allegedly guiding their judgments at the same time (Ch. 3).

As we might expect, criteria from outside the literary work are not accredited for evaluation. "Psychology," "sociology," and "philosophy" can have "artistic value" only if they "enhance coherence and complexity" (TL 93, 109, 123). "Philosophical," "psychological, or social" "truth as such has no artistic value" (TL 123). After all, "mediocre, average works" "may seem better to a modern sociologist" (TL 95). Moreover, "no biographical evidence can change or influ-ence critical evaluation" (TL 80). In sum, "applying some extra-literary stan-dards" is apparently as bad as "resigning ourselves to the meaningless flux of changing" "values" (TL 257).

In addition to value, Wellek and Warren uphold the correctness of possible readings for literary works. Predictably, they seek their standards inside the text (or "poem," as they like to say). "We can distinguish between right and wrong readings of a poem, or between a recognition or a distortion of the norms implicit in a work of art by acts of comparison, by a study of different false or incomplete 'realizations' or interpretations" (TL 154). When reading a poem aloud, "a reciter may or may not recite correctly," and the "selection of components implicit in the text" "may be either right or wrong," the "wrong readings" being "distortions of the true meaning" (TL 169, 145). "The normative character of the genuine poem" is due to "the simple fact that it might be experienced correctly or incorrectly" (TL 150).

Yet Wellek and Warren also imply that the right reading is difficult to attain. Even "the author," "when he re-reads" the text, "is liable to errors and misinterpretations" (TL 148). "Intelligent critics" may perpetrate single "misreadings" or overall "misconceptions of the artistic process" (TL 239, 259). The situation worsens when we admit the general public. "The sum of all past and possible experiences of the poem" "leaves us with an infinity of irrelevant individual experiences, bad and false readings and perversions" (TL 150). If "the genuine poem is the experience common to all experiences," this "common denominator" "must be the *lowest*," "the most shallow, superficial, and trivial experience" —the supposition being that "most men stay at a sub-literary level" (TL 150, 200). At times, correctness seems quite out of reach: "in every individual experience only a small part can be considered as adequate to the true poem" (TL 150).

Thus, Wellek and Warren define "the real poem" as "a structure of norms," which "together make up the genuine work of art," and yet stipulate that an individual reader can "realize" them "only partially" (TL 150f).[15] This outlook is hard to reconcile with a strong stand on correctness and evaluation. Their evident mistrust of "social and collective experience" forces the two critics to situate the "norms" in the text and bracket the problem of how to decide which actualization to prefer when these "implicit norms" get "extracted from every individual experience of a work of art" (TL 150f). On occasion, suggestions are made that it's wrong to insist on one particular reading, as when "some readers" of Frost are castigated for "giving to his plurisigns a fixity and rigidity alien to the nature of poetic statement" (TL 190).

The conception I advocated (Chs. 1 and 2)—that there is no "right" meaning, but an experience of feeling a meaning to be more or less right, and a performance of asserting this—was not recognized as an issue to be studied empirically, and still isn't by most critics. Wellek and Warren content themselves with the thesis that the work has a "dynamic" "structure" which both retains "substantial identity" "throughout the ages" and "changes throughout the process of history" (TL 155). Yet this "perspectivism," they hasten to add, "does not mean an anarchy of values, a glorification of individual caprice, but a process of getting to know the object from different points of view which may be defined and criticized in their turn" (TL 156). Moreover, "all different points of view are by no means equally right"; "it will always be possible to determine which point of view grasps the subject most thoroughly and deeply."

---

[15] The cited analogy to "langue" and "parole" (p. 29) seems appropriate here. The source of those terms, namely Saussure's (1916) theory of language (TL 294), would not have placed *any* text on the side of "langue." See Beaugrande (1987, in preparation) for discussion.

The traditional recourse for establishing the "right" reading by appealing to the author's intended meaning is handled here with circumspection. "The view that the genuine poem is to be found in the intentions of the author is widespread"; "though it is not always explicitly stated," "it justifies much historical research" as well as "many" "specific interpretations" (TL 148) (cf. Walzel, 1920; Coomaraswamy, 1944; Walcutt, 1946; Hirsch VAL). "Historical reconstruction has led to great stress on the intention of the author" —under the assumption that "if we can ascertain this intention" and "see" that it was "fulfilled," "we can also dispose of the problem of criticism" (TL 41).

Given their zeal to focus on the literary work itself, Wellek and Warren are hardly well-disposed toward this notion. "The whole idea that the 'intention' of the author is the proper subject of literary history seems" "quite mistaken"; "the meaning of the work of art is not exhausted by, or even equivalent to, its intention" (TL 42). "As a system of values, it leads an independent life." "The intentions and theories of artists" "say little or nothing about the concrete results of an artist's activity: his work and its specific content and form" (TL 128). "The artist does not conceive in general mental terms but in concrete material: and the concrete medium has its own history," "tradition," and "powerful determining character which shapes and modifies" "expression" (TL 129). By the same token, the "stratum" of "'metaphysical quality'" should be the "world view which emerges from the work, not the view stated didactically by the author within or without the work" (TL 245f).

Besides, "for most works of art we have no evidence to reconstruct the intention of the author except the finished work" (TL 148). And even the "contemporary evidence" of "an explicit profession of intentions" from the author "need not be binding on a modern observer." It "may be merely a pronouncement of plans and ideals, while the performance may be either far below or far aside the mark." "Divergence between conscious intention and actual performance is a common phenomenon" (TL 149). Therefore, "'intentions' of the author are always rationalizations" "to be criticized in light of the finished work." The author's actual "experience, conscious and unconscious, during the time of creation" is "a completely inaccessible and purely hypothetical" entity "we have no means of reconstructing or even of exploring" (TL 149). "If we could have interviewed Shakespeare" about "his intentions in writing *Hamlet*," we would "still quite rightly insist on finding meanings (and not merely inventing them) which were probably far from clearly formulated in Shakespeare's conscious mind" (TL 148).

On occasion, "artists may be strongly influenced" "by contemporary critical formulae" that are nonetheless "quite inadequate to characterize their actual artistic achievement" (TL 148). "Zola," for instance, subscribed to a "scientific theory," but produced "melodramatic and symbolic novels." "Sometimes a psychological theory, held either consciously or dimly by the author, seems to fit a figure or situation," but can "do so only incompletely and intermittently" (TL 92f). The "Elizabethan psychology" of the four humors or the like cannot explain such characters as Hamlet or Jaques to the degree that they are "more than types" (TL 92).

"Literary biography" often uses "the works themselves" as "evidence" about the authors (TL 76). This "assumption" is also "quite mistaken." "One cannot, from fictional statements, especially those made in plays, draw any valid inference as to the biography of a writer." "Authors cannot be assigned the ideas, feelings, virtues, views, and vices of their heroes" (TL 77). "The relation between the private life and the work" is not simply one of "cause and effect." An author may, of course, choose to "display his personality," and "draw a self-portrait"; but even here, the "distinction" remains "between a personal statement of an auto-biographical nature and the use of very same motif in a work of art" (TL 77f). "A work of art forms a unity" with "a quite different relation to reality than a book of memoirs, a diary, or a letter" (TL 78). As a matter of "simple psychological facts," "a work of art may rather embody the 'dream' of an author than his actual life, or it may be the 'mask,' the 'anti-self' behind which his real person is hiding," or "a picture of the life from which the author wants to escape." We must "distinguish sharply between the empirical person" and the "'personal'" quality of " the work"; what we call "'Virgilian' or 'Shakespearean'" is certainly not based on "biographical evidence" (TL 79). Such considerations are presumably a motive why, as noted above, "biographical evidence" is disbarred from "critical evaluation" (TL 80).

Even as a form of literary history, biography should be treated with restraint. "The biographical approach actually obscures the proper comprehension of the literary process" when "it breaks up the order of literary tradition to substitute the life-cycle of an individual" (TL 78). The approach may also cloud "the internal development of literature" in terms of what Henry Wells (1940) calls "'literary genetics'": "books imitate, parody, transform other books, not merely those which they follow in strict chronological succession" (TL 235). Still, biography might be helpful for determining whether a given "parallel" is due to direct influence or to "a common source" for the two works (TL 258). Thus, biography might shed light on "originality," "a fundamental problem of literary history," though it should look for the "intricate pattern" rather than the "isolated 'motif or word." A related application might be "the study of the genesis of the works: the early stages," "drafts, rejections, exclusions, and cuts," though this task too is "not, finally, necessary to an understanding of the finished work" (TL 90f).

Another way to study authors could be derived from sociology. "Since every writer is a member of society, he can be studied as a social being" (TL 96). We might explore "the social provenance and status of the writer," and his "social ideology" (TL 95f). Yet our two critics assign "the social origins of a writer" "only a minor part" in "his social status, allegiance, and ideology" (TL 97). We might prefer to inquire how "the writer" "has pronounced on questions of social and political importance." But here too, we are admonished that "pronouncements, decisions, and activities should never be confused with the actual social implications of a writer's works." Or, we might examine "the economic basis of literary production"; "much evidence has been accumulated" here, but "well-substantiated conclusions have rarely been drawn" (TL 95, 101). Writers are not "merely dependent" on "patron or public"; they "may succeed in creating their own special public" (TL 101f). "The writer is not only influenced by society," but also "influences it" (TL 102).

Wellek and Warren grant that "literature is a social institution, using as its medium language, a social creation" (TL 94). "Literature occurs only in a social context, as part of a culture, in a milieu" (TL 105). Also, "aesthetic institutions are social institutions" (TL 94) (cf. Tomars, 1941).[16] However, the stipulation is upheld that "the most immediate setting of a work" is "its linguistic and literary tradition"; "only far less directly can literature be connected with concrete economic, political, and social situations." At most, "the social situation" "seems to determine the possibility of the realization of certain aesthetic values, but not the values themselves" (TL 106).

The concern here is again how to "isolate the strictly literary factor" (TL 108) and how to deal with the general divergence between literary versus sociological methodology. "The 'sociology of knowledge'" as developed by Weber and Mannheim,[17] for example, though it can help "draw attention to the presuppositions and implications of a given ideological position" and "to the hidden assumptions and biases of the investigator," is mistrusted because of the "skeptical conclusions" arising from its "excessive historicism" and because of its "inability to connect 'content' with 'form'" (TL 108). So it cannot "provide a rational foundation for aesthetics and hence criticism and evaluation."

"The most common approach to the relations of literature and society" is to "study" "works" as "assumed pictures of social reality" (TL 102). Yet "though some kind of dependence of literary ideologies and themes on social circumstances seems obvious, the social origins of forms and styles, genres and actual literary norms have rarely been established" (TL 109). And "only if the social determination of forms could be shown conclusively could the question be raised whether social attitudes" can "enter a work of art as effective parts of its artistic value." Occasionally, "social truth" might "corroborate" "artistic values." But "there is great literature which has little or no social relevance"; "social literature is only one kind" and "is not central in the theory of literature unless one holds the view that literature is primarily an 'imitation' of life" —a view which (as we saw, p. 30) is energetically rebutted: "art not merely reproduces life but shapes it" (TL 102). We must "know the artistic method of the artist studied," for instance, whether it is "realistic" or "romantic" (TL 104).

---

[16] Even "traditional literary devices" like "symbolism and metre" are pointedly declared "social in their very nature" (TL 94), though such a view has hardly affected literary studies. Compare Plekhanov (1936) on symbolism.

[17] Mannheim's approach is cited with sympathy by Bleich (SC 25f) and Jauss (TAR 40), but with disapproval by Hirsch (AIM 147) and Jameson (PU 236, 249).

Finally, "the sociology of the writer" might be pursued in terms of "the profession and institutions of literature" (TL 95). The most conspicuous contributor would be "Marxist criticism," which "at its best," "exposes implied, or latent, social implications of a writer's work" (TL 107).[18] Not surprisingly, though, the overall estimation of such research is unfavorable. "Marxism never answers the question of the degree of dependence of literature on society" (TL 109). "Marxists" "attempt far too crude short cuts from economy to literature" and often "fail to deal concretely with either the ascertainable social content" of a writer's works, "his professed opinions on political questions," or "his social status as a writer" (TL 106). "The 'vulgar Marxist'" perpetrates the "curious contradiction" of a "determinism which assumes that 'consciousness' must follow 'existence,'" that a bourgeois cannot help being one," and an "ethical judgment which condemns him for these very opinions" (TL 107).

Marx himself is called in to testify that "'certain periods of highest development of art stand in no direct relationship with the general development of society, nor with the material basis and the skeleton structure of its organization'" (TL 107). Marx "understood that the modern division of labour leads to a definite contradiction between the three factors ('moments' in his Hegelian terminology) of the social process—'productive forces,' 'social relations,' and 'consciousness.'" "He expected" in a "Utopian" "manner" that "in the future classless society, these divisions of labour would again disappear" and "the artist" would be "integrated into" a "society" with "communal art" (TL 107, 100). In consequence, Wellek and Warren suspect "Marxist critics" of being "not only students of literature and society, but prophets of the future, monitors, propagandists" (TL 95). Some of this hostility may be aroused by the Marxist tendencies to be "essentially relativistic," to repudiate "humanism" and "the universality of art," and to apply "nonliterary" "criteria" (TL 107, 95).

If Wellek and Warren are skeptical about sociology, they are even more reserved about applying psychology to literature.[19] As literary scholars, they typically apply the term "psychology" to Freudian and Jungian psychoanalysis, though behavioral psychology is mentioned in passing (e.g. TL 154, 178).[20] Four

---

[18] Plekhanov's (1936) view of "'art for art's sake'" as a depair with social change is cited here (TL 101), though without the emphatic endorsement appended by Jameson (MF 386). Another commonality is the idea of combining Marx and Freud (TL 108f), to which Jameson devotes a whole volume (PU).

[19] Wellek says: "much in the Psychology chapter could not have been written by me" (letter). Spitzer (1958: 371) argues that "'psychological stylistics applies only to writers'" "'of the eighteenth and later centuries,'" who cultivated "'an individual manner of writing'" (TL 183).

[20] The "behaviorists" are decried for "defining as 'mystical' or 'metaphysical' anything which does not conform to a very limited conception of empirical reality"; and for holding "a bad theory of abstraction" plus an "absurd theory" of "reading" being done by "the vocal cords" (TL 153f, 144). Yet the view that "reading" does not "break" "printed words" "into sequences of phonemes" (TL 154) is not shared by a number of recent psychologists (cf. Beaugrande 1984a: 224 for summary and references).

possible objects of "psychological study" are envisioned: "the writer as type and as individual," "the creative process," "the psychological types and laws present within works," and "the effects of literature upon its readers" (TL 81). Only the "types and laws" are claimed to "belong, in the strictest sense, to literary study." The reader gets relegated to a later chapter on "literature and society," as if real readers should enter the picture only as a group or mass, and not, as in the work of Holland, Bleich, or Paris, as individual personalities.

Studies of the "writer" and the "creative process" may be "engaging pedagogical approaches," but must not encourage "any attempt to evaluate literary works in terms of their origins." This formulation reveals the root of Wellek and Warren's mistrust: psychology might relativize or undermine the passing of value judgments. Reservations are voiced against critics like Arnold and Saintsbury, "who elaborately confounded psychological problems with problems of literary evaluation" (TL 178). Following a "shift of interest to the individual taste of the reader," "most scholars" evinced an "astonishing helplessness" about "evaluating a work of art" (TL 139).

The author's creative personality is a complex issue. The Freudian outlook is handled with caution, because it projects a gloomy portrait—a descendant of the ancient myth that "the poet" is "productively mad" (TL 205). Freud "thought of the author as an obdurate neurotic, who, by his creative work, kept himself from a crack-up but also from any real cure" (TL 82). "'The artist'" "'turns from reality because he cannot come to terms with the demand for the renunciation of instinctual satisfaction,'" and "in fantasy-life allows full play to his erotic and ambitious wishes.'" "He moulds his fantasies into a new kind of reality'"—a process likened (as by Fiedler and Frye) to the composition of a "dream"[21]—but "'without creating real alterations in the outer world.'" Wellek and Warren are uneasy about considering "the poet" a "day-dreamer who is socially validated": "instead of altering his character, he perpetuates and publishes his fantasies." Unlike "the day-dreamer," the writer "is engaged in an act of externalization and of adjustment to society." Besides, writers "have not wanted to be 'cured' or 'adjusted'" in order to stop writing or to accept a "philistine," "bourgeois" "social environment" (TL 83).

No doubt the view of authors as neurotic is part of a commonplace reaction to people questioning established reality, or proposing alternatives (cf. Ch. 2, 6). But to explain literature away in this fashion is to deflect its major purpose of influencing everyday awareness. Moreover, we need to contemplate not just the actual personalities of authors, but the "persona" or image they project. One

---

[21] Wellek and Warren however "question whether a poet has ever been so uncritical of his images" as the "dream" process is (TL 207) (cf. Rosenberg, 1931). Nietzsche's "most influential of modern polarities" "between Apollo and Dionysus" is made parallel to that between "dream" and "ecstatic inebriation," whereas Frye puts "dreams" on the "Dionysiac" side (TL 85; AC 214). For Fiedler, a "dreamlike style" may excuse a book's being "maddeningly disorganized" (LD 155, 157).

author might cultivate the image of the "possessed," "obsessive, prophetic poet," driven by an "obsessively held vision of life,"[22] whereas another would try to appear a "trained, skilled, responsible craftsman," exerting "conscious precise care for the presentation of that vision" (TL 84f). Or, "in the work of a subjective poet, we have a manifest personality far more coherent and all-pervasive than that of persons as we see them in everyday situations" (TL 24). Yet "there are obvious reasons why self-conscious artists speak as though their art were impersonal" (TL 88).

As for writing itself, "any modern treatment of the creative process will chiefly concern the relative parts played by the unconscious and the conscious mind" (TL 88). "The experience of the author" includes not just "conscious experience" and "intentions," but "the total conscious and unconscious experience during the prolonged time of creation" (TL 148). "The poet" "speaks" "out of" an "unconscious" that is both "sub- and super-rational" (TL 81). "The Jungian thesis that beneath the individual unconscious—the blocked-off residue of our past" — "lies the 'collective unconscious,'" favored the notion that the author "retains an archaic trait of the race" and "recapitulates" or "preserves" a "strata of the race-history" (TL 83f) (cf. Jaensch, 1930; Eliot, 1933; Chase, 1945).

One such phenomenon might be "synaesthesia," the "linking" of "perception out of two or more senses," as a "survival from an earlier comparatively un-differentiated sensorium" (TL 83). Another might be a "special integration of perceptual and conceptual," allowing the "unconscious" to make a "central contribution" of "visual" and "auditory" "imagery" (TL 83, 208, 188). However, it would be "mistaken" to suppose that "the poet must have literally perceived whatever he can imagine"; or that the "imagery" constitutes "a hieroglyphic report" on his or her "psychic health" (TL 207ff).

Composition is roughly described as "the associative linkage of word with word," plus "the association of the objects to which our mental 'ideas' refer," "the chief categories" being "contiguity in time and place, and similarity or dis-similarity" (TL 89; cf. Ch. 1).[23] But we get few operational details about the "creative process" in its "entire sequence from the subconscious origins of a literary work to those last revisions which, with some writers, are the most genuinely creative part of the whole" (TL 85). The inclination to see the "sub-conscious" or "unconscious" at work during "origins" or "inspiration" (TL 85f) may be fostered by our lack of theories and data about that phase of mentation. The "authors" themselves prefer to "discuss conscious and technical procedures,

---

[22] In Poe's case, "obsessive themes" are said to be "provided" by "the unconscious" and "literarily developed" by "the conscious" (TL 88). Compare the description of writing later in this chapter.

[23] Saussure (1916) has a similar terminology. We may also recall Jakobson's division between metonymy and metaphor, which may however violate Wellek and Warren's warning that "the psychological question should not be confused with the analysis of the poet's metaphorical devices" (TL 195, 27).

for which they may claim credit" (TL 88). Yet even a full and accurate account of an author's thoughts might not resolve the problem of a possible "distinction between the mental structure of a poet and the composition of a poem, between impression and expression" (TL 86).

A different application of psychology would be to scrutinize the personalities of literary characters (cf. Ch. 11). We might examine the "connection between characterization (literary method) and characterology (theories of character, personality types)" beyond global contrasts like "flat" versus "round" or sentimental clichés like "blonde" "home-maker" versus "passionate," "mysterious" "brunette" (TL 33, 219f).[24] "One cognitive value in the drama and novels" would be to reveal "human nature," as Horney believed about the works of "Dostoyevsky, Shakespeare, Ibsen, and Balzac" (TL 33). However, the notion that an author's characters are all his or her "potential selves" (TL 90) needs clarification. If we learn that the "four brothers Karamazov are all aspects of Dostoyevsky" (TL 90), are we to read his novel as autobiography, or his life as novel, or both? Are we to assume a trade-off, such as: "the more numerous and separate his characters, the less definite his own 'personality'"? Lest "psychologists" "use the novel only for its generalized typical value," Wellek and Warren warn that "the writer must be doing far more than putting down a case history": "he must be either dealing with an archetypal pattern" "or with a 'neurotic personality' pattern widespread in our time" (TL 33, 82).

At the reader's end, the main focus ought to fall on the "concretizations[25] of a given work of art" (TL 155). We might "reconstruct" these "from the reports of critics and readers about their experiences and judgments." Critics are presumably "'the right kind of reader'" that I.A. Richards (1924: 225ff) considered the basis for a "psychological theory" (cf. TL 147),[26] provided we had a model for analyzing the origins and effects of such "reports."

Yet Wellek and Warren raise copious and emphatic objections against any such model. They avow that "the psychology of the reader" "will always remain outside the object of literary study—the concrete work of art—and is unable to deal with the question of the structure and value of the work" (TL 147). They exhort us not to "put the essence of the poem into a momentary experience

---

[24] "Flat" and "round" are Forster's (1927) terms; compare p. 216. This stereotyping of women by hair color is a recurrent theme in Fiedler's analysis of the "American novel," whose authors used such types to skirt the problem of protraying real women (p. 92).

[25] A citation from Jauss may be helpful: "by concretization, Vodička means the picture of the work in the consciousness of those 'for whom the work is an aesthetic object'" (TAR 73). Iser uses the same term in a comparably phenomenological sense (p. 140).

[26] For Wellek and Warren, Richards' "extreme psychological theory" is "in flat contradiction to his excellent critical practice" (TL 147). For Bleich, the "subjective factors that Richards acknowledged" are the main contribution to "literary hermeneutics," one that gets "omitted from conscious consideration in his practice" (SC 34). Wellek tells me that a refutation of Richards appears in the fifth volume of his *History of Modern Criticism*.

which even the right kind of reader could not repeat unchanged" (TL 147). Such an approach must "fall short of the full meaning of a poem" and "add inevitable personal elements," "something instantaneous and extraneous," "something purely idiosyncratic and purely individual" (TL 146f). The reader's "mood," "education," "personality," and "religion," along with "philosophical" and "technical preoccupations," thereby mix with the work. Grave perils are evoked here: not merely "the absurd conclusion that a poem is nonexistent unless experienced and recreated in every experience,"[27] and the inability to "correct" an "interpretation" or to "explain why one experience of the poem should be better"; but also "complete skepticism and anarchy," plus "the definite end of all teaching of literature which aims at enhancing the understanding and appreciation of a text" (TL 146).

The motive for such vehemence must be the intense commitment to values, as noted (p. 40), joined with the thesis that a "complete confusion of values is the result of every psychological theory" (TL 147). The emotional aspect within "the individual reactions of a reader" is especially disparaged as unreliable: "describing some emotional similarity of our reactions" will "never" be capable of "verification" and will never lead "to a cooperative advance in our knowledge" (TL 128). "Merely emotional 'appreciation'" is equated with "complete subjectivity" (TL 18). Conventional critics are chided for having "recourse to an emotive language describing the effects of a work of art on a reader in terms incapable of real correlation with the work itself" (TL 253). "Tears," "laughs," and a "thrill down our spine" are picked as illustrations.

The neglect of cognition in the psychology of that time no doubt encouraged the suspicion that "every psychological theory" "must be unrelated either to the structure or the quality" of a text (TL 147). The two critics grant as "true, of course, that the poem can be known only through individual experiences" (TL 146). But they argue that "we recognize a structure of norms within reality and do not simply invent verbal constructs" (TL 154). "The objection that we can have access to norms only through individual acts of cognition" "can be refuted with Kantian arguments." We are "liable to misunderstanding" "these norms," and cannot profess to "assume a superhuman role of criticizing our comprehension from outside," or to "grasp the perfect whole of the system." But we can still "criticize a part of our knowledge in the light of the higher standard set by another part" (an idea expanded by Hirsch, p. 109f).

As we have seen, Wellek and Warren's "theory of literature" is a transitional vision documenting the early stages of that domain, and is thus nicely suited to start off our survey. They were understandably anxious to keep theory close to its object, the literary work. This center of gravity supported their organization of

---

[27] Precisely this "conclusion" is Bleich's starting point: "no work even exists unless someone is reading it" (SC 109). A similar thesis, quoted in later chapters, is voiced by Hirsch (VAL 14), Iser (AR 34), and Bloom (BF 8f) (pp. 109, 196, 284).

concepts, but minimized the importance of certain issues that have since come to the fore. Similarly, a powerful interest in evaluation and correctness fostered a deep mistrust of theories devoted to the mental activities of people who produce and receive literary texts. When contemplating methods they do not favor, Wellek and Warren are moved to premonitions of "danger" and "anarchy" (TL 42f, 129, 142, 146f, 156, 182, 193, 212).

Nonetheless, the cautionary or conservative aspects of the book by no means signal its main achievement. It covered a breathtaking range of past work and offered a substantial list of future tasks that "have scarcely begun to be studied" (TL 109; cf. TL 102, 122, 129, 161, 260). Some of these seem conventionally literary endeavors, though rather ambitious, such as to produce "histories" of "English poetic diction," "genres," "national literature" (not using "simply geographical or linguistic categories"), and indeed of whole "groups of literatures" (TL 260f, 53, 268). The centrality and specialness of literature would be best preserved if scholars could "trace the history of literature as an art, in comparative isolation from its social history, the biographies of authors, or the appreciation of individual works" (TL 254). Other tasks extend far beyond literary studies, such as to probe "the wide diversity of standard pronunciations" and "stratified speech" in "different ages and places"; or to "trace the social status of the intelligentsia," "the prestige of the writer in each society," and "the degree of dependence of literature on society" (TL 161, 177, 98, 109). Still more imposing are these unanswered questions: "how ideas actually enter into literature"; "how" "literature affects its audience"; "how" "all the arts in a given time or setting expand or narrow their fields over the objects of 'nature'"; "how norms of art are tied to specific social classes"; or "how aesthetic values change with social revolutions" (TL 122, 102, 129).

"After all," Wellek and Warren conclude, "we are only beginning to learn how to analyze a work of art in its integrity; we are still very clumsy in our methods, and their basis in theory is constantly shifting" (TL 268). Now, several decades later, none but a hardy soul would declare we have left all this far behind us. But as I hope to demonstrate, we have attained a steadily more refined and comprehensive awareness of the scope and necessity of "theory of literature."

5

Northrop Frye[1]

Like Wellek and Warren's *Theory*,[2] Frye's *Anatomy* is a milestone in the advent of critical theory. Both books confront the problems of categorizing the diversity of literary issues. But whereas Wellek and Warren's types are for sorting out critical methods, Frye's types are both for methods and for literary works themselves, and are thus even more elaborately tailored to concrete instances. Classifying both methods and works exerts diverse, sometimes conflicting pressures on Frye during his spirited campaign to balance the general against the specific, or the universal against the idiosyncratic. His ambition to situate and label so many branches of literary creation and tradition without suppressing their individuality leads to more complicated schematics than any other among our sample critics has produced. He purports to present not a "system" or "theory" as such, but an "interconnected group of suggestions" concerning "the possibility of a synoptic view of the scope, theory, principles, and techniques of literary criticism" (AC 3).

For Frye, "the freedom of man is inseparably bound up with the acceptance of his cultural heritage," "culture" being "provisionally defined as the total body of imaginative hypothesis in a society and its tradition" (AC 349, 127). "Criticism" is "an essential part" of "liberal education," one without which the "public" "brutalizes the arts and loses its cultural memory" (AC 4). If "there is no real correlation between the merit of art and the degree of public response to it," "the critic" must be "the pioneer of education and the shaper of cultural tradition." And since "culture" "insists on its totality," "the social task of the 'intellectual'" is "to defend the autonomy of culture" against "subordination to a total synthesis of

---

[1] The key for Frye citations is AC: *Anatomy of Criticism* (1957). I use the third paperback edition (1973). As with Wellek and Warren's *Theory*, I limit myself to one major work because of its enormous impact.

[2] Commonalities with Wellek and Warren's book (which Frye's never mentions) are numerous: that literary study should be self-centered, and both is and is not scientific; that history and chronology have been the only systematic areas so far; that causal explanation is not appropriate; that literary creativity is partly unconscious, and psychology is chiefly psychoanalysis; that the literary work is a self-contained verbal structure whose truth is not factual; that poetry is the center of literature; that the author is not the best interpreter of the work; and that sociological values diverge from literary ones.

any kind, religious or political" (AC 127). For "criticism" to be "a field of genuine learning," "no definitive positions" should be "taken": they could be "the source of one's liability to error and prejudice." (AC 19). Instead, "intellectual freedom" lies in "transvaluation": "the ability to look at contemporary social values with the detachment of one who is able to compare them with the infinite vision of possibilities presented by culture" (AC 348).

Frye calls for a "comprehensive view of what" "literary criticism" "actually is doing" (AC 12). "The varied interests of critics" should be "related to a central expanding pattern of systematic comprehension." "Scholars and public critics" would then be "related by an intermediate form of criticism, a coherent and comprehensive theory of literature, logically and scientifically organized" and "fulfilling the systematic and progressive element in research by assimilating its work into a unified structure of knowledge" (AC 11). Although Frye recognizes many types of criticism, he is not content to "stop with a purely relative and pluralistic position," but argues "that there is a finite number of valid critical methods, and that they can all be contained in a single theory" (AC 72).

As an "'ideal reader,'" "the critic" can "reforge broken links between creation and knowledge, art and science, myth and concept" (AC 354). Hence, "literary criticism has a central place" in the "swirl of intellectual activities" in "communication, symbolism, semantics, linguistics, metalinguistics, pragmatics, cybernetics," and "dozens of other fields" (AC 350).[3] However, Frye (again like Wellek and Warren) does not expect such "fields" to take the place of a properly literary theory. He warns against the "undertow" whereby "all the neighboring disciplines have moved" into "the power vacuum" "created" by "the absence of systematic criticism" (AC 12). "The barriers" between various "methods of criticism" are blamed for making "a critic" "establish his primary contacts" "with subjects outside criticism" —"barriers" Frye proposes to "break down" with a program that "assumes a larger context of literature as a whole" (AC 341, 134). "The critic must enter into relations" with such "neighbors" in ways which "guarantee his own independence" (AC 19). Yet if "nearly every work of art in the past had a social function in its own time" that "was often not primarily an aesthetic function at all" (AC 344), a purely literary "criticism" that would not be "the application of a social attitude" (AC 22) seems problematic. Even "the question of whether a thing 'is' a work of art" is decided not by "something in the nature of thing itself," but by "convention" and "social acceptance" (AC 345).

This ambivalence about what to include or exclude extends to Frye's view of science. On one side, he portrays "criticism" as "an art" because its "subject-matter" "is an art" and because its "center" is an "incommunicable experience" (AC 27f, 3; cf. AC 8). Thus, "the critic" "need waste no time emulating the natural sciences" (AC 19). On the other side, he reassures us that "the mental

---

[3] An interchange with "mathematics" is prominently suggested at the conclusion of the book (AC 350ff). The other disciplines are not pursued at all.

process involved" in "seriously studying literature" is "as coherent and progressive as the study of science" (AC 19, 10f). "A precisely similar training of mind" and "sense of the unity of the subject" are entailed (AC 11). "The presence of science" "changes" "the casual to the causal," "the random and intuitive to the systematic, as well as safeguarding the integrity of that subject from external invasions" (AC 7). Hence, the "scientific element in criticism" can "distinguish it from literary parasitism" and "superposed critical attitude."

Frye grants that this goal is not yet realized. Whereas "science begins" with "naive induction" and then takes an "inductive leap" to a "new vantage ground" so as to "see its former data as new things to be explained," "literary criticism" persists in a "state of naive induction" (AC 15). "Its materials, the masterpieces of literature, are not yet regarded as phenomena to be explained," but rather as "the framework or structure of criticism" (AC 15f). There is no "coordinating principle," no "central hypothesis," and no "sense of consolidating progress which belongs to a science" (AC 16, 8). "Literature" is conceived as an "enumerative bibliography" and an "aggregate" of "discrete 'works' "; the only "organizing principle" "so far" is "chronology" (AC 16).

"A systematic study alternates between inductive experience and deductive principles"; but "in criticism," only "some of the induction" is provided by "rhetorical analysis," while "the deductive counterpart," namely "poetics, the theory of criticism," is "underdeveloped" —so that "the critic is thrown back on prejudice derived from his existence as a social being" (AC 21f). To rectify this situation, Frye vows to "proceed deductively" and to stress "the schematic nature" of his book despite the "strong emotional repugnance felt by many critics toward any form of schematization in poetics" (AC 29).

This project casts doubt on his palliative maneuver of denying that his highly original approach involves any "change of direction or activity in criticism" or any "new program for critics," but merely "a new perspective on their existing programs," which "are valid enough" (AC 354, 341). He says his "book" "attacks no methods of criticism" (AC 341), but my impression is rather different. He diagnoses a whole gallery of "fallacies" (AC 4, 6, 17, 21, 36, 63, 86, 88, 108, 113, 132, 230, 332, 349). Behind their portentous labels[4]—the "intentional fallacy," "the fallacy" of "determinism," "the Archimedes fallacy," "the representational fallacy," "the pathetic fallacy," "the fallacy of premature teleology," the "fallacy" of " 'existential projection,' " the "fallacy of misplaced concreteness," "the fallacy" of the "mythological contract," and the like—they consist mainly of relating literature to something external, either to outside reality or to some specialized

---

[4] Some of these are of course traditional, such as the "pathetic fallacy" of Ruskin (1856) (AC 36). The "intentional fallacy," which de Man is alarmed to find as a "methodological cornerstone" in Frye's "system" (BI 25), is explained as a "failure to make the most elementary of all distinctions in literature," that "between fiction and fact, hypothesis and assertion, imaginative and discursive writing" (AC 86). If so, Hirsch's method is aimed at the wrong discourse type altogether, which I shall indeed argue in Ch. 7.

theory (AC 86, 113, 6, 12, 132, 36, 17, 63, 89, 108; cf. AC 21, 332). The most basic fallacy is thus "imposing on literature an extra-literary schematism" (AC 7).

Despite his professed distaste for "anti-critical criticism" (AC 3), Frye launches a barrage of further charges. Some critics are "restricted to ritual masonic gestures," "cryptic comments and other signs of an understanding too occult for syntax" (AC 4). Some dispense "sonorous nonsense" in "generalities, reflective comments," and "ideological perorations" (AC 18). Others "have" "a mystery-religion without a gospel" and "communicate, or quarrel, only with one another" (AC 14). Still others suffer from imposing a "religio-political color-filter" or "a limited historical context" (AC 7, 62). Matters seem to get worse in modern times, when "the assimilation of literature to private enterprise" has "concealed so many of the facts of criticism"; and when the "provincialism" of our "ironic age" looks only for "objectivity" in "literature" and makes "major arts" out of "advertising and propaganda" (AC 97, 62, 47; cf. AC 65f, 135, 214, 323).

Frye's reversion to classical and medieval theories indicates a determination to avoid these modern flaws. Since "the Middle Ages, when a precise scheme" "was taken over from theology and applied to literature," "criticism" "has seldom" "squarely faced" the idea that "a work of literary art contains a variety or sequence of meanings" (AC 72). "Today," this idea is only "established" by the "simultaneous development of several different schools of modern criticism." And this development too has a negative aspect. Whereas "scholarship" "admits the principle of polysemous meaning," "pedantry" "chooses one of these groups and then tries to prove that all the others are less legitimate." In later chapters, we will see more "pedantry" than "scholarship" among our critics (cf. Ch. 3, 19). Even Frye has favorites (especially "archetypal" criticism), though he is unusually syncretistic.

The greatest vehemence of Frye's invective is aimed at the very activity Wellek and Warren declared the true goal of criticism, namely evaluation. Frye's motives are far more complex than the commonplace intent to hide one's own values. His project for imposing order and categories upon criticism hinges on "separating" the whole superstructure from the "relative and subjective" (AC 18). "Value judgments" constitute "casual, sentimental, and prejudiced" bits of "meaningless criticism" that "cannot help to build a systematic structure of knowledge" (AC 18, 20). "Our natural likes and dislikes have nothing to do" with "working on a solid structural basis" (AC 215). "Whatever vacillates or reacts" "cannot be part of any systematic study" and belongs only to "the history of taste, where there are no facts" (AC 18).[5] "The attempt to introduce a value-judgment into a definition," for instance of "poetry," only engenders fresh "confusion" (AC 71).

---

[5] "We cannot correlate popularity and value," since even a "person of critical ability" can "experience profound pleasure from something" of "low critical valuation" (AC 117, 28). "The direct value-judgment of informed good taste" can signal "the disciplined response of a highly organized nervous system to the impact of poetry"; but "the accuracy" of "good taste is no guarantee that its inductive basis in literary experience is adequate" (AC 27f).

Frye's motives for excluding evaluation evidently go beyond disavowing "the limitations and prejudices" of "contemporary taste" (AC 9). He conjectures that "every deliberately constructed hierarchy of values in literature" is "based on a concealed social, moral, or intellectual analogy" (AC 23). Like Fiedler and Bleich, Frye insists that criticism should not be a "moral" enterprise in the everyday sense, and that "moral" standards are inappropriate for literary works (AC 26f, 33, 50, 38, 120, 127, 156, 167, 181, 196, 211, 229). He prefers an "ethical criticism" striving for a "conception of the total and simultaneous possession of past culture" and a "steady advance toward undiscriminating catholicity" (AC 21, 24f). "The real level of culture and of liberal education" is "the dialectical axis of criticism," having "as one pole the total acceptance of the data of literature, and as the other the total acceptance of the potential of those data" (AC 25). "Aesthetics" could thereby "learn to do what ethics has already done" (AC 26).

A further, closely related, motive is to rehabilitate certain traditionally devalued kinds of literature by designing more suitable categories for them. Frye complains that critics have not appreciated works of a given type, but misprized them as bad examples of another. "In nearly every period of literature," for instance, "there are many romances, confessions, and anatomies that are neglected only because the categories to which they belong are unrecognized" (AC 312). "A novel-centered conception of fiction" led critics to diagnose "carelessness," "defects," and "shapelessness" in such forms (AC 310, 305, 313). Frye retorts that being "typical" or "central" for some "form of fiction" does not justify "an estimate of merit"; nor does being more "fully realized" and "distinctive" entail being "better" (AC 304, 265). However, "one great" work frequently provides the "norm" for "theories," as happened with "tragedy" (AC 212) (p. 18). Even works following "superficial and inorganic conventions" can be "of great value to archetypal criticism" (AC 104). Still, Frye's own values interact with his categories, which is probably inevitable.

Using such arguments, Frye declines to remedy the situation that "no critical theory known to me takes any real account" of "different systems of valuation" (AC 28f). He is content if "the theory of literature takes values for granted" and leaves them "silent," "not directly communicated," making no attempt to "establish or prove" (AC 23, 50, 20, 25). He does not try to correct the "graphic formulas" which tend to guide "value-assumptions," for example, that "the concrete is better than the abstract," "the dynamic better than the static, the unified better than the multiple," and so on (AC 336), though his own position on such categories is more circumspect.[6] He does, however, address evaluation when he surmises that "the profound masterpiece draws us to a point at which we seem to

---

[6] Frye firmly endorses "unity" (p. 74), but does not take sides on these other pairs. "The fusion of the concrete and the abstract" is attributed to "all ages of poetry," and the same pair is aligned with "symbolism" and "allegory," respectively, though the "mythical" is judged "abstract" (AC 281, 89, 134, 136, 139). The opposition between dynamic versus static corresponds to that between "mythos" and "dianoia" (AC 83).

see an enormous number of converging patterns of significance" (AC 17). Or, he says that "poetry" goes beyond being "merely incidental to various social aims, to propaganda, to amusement, to devotion, to instruction" if it attains "an objective and disinterested element" in its "vision of human life," and thus "gains" "an authority based, like the authority of science, on the vision of nature as an impersonal order" (AC 319).

Perhaps values like these are being silently applied when he refers to the "greatest" "examples," "the greatest poets" or "the most admired and advanced poets of the twentieth century," "the noblest diction," "the chief ironic epic of our time," and so on (AC 219, 221, 273, 210, 323). Or, high values may go to the works and authors that best exemplify Frye's categories, as when Milton's "best" "prose" is his most "musical" in the odd sense Frye gives the term (AC 266).[7] At least, aptness for illustration must have been the standard whereby he was "rigorously selective in examples" (AC 29).

Like most theorists, Frye both asserts the overall value of literature as an institution and offers a theoretical justification for it. Just as "art" is "central to events and ideas," "literature" is "central to the arts" (AC 243). "The archetypal view," which we will encounter later (p. 59f), "shows us" the "literary experience as a part of the continuum of life" (AC 115). The "anagogical view" is even grander: "literature" "contains life and reality in a system of verbal relationships"; and "'life'" is "a vast mass of potential literary forms" (AC 122). Similarly, "poetry unites" "unlimited social action" with "unlimited individual thought" (AC 120). "Poetry imitates" "the action of an omnipotent human society that contains all the powers of nature." "The vast encyclopedic structure of poetry" "seems to be a whole world in itself" and "stands in its culture as an inexhaustible storehouse of imaginative suggestion." This "perspective is not to be confined only to works that seem to take in everything"; "any poem" "we happen to be reading" can be "the center of the literary universe," "a microcosm of all literature, an individual manifestation of the total order of words" (AC 121). Hence, "we could get a whole liberal education by picking" "one poem" and "following its archetypes through literature" (AC 100, 121).

Though Frye concedes "we have no real standards to distinguish a verbal structure that is literary from one that is not," he proposes a division between "two modes of understanding" that "take place in all reading" (AC 13, 74). He describes them spatially as "two directions" in which "attention" "moves" (AC 73). One is "inward" or "centripetal," based on "a sense of the larger verbal pattern"; the other is "outward" or "centrifugal," based on "the representation of natural objects and ideas" (AC 73f). He suggests that "inward" is "the final

---

[7] In one of his more wilful terminological skirmishes, Frye ordains that "musical" shall apply to "sharp barking accents, crabbed, obscure language, mouthfuls of consonants, and long lumbering polysyllables" (AC 256). "A careful balancing of vowels and consonants and a dreamy sensuous flow" are "unmusical," and assertions to the contrary are merely "sentimental" (AC 255).

direction of meaning" in "literature," and "outward" is "final" in "descriptive" or "assertive writing" deployed by "the active will and the conscious mind" to "'say' something" (AC 74, 76, 5).

As he often does, Frye advances this division only to attenuate it again. If "grammar" is "words in the right" "order," and "logic" is "words arranged in a pattern with significance," then "assertive" or "descriptive" writing "attempts to be a direct union of grammar and logic" (AC 245). But this "direct union," projected by "the notion that logic was the formal cause of language,"[8] "does not, in the long run, exist" (AC 331). For Frye, "all structures in words are partly rhetorical, and hence literary" (AC 350). "Our literary universe" "expands into a verbal universe," evoking the prospect that "the verbal structure of psychology, anthropology, theology, history, law, and everything else built out of words" may have been "informed and constructed by the same kind of myths and metaphors we find, in their original hypothetical form, in literature" (AC 350, 352).

Still, literature has its distinctive place as "a body of hypothetical verbal structures" "standing between the verbal structures that describe or arrange actual events or histories, and those that describe or arrange actual ideas or represent physical objects, like philosophy and science" (AC 79, 71, 245). This "body of hypothetical creations" "may enter into any kind" of "imaginative" "relationship" to "truth and fact" (AC 92, 74). At one "pole" is "the mimetic tendency" toward "verisimilitude," and at the other "myth," the latter "gradually becoming attracted toward the plausible" (AC 51). Yet "mimesis" already enacts "an emancipation of externality into image, nature into art" (AC 113).

To Frye's surprise, "it has never been consistently understood that the ideas of literature are not real propositions, but verbal formulas which imitate real propositions" —"one could hardly find a more elementary critical principle" (AC 84f). "Literary works" "are not true or false": "questions of fact or truth are subordinated to the primary literary aim of producing a structure of words for its own sake, and the sign-values of symbols are subordinated to their importance as structures of interconnected motifs" (AC 74). "Literature" is thus "a specialized form of language," consisting of "autonomous verbal structures." Although "descriptive meaning" is among its "subordinate aspects," literature conveys "ideas" that are "dull when stated as propositions," yet "rich and variegated as structural principles" (AC 82, 103). By the same token, many "phenomena," such as "paranomasia," represent "an obstacle in discursive writing," yet "a structural principle in literature" (AC 332).

Frye follows the "authority of Aristotle" in using "poem" as a "synecdoche" for any "work of literary art" (AC 71). This broad usage lends force to the claims that "the events and ideas of poetry are hypothetical imitations of history and discur-

---

[8] Frye vows to "work as independently as he can" from "symbolic logic" when exploring "literary meaning" (AC 72). Tensions between speech-act logic and literary theory are discussed by Iser (AR 54-62).

sive writing respectively, which are in their turn verbal imitations of action and thought"; and that "the poet never imitates life," because "life" "becomes" "the content of his work" (AC 113, 63). But elsewhere, Frye seems to mean only poetry as the most tightly organized verbal structure: "the forms in which" "poetry organizes the content of the world" "come out of the structure of poetry itself"; "the poet" "aims" "only at inner verbal strength," rather than "morality, truth, and beauty"; "poetic ambiguity" arises because "the poet does not define his words but establishes their powers by placing them in a great variety of contexts" and by "associating words similar in sound and sense"; and so on (AC 102, 113, 334). For Frye, "the lyric" "most clearly shows the hypothetical core of literature, narrative, and meaning in their literal aspects as word-order and word-pattern" (AC 271). Befitting the idea that "poetry is a *disinterested* use of words: it does not address a reader directly," "lyric is the genre in which the poet" "turns his back on his audience" (AC 4, 271; cf. AC 249f).

In contrast to Fiedler and the Yale group, Frye makes it clear that criticism cannot equal literature or poetry. Trying to "bring the direct experience of literature" —"where every act is unique and classification has no place" —"into the structure of criticism produces the aberrations of the history of taste" (AC 28f). The converse, trying to "bring criticism into the direct experience, will destroy the integrity of both." The "experience" can't be "new and fresh" "each time "if the poem itself has been replaced by a critical view" of it. "Direct experience" is "the basis of critical apologetics" and "central to criticism, yet forever excluded from it," and "can never" be "recaptured or included" in "critical terminology" (AC 27, 10).

Reciprocally, "criticism is a structure of thought and knowledge existing in its own right" and claiming "autonomy" and "independence from the art it deals with" (AC 5f). "Criticism is to art what history is to action, and philosophy to wisdom: a verbal imitation of a human productive power which in itself does not speak" (AC 12). "Criticism" "has to exist" because it "can talk, and all the arts are dumb" (AC 4). This self-sufficiency is further buttressed by disbarring "the notion that the poet necessarily is or could be the definitive interpreter of himself" (AC 6). "The poet speaking as critic produces not criticism, but documents to be examined by critics" (AC 6).[9] "The more sharply we distinguish the poetic and the critical functions, the easier it is for us to take seriously what great writers said about their work" (AC 122).

If, as Frye ordains, in "the literary universe" "everything is potentially identical with everything else," and "all poetry" "proceeds as though all poetic images were contained within a single universal body" (AC 124f), he needs a highly flexible schematics for breaking literature down into types. The reviewer (quoted on the book jacket) who pronounced it "hopeless to attempt a brief summary of

---

[9] "Anagogical criticism," however, "is to be discovered chiefly in the more uninhibited utterances of the poets themselves" (AC 122).

Mr. Frye's dazzlingly counterpointed classifications" must have felt the vertigo of the book's exuberant, encyclopedic superstructuring. In trying to assign each type or phenomenon its own place, Frye risks a diffusion the mind can no longer survey or control.

My concern will therefore be to bring out some major tactics in Frye's "anatomizing," at the obvious expense of blurring details. I believe his procedures essentially oscillate between centripetal and centrifugal movements to concentrate or disperse masses of exemplars inside mainly spatial constructs. The creation of these constructs is another such oscillation, since their proliferation is balanced against an insistent suggestion of "parallels" from one to another (AC 35, 40, 116, 152, 177, 194). "Once we learn to distinguish," "we must then learn to recombine"; we can thereby capture "the subtlety of great literature" arising from "counterpoint" (AC 50f). Such methods seem to anticipate the later urgency, expressed particularly by Jameson and Culler, of transcending the static binary oppositions so rampant in structuralism, whose practitioners Frye seems to both resemble and overreach.

One of Frye's prime tactics is to avoid static piles or pigeonholes by devising an ingenious collation of metaphoric spaces wherein categories can move about and "merge" with others (AC 284, 302, 307, 312), for instance, via "hybrids" or "insensible gradations" (AC 312, 307). Or, things get placed in a "scale," "range," or "sequence" (AC 91, 177, 49, 72, 77, 115, 185, 198, 225, 244, 270). Or, certain categories emerge as we "move toward" or "away" from others (AC 42, 285, 328; cf. AC 117, 151, 156, 284, 291, 329). For instance, "as we go down the modes," "an increasing number of poetic images are taken from the actual social conditions of life" (AC 154).

Frye's spatial thinking goes in several directions. One is the "centripetal"[10] vision of some category positioned in the midst of its fellow constituents, rather reminiscent of the poem at hand being at the center of the universe (see p. 50). His obsession with "centers" and "central" entities[11] matches his concern that "criticism" must postulate "a center of the order or words" or else be mired down in "a series of free associations" "never creating a real structure" (AC 118). Paradoxically, though, the multiplying of centers eventually reverts to dissemination.

Sometimes, Frye envisions a central point "flanked" by two comparable categories (AC 12, 243, 250, 288), in the manner of an allegorical painting. In "the humanities," "literature" is "flanked on one side by history, and on the other

---

[10] As we saw (p. 50f), "centripetal" is a favored term for the dominant type of meaning in literature (AC 73ff). It is also used to describe "myth," "poetry," "the writer's intention," "the audience's attention," and the "high mimetic" "gaze" (AC 341, 80, 86, 112, 58, 153).

[11] On "centers," see AC 28, 91, 116ff, 121, 239, 285, 349. On "central" entities, see AC 12, 16, 22, 27, 37, 42f, 86, 95, 105, 185, 188f, 192, 209, 219, 223, 228, 243, 250, 284, 304, 315, 341, 350. Compare Note 10.

by philosophy" (AC 12; cf. AC 79, 83, 248, 287). In "the central area of literature," "epos and fiction" "are flanked by drama on one side and by lyric on the
other" (AC 250). In "the division of 'the good'," "the central" "area" of "art,
beauty, feeling, and taste" "is flanked by" "the world of social action and events"
and by "the world of individual thought and ideas" (AC 243). Here we add,
"reading from left to right," three groupings: the "human faculties" of "will,
feeling, and reason"; the "mental constructs" of "history, art, science and philosophy"; and "the ideals" of "law, beauty, and truth." Poe suggests "moral
sense," "taste," and "pure intellect" for these three, "taste" being "'in the middle
because it is just this position which in the mind it occupies.'" The total result of
"this admirable explanation" is one of the multiplex grids often implied in Frye's
schematics, as shown in Figure 5.1. At times, I feel reminded of a Ptolemaic or
Dantesque spiritual space where each concept has its confreres above and below,
and its counterpoints to the left and the right.

The complementary centrifugal vision is chiefly elicited by treating a category

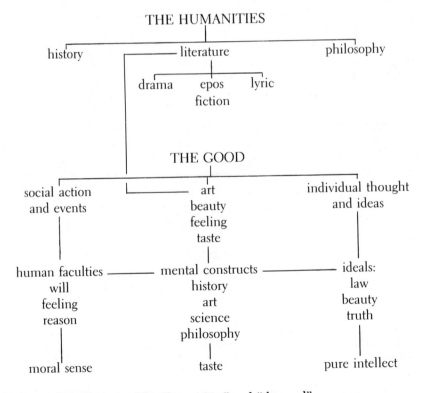

Figure 5.1. The division of the "humanities" and "the good"

as a space with two opposite "poles" (AC 25, 42, 47, 51f, 148, 187, 317f, 322f). The "two poles of literature" are "verisimilitude" and "mythos," with "plot-formulas" "moving" back and forth in between (AC 51f). In another space, "the contrast-epic," "myths accounting for the origin of law" "are at one pole and human society under the law is at the other" (AC 317). Or, "the characterization of comedy" relies on "two opposed pairs" that "polarize" the "action" and the "mood," respectively (AC 172). Such analyses might be called "dialectic," and Frye frequently uses that name (AC 106, 151, 155, 161f, 187, 192, 195, 217, 286, 317, 333), though he dissociates it, for his purposes, from the "social dialectics" a Marxist critic might stress (AC 24).

Another spatial contrast is a vertical polarity of high and low, or up and down (AC 45, 161, 187, 202, 318, 321ff, 337, 347). For example, "literature has an per limit" where the "imaginative vision of an eternal world becomes an experience of it," and "a lower limit in actual life" (AC 45). In parallel, the "Messiah or deliverer" "comes from an upper world" and the "demonic powers" from "a lower world," while "óur world" "is in the middle" —a conception also polarized by "assimilation to the opposite poles of the cycle of nature" (AC 187; cf. AC 161, 202ff, 237, 318, 322).[12] The "high" and "low mimetic modes" described later on seem to echo this arrangement when we behold "the central position of high mimetic tragedy" "balanced midway between godlike heroism and all-too-human irony" (AC 37). In another conception, this one dealing with "types of mythical movement," "the top half of the natural cycle is the world of romance and the analogy of innocence"; "the lower half is the world of realism and the analogy of experience" (AC 162). In this space, the "downward movement is the "tragic" and "the upward" is the "comic" (AC 162).

Frye conjectures that "all arts possess both a temporal and a spatial aspect" (AC 77), and he does occasionally indulge in temporal theorizing (AC 52, 105, 108, 287, 307, 344). But elsewhere he may either negate time by appealing to "the aesthetic or timeless moment" or to "simultaneous perception" and "apprehension"; or he may reshape time by making it not a linear progression, but a "cycle," the basic model being "the natural cycle" (AC 61, 77f, 318, 105).[13] Variants of the latter cycle include: "sleeping and waking life"; "life and death of the individual"; and "the slower social rhythm" of "cities and empires" (AC 105, 318). A still grander scheme accords with "cyclical theories of history" (AC 65). "Reading forward in history," the trend was from "myth" toward "verisimilitude" until "irony" became dominant, situating us now in an "ironic phase of literature," whereupon the trend "begins to move back" to "myth" (AC 52, 46; cf. AC 47, 62, 65f, 135, 214 323). Cyclicality may be combined with oscillation: the

---

[12] The Messianic analogy seems important also for Frye's account of the "mythoi" as a "quest" (see p. 74).

[13] This cycle is used, for instance, to account for the "form" of "the Classical epic" (AC 318). As the "life cycle," it serves as an analogy for Frye's "mythoi" (p. 70ff).

"general tendency" is "to react most strongly against the mode immediately preceding, and, to a lesser extent, to return to some of the standards of the modal grandfather" (AC 62).

Frye's classificatory project provokes his concern about the long-standing "problems of a vocabulary of poetics" (AC 79). He "finds particularly baffling" that the "technical vocabulary of poetics" doesn't even have a "word for a work of literary art" (AC 71). His own treatment of terminology betrays yet another oscillation, one between economizing and proliferating. He economizes by using a familiar term in an unusual or specialized sense, as is the case for "symbol," "desire," "naive," "literal meaning," and so on (AC 71, 106, 35, 82, 115f, 80). Or, he makes one term do multiple duty in different senses, as is the case with "fiction" (AC 365f), "satire" (AC 224 vs. 310) and "sentimental" (AC 35 vs. 179). He defends such practices as "a compromise with the present confused terminology" so as not to "increase the difficulties of this book by introducing too many new terms" (AC 248). He is also uneasy about "cacophonous jargon" and the "abuse of ordinary language" (AC 71).

But such sentiments clash with his cultivation of a luxuriant garden of technical neologisms appropriated in the manner of a "terminological buccaneer," among the most exuberant being "babble" and "doodle" as types of "subconscious association," or (borrowing from literary works) "Golux," "high Ydgrunism," and "deipnosophistical" (AC 275, 197, 232, 312). Also, his introduction of precise shadings between related words tends to terminologize, as when he pinpoints the difference between "enmity" versus "hatred," or between "skepticism" versus "cynicism" (AC 167, 230).

Frye diagnoses a theoretical lethargy in traditional criticism that used the ideas and terms devised by the ancient Greeks and showed little initiative to standardize any more (AC 13f, 65f, 206, 248). Though he has no qualms about coining new devices, he follows suit here in using a welter of Greek terms (thankfully transcribed into the Roman alphabet), such as "alazon," "eiron," "lexis," "melos," and "opsis" (AC 39f, 244). His treatment of "characterization in comedy," which he carries over to "romance" and "tragedy" (AC 172ff, 197, 216ff), is couched mainly in Greek terms. How closely he is following the original usage is not always made clear. The Greek may be kept distinct from its English counterpart, as with "epic" versus "epos" (e.g. AC 54f vs. 248, 263, 320), or with "myth" versus "mythos" (AC 33, 136 vs. 162), though Frye eventually decides the latter pair are "ultimately" the same (AC 341). Some terms have two technical senses, such as "archetype" (AC 99 vs. 291) and "mythos" (AC 53 vs. 162). Others have a technical sense alongside the everyday one, such as "myth" (AC 341 vs. 33) and "pathos" (AC 187 vs. 38).

All these cases suggest that Frye adapts his terms freely according to the context where he uses them. A comparable point might be made about his mania for enumeration. He keeps delivering parallel numbers of things, like the true love in carol of the twelve days of Christmas except that he doesn't relish sending more than six or less than two. His favorite numbers are twos, threes, and fours, though he has an assortment of fives and sixes too, the latter typically breaking down into two sets of three.[14] Twos and fours are good for making oppositions, for example, the centrifugal pairs of "poles," whereas threes and fives offer an obvious "center," for example, a centripetal point "flanked" by two confreres. Throughout, Frye is less concerned to fixate exact numbers than to show that literary forms and concepts are not monolithic units, but scales or sequences in which a given exemplar may be more or less typical, explicit, emphatic, and so on.

A few examples should suffice. On one occasion, he announces "three stages" of the "quest," matching the "threefold structure" "repeated in many features of romance," including the "three-day rhythm" of "Easter"; yet after his analysis, he decides "there are" "not three but four," this time matching the "four mythoi" ("comedy, romance, tragedy, and irony") he wants to incorporate inside "a central unifying myth" (AC 187, 192). Another time, he wants "four periods of life" to go with "the four seasons of the year," "four periods of the day," and "four aspects of the water cycle";[15] later, he wants "five stages" of "life" to go with his "five phases of comedy" (AC 160, 185). As his motives for creating or aligning patterns change, so do his enumerations.

Frye's point, reconfirmed in a letter to me, is that although "the demand for order in thought produces a supply of intellectual systems," "no one system can contain the arts as they stand" (AC 231). Frye champions "a comprehensive view of criticism," subsuming "the archetypal or mythical critic, the aesthetic form critic, the historical critic, the medieval four-level critic," and "the text-and-texture critic" (AC 341). He lists the types of criticism in several other ways as well. At one point, he whimsically enumerates three types of "learning" as "the most conspicuous": "fantastical" (= "mythical") "contentious" (= "historical"), and "delicate" (= "'new' critical") (AC 72). At another, he distinguishes between "biographical criticism" concerned with the author, and "tropical criticism" (unlike this chapter, not written near the equator) "concerned with the contemporary reader" (AC 20f). "The true dialectic of criticism" combines these latter two, uniting the "historical" with the "contemporary" (AC 24). The outcome is "ethical criticism," wherein "ethics" is not the "rhetorical comparison of social facts to predetermined values," but "the consciousness of the presence of society" and of "the total and simultaneous possession of past culture." This view ensures that

---

[14] Compare the following sources: twos (AC 37, 47, 140, 148, 161f, 166, 172, 191, 193, 209, 221, 224, 263, 267, 310, 315, 317, 334, 338); threes (AC 140f, 148, 151, 171f, 177, 187, 198, 209, 225, 243, 246, 319, 347); fours (AC 17, 50, 53, 145f, 160, 162, 192, 198, 206, 251, 308, 312, 317, 341); fives (AC 42, 141, 158, 185, 250, 319); and sixes (AC 52, 177, 198, 219, 225, 239, 312).

[15] To get four, he counts "snow" with "sea" rather than with "rain" (AC 160), God knows why.

historical criticism will not be merely biographical or "documentary," "dealing entirely with sources" (AC 109).[16] However, it becomes harder to justify the exclusion of "the history of taste" from "the structure of criticism," and the banishment to a non-theoretical limbo of "the public critic" whose "task" is "to exemplify how a man of taste uses and evaluates literature" (AC 18, 8).

Frye's most prominent typology of criticism is the "modern parallel" into which he transforms the "four-level critic's" "medieval" scheme and which he places entirely under the heading of "ethical criticism" in the broad sense just expounded (AC 116, 341, ix, 71). Again changing numbers, he converts the four into five "levels" or "phases" that form "a sequence of contexts or relationships in which the whole work of literary art can be placed" (AC 115f, 73). This "sequence" is not meant to go from "elementary" "first steps" toward "more subtle" ones, nor is it "a series of degrees of critical initiation" (AC 72f). But the *Anatomy* doesn't give a full-scale demonstration of the levels on a specific work to show what the exact nature of the "sequence" *is*.

Frye's first or "literal" level deals with the "simultaneous pattern of meaning" (AC 115f, 244), roughly a formalist approach. "Rhetorical" criticism ties in here by "returning us to the 'literal' level," though it is "illegitimately extended" if "value-judgments" result (AC 244, 21). The "rhetorical" is in turn associated with "New" criticism, "based on the conception of a poem as literally a poem" (AC 82, 86, 140, 273).

His "second or descriptive level" includes "everything that influences literature from without" (AC 116, 75). This definition, which sounds very broad and vague, suggests a more "centrifugal" scope than the "centripetal" first level's, matching his already described division between two "directions of attention" (cf. AC 73ff).

The old "allegorical[17] level of the Middle Ages" is Frye's "third" or "formal" level, where "criticism" dispenses "commentary and interpretation" by "attaching the imagery to the central form of the poem" and "rendering an aspect of the form into discursive writing" (AC 116, 86). This phase is "conceived of" "as aesthetic," since "art" is "an object of aesthetic contemplation" (AC 116, 349, 155). This phase also integrates the first and second by moving from literal to descriptive (AC 82, 86), again illustrating how Frye's distinctions flow back together. The main focus remains centripetal, the "final direction" in "literature" (AC 74): "good commentary naturally does not read ideas into poems," but only

---

[16] Frye can't decide himself how important the sources should be. He sometimes declares them irrelevant, at least as historical facts (AC 109, 148, 163f, 173, 188f), but he cites them frequently.

[17] On the one hand, "allegory is a structural element in literature" and "cannot be added by critical interpretation alone" (AC 54). On the other hand, "all commentary is allegorical interpretation" (AC 89). "Any great work of literature may carry an infinite amount of commentary," and "no structure of imagery can be restricted to one allegorical interpretation" (AC 341f, 120). Contrast this indecision with his "sliding scale" "from the most explicitly allegorical consistent with being literature at all" over to the most "anti-allegorical" (AC 91).

"translates what is there," the "evidence" coming from "the study of the structure of imagery" (AC 86). "Criticism" should "grow in the understanding of the work itself, not in the number of things one can attach to it" (AC 72).

The "medieval" "moral" "level" becomes the fourth, the "mythical," devoted to "the study of myths, and of poetry as a technique of social communication" (AC 116). Since its "symbol" is the "archetype," it is also called the "archetypal phase," defined as "social and part of the continuum of work" (AC ix, 95, 116). "The aesthetic" is thus not "the final resting place"; the tendency of the "formal phase" to "isolate the individual poem" can be transcended by considering how the "work of art" "participates" "in the vision of the goal of social effort" (AC 348f, 95). "Archetypal criticism" "comes to our aid" by projecting a "sense of the total form" that "art" possesses as "an ethical instrument participating in the work of civilization" (AC 349). Despite the warnings just aired against reading things into the work, Frye concedes that in our "copyright age," "most archetypes have to be established by critical inspection alone" (AC 101). But he implies they are "unconsciously" there all the time (cf. AC 17, 100, 271f).[18]

Finally, the old "anagogic" "level" or "phase" keeps its name and yields the still grander vista of "literature as existing in its own universe," "containing life and reality in a system of verbal relationships" (AC 122). "Literature" "imitates the thought of a human mind which is at the circumference and not at the center of its reality" (AC 119). Whereas in the "formal phase the poem is still contained by nature, and in the archetypal phase the whole of poetry is still" so "contained," in the "anagogical," "nature becomes" "the thing contained" "inside the mind of an infinite man" (AC 119). Thanks to the vast scope of the two final "levels" or "phases," "the structural principles of literature are to be derived from archetypal and anagogic criticism, the only kinds that assume a larger context of literature as a whole" (AC 134). The *Anatomy* is partly an attempt at such a derivation, as signaled by the thesis that we must "accept the archetypal" "element" in order to get "any systematic mental training out of the reading of literature" (AC 100).

Frye's table of contents marks a further breakdown of the field of criticism that he doesn't justify by discursive argument. "Historical criticism" gets the "modes," "ethical" gets the "symbols," "rhetorical" gets the "genres," and "archetypal" gets the "myths" (AC ix). "Historical criticism" is partitioned into "thematic and fictional modes," the latter further cut into "tragic" and "comic." "Ethical criticism" is divided into five "phases" paralleling the five-level typology adapted from the medieval scheme. Each "phase" has its special kind of "symbol." In the

---

[18] "In archetypal criticism, the poet's conscious knowledge is considered only so far as the poet may allude to or imitate other poets" or "make a deliberate use of convention"; "beyond that, the poet's control" "stops with the poem" (AC 100). Frye makes no distinction among "sub-," "pre-," "half-," or "un-conscious"; and is "reluctant to explain literary facts by psychological clichés" of this kind (AC 88), though he sometimes does anyway.

"literal and descriptive phases," the "symbol" is "motif" and "sign," respectively; in the "formal phase," it's "image"; in the "mythical phase," it's "archetype"; and in the "anagogic phase," it's "monad." "Archetypal criticism" is cut into three kinds of "meaning," "apocalyptic," "demonic," and "analogical"; and into four types of "mythos" named for the four seasons (I return to these, p. 70). Finally, "rhetorical criticism" is chopped into four "rhythms" fitted to genres: "association" to "lyric," "recurrence" to "epos," "continuity" to "prose," and "decorum" to "drama"; and into "specific forms": "lyric and epos" go together as "thematic," "prose" is "continuous," "drama" gets no name, and "encyclopedic" gets no genre (maybe the "satire," AC 322).

I have tried to situate the types of criticism summarized so far in Figure 5.2. Even more than in Figure 5.1, we get a multiply loaded grid whose untidiness reflects Frye's oscillation between dividing and recombining. Frye includes no such figures in his book, evading rigidity but also clarity. He feels no obligation to make his various schematics tally exactly, though his "postulate of total coherence" (AC 16) inspires him to propose "counterparts" of every sort (AC 16, 22, 44f, 150f, 194ff, 216ff, 228, 233, 284, 298, 300). The apparent "lack of ingenuity" (AC 29) in his organization conveys the insight that, depending on one's perspective, the various areas subdivide into diverse orders. Just as Frye asserts that "no set of critical standards derived from only one mode can ever assimilate the whole truth about poetry" (AC 62), he declines to devise a single, complete, all-purpose frame for critical methods.

"Modern criticism" has its own set of "schools," "each making a distinctive choice of symbols in its analysis" (AC 72). Some bear the names of their inspirers or originators: "Aristotelians, Coleridgeans, Thomists, Freudians, Jungians, Marxists," and the like (AC 72). Some reflect their source disciplines: "rhetoric," "history," "psychology," "anthropology," "theology, philosophy, politics," or "science" (AC 72, 7). "Moral criticism" tends to be "harnessed to an all-round revolutionary philosophy of society," as in "Marxism" and "Nietzsche" (AC 346).

Frye is generally skeptical about all these schools. They are "determinisms" "substituting a critical attitude for criticism" and "proposing" "to attach criticism" to "frameworks outside" "literature" (AC 6). They use "causal relationships" to "explain one's subject while studying it." If "mimesis" is to be the "emancipation of externality into image, nature into art," "art" "can never be ultimately related to any other system of phenomena, standards, values, or final causes" (AC 113). However, Frye's resolutely eclectic and erudite mind cannot ignore all these frameworks nor forego all ambitions regarding "science" and a "central place" for "literary criticism" in the "activities" of a host of other disciplines (p. 46).

One unmistakable influence comes from psychoanalysis, which, like many colleagues, Frye calls "psychology." This domain offers a means to reintegrate the author and the process of literary production, both of which archetypal criticism tends to marginalize. The "biographer" is to regard "his subject's poetry" as a record of "private dreams, associations, ambitions, and repressed desires"

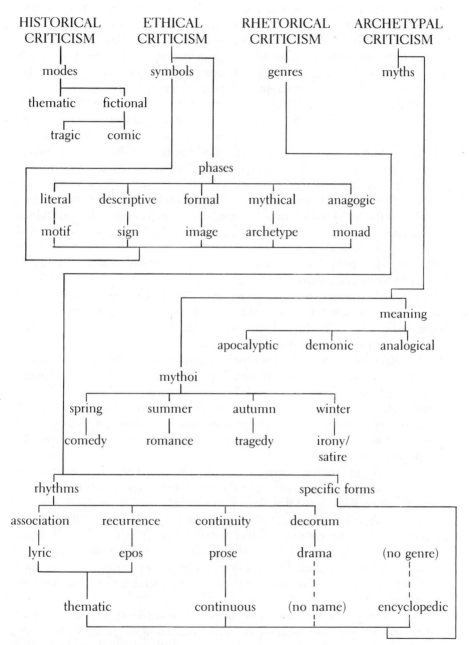

Figure 5.2. Types of criticism

61

(AC 110). Such criticism should include only "serious studies which are technically competent both in psychology and in criticism," as opposed to those which "simply project" the critic's "own erotica, in a rationalized clinical disguise, onto the author" (AC 110), though in practice, this distinction may be slippery. As the mutations in Holland's career demonstrate, even a fully competent psychoanalyst is constitutionally disposed to project.

In literary production, the division between "conscious" and "unconscious" becomes prominent, as it did in Wellek and Warren's "modern treatment of the creative process" (TL 88). For Frye, "poetry is the product, not only of a deliberate and voluntary act of consciousness, like discursive writing, but of unconscious" "processes" (AC 88). "Poetic technique" is "an increasingly unconscious skill" whereby "great poetry" "overcomes" all "difficulties" "at a subconscious level" (AC 88, 277). "Poetic creation" is "an associative rhetorical process, most of it below the threshold of consciousness, a chaos of paronomasia, sound-links, ambiguous sense-links, and memory-links very like that of a dream" —especially if "verbal association" "is subject to a censor," namely "the 'plausibility-principle,' the necessity of shaping itself into a form acceptable to the poet's and his reader's waking consciousness" (AC 271f, 276, 51f).

Such analogizing is put to multiple uses. "Plausibility" acts within a range from being a "perfunctory concession in a myth" to being a "censor principle in a naturalistic novel" (AC 52). "Elements of subconscious association" are diagnosed as the basis for "the associative concentration of poetry" that "prose" can hardly attain (AC 275, 277). Two such "elements" are "babble" and "doodle," "the basis for lyrical melos" ("musical" quality) "and opsis" ("visual" quality) respectively (AC 275, 255, 258). The most striking move occurs when the "absurd quantum formula" that "the critic should" "'get out' of a poem exactly what the poet may be vaguely assumed to have been aware of 'putting in'" is exploded with the thesis that "the poet unconsciously meant the whole corpus of his possible commentary" (AC 17, 342).

On the side of "reading," Frye diagnoses an omnipresent "unconscious" process of "expanding images into conventional archetypes of literature" (AC 100). Though we need not insist that "latent content is the *real* content," it remains a "factor which is relevant to a full critical analysis" and "which lifts a work of literature out of the category of the merely historical" (AC 158). "If we are reading the story for fun, some murky 'subconscious' factor in our response will take care of the association," such as between "hero" and "sun" (AC 188). But if "reading" "as critics, with an eye to structural principles, we shall make the association" explicitly.

Various uses of psychoanalysis are proposed for criticism. Frye's recommendations are detailed: "the literary critic finds Freud most suggestive for the theory of comedy, Jung for the theory of romance," and "the psychology of the will to power, as expounded in Adler and Nietzsche," for the theory of "tragedy" (AC 214). The "ternary action" of "comedy" is "psychologically" comparable to "the removal of a neurosis or blocking point and the restoration of an unbroken current of energy and memory"; the "last phase" of "the comic" can be "connected psychologically with a return to the womb" (AC 171, 186). The "archetype" is cited "in Jung's sense of an aspect of the personality capable of dramatic projection" (as compared to Frye's sense of "typical or recurring image") (AC 291, 99). "In the romance," "we find Jung's libido, anima, and shadow reflected in the hero, heroine, and villain, respectively" (AC 304).

As usual, the "parental origin" of "sinister figures" is assumed, such as the "antagonists" in "the quest-romance" (AC 193). "The 'terrible mother'" is "the witch" or the "black" "queen," "associated" by Jung with "the fear of incest" (AC 196). And of course, "the hated father-figure" makes his obligatory appearances (AC 158, 164f, 172, 180), getting "baited and exploded from the stage" (AC 165). He often figures in the "Oedipus situation," though Frye suggests it "would involve less anachronism to assume that the "myth" "informed and gave structure" to the "psychological investigations" of Freud, rather than the other way around (AC 181, 353).

This move of appropriating psychoanalysis while placing it on a mythical or archetypal basis is characteristic of Frye's procedures. A similar trend pervades the many analogies he draws to the "dream."[19] The notion of "displacement," in psychoanalysis a shift to make repressed content more acceptable (p. 161), becomes "the adaptation of myth and metaphor to canons of morality and plausibility" (AC 365; cf. AC 52, 136ff, 155, 188). If the myths themselves are "less displaced" or "undisplaced" (AC 190, 139ff, 151, 181, 185, 203, 223), they needn't resemble the actual story or content of literary works very closely. Also, "rituals" are placed alongside "dreams" as "two symbolic structures analogous to same thing" (AC 193; cf. AC 105, 107, 119, 179, 193, 243, 250). "Myth" is "the union of ritual and dream in a form of verbal communication" —precisely the definition later offered for "the work of literary art" "in the archetypal phase" (AC 106, 118).

Frye's conception of "desire" is ostensibly derived from the Freudian conception of "the work of the dream": "not simply the fantasies of the sleeping mind, but the whole interpenetrating activity of desire and repugnance in shaping thought" (AC 105, 359). The "dream" leads into "the world of fulfilled desire, emancipated from all anxieties and frustrations" (AC 119). We glimpse a Jungian, reassuring shift in Freud's darkly pessimistic view of the psyche when Frye eulogizes "the psychological discovery of an oracular mind 'underneath' the conscious one" and of "the nightly awakening of a titanic self" (AC 353, 105, 159). Frye's optimistic and allegorizing outlook precludes any "limiting" of "desire" to "a simple response to need" or "want," including that for "sexual fulfillment" (AC 105f, 156). Nor is he sympathetic to the attempts of "civiliza-

---

[19] AC 37, 45, 57, 100, 105-112, 118, 120, 159, 183f, 186, 193, 206, 214f, 226, 243, 250, 272, 277f, 354.

tion" to "make the desirable and the moral coincide"; "literature" "owes much of its status as a liberal art" to being "less inflexible than morality" (AC 156).[20]

Instead, Frye views "desire" broadly as "the energy that leads human society to develop its own form"; "the form of desire" is "liberated and made apparent by civilization," the latter being "the process" of "making a total human form out of nature." He can then construe "the conflict of desire and reality" as the "significant content" of "literature in its archetypal aspect" (AC 105). Although "desire" "tries to escape from necessity," "the archetypal function of literature" is to "visualize the world of desire not as an escape from 'reality,' but as the genuine form of the world that human life tries to imitate" (AC 156, 184). "Poetry" "expresses, as a verbal hypothesis, a vision of the goal of work and the forms of desire" (AC 106). It is thus logical to "begin our study of archetypes" "with a world of myth," since "in terms of narrative, myth is the imitation of action near or at the conceivable limits" of "human desire" (AC 136). More specifically, "the apocalyptic world, the heaven of religion, presents" "the categories of reality in the forms of human desire" (AC 141).

This last speculation is one among many signals of the pervasive presence of another major and obvious source for Frye, namely religion or theology. He postulates "the theological origin of critical categories" and owns that the *Anatomy* started from a decision "to apply the principles of literary symbolism and Biblical typology" (AC 76, vii). To his dismay, "the absence of any genuine literary criticism of the Bible in modern times" "has left an enormous gap in our knowledge of literary symbolism" (AC 315). Critical projects, such as "comparing Bunyan and Spenser," are "perverse" if done "without reference to the Bible" (AC 194). "Historical scholarship is without exception 'lower' or analytic criticism"; "higher criticism" would construe "the Bible" as "a typological unity," "a definitive myth, a single archetypal structure," its "two testaments" being "metaphorical identifications of one another" (AC 315; cf. AC 56, 325, and Bloom's opposite view, CCP 13). Frye pursues precisely that vision when he insists that "the Bible" is "probably the most systematically constructed sacred book in the world," "presenting an epic structure of unsurpassed range, consistency, and completeness" —not "the scrapbook of corruptions, glosses, redactions, insertions, conflations, misplacings, and misunderstandings revealed by the analytic critic" (AC 315, 325). Even "its editorial and redacting process must be regarded as inspired" (AC 315).

Yet in the *Anatomy* at least (*The Great Code* may be another matter), Frye wants to avoid any semblance of a Christian apologist. "The critic" "has nothing to say for or against the affirmations" of any "religion," but must "treat" it as "a human hypothesis" (AC 126). "In literary criticism, theology and metaphysics

---

[20] Compare p. 49f. The "ribald, obscene, subversive, lewd, and blasphemous have an essential place in literature" (AC 156). Fiedler has a similar view, though he does not stipulate that "they can achieve expression only through ingenious techniques of displacement" (AC 156).

must be treated as assertive, because they are outside literature"; and "typological constructs" "are simply reference tables" (AC 75, 359). "Every age of literature" has "some central encyclopedic form, which is normally a scripture or sacred book" —"in our culture," "the Christian Bible" (AC 315). Similarly, "nearly every civilization" sees one "particular group of myths" as "closer to fact and truth" and hence as "canonical" rather than "apocryphal" (AC 54). Yet for "literary criticism," "the Bible and Classical literature are equally mythological."

Frye's tactic for incorporating religion is thus much the same one he used for psychology: relating it to myths and treating the mythical version as more basic. "The informing" of "theological constructs by poetic myths is even more obvious" than that of "psychological" ones (AC 353). "The priority of myth to fact is religious as well as literary" (AC 325). "Historical fact" "in the Bible" "is there not because it is 'true' but because it is mythically significant." This tactic maintains the freedom of Frye's own position. He can hail "the transcendental and apocalyptic perspective of religion" as "a tremendous emancipation of the imaginative mind," while asserting that no "religious" "myth is either valuable or valid unless it assumes the autonomy of culture" (AC 125, 127). "Religions" "cannot as social institutions *contain* an art of unlimited hypothesis" (AC 127). "Culture" must "destroy intellectual idolatry, the recurrent tendency in religion to replace the object of its worship with its present understanding and forms of approach."

In this spirit, Frye avers: even "the loftiest religion" "gives" "the poet" "only" "metaphors for poetry" (AC 125) (cf. p. 31). What is "existential" in a "religious" context is merely "metaphorical" in a "poetic" one (AC 142; cf. AC 120). The "physical world" is set in opposition by "religion" to "the spiritually existential," but by "poetry" to "the hypothetical" (AC 148). Still, by arguing that "the structural principles of literature are as closely related to mythology and comparative religion as those of painting are to geometry," Frye can "use the symbolism of the Bible" "as a grammar of literary archetypes," the "Bible" being "the main source for undisplaced myths in our tradition" (AC 134f, 140).

On a small scale, individual works are interpreted this way,[21] as when "the first book of the Faerie Queen" is taken to be "the closest following of the Biblical quest-romance theme in English literature"; or when "the paradisical garden and the tree of life" are made "parallel" to "symbols in *Comus* and *Tannhäuser* (AC 194, 152). On a larger scale, whole genres are affected, as when we learn that "romantic encyclopedic forms use human or sacrimental imitations of the Messianic myth"; or that "the crudest of Plautine comedy formulas has much the same *structure* as the central Christian myth" of "a divine son appeasing the wrath of a father and redeeming" both "a society and a bride" (AC 317, 185). On a very grand scale, Frye attains the ultimate logocentric position: "anagogically, the symbol is a monad, all symbols being united in a single infinite and eternal

---

[21] At times the interpretation seems tenuous, as when the supposed historical times of *King Lear* and *Cymbeline* are aligned with events of the "Old Testament" and the New (AC 222, 219).

verbal symbol," "the Logos" (AC 121). Thereupon, "Christ" himself becomes "the Word that contains all poetry."

Frye's relation to sociology is far more tenuous than to psychology and theology. As noted (p. 50), he sees the "work of art" "participating" in "social effort" (AC 348), but he is rather sketchy about how this process functions. He links his favored "ethical criticism" directly to "the consciousness of the presence of society" and to "a broad estimation of social values," but wants the critic to be "under no obligation to sociological values," which might conflict with those of "great art" (AC 24, 348, 19).

Marxism is slighted when Marx gets tossed together with Plato of all people,[22] for having propounded "a revolutionary way of looking at culture" and suggested that "the artist ought to assist the work of society by framing workable hypotheses" (AC 346, 113), which sounds to me like what Frye also says. For another link, Frye is confident that "a Marxist or Platonic state would" "impose limitations on the arts" (AC 127). The stark contrast between the timelessness of Platonic concepts and the historicity of Marxist ones (cf. pp. 365, 386) is suppressed; anyway, "Marxists" are spurned for their "muddled version of some quasi-organic theory of history" (AC 343f). Nonetheless, Frye's thesis that "criticism has to look at art from the standpoint of an ideally classless society" (AC 22), though conflicting with the current core of Marxist criticism, points toward the utopian function of art expounded by Marx as well as Jameson.

Frye does express a strong interest in "primitive and popular" "literature" for "possessing the ability to communicate in time and space respectively" (AC 107f). He comes close to Formalism and structuralism by proposing to "extend the kind of comparative and morphological study now made of folktales" into "the rest of literature" (AC 104). He weighs "the possibility of seeing literature as a complication of a relatively restricted and simple group of formulas that can be studied in primitive culture," but keeping in mind that "complication" "is by no means" the only trend (AC 17). His main motive for favoring "popular literature" is plain: it "affords an unobstructed view of archetypes" and is "most deeply influenced by the archetypal phase of symbolism" (AC 116, 108)—much the same as Fiedler's motive (cf. WL 129; NT 232). "Archetypes are most easily studied in highly conventionalized literature: this is, for the most part, naive, primitive, and popular" (AC 116). "In a popular tale," "logical construction" "is a matter of the linking of archetypes" (AC 362). Similarly, "legend and folktale often contain" a "great concentration of mythical meaning," equal to that of such "canonical myth" as in the "Bible" (AC 188). Frye concludes that "archetypal criticism seems to find its center of gravity in romance, when the interchange of ballads, folktales, and popular stories was at its easiest" (AC 116). And in fact, his scheme of "modes," to which we now turn, centers on romance.

Frye derives his typology of "fictional modes" from a remark of "Aristotle" that

---

[22] For Jameson, "vulgar Marxism" "presupposes" "Platonic ideas" that "leave out" "the unique historical situation" (MF 193). But he doesn't blame Marx for this.

has "not received much attention from modern critics" (AC 33). "Fictions" are to be "classified" "by the hero's power of action" as compared to "ours." Five categories result, three of "superiority," one of equality, and one of "inferiority." "If superior in *kind* both to other men[23] and to the environment," "the hero is a divine being and the story a myth in the common sense."[24] "If superior in *degree* to other men and to his environment, the hero" is "human" and the story a "romance" (including "legend" and "folktale"). "If superior in degree to other men but not to his natural environment, the hero is a leader" "of the *high mimetic* mode, of most epic and tragedy" (AC 33f). "If superior neither to other men nor to his environment, the hero is one of us" and "of the *low mimetic* mode, of most comedy and realistic fiction" (AC 34). Finally, "if inferior" "to ourselves," "the hero belongs to the *ironic* mode." Frye cautiously debars "comparative value" from the designations "'high' and 'low,'" though he makes the "high" the "central" "sense" of "tragedy" (AC 34, 37).

The form of his definitions reveals several inconsistencies, even after I have made them more parallel here than they were in the book. The first two name one text type each, the second two name "modes" with two text types apiece, and the fifth names a mode with no specified text type. When the hero loses his "superiority," terms change: he doesn't get a label (later, "heroic" is used as the opposite of "ironic," AC 44, 219), "natural" is added to "environment," "other men" are replaced by "ourselves," and "power and intelligence" appear as standards in place of "authority, passions, and power of expression." We are left to wonder if the points of orientation have also shifted (and with what consequences) or merely been renamed.

Again in his characteristic way, Frye superposes a barrage of further criteria onto his "modes." He says "a distinction" between "naive and sophisticated literature" "will be useful in each mode," but he fully uses it just for "romance" and "irony"; only the "naive" is noticed for "high mimetic tragedy" and "melodrama," and only the "sophisticated" for "pathos" in the "low mimetic" (AC 35, 37, 41, 38, 47, 39). He also establishes a binarism of "pity and fear" as "two general directions in which emotion moves, toward and away" (AC 37). In "romance," these two "become modes of pleasure, usually the beautiful and the sublime respectively"; "in high mimetic tragedy," they "become, respectively, favorable and adverse moral judgment"; "in low mimetic tragedy," they are "communicated externally, as sensations" (AC 301, 38). What happens to them in myth or irony we aren't told. In comedy, though, they turn up in nicely "corresponding" forms as "sympathy and ridicule" (AC 43).

A historical criterion is added by taking the sequence as the order of phases of

---

[23] "Men" are clearly those ones identifying with the hero, who represents the "libido," has "fun with the distressed damsels" "tied naked to rocks or trees," and in his "triumph" gets "mistresses" or a "girl" as "a stage prop" (AC 304, 195f, 173, 164). How feminine readers would identify these "modes" is hard to tell.

[24] Which is of course not Frye's sense. Fiedler would call this "mythology" (NT 328; WL 131).

literature overall. "Looking over our table, we can see that European fiction, during the last fifteen centuries, has steadily moved its center of gravity down the list" (AC 34). We have "the pre-medieval period" of "myths," followed by the "romance" of "chivalry" and of "legends of saints." The "high mimetic" takes "the foreground" in the "Renaissance," and "the low mimetic" "predominates in English literature from Defoe's time to the end of the nineteenth century."[25] Our own time is the "ironic age" (AC 46f, 52, 62, 65f, 135, 214 323), as we heard (pp. 48, 55). However, "the return of irony to myth," in "modern literature" and possibly in "sacramental philosophy and dogmatic theology," shows how "our five modes evidently go around in a circle" (AC 42, 65, 48; cf. AC 135, 140, 151). Frye detects "the same progression of modes in Classical literature," though with an unmistakable strain he blames on "religion": he can't get the "the mythical, romantic, and high mimetic" to "separate," and admits the "low mimetic and ironic" were "abortive" (AC 35). So the "classical parallels" must reflect Frye's drive to reuse his patterns even when the fit is problematic.

A further criterion for defining "modes" is the role of the central figure in relation to society. In "tragedy," this figure is "isolated from society" (AC 37, 41, 54, 208, 218). The "high mimetic" uses "the fall of the leader"; the "low mimetic" uses the "pathos" of "the exclusion of an individual on our own level from a social group"; "irony" focuses on "the sense of arbitrariness" in the "isolation"; and so on (AC 37, 39, 41). "The theme of the comic," in contrast, is "the integration of society, which usually" "incorporates a central character" (AC 43, 218). In "mythical comedy" "the hero is accepted by a society of gods"; in "high mimetic comedy" "the central figure" "constructs his (or her) own society"; in "low mimetic comedy" "the hero" is "incorporated" "into the society that he naturally fits," "frequently" with a "social promotion"; and so on (AC 43ff). In the "ironic" mode, the main character tends to become a "pharmakos or scapegoat" (AC 41, 45). On the tragic side of irony, the "pharmakos" is "guilty" by being "a member of a guilty society," and his fate moves between "the opposite poles" of "the incongruous and the inevitable" (AC 42).[26] On the comic side, the "poles" are "melodrama" that "defines the enemy of society as a person outside that society," and "satire" that "defines the enemy of society as a spirit within that society" (AC 47). Fig. 5.3 shows the whole scheme.

For "thematic literature" (the opposite of "fictional"), this whole scheme of "integrate" versus "isolate" gets carried over to the author, who may "write" either "as an individual, emphasizing the separateness of his personality," or as "a spokesman of his society" that "needs" his "expressive power" (AC 54). The separatist attitude is said to yield "most lyrics and essays," plus "satires, epigrams," "'eclogues,'" and such "episodic" forms; the spokesman stance is said to

---

[25] In "French literature," this stage is dated "about fifty years earlier" (AC 34).

[26] The space measured by these poles is peopled with Adam on one end, Christ on the other, and Prometheus in the center (AC 42).

FICTIONAL MODES

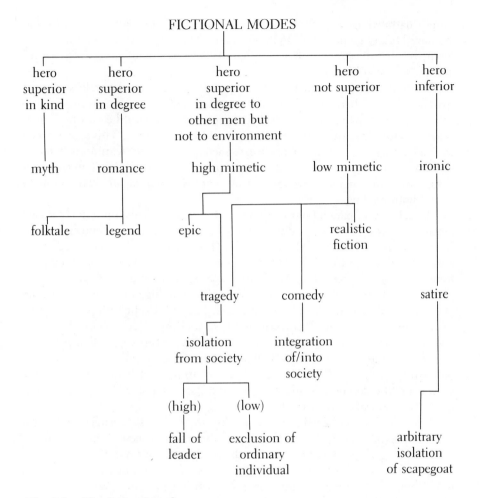

Fig. 5.3. The fictional modes

yield "educational" "poetry" of the "epic," "didactic," or "encyclopaedic" kinds (AC 54f). We see again how Frye strives to get maximum mileage out of the schemes he draws up, such that division within them oscillates with unification among them.

A still more striking case of this striving is the "forbidding piece of symmetry" when Frye goes from "modes" to "mythoi" (AC 177), where "mythos" chiefly means, in the Aristotelian tradition, "generic plot" and "structural organizing principle of literary form" (AC 162, 341; cf. AC 52, 82, 107). Of the six "modes" we saw, the "mythical" disappears because it in effect swallows all the others, which suggests that myth didn't really "return" after "irony," because it never went away. To match the seasons of the year, Frye compresses and reorders to get "four" "narrative categories of literature broader than, or logically prior to, the ordinary literary genres" (AC 162). "Romance" fits "the mythos" of "summer," "comedy" that of "spring," "tragedy" that of "autumn," and "irony" and "satire" that of "winter" (AC ix).

This temporal arrangement is then spatialized into an elaborate system of "parallel phases" shared by "neighboring mythoi" (AC 177). Frye "recognizes six phases of each mythos," split into two "threes" shared with the "mythos" right before or after it, as shown by the arrangement in Figure 5.4. This scheme may be read temporally, as the narrative sequence of actions within each form, roughly mirroring the cycles of seasons or human lives. Or, it might be a spatial array of different types of tragedy, comedy, and so on. Frye seems to intend both readings.

The scheme of parallel phases drawn in Figure 5.4 yields intriguingly mixed forms requiring "tenuous" "distinctions" between "romantic comedy" versus "comic romance," or the like (AC 177). "Innocence" and "experience" each cover two blocks of three; this order is reversed for comedy, leaving irony positioned to borrow both its blocks from "experience," represented in "mythical patterns" that "attempt to give form to the shifting ambiguities and complexities of unidealized existence" (AC 181f, 201, 221, 223, 237). The fifth phase is twice made a more "experienced" correlate of the second (AC 202, 222). Also, the first and sixth phases at either end are areas of high intensity. The "first phase" of "comedy" is the "most ironic," and that of "tragedy" involves "the greatest possible dignity" (AC 177, 219). The first phase of "irony" is of "nightmare," and the sixth is of "the demonic," "madhouses," and the "inferno" (AC 226, 238). But generally this scaling is sketchily executed.

"Romance" is subdivided such that its "first three phases are parallel to the first three phases of tragedy," and "the second three to the second three phases of comedy" (AC 198). "The first phase is the myth of the birth of the hero." "The second phase is the innocent youth" (AC 199). "The third phase is the normal quest theme," itself having "three stages": "perilous journey" ("agon"), "crucial struggle" ("pathos"), and "exaltation" ("anagnorisis") (AC 200, 187). "The fourth phase" focuses on "maintaining" "the integrity of the innocent world against the assault of experience" (AC 200f). "The fifth phase" gives "a reflective, idyllic view of experience from above" (AC 202). "The sixth or *penseroso* phase" shows "the end of a movement from active to contemplative adventure." This sequence runs roughly parallel to the hero's life as he is born and matures, finally figuring as an "old man"; the boundary between "innocence" and "experience" falls exactly at the center (AC 201f). This progress is also "erotic": "the rivalry of the son and a hateful father for possession of the mother"; "maternal sexual imagery" and "'chaste' love"; then "true love" placed "on top of a hierarchy"; and finally "lust and passion" ending in "perversion" (AC 202). "The natural cycle" is also close by, though Frye gives it special "prominence" in the fifth phase, as he does again for "irony" (AC 202f, 237).

TRAGEDY	ROMANCE	COMEDY	IRONY
1. hero gets greatest dignity	1. birth of hero	1. humorous society triumphs	1. satire of low norm: anomalies, injustices, crimes
I ←——— →I	→I	E ←——— →E	→E
2. innocence of young people	2. innocent youth	2. hero flees humorous society	2. ridicule conventions
I ←——— →I	→I	E ←——— →E	→E
3. success of hero's achievement	3. quest: agon, pathos, anagnorisis	3. humor gives way to young man's desires	3. satire of high norm: let go of ordinary sense
I ←——— →I	→I	E ←——— →E	→E
4. fall of hero through hybris and hamartia	4. protect innocent world from assault of experience	4. move between normal and idealized green world	4. moral and realistic perspective on tragedy
→E ←———	→E	I	E ←
5. lost direction, lack of knowledge	5. reflective idyllic view of experience from above	5. world more Romantic and pensive, less festive	5. natural cycle, wheel of fate
→E ← ———	→E	I	E ←
6. shock and horror	6. end movement from active to contemplative	6. comic society collapses, disintegrates	6. human life as bondage
→E ← ———	→E	I	E ←

Fig. 5.4. The mythoi and their phases—I: innocence; E: experience

Comedy is dissected with the same maneuvers. "The first three phases of comedy are parallel to the first three phases of irony," and "the second three to the second three of romance" (AC 177). "In the first or most ironic phase of comedy, a humorous society triumphs." In "the second phase," "the hero does not transform a humorous society but simply escapes" from it (AC 180). In "the third phase," "the normal one," a "humor" (a "character dominated" by an "obsession") "gives way to a young man's desires" (AC 180, 168). In "the fourth phase," the action "moves from the normal world" to the "idealized green world[27] and back again" (AC 182). In "the fifth phase," the "world" is "more Romantic," "less festive," and "more pensive," almost to the point of "containing" "tragedy" (AC 184). In "the sixth phase," "the collapse and disintegration of comic society" occur (AC 185). This time, the two groups of three move from "experience" toward "innocence" (AC 182), which seems odd with the last phase being so grim.

To match up with the patterning of romance after the life of the hero, the "first five phases" here are made to allegorize "a sequence of stages in the life of a redeemed society": "infancy," "adolescence," "coming to maturity," "being mature and established," and "settled order" (AC 185). This leaves "death" to parallel the sixth phase, though Frye's reversal of the romance-pattern and his cyclical plan oblige him to end with "a return to the womb" from where "the embryo" came in the "first phase" of "romance" (AC 186, 198). This life-allegory may be another foray to squeeze extra mileage out of a pattern better motivated elsewhere. I can't see why "infancy" is the most ironic stage in the life of anybody, "redeemed" or not; why "coming to maturity" is "ironic" and "experienced," whereas "being mature" is "romantic" and "innocent"; and so on.

As we might predict by now, "the first three phases" of "tragedy" "correspond to the first three phases of romance," and "the last three to the last three of irony"; and we're back to the progression "from innocence to experience" set up in "romance" and reversed in "comedy" (AC 219, 211). In "the first phase," "the central character is given the greatest possible dignity" by virtue of "courage and innocence" (AC 219). "The second phase" is "the tragedy of innocence," "usually involving young people" (AC 220). "The third phase" "emphasizes" "the success" of "the hero's achievement." "The fourth phase" is "the typical fall of the hero through hybris and hamartia" (AC 221, 213), though not necessarily of the conventional sort (AC 36, 38, 41, 210). "The fifth phase" centers on "the tragedy of lost direction and lack of knowledge" (AC 222). "The ironic increases" and "the heroic decreases," with "the character" entering "a state of lower freedom than the audience" (AC 221). "The sixth phase of tragedy" is "a world of shock and horror" (AC 222). The parallel to the hero's life seems to work fairly well this

---

[27] In this "green" world, "life and love" "triumph" "over the waste land," and "summer over "winter" (AC 182f). Compare this with the "green and golden" coloring of the second phase ("youth") in romance and tragedy (AC 200, 220).

time. A tragedy often centers on one phase, though the hero's whole life might be covered in the course of the plot.

By the time he gets to irony, Frye hopes we are "accustomed to our sequence of six phases" (AC 225). "The first three are phases of satire, [28] and correspond to the first three or ironic phases of comedy"; and the last three to those of "ironic tragedy" (AC 225, 236), so that, as I said, the whole sequence goes with "experience" (see Figure 5.4). "The first phase" is "the satire of the low norm," with a "permanent and undisplaceable world" of "anomalies, injustices, follies, and crimes" (AC 226). In "the second phase," "the sources and values of conventions" are "objects of ridicule" (AC 229). "The third phase" is "the satire of the high norm," "letting go even of ordinary sense as a standard" (AC 234). "The fourth phase looks at tragedy from below, from the moral and realistic perspective of the state of experience" (AC 237). In "the fifth phase," the "irony" has its "main emphasis on the natural cycle, the steady unbroken turning of the wheel of fate." "The sixth phase presents human life in terms of largely unrelieved bondage" (AC 238). "On the other side of this," "satire begins again" (AC 239). This stipulation of cyclical motion within the mythos may remind us of the merging of death into rebirth suggested at the end of comedy and romance (AC 186, 192), though like tragedy, irony ends with a counterpart, that is, "demonic epiphany" (AC 223, 239). [29]

As if all this uniting and paralleling of the modes were not enough, Frye decides that all "four mythoi," "comedy, romance, tragedy, and irony," can "be seen as four aspects of a central unifying myth" (AC 192, 215). This myth follows the "quest," which as we saw, was "the third phase" of "romance" —"romance" being in turn "the center of gravity" for "archetypal criticism" (AC 220, 116). The "three stages" of the quest now become four to fit the mythoi: "agon" for "romance," "pathos" for "tragedy," "sparagmos" for "irony," and "anagnorisis" for "comedy" (AC 192). [30] Within this configuration, "comedy can contain a potential tragedy" just as "resurrection" requires "death" (AC 215; cf. AC 184).

This argument is claimed to show how "myths explain the structural principles behind familiar literary facts": "to make a sombre action end happily is easy, and to reverse the procedure almost impossible" ("our natural likes and dislikes" can't be the explanation because they're not "structural") (AC 215). But the most

---

[28] "Satire" is distinguished from "irony" in having "clear" "moral norms" and "standards" (AC 223).

[29] "Epiphany" is elsewhere expressly connected to rebirth (AC 215, 316). On the "Messianic" implications of such a cycle, see AC 317.

[30] "Agon" originally meant "conflict," "pathos" "death struggle," "sparagmos" "tearing apart of the sacrificial body," and "anagnorisis" "discovery" (AC 187, 148, 52). This scheme here abstracts and allegorizes the terms for the occasion: "pathos" becomes "catastrophe"; "sparagmos" becomes "the sense that heroism and effective action are absent"; and "anagnorisis" becomes "the recognition of a newborn society rising in triumph around a still somewhat mysterious hero and his bride" and later "recognition as God's son" (AC 192, 316).

incisive motivation for putting romance and its "quest" at the center of the mythoi may be Frye's interest in "the heroic quest of the Messiah from incarnation to apotheosis," the "cycle of pre-existence, life-in-death, and resurrection" (AC 316f, 215). This parallel casts Christ in the role of a "dragon-killer," the emphasis of the New Testament falling on "the Book of Revelations" (AC 189f). It also pushes the stages back to three so as to fit "the three-day rhythm of death, disappearance, and revival" in "myths" of "dying gods" like "our Easter" (AC 187).

My bare outline of Frye's scheme with four six-phase mythoi is unfair in leaving out the clusters of examples and special cases he situates in nearly every phase. But we can at least see how Frye's elaborate architecturing of theoretical categories serves his plea for an "assumption of total coherence" in literary theory (AC 16). One traditional literary value he shares without reservation is "unity" (AC 11, 77, 80, 82, 125, 246, 314). The diffuseness of forms and variations is mastered by the sheer will for order, and any signs of stress or discrepancy we may detect are hardly surprising. The patterns of sequences and parallels work better in some areas than in others. Sometimes the structure seems to have a life and motivation of its own, so that the correspondences are not so much found as urged.

Perhaps the variegated, complex, and sometimes conflicting procedures in Frye's book might best be appreciated by relating its title to his admonition that "a clearer understanding of the form and traditions of the anatomy would make a good many elements in the history of literature come into focus" (AC 312). As a "literary form" —Frye's "favorite," according to Bloom (CCP 12)—the "anatomy" is a "dissection or analysis" with an "intellectualized approach" (AC 311). It pursues an "encyclopaedic" and "creative treatment of exhaustive erudition," and a "comprehensive survey of human life." Its "verbal exuberance" "piles up an enormous mass of erudition" about its "theme" (AC 236, 311). "At its most concentrated," it "presents a vision of the world in terms of a single intellectual pattern" (AC 310). Its "unity" may be "built up from an intricate scheme of parallel contrasts" (AC 314). All these characteristics belong to Frye's book just as much as to the works he is addressing in the passages just quoted, such as Burton's (1628) *Anatomy of Melancholy* (AC 236, 311) (curiously, also the model for one Fiedler's books, WL 34). And any "appearance of carelessness" or of "violent dislocations" of "customary logic" (AC 310) may simply reflect the pressures of seeking an "ideal order among" "the existing monuments of literature" (AC 18).

This reading of Frye's title would make him essentially a satirist in the learned tradition of Menippus and Varro (cf. AC 309). In some ways, his depiction of satire could indeed apply to his own book. "Satire" "continues encyclopaedic tradition"; "the containing form" of the "satiric epic" is "the pure cycle" of the "quest" being "made over again" (AC 322). "The satiric attitude" is "an expression of the hypothetical form of art" (AC 231). "Intellectual satire defends the

creative detachment in art" (AC 233, 231). "The satirist" can "break down customary associations, reduce sense experience to one of many possible categories,
and bring out the tentative" "basis of all our thinking" (AC 235) (a goal extolled
by Iser for all literature, p. 131ff). The outcome is "to prevent any group of
conventions from dominating the whole of literary experience," and even to
"break up" "all things that impede the free movement of society" (AC 233). Such
intents sound like Frye's own "goal" of "intellectual freedom": "the ability to look
at contemporary social values with the detachment of one who is able to compare
them with the infinite vision of possibilities presented by culture" (AC 348). This
"response to culture is, like myth, a revolutionary act of consciousness" (AC
344).

His range, depth, and complexity make Frye's presence on the theoretical
scene hard to ignore, even many years later. He is cited expressly in the works of
all the other critics I review except Millett. His conception of reading by expanding one's frames of reference is widely shared, notably by Iser, Jauss, Bleich,
Holland, Hartman, Hirsch, and Jameson (who even views his own scheme of
"semantic horizons" as "dialectic equivalents" of Frye's "phases," PU 75). The
fearful symmetry in Frye's balanced oppositions, his exhiliarated schematizing
and taxonomizing, his accumulation of generic parallels and contrasts, and his
bristling terminology, anticipate the methods of structuralism; and Frye's work
might well be saluted as the more comprehensive and insightful.

He deploys "deliberate shifts in context" (letter to me) as part of his design to
include everything without reducing its individual status or dissolving its uniqueness. This ambition anticipates deconstruction as well, especially his tendencies
to remain in oscillation, to invert hierarchical oppositions, and to assign centers
to marginal forms. So even if his terms and schemes may not reappear intact very
often within more recent critical theory, his total achievement might be seen as
one of the spatial models he likes so much, one with limitless room to expand,
absorb, and integrate.

6

Leslie Fiedler[1]

Though he might seem too inimitable and quixotic to be a prototype, Leslie Fiedler has decisively contributed to shaping the role of the critic in American letters. He is "convinced" that "criticism" "*must* not die, being a human response as ancient and essential as the story and song that prompt it" (WL 127). And he has accomplished much in his campaign to see that it won't die, as he reminds us: he "helped to create" a "new cultural climate"; he "made American literature seem more interesting and amusing" than it had in "most academic accounts"; he "provided the basis for a new understanding of our classic books and of our culture in general" and so on (LD 8; WL 34; EI ix). He "announces every new insight boldly," not "trying to speak" "objectively," but "writing in pure rage and love" "what at any moment" he "passionately believes" (WL 73; NT xivf; EI xiii). Yet he "likes to think" he "registers" through his "particular sensibility the plight of a whole group," and to "see" his "own ironies and dissents as a necessary part of an overall pattern" (EI xiii, 93). In retrospect, he is "pleased to discover how often I managed to tell what still seems" "the truth about my world and myself as a liberal, intellectual, writer, American, and Jew" (EI xiii).

At no time, however, did he pretend to be a conventional authority or infallible interpreter of literature. For him "the experience of a work of art" is "unique and untranslatable; to suggest that one has captured it in analysis is" "to falsify and mislead" (LD 10). "The best criticism can hope to do is to set the work in as many illuminating contexts as possible," to "locate the work" where it "exists in all its ambiguity and plenitude." To set the "object" "in *all* its relevant contexts" is "the never-completed communal task of criticism."

"The 'text' is merely" the "lexical or verbal" "context," "no more or less important than the sociological, psychological, historical, anthropological, or

---

[1] The key for Fiedler citations is: EI: *An End to Innocence* (1971 [1948-5]); LD: *Love and Death in the American Novel* (1984 [1960, 1966]); NT: *No! in Thunder* (1960); and WL: *What Was Literature?* (1982). For passages repeated from earlier books to a later ones, I try to give all sources. I removed some italicizing that didn't seem to the point for my summary (e.d. = emphasis deleted). I agree with Fiedler that any summarizing is apt to lose his "cadences" and thus a "part of the real significance" (letter to me). But he was "pleased to see" that my chapter had managed to preserve "much" of his "own style."

generic." Hence, Fiedler strove to "emphasize the neglected depth-psychological," "anthropological," "sociological, and formal" "contexts of American fiction." This move earned him the stature of a "theoretical critic," at a time when very few scholars sought it. He himself warned that pure "theorizing" "threatens to leave literature and its appropriate delights for the sake of amateur philosophizing," and preferred to proceed by "embedding" "full-scale readings" and "analyses" "in a context of more general theoretical explications" (NT 295; LD 9f).

His broad contextual method allowed him to function as a "general critic of society," critiquing "cultural" and "political events" in "the American scene" and attempting at times to "write a thumbnail moral history of our time" (NT x; EI xiv, 28). Indeed, the major work he addresses, whatever texts are cited, is none other than America itself, a place where "literature" can "influence 'real life' more than such life influences it" (LD 31).[2] Though he may treat America as a literary creation of novelists and philosophers,[3] he may have done as much as they to make it so. He has expounded the treatment of America, by its own authors and by Europeans, in literary and fictional terms few cultural historians of the nation can henceforth safely ignore.

One benefit of "telling the truth" not just "about literature," but "about the indignities and rewards of being" "an "American" (LD 16), is that Fiedler himself can join the prospective protagonists of literary America. His criticism has overtones of an "autobiography" portraying his "sentimental education" (NT xiv). His arguments are often clinched with anecdotes from his own life,[4] as if he were living out a modern allegory. He seems as much at home in the worlds of Huck Finn and Ishmael as in those of Twain and Melville—a critic-stowaway to "America," "the land for which we can only set out" (NT 152). This fate well befits a would-be author forced to turn critic by the distaste of "editors" for his "fiction and verse," consoling himself that "literary criticism" is "a form of literature," and *Love and Death* is a "gothic novel" (NT 295; LD 8). His comment that the greatest creations of authors like Poe and Fitzgerald were themselves (EI 177ff; LD 424) might be applied to him too, though whereas their careers fell under the motto "nothing succeeds like failure" (EI 174f; LD 427; WL 31), I later suggest (p. 96) that his own may be tending to illustrate the converse.

He considers himself *"primarily* a literary person," a reader of private and public life as if it were a text, using "a sensibility trained by the newer critical methods" (EI xivf). He offered "a 'close reading' of recent events" and "pledged"

---

[2] Illustrations include literary images of sentimental love and of the incorruptibly naive child (LD 31, 81; EI 253, 259).

[3] This doctrine was asserted in 1952 for "Montana," but the "Chateaubriand" and "Rousseau" version had long since yielded to "the sentimentalized Frontier novel" (EI 131; 164).

[4] For instance, the low status of the "critic" is revealed by how Fiedler had his "house" "snatched away" by "a local 'scholar'" in 1953 (WL 60). Or, his wide-ranging, generalizing essay about the "Negro" describes most of the few blacks he knew closely as a child (NT 245ff).

"to give certain political documents" "the same careful scrutiny we have learned to practice on the shorter poems of John Donne"[5]; but also to "approach" "poems" "with the sense that they matter quite as much to the self and the world" as political events like "the suspension of atomic testing" (EI xv; NT xvf). He professes "no expert knowledge in political matters" and himself "an indifferent researcher," although here, as often, he is adjusting his image to elude scholarly clichés (his research is extensive, but offhandedly presented). His claim upon the attention of his audience is his "deep" "involvement" (EI xv). His "interest in works of art is dictated by a moral[6] passion," and his "personal myth" is "The Intellectual Life as Moral Combat" (EI xiv; NT 6; cf. LD 16).

"To fulfill its essential moral obligation," "serious fiction" "must be negative" (NT 6f, e.d.). Hence, Fiedler expropriates, for his "last word" in "literary theory," as of 1960 (also in the 1971 edition of NT), the slogan "'No! in thunder,'" originally coined by Melville for Hawthorne's art (NT 296, 8; LD 505). "Insofar as a work of art is, as art, successful, it performs a negative critical function" (NT 7). Artists can "achieve" in a work "a coherence, a unity, a balance, a satisfaction of conflicting impulses" "they cannot achieve in love, family relations, politics." "Literature" is "the record of those elusive moments at which life is alone fully itself, fulfilled in consciousness and form" (LD 15f). The "intolerable inadequacy" of "radically imperfect human activities" is "revealed" when they are "represented in a perfectly articulated form" (NT 7). Even (or especially) in its "most magnificent portrayal," "the image of man in art" expresses "failure." "Telling the truth" is opening a "vision of an eternal gap between imagined order and actual chaos" (NT 11). "Having endured a vision of the meaninglessness of existence," "the negativist" "affirms the void" and "renders the absurdity which he perceives" (NT 20). To "abjure negativism" is to "sacrifice truth and art" and be not a "serious artist," but a "purveyor of commodity fiction" who "perishes as he pleases" (NT 20, 10f). To "pursue" "the positive means stylistic suicide" amid "unearned euphoria," "shapeless piety," "sentimental self-indulgence," "maudlin falsity," "heavy-handed symbolism," and similar "failures" (NT 19f).

Fiedler suggests that "censors" attack "serious fiction" not because of its "'dirtiness,'" but because of this "negative" quality (NT 6f). He recalls that "literary criticism" "was born of conflict, out of an attempt to dissuade those who would control or ban poetry as socially and morally dangerous" (WL 39). "Literature asserts," if "anything," "the impossibility of unqualified assertion, the ambiguity of all moral imperatives" (WL 129) (a notion de Man pursues for different

---

[5] "Donne" and "newer criticism" here, as well as "close reading" in the previous quote, are signposts for the "New Critics" whose influence on Fiedler and his 1941 dissertation will be discussed in a moment.

[6] This sense of "moral" applies only to the artistic function and "the moral effect of literary art" (cf. p. 81f); it is quite distinct from that of commonplace middle-class or Puritan morality, which may even foster "full-blown self conscious evil" and "lynchings" (NT 277; EI 82). Conflicts between the two kinds of morality are often suggested (EI 154, 196; LD 95, 425; WL 39f, 42, 50 122).

reasons, p. 261). "On its deeper, more mythological levels," "literature" owes its "most nearly universal appeal" to being "fundamentally antinomian" and "reinforcing no respectable pieties of any kind," "no matter what its superficial ideology." This function is necessary because "the burden of any system of morality becomes finally irksome even to its most sincere advocates, since it necessarily denies, represses, suffocates certain undying primal impulses" that "need somehow to be expressed" (WL 50) (compare Iser's view, p. 144).

Over the years, Fiedler's progress reminds one of a self-consuming artifact, a titanic Kronos-critic gaining sustenance partly by devouring earlier versions of himself. One such version, namely as a leftist promoter of "radical politics," was soon attenuated and disclaimed as an effect first of "pressure from friends on the Left" and later of "nostalgia for a lost revolution and my own lost youth" (NT ix; WL 147). He asks to be considered "by temperament apolitical," "politics" being "the opium of the liberals" (NT ixf). He "smiles" over "attempts at social realism" "in Europe today," and over literary portrayals of "the Class Struggle" in "American 'realism'" of "the 'thirties" (NT 198). He uncouples the "authors' politics" from the readers' "passionate" "response"; and (as just shown in his treatment of negativity) "superficial ideology" from the "antinomian" message (WL 133, 129; cf. WL 195).

He was already on the backswing when he published his first book. In that array of "polemical" "essays," he explains that "the typical initiation into the intellectual community" included "a brief bout of membership in the Communist party, fellow-travelling," or "collaboration" with people of such creeds (EI xiv, 67f; cf. EI 107).[7] "'In those days, anyone with guts and brains'" went that way (NT 164). The "Communist" "movement" "established itself in the intellectual community as an acceptable variant of the liberal-humanistic tradition" and a "test of political decency" in a time of "moral dissatisfaction" (EI 70; NT 165).

But by "1954," Fiedler saw in "Communism" only "the rationalization and defense of that which Russia and its agents do for the sake of expansion or self-defense" (EI 59f). Along with "the main body of liberals," he "recognized" the "Soviet Union" "as a symbol of social evil," and certified that "the human spirit is offended and maimed wherever Communist governments exist" (EI 67, 71). He even pronounced his own condemnations of Hiss and the Rosenbergs, though for "motives" "too complex to set before an ordinary juryman" (EI 6). He assailed Ethel Rosenberg's "painfully pretentious" attempts at "literary" "style" in her letters (EI 40ff), but never suggested it as grounds for capital punishment. For an instant, though, I felt oddly reminded of his legalistic dictum that, for their "sloppiness" and "submission to the decay of language," "pseudo-" or "anti-

---

[7] He also claims he went "radical" in "a desire to be delivered from the disabilities of being a Jew," and from a hope that "in the Marxist scheme of remaking society," he could "win" "freedom rather than buy it at the expense of somebody else" (NT 248).

stylists" "stand condemned in the court of high art for flagrant immorality of form" (NT 4)—whereupon they are presumably shot with an aesthetic cannon.

"Marxist critics" were still lauded for having taught Fiedler that "the class relations of a culture help determine the shape of its deepest communal fantasies, the obsessive concerns of its literature" (LD 14), although the Freudian drift is already getting the upper hand in this formulation. Even so, "Marxism" is blamed for the "quasi-religious messianism" of the "proletarian novel" that "projected violence" as a "method of deliverance" (LD 481f). When Fiedler later becomes an emphatic populist, he thinks to charge "Marxists" with "elitism in the arts" and Marx himself with having been a "genteel academic" (WL 27, 100).

"Marxist aesthetics as developed by "Marcuse" and "the Frankfurt school" (discussed in Chs. 17, 18), are dismissed as a "paranoid 'conspiracy' theory" (WL 101). This move is justified, in the grand Fiedlerian manner, with a personal anecdote (how an article of his got attacked) to show how "boards of directors" in "publishing and broadcasting" "detest and fear" "horror and porn"; they merely "seek to provide" "what they surmise the mass audience wants." But this claim overlooks his own earlier thesis (p. 79) that censors are really trying to suppress negativity—which is precisely Marcuse's argument, and Jameson's too.

Another early Fiedler was devoted to aesthetic and formal issues. He admired Matthew Arnold and the New Criticism, writing his dissertation on John Donne (NT x; WL 146, 88). He praised works for being "precisely imaged or richly phrased," and for attaining through their "richness and difficulty of involution" "reaches of meaning unavailable to perspicuity" (NT 66, 29). He rejoiced in discovering "oppositions," "antinomies," "contradictions," "paradoxes," "reversals," "ambiguity," "ambivalence," and "multivalence" (NT 32, 35, 50f, 102, 41, 39, 74, 129, 86, 98, 101). "Irony," "detachment," and "complexity" were hailed as bulwarks against "confession," "sentimentality," "self-pity," and "nostalgia" (NT 55; EI 178, 180, 206f).

The "total effect" of an "intricately constructed and immensely complex work" can make it "the most deeply moving" of its kind, though Fiedler once worried that a "complex" work may not attain "success" and "fame," or only if "simplified in the folk mind" (LD 414, 490, 263ff). "Our better novelists" are "un-popular" or else "misread" and "admired for the wrong reasons," since "the mass audience has stubbornly refused to catch up" even with "the techniques" of the "'twenties" (EI 200; NT 5). This lag might be an advantage if the "work of art can be wrecked" upon its own "popularities" (NT 104). Later, though, Fiedler sides with "mass audience" enough to disdain "modernism" himself, as will be shown below (p. 101).

Yet already in his early books, Fiedler was not at ease among the "embattled highbrows" he saw in the "New Critics" (NT 134). He distrusted "'formalism'" for its "gentility, overelaboration, and the sentimentalizing of detached insight" (EI 185). For such a "critic," the work is "at best a skillful and sophisticated

arrangement of words, a pleasantly intricate web of sensibility, which is judged good or bad in terms of how complex and various, though finally unified, in its abstract pattern" (LD 155).

Even while Fiedler averred that "a work of art is on one level about the problems of its own composition," he castigated "the notion" of the "work" being "absolutely self-contained, a discrete set of mutually interrelated references," as a "reductio ad absurdum" if not "a dangerous full-blown aesthetic position" (NT 48, 313). That notion is "even apparently applicable only to a lyric of the most absolute purity" (NT 314). The "formalists'" "extreme nominalist definition of a work of art" is "metaphysically reprehensible" (NT 311). Hence, even the New Critical "reforms in pedagogy" were conceded merely a "small usefulness" alongside having failed to "explain great novels of our own tradition" and "inhibited" "new experiments" "in poetry" (WL 71; cf. NT 316). Most recently, "New Criticism" is belabored for "proto-fascist" if not "fascist politics" (WL 42, 70; cf. NT 187)—though Fiedler, we saw, freely waves aside his own erstwhile "politics."

A more enduring version of Fiedler is the critic of "myths" and "archetypes." Indeed, he ranks with Frye as an archetypal proponent of this method and even draws from it a means of evaluation (NT 324). For Fiedler, the "archetype" is defined as an "immemorial pattern of response to the human situation in its most permanent aspects"; or as an "archaic and persisting cluster of image and emotion which at once defines and attempts to solve what is most permanent in the human predicament" (NT 319, 301). It "belongs to the infra- or meta-personal," "to the Community at its deepest, pre-conscious levels of acceptance" (NT 319). This "pattern of beliefs and feelings" is "so widely shared at a level beneath consciousness that there exists no abstract vocabulary for representing it" (EI 146). It "finds a formula or pattern story" to "embody it" and "conceal its full implications" about some "aspect of our psycho-social fantasy life" (EI 146; WL 15f).

A related concept—Fiedler can't quite make up his mind how far it's the same—is "myth" or "mythos."[8] Borrowing his remark on Pavese, we might picture Fiedler as "proceeding from speculation on myth to a general theory of literature" (NT 147). He finds in "mythos" both "an immediate intuition of being, pure quality without the predicate of existence," the "intuited" here equaling "the archetypes"; and a "mediator between the community and the individual, the person and his fate, the given and the achieved" (NT 301f). The "archetypal meaning" of a "myth" is "independent of any individual's conscious exploitation of it" (NT 49). Its "unity underlies the diversity of our acquired cultures"

---

[8] On one occasion, "Archetype" is substituted more or less as an equivalent for "myth" when the latter "becomes increasingly ambiguous" (NT 318; cf. WL 129f). On another, "Archetype" is judged "too modern and abstract to encompass the total richness of mythos," forcing Fiedler to "call mythos by its poor, prostituted cognate, myth" (NT 302). On yet another, "mythos" is "defined" "as the Archetype without Signature" (NT 304).

(NT 142) (Frye would agree). "Even in the most sophisticated communities, mythos survives below the margin of consciousness," "since all power" "must come from below reason" (NT 300). The "ancient Greek Myths" "preserve for us the assurance" "that what is done below is done above, what is done here and now is done forever, what is repeated in time subsists unbroken in eternity" (NT 302).

"Literature" "comes into existence at the moment" "the Archetype" is given a "Signature": "the sum total of individualizing factors in a work, the sign of the Persona or Personality through which an Archetype is rendered" (NT 319). The "great artist" must be "capable" "at once of realizing utterly the archetypal implications of his material and of formally embodying it in a lucid and unmistakable Signature" (NT 327). "When myth is uncertainly becoming literature," "the poet is conceived of passively, as a mere vehicle" for "the Muse," that is, for "the unconscious, collective source of the Archetypes" (NT 325). "But very soon the poet" "assumes a more individualized life-style, the lived Signature," thereby "making the first forays out of collectivity toward personality" (NT 325f). "The mass mind" "composes" an "image to punish the poet for detaching himself from the collective id" —thus the "Alienated Artist" we still visualize today (NT 325f).

"Poetry is historically the mediator between mythos and logos, the attempt to find a rationale for the pre-rational" (NT 300). "We experience the controlling perceptions of poetry as poetry" as "closer to mythos than to logos" (NT 301). "Philosophy" and "its heir," "science," are "representatives" of "logos" and think "there is no mode" except this (NT 300). The "hubris of science" is to "deny poetry which alone could become its conscience." Fiedler arrives at a "series" of formulas: "the Marvelous as Marvelous is mythos; the Marvelous as Credible, poetry; the Credible as Credible, philosophy and science; the Credible as Marvelous," "rhetoric, journalism, kitsch" (NT 303). "Much contemporary criticism has cut itself off from this insight" (NT 324).

Fiedler consistently attributes the "power" and value of literature to its "mythopoetic" qualities.[9] "The mythic work" can have "instant acclaim," whereas "great analytic or poetic works" "often have to wait long for their popularity" (LD 187). "A work of literature" "does not finally depend for its force and conviction on 'truth' of action, character, or detail, but upon how much daemonic energy of the myth survives its rationalization" (NT 147).[10] Yet though "consideration of the archetypal content of works" is "essential" to "evaluation" (NT 324), no simple equation or causality is implied here. On the one hand, "mythopoetic power" is "independent of formal excellence" and may be found in works that are

---

[9] See LD 62, 84, 156, 174, 191, 273, 474; WL 36, 125, 198, 217, 231; NT 324. Even Freud is awarded "mythopoetic power" (NT 308), which might explain why his reputation among literary critics has outdistanced that among psychologists.

[10] This view is assigned to Cesare Pavese (NT 147), with whom Fiedler showed extraordinary empathy, expostulating Pavese's ideas in ways that seem to capture his own as well.

"woefully inadequate by conventional literary standards" (WL 36, 165)—a key factor in Fiedler's later outlook. In *Uncle Tom's Cabin*, the "most mythically resonant tableaus" are "usually the 'worst' written," "yet so magically moving" as to "transcend" "the criteria of taste" (WL 165). On the other hand, using myth or archetype does not guarantee successful literature. If used self-consciously, a "myth" may be "degraded, profaned" (NT 49). "Archetypes" can enter a "fallen form" as "inherited and scarcely understood structures," "platitudes," "type characters," "'popular' stock plots," or "stereotypes" (NT 328, 274; WL 130, 141, 151; LD 166, 226, 310, 400, 420). "Subliterature" may subsist on "a shoddy, and cheaply popular evocation of archetypal themes"; or "comic strips" on "obsolescent" and "embalmed" "archetypes" (NT 80, 288).

Evidently, "myth" can get "secularized into 'entertainment'" or deployed as a "machine" "to lend the semblance of metaphysical depth to a half-imagined story," to "do the work of imagination, invention, and coherence" (NT 306, 107). The "anti-artist" "composes parables, pseudo-myths, to express not wonder and terror but sentimental reassurance" (NT 11). To "redeem" "debased popular archetypes," "the writer" may "rerender" them "for serious purposes" "through complex and subtle signatures"; or "ironically manipulate the shreds and patches of outlived mythologies"; or "invent a private myth system of his own"; or pursue his own "personality, past his particular foibles and eccentricities, to his unconscious core, where he becomes one with us all" (NT 328f).[11] But these tactics bring hazards: "plot" may "founder under the burden of overt explication"; "the popular audience" may be lost; "highbrow reworkings" may merely signal that the "archetypes" "are dying"; and so on (NT 328f; EI 136).

Another pervasive and controlling theoretical framework in Fiedler's writings, and the one that brings him the closest he comes to jargonizing, is "psychoanalysis," touted as "the science of our age" (NT 308). "Depth psychology" offers "a way of binding together our fractured world, of uniting literature and non-literature without the reduction of the poem" (NT 323, e.d.). "Psychoanalysis" as "a theory of the mind has been part of our culture for nearly half a century"; by now, "the procedures of pre-Freudian critics" are "hopelessly outdated" (NT 224; 311). Fiedler appropriated "much of his basic vocabulary" from "orthodox Freudianism and Jungian revisionism" (LD 14). In recent work, he still professes himself a "vestigial" "Freudian," "believing that character is destiny"; and an "anti-Jungian Jungian," holding that "archetypes are not eternal but socially determined" —a trace of the "vestigial Marxist" (WL 17).

Fiedler's version of Freud is less orthodox than Holland's, though more so than Frye's, Bleich's, Bloom's, or Jauss's. Jung's "further allegorization" is admitted, whereby "what Freud took to be final facts" are reconsidered to be "only symbols of a deeper-lurking reality" (NT 308). Such a step is congenial to the

---

[11] This argument serves to justify the use of "depth analysis, as defined by Freud, and, particularly by Jung," and, somewhat oddly, to advocate "the biographical approach" (NT 329).

literary critic because "the poetic overtones of the archetype," the source of the power of literature, are not "threatened" (NT 309). But Fiedler is too committed to the "bleak stoicism," "despair," and "tragic view of man" in Freudian thought to accept the "expurgation" of Freud into "a bourgeois prophet of social adjustment" for the "ideal image of society" (NT 224f, 310). The "revisionists" like Karen Horney with their "optimism" and "rationality" are rebuked for offering "platitudes" that "society cannot live by" (NT 310) (but see p. 208).

Fiedler's own depth-psychological depiction of literary experience wavers between hope and pessimism. "Psychic levels" form the center "from which works of art proceed and to which they seek to return" (LD 389). "All art, high, low or middling, of wide mythic appeal provides on the first encounter" an "unearned instant gratification" "necessary to our psychic well-being" (WL 138, e.d.). This event, he feels, is inadequately described by "anal Aristotle's" "catharsis," "Thoreau's" "in dreams awake," and "Freud's" "regression in the service of the ego." More "intriguing" is the conception of "a descent into, a harrowing of Hell," "a recourse to the dark powers in quest of salvation: a way out of the secular limbo," the "least-common-denominator consensus reality enforced in the name of sanity and virtue" (WL 138f). Through its "release of the repressed," "popular literature" makes us "more at home with" "the darker, more perilous aspects of our own psyches" (WL 49f).

Yet this process "triggers another primeval response: the fear of the unconscious and its tyranny," and thus of "the art which simultaneously releases and neutralizes its darker aspects" (WL 42). "Censorship" can then raise the "contention that art is incitement rather than therapy, reinforcing whatever a given era considers socially undesirable or morally reprehensible." This account gives the "negativity" previously judged to motivate "censors" (NT 6) a twist back toward narrower moralistic issues—a loss, in my view, fixating the artist on a certain mode of negating, much as Holland does within his lighter-hearted model.

Even more than Frye, Fiedler expounds literary phenomena in terms of "dreams."[12] Writing itself is repeatedly portrayed as a dreaming process.[13] "In literature," we learn, "myth and dream are made flesh" (NT 232; cf. LD 192). A main grouping of themes in these dreams includes "innocence," "purity," "virginity," and "remitted" "guilt" (NT 123ff, 158; LD 393, 274, 327, 353). Yet as befits Fiedler's propensity for the "darker aspects," the "nightmare" is invoked still more often than the dream.[14] Besides the usual "ancestral and infantile fears," such as "rejection, paralysis, castration, and death," these "nightmares" feature

---

[12] Compare NT 11, 30, 37, 61f, 84, 106, 123ff, 129, 139, 158; LD 26, 29, 59, 95, 128, 155, 157, 183, 224, 356, 393, 396, 399, 491.

[13] Compare EI 147; NT 84, 139; LD 157, 183, 276, 393, 396, 399, 491; WL 152, 175.

[14] Compare NT 10, 14, 37, 55, 57, 123ff, 130, 132f; LD 26, 52, 98, 127, 155, 164, 244, 260, 280, 314, 353f, 364, 369, 373, 375, 379, 393, 399, 435, 438, 493, 497; WL 16, 50, 160, 168, 194, 204f, 209, 222, 235, 245.

the suffering and revenge of groups downtrodden by white male Americans: the Indians, the Blacks, and the women.[15] The "American dream" of "innocence" and "purity" reverts to a "nightmare" of "guilt" and "evil" (NT 123f; LD 393; cf. LD 287, 315).

Fiedler also invokes the allegorical trio of ego, superego, and id (or libido), his own secret motto apparently being "Where Superego or Ego was, Id shall be" — the reversal of Freud's "demythifying" dictum, "Where Id was Ego shall be" (WL 37).[16] "Depth psychology" is hailed as the "'theology'" of the "Psychic Breakthrough, the Re-emergence of the Id" (NT 256). Our "age" is "characterized by the consciousness of the unconscious and by the resolve to propitiate and honor that dark force." The "major revolution" in the literature of "the mid-eighteenth century," inspired by Rousseau and encouraging "Pantheism, Deism, Sturm und Drang, Sentimentalism, Romanticism, etc.," is thought to make a "god" of the "id" in place of the "superego" previously "deified" "for more than seventeen hundred years."

The "novel marks the entrance of the libido onto the stage of European art" (LD 44). "The popular mind" "demands" a "villain" as a "dark projection of id or superego to be symbolically defeated" (LD 100, 198). But the id gets to be a hero as well. "The Good Bad Boy of Western culture" "represents the id subverting tired ego ideals, not in terror or anarchy" (as had been done via the "symbols of the gothic"), "but in horseplay, pranks, and irreverent jests" (LD 272, 131). "Lean Bean," "Huck," and "Nigger Jim" are all taken as "id-figures"; at one point Fiedler associates the "id" with "the symbolic Negro" at large (LD 174, 279; NT 239f). Perhaps Fiedler's skepticism about an eventual union of his racially divided society (e.g. WL 231f) matches his conviction that "profound and aboriginal" "forces in our life" "work against" conceiving "the relationship of instinct and ego," "black" and "white," as a "marriage of equals" (LD 368).[17]

A similar allegorizing pervades Fiedler's vision of family relationships. He offers an "archetypal metaphor" for the various aspects of authorship: "the personal element" is "the Son, the conscious-communal the Father, and the unconscious-communal the Mother" (NT 321).[18] He regards the "family romance" in Jungian terms: "the desire for incest with the mother symbolizes the desire to remain a child, to be unborn"; "the murder of the father signifies the rejection of

---

15 Compare LD 26, 128, 369, 373, 375, 399, 435; WL 16, 168, 194, 204f, 209, 222, 235. This revenge most often takes the form of murder or rape.

16 Freud is called a "defender-betrayer of myths," presumably because he "mythicized reason," yet "demythicized" by "rationalizing" a "figure of poetry" and by bringing myths to the awareness of the ego (WL 37; NT 307; cf. NT 299, 309).

17 "The rapid mobility of American social life" is said to make this "marriage" seem plausible (NT 368); but the "mobility" projected by American literature comes from running away from society.

18 Making the woman represent the "unconscious" (also LD 57, 339) implies that females read literature with more orientation toward the mythic or the id, but Fiedler portrays them doing just the opposite, as we'll find later (p. 92f).

fatherhood, of adult responsibility" (NT 308f). Alternately, Melville's vision sees "mother and father" as poles of "a fundamental conflict" between "two princi- ples, called variously earth and heaven, nature and spirit, id and superego" (LD 423). Or, "the battle with the dragon can be interpreted" as "an attack of the son against the father" as well as "the victory of light over storm and darkness," "a combat with the Devil or with God," or "an assault on the irrational in nature and an attempt to resolve the world's mysteries by liquidating them" (LD 384f).

More specifically, family roles figure in analyzing literary characterization. As in Frye, "the "despised Father" is perpetually cast as "enemy," "villain, "Evil," and so on (WL 227; LD 56, 100, 120, 463; NT 91, 272). "The beloved Mother" is more ambivalent: for the "boy" she is "the secret enemy, to be evaded even as she is loved," because she is "wholly committed to respectable codes of piety and success" (LD 212f, 352). The boy's Oedipal feelings are offered as the "secret" motive for the persistent fascination with "incest" as a literary theme[19]: the "bride" as "sister" is the "first surrogate for the mother" (LD 56; cf. Frye, AC 200). Remarkably "many early novels end with the discovery by the hero that the mistress for whom he has sighed is his sister" (LD 56; cf. AC 101). But the incest taboo may sometimes have been just a notoriously presentable pretext for the novelist to debar sexual union from the plot line without seeming merely pru- dish.

Central to Fiedler's overall conception is the role of the third family member, the child, whose awareness stands for that of both writers and readers of litera- ture. "A work of art is successful insofar as it can recapture for us the 'state of grace' which as children we live" (NT 147) (another insight where Pavese matches Fiedler). "Normally, the vividly experienced moments on which a poet feeds throughout his career belong to childhood and adolescence," "before the natural scene has lost its primal magic" (NT 75). Especially in "twentieth- century fiction," "writers" "depend" on "the child's fresh vision as a true vision, a model of the artist's vision itself" (NT 276). From "the joy of innocence," the child undergoes "initiation" as "a fall through knowledge to maturity," and as "the start of moral life" amid "full-blown, self-conscious evil" (NT 281, 277). "The confrontation of adult corruption and childish perception remains a con- temporary subject, though we no longer believe in the redemption of our guilt by the innocence of the child" (NT 277). Thus, "the child character," originally "made compulsory by restrictions of gentility and fear of sex," becomes a means to "confront rather than evade experience" (LD 345).[20]

Authorship is portrayed in accord with Fiedler's already demonstrated ten- dencies to personalize and psychoanalyze. On the personalizing side, Fiedler vows "it is impossible to draw a line between the work a poet writes and the work

---

[19] Compare LD 87, 98, 104, 111f, 120, 122, 125, 232, 241, 243, 338, 348, 414, 418f, 423.

[20] The "Primal Scene" is of course a case in point (LD 345; NT 284), though Fiedler gives it by no means the universal function Holland does (DY 110f).

he lives" (NT 317f).[21] If "a pattern of social behavior can be quite as much a symbol as a word," then a "symbolics" should be able to "analyze" both "poem" and "poet's life" in the same "terms" (NT 318). Indeed, "the poet's life" "with his work" "makes up his total meaning"; and "a sense" of that "life" "will raise" "to higher power" "the larger meanings" in "a whole body of work" (NT 317). "A work of art is a history," "a record of the scruples and hesitations of its maker" (NT 47). By offering "the connective link between the poem on the page and most of its rewarding contexts," "biography" can counteract "the endemic disease of our era": "the failure to connect" (NT 317).

In this spirit, certain passages are deemed to represent the author's own "sentiments," "fantasies," "memories" of "childhood" and "home life," and so on (LD 99; NT 30; WL 241; LD 226). Characters are taken as "images" or "disguised portraits" of the author's own self (LD 498, 115, 252). "Melville and Pierre are symbolically one" (LD 455). "Tom Sawyer" and "Mark Twain are alternative sketches of the same character" (LD 284). "Kenyon" is "Hawthorne's mouthpiece" (LD 418). "Quentin Compson" "represents the conscience of Faulkner himself" (LD 414). And so on. Or, characters are construed as figures of the "artist" at large, in such roles as "questing lover," "outsider," "pariah," and "taboo wanderer" (LD 114f, 239, 469, 360f). Poe and Fitzgerald fashioned their own lives to reveal the "alienated artist" becoming a "drunken" "failure" —welcomed by an audience seeking a "conventional public myth" (LD 424, 426ff; EI 126f, 176ff; NT 326; WL 30f).

On the psychoanalyzing side, Fiedler focuses on the author as a "personality, inferred or discovered," so that "biographical information" serves "the understanding" of "ego elements" (NT 317, 321, e.d.). Since, as we found, writing is compared to dreaming, the author draws from the "unconscious" or "half-conscious" mind (LD 52, 435, 451; WL 137f; cf. LD 63, 241; NT 299, 329); Characters can be formed by a "splitting," particularly of "the author's ambivalent self, like our surrogates in REM sleep," as befits "the divided state of the psyche in modern life" (WL 133, 200; NT 90; LD 91f, 218, 336, 384, 386f).

Special notice goes to the author's "obsessions," which may be "harmful to art," but may also, if "mastered" and "transcended," render a work the "most convincing and moving" (WL 179, 182, 184; NT 26ff, 30, 54, 58, 76, 100, 115, 118, 149f, 278, 129, 150, 143, 132). However, an author's "syndrome" may make the treatment of a "theme" "too personal and pathological to shed much light" on its "general meaning" "in American literature and life" (LD 416). The "works" may be merely "symptoms rather than achievements" (LD 423). A "portrait" may "fail to become mythic" if it "arises not out of the part" of the author's "uncon-

---

[21] Contrast this assertion with: "only the most despicable of our contemporaries confuse the value of a man's collected works with that of his life"; or "the biographical fact" "does not finally matter" (NT xv, 29).

scious continuous with the collective unconscious, but out of repressed resentments, very private and personal" (LD 170).

Still, for the "community," the author has the psychic function of an "avatar" for an ancient, "almost universal" "archetype" harking back to "Orpheus" and "Euripides" (LD 426; WL 29). The "exclusion and scourging" of "the artist" is "the psychodrama of us all," "played out in earnest" (EL 127). As noted in the treatment of "signature" and "archetype," "the community foresees" in the "poet" who "invents" "personal consciousness" "its own imminent fall from the unity and peace of pre-conscious communal life, and they condemn him" (LD 426). Moreover, "the artist as outcast or outsider" offers a "surrogate for all in himself that the common reader secretly regrets having to reject in name of morality and success" (LD 425). An "artist" who "enacts rejected values" and is "abused" for it can "free the community from the burden of its repressed longings and secret guilt" (LD 426).[22] This account makes the author an "ego destroyed by the representatives of the id." Yet an author voicing the "unconscious" and the "myth" should have an "id" role; and one crying "'No!' in thunder!" resembles the super-ego.

Within the archetypal and depth-psychological orientations outlined so far, Fiedler pursues his "desire to define what is peculiarly American in our books" (LD 11).[23] Since "Americans" "believe that what we dream rather than what we are is our essential truth," such concerns are "not mere matters of historical interest or literary relevance"; "they affect the lives we lead from day to day and influence the writers in whom the consciousness of our plight is given clarity and form" (EI 172; LD 12f). Moreover, "the essential fact of literature in our age" is "its inevitable 'Americanization,'" "as mass culture advances and the old systems of evaluation go down" (EI 210). The "achievement of the American novel" is "to have posed" "the question": "can the lonely individual, unsustained by tradition in an atomized society, achieve a poetry adult and complicated enough to be the consciousness of its age?" (EI 210).

The "native tradition of symbolism" was "born of the profound contradictions of our national life and sustained by the inheritance from Puritanism of a typical (even allegorical) way of regarding the sensible world—not as ultimate reality, but as a system of signs to be deciphered" (LD 29) (cf. Chs. 12, 13). "Perhaps in America alone the emergence of a tragic literature is still possible" (EI 127). "Only where the sense of the inevitability of man's failure does not cancel out the realization of the splendor of his vision" and vice versa "can tragedy be touched"

---

[22] Or, an "alienated writer" can "objectify" the "unconfessed universal fear" of a community such as the "Americans" that they "may not be loved," may be "rejected, refused" (EI 150f).

[23] His sense is acute enough to tell if a book's failure is due to being "too little concerned with the experience of America" or "a little too American" (LD 490, 494). Europe, in contrast, makes him confused and ambivalent (cf. EI 124, 32, 113; LD 272, vs. EI 114, 164).

(EI 128). "If he can resist the vulgar temptation to turn a quick profit" with a "best-selling parody of hope, and the snobbish temptation to burnish chic versions of elegant despair," "the American writer" "has, after all, a real function" (EI 128). "If it is a use he is after and not a reward, there is no better place for the artist than America."

Whatever the moral fiber of the nation,[24] it is the peculiar trait of American "novels" to seem "not primitive, but innocent, unfallen in a disturbing way, almost juvenile" (LD 24). The "credo of original innocence" arose to confound the Puritan one of "original sin" (LD 184, 27). This confrontation made "the ambiguity of innocence" a central "theme of the deepest American mind" (EI 197). Portrayals of Americans as "mythically innocent" or "innocent by definition and forever" (e.g., in the works of Henry James) cannot overcome the dualism whereby "natural innocence" "corresponds" to "natural depravity" (LD 312, 308, 454). Americans are cast out of "the garden of illusion": "the age of innocence is dead," taking with it "the lapsed American dream of innocent success" (EI 24; LD 315).

"Writers" may indeed profit from "believing in hell" when "the official guardians of morality do not" (LD 30). The negativity Fiedler prizes in art may be manifested in blasphemy, a deliberate affront to the doctrine of innocence (cf. NT 13; LD 30, 336, 432, 504). An author who does not believe in hell or sin is prone to fail in his art—a judgment passed on Stevenson, Cooper, and Poe (NT 89; LD 185, 430).

In a tribute to "the critical importance of childhood experiences" (WL 46), Fiedler adjudges America to be "a society whose values are largely set in boyhood" (NT 14). "All Americans like to think of themselves as young" (WL 65). "The myth" of "boyhood" fosters "the regressiveness, in a technical sense, of American life, its implacable nostaligia for the infantile, at once wrong-headed and somehow admirable" (EI 144). "America's vision of itself" is "the Good Bad Boy," a "crude and unruly" "roughneck," but "sexually pure" and "endowed by his creator with an instinctive sense of what is right" (LD 270; NT 265).

"Great works of American fiction" therefore convey the viewpoint of "a preadolescent," the "novelist" "compulsively" "returning to a limited world of experience, usually associated with his childhood" (LD 24). Such a "world" is "accustomed to regarding the relations between the sexes in terms of the tie that binds mother to son" (LD 271). So "all American boys belong to mother," and to "betray" her is "the unforgivable sin" (NT 263; LD 270). The literary "fate of the American male" is "his fall from potency and his return to the maternal embrace

---

[24] As remarked in Note 6, "moral" has two very different meanings for Fiedler, one for society and one for the artist (and himself). The second is probably intended when he extols America as "a nation" "continuing to act on a plane where moral judgment" and "real protest" are "still conceivable" (EI 33f). This morality is not broken, but camouflaged, by the "duplicity" of American literature (EI 172; LD 11, 15, 228, 288, 386, 504).

just before death" (LD 239). Or, he is "a delinquent boy" to be "reformed" and "restored to the Garden by the love of a good woman" (LD 270, 240). "Growing up is for the male not inheriting the super-ego position, but shifting it to a wife, i.e., a mother of his own choice" (NT 265; cf. NT 82; LD 275, 400).

One of Fiedler's gloomier generalizations is that "there is no real sexuality in American life and therefore there cannot very well be any in American art" (LD 30). At least, "the American psyche finds" no "satisfactory" "heterosexual solution between man and woman" "worthy of standing in our fiction for the healing of the breach between conscious and unconscious, reason and impulse, society and nature" (LD 339). Instead, fiction circles around "impotence," "sadist aggression," "innocent homosexuality, and unconsummated incest" (LD 345f, 348). The "utterly sublimated homoerotic passion," with its "subversion of home and marriage," was a special success, even "considered 'safe' reading for children" (WL 186). "The love of males" fills "the sentimental center of our novels" and boasts "a general superiority" "over the ignoble lust of man for women" LD 368f).[25] Splendid examples are *Moby Dick*, "perhaps the greatest love story in our fiction," its "innocent homosexuality" offering "Platonism without sodomy"; and *Huckleberry Finn*, "turning from society to nature" so as "to avoid the facts of wooing, marriage, and child-bearing" (LD 370, 375, 25; cf. LD 349).

In "the dark vision of the American," this "embarrassment before love" parallels an "obsession with violence" (LD 28). "The withdrawal of sexual passion from art leads to an increase of horror," "sadism," and "masochism" (LD 262). Upon "the suppression of sex" follows the endless "attempt to convince us of the innocence of violence, the good clean fun of horror" (LD 27). Where "taboo" makes "delinquency" "the declaration of maleness," "sexuality" is diverted into "aggression" (LD 270; NT 264). "Rape" unites the two and has "always been a staple of American popular fiction" (WL 183). Against the older mythical "rape from above" by "gods and heroes," the "uniquely American version" was "rape from below" by a "repressed race," mainly "Indian" and "Afro-American" (WL 184, 186f, 168, 190, 194, 203ff, 209, 222; NT 240; LD 14, 412). Over and over, American writers convey and exploit the fear of "miscegenation" (LD 207ff, 220, 368, 411; WL 16, 153f, 156, 183, 186f, 189, 233; EI 147). Such themes can feed "the self-righteous sadism" in "the barbarous depths of the white Gentile heart" and fabricate a pretext for "vigilante justice" and "lynch law" (WL 188ff, 235; NT 240)—just the conclusion suggested by Millett as well (SX 402ff).

In such an American "symbolic world," where "sex and death become one" (LD 296), the antifeminism and the "misogynist canon" (WL 157) also diagnosed by Millett (Ch. 16) are predictable enough. "All Americans," Fiedler avers,

---

[25] A "crush, idolized in innocent homosexual adoration" can commit only "'treachery'" by "heterosexual" acts, "the discovery" of which ranks alongside "the stumbling on the primal scene, mother and father caught in the sexual act," as the "major crises of pre-adolescent emotional life" "around" which "our literature" "compulsively" "circles" (LD 345).

"including girls and women," "at levels deeper than ideology, perceive white women as the enemy" representing "everything that must be escaped in order to be free" (WL 152f). However, this feeling was only one side of a dualism or "schizophrenia," again noted by Millett, which typecasted the female as both "angelic and diabolic" (LD 314). In an earlier trend, the "woman" was "idealized" and "glorified" as "fundamentally pure," even "divine" (LD 79f, 67). The "Sentimental Love Religion" rendered her a "savior," her "virginity" a "mystique," and "marriage" with her a "salvation" (LD 444, 77, 84, 132, 218, 255, 47f). "Sentimental archetypes" "made it almost impossible to portray adult sexual passion or a fully passionate woman" (LD 217, 291). Instead, the "heroine" is "a monster of virtue," "a dull and embarrassing figure," "pale," "dovelike," "humble, long-suffering" (LD 75, 221).

In a later trend, probably fueled by real women's refusal to act out such a part or to salute "the bourgeois redefinition of all morality in terms of sexual purity," "novelists" "symbolized" "the rejection and fear of sexuality" by creating "monsters" of "bitchery" (LD 71, 221, 24). "To marry" was no longer to attain salvation, but "to accept complicity, to recognize one's participation in universal guilt" (EI 188). This "ambivalence toward women" as either "goddesses or bitches" impelled "American writers" to devise "the pattern of female Dark and Light": "the passionate brunette and the sinless blonde" (LD 314, 200f; cf. LD 218, 296, 300ff, 309f, 417) (compare Wellek and Warren, p. 42). An "ethnic" "polarity" was translated into a "moral" one (LD 301). Finally, even the "blonde" became a "gold-digger" and "vampire," a "symbol of sexual aggression as cannibalism" (LD 325).

Fiedler himself did not always avoid taking sides in the "class war is between the sexes" (LD 90). He may have been guided by "simple machismo" to esteem the "myth" behind "'masculine' sentimentality" over "the equally valid archetype" behind "'feminine' pathos" (WL 150). Also, he became a partisan in "the struggle of High Art and low," "perceived as a battle of the sexes" (WL 29). He was fond of Hawthorne's epithet about the "horde of damned female scribblers" (WL 29, 155; LD 83, 91, 104f, 127, 225, 249). He depicted their authorship both as "a critical moment in the emancipation of women" and as a "kidnaping" that produced "anti-literature: bourgeois, timid," "banal," "not quite literate," sometimes "ungrammatical"[26] (LD 83, 92f, 97, 101, 105, 95). "After its capture by women," the "tradition" of the novel traded "forthrightness and vigor" for "the more delicate nuances of sensibility" that suited the "tenderness or squeamishness of the lady authors" (LD 85, 476, 261). "'Young ladies'" were also "the most

---

[26] Actually, the form "I have wrote" (LD 95) is dialectal and still current among some groups, though not in the "dialect spoken by a handful of White Anglo-Saxon Protestants in a few Eastern Seaboard cities" and "brainwashed" into "recent immigrants" like Fiedler (WL 69). "Grammatical errors" are also charged against James Jones and his character (EI 187), but not against Mark Twain or his.

light-headed of all novel-readers" (LD 117). So "our best fictionists" —a list of males comes here—"felt it necessary to struggle for their integrity and their livelihoods" "against" the "female audience (female in sensibility whatever the nominal sex of the readers who composed it)" (LD 93). Fielding already had to "rescue prose fiction from bourgeois ladies"; and in modern times, "the subject matter of popular ladies' fiction" is precisely not what Fiedler expects to find in a major novel (LD 167, 364) (nor does Iser, IR 284).

Throughout his career, Fiedler has espoused the view that "American litera-ture is distinguished by the number of dangerous and disturbing books in its canon—and American scholarship by its ability to conceal this fact" (LD 11). He feels it his job "to redeem our great books from the commentaries on them." He contravenes the "optimism" that, "since decline of orthodox Puritanism," "has become the chief effective religion" in "American" "society" (LD 27). He prefers the "direction" of the Puritan "heritage" he labels "tragic Humanism,"[27] for which "it is the function of art not to console or sustain, much less to entertain, but to *disturb* by telling a truth which is always unwelcome" (LD 430, 432). Fiedler's general postulate of "negativism" as the "moral obligation" of art is thus brought home as the "obligation" of "the American author," who must "project" "the blackness of life" and "the dark vision of America" —the "obsession with violence," the "embarrassment before love," "the hope on the surface and the terror beneath" (NT 6f; LD 502f, 432, 28).

In its "flight from the physical data of the actual world, in search of a (sexless and dim) Ideal," "our fiction" tends to be a "gothic fiction, nonrealistic and negative, sadist and melodramatic—a literature of darkness and the grotesque in a land of light and affirmation" (LD 29). "In gothicism, the American novelist not only finds opportunities to render inward experience symbolically," but also "ways of mythicizing the brutality and terror endemic to our life" (LD 503). "The America novel" is hence "pre-eminently a novel of terror," the "passion which could fill the vacuum left by the failure of love" (LD 26, 104). "It is the gothic form that has been most fruitful in the hands of our best writers": "symbolically understood" in "metaphors for a terror psychological, social, and metaphysical" (LD 28).

Having been originally a "European genre," the gothic was nativized for "America" —"a world which had left behind the terror of Europe not for" "innocence," but for "new" "guilts associated with the rape of nature and exploi-tation of dark-skinned people" (LD 31). What had been "an enlightened attack on a debased ruling class or entrenched superstition" became a "Calvinist exposé

---

[27] The other two descendants are pictured as: the "orthodoxy" or "hysterical evangelism" that "rejects learning and scholarship and intelligence" and "fears" "art" and "sex"; and the "sentimental liberalism" that "respects learning" and "promotes rationalism" and "bland cosmic optimism" (LD 430ff). These two are more widespread than "tragic Humanism" and to some degree its targets for attack.

of natural human corruption" (LD 160). "Nature and not society becomes the symbol of evil," and "the life of the unconscious" appears "destructive" (LD 160f). "The European gothic identified blackness with the superego and was therefore revolutionary"; "the American gothic" "identified evil with the id and was therefore conservative," "whatever the intent of its authors." Typical themes of American gothic include "flirtation with death," "the diabolic bargain," "incest," and the figures of the "redskin" and "black man," defensively mythicized from victims into evil powers.[28]

The "gloom of tragic vision" (Melville called it "blackness ten times black") could animate the gothic writer to his "greatest work" (LD 444, 27, 185, 299). Conversely, an author who "abandons" "the gothic mode" with "its negative message" and "blasphemy" can lose "his truest self" (LD 504). "The Faustian implications" of the writer's "enterprise" encourage the creation of "Faustian characters" that "satisfy the dimly perceived need of many Americans to have their national existence projected in terms of a compact with the Devil" (LD 433; cf. LD 68, 134, 217, 421, 428, 433, 446-57, 461, 471). "Yet even treated as symbols, the machinery and decor of the gothic" "seem vulgar and contrived," leading toward "abstract morality," "shoddy theater," "the rhetoric" of the cheapest" "melodrama," and the "theatrical debasement of the pure Faustian cry of terror" (LD 28, 421; cf. LD 466).

A "tragic note" is needed to "redeem" "gothic effects from triviality" (LD 445). "In our most enduring books, the cheapjack machinery of the gothic novel is called on to represent the hidden blackness of the human soul and human society" (LD 27). "The gothic mode is essentially a form of parody, a way of assailing clichés by exaggerating them to the limits of grotesqueness" (LD 421; cf. LD 394f). This tactic makes it possible that the "diabolic stance can be passed off as an amusing sham" whose "bugaboos are all finally jokes," though "we are never quite convinced" (LD 504, 26; cf. LD 142, 423).

Beside melodrama, another danger for the gothic is the "sentimentalism" which it displaced and to which it threatens to revert (LD 433, 436, 438, 445, 454, 479). Unlike "the gothic rebel," who "revolts against the will of God," "the sentimental populist" "dissents in happy innocence" (LD 441). Within "the anti-intellectualism of the sentimental code," "simple feeling is closer to God's truth than educated intelligence," and "tears" are "the truest testimony of faith" (LD 79, 86; cf. NT 257, 260, 268, 293). The distaste of critics for sentimentality as a regressive and displaced emotionalism (Ch. 2) was once shared by Fiedler: "sentimentalism" "proved almost everywhere a blight," and its "influence" a "calamity" in which "truth" was "yielded up," "the reality-principle" "sold out," and "pristine purity" "compromised" (LD 75, 466, 458, 445, e.d.).

In "the American novel," "the sensationalism of anti-bourgeois sentimen-

---

[28] See LD 14, 26, 197, 435f, 442f, and the references in Note 15. A need to distract attention from the white man's "rape of nature" (LD 31, 360) was presumably a motive.

tality" was joined by "the smugness of liberal gentility," whose "fear of sex" impelled it to "confuse civilization and bowdlerization" (LD 124, 344, 81; cf. LD 163, 199, 445; NT 271). This outlook was not "capable" of "tragic ambivalence,"[29] "radical protest," "irony," or "detachment," and "denied the ultimate reality of the demonic" (LF 199; EI 180; LD 195). Instead, the "sentimental" author offered "stereotypes," "melodrama," "travesties," and "reassuring" "pseudo-myths" (LD 325, 466, 483; NT 168; LD 104; NT 11).

If "sentimentality" undercuts "the reality-principle," then the proper "counterbalance" for "exposing" its "self-delusions" ought to be "realism" (LD 458, 229; NT 13; cf. LF 479f). But Fiedler is an equally staunch foe of this literary trend. The "obligation to negativism, which the sentimental genres cannot fulfill," is "converted" by "realism" to "mere pamphleteering" (LD 503). It is an "entrapment" to "believe that a work of art is equal to its raw materials"; and "a thoroughly absurd idea" that "the truth of a work of art is capable of documentary proof" (EI 196; LD 164; cf. LD 188; NT 132).

"Realism" and "Naturalism" did "perform in the beginning the essential function of art, the negative one of provocation and scandal," by "denying" the "liberal view of man" as "the product" of "a rationally ordered and rationally explicable universe" (NT 13). Yet they became "a triumphant orthodoxy," and soon a "game" of "pretending to create documents rather than poetry" by deploying a "falsely scientific writing which sought to replace imagination with sociology" (NT 13f; LD 486). Besides, "sentimentality" was "smuggled" in anyhow, along with "political propaganda" and "heavy-handed symbolism" (NT 14, 185). Fiedler is certain that "our fiction is essentially and at its best non-realistic, anti-realistic"; "the classic American fictionists" "instinctively realized" that "literary truth is not synonymous with fact" (LD 28, 486). "Recent writers" also find that "literary modes based on reason and superficial observation must falsify" contemporary "themes," such as "modern war and the twentieth-century city" (LD 479).

Of course, Fiedler has his own "cemeteries to defend" in this matter (to borrow his phrase, NT xiii). A myth critic has a vested interest in proclaiming that even in a "'realistic'" "age," "not the real but the mythic prompts our feelings and actions" (NT 158). The "archetypal" "survives" beyond "the objective 'realism' of a social observer," however much "the theory of 'realism' or 'naturalism' denies" it (WL 167; NT 320). A work "triumphs" by "mythicizing" and "liberating" from "the implicit judgment of realism" (LD 380). In addition, "realism" and "fact" are adverse to the "dream," another center of Fiedlerian theory, as we saw (p. 85) (cf. LD 260; NT 11; EI 176).

"For many years," Fiedler "sought to reconcile" "the contradictory ideals" of

---

[29] "Tragic" "ambivalence" is later identified as a "honorific in the New Critic's cant" (WL 148, 150). But it designates something Fiedler still expects of literature, under a more Freudian label ("the darker, more perilous aspects of our own psyches," etc., WL 50).

"a hierarchical culture" and a "classless society" (WL 146). His division of culture among "high," "middle," and "low" "brows" (an anatomical metaphor for the size of the brain inside) fitted the class structure only approximately. The link between "middlebrow" and "middle-class" (NT 216; LD 225, 431, 477; WL 59) cannot be absolute. After all, Fiedler himself, though middle-class, is a "high-brow," maybe higher than American authors like the "half-educated" Whitman, or the "ignorant" and "self-educated" "Fitzgerald, Hemingway, Faulkner, and Pound" (EI 173; NT 157)—he is a truly elevated "intellectual,"[30] a Fiedler on the roof.

The "'middlebrows,'" being "puritan," "righteous," "sentimental," "not-quite enlightened," seemed, "even more" than the "'lowbrows,'" "the real enemies of 'culture'" (LD 431, 500, 162; NT 168, 218; WL 146). A further subdivision separated "lower" from "upper" "middlebrows, the latter being more "genteel" (LD 243, 249, 257, 260f, 289, 485) (raising their eyebrows when they are constantly offended?). Though "pretending to honor" "standards," the "middlebrows" would prefer "stereotypes," "pretentious kitsch," and "melodrama" (WL 146; NT 352, 274, 168). Hence, "middlebrow" was taken to be the opposite of "serious" (LD 340, 477, 496).

Recently, Fiedler professes to hardly "remember that I once used such terms in deadly earnest" (WL 146). Whereas his membership in the class of "intellectuals" formerly put him in a group "notoriously set apart from the general public," "living" "by different values and speaking a different language," he now seeks "a sense of at-oneness" with "the majority audience I was long taught to despise" (EI 6, 68; WL 231). Gone is his assurance that "the mature writer must write" not for the "mass" nor "the 'average reader,'" but for "the ideal understander" "once called the 'gentle reader'" (EI 209). The "unfortunate distinction" of "High literature and low" or of "literature proper and sub- or para-literature" is now spurned in favor of a division into "'minority'" and "'majority literature'" (WL 13). This numerical terminology moves the advantage to the other side, striking a special chord when Fiedler exposes how far his role as "a writer" "is inextricably involved with making money" (WL 23); if nothing else, the "majority critic" will sell more of his own books.

One of Fiedler's favored mottos has been: "nothing fails like success" (EI 175; NT 202, 297). Now, he seems destined to illustrate it. Having met his ambition to "open communication with an audience, to exist for others" —maybe even "'to be great, to be known'" —he is dismayed to encounter the erstwhile "enfant terrible" at the heart of the same academy he once stormed (cf. WL 23, 202, 60ff). He is now a "'seminal' critic," however much his "books" were "scorned" in "academic and literary reviews" (WL 18). So he feels a "need to get through or

---

[30] See NT 217; EI 68. The "liberal-intellectual" "supported trade unionism, social security, and the rights" of "minorities"; thought "the recognition of the Soviet Union" "a 'progressive' step"; and took "the Loyalist side" in "the Spanish civil War" (EL 68).

around the official critics to my proper audience" that loves "popular authors" but "never reads anything labeled 'criticism'" (WL 19). He still longs to "speak to" "the mass audience," not to "our eavesdropping colleagues" (WL 140). Having been "utterly mistaken" in "predicting" that "the mass audience" would "grow closer to the elite" (WL 80), he counsels, like Mr. Pickwick, to shout with the largest crowd.

He proposes "to take the first steps" himself "toward creating a new kind of criticism" to "confront" and "deal with" both "popular" and "high arts" "in a style consonant with a sensibility" of the "popular" (WL 115). He hopes he had "long been moving in the direction of such criticism, though without quite knowing what I was doing." Now, he "chooses to try to become in full awareness that to which I have all along inadvertently tended: a pop critic learning" "to speak the language of popular literature" (WL 141; cf. WL 15).

He insists that popular literature excels in doing just what he always said literature should—reworking myths and dreams, tapping the collective unconscious, releasing the id, subverting social conformity, and so on. Like Pavese, he sustains a "democratic faith that a 'colloquy with the masses' might be opened on the level of myth" (NT 142). "Low literature," "whether in pre-print, print, or post-print form, aspires to return to pure myth" (WL 129)—a formulation that cannily subsumes other mass media. "In popular" "art forms," such as "freak shows" (an old Fiedler favorite quite out of date now), the "archetypes which inform printed texts are" "made flesh" (WL 36; cf. NT 232). "Hack" authors have "easy access to their own unconscious where it impinges on the collective unconscious of their time" (WL 137f). "'Trash,' rooted like our dreams and nightmares in shared myth and fantasy, touches us all at a place where we have never been psychically sundered each from each" (WL 140). "Popular literature" makes us "more at home with, in tune with, the darker, more perilous aspects of our own psyches, otherwise confessed only in nightmares" (WL 50). "All art which remains popular" "makes possible" "the release of the repressed," of "undying primal impulses." "Popular theater or comic books" are "works of art" "subversive of all unequivocal allegiances, all orthodoxies" (WL 41).

Such theses echo Fiedler's earlier studies while giving added emphasis to popular art. This continuity might be a cagey move to show he's the best qualified one for the role of "pop critic." Consider his syllogism. "The critic who desires to do" "justice" to "low literature" "in a way which emphasizes its resemblance to rather than its differences from high literature must be first of all a 'myth critic'" (WL 129). And not just any of the "many 'myth critics'" "in this century" will do—only the "particular kind" who "use the term" "as I do"; and since "none" of the others do, we are left with exactly one legitimized candidate for the job.

To safeguard his position, Fiedler might use a variant of the classic Freudian defense against dissenters by arguing that whoever shuns the themes of popular art as "abhorrent to civility and humanity" —such as "cannibalism," "incest, the lust to rape and be raped" —joins the "moralists" "eager to deny their own unconscious impulses to lawlessness" (WL 41f). Fiedler levels this weapon at "social reformers, do-gooders, and commissars, as well as presbyters and priests" who promote "mythocide" and "censorship," rather than at his fellow "critics," who generally remain "silent" on the whole issue (WL 39f, 42, 44). But the weapon is ready should the latter break their silence for the wrong side.

On the other hand, Fiedler needs to project a radical break with his previous policies if his "new kind of criticism" is to seem genuinely new. Some tacks here are easy gestures, as when he drops his "pretentious middle initial" (WL 14).[31] Also fairly undramatic is his change of terminology, as when he now says "song and story" instead of "literature," (WL 14, 42, 58, 84, 109, 113ff, 120, 127ff, 131) and "mass" or "majority audience" in place of such locutions as "the wide audience capable of only the grossest responses," or "the gum-chewing, popcorn-consuming hordes of the remotest hinterlands" (LD 475, 478).

A more obtrusive tack is to assail his most programmatic early work ("No! in Thunder," "Archetype and Signature," etc.) as "pretentious," "insufferably arrogant," and "unforgivably solemn and heavy-handed," really only a "put-on, a joke" (WL 14, 37; cf. NT x).[32] He laments his "concessions to pedantry" and complains he was "brainwashed" into "elitist attitudes" and "pride" (WL 18, 61, 88, 121, 86) (though I can't imagine anybody being harder to brainwash than he). With cordial venom, he remarks on "the grim rigor" of "proper literary criticism," the "patient documentation and mindless accumulation of fact which characterizes academic 'research' at its deadliest," and "the "recherché vocabulary of semiotics, Lacanian psychoanalysis, and deconstructionism" (WL 124, 119).[33] Though these failings are scarcely found in his own early works, his are presumably among the "modern or bourgeois criticism" which "judges literature" and "distinguishes" between "high and low," and which "has outlived its usefulness" (WL 52).

A still more incisive tack is his "passionate apology" (WL 21) for popular literature in the face of its inadequacy by traditional criteria. "Pop" makes "aesthetic" and "ethical" "standards" "irrelevant" (WL 122). We cannot expect "elegance of structure" or "distinguished style," aspects to which the "majority au-

---

[31] It's my middle initial too, and I don't see why it's pretentious unless Fiedler stitches it onto his shirtfront. However, he thinks the initial is a typical gesture of "academics" and "minor business executives" (letter); he still uses it in his signature, though his secretary types his name just below without it. It stands for "Aaron," his "priestly name, an indication of caste."

[32] Or rather, they do not have enough jokes. Fiedler "likes to think" of himself "as one of the few critics willing to make jokes" (letter).

[33] Lacanian psychoanalysis, which makes language an extended metaphor for every aspect of mental life, only vaguely resembles Fiedler's equation of text and life (EI xv; NT xvf) (compare the surveys in Lemaire 1977, and Ragland-Sullivan 1986). Deconstruction seems more directly anticipated at times: the "Artist as Patcher"; "the poem" "lives cannibalistically amid the ruins of other fables and rhetorics"; "all such oppositions are dangerous" (NT 60, 130, 258).

dience is" "as indifferent" as it is to "verisimilitude of plot and character" (WL 132f). "Ordinary readers do not demand that their protagonists be psychologically credible, or indeed that they have any 'inwardness' at all." In pop works, the "actions" of the "characters" "take place in a realm where probability and rationality are no longer relevant." "Gifted oneiric writers" may have "no understanding of human nature or of the functionings of society." "They are likely to prove trivial and banal, even pathological and perverse." "Nor does it matter," since "they move us viscerally rather than cerebrally." As if to clinch the point, he demonstratively bathes in the "mild vices" —being "sentimental, philistine," and "ingenuous" —he once "hoped" he'd never "come nearer" to after having been "taught to eschew" them by "modernism" (WL 141, 92; NT 163).

Fiedler's new "advocacy" calls for "an approach to literature" whereby critics can "speak for ourselves," not "in the name of some impersonal tradition," to "the mass audience" (WL 139f). This project will "ease" an "intolerable" "classroom situation" and "join together the sundered larger community" (WL 140). Both "popular literature" and "High Literature" will be "read" simply "as literature" (WL 140; cf. WL 115, 129, 138). A key step is that we "if not quite abandon, at least drastically downgrade both ethics and aesthetics in favor of 'ecstatics'" (WL 139). With "ekstasis" —"ecstasy or rapture or transport, a profound alteration of consciousness in which the normal limits of flesh and spirit seem to dissolve" —"rather than instruction and delight" as "our chief evaluative criterion," we can "abandon all formalist, elitist, methodological criticism" in favor of an "eclectic, amateur, neo-Romantic, populist one" (WL 140). "We will find ourselves speaking less of theme and purport, structure and texture, signified and signifier, metaphor and metonymy, and more of myth, fable, archetype, fantasy, magic, and wonder." And thereby sounding more like Leslie Fiedler. The "newest critics" will "set literature in the broadest possible contexts," including "history and biography, sociology and psychology" (WL 115), just what Fiedler advised in *Love and Death* (p. 77f).

"In order to survive," we are told, "criticism must avoid the creeping professionalism endemic in our post-industrial world by eschewing jargon, the hermetic codes which secular hierophants use to exclude the uninitiated," and "speak with the authority not of experimental science or systematic philosophy," but of "a colloquial demotic poetry, vulgar enough to fear neither humor nor pathos" (WL 115). Whoever salutes this goal might be troubled to imagine the mass audience trying to read such a passage studded with an erudite vocabulary more like an "artificial tongue" than "the language of the people" (cf. WL 68). To appreciate *What Was Literature?*, the masses are liable to need some background in classical Greek, and a bit of Latin, Hebrew, Yiddish, German, and especially French (the idiom of "troubled elitists", WL 15). Plus of course a fair grounding in world literature, and in the the theories of Freud and Jung.

In fact, the most qualified audience for the book would be recruited from those like Fiedler, whose "high regard" for popular literature came "after having passed through an initiation into the world of elitist standards" (WL 212). This "readership" would be mostly "teachers and students," who encountered "'litera-ture'" primarily in "departments of English" (WL 63, 58). Some of us there, I for one, discovered that intense and extended experiences with "high art" had not narrowed our taste, but expanded our awareness and receptivity for all art and culture.

Still, Fiedler is obviously not satisfied with the academic audience, who already read his books. Yet even his pleas for a mass audience do not stop him from warding off several readerships. "Elitists" are barred for fostering a "canon" that grew "more self-consciously exclusive, more self-righteously narrow" (WL 61). Advocates of an "elitism" "stood on its head," who accept only "majority art" and "ban" "minority art" are likewise rebuked (WL 116f). "Solid middle-class citizens" won't do, insofar as they are "terrified" by "all manifestations of antino-mian or dionysiac impulses" (WL 48). Foes of "pornography" are counted out too, if all "forms of subliterature" that "have most pleased the mass audience" "can be regarded as 'pornography'" (WL 48, 133ff). "Revolutionary blacks and radical feminists" are also out, since they not only oppose porn, but refuse to celebrate Fiedler's favorites, *Uncle Tom's Cabin* and *Huckleberry Finn*, and don't relish hints that women "like being raped," especially black slaves by white masters (WL 208, 48, 42, 225). What remains, at least until Fiedler can write criticism in genuinely popular language, appears to be an audience of Fiedlerian readers waiting to hail the "newest" wave of Fiedlerian critics.

Suppose the battle is won, and "majority criticism" and "ecstatics" become the order of the day. What tasks does the critic have then? One might be to "open up the canon," whose list of accredited works Fiedler had once accepted on the authority of D.H. Lawrence and F.O. Mathiessen (WL 143, 27 145ff; NT 161; LD 14, 181). The authors were all "WASP males"; not "a single book by a woman," and "No Negroes Allowed" (WL 147; LD 398). But as Fiedler now owns, "the very notion of a 'canon' has been called into question by the rise of mass culture" (WL 146). A merely revised canon with a few works of popular literature "smuggled" in would bring no advance, being in essence what we already have (WL 123, 147, 238). Fiedler seems rather to intend a complete openness toward "all art, high, low, or middling" (WL 138; cf. WL 115, 129, 140). "Majority poetry," for instance, is said to include song "lyrics," "graffiti inscribed in public toilets, children's game chants, and greeting card verse" (WL 85). Moreover, since "all popular art" is "distinguished" by its "ability to move from one medium to another without loss of intensity or alteration of meaning," the majority critic will be dealing with "movies, radio, and TV" as well (WL 177f). If "in popular art, books are as independent of their authors as of their medium" (WL 178), authorship will receive less consideration than it tradi-tionally has, aside from the usual salute to "mythopoetic powers" (WL 36, 125, 198, 217, 231).

Despite this breadth and tolerance, modernism at least seems marked for the heave-ho, along with the "'aesthetical' criteria" it "defined" (WL 149). For

Fiedler, "modernism in poetry has reached a dead end, and the attempts of the so-called post-modernists to escape its limitations are doomed to failure as long as they continue to pursue originality" (WL 93). "Modernist writers" are blamed for the "split in literature" between "'serious books' and 'best sellers'"—"an especially unforgivable error for American writers" (WL 64). They "produce" only for "libraries" and "write as if for exegesis," "addressing merely themselves and their post-modernist critics," who "address only each other" (WL 64, 106, e.d.). "'Art novels'" "are no longer viable models for living fiction" (WL 64). "Modernist taste" sins by "tolerating" "the most extreme incoherence, provided it is high-toned, learnedly allusive and obtrusive enough to put off the ordinary reader" (WL 90).

Such denunciations of modernism not because it isn't classical but because it isn't folksy enough almost bring Fiedler near the utterly unexpected company of the cultural watchdogs of Stalin and Hitler (cf. WL 117, 150; LD 484; EI 204), though they would disapprove of much pop art he favors. Of course, Fiedler sincerely disavows the intent to "ban" "the high in favor of the low" or to "restrict the full freedom of literature" (WL 129); but he delivers arguments that could serve such a cause. Ultimately, his campaign against the "brainwashings" of "modernism" and "elitism" threatens to engender another "paranoid 'conspiracy' theory," the inverse of the one he blamed on "left-wing academics" (WL 61, 88, 121, 20, 101).

The favored "forms of subliterature" are recognized by their "having most troubled elitist critics" through "sentimentality," "horror," "hard-core pornography," and "low comedy" (WL 133f). These works fulfill "the essential function of literature to release in us unnatural impulses—including the need from time to time to go out of our heads—which we otherwise repress or sublimate for the sake of law and order, civilization, sweet reason" (WL 136). "We seek" "privileged insanity" in "mythic art" (WL 137). "The pleasures of pop train us to indulge impulses which morality and mental hygiene warn us are dangerous." Indeed, as I already quoted, "all four" "forms of subliterature "can be regarded as pornography, since they titillate by infringing deeply revered taboos" (WL 133f)—this too fitting Fiedler's older theses that great American works were "dirty books," and that "the line between 'pornography' and respectable literature has blurred" (LD 77, 85, 29).

However, Fiedler has not taken the step we find in Holland and Paris of viewing his own theory as partly an artifact of his particular personality. He certainly seems to match the Freudian pattern of ambivalence, with one side of his personality forbidding the pleasure of the other. He consistently assumes that the normal response to emotion is to repress it; and that pleasure is typically linked with inflicting or receiving pain.[34] Yet this internal division, or at least its

---

[34] Hence the insistence on "sadism" and "masochism" (LD 29, 262, 328, 346, 502; WL 190, 203, 209)—emotions of which he is "ashamed" (WL 231). Such "shame" is blamed on the influence of "elitist criticism" (WL 121, 13f).

intensity, might stem from a conflict between his populism and his peculiar elitist and modernist training (cf. WL 91f, 141).

His chapter on *Roots* is vastly instructive in this regard. As a demonstration of "ecstatics," it would be a flop. Only in the penultimate paragraph can Fiedler manage to admit that *Roots* "moves me deeply," "because" "it takes me into a world of primordial images" (WL 231). Even then, he "confesses" himself "still enough of a vestigial elitist to be ashamed of my own vulnerability" "to so gross an appeal" to his "sentimental and sado-masochistic" response.

As if to forestall that confession, he spends most of his 19-page chapter changing the subject over to things he feels more comfortable with: authors versus editors, other books (above all *Uncle Tom's Cabin*), and other authors (Stowe, Henson, Dixon, Wolfe, Yerby, Reed, Wright, Malcolm X). The approximately four pages where he really talks about *Roots* are crammed with barbs and slurs. The book is "pitifully naive," "awkwardly structured," and "ineptly written," presenting "shameless" "kitsch," "stereotypes," "banality of ideas," "palpable absurdity," and "perverse lust in violence," plus "sexist" and "inverted racist" characters (WL 219f, 223ff, 227f). Haley, the author, is an "Uncle Tom," "a 'good good nigger,'" "'a professional Negro,'" "bland," "squeamish," "reticent about sex," "timid" in "politics," and "committed to monogamy and bourgeois values" (WL 211, 223, 227, 225, 219). To avoid joining the "hysterical rightists" that "raised" their "voices" "against *Roots*," Fiedler craftily borrows most of these comments from leftist radicals and, yes, the "elitists" and "highbrows" he elsewhere disdains (WL 219, 223). The only favorable opinion, James Baldwin's, is at once rebutted with views from Baldwin's earlier work and that of Richard Wright (WL 220), both accredited highbrow black writers.

Fiedler contradicts himself in his frenzy of "vestigial elitism."[35] He concedes Haley's "mythopoetic power," but allows him only one "even approximately mythic character" (WL 231, 224). After noting the book's "universal acclaim," its "astonishing popularity" with "the majority audience," Fiedler suddenly declares Haley's "audience" "chiefly white" by citing statistics on "letters he got in response to the *Reader's Digest* version" —worthless evidence, since that periodical is the "secular bible of white Middle America" (WL 217, 225f).

Moreover, Fiedler's long-standing thesis about the irrelevance of historical truth to art (e.g., in his attack on realism and naturalism) collides with his drive (another tactic of "elite critics," WL 229) to establish, on the authority of "anthropologists," that Haley has "flagrantly falsified the record" or was "taken in by a notably unreliable" "historian" (WL 224f). "How pointless" "the debate about the historical veracity of Haley's book!" is the nervous refrain; "it scarcely matters how true to scholarship or the living Africans' perception of their past"; "it

---

[35] He is not certain whether it *was* or *is* "vestigial": "then" (WL 20, 42) or now (WL 231). Similarly, the idea that "all subsequent literature has come" out of "*Huckleberry Finn*" *is* endorsed on WL 48, but assigned to the past on WL 243.

matters little how selective and skewed" (WL 228, 224, 227). Yet before we agree, we are warned that "the question of historical truth cannot be avoided altogether"; after all, Haley and some of his "admirers" take the "fiction" for "fact" (WL 229f, 223, cf. WL 216). Why it should matter so much that the book is not "documented history" is hard to see, since "even scholarly, 'objective' historians disagree about what happened in those irrecoverable times" (WL 226, 230).

To top it all off, Fiedler harps upon Haley's use of "ghostwriters," "editors," and "collaborators," and brings up the "highbrow" and "modernist" view that this "matter" is "a dirty little secret" (WL 211, 217, 226, 216). He leaves it open whether Haley was legally guilty of "plagiarism" (a crime of which "Mrs. Stowe" is cleared, WL 218, 228f), but reminds us that it is "in law a punishable offense" and for "the popular audience a betrayal of trust" (WL 213). Fiedler may not think so, since Wolfe, Fitzgerald, and Caldwell relied on editors—even he shared an editor with "Leon Edel and Saul Bellow" (WL 215f). Besides, he says "popular" books are independent of their authors (WL 178). Yet at the announcement that "a black American" "succeeded for the first time in modifying the mythology of black-white relations in the United States for the majority audience," we are told to "never mind" (i.e., keep in mind) "his white editors, ghost-, and scriptwriters" (WL 229).

Fiedler "rereads the last page" of *Roots* and is "left with a sense of at-oneness not just with the majority audience," "but with much in myself I was long afraid to confront" (WL 231). But his chapter rather reveals how afraid he still is; and how far he responds like the elitists, not like the masses. Why does his intended "redemption" of *Roots* turn into a proof that it is still "a prefabricated piece of commodity schlock" (WL 212)?

Various motives might be imagined: his elitism being not so "vestigial" after all; his envy of the book's popularity and sales, including in its life as a film; his aversion to the "Home as Heaven" myth it "celebrates"; its "blessing by the PTA"; its rivalry with his beloved books by Stowe and Mitchell; its failure, right down to the "Happy Ending," to project the dark vision he demands of American novels; its author's "Christian" and "bourgeois values"; and so on (cf. WL 216f, 212, 220, 224, 223, 225). Perhaps the strongest motive is far simpler: it doesn't belong to Fiedler's childhood as do the pop books he genuinely reveres (cf. WL 85, 87, 141, 151, 164f 212). He might try his hand on a really recent mass art form, such as music videos, some of which, even finely crafted ones like Duran Duran's *Save a Prayer* or the Cars' *Hello Again* (directed by Andy Warhol), have been seen and loved by millions of Americans who were never deeply touched by Twain or Stowe, the "literary father" and "mother" "to us all" (WL is dedicated to "Sam and Hattie").

Perhaps too, Fiedler can abjure elitism more easily than pessimism. His works generally agree with "most of our present-day writers," who "feel that there are deeper perceptions of man's plight" than "optimism" can attain, even that of "a

Rousseau" (EI 197f). Throughout his critical sojourns, Fiedler uncovers the darker side, even in the most light-hearted scenes; and if it isn't dark enough, he is apt to misprize the work. Despite its "Happy Ending," *Roots* at least has its share of violence, lust, rape, and miscegenation, staples in Fiedler's recipe for proper American fiction. A real acid test for his "ecstatics" would be to deliver an unreservedly favorable critique of some smash hit with an optimistic ideology, like *Jonathan Livingston Seagull* (which he hates, WL 78, 126). For indulging in "ecstatic" writing, Fiedler once called Kerouac a "schoolgirl" and a "coward" (NT 4). Now, even a transmogrified Fiedler, the friend of the people, is tough to visualize in transports of happiness about the issues he has always felt drawn to address.

Or, a general rather than merely personal impasse may be the blocking agent: that so far, the actual function of the "majority critic" is unclear. "Low literature at its most authentic" is "loved by majority audience generation after generation, without ever having been embraced by the minority one" or by the latter's "literary critics" (WL 122, 200; cf. LD 41, 43, 72; WL 55). Why should the blessing of reformed highbrows be wanted now? If the "manipulation of popular taste" by "'the masters of the media'" is just a "paranoid" "theory" of "left-wing academics" (WL 101), then best-sellers must be what "the mass audience wants," and hence good by definition. The pop critic can only add a voice to the general acclaim, and perhaps spoil the fun by doing so. If the "story which long endures and pleases many does so with the 'vulgar' satisfactions of terror, sexual titillation and the release of tears" (WL 210), what happens when the story is certified and commended by critics and teachers? Might it not seem monotonous and point-less to an approved voyeurism free to stare and find nothing worth seeing? Fiedler senses "a need on the part of the majority to believe that what they read by preference is in some sense taboo" (WL 99), but overlooks the prospect that his project might violate that need.

The job of the "majority critic," we hear, is to "awaken" the "true archetype" that "sleeps" "in every stereotype" (WL 141f); but Fiedler performs no such office for *Roots*. In fact, has he not himself insisted on "the invisible character of the true archetype," its "explicit analysis" being "inhibited" by "unexamined, irra-tional restraints" (EI 146)? "The myth, by definition, cannot be conscious, and the moment we take pains to know it, it is degraded, profaned" (NT 49). "Our errors arise from too much knowledge of what the archetypal is rather than too little" (NT 306). "Bodies of story of whose mythic basis we have become fully aware" constitute "mythology" and "die as myth" (WL 130).

Fiedler concedes he has "helped turn living myth into dying mythology, if not archetype into stereotype" (WL 131). But he's still "convinced that there is a chance to raise such material to consciousness without utterly falsifying it": "the critic who does so" must "write literature about literature, fiction about fictions, myth about myth." We must not seek "the methodological rigor of the sciences," nor "attempt" "to prove or disprove, construct or deconstruct anything, but to compel an assent, scarcely distinguishable from wonder, like the songs or stories which are their immediate occasion." Perhaps Fiedler can now become the author he has longed to be "since he was seven years old" and finally join the company of "our most eminent novelists," who "first flirted with, then rejected, the temptations of High Art" (WL 14, 68). Yet his examples of this "anti-method," Nietzsche's *Birth of Tragedy* and Tolstoi's *What is Art?* (cf. WL 116f, 131), are rare and difficult displays of immense talent, far beyond the reach of a whole profession of pop critics or an entire majority audience.

Still, Fiedler's goal probably requires a criticism that pursues not high and low art, but high and low awareness. The works won't do the job by themselves, though some seem to help more than others; what criticism can contribute is so far poorly shown, as Fiedler says; and freedom in responding is undoubtedly the key. But a totally different gallery of signals will be needed, whether or not the profession of critics we now have can ever master or transmit them to the mass audience.

Fiedler irreverently gives his "motto" as "often wrong, but never in doubt" (WL 22).[36] Long ago, he professed the serious aim of "creating" "the difficult pleasure possible only to one recognizing a truth which involves a personal humiliation or a surrender of values long held" (NT xiv). He also opined that "real seriousness" and "actual greatness" are "approached" by a "writer" denouncing the "cause that is dearest to him" as "imperfectly conceived" and "bound to be betrayed" by "its leading spokesmen" (NT 9). Now, he may have the opportunity to prove all this upon himself. As yet, his struggle hangs in the balance, despite his manifest sincerity and commitment to the populist cause. Perhaps his ambivalence arises from his uncertainty about what the brave new world looks like and how we can recognize it if we approach it. *La lutte continue.*

---

[36] Fiedler said this motto is a "joke" I shouldn't take in "deadly earnest" (letter); but it's no less apt for being funny. I asked him if scholars or teachers who are "never in doubt" about what a work or author means might discourage ordinary readers from enjoying literature. He replied that "it is always good for a teacher to seem utterly committed," as were those "from whom I learned the most," "whether or not I shared their belief."

7

Eric Donald Hirsch[1]

Don Hirsch entered the field of "general hermeneutic theory" in order to confront "the problem of validity," which "has been neglected in recent years" (VAL viii). He avowed that "valid interpretation is crucial to the validity of all subsequent inferences" in "all human studies." "The theoretical aim of a genuine[2] discipline, scientific or humanistic, is the attainment of truth, and its practical aim is the agreement that truth has probably been achieved" (VAL viiif). "The practical goal" is therefore the "consensus" that "one set of conclusions is more probable than others" (VAL ix). Though "the subject matter of interpretation is often ambiguous and its conclusions uncertain," "valid interpretation" is needed for "any humanistic discipline to claim genuine knowledge" (VAL viiif, e.d.). Hirsch wants to reaffirm the "intellectual respectability" of "the activity of interpretation" by demonstrating how "its results can lay claim to validity" (VAL 164).

Hirsch envisions nothing less than a "general hermeneutics" "for all textual interpretation" (AIM 17).[3] To that end, he denies we have any "reason for isolating literature and art" from "other cultural realities" (AIM 109). "The literary text has no special ontological status" (VAL 210).[4] His project depends crucially on this thesis and could succeed only to the extent that we can set aside the special functions of literature described by most of the critics I review, particularly Wellek and Warren, Frye, Fiedler, Iser, Jauss, and the Yale group.

For related motives, Hirsch judges the traditional opposition between the "hard" or "exact" sciences versus the "soft" or "inexact" humanities to be a "nonsequitur" (AIM 149). "The cognitive elements in both have exactly the same

---

[1] The key for Hirsch citations is: AIM: *Aims in Interpretation* (1976); IE: *Innocence and Experience* (1964); PC: "Privileged Criteria in Literature" (1969); and VAL: *Validity in Interpretation* (1967).

[2] Hirsch's critical vocabulary is loaded with terms that imply a judgment of what is authentic ("genuine," "serious,"). The actual state of literary studies appears spurious; the real is made to seem unreal.

[3] On the history of the controversy over hermeneutics in science versus humanities, see AIM 150f. The fact that hermeneutics was originally practiced on sacred texts whose authors claimed divine authority is interesting in light of Hirsch's exaltation of authorial meaning and intention.

[4] Hirsch's suggestion that any claims for the special status of literature have a "mystical" nature (VAL 210; AIM 109) is quite unfair to stylistic and linguistic theories, which he spurns precisely because they are too deterministic (cf. AIM 50f).

character": "the progress of knowledge and its consolidation are governed by the critical testing of hypotheses with reference to evidence and logic" (AIM 149, 151). "Knowledge in all fields thus turns out to be a process rather than a static system" (AIM 152). Every "discipline"[5] is "a communal enterprise" for whom "the logical relationship between evidence, hypothesis, and probability" "remains the paradigm (or ideology!)." The "enterprise" must make sure "past evidence is stored" and "unfavorable evidence" is not "suppressed," but brought to bear "upon a hypothesis to which it is relevant." "The process of knowledge ceases" when "the consolidation and discovery of evidence decline" along with "the commitment to the critical testing of hypotheses against all known relevant evidence" (AIM 153).

This portrait of "knowledge" as a "process" is widely shared, even by the subjectivist Bleich (p. 183).[6] The performative nature of cognition is, as I argued in Ch. 1, steadily gaining recognition in many disciplines. Hirsch proposes to resolve the subject-object division with the thesis that "objectivity consists in the universality of the subjective experience" (AIM 99). But his whole method reveals the anxiety that no such "universality" prevails, so that it must be imposed by painstaking procedures for choosing and rejecting. The outcome would tend to drive a still greater wedge in between subject and object by objectifying various stages and results in the process of knowledge so as to blot out the issues of subjectivity: bias, selectivity, motivation, disposition, interest, and so on. These issues are extremely relevant for many uses of literature in society, and the reasons for severing them from interpretation need to be justified.

Hirsch rests his hopes on logical procedures that attain "validity" by "relating hypotheses" to a "body of evidence" (AIM 151) and deciding which meaning is the most probable. The concept of "probability" applied here is derived not from the "statistics" of "numerical quantities," but from "the logic of uncertainty" (VAL 173f). The main tactic is to narrow down the "classes" to which a disputable "object" belongs (VAL 176ff). Since "the idea of the class in itself entails an idea of uniformity" based on "the defining characteristics of the class," "anything we can do to narrow the class" will make the characteristics more specific and "increase the likelihood" of our "judgment" being "true" (VAL 176, 179). For instance, if a word-meaning is in dispute, we could work through classes like these: (a) uses of the word in English at large; (b) uses in the historical period of the text; (c) uses in both historical period and genre of the text; (d) uses by that same author in that genre; (e) uses in that same text; and (f) uses in that same

---

[5] "Discipline" is intended to render the German term "Wissenschaft" applied to both the sciences and humanities, though the "equivalent is not close enough" (AIM 150).

[6] Despite their diametrically opposed philosophies, several parallels between Hirsch and Bleich can be found. They both advocate negotiation of individual meanings in order to attain consensus. Both hold that the text exists only when it is read. Both consider subjectivity the norm in reading. Both draw on Piagetian psychology. And both show great respect for the author, though this move fits Bleich's scheme rather badly (see Ch. 10).

passage (cf. VAL 184ff). However, neither disputes nor evidence are usually this clear-cut.

Somewhat paradoxically, the narrowing of classes is to be achieved by expanding one's materials. The interpreter "should base his decision on all the relevant evidence available" in order to make "a grounded choice between two disparate probability judgments on the basis of common evidence which supports them" (VAL ix, 180). Hirsch concedes "it would be unfeasible and undesirable to publicize all the evidence relative to every interpretive problem" (VAL x). However, he conjures literary scholars to "take the responsibility of adjudicating the issue in light of all that is known"; the fact "that few such adjudications exist merely argues strongly that many more should be undertaken" (VAL 171). Hirsch himself, though, has not "undertaken" any, for reasons which may become clearer in the course of my review.

Repudiating the objectifying notion that the meaning is "in" the text, Hirsch acknowledges that "the text does not exist even as a sequence of words until it is construed" (VAL 13) (this too a thesis of Bleich's, p. 196). But Hirsch encounters a dilemma between two wholly disparate notions about how that "construing" takes place. On the one hand, he wants to make the processes of comprehension look disorderly enough that his stringent methods of interpretation will seem vitally necessary, like a deliverance in an hour of dire need. On the other hand, he wants to suggest that those processes are elaborately controlled, because his methods require determinate and stable meanings to work on.

In the 1967 volume (VAL), the disorderly version gets prominent coverage. In contrast to many theoretical critics, Hirsch declares that "the process and psychology of understanding are not reducible to a systematic structure" (VAL 170). This judgment is reached by applying a rigorous standard: "there is no way of compelling a right guess by means of rules and principles." He observes "there would not be any problem of interpretation" if "public unanimity" "existed generally" about the "meaning of a text" (VAL 12f). "The variability of possible implications is the very fact that requires a theory of interpretation and validity" (VAL 123).

Hirsch follows Schleiermacher (1959 [1838]: 109) in dividing literary response into two stages: a "divinatory moment" that is "unmethodical, intuitive, sympathetic"; and a "critical moment" that "submits the first moment" to a "high intellectual standard" by "testing it against all the relevant knowledge available" (VAL x).[7] These two "correspond to two distinct moments in knowledge which Whitehead aptly calls 'the stage of romance' and 'the stage of precision.'" Hirsch's theory "is mainly concerned with the second moment," the only one

---

[7] Schleiermacher quaintly labeled these "functions" "female" for the "divinatory" ("transforming" oneself "into the author") and "male" for the "comparative" (moving from "general" to "unique") (VAL 204). Mercifully, Hirsch does not adopt this terminology.

able to "raise interpretive guesses to the level of knowledge." The first moment resembles "a genial guess" and is not determined by validity: "there are no methods for making guesses, no rules for generating insights" (VAL 204). "The methodical activity of interpretation commences when we begin to test and criticize our guesses."

This proposal resolves Hirsch's dilemma by splitting reading into a disorderly initial phase and a totally ordered final phase. He grants that "these two sides of the interpretive process, the hypothetical and the critical, are not of course neatly separated when we are pondering a text, for we are constantly testing our guesses both large and small as we gradually build up a coherent structure of meaning" (VAL 203f). Yet his theory is expressly justified with the purported opposition between "the whimsical lawlessness of guessing" and the "ultimately methodical character of testing": "both processes are necessary in interpretation, but only one of them is governed by logical principles."

In the 1976 volume (AIM), Hirsch attenuates the split: "the private processes of verbal understanding have the same character" as the "public activity" of "validation," the "objective marshalling of evidence in the cause of an interpretive hypothesis" (AIM 33). Hence, "the process of validation is not easily separated from the process of understanding in either theory or practice." He does not think this change of perspective demands "substantive revisions of the earlier argument" (AIM 8). Yet if his two stages of reading have "the same character," his elaborate enterprise of validation, advocated on the grounds of their difference, seems far less compelling.

He also owns that he had previously "almost" "ignored the whole question of the process of understanding" (AIM 33). By dividing reading into two "moments" and offering a theory only for the second, he essentially proposed a theory that deals with effects, yet pays no attention to causes. It seems illogical to classify and judge competing hypotheses while disregarding how they are engendered in the first place. That way, we can only objectify them as entities which abruptly emerge ready-made from a spree of "lawless guessing." Hirsch remarks that "meaning" "is not a physical object," and to treat "meaning as an object" is merely "a short-cut" or "convenience" to designate both "intentional objects" and "intentional acts" (AIM, 8). But this short-cut conceals precisely what most theoreticians on the current scene consider the vital issue: how "objects of knowledge" or "objects of our construing" (VAL 176f) are created by the human subject participating in literary communication.

Hirsch stipulates that personal interests in formulating hypotheses should be completely discounted. He finds it "obvious" that "the consolidated knowledge

---

[8] Perhaps the expansion of rhetoric in the theorizing of the Yale critics (Ch. 13-15) is one motive why Hirsch attacks the "American disciples" of "Derrida and Foucault" (AIM 147, 13). His campaign against these "cognitive atheists" will be described later (p. 119).

within a discipline has nothing to do with its rhetoric" (AIM 153). Through its means of "persuasion," "rhetoric" influences "the communal acceptance of hypotheses" and "can subserve both knowledge and intellectual chicanery."[8] Although "the spirit of vanity and advocacy" always endangers the "selfless devotion to the communal enterprise," "the direction of knowledge goes forward at the level of the discipline" (AIM 152f). It is "essential to distinguish hypotheses from the rhetoric used to convey them," since they "are not bound to any single expression of them" (AIM 153f). This demand might be met by stating every hypothesis in several forms, then proving them partially equivalent, and finally extracting only what is common to them all. This task looks intriguing, but we do not find it performed in Hirsch's books beyond brief demonstrations for a few parts of texts.

Given the arguments summarized above, we would not expect Hirsch's orderly version of reading to be depicted in psychological terms. Nor can it be a product of "linguistic norms," since they constitute "the possibilities, not the actualities of language," and may therefore "be invoked to support any verbally possible meaning" (VAL 69, 226). Instead, he proposes an essentially set-theoretical concept of the "intrinsic genre"[9] as an "overarching notion" which "embraces a system of expectations" and "conventions," including "the entire system of usage traits, rules, customs, formal necessities, and properties which constitute a type of verbal meaning" (VAL 78, 92). If "genre" is defined as the "type which embraces the whole meaning of an utterance" and "controls the temporal sequence of speech," then "all understanding of verbal meaning is necessarily genre-bound" (VAL 71, 78, 76). "The intrinsic genre of the utterance" is thus "the essential component of a context"; "everything else in the context serves merely as a clue to the intrinsic genre" (VAL 87). The "shared genre conception" is "constitutive both of meaning and of understanding" (VAL 80f). These theses lead to a "universally applicable" "principle": "valid interpretation depends on a valid inference about the properties of the intrinsic genre" (VAL 121).

Hirsch stresses that his idea of "genre" is far more specific than traditional literary genres like "Christian-humanist epic"; indeed, "there is no ready-made vocabulary for describing the intrinsic genres of particular utterances" (VAL 84, 82). Hirsch is willing to admit the old "broad genre concept," as long as it does not "pretend to be a species concept that somehow defines and equates the members it subsumes" (VAL 110). But he rejects "the notion that the larger classifications of texts represent an adequate foundation for defining different types of interpretation" (VAL 113). "There are no clear and firm boundaries" among those "classifications," and their "categories" are "not everywhere equally

---

[9] Saussure's old dichotomy of "langue versus parole" is invoked, but the "intrinsic genre" is not to be "subsumed under either category" (VAL 69, 111). It seems to emerge during a movement from the former to the latter.

appropriate" (VAL 115ff). The "broad genre concept" tends to rely on "conclusions about recurrent patterns" "subsequent to interpretation," as opposed to the intrinsic genres actively applied for and during interpretation (VAL 110).

We can see that even on the theoretical plane, Hirsch is already practising his precept of narrowing down classes (in this case, "genres"). In principle, he "objects to the dangerous practice of using abstract categories or monolithic 'approaches' and 'methods' to interpret a wide variety of texts" (VAL 88f). He feels that a "description" of "the common elements in a narrow group of texts which have direct historical relationships" "becomes less useful to interpretation" as its "scope becomes broader and more abstract" (VAL 110).

The "intrinsic genre," in contrast, "emerges" during communication "only after a narrowing process," going from "vague and empty" toward "more explicit" (VAL 103, 77). Indeed, his notion of "genre" appears so specific that Hirsch reassures us it is not "identical with the particular meaning of the utterance" (VAL 86). "An interpreter's preliminary generic conception of a text is constitutive of everything else that he subsequently understands" and provides an "anticipated sense of the whole by virtue of which the presently experienced words are understood in their capacity as parts of a whole" (VAL 74, 82). Therefore, the "intrinsic genre" is definable as the "sense of the whole by means of which an interpreter can correctly understand any part in its determinacy" (VAL 86)— precisely the construct needed to support a "valid interpretation."

The "intrinsic genre" also "determines" "the implications of an utterance," a "crucial issue" "when our central concern is validity" (VAL 89). The genre is not merely the "additive" "set of implications" postulated in logic, but a means for "structuring" and "unity," and an indicator of "purposes," "emphases," and "relative importance" (VAL 98f, 117, 102). Control is thereby maintained without total determinism. "Minor alterations can always be made" in the text "without changing the intrinsic genre" (VAL 85). Conversely, the same "word sequence can represent more than one meaning" because it "can be subsumed by more than one intrinsic genre and therefore can carry different implications" (VAL 98). It follows that "the correct determination of implications" is "crucial" for "discriminating a valid from an invalid interpretation" (VAL 89). By the same token, "disagreement about an interpretation is usually a disagreement about genre" and "centers on details of implication" (VAL 98, 89).

This conception of a "genre" yielding a "sense of the whole" is disrupted somewhat when Hirsch disclaims "coherence" as a measure for validation. His reasoning follows logic: "appeals to coherence" are "useless because they are circular" (VAL 194, 237). Though "the hypothesis which makes functional the greater number of traits must, in relation to that limited evidence, be judged the more probable," this adjudication is "unsatisfactory" because "one hypothesis will make functional different traits from the other" (VAL 190). Hirsch wants the interpreter to "consider all the known relevant data" (VAL 192), as if relevance itself could be decided by any other criterion than the coherence among the items it is assigned to.

In the orderly version, reading generates meanings that, in Hirsch's view, are always determinate, because "determinacy is a necessary attribute of any sharable meaning" (VAL 44). This conception is supported with the logical principle of identity: "if a meaning were indeterminate," "it would have no boundaries, no self-identity, and therefore could have no identity with a meaning entertained by someone else." "Verbal meaning" "is what it is and not something else, and it is always the same" (VAL 45f). "Determinacy does not mean definiteness or precision" or "clarity" (VAL 44, 85). As we see, Hirsch postulates inevitable determinacy by construing the concept in a very weak sense, as compared to the everyday sense of "definitely settled," "conclusively determined," "unequivocally characterized" *(Webster's New Collegiate Dictionary)*.

Logicians have yet to prove that the principle of identity applies as straightforwardly to meanings as to physical objects. Hirsch makes a foray in this direction when he defends "the existence and importance of synonymity, that is, the expression of an absolutely identical meaning through different linguistic forms" (AIM 50). He argues that "form does not compel meaning," so that "the relationship" between the two is "essentially indeterminate" (AIM 10, 50f). He opposes "linguistic determinism" with something he styles the "Gödel's theorem of language": "the intrinsic undecidability of the correlations between linguistic levels" (AIM 50f, 66; cf. Bazell 1953, 1966). This attitude might explain why Hirsch rejects stylistics as a "reliable method of confirming an interpretation" (AIM 22, 50, 72).

Synonymity also is construed in a weak sense. For Hirsch, it requires that expressions can be "substituted" for each other only "occasionally" rather than "universally" (cf. AIM 54). Expressions may appear different in isolation, but equivalent in a particular text (cf. AIM 61).[10] This proviso removes the obstacles that "language" allows "the same words different meanings" and "different words the same meaning"; and that "meaning postulates" are "only provisional," subject to change during "actual use" (AIM 62f). Even poetry gets included by reasoning that we "cannot reliably assert" "absolute synonymity is impossible" in "poetry" "unless we can also assert nonsynonymity for all speech" (AIM 58f). This reasoning depends on Hirsch's original denial of a "special ontological status" to "the literary text" (VAL 210) (see pp. 107, 119, 123, 126).

No matter what a dispute may concern, a scholar cannot compare objects and classes without first constituting them. This process cannot be taken for granted, and Hirsch provides no directions for performing it upon complex materials. Empirical studies reveal that humans have only fuzzy notions of the criteria for

---

[10] He cites a "test" or "experiment" he did on synonymity by "showing" "documents" "to a number of literate native speakers" (AIM 60f).

defining even familiar, concrete classes of objects; and that class membership is not uniform, but arrayed along a gradation of more or less typical (cf. Rosch & Mervis 1975; Rosch 1977). If so, the far less ordinary or tangible objects of creative literature could hardly fall into orderly and homogeneous classes. Hirsch would restrict innovation to "novel subsumptions under previously known types" (VAL 105).[11] Yet he elsewhere depicts literature as "an arbitrary classification of linguistic works which do not exhibit common distinctive traits" (AIM 135). So this domain should be the least amenable one to logical classification based on the "uniformity" of "defining characteristics" (VAL 176).

To forestall such problems, Hirsch further constricts and stabilizes the objects of "interpretation." He limits them to what he calls "verbal meaning," as opposed to: "significance," the "relationship between that meaning and a person, or a conception, or a situation, or indeed anything imaginable"; "subject matter," "the 'objective' character" of what a "verbal meaning" "refers to"; "response," "the more or less personal meaning" a reader "attaches to a verbal meaning"; "unconscious and symptomatic meaning," "involuntary accompaniments to meaning"; and "implication," "any submeaning belonging to the whole array" of meanings "carried" by "an utterance" in the same way that "a trait belongs to a type" (VAL 8, 59, 39, 52f, 62, 71). The problem now is that "we cannot isolate the act of construing verbal meaning from all those other acts, perceptions, associations, and judgments that accompany that act and are instrumental in leading us to perform it" (VAL 140). "Such aspects of a context as purposes, conventions, and relationship to an audience are not outside the meaning of the utterance but are constitutive of it" (VAL 87). Besides, we already heard how Hirsch stressed the "crucial" role of "implications" for telling what is "valid" (p. 112).

A skilled interpreter might try to sort out different kinds of meaning after having already arrived at a provisional interpretation. But quite apart from the difficulty of attaining such specialized skills, the interpreter would be in the odd position of discarding for theoretical motives some elements of meaning that he or she had depended on in practice, rather like a magician disclaiming the mechanisms behind the act. If the purported "verbal meaning" could not have been attained without using these other types of meaning, it can hardly have a sufficiently independent status to provide the structural base for an elaborated process of validation. Even if subjectivity can be trimmed down close to objectivity, subsequent inferences are not automatically objective.

Nonetheless, Hirsch draws a line between "interpretation, whose exclusive object is verbal meaning," and "criticism," whose "proper object" is the text's "significance" —a domain he considers "boundless," invested with "countless dimensions" (VAL 57). Though he says "all textual commentary is a mixture of

---

[11] The possibility of "unique meaning" is denied because "understanding" depends on knowing what "type of meaning" to expect (VAL 80). Wellek and Warren (TL 18, 151) offer a similar argument. Iser suggests on the contrary that each experienced meaning is "unrepeatable" (AR 150).

interpretation and criticism," he thinks that "usually a choice has been made as to which goal is to receive the main emphasis" (VAL 140). He advertises this "distinction" as a "charter of freedom to the critic, not an inhibition" (VAL 57). But this freedom is rescinded again when Hirsch declares that "the discipline of interpretation is the foundation of all valid criticism" (VAL 156). Here we have the typical move of the critic portraying his theory as central and indispensable. The implication should be that a large portion of available criticism is "invalid" because it doesn't conform to Hirsch's methods. But in my discussions with him, he has repeatedly claimed to be merely providing a theoretical rationale for what interpreters have been doing all along.

The problem of ambiguity is treated not as flux or dispersal, but merely as an array of alternate determinate meanings awaiting a decision. "Whenever a reader confronts two interpretations which impose different emphases on similar mean-ing components," he says, "at least one of the interpretations must be wrong" (VAL 230). This assertion reverts back even before the work of the New Critics, notably Empson's (1930) classic study showing that ambiguity can be systemat-ically present in literary communication without pressure to decide which read-ings are "wrong." Hirsch imagines that Empson's argument depends on the text being "conceived" as a 'piece of language'" (VAL 62, 224). But interpretive hypotheses must become such pieces too before they can be adjudicated; and how to make sure they convey only "verbal meaning" without "significance" is far from obvious.

Whether the orderly or the disorderly version of reading is accepted turns out to be inconclusive, because Hirsch situates the ultimate recourse not at the reader's end, but at the author's. The "philological effort to find out what the author meant" is "the only proper foundation of criticism" (VAL 57). "The only object of cognition having an implicit claim to be 'a universal point of reference' is the sharable object cognized by its maker" (AIM 105f). "All valid interpretation of every sort is founded on the re-cognition of what an author meant" (VAL 126). The term "re-cognitive" was adopted from Emiliano Betti (1955), who contrasts it with "presentational" and "normative" interpretation (VAL 112). Though Hirsch asserts that "only a re-cognitive interpretation is a valid interpretation" (VAL 122), his own standards are heavily normative, at least in the sense that "the normative dimension of interpretation is always in the last analysis an ethical dimension" (AIM 77). But the ethical basis of his enterprise was not fore-grounded in his earlier formulations. We return to this shift later (p. 120).

As we might predict, Hirsch finds the decisive act is not so much in speaking or writing, but in selecting an "intrinsic genre." "Once the speaker has willed 'this particular type of meaning,' the further determination of his meaning de-pends entirely upon his subsequent choice of words and patterns falling within the tolerance of the intrinsic genre" (VAL 86). Hirsch presumes that the author's original act of "will" to convey a "type" (VAL 31, 51, 86, 124, etc.) always has a specific result. We are categorically told that "an author cannot mean what he does not mean"; that "no example of the author's ignorance with respect to his meaning could legitimately show that his intended meaning and the meaning of his text are two different things"; and that "either the text represents the author's verbal meaning or it represents no determinate verbal meaning at all" (VAL 22, 234). These are interesting claims about psychological states, although Hirsch offers no empirical evidence to support them, and I wonder if any could be found.

He sidesteps the "distinction between a mere intention to do something and the concrete accomplishment of that intention" by transferring it from the domain of "verbal meaning" over to that of "evaluation" (VAL 11f). There too, the author is the point of reference. "The only values which can be considered intrinsic properties of a work are those which attach by subjective necessity to a re-cognition of the author's work" (AIM 106). In contrast to Frye, Hirsch supposes that "evaluation" can "qualify as objective knowledge" if it is "accurate with respect to" "explicit" "criteria being applied" (AIM 108). Such "judgments" "furnish the grounds of their own validation" and can attain "as much objectivity as accurate interpretations." Reciprocally, "those which are necessarily implied in interpretation" are "the only unavoidable judgments of value in literary commentary" (AIM 106). "It is quite possible to eschew other kinds."

Such a strong stand for the author is highly atypical, and we should consider the difficulties (beyond mere fashions of the day) that make it so unpopular. One difficulty is the sheer size of the "philological effort" involved. In order to find out what the author meant, we are enjoined to consult "all clues" about the "cultural and personal attitudes the author might be expected to bring to bear in specifying his verbal meanings" (VAL 240). Interpreters might have to sift through a staggering mass of historical, biographical, and psychological evidence on the good faith that it will apply to the issues being adjudicated. But the assembled evidence might be inconclusive, contradictory, or unrelated to the text or passage in dispute. Besides, we have no reliable way to tell exactly when "all" the evidence is in. For some authors, an entirely scholarly career might be spent digging and gathering without producing the necessary certainty.

A second difficulty is the incongruity of trying to extract the narrowest possible meaning from the widest possible scope of evidence. To make meaning decidable, we are asked to make it undelimitable. Hirsch agrees with Wellek and Warren's "programmatic idea" that "literary interpretation must be intrinsic" (VAL 113). But the mass of "clues" are highly likely to spill far outside the boundaries of the clearly determinate "verbal meaning" Hirsch would make the sole basis for interpretation. Such clues could easily belong to "significance," "implication," and all the other types Hirsch set aside; even "autobiographical meanings" are discounted (VAL 16).

Therefore, the ostensibly "objective" evidence only becomes evidence at all when the interpreter subjectively elects to consider it as such. Hirsch himself admits that since "the intrinsic genre is always construed, that is, guessed, and is never" "given," "the interpreter can never be completely certain" what "genre" the speaker[12] has "willed" (VAL 88, 94). "We have no direct access to the author's mind" (VAL 99). "The speaker's attitudes are not given but are construed from the utterance itself" (VAL 87). The investigator often has to rely on an "arbitrary supposition" derived from a "psychological reconstruction" of the author (VAL 123, 240). We seem to be trading a community of unreliable readers for the single authority of an inaccessible author.

A third difficulty is that text production is being pictured as stable and reliable, even though text reception has been portrayed as "whimsical" and "lawless" (VAL 203f). There is no empirical support for the idea that when people turn from reading to writing, their mental processes abruptly become more determinate. Available findings indicate rather that authors typically work from a highly approximate mental representation of intended meanings and, for a whole spectrum of reasons, may fail to execute their intentions.[13] We might therefore incur the additional labor of proving that whatever authors say about their meanings —even explicit paraphrases, which would presumably constitute the most directly applicable evidence—is indeed dependable. The consensus among our critics (notably, Fiedler, Iser, Holland, Paris, and de Man) is more the contrary. Even Hirsch admits that in literature, the author "submits to the convention that his willed implications must go far beyond what he explicitly knows" (VAL 123).

A fourth difficulty is that the author's intention might be precisely to evade determinacy. As several of our critics point out, Iser in particular, modernism is distinguished by a split or circuitous relation between expression and intention, a deliberate withholding of clues for readers who wonder where the author's real opinions lie. It is no accident that none of Hirsch's samples are taken from modernist texts, a problem I return to (p. 122). In effect, we are urged to revere all authorial intentions except those which prove inconvenient for the project of validation. And this injunction too seems illogical, or, from an ethical standpoint, inconsistent.

Hirsch's theory implies the general hypothesis that the literary author uniformly intends to convey a single "valid" "verbal meaning," no matter how much interpretive effort might be required to establish it. This assumption looks dubious when we consider the overwhelming diversity of intentions that lead authors to compose a work. If we juxtapose Homer and Milton, Richardson and

---

[12] Probably influenced by ordinary-language philosophy, Hirsch uses the term "speaker" in much of his argument and alludes to Saussure's view that "writing is a lately developed surrogate of speech" (VAL 101f). But in fact, writing poses problems of interpretation that speech does not, or in different ways (cf. survey and references in Beaugrande 1984a). For one thing, getting validation from a speaker should be easy.

[13] On the processes and problems of writing see Beaugrande (1984a). The failure of authorial intention becomes systematic in the theorizings of de Man, Bloom, and Hartman (Ch. 13-15). Compare Notes 8 and 16.

Fielding, Goethe and Sterne, Zola and Kafka, Wordsworth and Berryman, Twain and Joyce, or Hauptmann and Ionesco, we may seriously doubt any uniformity of intentions regarding determinate and decidable meaning. Instead of just amassing clues about "verbal meanings," we might seek clues about whether authors did or could have intended standards of "validity" in the first place. Like Wellek and Warren, Hirsch offers us only his warning that the alternative to his own view is mere anarchy—the absurd doctrine that an author or text "does not mean anything in particular" (cf. VAL 4, 11, 13, 45, 234).

Hirsch is sufficiently aware of the problematic character of his basic assumptions to have anticipated some possible objections to them. In his earlier book, he professes to refute his adversaries with logical argumentation. He charges them with various forms of "skepticism" that "implicitly deny the possibility of validity in any absolute or normative sense of the word" (VAL viii). His refutations rest mainly on the same tendencies we have seen in his whole model: splitting of subject from object, and adducing relative probabilities.

In one form of "skepticism" called "psychologism," "textual meaning" "changes from reading to reading" (VAL 6). He retorts that it is a "mistake" to "identify meaning with mental processes rather than with the object of those processes" (VAL 32). "The objects of awareness are not the same as the subjective 'perceptions,' 'processes,' or 'acts' which are directed toward those objects" (VAL 37). If "an unlimited number of intentional acts can intend (be averted to) the very same intentional object," they can also "intend the same verbal meaning" (VAL 38). Thus, it is "possible to reproduce a verbal meaning," even though "one man's mental life is not the same as another's" (VAL 38, 32). "It is far more likely that an author and an interpreter can entertain identical meanings than that they cannot" (VAL 18). Of course, it is narrow "verbal meaning" rather than wide "significance" that is "in principle reproducible" and "sharable" (VAL 38, 40).

In a second form of "skepticism" called "radical historicism," "the meaning of the literary text is 'what it means to us today'" (VAL viii). Hirsch replies that a "reinterpretation is not the same as a different understanding" (VAL 42). After all, "all understanding of cultures past or present is 'constructed'"; "there is no immediacy in understanding either a contemporary or a predecessor" (VAL 43).[14] He admits that "generally, we are more likely to get a contemporary text right" than "a text from the past"; "but this general likelihood does not automatically hold in any particular instance (where factors of temperament, knowledge, diligence, and luck are decisive)" (VAL 44). This argument plays upon the "distinction" between "the general probability" versus "the particular probability that may obtain in a particular case" (VAL 42f). Apparently, the most probable meaning is to be uncovered by improbable acts of scholarly diligence.

---

[14] The somewhat fanciful attempts of Roland Barthes and Jan Kott to make Racine and Shakespeare into our contemporaries are used to prove that the contemporary mind is always a "construction" (AIM 41, 88).

In a third form of "skepticism" called "autonomism," the "central tenet" is: "it does not matter what an author means—only what his text says" (VAL 10). This time, the rebuttal is that a text doesn't "say" anything; there is only "the saying of the author or a reader" (VAL 13). "Signs can be variously construed, and until they are construed the text 'says' nothing at all" (VAL 14). Although Hirsch presents the "empirical fact" that "public consensus does not exist," he attributes this not to "private meanings," but only to "improbable" or "wrong" ones (VAL 13ff). Also, the idea that "meaning is independent of authorial will" would require the supposition that "literary texts belong to a distinct ontological realm" (VAL viii) —a thesis Hirsch has to reject, as we have noticed (cf. VAL 210; AIM 58f) (p. 107).

In more recent times, Hirsch adopts a different defense after transferring the main rationale of his theory from the *logical* over to the *ethical*. He may have felt angered by the refusal of criticism to adopt his proposals. Or, he may have realized that the latter entail an arduous task with an uncertain outcome. Either way, he elects to meet any doubts about whether his "validation" is being done or can be done by avowing with rising shrillness that it jolly well ought to be done in the name of ethical responsibility. Even he can see how hard it is to find explicit model interpretations that genuinely fulfill his criteria.

In the *Validity* volume, this lack of model interpretations was acknowledged with equanimity. We "will be disappointed" if we "expect to discover" there "a new interpretive program or 'approach'" (VAL x). Nor should we "expect to find complete and exemplary demonstrations of the validating process." "The practical consequences" of such a theory "are bound to be largely indirect"; he "believes" they will "take care of themselves" (VAL xf).

In *Aims*, however, Hirsch finds they haven't. He is mightily "indignant" to see how "the anxiety-ridden insistence on distinguishing itself from natural science" has led "literary study" to become "the most skeptical and decadent branch of humanistic study" (AIM 13, 149). The "skeptics" of the earlier volume are restyled "cognitive atheists" for "assuming that all 'knowledge' is relative" (AIM 36). Though he denounces his opponents as "theologians" (AIM 13; cf. VAL 44), his own term "atheism" implies not a failure to be objective, but a failure to make a leap of faith—in this case, the faith in "validation." Theological overtones pervade a project which began with an emphatic salute to scientific method (just what Bleich would predict, p. 184). Its "patron saint" is none other than Matthew Arnold, who "was profoundly right to set the aims of criticism on foundations that can ultimately be described in ethical terms" (AIM 139).[15]

---

[15] Hirsch is one of Arnold's few supporters in our survey. Wellek and Warren complain that Arnold "confounded" "psychology" with "evaluation" (TL 178). His rationale for measuring the "greatness" of works is pronounced "nonsense" by Frye (AC 22). His "elitism" is assailed by Fiedler (WL 104, 128) and Bleich (AX 111f). His "intellectual position" is transformed by Holland into an "unconscious" "wish to avoid sexual touchings" (DY 156). Hartman laments the "Arnoldian concordat" that cut off "criticism" from "the creative" (CW 6). And so on.

Aims at least is quite explicit about the ethical grounding of the enterprise. "The choice of an interpretive norm is not required by the 'nature of the text,' but being a choice, belongs to the domain of ethics rather than the domain of ontology" (AIM 7). If we cannot depend on "neutral analysis in order to make decisions about the goals of interpretation," "we have to enter the realm" of "ethical persuasion" (AIM 85), which presumably brings us back from logic to rhetoric, the domain we saw disbarred before. "Even understanding" itself "as contrasted with misunderstanding has only an ethical and not an ontological claim to privilege" (AIM 135)—again, a strongly performative view of knowledge.

Hirsch says "this observation had been made in the earlier book, but so briefly that it was generally overlooked" (AIM 7), namely in the passage about "the interpreter" "deciding what he wants to actualize" (VAL 25). But *Validity* is not argued in ethical terms, except in its waspish asides, as when a scholar with a "tolerance to a wide variety of readings" is denounced for "abject intellectual surrender" and "abandonment of responsibility" (VAL 168). Still, the earlier book implied a systematic leap of faith from the *logical gradation* of *more versus less probable* over to the *ethical dichotomy* of *right versus wrong*. Few logicians would be inclined to designate classification and hypothesis-testing as ethical operations. "Validation" procedures can at best determine probability. The assertion of "correctness" is a crucial additional performance on the critic's part, and one that steadily fewer critics on the contemporary scene are eager to enact—a stance which Hirsch may call "unethical," but hardly illogical. He raises his vehemence to arouse them from a state which he considers lethargy and irresponsibility, but which may well be a concern for other uses of literature than his.

As would be predicted, Hirsch draws his most powerful ethical mandate from fidelity to the author. He now calls the author's intended meaning the "original meaning," and designates it "the 'best meaning,'" whereas any other is "anachronistic meaning" (AIM 92, 77, 79, 88f).[16] So the "ethical maxim for interpretation" is: "unless there is a powerful overriding value in disregarding an author's intention (i.e., original meaning), we who interpret as a vocation should not disregard it" (AIM 90). Such an ethic presupposes that we *know* what the author's intention was; and the ethical emphasis invites scholars to exaggerate the degree of their own certainty on this point. An *authorial* orientation too readily becomes an *authoritarian* one when the most probable reading becomes the "valid" one for which we must surrender all others.

Hirsch is so convinced by his own arguments that he can only comprehend the opposition of other critics as a sign of "decadence" (AIM 13, 149). He accuses the "cognitive atheists," deconstructionists in particular, of two kinds of errors. In

---

[16] Hirsch says the latter term is "a shorthand, not a pejorative term"; but it is the converse of "'the best'" (AIM 163, 92). This return to origins may be yet another point of friction with the deconstructionists (cf. Notes 8 and 13).

the first place, "it is ethically inconsistent to batten on institutions whose very foundations one attacks"; "it is logically inconsistent to write scholarly books which argue that there is no point in writing scholarly books" (AIM 13). But the implication that academics must believe what their institutional overseers demand seems more apt for theologians than disinterested scholars. And the "scholarly books," of which the "atheists" produce more than Hirsch does, do not, as we will see in Chs. 13-15, deny their own purpose, but their traditional functions.

In the second place, he bars "universal relativism" from claiming "absoluteness" in "a world devoid of absolutes." But this argument falls apart too. Applied to itself, relativism generates not "absoluteness," but an ever-finer scaling of greater or lesser relativity. By the same token, an increase in inconsistency will not lead ultimately to consistency, but to greater diversity and nuancing. Whatever logic may dictate, every system is operationally relative and inconsistent in some aspects. At the conclusion of this chapter, I review the inconsistencies in Hirsch's own position, wherein they are at least as disruptive as any a deconstructionist would commit.

A better way to estimate Hirsch's claims than philosophical or ethical disputation might be practical demonstration. Hirsch admits he has never provided one for an entire literary work (interview, 1984). He is content with sporadic illustrations whose simplicity conceals the problems I have raised. His example for narrowing down classes is a dispute over two competing versions of an Old English manuscript (VAL 187f). The objects of contention ("thwyrlic" versus "thrymlic") were already produced by two different scribes of the text and thus came ready-made for the interpreter to adjudicate.

When his objects are interpretive hypotheses, they are also fall into neat, straightforward contrasts: an optimistic versus a pessimistic way to construe Wordsworth's "A Spirit Did My Slumber Seal"; death versus physical departure as the topic of Donne's "Valediction Forbidding Mourning"; an Oedipal versus a non-Oedipal reading of *Hamlet*; and so on (VAL 190ff, 122ff). Hirsch cheerfully concedes that his demonstrations "work well" when one reading is "a sitting duck" rather than an "expert reading" (VAL 192). But he sees only a quantitative problem here that would be solved with more evidence—"all the known relevant data." He does not foresee a qualitative jump in complexity and indeterminacy that could undercut his methods.

In my estimation, the really straightforward disputes tend to be rather uninteresting ones, hardly worth amassing heaps of data. Consider Spenser's lines in Faerie Queen, (I, ii, xix)[17]: "And at his haughtie helmet making mark, / So hugely stroke, that it the steele did rive / And cleft his head." I am uncertain whether the "it" refers to "stroke" and is thus the grammatical subject, while the

---

[17] This example was brought to my attention by George Dillon's (1978) useful book on linguistics and the reading of literature.

"steele" is the foe's helmet; or to "helmet" and is thus the direct object, while "steele" is the sword. Gathering "all relevant evidence" —on 16th-century syntax, Spenser's usage, other passages in the same work, and the like —seems unreasonably arduous in light of what I stand to gain by clarifying such a minor point. The "head" is "cleft" either way, and probing the syntax of the passage is hair-splitting of a far less valorous kind.

Moreover, even straightforward disputes may have to be settled in devious ways. Frost's poem about "The Road Not Taken" says that one road "was grassy and wanted wear," but just afterwards that the "passing" "had worn them really about the same." A logician would object that both statements cannot be literally true at the same time. To assume the author was just being careless would violate Hirsch's very center of authority (as we will see in a moment, he bends meanings every which way to save some jarring passages of Blake's). If we undertake a validation, the most relevant evidence would be found in the theme and lesson of the poem, both of which convey the idea that "taking the road less travelled by" has made "all the difference." My students, who pick this poem a lot, usually solve the conflict by assuming that the speaker is in a divided state of mind. This interpretation, though reasonable enough if we want to rescue the point of the poem, is reached not by virtue of verbal meaning of the incongruous statement, but in spite of it.

In another famous poem, William Carlos Williams says that "so much depends upon a red wheelbarrow beside the white chickens." An anecdote has been preserved that this poem was inspired when the author, a doctor by vocation, was gazing out from the window of a gravely ill patient's house at a certain wheelbarrow (cf. Rhodes, 1965). This fact might qualify as authorial evidence to "validate" the reading of "so much" as "the chance of recovery, survival," and so on. Yet the evidence places the poem in so specific a context as to severely impoverish its potential meaning. The poet certainly isn't asking us to believe that a wheelbarrow cures illnesses, assisted by chickens in white uniforms. I would construe the connection in terms of how mundane objects can seem vital and significant. This effect no doubt increases when the prospect of death is imminent, but I do not get this specification from the poem as it stands. So I am inclined to treat the anecdote as a curious sidelight, but by no means a motive for enforcing a specific meaning.

These examples are still deceptively elementary. I can scarcely imagine how Hirsch's method would deal with really complex passages, such as: "And the hapless soldier's sigh / Runs in blood down palace walls" (Blake); "A breeze like the turning of a page / Brings back your face: the moment / Takes such a big bite out of the haze / Of pleasant intuition it comes after" (Ashbery); "And once below a time I lordly had the trees and leaves / Trail with daisies and barley / Down the rivers of windfall light" (Dylan Thomas); and so on. To "validate" interpretations for these, the critic has no tidy rows of comparable "objects" to work with. Considerable skill would be needed to manufacture the objects by translating the hypotheses of various readings into some format that would group them under roughly similar categories. This process would be interesting to observe, but I doubt it would resemble Hirsch's "objective" methods very closely. Moreover, all the evidence we could gather about the authors might only diversify rather than unify our hypotheses.

I could multiply examples indefinitely, but my point would always be the same. The most important factor Hirsch loses by denying the "special ontological status" of literature is the experienced pressure to shape and reshape its "verbal meanings." Indeed, certain types of literature are expressly constituted by deliberately abdicating authorial control over meaning. "Concrete" or "visual" poetry presents configurations of letters and nonwords rather like inkblots designed for free association. "Found" poems depend on the determination of the presenter and the reader to disregard the original author's intention and "will." Hirsch again prescribes an unintended and inappropriate response when he suggests that a "definitive interpretation" of a found poem requires "access to the texts from which they were excerpted" (VAL 97). He refers us back to the nonliterary domain because his model discounts the special focus that converts the "found" text into a poem.

I find it revealing that when Hirsch does embark on large-scale interpretation, he by no means stays within the limits of his own theory. In his study of Blake's poetry,[18] Hirsch has occasion to ask whether the phrase "Gave thee clothing of delight" should be read as "God clothed the lamb with delight," making "delight" a substance; or as "God gave the lamb delightful clothing," making "delight" a descriptive modifier—and he accepts *both* readings (IE 178). This sort of solution, spurned in his theory as an "abandonment of responsibility" (VAL 168), seeks the "rich variousness" he rejected in his argument on "determinacy" (VAL 45).

Hirsch may transform the "verbal meaning" or contravene it if it collides with his reverence for the author. In the *Songs of Innocence,* the "childish simplicity of language utterly belies their adult profundity of insight" (IE 21). Blake "must have made an implicit moral judgment on cruelty and injustice which was at odds with the benign and accepting surface tone of his poems" (IE 18). Whatever authorial evidence Hirsch may have for these assertions must relate not to "verbal meaning," but to "significance."[19]

As we see, Hirsch finds it expedient to interpret by overstepping the restric-

---

[18] Hirsch cannot have simply changed his mind between 1964 (Blake study) and 1967 (VAL), because his original essay on "verification" was already published in 1960. He admitted apologetically that he failed give a "model of adjudication" for choosing between "two disparate modes of interpreting Blake's *Songs of Innocence and of Experience*" because he did not consider "all the important relevant evidence" (VAL 182).

[19] "Irony" is a case where "two different mental sets" are "simultaneously adopted" (AIM 107; cf. AIM 23ff). But since the two pertain to "verbal meanings" in very different ways, I wonder how Hirsch's validation might proceed.

tions prescribed in his theory for validation. He expounds "significance," "implications," "unsaid meaning," "symbolic meaning," "sacramental meaning," "prophetic meaning," "images," and "imaginative identification" (IE 42, 30, 30, 43, 38, 40, 22, 249). He reminds us that Blake's poems are not uniform objects: "each poem for him was a new start" and thus must not be made an "intellectual counter" in a "dialectical system" (IE 5ff)—yet his own logic of classes is presumably one such "system." And he ventures interpretive statements that could not be validated in *any* logic, because their own verbal meanings contain stark contradictions, for example: "Man is a Child, and a Lamb, and to others, a Shepherd. Ultimately, Shepherd and Sheep, Father and Child, are the same" (IE 29). The issue of synonymy, about which he was so confident, cannot be sensibly raised here.

Also instructive is Hirsch's fabrication of a "reader" who construes the text the way Hirsch does. We get told what "the adult reader implicitly knows"; what "the sensitive reader will feel"; or what "all sympathetic readers of the poem have experienced" (IE 178, 246). Such attributions imply an immediately attained consensus among readers, though his theory predicts just the opposite principle.

Or Hirsch adopts the familiar expedient of standing aside to let the text act out the meaning on its own, even though he does not subscribe to the independence of the text asserted by the New Critics (VAL 11f).[20] For Blake's "Tyger" (IE 244-252), he delivers a detailed hypothetical account of the poem in action, for instance: "these staccato beats of controlled fury are succeeded by a stanza of immense calm that enormously widens the imaginative range of the poem" (IE 248). This practice goes against his precept that "the 'text' says nothing at all" by itself (VAL 14). And when he gets to his value judgment, he gives none of the "explicit criteria" he prescribed for "evaluation" (AIM 108), but merely opines: "it is the most inclusive poem Blake ever wrote," and "its spiritual scope is immense" (IE 252).

The point here is not that Hirsch's readings are vulnerable. That risk must be taken in stride for any poetry as abstruse and uneven as Blake's. The point is that such challenging texts can scarcely be interpreted in any productive or revealing way with a weighty apparatus of validation confined to "verbal meanings." Hirsch's interpretations of Blake can claim validity because they succeed in "making functional many elements of the mute text" (cf. VAL 190).

In sum, Hirsch's enterprise is not an intrinsic and logical one after all. Rather, it is an attempt to impose an extrinsic ethic upon a diffuse and diversified activity by forcing the latter into a reduced, normatized, and idealized mold. "Clues" about an author's "meanings" need not "compel a right guess" any more than just reading the text and trying to formulate "coherence" (cf. VAL 240, 170, 194).

---

[20] The "intentional fallacy" gets rescued by claiming that its "careful distinctions and qualifications" got lost in a "false and facile dogma" (VAL 12); but compare de Man's meticulous argument (BI 24ff). *Validity* is dedicated to Wimsatt, as is its antithesis, Bloom's *Anxiety of Influence*.

Only the critic's prior interpretation will decide what the clues are and what they prove. As Hirsch says, "the interpreter" "decides what he wants to actualize and what purpose his actualization should achieve" (VAL 25). The circularity of understanding within context can only be traded for a greater circularity of selecting and using external clues: greater because the author evidently did not think the text needed the clues, but did compose a context by including what seemed relevant and necessary.

The usefulness of validation seems limited to the kind of obstacles that confront editors of definitive editions or compilers of variorum (cf. VAL xi; AIM 89). The method has failed to gain wide application not because today's literary critics are prey to "decadence" and "atheism," but because it assigns to the interpreter tasks that demand extreme efforts for meager rewards. Besides, even as pure theory, it is rife with inconsistencies: studying effects without causes; narrowing interpretation by broadening the evidence; arguing for the self-identity of meaning but relying on outside clues; seeing reading as both orderly and disorderly, but writing as fully determinate; seeking uniform traits while denying that literature has any; distinguishing between interpretation and criticism yet saying they are always intermingled; defending the author's intended meaning but disregarding the author's intentions about determinacy; and so on. When Hirsch puts "true" or "correct" in the place of "most probable," he commits the "logical error" of "erecting a stable normative concept" "out of an unstable descriptive one" (VAL 13). Even a devoted apostle of "validation" would be torn by contrary pressures.

Hirsch's theoretical arguments are also beset by relativism, the failing of which he convicts the "atheists." He claims that science and humanities have the same "cognitive element" (AIM 149), but instead of stating laws, regularities, or testable predictions, he prefers to look for "maxims" and "rules of thumb," which he says "cannot be relied upon in any particular instance" (VAL 203; AIM 59)—so that his claims are insulated against refutation by counter-examples.

However, the impossibility of proof is used as a shield against arguments contrary to his own. "That one man's verbal meaning is always necessarily different from another's" is a "hypothesis" which cannot be "falsified by empirical tests"; "the inaccessibility of verbal meaning is a doctrine" whose "falsity" "neither experience nor argument can prove"; "that an author's verbal meaning is inaccessible" is "an empirical generalization which neither theory nor experience can decisively confirm or deny"; and so on (VAL 39, 33, 18f). Such hedges are apparently thought sufficient to dispose of these arguments while discouraging empirical research that might endanger Hirsch's own position.[21] But the superiority of literary scholarship or philosophical logic over empirical tests has itself yet to be proven.

---

[21] Hirsch told me in 1978 that he really isn't happy unless he's being attacked, which may have to do with his championing of unpopular stances and his neglect of substantive evidence.

In fact, current research in cognitive psychology reveals some noteworthy parallels with Hirsch's deliberations. His concept of the "intrinsic genre" is quite close to what is now usually called the "schema".[22] The term "schema" appeared marginally in his earlier book and prominently in the later, where Piaget is cited (VAL 109; AIM 31ff). And Piaget's "schema" is explicitly compared to Gombrich's "genre" (AIM 32; cf. VAL 104). Perhaps a more empirical orientation might eventually be reached, though several important points of divergence should be kept in mind. So far, psychological probes of the "schema" have hardly dealt with literary or poetic communication. Authorship and writing have been probed in far less detail than reading. And schema theory (including Gombrich) is less concerned with validation than with broader issues of expectation and coherence.

We need to consider here the interests of both the reading and the criticism of literature, whose fate is at stake in all literary theory (Ch. 3). If established, Hirsch's methods could severely worsen the already alienating gaps between the subject and object, and between the trained critic and the ordinary reader. Hirsch never spells out what we are to do with a "verbal meaning" once it has been "validated," though he readily assumes that a "student's reading" is "probably wrong" in comparison to "his instructors'" (VAL 237f). Presumably, what is validated gets duly published and enforced in critical discussions, including those of classrooms and textbooks. I can think of no more efficient way to close and devitalize the literary experience, and to project an image of literature as reserved for authorized insiders. The danger is not merely that Hirsch wants to "throw out the experienced work of art and retain only the scholarly apparatus," as Louise Rosenblatt (1978: 110) has remarked; but that the apparatus would marginally useful and eventually suffocating. It would mandate what Wellek and Warren call "a fixity and rigidity alien to the nature of poetic statement" (TL 190).

At the same time, the ontological status of literature would be leveled by the doctrine that "genuine knowledge in any field, that is, sharable and usable knowledge, depends on the communication of propositions about reality" (AIM 72). The study of literature would be hard to justify on that basis; we would seem to be dealing with a medium so inefficient, if not misleading, as to scarcely reward the interpreter's efforts. Already embattled on many fronts, criticism can scarcely afford a stupendous investment in a mode of research whose specific relevance for literature has yet to be demonstrated.

In the meantime, we have at least the performance of a theoretician attempting to found the purpose and prestige of literary studies on objectivity and ethical commitment to a certain form of truth. So far, he has not followed up with the

---

[22] In recent years, Hirsch has been following with interest the discourse studies of the renowned cognitive psychologist Walter Kintsch, to whom I introduced him in 1978. For a review of models in text research, see Beaugrande (1980-81, 1982a, 1982b).

far more strenuous performance of putting the program into action on a complex and large-scale work of literature. This lack provides a counterpoint to those theoretical critics, such as Fiedler, Jauss, Holland, Paris, Bloom, de Man, and Millett, who work their theories out in close correlation with the issues of confronting specific texts. Hence, validation remains only a goal, or rather an attitude about a goal we cannot finally judge. The trends of the times are adverse to the attitude for motives I have tried to outline. In a different scholarly climate, however, we might profit from observing the experiment of stringently attempting to put such procedures into practice.

8

Wolfgang Iser[1]

Among the critics who are strongly concerned with reading, Wolfgang Iser's approach is rather distinctive. His major sources include phenomenology and gestalt psychology, as well as aesthetic theories derived from these. His approach is correspondingly mentalistic, attributing lesser importance either to the observed behavior of literary participants or to the surface text of the literary work. He envisions an elaborate mental construct elicited by the work and subjected to continual transformations as reading proceeds. The utopian aspect of this process, though not expressly acknowledged by Iser,[2] lies in its power to restructure the reader's awareness and in its fundamental openness.

In his earlier book (IR), surveying "patterns of communication from Bunyan to Beckett," Iser's "theoretical ideas" are mainly "developed through examples" which he uses again in the later book (IR iii; AR xif). His principles may have been influenced by this selection of texts that evidently inspire him. Being mainly transitional works designed to break away from prevailing conventions and expectations, they do not provide a complete cross-section. Literature as a whole is made out to be more creative and demanding than conventional works would suggest. Such a tendency is common in theoretical criticism, but should alert us to the utopian drift in describing as normal or appropriate the proceedings of intensely active and progressive authors or readers, and in making a critic such as Iser himself the test case.

Like Culler (p. 240), Iser feels that "the traditional expository style of interpretation has clearly had its day" (AR 10). (He claims his own are "not meant as interpretations," but as "illustrations," AR xi). "Through interpretation, literature is turned into an item for consumption" —a "fatal" outcome "for the text"

---

[1] The key to Iser citations is: AR: *The Act of Reading* (1978, original 1976); and IR: *The Implied Reader* (1974, original 1972); plus LL: *Lesen auf dem Lande* (Hömberg and Rossbacher 1977). Iser repeats extensive passages verbatim not only from book to book, but within the same book (IR), hence the multiple citations. I have tried to use cutting techniques to lend the quotes a smoother form. Note the dilemma of translating "Wirkung" as "effect" or "response" when the German includes both (AR ix).

[2] Though he is evidently conversant with the Frankfurt school, Iser uses the term "utopian" only pejoratively for what is too good or remote to be possible (IR 135, 150, 189; AR 229).

and "for literary criticism" (AR 4). "To impose one meaning" as "the right, or at least the best, interpretation" is a "trap" that discounts "subjective contributions and context" (AR 18f). "Literary texts" get "reduced to the level of documents" (AR 13). "At least since the advent of 'modern art,' the referential reduction of fictional texts to a single 'hidden' meaning" "belongs to the past" (AR 10). Iser admits, however, that the "historic and invalid" "norm of interpretation" whose "demise" he announces enjoys "continuing application" "right up to the present" (AR 6, 3, 12, 14).

The historical evolution of this state of affairs has been complex. "Classical norms" like "the totality, harmony, and symmetry of parts" "guarantee a high degree of assurance," support the "building" of "consistency," and "make the unfamiliar accessible if not controllable" (AR 15, 17f). As "modern art" "reacts against" those "norms," "interpretation" tries to save the situation by "taking over" "the old claims of art" to be "universal" and "closing its eyes to the historical break manifested by modern art," or "describing" the latter as "decadent" (AR 11ff). Such "'interpretation' is a form of refuge-seeking—an effort to reclaim the ground which has been cut from under" the "readers" (IR 233).[3] "The absolutist claims of art have tended to dwindle, while the expository claims of interpretation have become more and more universal." Hirsch's method (Ch. 7) is a culmination of the latter trend.[4]

Iser considers it "far more instructive" to attempt "an analysis of what actually happens when one is reading a text," as "the text comes to life" and "begins to unfold its true potential" (AR 19). "The traditional form of interpretation" "set out to instruct the reader" and "tended to ignore both the character of the text as a happening and the experience of the reader" (AR 22). Iser contends, again like Culler (p. 241): "the interpreter" should undertake "not to explain a work, but to reveal the conditions that bring about its various possible effects" (AR 18). One should "elucidate the potential meanings of a text, and not" "restrict himself to just one" (AR 22, 18). "It is time now to change the vantage point and turn away from results produced" toward the text's "potential" to "trigger the re-creative dialectics in the reader" (AR 30). In this manner, "a theory of aesthetic response" ought to "facilitate intersubjective discussion of individual interpretations" (AR x). "Any one actualization can be judged against the background of others potentially present in the textual structure of the reader's role" (AR 37).

---

[3] This verdict, like a number of others I will cite, is passed upon a specific work, in this case Joyce's *Ulysses*, so that I cannot tell how generally it applies. But many such assertions are delivered as generalizations about art, literature, life, reality and so on; and Iser expressly wants his "interpretations" understood as "illustrations" of "theoretical ideas" (AR xi).

[4] However, Iser believes, like Hirsch, that "meaning and significance are not the same thing," the former being "intersubjective" and the latter having "many forms" (AR 150f). But Iser's concept of "meaning" as "the referential totality which is implied by the aspects contained in the text" is far broader than Hirsch's "verbal meaning" (p. 114).

The usual "pronouncements" of "literary critics" "invoke" either "the contemporary reader," "reconstructed" from "documents"; or else "the ideal reader," who "cannot be said to exist objectively" (AR 27f). The "ideal" one "tends to emerge from the brain" of "the critic" (AR 28). "An ideal reader is a structural impossibility" as someone "able to realize in full the meaning potential of the fictional text" "independently of his own historical situation" (AR 28f). Even if it could be achieved, such an "exhaustive" "result would be total consumption of the text" and "ruinous for literature" (AR 29). Or, the "ideal reader" might be defined as having "an identical code to that of the author" and "sharing" the latter's "intentions"; but "communication would then be quite superfluous" (AR 28f). A similar problem applies if "the author himself" is asserted to "be his own ideal reader," since the author "does not in fact *need* to duplicate himself" (AR 29). Besides, this assertion is "frequently undermined by the statements writers have made about their own works."

"The 'real' reader" is also set aside, that is, relegated to the "history of responses" (AR 27, 29), as studied by Jauss (Ch. 17). Iser prefers to deal with "the implied reader": "a construct" "in no way to be identified with any real reader" (AR 34). Nor does it "refer" to "a typology of possible readers" (IR xii). Instead, "the implied reader" is based on "the structure of the text" and "embodies all those predispositions necessary for a literary work to exercise its effect" (AR 34). "Thus the concept" "designates a network of response-inviting structures which may impel the reader to grasp the text." This "textual structure anticipates the presence of a recipient without necessarily defining him." "The real reader is always offered a particular role to play," "even when texts deliberately appear to ignore" or "exclude him." "The reader is stylized" by "being given attributes he may either accept or reject" (IR 114). His "role" is "potential, not actual," allowed to "make his choice" within "a framework of possible decisions" (IR 55).

Iser is anxious to demonstrate that "the structure of the text allows for different ways of fulfillment" (AR 37, e.d.; cf. AR 29, 118, 231; IR xiii, 56, 281, 293). His central argument comes from phenomenology (though we see it also in deconstruction),[5] namely the unattainable nature of stability and completeness in either life or literature. Human awareness is everywhere beset by "multiplicity" and "multifariousness" (IR 89, 186, 203, 278; AR 125, 49, 76). "Empirical situations" are "generally too complex" for "applying one set formula" (IR 45). The "multifarious possibilities" of "human nature cannot be reduced to a single hard-and-fast principle" (AR 76). "Humanity never coincides completely with any of its historical manifestations" (IR 183). "If reality is nothing but one chance track, then it pales to insignificance beside the vast number of unseen and

---

[5] Lentricchia (1980: 159) remarks that critics "fascinated in the 1960s by strains of phenomenology" readily "shifted to post-structuralist direction and polemic" —de Man, Miller, and Hartman, plus Edward Said and Joseph Riddel.

unfulfilled possibilities" (IR 206). "The mode of conduct demanded by convention" is "just one special case out of many possibilities," or "one restricted, pragmatically conditioned form of human reality" (IR 156, 163).

Such theses lead to a corollary for "all literary texts": "the potential text is infinitely richer than any of its individual realizations" (IR 280). "Each actualization" "represents a selective realization" (AR 37). The "concept of the implied reader" is therefore offered as the "frame of reference within which individual responses to a text can be communicated," and hence as a "transcendental model" for "describing" "the structured effects of literary texts" (AR 38).

To stress the urgency of his approach, Iser almost outdoes the deconstructionists in insisting that "indeterminacy is irreducible" and "reality" "unexplainable" (IR 221). He obsessively evokes "the indeterminability" of "all phenomena"; "the "intangibility" of "observable reality"; "the impermeable potential of human reality"; "the unplumbable depths of the self"; "the impenetrability of human motivation"; "the unfathomableness of human actions and reactions"; "the imponderability of history"; "the imponderability out of which speech arises"; and so on (IR 221, 212, 192, 256, 152, 92, 243; AR 193). We might detect the influence of Maurice Merleau-Ponty, for whom the " 'world' " is " 'experienced' " as " 'an open totality the synthesis of which is inexhaustible' " (1962: 219) (IR 226, 281). When Iser proclaims "the impenetrability of the reader's subjectivity" (AR 124), he even seems to disavow his own project of describing the mentations of reading.

Literature both designates the infinitude of humanity and reality and counterbalances it with organizational techniques. The very act of reading offers the "experience of a reality which is real precisely because it happens" (IR 227). "Since his reactions are real, the reader" gains "the impression" that the "fictional" "world" is a "reality" (IR 113). "The unfolding of the text as a living event" creates "the impression of life-likeness" (IR 290). These theses suggest why Iser emphasizes processes more than results: in his model, the reader's activities offer the most direct contact with reality.

So paradoxically, "fiction" can make "facts" "probable" and engender "the illusion" of "reality" (IR 92). The content of "fiction" offsets "the incomprehensibility of reality" and of "the ego," and "the apparent senselessness of everyday life" (IR 268, 197). "Indeterminability is only to be removed by means of fiction" (IR 221). "The continual invention of images" is a "means of coping with" "a basic dilemma of life": "we do not know what it means to be alive" (IR 266f). Whereas "historical reality is continuous and indeterminable," "fiction permits "integration," "self-containment," "completeness," " 'concord,' "[6] and "consistency," as shown for example by "the nineteenth-century realistic novel" (IR 100, 236, 264, 93; AR 225). "No literary text relates to contingent reality," "but to models or concepts of reality, in which contingencies and complexities are

---

[6] On the notion of "concord" in "fiction," see Kermode (1967).

reduced to a meaningful structure" (AR 70; cf. Blumenberg 1969; Schmidt 1973).

However, literature can just as well adopt the converse approach and try to seem "realistic" by presenting "chance associations" (IR 68). "By constantly varying the angle of approach," "the potential range of the 'real-life' world" can be "conveyed" (IR 194).[7] Through an "array of possible conceptions," "the reality of everyday life will come alive in a corresponding number of ways" (IR 68, 232f).

As these remarks indicate, whether literature seeks reality through integration or dispersal, the dynamics of the reader's experience constitute the rewards of literary communication—a factor that may render more palatable Iser's portrayal of "the meaning of the text" as "not a definable entity, but" "a dynamic happening" (AR 22). If "the production and subsequent negation of fictions" is "the condition for establishing an open situation as regards life in general," "the usefulness of fiction cannot be dispensed with" (IR 268). "Human potentials" "can only be brought to light by literature, not by systematic discourse" (AR 76). A reader can "exercise" his "emotional" and "cognitive" "faculties," gain "an enhanced awareness" or "an expansion" of "experience," and "sharpen his sense of discernment" (IR xiii, 39, 59). "He can" "discover a new reality" or see "familiar reality with new eyes," and "bring to light a layer of his personality that he had previously been unable to formulate in his conscious mind" (IR xiii; AR 181, 50). He can "escape from the restrictions of his own social life" and "discover deficiencies inherent in prevalent norms and in his own restricted behavior" (IR xiii). "In seeking a determinate meaning, the reader loses possibilities of meaning," yet thereby "becomes aware of the freedom" of "his faculty of understanding" (AR 177).

The necessarily provisional character of literature thus endows it with life and lifelikeness. "Dynamism" is attainable via "virtuality," "indeterminate position," "inevitable omissions," or "inherent nonachievement of balance" (AR 21, 70; IR 280, 287). The "absence of finality" "drives us continually to go on being active" (IR 269). "The number of blanks that break up the good continuation" determines "the liveliness of the images" and "the vividness of the meaning" (AR 189, e.d.; cf. AR 192). "The shifting of perspectives" "makes us feel that a novel is much more 'true-to-life'" (IR 288). "The split-level technique conveys a far stronger impression of reality than does the illusion" of "the novel corresponding to the whole world" (AR 112). "The very fact" that "mythical patterns[8] cannot

---

[7] Iser vows that "constant varying" is the "only" way to "convey" this (IR 194). But surely the common sense notion of the "real-life world" denotes precisely what is relied upon *not* to vary from one observation to another (cf. Gombrich 1960). I would raise the same reservation against Merleau-Ponty's vision (shared by Iser) of "the world" as an "open totality" (IR 281).

[8] In such passages, "myth," like "archetype," figures as an abstract framework to be filled in many ways; Frye has a "very different conception" (IR 230), presumably because the society devises his "archetype" more than the reader does. In Fiedler's conception, the "unconscious" is the productive agent (NT 321).

incorporate everything endows the nonintegrated material" with a "live tension" which "makes us immediately aware" of "the modern world" (IR 200). "A conversation" "so different from the normal familiar forms" "provokes" "attentive involvement" (IR 154). "The "surprising" "oddness" and "unexpectedness" of the "picture" "stimulate those reactions that bring the character to life" (IR 41). "The characters seem real" when the reader is "constantly under obligation to work out all that is wrong with their behavior" (IR 112; cf. IR 9). And so forth.

These strategies become particularly crucial in modern literature. Whereas the "wealth of details" in "the realistic novel" had formerly "reflected" the "world of experience," "details no longer" "stabilize the illusion of reality" (IR 198). But the newer techniques can still elicit insightful outcomes. The "disoriented reader" "begins to be aware of the elusiveness of reality" and can draw the "conclusion" that "any claim to knowledge is an automatic reduction of the infinite and discounts the changeability of phenomena" (IR 255, 208). "The construction of the novel"[9] can reveal "the fundamental fluidity of human conduct" and the "unpredictability of the self" (IR 163). A mixing of "different styles" can fit "each style" to "one possible facet of everyday reality" and "convey the potential range of the 'real-life' world" (IR 225, 194). Deliberate "irrelevance" can "accentuate the conditional nature of all intentions" (IR 163). "The senselessness of life" can be "transplanted into an *experience* for the reader" (AR 222).

This line of argument suggests a history of literature in terms of how the openness of reality is treated in various periods (cf. Gombrich, 1960 on painting). However, we would be dealing with idealized responses wherein the readers appreciate variations in technique, even disturbing ones, and react in appropriate and gainful ways. We would thus have a history of imperatives that may or may not have been met in concrete instances. Recent empirical tests (e.g. Mauser et al., 1972) reveal what the persistence of traditional interpretation also signals, namely that many readers refuse the role offered by modernist literature. They expect a clear-cut message or meaning and an integration of reality already perfected for them by the author. Consequently, a history of response is likely to uncover a diffusion of competing tendencies among projected and actual ways of reading.

We can tell by now why Iser would feel that a "textual model cannot be equated with the literary text, but simply opens up a means of access to it" (AR 53). Such "models designate only one aspect of the communicatory process" that has "two poles": "textual structures and structured acts of comprehension" (AR 107; cf. AR 35, 163). "The text represents a potential effect that is realized in the

---

[9] The novel is the exemplary literary form for Iser, as it is for Fiedler, Paris, Millett, and Jameson. He extols "the novel" as "the genre in which reader involvement coincides with meaning production," ostensibly because it "was concerned directly with social and historical norms" and thereby "established an immediate link with the empirical reality familiar to its readers" (IR xi). This technique "helped" them "understand" their "own world more clearly."

reading process" (AR ix; cf. AR 21). If "literary texts take on their reality by being read," they "must already contain certain conditions of actualization" (AR 34). "Rather than actually formulating meanings themselves," "literary texts initiate 'performances' of meaning" (AR 27). "The formulated text" "represents a pattern, a structured indicator to guide the imagination of the reader" (AR 9). Moreover, "the structure of the text" "must" "bring about" a "standpoint" "able to accommodate all kinds of different readers" (AR 35, e.d.).

To depict what happens to the text, Iser presents the metaphor of an "unwritten text" "constituted by a dialectic mutation of the written" (AR 229; cf. IR 42, 44, 282f; AR 147, 182, 226). The author's "formulated" version of the text "shades off" "into a text that is unformulated though nonetheless intended" (IR 31; cf. IR 42, 45f, 287, 294; AR 17, 46, 82, 99, 182, 225ff, 229). "The uniform meaning of the text" and its "aesthetic value" are "not formulated" (AR 17, 82). The "process whereby the reader formulates the unwritten text requires active participation," and "the formulated meaning becomes a direct product" and "experience of the reader" (IR 45). Indeed, "the production" of the "unformulated" "meaning of literary texts" "entails" "the possibility that we may formulate ourselves, and so discover what had previously seemed to elude our consciousness" (IR 294) —another benefit of openness.

The notion of an "unwritten text" is plainly problematic. Iser is acutely aware of this, the more so as every "reader-oriented theory" will be accused of "uncontrolled subjectivism" (AR 23). A "theory of aesthetic response" faces the "objection that it sacrifices the text to the subjective arbitrariness of comprehension." He proposes several lines of defense to disclaim the "arbitrary" (cf. AR 24, 85, 140, 195, 201f).[10] One is that even traditional "single-meaning" "interpretation" arises from a "sophisticated subjectivity," and "would-be objective judgments" from a "'private' foundation"; "the compilation of meaning" was "simply" "taken for granted" (AR 23f). A second is that "the very existence of alternatives makes it necessary for a meaning to be defensible and thus intersubjectively accessible" (AR 230). A third is that "the subjectivist element of reading comes at a later stage," "where the aesthetic effect results in a restructuring of experience" (AR 24). The "affective fallacy" does not apply to "a theory of aesthetic response" "concerned with the structure of the performance which precedes the effect" (AR 27). The second and third defenses are not too satisfactory, though, because they entail practical difficulties. Readers often enough create meanings they couldn't defend, and exhibit no demarcation at the point when they begin to be subjective.

The best defense therefore, and the one to which Iser devotes by far the

---

[10] Among the things Iser claims are not "arbitrary" are: "the lines along which text is to be actualized"; the "equivalences" or "reciprocal transformations" among "segments"; "the sequence of positions in the time-flow of reading"; and "the combination of signs made present in the image" (AR 85, 185, 201f, 140).

greatest care, is to demonstrate that "acts of comprehension are guided by the structure of the text," although "the latter can never exercise complete control" (AR 24; cf. AR 108). The "indeterminacy arising out of the communicatory function of literature" "cannot be without a structure" (AR 182). The "spectrum of actualizations" that can result from "the interaction of text and reader" is "conditioned" by a "mixture of determinacy and indeterminacy," and "such a two-way process cannot be called arbitrary" (AR 24). "If communication between text and reader is to be successful, clearly, the reader's activity must be controlled in some way by the text" (AR 167). With such statements, Iser warily drifts back toward a conception of the text as a guiding entity. "The written text must employ certain modes in order to bring about and simultaneously guide the conceivability of the unwritten" (AR 147).

A key point is that a "sameness of processes" underlies "differences in realization" (AR 143). All readers are influenced by the fundamentals of human awareness. Iser invokes the "mechanisms" and "basic rules of human perception," "the imaginative and perceptive faculties of the reader," "the structure inherent in all systems," and the like (AR 98, 38, x, 71). "We cannot conceive without preconception"; "pure perception is quite impossible" (AR 166). "Consistency-building is the indispensable basis for all acts of comprehension" (AR 125; cf. IR xiv). "Recognition" and "grouping" are "elementary activities in reading" and "part of" "the reader's" "natural disposition" (IR 228). Such assertions imply that Iser's model is derived from general mental principles and is in that sense realistic.[11] Yet this strategy competes somewhat with his contention that the literary experience is exceptional, as when it makes "the subject-object division essential for all cognition and perception" "disappear" (AR 154, 135).[12]

Iser also appropriates the conceptions of gestalt psychology. "Apprehension of the text is dependent on gestalt groupings," during which "the reader" "identifies the connections between signs" and thereby "endows" them with their "significance" (AR 120f; cf. IR 40). It "is essential to our own understanding" that "the 'gestalt' of a text normally takes on" a "fixed or definable outline" (IR 284). "The 'gestalt' is not the true meaning of the text," but "a configurative meaning." The

---

[11] And Ingarden is criticized because his "concretization" is "used as if it denoted an act of communication," yet it involves "a one-way incline from text to reader" (IR 173). He thus "implies that each schematized aspect represents a facet of the object" (AR 98). Compare Jauss's view of "concretization" adapted from Vodička (p. 360).

[12] Starobinski (1973: 78) is cited for this view (AR 135). But Jameson points out that "the adequation of subject to object" is "virtually Hegel's intellectual invention" and recurs variously in the theories of Adorno and Bloch (MF 44, 38, 141, 146). Bloch portrays this "adequation" as a "Utopian fulfillment" (MF 146), which seems more plausible than taking it for granted, as Iser seems to do here. For Jameson, "a concrete reconciliation between" "the subject and the world would be possible only in a society in which the individual was already reconciled in fact with the organization of people and things around him," which is why "Hegel's system fails" (MF 49). Iser has to admit that "the division between subject and object" is in fact upheld by the traditional "critic," whose "expectations" are also attributed to "most readers of literary works" (AR 9, 5).

"primary" or "initial open gestalt" can apparently encompass "all referential contexts" of "the sign," plus "all ramifications"; but it is soon succeeded by a "closed" one that increases "consistency" (AR 121ff). The "interdependence" of the two gestalts is "an intersubjectively valid structure," even though the later "gestalt must inevitably be colored by our own characteristic selection process" (AR 123; IR 284).

"Gestalt psychology" also supplies "the concepts of 'schema and correction'" "developed" by Gombrich (1960) (AR 90). "The schema functions as a filter which enables us to group data together," so that we can "'grasp the infinite variety of this world of change.'" "The schema reveals not only the economy principle, which gestalt psychology has shown to regulate all our everyday perceptions,[13] but also a drastic and necessary reduction in the contingency of the world," that is, in the "unpredictability" of event configurations (AR 90f, 163f). "The structure of the schema" "dialectically" "balances" "economy" "against its own increasing complexity" (AR 91). "When something new is perceived," it is "captured and conveyed" by means of a "correction to the schemata," that is, a "restructuring of points of significance" (AR 91f, e.d.). The "imagination of the observer" is "set to work" to "discover the motive behind the change in the schema" (AR 92). In such ways, "the schemata of the text" "stimulate the reader" to "establish the 'facts'" and "assemble a totality," but "he will occupy the position set out for him" (AR 141).

The "sequence of schemata" is "built up" by a constellation Iser calls the "repertoire" (AR 141). Its constituents are already "familiar" to the reader, mainly "social and historical norms" and "literary patterns and themes" (AR 69f, 191, 200, 211f; IR 34, 37, 182, 288). "The repertoire has" the "function of incorporating a specific external reality into the text" so as to "offer the reader a definite frame of reference" (AR 212). This "determinacy supplies a meeting point between text and reader," but the latter "must construct for himself the aesthetic object" (AR 69, 107). "The reader's ideation" is "linked" to the "thought systems" and "social systems" for whose "problems" the "text" "attempts" an "answer" (AR 199, ix, 212, 79). These "systems" are "recoded into a set of signals that will counterbalance" their "deficiencies" (AR 74). The "conventions, norms, and traditions" that enter "the literary repertoire" are thereby "reduced," "modified," "depragmatized," and "transformed" (AR 69, 109, 184, 212). In this way, the "repertoire" "forms an organizational structure of meaning" waiting to be "optimized by the reader" "willing to open himself up to an unfamiliar experience" (AR 85).

Another aspect in mapping out the reading activity is its "'temporal quality'"—according to Husserl (1928), "'the only case where'" "'the imagination'" "'creates something truly new in ideation'" (AR 148). Since "the whole text can

---

[13] Yet Iser stipulates that "in literature, the principle of economy is broken more often than followed" (AR 186).

never be perceived at one time," "the reader must inevitably realize" "a potential time sequence in every text" (AR 108; IR 280). The order of words is of less interest here than are the "arrangement" of "perspectives" and the "sequence of schemata," "imaginary objects," or "images" (AR 100ff, 141, 227, 148, 203; cf. AR 97, 189; IR 280f). Unlike words, "perspectives do not follow on in any strict sequence—they are interwoven" within "an uninterrupted synthesis of all time phases" (AR 184, 149). The "basic types of perspective arrangement" can be ranked according to whether and how one perspective is allowed to dominate the others (AR 100-03).

Iser portrays the reader maintaining a "wandering viewpoint" "situated in a particular perspective during every moment of reading but" "not confined to that perspective" (AR 114). "The text" "passes through the reader's mind as an ever-expanding network of connections" (AR 116). As the "viewpoint" "constantly switches between the textual perspectives," their "combination" "establishes" "the reader's position" (AR 114). The "reciprocal spotlighting" of "perspectives" creates the pattern of a "foreground" continually "merging into the background," or of a "theme" becoming current and then fading into the "horizon" (AR 148, 116, 96-102, 198ff, 203).

This process lends "the imaginary objects" their "individualized" "identity" and "gives us the illusion of depth and breadth" and hence "the impression" of "a real world" by "producing the very conditions under which reality is perceived and comprehended" (AR 148, 118, 116, 103; cf. IR 281). The "synthesis" of the various "manifestations" of "the aesthetic object" throughout "the journey of the wandering viewpoint" leads to an event Iser likes to call the "transplanting" or "transfer of the text to the reader's conscious mind" (AR 109, 135; cf. AR 38, 211, 226). This metaphor is a bit mysterious, not merely because no actual change of location is involved, but because what arrives in the "mind" is plainly not the text as such.

The "time dimension" of "meaning" being contemplated by "the wandering viewpoint" is fraught with "transformations" (AR 148f). "The term 'structure'" is used by Iser "in the sense outlined by Jan Mukařovský" (1967 [1941-48]: 11): "'energetic and dynamic,'" in a "'ceaseless state of movement'" and "'continual transformations'" (AR 85). For instance, "textual perspectives" and "positions are set up and transformed by the structure of theme and horizon," a process which generates "the aesthetic object" (AR 98, 198, 203, 205). Or, "familiar knowledge" is "transformed into material for the exposition of that which had been hitherto concealed" (AR 227; cf. AR 169, 218, 227). Or, "events" are "transformed" "into the 'discovery of virtual causes,'" a "process that endows the meaning of the literary text with its unique quality" (AR 228). Or again, "expected functions" are "transformed" "into blanks," which are in turn "transformed" "into stimuli[14] for acts of ideation" (AR 208f, 194), as we will be seeing in a moment.

---

[14] "Stimuli" are "sent out" by "every reading moment" and "evoke" "perspectives" both "immediate" and "past" (AR 115f). This might sound vaguely behaviorist if Iser did not stipulate that "it 'is the

All these changes befit Iser's convictions that "the aesthetic object is constantly being structured and restructured"; that "experience" occurs only "if our preconceptions have been modified or transformed"; and that "the individuality of the text" "depends largely on" the "transformation" of the "elements" of "the repertoire" (AR 112; IR 262; AR 69). Indeed, "we" ourselves "are to undergo" a "transformation" "in the act of reading" so as to "become" "the author's" "image of his reader" (IR 30).

"The process of serial transformation" has "a catalytic function: it regulates the interaction between text and reader" "through a history" "actually produced in the act of reading," "the history of changing standpoints" that enables "the production of new codes" (AR 212). Via a "serial" "restructuring of established connections," "everyday life can be experienced as a history of ever-changing viewpoints" (AR 210). This history is divided into a "past," being the "background" or "horizon," a "present," being the current "theme" or "moment of reading," and a "future," being the "expectations" (AR 114, 116, 97, 99, 112, 115).[15] "Reading has the same structure as experience" insofar as "our entanglement" "pushes" our "criteria of orientation" "into the past" and "suspends their validity for the new present" (AR 132).

"Negation" intensifies this progression by making "the familiar" "appear" "obsolescent" (AR 212f; cf. AR 70). As "the reader's past experiences become marginal," "he is able to react spontaneously" (AR 158). The reader is "actively involved" in "synthesizing" "constantly shifting viewpoints" that "influence past and future syntheses" (AR 97).

"Images" are further entities that "take on" a "time dimension" and "are transformed through ideation" (AR 149). "Image" is here defined as "the manifestation of an imaginary object," and is "a hybrid" of "pictorial" and "semantic" (AR 140, 147). It "is basic to ideation" and "endows" the "absent" "with presence" (AR 137). "In reading literary texts, we always have to form mental images" via "ideation." "The instructions provided stimulate mental images, which animate" what is "implied, though not said" (AR 36). "The sequence of mental images" "leads to the text translating itself into the reader's consciousness" and permits "the text" to "come alive in the reader's imagination" (AR 36, 203).

In this fashion, "the liveliness of images" supports "the vividness of meaning" (AR 189). "The process of image-building begins" "with the schemata of the text," works through "theme and significance," "gives at least the illusion of perception," and "eventually results" in the "reader" "constituting the meaning of the text" (AR 141, 147, 176). Indeed, Iser avers that "the meaning can only be

---

prerogative of the receiver, not a characteristic of the stimuli, to decide which differences shall be significant'" (AR 119; Smith, 1971: 133).

[15] At one point, Iser says the "past" is "fading," and at another that is "not fading" (AR 112, 149). Elsewhere, Cavell's (1969: 322) "'presentness'" is described as a state when "the past is without influence, and the future is unimaginable"; Iser includes this in his account of how "the subject" "makes himself present to the text," despite an earlier insistence on "an uninterrupted synthesis of all the time phases" (AR 155f, 149).

grasped as an image" produced by "the imagination of the reader" (AR 9). This claim seems overstated, but as the previous quotes reveal, Iser's concept of "image" —etymologically close to "imagination" —designates much more than a mental picture.[16]

All these temporal dynamics outlined so far help Iser account for the potential of literary texts to be read over and over without loss of momentum. "The structure-determined unrepeatability of meaning" enables "the repeatability of the newness of the identical text" (AR 150). Since "a second reading of the text" is "influenced" by "the originally assembled meaning," and "our extra knowledge" "results in a different time sequence," "a text allows and, indeed, induces innovative reading" "on repeated viewings" (AR 149; IR 281). "Each concretization of meaning results in a highly individual experience," "which can never be totally repeated" (AR 149). The "change" of "the time dimension" also "changes the images" and "the way" they "qualify and condition each other in the time flow of our reading." "The literary critic" needs to consider this situation when "using hindsight to analyze the techniques which brought about the 'first' meaning."

To describe the "structures of indeterminacy" (AR 182), Iser presents an elaborate spatial metaphorics of emptiness, in which "gaps," "blanks, "gulfs," "vacancies," and "empty spaces"[17] cue the reader to become active by completing them. This model agrees with Merleau-Ponty's (1967: 73) remark that "'the lack of a sign can itself be a sign'" (AR 169), and implies a hierarchical reversal ranking absence over presence, as in deconstructionism (p. 235). The image of the reader "filling in a hollow form" is repeatedly evoked (AR 143, 213, 216).[18]

The "empty spaces" act as a "vital propellant for initiating communication" (AR 195). "Gaps" are "elements of indeterminacy" where we can "use our imagination"; and "points at which the reader can enter the text" to "create the configurative meaning of what he is reading" (IR 283, 40; cf. IR 280). "The blank" "functions as an elementary condition of communication" by "intensifying the acts of ideation on the reader's part" (AR 189). "Gaps" "heighten our awareness," "give the reader motivation," and "focus" his "attention on the interaction between perception and reality" (IR 33f, 210). They are also "textual positions" the "reader" can "fill with mental images" (AR 226, 9, 189, 220). In sum, "an indeterminate, constitutive blank" "underlies all processes of interaction" (AR 167). The text looks like a Swiss cheese whose holes yield the most nourishment.

---

[16] Iser's opposition between the "imagistic" and the "referential" (IR 9) appears to me too strong, as does his claim that "imaginary objects" elicit a "position" that "can never be subject to any frame of reference" (AR 150). That would make them unimaginable, at least for many readers (Gombrich 1960).

[17] "Gaps," "blanks," and "empty spaces" are apparently the same, since they are used interchangeably (AR 167ff, 195, 198, 220; IR 226). But see Note 19 on "vacancies."

[18] Sartre (1971: 207) too offers this rather objectifying image, implying a rigid entity with a fixed shape and capacity.

Gaps or "blanks" may "assume different forms" (AR 167). A "gap" or "gulf" can appear "between" "two passages" or "chapters"; "between illusion and reality"; between "images formed by acts of perception"; "between unconnected allusions"; "between monologue and overall situation"; "between what the character does" and "is"; "between the characters' actions and the narrator's comments"; and so on (IR 208, 226, 111, 210, 213, 162, 108). Other cues include: "asymmetry, contingency," "archetype," "nondescription," "cuts," "interruptions," "unexpected directions," "abbreviations," "abrupt juxtapositions" or "suspension of connectability" among "segments," "alternation of stylistic devices," "invalidation" of "norms," and "minus functions" (i.e., "nonfulfilled, though expected functions") (AR 167; IR 230, 38, 213, 280; AR 195, 202; IR 213; AR 217, 209). When Iser suggests a correlation between "the number of blanks" and "the number of different images," "segments," or "minus functions" (AR 186, 209), a quantitative measure of indeterminacy seems to be inferrable; but with so many diverse types, counting blanks is hardly practicable, even if they are indeed "present in the text" (AR 216); and Iser tells me no attempts have been made.

Iser enumerates three "functions of the blank," depending on whether it occurs as an intersegmental space, a large-scale framework, or a tension between the current viewpoint and previous ones (AR 196ff). In their first function, "blanks open up" a "network of possible connections" between "segments of the literary text" (AR 196). As the "reader's" "viewpoint" "wanders" and "switches" among "segments," it "forms" "the referential field," "the minimal organizational unit in all processes of comprehension": "two positions related to and influencing each other" (AR 197). "The segments of the referential field" are then "given a common framework" wherein "the reader" "relates affinities and differences" and "grasps" the "underlying" "pattern" (AR 197f).

"The second function" now becomes active, because this "unformulated framework" "is also a blank" "requiring an act of ideation to be filled" (AR 198). "The third and most decisive function" is the "blank" or "vacancy"[19] created when the "theme," that is, the "viewpoint" in "focus," becomes the "horizon" for the next one. Thus, "blanks" "regulate" "the structure" of "interconnections" that "produce" the "imaginary object"; "control" "all the operations that occur within the referential field of the wandering viewpoint"; and "guide" the "building" of "the aesthetic object" out of "transformed textual perspectives" (AR 197f). In all these capacities, "the blank in the fictional text induces and guides the reader's constitutive activity" (AR 202).

The division into form and content is mirrored in Iser's model by "two basic structures of indeterminacy in the text—blanks and negations" (AR 183). Whereas "blanks" "organize the syntagmatic axis" "relating to structure," "negation" does the same for "the paradigmatic axis" relating to "content" (AR 212,

---

[19] Iser differentiates: "blanks refer to suspended connectability in the text, vacancies refer to nonthematic segments within the referential field of the wandering viewpoint" (AR 198).

215).[20] Every "model of reality" implies "a division" of the "possibilities" of "the world" into "dominant" versus "neutralized and negated" (AR 71). "The literary text interferes" by making this second category "its dominant meaning" and "negating" the "repertoire" of "familiar knowledge" (AR 71f, 147, 217f, 227). "Literature applies itself" to "the deficiencies" arising "automatically" because "all thought systems are bound to exclude certain possibilities" (AR 73). "Carefully directed partial negations" "bring to the fore the problematical aspects" and encourage "a reassessment of the norm" that is "retained as a background" (AR 213). The "text" thus "starts" from "the borderlines of existing systems" and "activates" what the latter have "left inactivated" (AR 72). The "text" "draws attention to" "the system's limited abilities to cope with the multifariousness of reality." "Existing patterns of meaning" are accordingly "rearranged" and "reranked."

Since "negation" "is formulated by the text," Iser coins the (confusingly similar) term "negativity" for the text's "unformulated double" (AR 226), rather like the "unwritten text" already described. This "negativity" forms the "unwritten base," and "conditions" "the formulations of the text" by lending them "multiple referentiality" (AR 226). This "expansion" is "necessary to transplant them as a new experience into the mind of the reader." In this way, "blanks and negations" paradoxically "increase the density of fictional texts" (AR 225).

Such a wide range of powers is assigned to "negativity" that it threatens to walk off with the whole show "as a basic constituent of communication" and "an enabling structure" underlying both "the interaction of text and reader" and "the invalidation of the manifested reality" (AR 229f). It "makes possible the comprehension" resulting from "constitutive acts of the reading process"; "traces out the nongiven by organizing things into meaningful configurations"; is "the nonformulation of the not-yet-comprehended"; is both "the conditioning cause" and and "potential remedy" of "deformations"; "embraces both the question and the answer"; "gives rise to" "the fecundity of meaning" that leads to the "aesthetic"; and so forth (AR 226, 228ff).

As we see, the negative has many rewards. The "reader's constitutive activity" has "blanks and negations" to thank for its "specific structure" that "controls the process of interaction" (AR 170). "The efficacy of the literary text is brought about by its evocation and subsequent negation of the familiar" (IR 290). "Only when we have outstripped our preconceptions" can we "gather new experiences" (IR 290; cf. IR 58; AR 131f) —an idea Jauss and Jameson also advance (pp. 371, 387). The "reader" can "perceive consciously" "the norms of society" in which he was "unconsciously caught up"; and "his awareness will be all the greater" if their "validity" "is negated" (AR 212). "The negation" requires that something "out-

---

[20] Yet Iser clouds the distinction again when he pictures "negation" as being or "producing" "blanks" (AR 212f, 215).

lined but concealed by the text" should "be formulated"; this process "draws the reader into the text" and "away from his habitual disposition" (AR 218).

The reader now faces "a choice." "If he adopts the discovery standpoint, his own disposition" can "become the theme for observation; if he holds fast to his governing conventions, he must then give up his discoveries." "Balance is achieved when the disposition" undergoes a "correction" and is "temporarily suspended." Such "balancing operations" "form the aesthetic experience offered by the literary text" (AR 286). Others include "balancing" "consistency" or "convergence" against "'alien associations,'" "contradictions," or "ambiguities"; and "integrating" "illusion-building" with "illusion-breaking" (IR 286, 52; AR 129, 127).

"Balancing" to "establish consistency between contrasting positions" is also said to support yet another mentalistic entity Iser terms "the virtual dimension of the text" (IR 42; cf. IR 49). As we'd expect, "virtual themes" are "denoted" by "blanks and negations" (AR 225). "The selections we make in reading produce an overflow of possibilities that remain virtual" (AR 126).[21] Indeed, Iser asserts that the "work" as such "must inevitably be virtual," "as it cannot be reduced to the reality of the text or the subjectivity of the reader" (AR 21). "This virtuality" or "indeterminate position" is deemed the source of the work's "reality," "dynamism," and "aesthetic value" (IR 279; AR 21, 70; IR 275). These functions overlap with those claimed for "fiction," "unwritten text," "structure," "wandering viewpoint," and "negativity," as we have seen. So far, Iser's books present no grand design in which all these concepts are precisely differentiated.

As we might have surmised by now, the typical gesture whereby the theoretical critic offers his model as an account for the essential value of literature has a special tension in Iser's case. He raises to the top of his value scale the potential of literature to be indeterminate and destabilizing. His aesthetics is correspondingly dynamic, defined "only through its effects" (AR 70; cf. Kalivoda, 1970: 29). He consistently develops the view that "the aesthetic quality" of "literary texts" "lies in" the "structure" of "performances of meaning" (AR 27). The "aesthetic object of the text" stems from "transforming" "textual perspectives through a whole range of alternating themes and horizons" (AR 198; cf. AR 98, 203, 205). The "aesthetic experience" is an "operation," "oscillating between consistency and 'alien associations'" (IR 286). "Aesthetic provocation" is aroused by "undefined and undefinable" "action" (IR 238). "Aesthetic appeal" can be attained by "working out alternatives," "allowing" "latitude," "compelling specific reactions" "without expressly formulating them," and not "loading" "judgments" "in advance" (IR 118).

A particularly "essential quality of aesthetic experience" is "the ability to

---

[21] If this "overflow" is "eclipsed," "the text takes on a didactic tone" (AR 126f). The treatment of didactic literature as a marginal type is covered below (p. 144).

perceive oneself during the process of participation" when stimulated by "discrepancies" "produced during the gestalt-forming process" (AR 133f). "'Aesthetic'" "designates a gap in the defining qualities of language"; its "experience" is fostered by "the gulf between illusion and reality" (AR 22; IR 111).

In exchange, Iser misprizes whatever falls short of such standards. "If a literary text organizes its elements in too overt a manner," "we as readers will either reject the book out of boredom, or will resent the attempt to render us completely passive" (AR 87). "The 'continuously' patterned text" gives an "impression of comparative poverty," "as opposed to the vivid complexity of the 'impeded' text" (AR 189). The "fulfillment of expectations" can render "literature" "totally functionless" (AR 208). "Any confirmative effect" "is a defect in a literary text" (IR 278). When "the reader's assumptions are confirmed," "tension is relaxed" and "he will invariably lose interest" (IR 141). An undersupply of "blanks" and "gaps" leaves only "minimal scope" for the "participation" of the reader, who "feels the 'let-down' of banality" (AR 190; IR 214). Hence, "filling in the 'places of indeterminacy'" can even "transform high art into kitsch" (AR 174).

Marginal forms of literature are also characterized along these lines. "The didactic text," as in "thesis novels," "propaganda, and publicity," "achieves its control mainly by restricting its blank references to a simple yes or no decision"; "the wandering viewpoint switches far less frequently" (AR 190f). "Light literature" "formulates" its own "solution," "confirms one's disposition," and is made to be "totally consumed" (AR 46, 219, 29). "Trivial" "works" "support prevailing systems,"[22] administer "an overdose of illusions," and seek "commercial success" by "controlling" the "proliferation of blanks" and not "making too many inroads into the repertoire of norms and values" (AR 77; IR 294; AR 191). They "offer nothing but a harmonious world, purified of all contradiction" and "disturbances" of "the illusion" (IR 284).

In his "concern" for "the interaction" "between text and reader," Iser has scant reason to uphold a division between "'right' and 'wrong' reading," and he faults Ingarden for doing so (AR 210, 171). The "aesthetic" "fecundity of meaning" is due precisely to the lack of a "frame of reference to offer criteria of right or wrong" (AR 230). The "true meaning" of "language" in a "literary work" is "what it uncovers" rather than "what" it "says" (AR 142). "The text provokes continually changing views in the reader," who "can never learn from the text how accurate or inaccurate are his views of it" (AR 166f; cf. IR 273).

Still, the very fact that Iser's model foresees particular activities for the reader implies these may be more or less appropriate. Particular qualifications must be met beyond just a "basic knowledge" and "familiarity" in regard to "literary texts" (IR 187; AR 207). The "optimization" of the "organizational structure of mean-

---

[22] "The courtly romance of the Middle Ages" did so, however, and was still "serious" "literature" (AR 77). Jauss makes the same exception (AL 18), but Millett finds only another evasion against genuinely improving the social status of women (SX 50f) (see pp. 344, 372).

ing" "depends on the reader's own degree of awareness and on his willingness to open himself up to an unfamiliar experience" or to "a creative examination" of the self (AR 85; IR 290). "The real reader "must" "adapt" and "'modify himself' if the meaning he assembles is to be conditioned by text and not by his own disposition"; "to exert a modifying influence" upon the latter is "ultimately the whole purpose of the text" (AR 153).

So Iser, who "doubts" whether "criteria of adequacy or inadequacy" can be applied to "each reader's individual concretization" (AR 171), introduces some anyway. The reader must do certain things "if his viewpoint is to be properly guided," or if he "is to be maneuvered into a position commensurate with the intentions of the text" (AR 152, 213). He must welcome being "manipulated" and "reoriented" (AR 95, 152, 125f). Although "successful communication" "depends on the reader's creative activity," it also requires that "the text" "control" that "activity," activate the "reader's faculties of perceiving and processing," "establish itself as a correlative in the reader's consciousness," and elicit "changes in the reader's projections" (AR 167, 107, 112).

Conversely, a "failure" of "interaction" comes from "filling" a "blank exclusively with one's own projections" (AR 167). Also disbarred is an undue "commitment to ideology," which would make "the reader" "less inclined" "to accept the basic theme-and-horizon structure of comprehension" (AR 202). Moreover, "the reader cannot" "reestablish the nonfulfilled function" so as to "produce a unified evaluation of events" or "a consistent attitude toward positions in the text" (AR 211). Otherwise, "the text will always become senseless or abstruse."

Even more is demanded of the reader by modern literature. Its requirements may exceed one's "powers" of "perception," "absorption," "vision," and "memory" (IR 231f, 225, 211). "The reader" is likely to become "disoriented" when his "expectations" are "productively destroyed" by "monstrous things" or by "overprecision" (IR 255; AR 207). Though such effects are no doubt part of the intention to foster an awareness of one's own "faculty of understanding" (AR 177), readers might react quite differently. They might take "shelter behind their preconceptions of meaning"; or "resist the pressure" and see the work as "chaotic and destructive"; and so forth (IR 262; AR 210).[23]

As long as Iser occupies the reader's role, such problems are not unduly acute. He reads, for instance, Beckett's novel *Murphy* as "an attempt to expose the truth behind the commonplace," and "to reveal the basis of fiction through fiction itself" (IR 262). The opening sentence, "'The sun shone, having no alternative, on the nothing new,'" is taken as "a form of words devoid of content and of function" (IR 262f). If in such cases "the reader" tries "to supply the meaning which the author has removed," "the whole thing becomes abstruse, but only so

---

[23] Iser defends the "esotericism" of "modern texts" as preferable to the "fulfillment of expectations" that would render "literature" "functionless" (AR 208).

long as one insists on regarding the novel as a representative portrayal of reality" (IR 263). Murphy's plan "to go into a lunatic asylum" and "go mad" is read as a "representative" "withdrawal from his social environment," perhaps into "the depths of his spirit," where "'there was nothing but commotion.'" Iser likens this to Merleau-Ponty's idea that "'absolute self-evidence and the absurd are equivalent.'" Beckett's novel is thought to address "the synchronization of the ego with itself" and to show that "no statement, not even a hypothetical one, can be made about a reality that is detached from human perception" (IR 264). "Our compensation for what cannot be perceived is the knowledge pretended by fiction, which is 'consciously false'"—a thesis expressed in different terms by de Man (p. 261).

This reading fits Iser's theoretical orientation very well, but may not be representative for readers in general. We might be uneasy about the lack of "empirical tests" for his "theory," which he says could "help to devise a framework" for "guiding empirical studies" (AR x). One research group at the University of Salzburg took him at his word (Hömberg & Rossbacher 1977, hereafter LL).[24] They had ordinary citizens from a rural Austrian area read a story by Christoph Meckel in installments and answer questions like "what happened?" and "what will happen?" The story is set in an environment similar to that of the readers and depicts the failure of an outsider to hold a job delivering baked goods to remote mountain villages. The story "combines familiar narrative techniques with innovative ones" (LL 70). But it had to be "shortened" and "simplified in places," and "the narrator's reflection on the poetic was cut" —just the material Iser would want to foreground.

The conventionally narrated first part of the story was "received according to Iser's description of response potential" (LL 77). "Text structure and reading-act structure did not diverge significantly" (LL 78). This ratio changed when the outsider suddenly disappears and readers had to predict what would happen. The actual course of the story, in which the outsider falls into a state of mental disorientation narrated in a more modernist style, was not guessed by any of the 181 readers, who mundanely imagined he'd run off or been hurt in an accident. These predictions were construed to show an "'imaginary resolution of deficient realities'" and "a need for order and normal behavior" (LL 82).

The same tendencies appeared in the final retrospections about the author's intention: to "show how a nonconformist can't fit in" (28% of the readers); to "show the fate of a dreamer" (21%); to "show the lack of understanding toward outsiders" (17%); to "show how a person rebels against his monotonous job" (14%); and so on (LL 89). The main "'message' of the story" was thus to make "the problem of the outsider" show "the formation of norm and violation" "in our social life" (LL 90)—a reasonable confirmation of Iser's model. But the data

---

[24] All quotes are my translations. The book is available, if at all, from Fotodruck Frank, Gabelsbergerstrasse 15, 8 Munich 2, West Germany.

indicated that "some 49% of the readers had difficulties with the 'modernness' of the text" (LL 86). And making the protagonist a "dreamer" seems to ignore the social message.

We thus return to a point raised before (p. 134): that Iser's theses may lead to a history of reading as a series of implied imperatives problematically related to documented responses. This factor might provide a useful expansion of perspective, especially if we assume, along with most of our critics, that particular readers can actualize only some aspects of a literary work's potential. In return, though, Iser cannot expect his own necessarily partial reading to cover that potential. He needs a much broader framework.

He can obtain some guidance from the history of ideas. For example, he traces the impact of the "seventeenth century" "doctrine of predestination," or of "eighteenth century" "associationist psychology" and "Scottish empiricism," though he does not favor "an aesthetics" "prominently" "derived and conditioned by philosophy rather than by literature" (IR xiii, 78, 70, xif).[25] Such ideas belong to the "historical background" or "repertoire" which literature "counterbalanced" (AR 130). "Such processes certainly occur more in modern literature," as compared to "the classical norm" stressing "harmonization" and "removal of ambiguities" (AR 130, 15). This focus enables Iser's approach to deal with modernism expansion from work to context.

A "history of narrative prose" should above all uncover the "literary devices" "built into the structure of the text to stimulate the production of discrepancies" (AR 130). "Such processes certainly occur more in modern literature," as compared to "the classical norm" stressing "harmonization" and "removal of ambiguities" (AR 130, 15). This focus enables Iser's approach to deal with modernism better than those of other critics like Fiedler or Hirsch. Since every work is at the time of its appearance at least modern, if not expressly modernistic, this capacity is a meritorious gain.

Iser's literary history could also retrace the progression in techniques that steer reader response. With "traditional texts," the "process" of "forcing" "decisions" in the face of the "inexhaustible" "was more or less unconscious, but modern texts exploit it quite deliberately" (IR 280). "The transition to modern times" was marked by "a fundamental questioning of identity," and an "attack on the prevailing myth of the self-sufficiency of the individual" (IR xiii). Reacting against the "religious despair of the Calvinists" who upheld "predestination," "the pattern of the eighteenth-century novel" dealt with "human self-assertion" (AR 100f; IR xiii, 2, 4, 17f, 24). Yet "novelists" remained "morally oriented" and "cast" the "reader in a specific role" to "guide" him "toward a conception of human nature and reality," often issuing him "direct addresses" (IR 81, xiii, 29). "The segments

---

[25] "Literature" differs from "philosophy" in "not making its selections and its decisions explicit" (AR 74) (cf. p. 13).

of the reader's viewpoint consisted mainly of the different character perspectives" "in a hierarchical pattern" (AR 203f). "The narrator" stayed "firmly on the top," so that his "perspective" "guaranteed" "the right appraisal" (AR 204).

"The end" of this approach was "marked" by a "complex technique" to "induce the reader" "to take a fuller part in the coordination of events" (IR 78). "The nineteenth-century reader," not given a "part," "had to discover" that "society had imposed a part" and to assume "a critical attitude" (IR xiii). "The implied author" was separated from "the unreliable narrator," and "no authoritative orientation" was "supplied" (AR 204f, e.d.; cf. Booth 1961).[26] "The reader" was to be made "more ready and able to react" and to "rise to the level of his own discoveries" in "a world" "grown more complex" (AR 206). "Literature" undertook to "balance deficiencies" in "conflicting religious, social, scientific systems of the day" (AR 6).[27]

A further change ensued when literature entered "the modern world," wherein "we are denied direct insight into the meaning of events" (IR 180). Works showed a corresponding rise in "the number of blanks," "negations," and "unfulfilled qualities," (AR 206, 219, 172).[28] "The modern novel thematizes" "blanks" "in order to confront the reader with his own projections" (AR 194). "The components" of "narrative techniques" are "deliberately revealed" so as to encourage "the discovery" of "the functioning of our own faculties of perception" (IR xiv). "The presentation of the object is refined" so as to "multiply schematic aspects" (AR 171f). "Old connotations of form, order, balance, harmony, integration" are "invalidated" (AR 12). When the reader "links" a "primary negation" to "his own disposition," "secondary negations" become "preponderant" and allow "a defamiliarized world" to be "incorporated into the reader's store of experience" (AR 219, 221ff).

Psychoanalysis offers another framework for Iser's project. He remarks that "a large area in the subject" "is closed to the conscious mind" and "manifests itself in a variety of symbols" (AR 158). "Reading plays a not unimportant part in the process of 'becoming conscious'" (AR 159).[29] Freud's notion that "there are no negations in the unconscious" indicates that "their intellectual function can only

---

[26] Like Paris (PAF 16-20), Iser refuses to join the "literary critics" such as Wayne Booth who "bewail" the "loss of the narrator" (AR 207). What was lost was rather "an expectation" for "some form of orientation" provided by "the traditional novel."

[27] This project made "the critic" "a man of importance" in "the nineteenth century" (AR 6)— surely a main motive for retaining the old style of interpretation (cf. p. 130).

[28] "Modern literature" is said to achieve "greater determinacy" and yet to "increase" "the degree of indeterminacy" (AR 171, 206).

[29] Freud's motto "Where id was, ego shall be" (or rather, an odd translation of it) is therefore approved as a description of "'becoming conscious'" (cf. Ricoeur 1973: 142; and compare Fiedler's use, p. 86). Poulet's "materialization of consciousness," on the other hand, is essentially rejected (AR 154f); Holland is more favorable to the idea, though he imposes a bodily metaphor: "some form of mother and fetus perhaps" (5RR 51).

come about through a conscious act" (AR 224). Iser envisions a number of operations whereby things emerge from the "unconscious": "our own decipher-ing capacity"; the "expectations that underlie all perception"; the "process of consistency-building"; the "system" of "norms" in "society"; and so on (IR 294, xiv; AR 212).[30]

Iser also concurs with the psychoanalytic implication whereby "reading" shows that "the certainty of the subject can no longer be based exclusively on its own consciousness" (AR 159). His phenomenological orientation fits "the psy-choanalytic theory of art" about the "contrapuntally structured personality" "re-sulting from the split between the subject and himself"; and about the "hidden" "layer of the personality brought to light" via "the text" (AR 156). In this view, "the self is essentially incapable of completion"; "cannot comprehend itself as the synthesis of its manifestations"; "cannot ensure its own identity through memo-ry"; and "needs a specific reality to take on a concrete form of its own" (IR 145f, 122).

Yet this very "inadequacy" promotes "richness" (IR 145; cf. IR 149). "Inven-tion enables the self to confront itself with its own image" (IR 169). "The self grasps historical reality through the perspective it brings to bear," "relates" to "itself" by "mobilizing its standpoints," and "reflects on its own subjective judg-ments" (IR 134). In "heightened consciousness," "the self can only experience its own reality through an unending sequence of unintegrated and unintegratable images"; it can thereby "acknowledge its own unfathomableness" (IR 175; 171). Once more, multiplicity and instability are seen as potential advantages leading toward new experiences—an un-Freudian conception closer to third-force psy-chology (cf. Ch. 11).

Iser is evidently more wary about psychoanalysis than critics like Frye, Fiedler, Holland, and Bleich. He grants that "a psychoanalytically based theory seems eminently plausible, because the reader it refers to appears to have a real existence of his own" (AR 28).[31] But he complains that in the work of Lesser (1957) or Holland (1968), Freud's "original hermeneutic perspective" is "buried,"

---

[30] The processes Iser calls "automatic" may belong to the "unconscious" as well: "observation" "involving" "preconceptions"; "one meaning" "bearing" "the seeds of several others"; "a speech act" "carrying implications"; "thought systems" being "recoded into a set of signals"; "a blank" "increasing" "disorderliness"; thematized "norms" being "open" to a "critical view"; and so on (IR 209; AR 210, 60, 74, 209, 202). But these processes hardly resemble the drives and fantasies Freudians assign to the unconscious (cf. Ch. 9).

[31] In his vehement attack on Holland, Iser repudiates psychoanalytic ideas I find similar to his own. He denies that "reading is" "a therapy to restore to communication the symbols that have separated themselves from the conscious mind" (AR 158f). Or, he derides as "far-fetched" the "idea of literary texts changing the psyche of readers" as the "true meaning is uncovered" (AR 42), yet asserts that "the whole purpose of the text is to exert a modifying influence on" the reader's "disposition" (AR 42, 153). Holland actually says just the opposite, namely that the psyche of the reader does *not* change, but duplicates itself and its style in whatever is read (cf. pp. 162ff).

and "the heuristics" "congeal into a system," creating "an 'imperialistic philosophy'" with "a jumbled, bloated terminology" (AR 39). "Insights" are "obscured" and "distorted" by "categorizing in orthodox psychoanalytic terms" and by making "reified use" of the latter (AR 39, 41).

Besides, Iser feels reminded of "eighteenth-century classical aesthetics" (recurring in the "emotive theory of I.A. Richards," AR 44), when Lesser (1957) suggests that "the solution" to "conflict" is "manifested in the act of presentation"; or when Holland (1968) claims that "literature should provide pleasure" by means of "a rhythmic alternation of disturbance and solution" (AR 43f, 46; cf. AR 223). Adorno's (1970: 25) reproach is quoted: the "'psychologism of aesthetic interpretation'" entails an "'aesthetic hedonism which banishes all negativity from art'" (AR 47). Or, if literature "merely" "demonstrates the functioning of our psychological dispositions," as Holland avers, it "must lose its aesthetic quality," and its "study" becomes "superfluous" (AR 40).

Iser is also skeptical about "the instruments of linguistics," including "generative-transformational grammar" (AR 31f, 34). Linguistic models insist on "the surface structure of the literary text," and the furthest they get from it is a "deep structure" couched in much the same categories and badly suited to "clarifying the processing of literary texts" (AR 32).[32] Such models resist the idea that "the extent and nature of the context" "established by the retentive mind of the reader" "are beyond the control of the linguistic sign" (AR 116). The "system of equivalence" postulated in those models (by Jakobson for instance) is not "indeterminate" or "unformulated" (AR 85), but situated in the material of language. Even the "Russian Formalists'" notion of "protracted perception" of "art," though stated as a "process," implies a stable text to perceive, and hence "the determinate comprehension of an object" (AR 187). This process could occur "only" "once," whereas the "impeded ideation" and "image-building" foreseen by Iser "make continual use of our disposition" and "lead to the repeatable diversification of innovative gestalts of meaning" (AR 187f).

Iser is more favorably inclined toward "General Systems Theory," wherein "each system has a definite structure of regulators which marshal contingent reality into a definitive order" (AR 71). "Each system must effect a meaningful reduction of complexity by accentuating some possibilities and neutralizing," "negating," or "deactivating" "others." "The reader's communication with the text" can be described as "cybernetic," "involving a feedback of effects and information throughout a sequence of changing situational frames" (AR 67). "The relation between text and reader" might be a "self-regulating system," "the text" being "an array of sign impulses" whose reception is subject to "constant 'feedback' of information already received." A similar account is propounded for

---

[32] Speech-act theory might be more helpful in exploring the "pragmatic function" of "fictional language" to "depragmatize the conventions it has selected" (AR 61). But the work of Austin and Searle would have to be revised, since they "excluded literary language from their analysis."

"the transformations brought about by the theme-and-horizon interaction" (AR 200f). "Blanks" are also said to "function as a self-regulating structure" "operating according to the principle of homeostasis" (AR 194).

However, this framework, which Holland too now favors (pp. 179f), is yet to be worked out in detail. My own view outlined in Chs. 1 and 2 is also compatible, though I suggest that complexity is ideally integrated rather than reduced, especially in regard to art works. Iser seems to concur when he warns that "reduction" "should not be equated with simplification" and "should not" "eliminate possibilities" (AR 71).

To make an overall estimate of Iser's work, we must appreciate his drive to venture into difficult or uncharted areas. When I once edited and published a summary of Iser's *Act* in a special issue of *Discourse Processes* (3/4, 1978), he was impressed by the number of offprint requests he got from psychologists and psychiatrists. Further empirical research is obviously needed before his work can be more than a possible map of new territory. But when the neglected terrains of language and cognition are finally fully opened to free exploration, the far-sightedness of Iser's theorizing will no doubt be manifest.

9

Norman Holland[1]

Norman Holland displays no hesitation about the proper source for literary theory: "psychoanalytic psychology" is "our most fruitful way" of "relating literature to human beings," and "the only psychology useful for studying literary response" (DY v, xiii). "Modern psychoanalysis" "offers the only psychology I know that can explain the choices of particular words which are, after all, the *Stoff* which I as a literary critic seek out, as well as a particularly important type of human behavior" (PIP 135). "At the same time, psychoanalysis provides at least some insights into the larger aspects of human experience: learning, politics, the arts, religion, sex, science, love, youth, age, and all the things that make our lives lively. Until some other psychology offers such an extraordinary range from the particular to the general, I do not see how the literary critic has any other choice."

The typical salute to literature is performed in very broad terms. The "new psychoanalytic look" sees "literature as a human experience" with "a series of rich analogies and connections" to "life" (PIP 169, 134). "Once we insist" that "literature" is "an organic experience in the minds of men[2] and a part of the great continuum of human experience," we are led into "very large questions indeed" (PIP 161). By acknowledging that "people are the natural habitat of literature" and of "literary theories," we may find "ways to understand the most central processes of human life." A reader who is "learning more about literature" also "learns more of his own inner dynamics" (PIP 134). "We feel the ordering and structuring powers of literature" "as though they were our own"; and become "a larger, wiser self, both deeper and higher—at least for the long moment of a

---

[1] The key for Holland citations is: BRF: "The Brain of Robert Frost" (1983-84); CRAP: "Carlos Reads a Poem" (Holland & Kintgen, 1984); DGF: "Driving in Gainesville, Florida" (1984); DY: *The Dynamics of Literary Response* (1975 [1968]); 5RR: *5 Readers Reading* (1975a); I: *The I* (1985); PIP: *Poems in Persons* (1973); and UITS: Unity, Identity, Text, Self" (1975b).

[2] For Freudian critics, the reference to "men" is no mere generic indefinite. Freud's thinking was heavily determined by the male viewpoint. Holland, in turn, tends to introject the male child's fantasies, as in: "even in early infancy, the child has longed for exclusive possession of his mother" (DY 47). I return to this problem later (p. 166).

work of art" (DY 101, 103). We encountered the same thesis in the theorizing of Iser (Ch. 10), who is closer to Holland than he acknowledges.[3]

Again typically, Holland portrays his preferred theory not merely as attractive, but indispensable. "All literature has this basic way of meaning": to "transform the unconscious fantasy discoverable through psychoanalysis into the conscious meanings discovered by conventional interpretation" (DY 28). Hence, "the fantasy psychoanalysis discovers at the core of a literary work has a special status," "occupying a special prior and primitive place in our mental life," and "involving the deepest roots of our cumulating lives" (DY 27, 31, 29).

So "the psychoanalytic meaning underlies all the others" (DY 27). "It is impossible to understand the 'higher' levels," such as "verbal form," "unless we first recognize the deeper fantasies they are designed to deal with" (DY 238). "We can only talk intelligently" about "form, language, character, plot, genre, sound" "if we recognize that they shape and balance a core of fantasy material" (DY 316). Other critical theories (who must be talking unintelligently) are accorded a derivative place: "a psychoanalytic reading of a literary work" is "not simply a reading parallel to other readings from ideologies, Marxist, Swedenborigan, Christian humanist, or whatever; it is the material from which other such readings are made" (DY 31).

Holland's career has been shaped by a long struggle with a "bête-noire: the problem of subjective and objective" (DY 108). Originally, he was one of those "people" who "become distinctly uneasy at the idea of finding self-expression or personal style or subjectivity in the literary experience"; and who "would like that experience to be objective" (PIP 1). But if "it is impossible" "to look only at the words on the page without modifying them by one's own perceptual matrices," "reading can never be impersonal and objective" (DY 108; PIP 117). Freud is hailed for his "great achievement" of "setting in motion" the "systematic study of subjectivity" (I, xiv).[4]

For a time, Holland's solution was to divide reading into the "objective text" and the "subjective experience" (DY 108). The task was "not to sort out subjective from objective but to see how the two combine when we have experiences" (PIP 2). "We, as humans, live in a world which is both objective and subjective, a world where, in some way we have not yet understood, we are able to share subjectivities which remain nevertheless completely private and individual" (PIP 99). "Thus, paradoxically, only by beginning with different subjectivities can we

---

[3] Both critics reassure us that not just any reading will work. Both distinguish a more uniform and a more diverse stage of reading. Both have a nonpredictive conception of the reader. Both have a metaphoric idea of the text entering the reader's mind; Holland agrees more readily with Georges Poulet about this than Iser does (cf. 5RR 18 vs. AR 153ff).

[4] Bleich salutes Freud for exactly the same reason (SC 30f). Yet Bleich is ambivalent about resemblances between Holland's theory and his own (Ch. 10). On one side, he told me Holland's main "ideas" were "gotten" from him (an accusation I cannot confirm from studying their works); on the other, he swears that Holland's ideas are badly mistaken, whereas his own are correct.

arrive at that consensus about experiences that constitutes all the objectivity subjective beings can have" (5RR 231). "It is only by having objectivity limited that we can have any objectivity whatever."

These remarks from steadily later books signal a progression we find among numerous theorists on the contemporary scene—Fish, Bleich, Culler, and even (without admitting it) Hirsch. The subject-object division is attenuated by combining the cognitive conception of having knowledge with a performative conception of claiming to have it (Ch. 1). If "'objective reality' and 'pure experience' are themselves only useful fictions, vanishing points we approach but never reach" (PIP 2), asserting we know them must be an action in progress, a utopian projection. A critic who "claims his reading is 'objective' or 'authoritative'" is "really" making the hopeful "assertion that others can *share* his private synthesis, using a communal acceptance to achieve personal mastery for themselves—and for the critic" (PIP 130). Still, Holland did not so much abandon his ambitions of objective mastery as shift them from one domain to another, as I shall try to make clear.

Early in his career, Holland was "enormously influenced and pleased by the so-called 'New Criticism'" and became devoted to "the close examination of particular texts for plot parallels, repeated images, figures of speech, structure, myths, points of view" (DY xiii). He misprized traditional criticism as "literate, urbane chatter," "emotional effusions," "maundering about in literary history or anecdote," "morocco-bound and old-madeiraed musings," and "a private sanctum" for "mandarins," "scholiasts," and "panjandrums" (DY 309, 196; PIP 134, 101).[5]

In contrast, the New Critics performed "the one great achievement" in "literary studies of the past forty or fifty years" by introducing "the careful 'objective' study of the literary work as a thing in itself" —"an analysis that often became as objective" as "behaviorist psychology or analytic philosophy" (PIP 101; DY 196).[6] All this was "compelling and attractive" to Holland's own personality, and still is: "I *like* examining the verbal surface of a text," he confesses, "looking particularly for an 'organic unity'" (PIP 112).

During his early period, he felt we should "talk, at least initially, about literary works as purely formal entities," "without reference to author's intention, value, historical background, or anything except the text itself and some dictionary

---

[5] This low estimation clashes with the move whereby Holland finds "confirmation" in the way his "model" "returns us finally to the very things literary critics have always talked about" (DY 316).

[6] Holland was for a time impressed by behaviorist psychology, perhaps because it suited his own bodily orientation. But he soon became disenchanted with its mechanistic mentality (cf. PIP 158f; 5RR 228, 275). The classic "physiological variables" such as "galvanic skin reaction" "are too crude, too limited in dimension and number, to correspond to something as subtle as affect" (DY 281). He pictures as "comedy" an experiment measuring the frequency of "fidgeting" in an audience (PIP 154), but elsewhere includes "fidgeting" among the "words people make with their bodies" and among the evidence available to "objective criticism" (5RR 215, 232).

knowledge" (DY xvii). He focused on "observable elements in the literary text," and "proposed to describe works of literature objectively, as so many words on a piece of paper or spoken aloud" (DY xiii, xvi). Only "then" would he "describe psychologically my own response to that objective stimulus" —presuming that "the stimuli are, after all, the same" "for me" and "for you."[7]

Later on, this project seemed unpromising: "the more I worked with real readers, the more I was reminded that a literary work is not a fixed stimulus" (5RR 43). "It is merely" the "language of formal explication which follows the less-than-candid convention that what I attribute to the poem is 'in' the poem" (PIP 124). He recognized that his formalist training had given him "the habit of hiding behind a polite fiction, namely, that books do things to people, and critics merely witness their actions like innocent bystanders" (PIP 131, 3). He sees this tendency as a "modest, self-effacing convention," whereas I see it more as a self-aggrandizing tactic to expropriate the authority of the work for one's own reading (Ch. 3).

Breaking this "habit" cost him considerable effort. "It has been hard for me to look at what goes on 'inside' readers instead of simply confining my attention to the surface of the text and presupposing a response" (PIP 113). In the period when he used only his own responses, he did not uphold his promise to "use 'I' and 'you' and 'we' with some care to keep these three levels of discourse clear: subjective, objective, and commonly experienced" (DY xvii). His analyses reveal a mixture instead: "the poem is evoking in *me*" "primitive feelings"; "*we* experience sound as a distancing from a parent"; "*one* can find fantasies from all the levels of child development in this poem"; and so forth (DY 120f, 109, e.a.). Or he'd assign his version to the author: "in fiction" and "in narrative poetry, too, *the writer* presents a fantasy" (DY 159, e.a.). Or he'd hide behind text: "*the poem* defends against the wish to see," or "tries to re-create in the relationship with a lover a simplified, more childish, but more satisfying version of an adult sexual love"; "*the Tale* starts with phallic, aggressive sexuality, regresses to a more primitive relation between taboo mother and passive son, and finally progresses to genital mutuality"; "*the final line*" "carries out a typical fantasy"; and so on (DY 111, 129, 16, 36, e.a.).

Though he readily conceded that "meaning is not simply 'there' in the text," but "is something we construct for the text within the limits of the text," he was fond of saying that meanings, fantasies, or processes were "embodied" in or by the work (DY 25, 58, 67, 72, 75, 95, 139, 144, 202, 221, 222, 223, 274, 282, 294, 307, 310, 335)—a fine Freudian locution circumventing the question of interpretation. In *Poems in Persons*, his diction was more cautious: "novels do not embody defensive strategies; people find them in novels"; "poems do not"

---

[7] The phrasing "objective stimulus" again signals a behaviorist outlook which is undermined elsewhere (see Note 6). Holland felt "the very notion of 'response' presupposes a fixed stimulus" (5RR 43); but behaviorism never related the stimulus to a fantasy.

"fantasize; people do" (PIP 98). In 5 *Readers Reading*, his former notion that "these fantasies" "were embodied in the literary work" is cast off as a "fiction" he no longer thinks "useful" (5RR 19).

As we see, he only gradually repudiated the "older psychoanalytic concept of literature" wherein critics write "as though each literary work had a fixed fantasy content" (5RR 117). To be sure, "one has only oneself for a sensing instrument. I can respond and by a kind of self-analysis get at the things in the literary work that shape the less conscious aspects of my response. I can then guess the same or similar things are shaping the response of others" (DY 134). Yet "I do not mean to imply" that "my own responses" are "'correct' or canonical for others"; "I simply hope that if I can show how my responses are evoked, then others may be able to see how theirs are" (DY xvi). His diction shifted accordingly. Early on, he'd say: "I assume you share" "the nuclear fantasy which I am experiencing" (DY 181). Later, he'd say: "naturally, I hope you share my reading, but I know that you may not" (PIP 124). Later still, he'd say: "the reader will use the materials in the story to build, not some fantasy ostensibly 'in' the story, but his own characteristic fantasy" (5RR 119).

And so Holland eventually discarded the idea that "the poem evokes the same experience in different readers —it doesn't" (PIP 116). He had to revise his "simple credo" in order to face "a salient fact": "different readers read differently, and there seems to be no way of laying the differences to rest" (PIP 113). Although "consensus" may occur because "different readers are using the same material," any "consensus" "must begin, not with the poem," "but with the reader" who "reaches into the poem and takes materials from it with which to achieve an experience within the characteristic pattern of ego choices he uses to minimize anxiety and cope with reality" (PIP 115f).

Once again typically, Holland, like Iser and Bleich, reassures us: "recognizing the reader's creative role" "does not imply that all readings of a poem have equal merit" (PIP 148). "Any given reader may neglect part of the text, assign idiosyncratic meanings, and be inconsistent or arbitrary." Also, "if we introject a literary work at all, we introject a ready-made psychological process to which only certain responses are possible" (DY 283). "Only some possibilities" "truly fit the matrix" that is "the literary text" (5RR 12).

As a corrective recourse, "one can judge a reading by a variety of objective criteria: completeness, unity, accuracy, directness," "logic, coherence," and "universality" (PIP 148). We might then recognize when a reader is perpetrating "bizarre reworkings" and a "contortion of the words and the plain sense," or "doing violence to the text or ignoring it" (PIP 116, 118). "The theme or content of a poem has to be something one can achieve with a minimum of shoving, heaving, and hauling of the actual words." A "failure" may occur if the reader "lacks the skills" to "build up his psychological process from the work," or "he may be confronting a work which has features he simply cannot accept" (PIP 85f).

Holland might have been content to let matters rest when he had "succeeded in mastering" literature to his "own satisfaction" (PIP 125). He might have found it sufficient to give readings that "combine" his "very personal feelings and intuitions toward the poem with more logical and objective analysis." His model would then be a primarily personal construct, an account of what Holland himself, or critics with similar backgrounds, personalities, and interests, do with literary works. Such is the solution Bloom at least purports to adopt (Ch. 14).

But Holland must contend with his "own characteristic demand for generality of explanation" —related perhaps to his inclination "to cope with the interactions of people" around him "by finding generalizations from a safe distance" (5RR 277, x). So he decided that even if his *response* could not be correct or objective, his *model* could be. He displaced his search for mastery to the level of theory and appropriated a "psychology" he considered "adequate to the problem" of "what goes on in the mind of the reader" (PIP 60).

His New Critical orientation persisted with a changed focus. He extolled his theoretical framework as "the only general psychology that can talk about an inner experience with as much detail and precision as a New Critic can talk about a text" (DY xvii). In this endeavor, "a reader uses the fine subtle listening" of the New Critics to "listen to himself and to others with the same attention to detail and nuance that formerly was reserved for literature" (PIP 134). By "looking at" "a person" "as if he were a text," Holland would see a "unity" he called "identity" (5RR 259) (see p. 173).

The reading of a poem thus resembles psychotherapy, since in both acts, a "unifying scheme of meanings" is "brought to bear" "by the one who interprets" (5RR 260; Fingarette 1963). Diesing's (1971) "holistic" "case-study method" for "social scientists" is also thought to "look more and more like literary analysis as described by Frye or Spitzer" (5RR 261f). Such pronouncements indicate how Holland's career illustrates the application of the same interpretive acumen to a series of changing issues.

Unlike most critics, Holland was actually trained in psychoanalytic method, rather than merely importing a few psychoanalytic notions that suit his purposes. He moved his center of gravity to the other side by adopting classic Freudian psychoanalysis as an essentially correct, though incomplete, critical approach. He was resolved to revise literary theory as far as necessary to obtain a match with the Freudian outlook. He thus combined a radical critique of conventional literary theory with an orthodox credence in Freudian ideas. He developed a literary theory as faithful as possible to psychoanalytic theorizing. Most of the cited authorities besides Freud followed the latter fairly closely, such as Karl Abraham and Otto Fenichel.[8]

---

[8] Abraham (1927) "constructed the 'oral character,'" so important for Holland, by analogy to Freud's "'anal character'" (Fisher & Greenberg 1977: 82). Rivals to the orthodox Freudian camp, including "existentialists" and "third force psychologists," and, specifically, "Reich, Marcuse, Laing,

The privileged postulates in Holland's model were therefore destined to be the classic Freudian ones. Great emphasis was placed on infantile experiences and imaginings. "Clinical psychoanalysis" "traces the influence of early issues even to the end of life" (DY 32). "We know that character is formed largely in the oedipal and pre-oedipal stages" (DY 334). Moreover, the explanation for "art and life" and "virtually all that we know as living" was to be sought in the "compromise between the mighty opposites of drive and defense" (DY 53). "Any human's act satisfies for him some combination of pleasure-giving and defensive needs, inner inertia and outer pressures to change, personal demands and society's stringencies" (PIP 57). "It is a basic pattern in human behavior to relate to the rest of the human and non-human world by constructing it from one's characteristic pattern of adaptations through which one then projects and introjects wishes and fantasies" (PIP 149f).

Holland re-evaluated literature by extending these theses. "Writing itself—even the very manner and matter" can be seen as the "ego's solution to the demands set by inner and outer reality" (PIP 57). "In the literary transaction, one's fantasies at 'higher' levels represent transformations of more primitive fantasies associated with the earliest levels of human development" (PIP 167). "Literature transforms our primitive wishes and fears into significance and coherence, and this transformation gives us pleasure" (DY 30).

This line of reasoning brings us back to Holland's main hypothesis: "the psychoanalytic theory of literature holds that the writer expresses and disguises childhood fantasies; the reader unconsciously elaborates the fantasy content of the literary work with his own versions of these fantasies" (DY 52). The most basic content of literature is not "conscious and adult and intellectual," but "infantile, primitive, bodily, charged with fear and desire" (DY 27, 29). "It is from such deep and fearful roots of our most personal experience that literature gets its power and drive" (DY 30).

Freudian criticism faces the problem that Freud did not develop a special theory of language, perhaps because he assigned a determinate function to the early stages of infancy, when language is hardly developed beyond a few demands and commands. Holland remarks that "infant" is derived from "infans," which "literally means 'unable to speak'" (DY 79). Mentally disturbed patients, Freud's main subjects, also tend to have a limited or disrupted control of language. The Freudian perspective therefore projects language in the subsidiary role of an expression, commentary, or disguise for mental images or fantasies related to drives or defenses, as when the "analyst" "transforms the patient's words

---

Lacan, Perls" are dismissed as "gurus" (PIP 164). Jung is snubbed, perhaps because Holland is anxious to dissociate his own method from "myth criticism" (DY 25ff, 260f), which it resembles more than he would like, as when it "claims a kind of validity or authority for" the myth it "prefers" (DY 245). Holland twists Jung's "collective unconscious" into a bodily concept assuming that "RNA and DNA" or "brain traces" "carry Grimm's fairy tales" (DY 244, 260).

into pictures and feelings" (5RR 257; Greenson 1960). Language appears less as a system with independent principles than as a superstructure imposed upon body-language and body-imagery—something to be "approached through the libidinal phases" (DY 34).

A striking demonstration is Holland's straight-faced endorsement of Edmund Bergler's (1950) "suggestion: that writers may acquire their predisposition to become writers because in early infancy they use words coming out of their mouths as an important defense against masochist impulses aroused by their mothers' putting food in" (DY 79). Conversely, "as readers, we do the opposite: we do not emit words to defend against passively being fed." Bergler also speculated that "writers emit words as a way of defending against the fearful desire to obliterate oneself in a total at-oneness with some primal mother" (DY 38). Another bodily explanation is that "the ear may come to stand for the anus—sounds are common anal images" (DY 40).[9] This association is argued on the grounds that "attitudes toward language are formed" in the "anal stage," when "a good deal" of "language" is "devoted to commands and decisions" about "toilet training" (DY 39). By a further extension, "a writer, often, will collect jargons—take them into himself and then excrete them in his works" (DY 40).

Such explications show the reductivenss of using infantile body functions to derive language, crudely pictured as the movement of sounds in and out of bodily orifices. Among the most important factors that get lost (or Berglerized) are the specifics of meaning and the difference between speech and writing, the latter not being done with the mouth (not even by Flaubert when he drank ink in order to describe Emma Bovary's agonies). Since infants don't read or write (not even about food or excrement), these acts get forced into dubious analogies with the things kids do do.

A less reductive approach would be to "extend" Freud's "linking of dreams and jokes into a model for literature in general" (DY 54).[10] These sources at least deal directly and subtly with symbolic imagery. Following "Freud's essay on jokes," Holland places "condensation," whereby "two or more lines of thought combine in a single representative," "at the root of all particular linguistic effects of literature," such as "rhyme, alliteration, stanza-form," "ambiguity," and "wit" (DY 58f). Similarly, "in dreams, any particular element in the manifest dream generally expresses several elements in the underlying dream thoughts," and

---

[9] Holland's interpretations tend to rate "sound" rather low ("disillusioning," "harsh," "agitated," etc.) as compared to "sight" ("hopeful," "sweet," "calm," etc.) (DY 116, 119ff, 212; PIP 123). For him, "sight becomes linked in our minds with being fed, with a nurturing mother," whereas "we experience sound as a distancing from a parent" (DY 119f). However, Freud testifies that the "repetition" of word sounds is "a source of pleasure in itself" (DY 145).

[10] A joke is the lead example in *Dynamics*, (DY 3f, 8-12), and many more are treated in *Laughing* (1982), which is not proffered as literary theory. Holland suggests that jokes qualify as "literature," since they are "language with a literary form" (letter; cf. the juxtaposition of "joke" and "lyric," DY 144). But for reasons argued in Ch. 2, I wouldn't accept such a definition.

vice-versa (DY 59). Such parallels offer a bridge between presumed psychic events and the New Critical project of detailed interpretation.

From the same Freudian sources came Holland's central proposal to construe the "intellectual meaning" of language (his name for what Hirsch might call verbal meaning) as a "transformation of the unacceptable fantasy content" (DY 180f; cf. DY 128).[11] Meaning is (or "is analogous to") the "sublimation of an infantile" or "primitive" "fantasy" "transformed" into "social, moral, and intellectual themes which are consciously satisfying to the ego" (DY vi, 12, 104). This "act of meaning" provides "pleasure" in several ways (DY 184). In addition to "economy," "condensation," and "mastery" over the "fantasy," the "feeling we are engaged in a socially, morally, or intellectually responsible enterprise assuages guilt and anxiety." Holland grandly declares "meaning" "a sop thrown to the superego," here too a peripheral phenomenon or a pretext. In this scheme, we cannot analyze meaning without a critic who "listens with the analyst's 'third ear'" (DY 317).

The Freudian concept of "defense" denotes "the unconscious process" "the ego puts into action automatically at a signal of danger from the external world, the id, or the superego" (DY 57f). Several types are distinguished (DY 53-56). "Repression" "keeps an idea or feeling from consciousness." "Denial" prevents "seeing something in reality we don't want to see." "Displacement" moves a "value" from "one thing" to "another." "Symbolization" connects via "physical or psychic similarity." "Reversal" and "reaction-formation" convert into "opposites" an "object" or a "response," respectively. "Projection" changes an "internal perception" into an "external" one. "Introjection" "brings inside" an "impulse initially perceived as outside the self." "Splitting" "breaks up one thing into several." And so on. Holland associates these "defenses" with traditional literary concepts. He links "symbolization" with "figures of speech," such as the "trope" of the "simile"; "reaction-formation" with "irony"; "splitting" with the "complex, multifaceted work of art";[12] and so forth (DY 54, 57, 56).

This line of argument leads to his major notion of "form as defense" previously proposed by Lesser (1962). For the writer, the "hard work of formally shaping the medium also satisfies multiple needs of drive and defense" (PIP 56). For the reader, "many meanings are possible; many forms are not," because "form operates defensively, against the press of the fantasy toward expression" (DY 189). So "form must be much more precise than meaning" (DY 314). In fact, "the slightest tinkering with the wording of a joke or a lyric radically changes its effect" (DY 144). This tenet pays homage not only to the formalist orientation of the New Critics, but also to the determinism of Freud, for whom "'our

---

[11] Holland also designates meaning as "the idea that informs" the text (DY 5, 21, 236, 306).

[12] "Splitting off different psychological positions into different characters" is detected in "myriad works," where the "common ancestry" is "symbolized by kinship or juxtaposition" (DY 56). Fiedler makes much of splitting (WL 133, 200; NT 90; LD 218, 384).

psychoanalytic training forbids our assuming that these words can have been without significance or chosen at haphazard'"; "'an explanation must be found for every detail'" (PIP 157; cf. 5RR 257).[13]

Thus, Holland can be a servant of two masters and still attain his own mastery when he feels his "analysis" of the poem has both "justified" "the presence of every image and word in the poem" and "rationalized" his "pleasure" (PIP 124f).[14] He has assuaged his anxiety that "'close reading'" "often seems overly intellectual, even sterile, certainly far removed from the roots of our pleasure in literature" (DY 7).

Holland divided his model into "four closely meshed principles" "governing the way a reader re-creates a literary work" (PIP 76-78; cf. 5RR 114-22; UITS 124-26). The model projects a "full circle" of confronting the text, moving away from it, and returning to it. First, "style creates itself: the reader tries, as he proceeds through the work, to compose from it a literary experience in his particular lifestyle" (PIP 77). Second, "defense must match defense": "the reader" "must re-create for himself from the text rather precisely all or part of the structures by which he wards off anxiety in real life." Third, "the reader can very freely shape for himself from the literary materials he has admitted a fantasy that gives him" "the pleasure he characteristically seeks." Fourth, "the reader 'makes sense' of the text: he transforms the fantasy he has created from it to arrive at an intellectual or moral 'point' in what he has read." Though Holland suggests that the "four principles" "all go on together" (UITS 124), they seem to interlock in a real-time sequence or series of loops, each operation apparently needing the results of the one before it.[15]

Making "aesthetic,[16] intellectual, and moral 'sense'" of the text (PIP 81)

---

[13] Waelder's (1930) "theory of multiple function" also is deemed to show "how every psychic act is over-determined," because "any ego choice represents a new compromise among eight groups of problems" (PIP 47). Explaining the production or reception of an entire literary text in those terms would be an immense task.

[14] This result wouldn't be terribly elevating if "rationalization" is "finding intellectual reasons for something patently illogical" (DY 57). I would rather define it as displacing one's real reasons with those more satisfying to the ego.

[15] Compare the uses of the temporal "once": "once" the reader "has achieved the defensive forms and admitted at least part of the story into his psyche, he easily goes on to transform . . . "; "once the reader has achieved both the delicate matching of all or part of his defensive structure and the much more open adaptation," "he will 'make sense' of the text" (5RR 121; also in PIP 79; UITS, 125, 126). In the "feedback" model of DGF, timing would be organized in flexible configurations of loops, which looks more plausible.

[16] The "aesthetic" is thus included in the unification of content. The concept of "beauty" has no role in this model; it could only be some variant of "pleasure," presumably elicited by a successful transformation of fantasies that would not consciously be considered "beautiful." Kant's conception of beauty as pleasure without interest is ruled out. On Freud's neglect of "beauty," see Note 22 to Ch. 17.

occurs fairly late in this model of the reading process, and in a subsidiary way—to "consolidate and affirm" a "response" mainly determined by "the fantasy level" (5RR 286). Form figures strongly in initial reading, whereas content in the usual literary sense figures strongly in final reading; in between, the major activity is a defensive associating and transforming of fantasies. Where other critics envision a direct surface route from reading to verbal meaning, Holland envisions a deep and circuitous "tunnel" for much of the route (cf. 5RR 222); and his strong claims resemble a stringent ordinance that all traffic must pass through the Holland tunnel. This commitment in turn favors a characteristic "tunnel vision" whereby Holland skillfully zeroes in on precisely the aspects of reading most amenable to his procedures.

The design of Holland's model situated meaning "in a space which reader and work create together" (PIP 98). "It does not matter whether the meaning is 'in' the text or whether the reader supplies it"; "either way, meaning opens up a kind of sublimatory path for fantasy gratification" (DY 185). Since the reader "has duplicated his own style of mind, neither he nor we can see any difference between his characteristic mental processes and those that seemingly belong to the work" (PIP 98). Hence, "the question 'Where is the fantasy and defense, in the work or in the reader?' ceases to have any meaning." But this "question" was not laid to rest so easily, and Holland keeps revising his thinking as he tries to answer it.

Like Iser and Bleich, Holland views reading as composed of a more uniform and limiting stage followed by a more personal and freewheeling stage. "The reader reconstructs" "part of his characteristic defense pattern of adaptive or defensive strategies from the work, and this re-creation must be rather delicate and exactly made" (PIP 98). Thereafter, the reader can use "material" from "the work" in order to "very freely create the kind of fantasy that is important to him. He then (again, with great freedom) transforms that fantasy by means of the defensive strategies he has created toward the coherence and significance he consciously demands."

We again obtain a hybrid design. Fidelity to the text and its verbal forms, the New Critical response, goes to the earlier stage of reading. Freedom to create associations, the Freudian response, rules the other stages. The stability of the text is thereby prevented from clashing with the variation of responses.

In this manner, Holland escaped his original dilemma of different readings for the same work. If "all, really, that meaning-as-defense need do" is "offer a mastery of fantasy content," then "a reader does not" "need to settle for himself the exact, stringent" meaning of the text (DY 185). Nor "need there be only one central meaning; almost any kind of coherent thought about the work will open up paths of gratification, so long as it 'makes sense' of the text" —that is, "makes it acceptable to the conscious ego and so permits the fantasy content a disguised and sublimated gratification." "We can accept a wide variety of possible meanings to achieve literary pleasure; almost any kind of interpretation we derive from a text will get it past the censor and permit our egos to enjoy the fantasy content" (DY 314).

Such tolerance toward meaning may seem reckless in a literary critic; but Holland could afford it because he had taken over the privilege of determining the (allegedly more important) fantasy. Later on, the marked variety of fantasies he detected in his readers forced him to relinquish this privilege in favor of the power to decide the reader's "identity theme," a concept we examine soon (p. 173). This theoretical development steadily shifted the critic's authority from one mode of ostensible stability to another: from textual meaning to central fantasy to identity theme.

In Holland's "transformational" model, the fantasy is primary on the author's side as well. Instead of having formulated an "intention" "latent in the work as a 'message'" for the reader to "recover," the author is claimed to have "begun with a fantasy," such as "feminizing a phallic symbol" (PIP 117; DY 28). The author's job is to deliver "building blocks" or "raw materials" for readers to use (PIP 143, 96, 117, 126; 5RR 201).[17] "The fantasy a reader creates may or may not coincide with the fantasy the writer had while writing" (5RR 117). "The poet does not speak to the reader directly so much as give the reader materials from which to achieve the poem in his own style" (PIP 99). "The maker cannot impose his meaning on any reader who does not wish to accept it"; "he can only exclude certain possibilities by the choices he makes which limit for once and for all the raw materials from which his audience will create its experience" (PIP 117). "Many writers, as they write, imagine a reader," a process that "assuages the writer's inner needs"; but this construction (as Iser also notes, AR 29) "does not predict the ways of real readers" (5RR 219).

The overall purpose of "literary creativity" and "writing" is to attain the "ego's solution to the demands set by inner and outer reality" (PIP 57). Holland follows Robert Waelder's (1930) conjecture that "every psychic act results from the ego's actively and passively seeking an optimum balance of the forces impinging on it" (PIP 46). Hence, an author's "creative writing" "satisfies" a "combination of pleasure-giving and defensive needs" as well as "personal" and "social" "pressures" (PIP 57). This thesis seems to deny the special ontological status of literature, a move made by Hirsch for quite different motives. Holland was assailed by Iser for dissolving the "aesthetic quality" of literature (AR 40) (p. 150).

"Creative style" "stabilizes the psychic economy" peculiar to the individual: it "is his and his alone" (PIP 57). "Writing" can become a permanent and preferred solution" if it "functions multiply for us." Though finding "the various attempts to define artistic creativity as a function of 'neurosis'" "clumsy and misinform-

---

[17] Holland recently favors the term "promptuary," "a type of book in the sixteenth century that stored quotations and other structured information from which one could copy to construct one's own book" (letter; cf. 5RR 286). See Note 20 to Ch. 17.

ing," Holland believes "mental illness" and "creative writing" share a common impulse, namely to "act out the same underlying myth"; "the key variable is *style*" (PIP 47, 58).

The author's biography enters when we "read back from literary style to life style" (DY 241). "We can go from the text" to the "mind" of the "writer" and "from thence to his life to confirm a pattern of fantasy and defense" (DY 242). Again, New Critical formalism gets a Freudian turn: "a writer's biographer ought to be able to read back from his subject's preferred formal devices to the defenses they represent to the circumstances in life that charged those defensive modes with pleasurable possibilities" (DY 240f).

However, Freudian research emphasizing infantile experiences is hard to integrate with the customary historical documentation dealing mostly with adult ones. "One does not come easily by materials from so early in life, and only a great deal of research could tell the full story of the poet's early development" (PIP 54). The critic may proceed by "inference," or at worst, by "totally unprovable statements about authors' lives" (DY 241; PIP 165). Early childhood records would probably be unenlightening anyway, because, as I have said, the activities of infants are poorly differentiated in comparison to those of adults or to the layout of a literary text or corpus.

In practice, Holland uses occasional biographical facts rather informally. The timing of H.D.'s "most distinguished creative work" during the world wars is made into a "graphic illustration of the theory that artistic creativity stems from the wish to reconstitute what has been lost in aggressive fantasy" (PIP 38). "Frost's attempted suicide" in trying "to drown himself in the Great Dismal Swamp" is read as a "submission to a big mysterious entity," in accord with Frost's "identity theme" (BRF 370). The "evidence that Conrad himself attempted suicide," on the other hand, is to indicate what a "swamp or sea might have stood for in Conrad's mind" —"irrational or self-destructive aggression" (DY 233f). As "confirmation" for the thesis that "the sea in 'Dover Beach' evokes feelings like those toward a nurturing mother," Holland adduces "Arnold's letter" "describing himself as 'one who looks upon water as the Mediator between the inanimate and man'" (DY 122f). These accounts show the the problem I raised against Hirsch: that authorial evidence does not bring independent confirmation of verbal meaning, but only confirms what the critic has already postulated (pp. 116, 125).

Holland is delighted to have a better groundwork when an author, H.D., left an "account of her analysis by Freud" himself, which with "a little reading between the lines" can be "unscrambled" "to give an absolutely unparalleled picture of the infantile forces that engendered a poet's life pattern" and "the very style of her writing" (PIP 9). Her "longing" to "create a work of art" resulted from an intention to "immortalize an inner wish" and to "re-create a lost masculinity or a 'hard' ungiving mother" (PIP 43). "Hard, firm works of art" might serve to "replace the missing part" and "the masculinity it represented" (PIP 52). "'Signs' evidently achieved, with the least effort, the most effect in closing the gap" "between herself and her mother, her father, her brothers, a gap in her body" — "and she became a writer" (PIP 56).

The most salient fact in this biographical sketch is that H.D. was a woman. Undeniably, by any contemporary standard, orthodox Freudian theorizing is vehemently sexist—virtually a phallic mythology of male superiority, as Millett demonstrates in detail (Ch. 16; cf. Irigaray 1974, 1977). Holland no longer holds the attitude wherein he once cheerfully wrote: women "have as it were, already been castrated"; "the little girl" "feels, as it were, that the damage has already been done"; "the mother is contemptible in that she too has lost the precious organ" (DY 48). But though "Freud was wrong about women in general," he may have been right about this "one woman" (letter from Holland).[18]

The problem of sexism is somewhat attenuated by relating literary response to "the developmental phases prior to latency, before fantasies and reading choice became markedly different for boys and girls" (DY 51). But the model definitely projects the male reader's response, notably in the oral and oedipal fantasies about the desired mother; the few references to the father portray him mainly as figure competing with a male child, or threatening to castrate him (e.g. DY 42, 46).

As an interpretive aid for his approach, Holland presents a "dictionary" of the "fantasies" "we find" "very generally in literature and in both men and women" (DY 62). This list is to illuminate how "the text" "presents us with a central core of fantasy that is evidently much more universal" than our "very personal and idiosyncratic" "associations to small details of the text." The "dictionary must be confined" to "the libidinal phases," and thus to "oral, anal, urethral, phallic, and oedipal fantasies" (DY 33). The justification is that "the reference of literature to the child suggests the universality of its appeal better than does referring to the more individualized adult." Young children readily fall into "personality types," whereas "by the time we reach latency or puberty, we have become quite individual"; "adolescence" is a time for "trying out a variety of identities" (DY 33, 334). Hence, the "fantasies of latency or puberty" and "in the adulthood beyond, are far too various to be generalized about."

This argument makes a virtue out of the standard Freudian liability of fixating all explanation on infancy. The undifferentiated nature of the categories is deployed to assert their universality. The same fixation obliges the critic to see reading as a regression sending the reader back to an age where Freudian concepts can take hold. For interpretation, the infantile phases handily limit the repertory of themes and images.

Holland felt "stung by a comment" that every "traditional Freudian literary

---

[18] "The research literature" summed up in Fisher and Greenberg's (1977: 395) comprehensive survey "does not indicate that the female has a more inferior concept of her body than the male." Nor does it "support Freud's notion that the male has a dramatically more severe set of superego standards than the female." Contrast Holland's remark: "Freud was fond of saying that in women the conscience was less developed" (DY 48).

analysis" "turns out to say the same thing" (PIP 139). Though Holland's works disprove this charge, the set of childhood fantasies his "dictionary" contains is certainly far smaller than the set of literary topics, plots, and images avid readers could find in literature. This few-versus-many structure compels the interpreter to struggle with utmost ingenuity against reductionism and blurring of detail.

Holland readily admits that "there are few symbols with universal unconscious meaning"; Freud himself "cautioned" "against one-to-one symbolic decodings," wrily observing that "sometimes," "'a cigar is just a cigar'" (PIP 29; DY 60). Disdain is expressed for "the old-fashioned kind of symbol-twirling that used to pass for psychoanalytic criticism" (5RR 218). "Symbols are flexible and dynamic: they vary with the context. They do not represent a code of one-to-one correspondences that can be looked up in some 'Freudian' dreambook. The only one who can really tell what unconscious meaning a symbol has is the one who is using or responding to it" (DY 57).

Yet in his New Critical drive to "justify" "every image and word" (cf. PIP 125), Holland assumed that "all important objects" have the "dual reality" of "thing and symbol" (PIP 151). He had no doubt that "any plot or symbolism" "'will express for us fantasies derived from our experience of our own bodies and our parents'" (DY 261). Living up to that motto led to disturbing generalizations. He averred that "every woman in our lives is partly a mother, every man partly a father," so that "almost any interpersonal relationship has oedipal elements"; and drew the "general rule" that "a work of literature builds on an oedipal fantasy whenever it deals with a relationship involving more than two persons"; or that "any work of art dealing in depth with relations of love and hate between people is likely to contain some oedipal fantasies" (DY 46f). Though these "fantasies" may be "especially various," we can "easily" "identify" them "by looking at the fictional women as mothers and the fictional men as fathers and sons" (DY 50) (no daughters?). We can be particularly sure that "dark, unknown, obscure, banished, or debased persons" "symbolize" the "forbidden love object" (DY 49f).

This generality is typical of much of Holland's "dictionary." Again privileging the male viewpoint, he says "the phallus can be expressed in an astonishingly wide range of symbols" (DY 60). "The entire body" or "the hands" or "anything that keeps the hands busy," such as "camera," "tools," or "playing cards," "can be defensive substitutes for a phallus" (DY 59f). Moreover, "because the child's interest in his genitals is involved with his sexual knowledge and discoveries, his mind itself can sometimes serve as a symbol for these parts of his body" (DY 43). Indeed, "the "eyes, hands, legs, head, or mind can all symbolize the phallus in castration fantasies." Or, "the phallus becomes the visible narcissistic embodiment of one's own autonomy." In literature, "almost any strongly aggressive or assertive plot is likely to be phallic," as well as "stories that sharply distinguish the sexes," or even stories that don't, for instance, by "bringing in homosexuality" (DY 43). The "threat" of "castration" is "symbolized" by "cutting off the head, loss of self-determination, loss of sanity" (DY 15).

The "primal scene fantasy," wherein the child "watches what he takes to be the sadistic, bloody violence of his parents in the struggle of love ending in a death-like sleep," is to be assumed for such "clusters of images" as "darkness, a sense of vagueness and the unknown, mysterious noises in night and darkness"; "vague movements, shapes shifting and changing, nakedness, things appearing and disappearing"; or "images of fighting and struggling, blood, the phallus as weapon" (DY 111, 46).[19]

Equations of such breadth should be applicable to nearly any literary work. But should something appear unrelated, it can be interpreted as a defense against the images one wishes to find. For example, "fog, mist, sweet smells, pure air, light, even, ultimately, *logos*, the word of God" are all classified as "transformations" of an "anal" "preoccupation with dirt" (DY 40). The "primal scene" fantasy is diagnosed not merely in "images of fighting and struggling," but in "images of quietness" and "motionlessness" (DY 46). The "urethral" focus on "fluids" is extended to "their opposites, such as fire" (DY 41). This tactic further extends the critic's leeway to get a Freudian reading even when textual evidence appears contradictory or missing.

Since Holland believed the "primal scene" to be the "well-documented and well-nigh universal unconscious meaning" of "watching stage performances" (DY 110f),[20] he set to work showing that Shakespeare's "To-morrow" soliloquy (*Macbeth*, V, iv, 19-27) is a "handling" of "a familiar fantasy: perceiving and denying the primal scene" (DY 114). I wasn't surprised to see the "candle" enlisted in "phallic symbolism" (DY 111)—par for the (inter)course.[21] But I was nonplussed to read that "walking distances sexual activity into another kind of erect action," on the grounds that "the phallus with its power to stand erect becomes identified with the boy's own recently acquired power to stand up" (DY 111, 42).[22] To extract the "primal scene," Holland converts "days" into "nights," and the "player" into a "parent" (DY 112). Far from feeling that Shakespeare's imagery has been explained, I am more perplexed than before at the new text that has supplanted the original.

Holland says his reading can resolve the "illogical" movement of the passage "from metaphor to metaphor" by uncovering "the basic pattern of impulse and defense" (DY 107). In Elizabethan rhetoric, though, the mixing of metaphors

---

[19] And any weapon gets interpreted as a phallus as a matter of course, even that of Sir John Fallstaff (Phallstaff?) (DY 59), whose amorous initiatives always miscarry as badly as his martial ones.

[20] If so, its's odd no play I can think of—not even by authors who reveled in presenting sexuality and brutality for shock effect, such as Hebbel, Jahnn, and Artaud—shows a child watching parental intercourse as murderous rape. Novels would be a better place to search, as Fiedler remarks (LD 345).

[21] Probably in his classic book on dreams, Freud refers to the use of candles in female masturbation, in connection with a student song.

[22] This "identification" seems to conflate disparate senses of the term "erect," one spatial (as in "rectangle"), one anatomical (as in "rigid").

was so common and luxuriant that such a passage would hardly seem incoherent enough to require translation into a different construct.

Besides, Holland ignores the lines immediately preceding the speech, where Macbeth is told of the queen's death and says "she should have died hereafter": "there would have been a time for such a word" (V, iv, 16-18). The theme is therefore set as junction and disjunction between "time" and "word" in regard to death. The passage can be read by constructing a network of conceptual associations among its terms: time ("to-morrow," "yesterdays," "time," "day," "hour"), word ("syllable," "tale"), sound ("heard," "told," "sound," "fury"), movement ("creep," "pace," "way," "walking," "struts"), illumination ("lighted," "candle," "shadow"), end ("death," "out," "last," "no more"), and insubstantiality ("petty," "brief," "poor," "shadow," "fools," "idiot," "signifying nothing") (cf. Beaugrande 1979a). I feel reassured to hear that the loss of life—not "the tense terrible sexual imaginings of the night" —"signifies nothing" (cf. DY 111f). I can only conclude that Holland himself happens to be strongly "interested" in "seeing and then not seeing primal scenes" (DY 143).

Holland seemed willing to call such "readings" "farfetched," or "strange," "astonishing," "lame," etc. (DY 112, 156; PIP 121; DY 32, 137). ("Positing farfetched connections" is at one point listed as a "sin" that does "violence to the text," PIP 146.) But these admissions were usually preludes to a series of defensive maneuvers during which his reading was not retracted. One "farfetched" reading received "confirmation" from the "faintest echoes" detected in the "more conventional readings" of "other critics"; another "peeped through" their "phrasing" (a good Freudian locution too) (DY 112f, 271). If a critic doesn't get the same reading, then such "fantasies are less available or less threatening to him"; to find out why, we need to "know unseemly things" about his "personality" (DY 114). This prospect might well discourage a critic from disputing a Freudian reading.

Holland is extremely gratified when a work "coincides quite strikingly with clinical phenomena"; H.D.'s poem "There is a spell" uses "shellfish" imagery that "in a dream" or a "free association" would be "almost certainly drawing on fantasies, themes, or issues from that first chapter of infancy when the mouth was our chief way to meet the world" (PIP 107f). But Holland digs further down when such coincidences aren't manifest. Reading Matthew Arnold, he says that "though they are very deeply buried, words like 'organs', 'ends,' and 'serve' have sexual connotations" which "Arnold did not consciously intend" (DY 156). Nonetheless, the words suggest that "Arnold's quite reasonable intellectual position, that criticism should eschew practicality, has unconscious roots in a wish to avoid sexual touchings." The inverse of this claim should be that critics who stress practical ends, such as Fiedler, Bleich, and (in a special sense) Bloom, must be unconsciously eager for sexual touchings—an "unseemly" theorem indeed.

Certainly, Freudian readings seem apt for works with appropriate themes and expressions. The selection of explicitly sexual materials, such as a *Playboy* joke, or the Wife of Bath's tale, greatly enhances the plausibility of Holland's libidinal interpretations —no doubt the reason he put them at the beginning of his *Dynamics* (DY 3-4, 8-27). *A Rose for Emily*, the featured text for *5 Readers Reading*, is eminently designed to bring up Freudian issues, such as anal fixations on dirt, Oedipal wishes between daughter and father, primal scenes with love enacted as murder, and so on. The scene in *On the Road* where the characters "urinate off the back of a speeding truck" is enlisted for the idea that "the early restless novels of Jack Kerouac instance quite fully the urethral in literature" (DY 41).

Yet overt correspondence is problematic if our theoretical premise is that libidinal content must get transformed before it can be expressed. Explicit representations of fantasies should logically count as refutations rather than as confirmations of the premise. The recourse of assuming that the fantasies escaped the writer's vigilance is hardly plausible if writers are masterfully defensive in their control of literary form. The presented fantasy might be the transformation of some other fantasy, for instance, Kerouac's urination image being a disguised homosexual fantasy; yet in that case, it would not "instance the urethral," but the "phallic" (cf. DY 43).

The only genuine solution I can see is to limit the universality and probability of fantasy responses, by gauging the design and themes of the works as well as the identity and predispositions of the readers. Certain works encourage readers to associate with infantile fantasies more than others do; and writers may consciously and deliberately exploit that aspect, especially after Freud's theories were popularized (D.H. Lawrence, for instance, cf. SX 346f, 353f). We might obtain some gradients for measuring how likely Holland's "transformational" model is to apply in particular cases. So far, though, he resists this reservation.

Holland once condemned criticism that makes "psychological assumptions about the impact of poetry and fiction on men's minds," but no "attempt to validate them" (DY xii). "Inevitably, the critical conclusions" "are the weaker," a complaint he apparently lodges against a whole series from Plato to the New Critics (DY ix-xii). Like Robert Lane (1961), Holland "takes literary critics to task" for their "almost willful refusal to use ordinary systematic procedures of classification, theory testing, or methodology" (DY xviii).

In contrast, Holland's *Dynamics* vowed to "create" "at least a testable hypothesis" (DY xvii). "Experimentation" can determine "whether the model itself" is "correct"; "a psychologist skilled in designing experiments could confirm or deny the conclusions reached here" (DY 316, xvii). This factor was thought to make his model "unlike most literary theories" (DY xvii), but I think every literary theory may *imply* a testable hypothesis which the critic usually fails to see as such, let alone to look for empirical confirmations from representative groups of authors or readers.

Before he began testing, Holland sought to confirm his model by invoking previous findings of "psychoanalysis," which, he avowed, "is not an ideology" because it is "clinical and experiential" (DY 31). He felt "very close to the immediate data of couch and clinic," to the "mass of evidence" from "thousands of case histories" (DY 32, 245, 27). The "impulses" and "defenses" he postulated "are not 'constructs' or 'hypotheses'" but "things that many people have directly observed in dreams, in children's play, and in the psychoanalyses of both children and adults" (DY 32). He reassured us that "psychoanalytic studies by the hundreds demonstrate the presence of these fantasies in literature" (DY 52). "Because we know these fantasies clinically, because they have to do with the primitive, unconscious part of our mental life, we can safely say they are what gives literature its astonishing power over us" (DY 310).

This argument raises three serious problems. The first is that, as far as I can discover,[23] the clinical evidence is not literary, and the literary evidence is not clinical. Virtually all these "demonstrations" consist of psychoanalysts or literary scholars discovering "fantasies" in literary works much the same way Holland did, by magisterial assertion. Since these analysts were extremely interested and skilled in detecting such fantasies, the evidence is circular. What is proven may be not that the works contain infantile fantasies, but that the latter can always be projected by people highly trained and determined to do so. As we have seen, the categories are flexible enough to apply to almost anything, and the procedures of application offer wide leeway for finding correlations. Holland should have warned us that his "clinical" "evidence" included few experiments with representative reader groups experiencing literature.[24]

The second problem emerges when Holland explains how to look for "fantasies" in "dreams, slips of the tongue, clichés, jokes, advertising, myths, folklore, proverbs, and of course, in works of art of all kinds (even philosophies and scientific disciplines)" (DY 51f). We can get "quite overwhelming" "evidence" "for these fantasies" if we "look" at "the world of human behavior around us" in "a disinterested, scientific frame of mind" (DY 51). Precisely this "frame of mind" is what Freudian theorizing denies: "we are not quasi-scientific observers of a phenomenon outside ourselves" (DY 272). "The scientifically minded man will see verifiable realities" which are actually a product of "transforming" a "fantasy" "into a synthesis and unity that he finds consciously integrating and satisfying" (5RR 125). An analyst who, like Freud and Holland, already believes that at "virtually every moment of our lives we manage fantasies defensively" (DY 161) will be "satisfied" by bringing the "realities" into line.

---

[23] I am indebted to Michel Grimaud of Wellesley College for his comprehensive and expert opinion on this question.

[24] Such evidence is not for instance provided by either of Holland's most favored source works, Kris (1952) and Lesser (1957) (cf. DY xii; PIP 174). And evidence in older research may not support a model that renounces the basic procedures, such as sifting "works of art" for "clues to the writer's childhood, neuroses, or sexual idiosyncrasies"; or assuming that art "transmits" "drive gratification with relatively little modification from form" (PIP 142; DY 296f; cf. Alexander, 1963).

The third problem is to portray this model as a result of making a universal principle more specific. "To explain a phenomenon is to relate it to principles more general than itself"; therefore, "to say one can analyze literary experiences by principles applicable to all human experiences is simply to say one can 'explain' literary experiences" (DY 309). This argument has force only if Holland can genuinely show that "we absorb literature like the rest of the outside world" (5RR 210), an assumption contradicted by most aestheticians (Ch. 2). Even he may say the contrary: "the most basic of artistic conventions" is that "literary or artistic experience comes to us marked off from the rest of our experiences in reality," by virtue of a "far more orderly structure," "a longer, deeper range of response," and so on (DY 70, 101, 283). If this assessment is valid, then we cannot so easily jump from "the world of human behavior" over to literary response.

The problem remains if that response is instead compared to abnormal behavior. This tactic surfaces when Holland offers "clinical evidence," not merely as "analogies," but as "confirmations" —the processes of "psychoanalysis, hypnosis, and dreaming," involving a "persistence of adult ego-functions along with an encapsulated regression" (DY 89). "We might well be in the same schizoid state when we are engrossed in a literary 'entertainment'; certainly, the behavioral signs of that engrossment resemble our behavior in analysis, hypnosis, and dreaming." "Absurd" theater in particular "creates in us a state approximating schizophrenia, affectlessness, concretized metaphors, klang associations, depersonalization, an unclear relation of self to object"; "intellection" can then be applied as "a self-defeating way of dealing with this miniature psychosis" (DY 177).[25]

The same mode of comparison adduces "motor inhibition" to explain the "basic convention" that "we do not expect to act as a result of literary or artistic experience"; "the work of art" "presents itself as divorced from usefulness" (DY 70). Such analogies preserve the difference between everyday behavior and literature by situating the latter in the domain of the neurotic; and this thesis too is far from proven (cf. Wellek and Warren, p. 40).

In any case, Holland's argument by "clinical evidence" fades when he repudiates the "older psychoanalytic concept of literature" whereby "each literary work had a fixed fantasy content" (5RR 117). Psychoanalysts are understandably reluctant to admit that their diagnoses project their own fantasies into the patient. But Holland gradually acknowledged as much for the literary works he interpreted. "I much prefer to look at the fantasies in literary works through what we know of the fantasies typical of the various libidinal phases associated with child development" (DY 33). This preference is "close to clinical observation" in a more

---

[25] If the "crisis of self-object differentiation" is "described" as "an inability to distinguish between subjective states and objective reality" (DY 176), then Holland's career might be a continuing attempt to master such a "crisis."

unflattering sense than he realized: by putting the fantasizing analyst at the center of the transaction.

To describe the role of personality in response, the reader was assigned what Heinz Lichtenstein (1965) called an "identity theme": an "invariant style running all through a person's chosen behaviors" (DY vif). "Once a person's identity theme is established, it never changes"; "but the individual can grow and change infinitely within that style" (5RR 60). "Adding variation" to an "identity theme" is thus a "general model" of how "a human being experiences" (5RR 231). "Identities in this sense begin very early, presumably with one's biological endowment and prenatal influences" (5RR 58). The theme might be "inherited" (Freud) or "imprinted on the infant" by "the mother" (Lichtenstein) (5RR 58, 223).

Again, Holland jumps from general experience to literary response. During reading, "we each transform the resources the work offers us so as to express our different identity themes" (5RR 231; DY vii). For every reader, this "reading style" is "deeply ingrained, more deeply than even a professional's training as a reader; far from changing one's reading style, critical skills, specialized knowledge, and the experience of many books will all serve as ways of fulfilling it and carrying it into practice" (PIP 114).

Holland's own style manages to invest his professional training very handily: he finds identity themes with the same methods he uses for analyzing texts. "One abstracts an identity theme from the myriads of ego choices a person reveals much the way one abstracts a central theme to express the unity of all the many words in a literary work" (5RR 111). "I can abstract, from the choices in life I see, facts as visible as words on the page, various subordinate patterns and themes until I arrive at one central, unifying pattern" (UITS 121).

To verify his model conclusively, Holland "hoped to do an 'experiment' in stimulus and response, complete with rigorous hypotheses, predictions to be confirmed, measurements, repeatable data, isolation of the experimenter from his material," and "objective tests like questionnaires that could be analyzed statistically" (5RR 42). "Abruptly, and rather painfully," he "realized that none of this fit the problem." So he "gave up questionnaires and group experiments with statistical possibilities" (5RR 43f). Indeed, if "psychoanalysis" is "the science of human individuality," he says it must "necessarily give up repeatable experiments" (5RR 10). His research would not be "looking for classes or categories of behavior that could be considered the same," but for "the uniqueness of each response" (5RR 63). Efforts to "correlate" "responses" with "characteristic patterns of adaptation, discovered by interview or projective test," will not lead to successful "predictions" (5RR 48f). "One cannot predict" what a reader "will say or do, although one can understand it quite exactly in retrospect" (PIP 127).

Holland elected for the "holistic" method used in the social sciences. According to Diesing (1971: 258), a "holistic theory" need not "contain rigid formal definitions" or "yield predictions or deductive explanations" (cf. 5RR 270).

"Where the experimentalist puts method before matter, the holist puts his unique subjects first" and thus grants a "primacy of subject matter over method" (5RR 273). Yet "the psychoanalytic study of cases" is still asserted to "have led to a truly universal theory of human psychology, markedly more general than the fragmentary 'laws' of experimentalists" (5RR 274).

Holland "decided to fish for a method by seeing what issues emerged" from "more or less undirected interviews with a few readers who had taken standard personality tests," the "Rorschach" and the "Thematic Apperception Test," in which people describe what they see in inkblots and pictures, respectively (5RR x, 52).[26] "The interviews" were treated "as the primary source of data on personality," and "the tests as only supplementary," subject to being "overruled" (5RR 52). The "crucial data" were "the words the readers used about what they had read" (5RR 46; cf. PIP 161). Holland would pose questions like: "what did you think of it?"; "what does he seem to be saying?"; "are there any phrases that appeal to you?"; "what catches your eye?"; "do you like that?"; "does that statement make you feel good"?; and so on (PIP 70-74).

The "phrasings" of the answers were the main "evidence" about "each reader's synthesis and achievement" (5RR 46). "The problem became interpreting what he said." Holland tried to listen in the way he recommended for the "analyst's 'third ear'": "with some knowledge of the issues clinical experience has found important," and "with an open, free-floating attention to the kinds of things people are likely to say or think about parents, their own bodies, authorities, desires, or fears" (DY 317; 5RR 52). He sifted his transcripts for "misrememberings," "opinions usual and unusual, misreadings, slips, special wordings, body symbolisms" (5RR 64f, 45)—pretty much what a psychoanalyst looks for. It "was not essential" that "what my readers said about their feelings at the time they read the story was true"; "free associations reveal the synthesis and creation" behind the feelings, whether they are being "invented" or "recalled correctly" (5RR 45). Thus, the reliability of the data was not endangered by the possibility of his test persons, or "testees" as he calls them, being evasive or defensive during the interviews.

The test materials in these interview studies were all literary texts reprinted often enough in anthologies to qualify as representative. This choice removes one problem I found in the earlier work, where his demonstrations were often not done on literary texts at all.[27] *Dynamics* is illustrated repeatedly with films (DY 74, 82f, 94, 150, 162-174, 211, 218-223, 253ff, 272, 282f, 294, 333), perhaps because Holland was for some years a film critic on television. He "likes to work" with films "because they are all surface"; and because audience response

---

[26] Most recently, he uses his own "I-test," where "the testee is asked to say which two" in a group of three items "seem more alike, and which one less like the others, and why" (CRAP 479).

[27] Holland might want to include them in a very broad definition of "literature," as proposed for jokes (Note 10). But the broad claims of his model should cover many other text types.

is observable in a "curious collectivity" (PIP 111, 128). Yet films differ crucially from the literary text (cf. Iser's remarks, AR 137ff). They appeal to fantasy content much more strongly. As Fiedler also observes (cf. WL 50, 137f, 140), "entertainments" are generally more apt to provoke regressive responses and to provide "fairly primitive artistic experiences" centered on "pleasure" (cf. DY 74). Absorption in the experience is likely to be very powerful, whereas "harder literature usually requires an effort that keeps one aware of oneself" (PIP 84) (cf. Chs. 8, 13, 17).

Holland's interview transcripts (5RR 130-200, 300-393) contain a rich documentation of associations, mental images, affective responses, and personality traits. Of course, the testees did not report responses to all words or elements from the text; they focused mainly on the portrayal of characters and scenes, especially where dramatic incidents were involved. This result fits Holland's supposition that "most" "defenses (or displacements)" "shape plot" more than "purely linguistic form" (DY 58). We could thus formulate another reservation: that fantasy transformation is selective in preferring not only one work over another, as I maintained, but also certain elements or aspects within the same work.

For each of his five student readers, Holland hypothesized an identity theme (5RR 201-03).[28] Sam "wanted to be helpless so as to take in supplies of love or admiration from outside; but then, by identifying with the source of those supplies, he would make himself strongly, safely, and separately male." "Sandra sought to avoid depriving situations and to find sources of nurture and strength with which she could exchange and fuse." "Saul sought from the world balanced and defined exchanges, in which he would not be the one overpowered." "Sebastian wanted to unite himself with forces of control, to which he would give something verbal or intellectual, hoping to sexualize them and get back something warm, dirty, or erotic." "Shep charactertistically evaded human relationships, which were charged with aggression for him, by polarizing them into extreme opposites."

These descriptions are far more individualized and less reductive than the "characterology of early psychoanalysis," according to which "Sam and Sandra" are "'phallic' characters," "Saul and Sebastian" are "'anal'" "characters," and "Shep" is an "'oral' personality" (5RR 110). But the newer terminology still reflects Lichtenstein's (1965) definition of "identity theme" as an "infinite sequence of *bodily* and *behavioral* transformations" (5RR 201, e.a.).

Holland soon made the "surprising" and "troubling" "discovery that my critical method, disciplined, professional, accredited, also acts out my identity theme" (PIP 112). He conceded that "identity themes" "are drastically open to the biases of the interpreter's own style" (5RR 110). In the 1975 volume, he finesses

---

[28] The Index of the book makes it clear that these statements convey the readers' "identity themes"; the term also appears earlier in a similar context (5RR 110).

the problem by splitting himself into a reader he liked to call "Seymour"[29], whose interpretation was no longer claimed to be representative; and a theoretician whose model of the act of reading is ostensibly universal and correct. He oscillated between these two egos while he supervised his interviews, offering his interpretations as mere suggestions, but never doubting the validity of his search for childhood fantasies and identity themes. By 1984, he no longer assumed that these themes are "in" readers; they too are his own "representations" (BRF 380). "My formulating a theme and variations for you or any other reader is just as much my act of interpretation as your reading of a poem is yours" (DGF 11).

If we tried to find Holland's *own* identity theme in his books, we would most likely classify him as an oral type. He eagerly assumes that "it was through the mouth" and "out of the rhythmic cycles of hungering and being fed by another that each human being set up his identity theme" (PIP 108) (if so, everybody should have much the same identity). Even sexuality is subsumed: "fantasies about male and female interaction as the balancing of strengths derive from still earlier fantasies about being fed" (PIP 80).

By the same token, the "aesthetic pleasure" afforded by works of art is traced back to "our first experience of pleasure, being held by a nurturing mother and being fed" (DY 75). "We take in the literary work, all literary works, in a very primitive oral way: what is 'out there' is felt as though it were neither 'out there' nor 'in here'—boundaries blur" (DY 83). "No matter what other issues from later stages appear in a literary work, one almost always finds at the core some fantasy of oral fusion and merger" (DY 38). This description of reading links it with a "regression to our earliest oral experience of a pre-self in which we are merged with the source of our gratification" (DY 89). "We approach a literary work with two conscious expectations: that the work will give us pleasure; it will not ask that we act on the external world"; "these two conscious expectations find a matrix in us, a memory of the primal at-oneness with a nurturing other," "the giving mother" (DY 260; PIP 85).

Such theses suggest how "literature seems to build on orality": "of all the different levels of fantasy in literature, the oral is the most common (at least in my range of reading)" (DY 38).[30] "Much" of *Poems and Persons* is "built" "around this one type of fantasy, the oral"; "obviously, I have reasons for doing so which stem from my own personality structure" (PIP 139). Holland is certainly talented in detecting orality beneath all sorts of activities and expressions. The "fantasy" of a "wish to eat mother" or a "fear" that "she will eat you" is argued

---

[29] Inventing names beginning with "S-" "testifies to an ex-engineer's nostalgia for the rigor of statistical work with objective Ss that so sternly commands attention in psychological journals" (5RR 44).

[30] Elsewhere, he says that "the single most common fantasy-structure in literature is phallic assertiveness balanced against oral engulfment" (DY 43). If "absolute words" like "all" "often go with oral fantasies," (DY 37), then Holland's use of "all" in his generalizations (DY 15, 28, 77, 83, 99, 103, 105, 172, 174, 244, 269) could further signal his oral emphasis.

from locutions like "'Sweetie,'" "'Honey,'" and "'You're so cute, I could eat you up'" (PIP 136f; DY 35). "'Feasting one's eyes'" and "'taking in' through our eyes" are listed to show that "unconsciously, to look at is to eat, as when we 'devour' books" (DY 37).[31] "Even as adults we associate reading with eating": we say "a man 'devours books'" or is "a 'voracious' reader"; "a certain novel may be a 'treat'"; "a parody may be 'delicious'"; and so on (DY 75; cf. PIP 85). The logic is the same when "orality explains the open-mouthed wonder with which we 'absorb' a theatrical performance" (DY 76) (though I suspect the reference was to the gasping for air in astonishment).

Turning to literary works, Holland finds Wordsworth "saying": "something that would ordinarily be felt as an unpleasant, anally toned restraint can become a source of oral pleasure and merger" (DY 239). Holland thinks it "striking that the same pattern occurs in Keat's less well known 'Sonnet on the Sonnet.'" But the coincidence is hardly remarkable for an analyst with such an oral fixation.

Orality dominates again when Holland avers that "particular sounds" in "poetic language" "involve muscular actions that somehow match the sense" (DY 136). The mere "repetition of vowels or consonants" is "a source of pleasure," according to Freud (who is "no doubt" "correct") (DY 145). "We ask that the sounds act out for us some management of the fantasy the sense embodies" (DY 139). Holland's illustrations of "movements of the mouth that simulate muscular ways of dealing with fantasy content" —"spitting out, hissing at, biting off, striking, stopping, and so on" —(DY 142, 158) are among the most breathtaking romps of his Freudianized New Critical ingenuity. A "stanza with its *s*'s, *t*'s *th*'s, and *f*'s" "makes the mouth spit out a hurly-burly of sensual aggression and love"; "the deletion of the *d* from 'elated' does something" "to control the feminizing of the masculine train"; in Prospero's announcement that "'our revels now are ended'" *(Tempest, IV, i, 148)*, "the double *d* that stops these revels acts out the psychological denial" of a "primal scene"; and so on (DY 208, 328, 143).

These oral tendencies bear out Holland's recognition of the role of the researcher's personality in postulating and generalizing a model. Orality and related fantasies become the framework for describing not merely the hidden content of works, but the functions of language and reading as such. The reader accordingly seems to regress back to infancy through multiple channels that reinforce each other in much the way a New Critical interpretation shows the art work thematizing its own composition and structure. This resemblance is no accident, given Holland's dual loyalties and his shift from text over to reader. The "identity theme" is a strategic concept for suggesting that the regression varies a parameter that is essentially constant anyway.

The darkest implication of such a vision is that higher culture looks ultimately

---

[31] Fenichel (1953) is the authority for this equation of looking with eating, the logic again probably being that "pre-verbal life consists mostly of looking at mother, taking her in" (DY 76, 219f) (see Note 9).

hollow and phony,[32] like a collective superego legitimizing intellectual disguises for shameful fantasies. Holland's references to "intellectual" acts routinely portray them as a devious or defensive veneer (cf. DY 57, 104, 128, 156, 171, 177, 184, 187, 222; PIP 47, 77, 81, 160; 5RR 116, 122, 201). Public institutions devoted to art—museums, academies, and even criticism—would be communal laboratories for defending against, or transforming, ideas and images which everyone is obsessed with, but which no one can bear to confront. The various arts and genres are merely "different ways of managing fantasy content" (cf. DY 315).

To be consistent, Holland should predict that extremely active and diverse epochs in the arts would develop in correspondingly repressive, defensive cultures. Yet this ratio does not hold. Licentious periods such as the Elizabethan era or the 1920s brought culminations in the arts; the prudish, repressive systems of of Stalin and Hitler left almost no art works of merit. Moreover, repressive people like the modern "Puritans" Fiedler portrays entertain a "deep" "fear of art" (LD 430), whereas they ought to seek it as a respectable disguise for an otherwise forbidden release—Holland, "something of a Puritan," does (DY 222).

In his letter responding to a draft of this chapter, Holland challenges me to give "evidence" that "literature is a progressive social force." I could cite his own credo that through "the work of art" we become "a larger, wiser self" (DY 103), but that opinion is not well borne out by his analyses. I could cite the models of Iser, Bleich, Millett, Jauss, and Jameson, or of critics outside my survey, such as Lukács, Sartre, Adorno, Bloch, and Marcuse, all of whom assert that art holds at least the potential for progressive action. That potential is the strongest claim we can make, because nobody can actually force art to be used in one specific way.

Freudian models, also scant on "evidence," issue the self-fulfilling prophecy that art is regressive and offer all-too-patent alibis for the failure of culture to mature and develop, to get beyond the basic but monotonous drives of infancy, or to openly and honestly satisfy human desires. If art only serves to "hallucinate gratification" and "'ego mastery'" (DY 181, 202), the only progress could be hedonistic and private: finding better ways to maximize pleasure and minimize anxiety or guilt. Art could not engage the history of ideas or the ideologies of society in the ways our other critics demonstrate.

Another troubling implication of Holland's approach is that the literary transaction should be fundamentally altered when a critic consciously perceives and explicitly exposes the normally unconscious fantasy content. The whole mechanism of defense and denial should break down when the materials are brought to the surface. Holland proposes that "critics" can "give us new intellectual associations which we then preconsciously or unconsciously add to our analogizings to a given literary work" (DY 332). But, quite aside from the practical problems of

---

[32] Holland conjectures that "an individual's own psychic structure makes much more of a difference in response" than "culture" does (DY 335). This idea might suit Bleich, Paris, and Bloom, but hardly Frye, Fiedler, Hirsch, Culler, or Jauss.

making such a transfer, the "unconscious" is not an "intellectual" domain in Freudian theory, and the associations Holland supplies are mainly libidinal ones.

Freud originally assumed that the conscious recognition of the fantasy causing a neurosis promoted therapeutic insight. Holland's criticism might thus have a quasi-therapeutic function. He does envision "teaching actively" by "suggesting a slant on a particular work" that can enable students to "absorb it through their defenses" (5RR 217). Moreover, "with a positive and supportive discussion," he has "seen students—out of their own curiosity about themselves—become strikingly aware of their own feelings and associations, and from that awareness followed an understanding of their synthesis of the work" (5RR 218).

Yet Holland would not call this process "therapy": it is "only understanding within and for a limited, literary purpose." Besides, what he says of the author should go for the critic as well: "when a writer chooses to air his fantasies, he is likely to arouse the reader's defenses" and elicit "a negative reaction" (5RR 221). To avoid such dangers, Holland's approach "requires sophisticated students, ideally those with some insight into themselves arrived at in a clinical setting." And the "insight" that "enables a teacher to direct what he is saying" to a particular "student" can be "not easily won and rather exhausting to live with" (5RR 217f).

Throughout his career, Holland has sought to resolve his original dilemma of different readings by combining two frameworks that are heavily deterministic. For New Criticism, the text is decided by the writing on the page. For Freudian theory, the personality is decided by early experiences. Holland concurs: "the words on the page and the character patterns a reader brings to them," as well as "the psychological transformation in the work itself," are "fixed" (PIP 127; DY 329). These "fixed" or invariant aspects were to be the critic's concern. "A psychoanalytic reading can reveal 'deep' fantasies that many people are likely to experience in a literary work, but it cannot generalize about certain very intense sources of pleasure at a relatively conscious level" that "come from one's own highly individual experience" (DY 50). He later propounded a corresponding inner-outer duality: "facing outward," readers' "experiences point to a shared reality having a centering theme"; "facing inward, their experiences become private assimilations to a series of individual centers" (5RR 291).

Most recently, he invokes the cybernetic concept of "feedback," which had been mentioned only marginally before (DY 132; 5RR 288). (Perhaps he likes the term for its oral and anal undertones.) In a "feedback loop," "input" is registered and compared to a "standard or reference signal"; any "difference" leads the system to adapt (cf. BRF 372). In DGF, his example is driving on the pavement by adjusting to road conditions (a "cliff," a "puff of wind," a "pick-up truck"), which still suggests a fairly deterministic conception. "Identity" is now depicted as "a theme with its history and its variations, which governs and permeates" a "hierarchy of feedback loops" by "generating" "hypotheses," "hearing the return," and "feeling the discrepancy" regarding "inner standards" (DGF 10f; cf. BRF 380).

In this new scheme, the "loop part," associated with "lower-level physical and physiological" acts, is "more or less the same for all of us"; "the standard is individual" (DGF 7f). Also, "higher" "levels" such as "skills we use in reading, especially literature," are "more personal" (DGF 9). Or, in the "comparison" "against" the "standard," "the cognitive part may be automatic and physiological, not individual, while the emotional part is likely to be quite personal" (DGF 7). I'd say just the opposite: people differ more in their cognitions than in their emotions, though maybe not in the mental operations of driving a car.

Holland would like to think, along with Ernest Jones, the champion in Freudian hyperbole, that master Freud "anticipated the whole science of cybernetics" (DGF 2f). But I can see a parallel at most between Freud's mechanistic notions of mental energy and the part of cybernetics dealing with servomechanisms.[33] All such mechanisms lack the "active, creative element" Holland assigns to "identity" (DGF 13). He doesn't explain how "creativity" got there (identity was derived from being fed, a hard act to do creatively), nor how it can evolve if identity always duplicates its own style. In his cybernetic model creativity would have to be introduced through some new "standard or reference signal" against which to measure performance; and he hasn't explained how that might occur.

Still, the feedback model is more neutral and general than Holland's earlier ones. "Social and cultural codes" and "interpretive communities" can now be represented in the "hierarchy of feedbacks" wherein "the higher loops provide reference signals for the loops below them" (BRF, 381, 373). This expansion might help him align his research with that recently carried out in the "psychology of perception, cognition, and memory," "brain physiology," and "artificial intelligence" (BRF 379; cf. 5RR 252).

But these disciplines do not share his fundamental thesis that "psychoanalysis is a general account of humans, including literature" (letter). Holland brackets this problem in recent papers (CRAP, BRF, DGF) by avoiding the "old fashioned tone, the body-language about fantasies" of DY and considering these things "matters of style rather than conceptual problems." For example, he devises fairly abstract and symbolic "identity themes" for an author like Frost ("to manage great unmanageable unknowns by means of small knowns," BRF 367) or a reader like "Carlos" ("to be active, dominating, distinguishing, and distinguished," CRAP 490). Yet he feels he is merely "talking" in the "transformed forms" of "a language that translates body terms into" the kind of "theoretical

---

[33] Such mechanisms have already been built by Japanese engineers to steer a car with a vision and computation system (Tsugawa, Yatabe, Hirose, & Shuntetsu, 1979), a fairly simple design apart from the problem of visual recognition. "Driving a car" was also Holland's "analogy" for Waelder's concept of the "ego balancing forces," whereby the driver at least got some "pleasure" (cf. PIP 46).

discussion" "encouraged" by "our profession" (letter). This evasion is surely not what most researchers on cognition believe they're doing.

Holland opines that "psychoanalysis grows not so much by dropping earlier positions as by incorporating them into a larger and more all-embracing conceptual framework" (letter). This proceeding befits "the holistic both-ands of psychoanalysis" that cause "difficulty" for "logically inclined people" like me operating with "either-ors or if-thens." Dreams, desires, and emotions can evidently embrace all manner of contradictions and opposites; and literature seems to share this capacity. But I doubt if the *study* of cognition can be content to proceed the same way. Contrary to popular belief, there is a huge body of empirical tests for Freudian theory (summarized in Fisher & Greenberg, 1977), and a number of his "positions" have fared quite poorly: that infantile experiences accurately predict character traits; that every dream is motivated by a repressed wish; that women consider their bodies inferior; and so on.[34] Such "positions" should now be "dropped," not maintained out of nostalgia or reverence to Freud.

All the same, the most interesting aspect in Holland's work may be his own lengthy and intricate maneuvering to adopt new positions without vacating old ones. He has translated his theses from model to model with a minimum of recantation. Without much impairment, his authority shifted from analyzing meanings to uncovering fantasies to diagnosing identities. He refocused his preoccupation from testes to testees, from id and titties to identities, in defiance of all the headaches entailed in trading fantasy for empiricism.

Whatever proved not to be universal for all humanity or all reading was salvaged over into Holland's personal style. And even this tactic conserves more than it renounces, since he still regards himself as a typical enough reader to merit public description. Most of our theoretical critics have this divided ambition to be both representative and yet very special, to be the epitome of reading yet set apart not only from ordinary readers but from their nontheoretical colleagues. However, in few of those critics are the results of this tension so intriguing and elaborated as they are in Holland's case.

---

[34] Compare the important revisions in views on dreaming (e.g. Lipton, 1960; French & Fromm, 1964; Rycroft, 1979). Work in progress by Francis Crick and Graeme Mitchison suggests that dreaming may simply be the way to clear brain cells of stored information; the imagery is generated when the forebrain attempts to interpret nonsensical signals from the brain stem (cf. Melenchuk 1983).

10

David Bleich[1]

David Bleich announces a "new paradigm" whereby "our present conception of language may be productively altered" (SC 9). We are promised not merely "new ways to understand the human ontogenesis of language and symbolic thought," but also "new conceptions of the act of interpretation, the act of reading, and the pedagogy of language and literature" (SC 37, 9). Bleich asserts the generality of his "paradigm" on the grounds that human access to the world is necessarily subjective. "'Objective reality' is a construction of, and hence *a subordinate function* of, our subjective perspective" (SC 15f, e.a.). "Any perspective as well as the possibilities for new perspectives are determined by the subjective capacities for perception and cognition" (SC 111f). By themselves, such theses hardly amount to a "new paradigm," since some version of them is adopted by most of our other critics, especially Iser, Holland, Culler, Jameson, and the Yale group, plus many philosophers of science. Novelty can only be claimed if one draws genuinely innovative consequences for theory and practice.

Like Hirsch,[2] Bleich envisions a basic movement from individual toward communal, and, in parallel, from diversity toward consensus; and reserves the term "knowledge" for the outcome of this movement. This consensus disallows both impersonal objectivity and unguided subjectivity,[3] and calls for a negotiation not of verbal meanings, but of personal perceptions, feelings, and thoughts. Bleich stresses the extent to which "knowledge" is "strongly influenced by unspoken, collectively held psychological paradigms" (SC 283f). "The contexts of knowledge formation are always communal," so that "knowledge depends ultimately on how individuals form groups"; "to know anything" is "to have assigned a part of one's self to a group of others who claim to know the same thing"

---

[1] The key for Bleich citations is: LEE: "Literary Evaluation and the Epistemology of Symbolic Objects" (1981); RF: *Readings and Feelings* (1976); and SC: *Subjective Criticism* (1978).

[2] For a list of commonalities with Hirsch, see Note 6 to Ch. 7. These parallels are interesting in view of Bleich's thesis that Hirsch's "principle" "is inapplicable to literary study" (SC 94).

[3] At times, Bleich seems overly schematic in equating objectivity with sameness and subjectivity with difference or individual variation, as in: "rendering a reading experience as representative of a general human principle omits" "subjective immediacy" (SC 7f; cf. RF 3, 9; SC 19, 102, 116, 284, 295). His whole project after all assumes that subjectivity can and should be shared.

183

(SC 133, 264, 296). Since "even" "professional psychological circles" are "uncertain about how individuals function in groups" (SC 81), Bleich tries to construct his model as he goes along.

Probably to accentuate the urgency of his program, Bleich invokes the wide diversity of subjective experiences. He avers that "perceptual processes are different in each person"; "what is perceived is determined by the rules of the personality of the perceiver" (RF 3). A "major reason for the formation of the subjective paradigm" was the insight that "mutuality and collectivity made no sense without a prior awareness of individual subjectivity" (SC 264). Bleich's project is thus intended to help people "understand how and why each person sees differently" and make "public reality correspond to private reality" (RF 32, 95). "The synthesizing of communal knowledge" always "begins" with "the substrate of individual subjective knowledge" (SC 151). "Shared interests" are then "established" as a foundation for "authorizing" "new knowledge" (SC 283).

Bleich attacks objectivity with some resourceful arguments. To deflect the commonplace charge that subjectivity is solipsistic, Bleich turns the tables by maintaining that "the objective paradigm" is the "solipsistic" one (SC 295). It "reiterates one's perceptions to no end" and "is considered independent of human ethics" in that "the individual" "suppresses" his or her "active role in creating" and "bears no responsibility" for "only affirming true things" (SC 295; RF 9). "The assumption derived from the objective paradigm that all observers have the same perceptual response to a symbolic object creates the illusion that the object is real and that its meaning must reside inside it" (SC 98). This illusion can be deployed to suppress negotiation (Ch. 1).

A still more striking move is to discredit objectivity by attributing to it essentially the same foundation as religion.[4] The "religious" or "theological" "dimension of the objective paradigm" (SC 19, 21, 24) resides in assigning "the notion of objective truth" "the same epistemological status as God": "an invented frame of reference aimed at maintaining prevailing social practices" (SC 15). Historically, the "predictability" that "Newtonian mechanics" provided for "terrestrial and celestial" motion, combined with "the certainty of mathematical logic," is said to have "boosted science" into "the status of absolute truth," which "in turn demonstrated the certainty of divine control of the universe" (SC 14). This process engendered "the long-standing association of religious interests and the objective paradigm" (SC 34; cf. SC 12, 24, 26, 154, 158, 178; LEE 123f).

We might protest here that organized religion fiercely opposed the rise of science, and that the "objective truth" of science enabled a technology that profoundly transformed "prevailing social practices." Actually, though, Bleich is not denouncing science, but only shadow-boxing with it; as we will see in a

---

[4] Culler too suspects "the concepts and structures" of "criticism are a displaced theology" (PS 160). Bloom and Hartman are quite frank about this. Frye purports to take theology as an object to study rather than a method (compare Note 5).

moment, he is eager to support his own enterprise with scientific conceptions. He is more concerned with protesting the authoritarian metaphysics popularly associated with scientific claims to privileged truth, especially when these are imported, implicitly or explicitly, into his own field. He decries the "common critical practice" of combining "the religious assumption that ministers have a special access to the absolute truth and the scientistic assumption that an object of art is independent of human perception" (SC 33f), although again, this latter thesis is not held by many critics today, and by none at all in my survey.

Bleich ends up with two major critical positions as antagonists: objectivism and moralism. Purported practitioners of these two are readily called to account, such as T.S. Eliot, Northrop Frye,[5] and the New Critics (SC 33, 35, 8). But advocates of other approaches are also taken to task. I.A. Richards advanced an "argument" "in accord with the subjective paradigm," but did not follow it "in practice," "using only his assumption of his expertise in taste to authorize" his "judgments" (SC 34).[6] Proponents of "Rezeptionsästhetik" are given scant notice, because "they present models of the reader without studying specific responses of specific readers, and without inquiring into their own mental processes as readers" (SC 101), though of the critics he mentions, these charges apply only partly to Ingarden and Iser, and still less to Jauss and Groeben.[7]

Perhaps for motives of rivalry,[8] even the well-known subjectivists Holland and Rosenblatt are made targets of the suspicion, formulated by Whitehead (1925: 88f), that "everyone wants to struggle back to some sort of objectivist position" (SC 19, 112, 114, 124); and Rosenblatt is rebuked for being "moral" (SC 110). Philosophers are criticized too. "The religious interests" that "fostered the separation" of "subject and object" are said to have "limited the thought of Whitehead, Popper, Muller, and Polanyi" (SC 26), though Bleich acknowledges their concern for the problem of "subjectivity" (SC 19, 15, 18, 24).

In exchange, Bleich recruits some more remote authoritative predecessors for

---

[5] Bleich suggests that Frye keeps "knowledge" "objective" by situating the "subjective" in "value judgments" (SC 35), which, as we saw in Ch. 5, Frye would exclude from criticism. Bleich thinks it "no coincidence that Frye is an ordained minister," though Frye is no ordinary Christian apologist, much less a salvational critic like Philip Wheelwright (1954).

[6] Wellek and Warren, however, praise Richards' "practice" and castigate his "psychological theory" (TL 147). De Man also prefers the practice, rejecting the theory for "postulating a perfect continuity between the sign and the thing signified" (BI 232).

[7] Groeben (1980a, 1980b, 1982) has studied numerous reader responses, including those of critics. But much of this, like Jauss's attempt to report his "own mental processes" (pp. 375ff), was published after Bleich's book. Iser and Ingarden use their own processes in more concealed ways.

[8] On Bleich's confused relation to Holland, see Note 4 to Ch. 9. The rivalry impels Bleich to distort Holland's ideas into more vulnerable versions, and to denounce even some ideas they both hold. Points of agreement include: personality is the most fundamental fact of life; individual style controls reading; reading proceeds through stages, first staying close to the text, then working through associations; intellectualizing tends to disguise or conflict with genuine response; response can be detected through interviews; and Freud legitimized the study of subjective response.

his paradigm, though not without suggesting that they failed to realize or follow through the crucial line of argument. The paradigm is attributed to Kuhn, who "does not announce" it, and to Einstein, Bohr, and Heisenberg, whose "formulations" "make sense as a manifestation of the subjective paradigm," because "the role of the observer is paramount" (SC 11, 18). Mannheim is said to have "outlined" "the form of the subjective paradigm without its content" (SC 25). Bridgman, Freud, and Fish are judged to subscribe to the paradigm rather in spite of their contrary intentions (SC 22, 30ff, 122ff). Freud gets special praise because his "interpretation of dreams" provided "rational systematic knowledge without objective epistemology" and established that "interpretive knowledge is as scientifically authoritative as any other knowledge" (LEE 126; SC 69).

Of the sources discussed in any detail, only a few are apparently accepted as full-fledged predecessors: Waddington, Eddington, Heisenberg, Poole, Piaget, and Gombrich (SC 13, 17, 20ff, 27f, 30, 32f)—plus Leon Edel, Bleich's revered teacher and (as we find out elsewhere) father figure (SC 35f; RF 76). "Marxism, psychoanalysis," and "structuralism" are acknowledged as "independent systems of thought" offering a means to eliminate the "moral character" of "judgments of meaning"; but in order to "gain an explanatory dimension" and not be a mere "formulaic application of a received dogma to literature," they must be "articulated in conjunction with a response statement" (SC 156, 158).

By disqualifying ostensible subjectivists and marshalling sources from less proximate areas, Bleich conveys the impression that he has personally discovered and elaborated the "subjective paradigm." In case this ambition might collide with his broad claims for its generality and necessity, he likes to present his own views as if the paradigm itself were addressing us. We read, for example, that "the subjective paradigm" "views," "aims," "says," "assumes," or "holds" (SC 13, 19, 88, 98, 110f). This tendency softens Bleich's own subjective intrusions without having to share the paradigm with other bonafide creators and contributors. To keep his territorial instincts in the background, he paradoxically objectifies subjectivity itself.

Though he vows to have turned away from the search for "objective" or "religious" truth in favor of a "subjective criticism" that "supersedes the traditional authority of quantitative science" (SC 297), Bleich essays to base his framework of explanation and motivation on two sciences that emphasize objectivity, namely, genetic biology and developmental psychology. The act of "paradigm formation" is judged "Darwinian": "a human form of organismic adaptation" whose "purpose is to better insure human survival as a species" —a view Bleich attributes to Kuhn (1970) (SC 12).[9] Bleich makes the Darwinian outlook a further criterion for choosing his allies: Poole and Piaget are annexed on these grounds, while Habermas is repudiated as "utopian," not "Darwinian" (SC 27, 30, 26).

---

[9] This attribution is not well justified. For Kuhn, the Darwinian process applies best to the survival of scientists, even despite the unfitness of their theories.

Bleich seems relieved that "the Darwinian paradigm" renders the "notion of objective truth" "unnecessary" and "evolution toward an ideal" "not viable" (SC 12, 26). Now, actions and views can be disparaged not as untrue or immoral, but as "maladaptive" —the misprized "objective paradigm" in particular (SC 27, 13). Yet a utopian aspect persists in the injunction to select a recommended course of evolution. In a genuinely Darwinian paradigm, evolution follows not choice or persuasion, but hard necessity. Bleich is obliged to argue on the one hand that his paradigm must evolve from all others, even such objectifying ones as operationalism (SC 22f); and on the other hand that a major deliberate effort will be needed to establish and uphold it against the "fraudulent" paths of evolution that actually occurred and were so successful that they "have not changed appreciably over the centuries" (LEE 123, 110). Such a survival of the unfittest is unaccountable within strictly Darwinian models.

Aligning Darwinism with psychology, Bleich sketches a parallel between the evolution of the race and the development of the person from child to adult. Piaget's (1967: 368) contention is cited that "the social environment" does "for the intelligence what genetic recombinations of the population did for evolutionary variation of the transindividual cycle of the instincts" (SC 29). The same alignment is repeatedly projected in Bleich's books: "the activity of developing knowledge is as phylogenetically founded as the formation of new families"; "the construction of meaning is motivated by organismic adaptation"; "the need of symbolization is analogous to the needs for food, air, or exercise"; and so on (SC 133, 30, 44).

Biology and psychology are further linked by Bleich's thesis, again ascribed to Piaget, and this time to Chomsky too, that "intelligence" "is best conceived as an organ of the body" (SC 29, 40). That Bleich would link subjective capacities to body parts and processes seems curious for at least two reasons. First, the same problem recurs that I noted regarding Darwinism: Bleich has to advocate the explicit development of knowledge which, if a genuine organic or genetic process were at work, would emerge of its own evolutionary necessity. Second, he falls right back into objectification by conflating the mental with the physiological, e.g. "intelligence" with "an organ." In that view, intelligence should grow automatically just as an "organ" reproduces cells, and we wouldn't need "new paradigms."

The way "the organ of consciousness functions" is offered as proof that "the level of primary reality is symbolic" (SC 88). "Only subjects are capable of initiating action,"[10] and "the most fundamental form of that action is the motivated division of experience" into "three classes": "real objects, symbolic objects,

---

[10] Equating "subjects" with "people" (SC 111) oddly debars animals from actions, a thesis no biologist, however Darwinian, would accept. Compare Bleich's idea that "self-consciousness and the capacity for objectification" are "developed" in a way that is "species specific for human beings" (SC 42).

and subjects (i.e. people)" (SC 110f; cf. LEE 101). "Reality is defined subjectively," because "subjects" "decide what shall be real objects and what symbolic objects" (SC 88). "Consciousness" "takes real objects for granted and directs its efforts" toward "symbolic manipulation" of "real" or "symbolic" "objects." "The symbolic object stands not for a real object or person, but for a person's concept of that object or person" and is "always" "'detachable' from experience" (LEE 102, e.d.). Until "the end of the second year of life," the "object" retains an "attachment to the body," in much the same way as "real objects" and "people" elicit only "sensorimotor comprehension" (LEE 101). After that, the "category" of "symbolic objects appears" "at the same time as the acquisition of syntactic language." This temporal scheme is a main argument for assigning priority to child experiences in the functions of language (see below).

Since this three-part classification is not logical (what the entities are), but functional (how people deal with them), the possibilities for shifting among the classes are a problematic factor that causes Bleich some inconsistencies. When assailing his rival subjectivists Rosenblatt and Holland, Bleich avers that the classes do not get confused: "the distinction a subject feels between himself and the symbols he uses is the basis of sanity and conscious functioning"; in a "linguistic person," "there is never a blur between real objects and symbolic objects, or between either of these and people (subjects)"; "the reader already has a well-established sense of just which objects are real and which are symbolic"; and so on (SC 111, 113f).

At such moments of attack, Bleich overstates the matter. Elsewhere, he keeps admitting how unstable the three classes are. He acknowledges "our natural tendency to objectify experience" and "to confuse the effects of symbolic and real objects"; and "the commonsense attitude that both the responding subject and the aesthetic object may be conceived as real objects" (SC 37; LEE 106; SC 107). Indeed, he avers that "the habit of objectification is fundamental in human mental functioning, and no one does without it" (RF 48). He speculates that this "habit of viewing the world objectively" is "connected with though not caused by" "the acquisition of the ability to objectify experience which appears in the infant at about eighteen months of age" (SC 15)—another appeal to timing.

Plainly, Bleich thinks people can and do confuse the three classes, but chiefly for motives that are alienating or maladaptive. The conversion from "symbolic" to "real" can help to secure "value judgments," to "guard against emotion," and "to conserve political, economic, and religious authority" exerted by "the judge, the censor, and the priest" (LEE 120, 123, 110; cf. LEE 105ff). If "literacy is knowing how to use symbolic objects" and "to distinguish between real objects, symbolic objects, and people," then "only universal literacy can de-authorize" such practices (LEE 125, 110). In the meantime, readers might be made less vulnerable through Bleich's program for explicitly negotiating subjective experiences about objects.

Bleich's use of organic development and Piagetian psychology emphasizes the determining role of childhood. The child's "first eighteen months" merit special scrutiny as a time when "life is almost entirely physiological and emotional" (RF 4f). "Thought and knowledge do not begin until some time after" "the ongoing experience of peremptory feelings." Hence, "the personality is grounded in the emotional history of an individual." "This basic developmental fact finds its aftermath in adult life in the peremptory nature of emotional experience, its automatic presence in our consciousness" (RF 5). Bleich insists on the continuity from infant to adult so much as to suggest that despite his respect for emotions, he can't quite help seeing them as a primitive or regressive aspect of adulthood, rather than as a mature or productive one.[11]

Using the infant as a model wherein we need not "distinguish between the affective and the cognitive," Bleich proffers a motive for closely integrating feelings with our readings: "language is the means through which we provide ourselves with an emotional orientation in life" (SC 48; RF 112). "Language" is predictably treated in terms of organic evolution, as "part of the human means of adaptation in nature" (SC 28f). Along with Piaget, Bleich thinks that "the child's body,[12] and his consciousness of it," play an "important role" in the "motives for and the means of symbol formation" (SC 52). Before "the onset of language and symbolic representational thought in the infant," both "the affective and the cognitive" are "directly dependent on experience"; afterwards, only "affect remains experience-dependent," "while conceptual thought takes place independently of experience" (SC 45, 48). "Representational intelligence" is depicted as "an internalization, or mentalization," of the child's "sensorimotor behaviors" (SC 29). More specifically, the "overall emotional condition" of "infantile frustration" regarding "absent objects and people" is designated "the motive for the development of representational thought" (SC 50, 53). This referral of the conceptual to the sensorial parallels that of the mental to the physiological and implies that feelings afford the closest contact with reality.

Another strategic referral is the claim that "large-scale intellectual construction is achieved" via "methods identical to those used by infants in small-scale constructions" (SC 30). Similar derivations appear thematically: "reading is an outgrowth of childhood conversational activity; commenting on reading experiences is likewise derived from infantile talking habits and motives"; the "reading activity" "grows from interpersonal language contexts of early childhood"; "more complex adult functions are psychologically shaped in the example of early syntactic predications"; "the principles of taste development are the same in child and adult" (SC 297, 135, 155).

---

[11] In one, passage, the show of emotions is linked to "bad manners" (RF 10). Or, "collectivity's best image" is said to exclude "conflictual or painful feelings" (SC 278). Bleich's students also worry about seeming "corny or melodramatic," or "lowering" themselves to a "sordid level" (SC 278; RF 84).

[12] As a basis for an "ethics" without "religion or Marxism," Bleich looks to "the human body," "the primary unit" in Roger Poole's (1972) notion of "ethical space" (SC 26f).

These derivations invite us to regard a temporally prior stage as a miniature model or reduced correlate for the later ones, despite changes in functional complexity —a problem I raised for the orthodox Freudian framework embraced by Holland (p. 166f). Darwinian and Piagetian theorizing are not sufficient to support any such implication, according to which the mind of the fetus or the ape ought to be a still more basic model than the infant's, being prior in evolution. Motives of expediency in designing simpler theories of cognition and affect favor the belief that the difference between the child and the adult is more quantitative than qualitative.

Bleich himself occasionally gives reasons to suspect incisive divergences between child and adult. He allows that in "a child's language," "meanings are arbitrary and idiosyncratic much of the time"; and in infancy, "each demand is signalled in the same way—by crying" (SC 49, 155). If so, the child's language system is significantly different in regard to negotiation and differentiation, factors to which Bleich's theory assigns much prominence (cf. SC 168f, 184f, 32; LEE 127). If "it is easier to understand the connections between subjectivity and taste" (SC 155) in the child, the latter would also be less likely to manifest the "personal style" which determines one's "special way of seeing things" (RF 32) and which is supposed to make Bleich's project so urgent. If adult minds were really so childlike, Bleich's project would be pointless.

As we saw, Bleich views the adult's language as an enlarged derivate of the child's. In fact, the same "affective frustration"[13] to which Bleich attributes the rise of cognition is credited with "motivating into existence" "the first acts of predication" (SC 50). We are referred to the "widely held" thesis that "all human languages seem to be founded" on this kind of "act," which is "not simply a linguistic structure," but "the elemental form of conceptual thought" (SC 50). Unlike Holland's more Freudian approach, Bleich's sees language forms providing satisfaction more than defense.

Bleich follows standard linguistics when he divides the predication into two constituents, "topic" and "comment," but not when he claims that their "linkage" "creates a dependent relationship between two ideas that reduces the frustration of, and substitutes for, each idea's dependency on real experience" (SC 51). As evidence, Bleich contrasts "the transience of the object" with "the invariance of the name" (though this view would occur to a nominalist or idealist philosopher sooner than to a child), and notes the timing "at eighteen months" of the "change" from "one-word utterances, usually naming, to two-or-more-word grammatical usages" (SC 49, 46). "In the presyntactic period, the naming activity is at first only a coordination of vocal schemata with perceptual or motor

---

[13] Bleich's connection between "frustration" and "controlling the use of excremental matter" (SC 52) recalls Holland's link between the rise of language and "toilet training" (DY 39). But mercifully, neither critic suggests that effusive writers must have suffered from diarrhea as infants, or laconic ones from constipation.

schemata"; then comes the stage of "symbolic formation" requiring "predication" (SC 51). Bleich allows that "the comment" of a predication may be only a "behavior" and uses one such case (from Piaget) as his prime example (SC 51f). Yet he stipulates that the "comment" must be "verbal" in order to "complete the prototypical adult predication by rendering the topic independent of sensorimotor experience and establishing the autonomy of mental action" (SC 51). Still, his linguistic criteria are not too rigid: for a response statement, "just as in infantile speech, the two parts of the predication need not be grammatical in the traditional noun-verb sense" (SC 217).

These maneuvers show Bleich's ambivalence about linguistics. On the one hand, he cites the "number of linguists who have begun to question whether formal linguistic description leads to the kind of knowledge demanded by many observers' intuitive experiences of language" (SC 100). He endorses pointed critiques of the discipline: "the better a description is from a linguistic point of view, the less likely it is to reflect subjective processes" (Kintgen 1977: 11); and "the objectively descriptive language" in "linguistic philosophy is shown to be a fiction" (Fish 1973: 50) (SC 100, 123). Such problems are only to be expected, because despite its advertized concern for human intuition, post-Chomskyan grammar is a strongly objectifying theory "in the tradition of positive science" (LEE 125f). The "epistemology of transformational linguistics" is thus deemed "the same" as "the epistemology" of the "formalist criticism" Bleich roundly rejects, in which "textual evidence is gathered" "without consideration of the motivated character of each opinion" (SC 130f, 178).

On the other hand, he needs some linguistic concepts for his own project. His solution is to borrow what he requires, while dissociating it from its original theoretical contexts. "Sentences are describable with transformational rules," he concedes, but "logical explanations" are "least convincing with psychological events" (SC 131). Also, he takes care to deflate a presumption which, I surmise, few scholars defend today: "at the complex level of functioning where interpretation takes place, the subject/predicate breakdown of all sentences will not necessarily add up, through transformational calculations, to the fundamental judgment" (SC 217).

A similar linguistic ambivalence emerges in Bleich's tendency to objectify language, just the practice he ought to disown. He calls a text "an objective set of sentences" (SC 129). He tells us that "the main clause of the sentence is clear as a piece of knowledge" (apparently without communal negotiation); that "doubleness" "appears in a variety of grammatical forms," such as "two-part sentences"; or that "a pair of ambivalent feelings" inheres "in the semantic predicate" (SC 218, 129f). He casts "sentences" as independent agents that "announce" or "formulate" the "meaning," "reflect feelings," have "a superstitious character," or "represent" "different psychological initiatives" "taken with the main perception" (SC 225, 232, 129, 130). Even nontextual entities get translated into sentence categories (after the fashion of structuralism, cf. p. 234), as when "the actual interpretation" becomes "a subordinate clause in the implicit predication 'The novel means that..'"; or when "a subjective dialectic eventuates in a motivated piece of new knowledge that is observable as a predication"; or when "the act of explanatory symbolization is the same as an act of linguistic predication" (SC 217, 137; LEE 104).

This tendency is interesting because it reveals how deeply ingrained the objectification of language is in both linguistics and criticism. Even an avowed subjectivist cannot manage to escape it. A deconstructionist might discover here an instance of an "unreadable" criticism which continues to use the concepts it attacks, and which undercuts at some points what it asserts at others (p. 257). However, Bleich does not pretend to have devised a new mode of nonobjectifying discourse. On the contrary, he acknowledges that the very "foundation of language is its continual development of new objectification"; in order to "function," "the mind" requires that "the subjective construction" of "meaning" be "removed from consciousness," encouraging the "normal capacity for objectification" (SC 237, 149f). He only intends to make readers more aware of how this factor is essential for applying language to any symbolic object—an intent perhaps akin to the deconstructionist project of making readers aware how the literal is an imposition upon the figural (p. 259f).

Bleich diverges again from standard linguistics when he states that "every individual has his own idiosyncratic language system determined by the relationships in which his language developed" (SC 149). This claim befits Bleich's concern for subjective variation (that demands negotiation) and for "the emotional importance of the situations" where words "are first learned" by a "child." Bleich seems to postulate a fairly uniform language core he calls "denotation" or "nominal verbal meaning," about which "consensus" is a fairly "trivial" matter (LEE 102f; SC 95; cf. SC 112, 131) (so that Hirsch's project is superfluous). This core can be documented by "dictionary definitions," which "have no reference to particulars" (SC 149).

But aside perhaps from "formal expository discourse," "the functional meaning" of a word is rarely of this kind: "any time a word is used anew, there is a slightly new meaning for it." Bleich's "interest" is in "unique contributions" during an "act of reading where comprehension of nominal meanings is not an issue" (SC 131, 96),—e.g., for an "artistic symbol," whose "purpose" is "connotation" rather than "denotation" (LEE 103).[14] He wants readers to explore their "peremptory memories and thoughts" and "bring to consciousness" their "subjective etymology" of "words," especially those that "name" "feelings" and "affects" (SC 149).

It is uncertain just how many "language systems" Bleich postulates. His usage

---

[14] Bleich splits "denotation" from "connotation" along the axis of "real" and "imaginary" (LEE 102). This division is not the usual sense of the terms, and would be decidable only through an impractical reality test.

variously assigns such a system to a whole "community," to a "family," to one "author" or "reader," or to a single "new experience" or "poem" (SC 160, 166, 137). A "system" is said to inhere in the author's "work" or in his "biography," or in both (SC 165, 161, 160). Bleich hypothesizes occasions "when a person is motivated to make another's language his own" or to "fully integrate" the "reading experience into one's own language system" (SC 165, 137) —considerable operations if the systems are substantially idiosyncratic. Contrarily, if "knowledge of the language" of "another mind rests on knowledge of the language of one's own" (SC 263), convergence might be trivial. Bleich may, of course, be exaggerating multiplicity and difference in order to make his project of explicit negotiation seem more urgent.

The proliferation and fractionation of social and linguistic systems leaves it unclear how the author fits into an ostensibly reader-oriented theory. Sometimes, Bleich demotes the author's intention outright. "The logic of interpretation excludes consideration of whether and how the author is communicating anything to us and explains, instead, the motives and processes developed by the interpreter(s) on the interpretive occasion" (SC 95f). "The interpretation of an aesthetic object is not motivated by a wish to know the author's intention— though this is an admissable enterprise in a different context—but by the desire to create knowledge on one's own behalf and on behalf of one's community from the subjective experience of the work of art" (SC 93).

Bleich disposes of Hirsch's "validation" project with the observation that "any procedure for recovering the author's meaning is necessarily either personally or culturally subjective"; besides, "the concept of intention is different in each language relationship" (SC 94, 238). Bleich further argues that the "real" author is "permanently unavailable"; that "the reader symbolizes the author," an act "as much a perception of the text as the isolation of formal or thematic units"; and that "'knowing an author' means knowing one's own conception of the author" (SC 263, 159, 161, 259). These claims add up to a logical corollary of his thesis (cited above) that knowing a symbolic object means knowing one's concept of it—provided we overlook his denial that persons (authors) and symbolic objects get confused.

On the other hand, Bleich can't completely dispense with the author, having been initiated into his profession by Leon Edel, whose compendious research on Henry James's life must have promoted Bleich's unexpected declaration that "for me, biographical understanding becomes the starting point for response, interpretation, and literary pedagogy" (SC 160).[15] Bleich projects three schemes for solving the dilemma of how to bring the author back into a method focused on readers' experiences.

---

[15] Bleich attained "a different conception of the author" by using "the same" "documentation" as Edel (SC 262, e.d.)—the point here apparently being the subjective aspect of using biographical facts.

The first scheme is derived from the general motto: "the role of personality in response is the most fundamental fact of criticism" (RF 4). "Analogously" to his principle that "understanding" "a work of literature" can be seen as an "expression of the personalities of the readers," Bleich says: "biographies of important authors have shown that even the greatest works of literature are most comprehensively understood as expressions of the personalites of the authors." Even if we discount the self-serving desire of such "biographies" to "show" this, we find sparse evidence in Bleich's books for the dictum. He claims for example that certain "poems" of Jonathan Swift "were written in consequence" of "attempts to reconstitute parent-child relationships," Swift "being an author by profession" with "satiric talents" (SC 292). The diagnoses of psychoanalytic critics that Swift was acting under "'anal fixation'" due to "regression" are accepted as "similar conclusions in more technical terms." In either form, such accounts hardly deserve to be called the "most comprehensive": they adduce broad motives for picking a theme, but not for creating the specific poem in its attested form.

Also quite general is the thesis that a "work may be conceived" as an author's "effort to consolidate his sense of self" "at that developmental phase of his life" (SC 160). Bleich hopes that if "biographical material" is "believed to have motivated this author," "the initial acts of perception and response are that much more integrated with natural communal interest in the motives it can associate with the symbolic object" (SC 161) (a turgid way, I guess, of saying that if readers could find out the work's original motivation, their reading would be more engaging). In my view, this scheme for reimporting the author as a personality doesn't carry much conviction. Hardly anybody studies biography before "the initial acts of perception and response" to the work. Besides, Bleich implies that a biographically-oriented subjectivity is better or more legitimate—a jarring element in a theory saluting the immediate reactions of naive readers.

The second scheme is to split the author into a symbolic and a historical component. Bleich vows that "public knowledge cannot proceed" "unless there is a deliberate separation of the individually symbolized author from the author synthesized by communally accepted documentation" (SC 162). "Most criticism" "formulates interpretive judgments" "as if they were deliberately intended by the author," and does not "separate" "biographical facts from perceptual inference" (SC 159).

But this scheme doesn't fare terribly well either. For one thing, "there is no final way to decide that a particular biographical formulation" is "objectively true" (SC 259). If a "biographer" can only produce a "motivated resymbolization of 'the author,'" and the result has only the "value" of the "subjective interest the biographer has applied to the task" (SC 262f), then it's hard to imagine how "biographical facts" can be delivered at all, and hence how history could be separated from subjective projections of it. Bleich stumbles over this problem when he declares that one aspect of "Victorian" literature is "a matter of fact and not of judgment," yet a few pages later that "what is meant by 'Victorian' can only be defined as a reaction to unspoken, collective, and subjective values" (RF 90, 94; cf. RF 87).[16]

Bleich's third scheme is to blur the split again between historicizing versus symbolizing access to the author. The inspiration this time is the work of Freud, whom Bleich eulogizes, as we saw, for having made an early "attempt to change our conception of knowledge in the direction of subjectivity" (SC 31). Bleich likens the "historicity" of "authorship" to "the exact past of a patient in therapy, or the exact cause of a dream" via the reasoning that each is "a matter secondary to the productive handling of an ongoing relation" (SC 146). "Interpretation" does "not function as the recovery of original factual causes of feelings and behaviors"; it should be "conceived as independent of actual facts and as a subjectively motivated construction by both patient and therapist *after* either fact or fantasy" (SC 30f).

This "logic of interpretation" is in turn "applied" to "aesthetic objects": "the interpretation explains the effect" on the perceiver, "regardless of the artist's intention" (SC 89, e.d.). The logic is the same when Bleich insists that a "feeling is not produced by the author *telling* us anything," but by our own "capacity for response" (RF 53).[17] An analogy is proposed: "the work of art corresponds to a dream; the artist's intention to the wish motivating the dream" (SC 89). Here, the activity of imagining authors' intentions becomes an object of inquiry without worrying about historical proof or "validity" in Hirsch's sense.

In this third scheme, biographical data can hardly be as crucial as Bleich, in reverence toward Edel, said it was for responding to Henry James. Such data can help to mould one's affective reaction to the text: "respondents perceive their feelings as being regulated by an authoritative person"; "the response is caused by the individual's perception of what the statement represents about the person making it"; and "if you don't like the author as a person, you can't like the novel" (RF 92, 14). Yet if these speculations[18] are too literally combined with Bleich's notion that it is "impossible to recover an author only by reading his work" (SC 163), we get the odd conclusion that you have to read the author's biography before you can properly "respond to" or "like" the works.

All in all, Bleich's three schemes to restore the author fit neither each other nor the rest of his theory. Just as he bends one way to move away from Holland, he bends another to get closer to Edel; and neither move improves the coherence of his model of reading, to which we now turn in detail.

---

[16] Wellek and Warren, as well as Paris, consider the trait in question —authorial intrusions—a peculiar habit or personality of Thackeray, not a general one of the Victorian age (TL 223; PAF 86ff; cf. p. 219).

[17] But: "subjectively, it is not the words themselves which either conceal or reveal, but the *author*" (RF 92).

[18] Surely the "liking" of an author is hardly relevant. I like the novels of James Joyce and Thomas Mann, but believe them to have been very unlikable people. Conversely, I like Gunther Grass and Heinrich Böll as people, but not their works.

This model matches his view of "language" as "the instrument of subjectivity and intersubjectivity" (SC 28). With "symbolic works," "*all* aspects of their existence, function, and effect depend on the processes by which they are assimilated by an observer" (RF 3, e.a.). Hence, "no work even exists unless someone is reading it"; the "text" has to be "conceived as a function of some reader's mind" (SC 109). However, Bleich does not always manage to maintain so extreme a position. If a reader "converts the text into a literary work" or "produces a subjective change in the text" (SC 111; RF 21), something must have "existed" before the reader got started. Calling it a "stimulus" in behaviorist parlance (RF 5, 12, 69) only repeats the fundamental objectifying misconception of Bloomfield's (1933) linguistics, one Bleich of all people should avoid: that the comprehension of a text can sensibly be compared to the physical stimulation of a lower-order organism, with no regard for intervening cognitive processes. If Bleich genuinely can't believe that "a text actually does act on the reader" (SC 110), then "stimulus" is an egregiously unfitting designation for a text.

The "subjective re-creation" of the "work" "by a reader" is "divided into three phases—perception, affective response, and associative response" (SC 21). The initial "sensory perception of words" gets "translated" "into consciousness," that is, "converted into an imaginary context or system that is clearly within the purview" of the respondent's "subjectivity" (SC 97, 113). "The second level of feeling," the "affective response," subsumes "whatever the reader actually felt" "while reading" (RF 33). Finally, "associations" "complete the subjective definition of the affect by bringing to mind" "personal and interpersonal relationships," including the "personal meanings" of words (SC 149f).

Apparently, Bleich envisions a more text-centered initial stage of reading "the text as immediately and evaluatively perceived" (SC 125), followed by a more self-centered stage. "The first perceptual initiative toward a symbolic object" expands into "the more deliberate conceptualization" (Bleich terms it "resymbolization") which "we try to synthesize from these initiatives" (SC 96). Thence, "readers of the same text will agree" about "their sensorimotor experience of the text" and "the nominal meaning of the words" (SC 111).

This vision of the first stage is similar to that propounded by several of our critics. But the events in later stages are pictured in different ways. Bleich expects an increase in consensus, although his "associative" phrase should encourage greater diversity among individual readers. For Iser and Holland, the sequel moves ever further into the private sphere. For Jauss and Jameson (and maybe Frye), the sequel is instead a rising historical and social awareness. Thus, our critics dispute less about reading in the everyday sense than about its effects and consequences.

This divided model of reading, as well as Bleich's divided loyalty between biology and subjectivity, occasions some ambivalence about how evidence can be gathered. On one side, Bleich acts confident: "there will always be a direct correspondence between the nature of the response and the manner in which it is offered"; "there is a discoverable causal relationship between the conscious judgment and the earlier subjective reaction"; "the affective evaluation of any perceived literary unit can be observed and recorded"; "the feelings" of "affect" "are usually accompanied by physiological correlatives" including "changes in heartrate, perspiration, respiration" that are "easy to spot" (RF 10, 19; SC 148; RF 11).

But on the other side, he expresses reservations: "the actual reading experience is as unsusceptible of recording as the actual dream"; "it is not easy to distinguish immediately the exact causes of these responses"; "it is difficult to estimate the role that perception of the reading experience plays in the response"; "it is usually not possible to observe exactly" what "objects" "mean to children at any given moment"; "there is no way we can tell if the language of the work occasions Ms. B.'s thoughts" (SC 148; RF 10; SC 173, 113, 188).

We are thus left in doubt about the means for "learning to disclose the series of subjective events which always precedes the announcement of a judgment" and for "demonstrating their causal relationship with this judgment" (RF 9). Bleich must know that it is hardly feasible to *observe* a meaning, or the cause of a meaning; at most, we can observe human actions which, in our interpretation, indicate or presuppose that a meaning has been activated. As he says, "interpretation is not a decoding or an analytical process; it is a synthesis of a new meaning" within "the experiential circumstance" "created" by "the present perception" (SC 95, e.d.).

I can't help wondering if Bleich's emphasis on feelings and bodily correlates might not after all betray a concealed desire to trade meaning for a more readily observable and, in the traditional sense, objective, substrate—just what he accuses other subjectivists of wanting to do (cf. SC 19, 112, 114, 124). Certainly, positivistic biology and psychology deemed it more scientific to study emotions and organic responses than meanings.

Unlike Fish, Bleich doubts that "any interpretive communities exist as organized, ongoing forums for the development of new knowledge outside the quantitative sciences" (SC 164f). However, "interpretive communities and other societal groupings" might be "defined" by "collective interests" whose "complex fluctuations" can be explored by means of "response statements" (SC 265). "Habits of thought" might be the "instruments" for this project, such as: "the fundamental human tendency to perceive automatically" through "unconsciously established patterns of perception"; the "cultural habit" of "announcing interpretive judgments in moral terms"; "the universal wish to validate" "our own feelings by discovering them in others," fostering "the collective establishment of values"; the "universal psychological habit" of "depersonalizing" when reporting a "response"; the "common" "psychological habits" of "shifting the discussion" to "large terms" in order to "dissolve the personal issue," or of "breaking up" one's "experience of the story" into oneself, "the author, the author's opinions, and the 'facts' that the story relates"; "the natural tendency" "to see the work in terms of one overriding thought" "and then to reconstruct the poem according to this thought"; and so on (SC 265, 158; RF 67, 81, 48, 47, 52, 28).

Since these "tendencies" or "habits" are typically invoked when Bleich wants to account for respondents' reports, his discovery of cultural parameters appears chiefly heuristic, drawing on plausible motivations for specific data. Whether these parameters are "common" or even "universal," as he claims (cf. RF 45, 47, 52, 88, 91), is not demonstrable on that basis alone; they may be extrapolated from "professional criticism" (cf. RF 48). In any case, the implication would be that negotiation is called for not merely because responses vary, but because they coincide in ways that deny or conceal one's own creative contributions. Readers can profit by becoming aware of such "habits," and trying to counteract them by injecting more creativity and personal nuance into their experiences.

To probe the empirical status of response, Bleich is developing a detailed practical methodology for "actively integrating" the "*study* of reading and interpretation" with the "*experience*" (SC 99). He declares his willingness to recognize "a truth value in any seriously given reading," according to the categories "disclosed by" the "response statements" (SC 112, 266). Like most of the critics I survey, he feels that "to find complexity and value in a variety of readings" is "more relevant to literary study than the use of standards of interpretive accuracy" (SC 104). Moreover, he views "motives" as "more decisive in determining correctness" than the "objective perception of meaning" (SC 95). "Idiosyncratic readings" —those which, for instance, "stress certain features over others" or include "personal embellishments of something which most professional critics agree is there" —offer "instances of negotiable subjective knowledge and collective interest" (SC 273, 285; RF 28f). "So-called 'mistakes' are a part of the individual's perceptual style just as are the omissions, the exaggerations, and the superfluous material that almost everyone will insert" (RF 32; cf. RF 25f). This conclusion may sound vaguely Freudian, although Bleich, unlike Holland, does not propose to infer and analyze the reader's personality from the response (cf. RF 12f).

Despite his proclaimed tolerance, Bleich won't accept all responses indiscriminately. "Once the personal dimensions of literary meaning constructions are introduced," he reassures his colleagues, "it is an utter necessity to discipline their presentation"; otherwise, the "discussion" may become "irresponsible or lawless" and "any claim would be permissible" (SC 227, 189). "One cannot write just anything and expect it to be received as a genuine emotional response"; "superficial or trivial" material indicates a failure to "respond" (RF 107).

Although Bleich warns that "all feelings and responses are not equally valuable," "honest," or "consequential" (RF 15), his demonstrations provide only very rough criteria to judge response statements. He is impressed when a response is produced with "fluency and eagerness," or when it seems "articulate," "thoughtful," "careful," "intelligent," or "observant" (SC 109; RF 51, 54)—much the same criteria English teachers traditionally use to judge compositions about literature. Yet he realizes he may be relying on indicators of "verbal skill" rather than of a "strong desire to express" oneself, and can't see how "teachers" might "distinguish" between these factors (RF 37).

The importance of authenticity in response is plain. Bleich sounds optimistic: "once an experience is subject to articulation, it loses its intractable quality and becomes susceptible to systematic comprehension" (RF 112). "The thoughts following the recording of an affective response" may not be the latter's "subjective definition," but "when thoughts appear, the conscious mind will test through simple acts of memory to see if the new thoughts do symbolize the named feeling" (SC 150). As further guidelines, Bleich opines that "long and substantial responses cannot be produced by someone who is 'lying' emotionally"; and that "the authenticity of the response is documented by the fluency of the associations, their conversational presentation, their line-by-line sequence, and most importantly, by the single theme they present" (RF 107, 43).[19]

Still, I can't tell if these are the criteria Bleich really uses when he claims a respondent is "describing the actual effect he felt while reading the poem" and "reporting directly on his perceptions during the reading experience" (RF 33; SC 178); or whether Bleich is just relying on his own "authority" as an "observer" with "experience in this kind of situation" (SC 169). As an added resource, he feels able to "check" and "validate" "inferences" and "proposals" about "a reading experience" through "discussion" with the respondent (SC 178, 188, 236; cf. SC 198). For example, he might learn from "further discussion with her" whether a student "felt more deeply and complexly" than she reported (RF 35).

All this presupposes that people are able to express what they feel in reliable ways. My own impression from studying readers' protocols is that the reporting is quite capable of shaping or transforming the cognitive and emotive activities it purports to present. Several reasons may apply: unfamiliarity with such reporting, wishful thinking about one's own mind or personality, desire to impress the interviewer, or simple lack of clear data about one's own mentations, past or present.

Even Bleich's own books contain numerous theses implying problems for respondents. A "difficulty" can "appear in trying to distinguish original feelings from feelings about feelings" (SC 236). Moreover, if Bleich subscribes to Freudian theory, he would have to assume that reports involve repression and defense, as he seems to do when admonishing that "feelings appearing in response to symbolic objects are frequently not to be taken at face value, since feelings of pathos and fear are commonly the motives for our perceptual initiative" (SC 120). If "conflictual or painful feelings," such as "adolescent loneliness in American culture," "are rarely included" among "a society's collective interests" (SC

---

[19] A student's "answering my initiating questions comprehensively" provides a "narcissistic reason" to "consider it psychologically authentic" (SC 141).

278, 281), people's "natural resistance" against giving "major credit" to "emotional" events (RF 67f) should be particularly strong here. A comparable dilemma is implied by Bleich's thesis that "certain collective values inhibit the search for facts" (SC 266).

If "perceptual distortion and idiosyncratic interpretation" are "universal facts," as Bleich contends (SC 110), then he is again deconstructing himself by using his own version as the undistorted one for rating others. Sometimes, he singles out students' "misinterpretations," remarking that "the 'real' parts of the poem got distorted,"[20] "exaggerated," or "altogether misinterpreted" (SC 103f; RF 29, 31, 28). Other times, he decides the "poem" has been "perceived correctly" (RF 24). He must also be applying his personal expertise to detect practical obstacles: a "denial" "covers up the real analogy"; an "individual's preoccupations interfered with perception"; "the need for an intellectual thesis created an intervening idea that was untrue to her response"; and so forth (RF 38, 31, 69).

Bleich's global thesis that "the true scope of feeling" is "essentially denied by intellectual reformulations" (RF 69) seems indeed to drive a wedge between the childlike responding and the adultlike reporting—and possibly to split off "feelings" from critical discussion altogether. If readers must "abandon customary habits of abstractive definition" and "revoke" "familiar social constraints of conversation" in order to "report without censorship" (SC 150), then they will need to learn to navigate unfamiliar tasks—whether or not "the use of perception, affect, and association as a means of determining interpretive responsibility is rooted in the normal function of language" (SC 189, e.d.).

Hence, Bleich has to train his readers, not just observe and record them. Though he deprecates Holland for "ruling out" the "relationship between himself and the respondents as a salient factor in the creation of response" (SC 116), he concedes the "importance" of his own "image and relationship to the respondent" (SC 116, 215, 174). He allows that "most respondents" "have no way of translating the vague idea of response into an actual document without discussing the matter" (SC 198). On occasion, he notes when a respondent's "cordial relationship with me and a cooperative attitude toward the ideas I propose obviously contributed," especially when "she read my book" and "heard my discussions of it." Bleich may not pay his respondents as Holland did, but students are after all performing for a grade. At the very least, they are likely to be selective in preferring certain kinds of materials to report.

After Bleich's students read, they get requests like: "record all your feelings about the story—your affective and associative responses" (RF 101).[21] A protocol

---

[20] Bleich warns that "'distortion'" "is just the word to be avoided" (RF 32).

[21] Bleich elicits two sets of responses, one he considers "affective" (RF 33-39) and one he considers "associative" (RF 39-48). The latter are adjudged "the most complex but the most useful form for expressing feelings about literature" and the clearest exhibition of the "demands of the personality at the time of the reading" (RF 48).

is made as a second text about how it felt to read the original text, the central problem now becoming the relationship between these two texts. To be consistent, Bleich should expect his students' protocols to manifest the same high degree of subjectivity as their responses to a poem or a story. But Bleich is optimistic, as we noticed, that the report can be a fairly close approximation of what happened while reading. Provided that the "response statement does not have an independent logic or meaning" (SC 198), as Bleich thinks (and I don't), it should be a transparent derivative of the original.

Similarly, he feels we can "safely assume" that "the prose presentation of a poem represents the reader's subjective perception of it" (RF 21). As long as "the original perception" of some "motif" was "spontaneous," an "increase in consciousness" "does not detract from involvement" (RF 56). If a "delay in recording the response" intervenes, "a judgmental overlay will become part of what seems to be the response" (SC 236). Just as Freud regarded dreamers' reports as integral parts of their dreams, Bleich can include his students' protocols within their total experience. Yet since, along with Wittgenstein, Bleich would include the entire work of interpretation in the dream (cf. SC 69-84), he ought to incorporate his own analysis and commentary for student responses as part of his theory; and he does so only marginally in his books.

Bleich's avowed goal is "the development of knowledge about a reading experience," not about the "reader" or "some 'reality' outside" (SC 169). He wants "to establish a conceptual constraint on the tendency to discuss each reader's personal problems," and to avoid "clinical judgments in the classroom" or "clinically articulated intrusions into personality" (SC 169, 150). "In no instance is one ever analyzing a person," he warns; "no respondent is a patient" (RF 13). But he admits the difficulty of "developing knowledge from their responses without making the respondents themselves" "the primary objects of investigation" and "attention" (SC 188, 179). Such is likely to occur once we assume that "associations" "represent a sample of what aspect of the personality was engaged in this experience" (RF 15).

Bleich's analyses do contain statements which resemble judgments about persons (though he may not offer them to the students): "Ms. M. is in Erikson's 'intimacy-isolation' stage"[22] and "must feel that part of her child-rearing responsibility is 'displaced' onto the importance of finishing at the university"; "Ms. R." feels "frustration as a result of masculine shortcomings"; when "Ms. A." "observes aggression and hostility emerging, guilt and fear follow immediately"; and so forth (SC 200, 186, 233). Nonetheless, these occasional remarks are side-products of an intensely experiential focus on reading, rather than, as in Holland's research (5RR), the central findings of a deliberate personality probe.

The respondents report profusely on their childhood. They talk about "when I

---

[22] Bleich expresses a reservation here: "in general, such judgments should be reserved for the discussion of children's responses," or for "face-to-face negotiation" (SC 201).

was a little kid" or "when I was a small child," giving such ages as "five" and "eight" (SC 182, 140, 177). They tell about their parents, ranging from the prosaic ("my mother never shouted at me") to the fantastic ("I did have fears of my mother turning into a werewolf") (SC 207, 203). They make admissions, such as: "I'm extremely ashamed of this, but I am still unable to escape the nostalgia of childhood daydreams" (SC 220). I suspect the influence of Bleich's training when a student makes an announcement like: "notably, my responses are childhood recollections" (SC 231). One respondent who brings in a flurry of personal incidents finally gets stuck: "I've been trying desperately to come up with some kind of counterpart incident in my life," "but I can't" (SC 247). Such statements hint at the pressure Bleich's students sense to report private associations, whether or not the latter occurred spontaneously during reading.

Some reports suggest that readers improved their attitudes, in conformity with Bleich's thesis that "the recording of response" can be "the agency of change" or an "instance of growth" (SC 211). Here too, an un-Darwinian "progress toward an ideal" may be implied (cf. SC 26) "Knowledge of one's taste greatly increases its versatility" and renders it an "instrument of self-enhancement and self-possession" (SC 210f). People who realize the "relativity" of "judgment" can "minimize the number of negative value judgments" and "reduce the tendency to communicate" "taste" "in moral terms" (SC 210). In one case, the therapeutic benefit was clear: "repeated contact with me" "helped to precipitate in Mr. D. a shift in self-identification from author to teacher, a profession he subsequently followed" (SC 258).

However, most of Bleich's illustrations of benefits are more specifically concerned with literary appreciation, maybe so as to attract teachers to his method. After "recording the response," one reader attained "fascination, and 'perhaps satisfaction and enjoyment'" in place of "her previous dislike" for the work (SC 200). One asserted: "my imagination transports me beyond reality into a creation of my own making" (SC 175). Another reader found "her interest is now more commensurate with her belief that the work is a masterpiece" (SC 208). Still another got the "clear premium" of a "more satisfying sense of why he was interested in the author and his work" (SC 245). And another had the "enormous comfort and pleasure" of "knowing that the world-famous artist James Joyce had had a boyhood" like his, and that "his analogous frustrations" might well be "the origins of great success" (SC 240).

A different benefit might accrue if a reader "uses the response to 'confess'" (SC 243), or to analyze one's preoccupations (a commonality, as Freud perceived, of Catholic confessional and psychotherapy). One reader admitted "the urge to surrender myself" "to the most demonic and evil wishes of my mind" (SC 252). Another diagnosed "two fiercely irreconcilable strains which run through my character" (SC 253). Bleich's theory got dutifully played back when a student commented that "through a subjective approach, I accept the responsibility for focusing on particular features of a story and attempt to understand why I have done so" (SC 197). Students also offered lay psychoanalysis: "the quest for peak experiences"[23] in a Hawthorne story "can only be a defense for the real wish for total regression"; or a James story "allows me to identify with strength, purge some guilt, and displace some personal responsibility" (SC 177, 197).

Though Bleich's theory may cite Piaget more than Freud, the latter's ideas turn up in practice. However, since Bleich denounces "intrusions" into the "personality" of students, (SC 150), he, like the early Holland, practices on himself. His response to a Lawrence story includes such Freudian self-displays as this: "when Paul names the horse, he brings my unnamed fears to consciousness and thus into control"; "to preserve" a "psychological pleasure" "which exists on a permanent basis in my personality," "I hide the nature of my own fears" (RF 59, 62). Bleich assumes that "in a boy or young man, there is a special guilt associated with the death of his father, the suspicion that he wished it all along" (RF 60).

Bleich has a field day with *Turn of the Screw*. Though he doesn't play upon the story's title (which seems to invite it), he reads "Peter Quint" as "male and female genitals" "(Peter, a slang word for penis, and Quint, from the Chaucerian 'Quainte' for cunt)" (RF 76).[24] He fantasizes himself "tremendously involved with a powerful sexual woman" (the governess) "who does not admit her sexuality to me"; this "represents" "in real life" "the feelings of the oedipal child toward his mother, conscious of her sexuality, yet confused by it" (RF 76). His "solution" is "the usual oedipal" one, "identifying with father," represented here by Leon Edel, "the same age as my father" and "evoking the same response in me," also being "my first source of enlightenment about the story" (RF 76f, e.d.). At the conclusion, Bleich has "transformed" himself "from a naughty boy to knowledgeable man" (RF 78)—an oddly happy ending for James's sinister tale.

If "it is not possible to have an interpretation of a work in isolation from a community" (SC 296), then it would be useful for readers to negotiate their responses with their teacher and with each other. "The assumption of the subjective paradigm is that the collective similarity of responses can be determined only by each individual's announcement of his response and communally motivated negotiative comparison" (SC 98). "It is not likely that the development of subjective knowledge can proceed without a verbal document and its verbal negotiation" (SC 167). "Only the gradual disclosure of perception, response, and interpretation on each reader's part can maintain the discipline of an acknowledged subjectivity capable of being held in common" (SC 138).

Since "language requires the least specialized interpretive skill," "subjective criticism" might "involve every interested individual" (SC 167, 297). "Any state-

---

[23] "Peak experiences" is a conception of Abraham Maslow's (cf. pp. 207-12).

[24] Fiedler's opinion of James being "reluctant to make explicit the genital facts" of a story (LD 307) seems more plausible than that of James devising sexual anagrams from slang and philology. As Fiedler also says, James is "hopelessly innocent, an innocent voyeur," "a child" (LD 344).

ment that a reader considers a response is negotiable into knowledge" (SC 168). "The principle of negotiation is that each new public perception of judgment is given in its subjective dimension and each new pedagogical purpose is considered acceptable by the community" (SC 189). Ideally, "each reader will alter his sense of reading as negotiations proceed," and take advantage of "a separate occasion for knowledge" (SC 188).

One reward could be to become more aware of values. "Evaluation is a natural and automatic feature of perception," especially of "symbolic objects" (SC 153). The "affect" of "response" is a "visible form of valuation that cannot be separated from perception" (SC 120). Also, "motivation is more clearly seen" in "evaluative acts" than in "interpretive" ones (LEE 105). Even if we suppose that "the critic always consciously serves personal and collective purposes by presenting his evaluative propositions" (LEE 101), these "motives" are "usually" "purposely ignored" (SC 266), particularly by critics who lay claim to an objective stance. As a result, "Plato's attitudes" were able to continue functioning as "automatic and unconscious[25] intellectual factors" in "literary evaluation" (LEE 105), engendering a tradition of elitism, misogyny, and mistrust toward emotions, from Aristotle down to Arnold and Eliot (cf. LEE 106, 108ff, 112, 116f, 119). Bleich evidently hopes that a public negotiation of values may help dislodge this tradition and give people better insights for forming and regulating their taste—more a utopian than a Darwinian projection, as I already suggested.

Unlike many theoreticians, Bleich makes a direct appeal to teachers of literature. He cites studies showing "epistemology is decisively tied to how each teacher conceives his classroom authority" (SC 106). "Mutual awareness of the motives in the development of objective knowledge" would "involve significant changes" in "pedagogical relationships" and "institutions" (SC 146)—of whose current state Bleich paints a bleak picture. "We expect that only in rare instances will students come to 'enjoy' what we are teaching" (RF 1). "Classroom routine diverts the emotional demands of the classroom situation" (RF 2). "Even in graduate school, the process of learning is still through emulation rather than instruction" (RF 73). "The preestablished authority of the teacher to pass judgment" makes him "feel he need not give reasons for his evaluations" (SC 151). "The *authority* is automatically objective, which is authoritarianism."

For Bleich's new method, teachers should have some "work in personality development and relevant psychologies,"[26] but should not make any "prolonged classroom presentation of personality theory"; "it is far more important to demonstrate the importance of emotional response than to articulate it" (SC 155; RF 5). "Subjective knowledge" should optimally be "developed independently" by the learner "without coaching or training" (SC 191).

---

[25] A moment ago, we were told that "collective purposes" were "consciously served" (LEE 100), but this later formulation seems more believable.

[26] Elsewhere, "special psychological knowledge" is declared unnecessary—"only traditional amounts of reading and patience are required" (SC 198).

Bleich's "course of study" "proceeds outward" "from the most primitive, automatic, and unconscious experiences to the most complex and lately developed
capacities" (RF 5)—imitating the putative evolution of mental development
along Darwinian and Piagetian lines. It is "reassuring to most students to delay
the application of traditional intellectual categories until the emotional groundwork has been laid" (RF 71). This tactic might help to "reduce or eliminate the
normal diffidence most students have about intellectual or academic enterprises"
(RF 70f).

Specifically, teachers are advised to pose certain tasks for their students. The
latter can explore their emotions by describing a "dream," an "argument with a
parent," "the most successful moment in your life," a "moment of great embarrassment or shame," or the times when "you cried in a movie" or "rooted for a
team"; or they can dwell upon their attachment to a "favorite doll" or "item of
clothing" (RF 97ff). In a more literary domain, students might identify the "most
important word," "passage," "aspect," or "element" in a text (cf. RF 50ff, 63ff,
70ff, 101); and the teacher can participate as well. The subjective viewpoint can
be reinforced with further tactics: by testing whether students "put" the "meaning
in the story"; by finding "opinions" in "critical interpretations" of a work; by
sensing "the author's presence in the story"; by "drawing" an "object" "along with
four or five other" students and seeing the "differences"; and so on (RF 100ff).

Undoubtedly, this practical side must be considered when estimating the
status of Bleich's model. His theoretical claims for his approach are somewhat
too strong. He is forced into the self-deconstructive position of awarding his
theory a degree of truth and validity the theory itself undercuts. He sees his
"paradigm" as the right one; others, like the objectivist, theological, and moralist
ones, are "fraudulent," "false," and "dangerous" (LEE 123; RF 3, 49). His stance
is like purporting to hold the truth about the impossibility of purporting to hold
the truth—of giving the true reason why, "in literary response and judgment,"
"truth is not a viable goal," but at most something "all parties *feel* when an
interpretation is accepted" (RF 48; SC 85). If "in subjective criticism, no existing
standards are necessarily right or wrong" (SC 159), the rightness of his paradigm
can only be the outcome of negotiation with other theorists and paradigms. So
far, he has shown far more inclination to attack them than to negotiate, as we
saw. Another duplicity might be sensed in leveling ethical arguments against
moralists (cf. SC 110, 156ff; LEE 105ff, 118f); but he views his positive, adaptive
ethics as the opposite of traditional constricting morality.

In my view, all his biological and psychological latticework can't conceal the
utopian nature of Bleich's undertaking. Like Arnold, he aspires to be "a critic"
who acts as "a servant of evolution" (LEE 111), though the declared goals are
radically different this time: not Arnold's elitist refinement of taste, but an involvement of "every interested individual—of any age—in the formulation of
consequential knowledge" (SC 297). "Each person's most urgent motivations are
to understand himself"; and "the simplest path" is the "awareness of one's own
system as the agency of consciousness and self-direction" (SC 297f; cf. Ch. 2).

If "we commonly read the work of others to know our own minds," "reading can produce a new understanding of oneself," and "a new conception of one's values and tastes as well as one's prejudices and learning difficulties" (RF 3f). And if "the cumulative nature of the reading experience acts out in miniature the cumulative nature of all subjective experience," the "cycle of literary evaluation" "creates new language initiatives" that are "contributions to the epistemology of language" (RF 67; LEE 128). We might "transform knowledge from something to be acquired into something that can be synthesized on behalf of oneself and one's community" (SC 99). In this manner, "subjectivity does not do away with the social goal of interpretive work," but "gives" it "new authority and binding power" "while reducing its pretended scope to more realistic size" (RF 70).

11

Bernard Paris[1]

During the last century or so, psychological research was dominated by two major "forces." "Behaviorism" viewed the human being as an "organism" whose activities are shaped by "conditioning" in repeated encounters with its environment. Freudian "psychoanalysis" viewed the human being as a "psyche" whose activities are patterned by infantile experiences within the family (cf. Ch. 9). Both views were heavily pessimistic and reductive, suggesting human life is formed by powerful agencies we can scarcely control or change—and thereby providing alibis for human inadequacy. The creativity of the intellect was considered a marginal or compensatory superstructuring on top of one's biological constitution. Hence, neither view had much to say about the utopian imperative of art toward an enlarged understanding of the human situation (cf. Ch. 2).

"Third force psychology" is a "humanistic" alternative to these two "forces." Its "different philosophy of human nature" projects "greater optimism" and "a more holistic approach to human behavior" (3FL 11). Its emphatic concern is the "evolutionary constructive force" that "urges us to realize our given potentialities." We should seek "self-knowledge" as a "means of liberating the forces of spontaneous growth" (Horney 1950: 15). The ultimate goal is "self-actualization," an "episode" in which "the powers of the person come together in a particularly efficient way" (3FL 35).

The "third force" is utopian (in the sense of Ch. 1) because it is always moving toward realization. Unlike Freud, third force psychologists assert that our "basic needs are not in conflict with civilization and our higher values" (3FL 30). A "conflict" between "reason and impulse" only "comes from deprivation." Hence, the "possibility of health," of being "happy, harmonious, and creative" (PAF 36) is not foreclosed, though it cannot be taken for granted (cf. JA 36). "Basic" "needs" are "built into the nature of all men" and "must be gratified" if "development" is to be "healthy" (PAF 31). But these needs are "easily suppressed, repressed," "masked, or modified by habits, suggestions, by cultural pressure, by

---

[1] The key to Paris quotations is: HAR: Experience of Thomas Hardy (1976); HEA: "Hush, Hush! He's a Human Being!": A Psychological Approach to Heathcliff (1982); JA: *Character and Conflict in Jane Austen's Novels* (1978); PAF: *A Psychological Approach to Fiction* (1974); and 3FL: *Third Force Psychology and the Study of Literature* (1986).

guilt, and so on" (Maslow 1954: 129). The "real self" is continually threatened, and every choice made against its "interest" incurs "self-hatred" (3FL 52). Hence, the optimism of third force psychology, often reproached with shallowness, for instance, by the pessimistic Fiedler (NT 310), is quite subdued and far from naive.[2]

Deciding the "truth" in the theories of Skinner, Freud, Horney, or Maslow is quite problematic. In the human sciences, to which psychology irretrievably belongs, every theory entails a decision to regard the human being in a certain way. The vital question is what consequences a particular view entails. The behaviorists produced a simple and unified theory by purporting to assert only what anyone can directly observe who does an experiment. They resolved the problem of the mind by ignoring its essentially mentalistic aspects. Freudians preferred to see the mind as complex and divided; they postulated, and concentrated on, another mind, beyond (or "under") the conscious one, which cannot be directly observed but only detected through certain channels, such as dreams and slips of the tongue.

The methods of proof accredited by these two forces were correspondingly different. Behaviorism used brief, timed stimulus-response experiments with tight controls and immediate results. Freudianism used long-term analyst-patient therapy in informal settings and with very gradual results. Both approaches assumed deterministic causalities, but the Freudian one interposed an elaborate hermeneutics for images and emotions in between an experience and a patient's action. Hypotheses were accordingly vulnerable if taken as factual statements about the patient's life history. And as I noted (p. 181), later empirical tests disconfirmed some of Freud's major theses.

Third force theorizing seeks to navigate in between simplicity and complexity, between unity and division. Indeed, its humanism and optimism includes the tenet that just such a balancing of extremes leads toward mental health. In place of the predestined triumph of biological or infantile determinism, a "hierarchy" of human needs is postulated that "will determine what we want, but not how we will act" (3FL 27). "Most behavior" is recognized to be "multi-motivated." Hence, third force analysis does not purport to predict or uncover causalities between the personality and some specific action or incident (such as the "stimulus" or "trauma" of the older psychologies). Its hermeneutics remains fully heuristic, a mode of understanding motivations rather than an explanation of causes and effects.

---

[2] Naive optimism is indeed critiqued through Horney's analysis of the "idealized images" that impel people to "reach out for greater knowledge, wisdom, virtue, or powers than are given to human beings" (3FL 53f). This "falsification of reality" is contrasted with how the "healthy individual reaches for the possible" and "works within cosmic and human limitations" (3FL 54). Horney quaintly equates "pride" and "the search for glory" with "the devil's pact" wherein "the individual" "loses his soul—his real self" (3FL 54).

Turned back on themselves, the three psychologies look very diverse. Behaviorists would believe in their theory because they have been conditioned to do so. Freudians would believe in theirs in order to gratify wish-fulfillment fantasies. Third force theorists would mount a project to actualize themselves by perceiving the world through the perspectives of other people. Hence, the third force approach can apply to itself with a more plausible motive and authority than can the two older approaches.

In the third force vision, the personality is a unit containing conflicts, yet more coherent than shattered. "Needs" form an orderly "hierarchy," all of whose constituents require gratification, the lower ones ("physiological satisfaction," "safety," "love," etc.) before the higher ones (especially "'intellectual issues'"); the latter are not, however, simply "reducible to the lower" (PAF 31ff, 37; HM9f). The personality develops in a healthy way by balancing as many needs as possible, and becomes fixated or neurotic when it ceases to do so. Freud's "pleasure principle" (focused on "lower needs," PAF 34) is revised to include the "'pleasure and fulfillment found in the encounter with an expanding reality and in the development, exercise, and realization'" of "'growing capacities, skills, and powers'" (Schachtel, 1959: 9) (3FL 42). These new "values" are "conducive to a fuller realization of human potentialities" (3FL 34).

"Self-actualizing" persons feel no "inhibition" in "experiencing and expressing the real self" (3FL 39). They "press toward" "good values": "truth, goodness, beauty, wholeness," "uniqueness, perfection," "justice, order, simplicity, richness, effortlessness, playfulness, self-sufficiency," "serenity, kindness, courage, honesty, love, unselfishness" and so on (3FL 37, 39). These values reflect the standards people would choose if "their natures" "were highly enough evolved to give them the opportunity for choice" (3FL 34). "The rewards of self-actualization" are the driving impulse in human motivation, rather than the striving for sensory rewards envisioned in Freudian and behaviorist approaches.

Also utopian is the description of "essential human nature" via the "observation" of "the people in whom this nature has achieved its fullest growth," giving "an idea what would be good" for "all people."[3] Paris sees some "difficulties" with the notion that "an adequate conception of human nature and human values can be derived only from the perspective of the most fully evolved people" (3FL 28). He "believes" this notion "but doesn't know how you validate your selection" of "people" (letter to me). The "misguided values of individual societies" make it hard to define "a universal norm of psychological health" whose values are "generated by the nature of the species" (3FL 93).

Paris notes that "all value systems" based on an "essential human nature" entail a "leap of faith"; "there is no one perspective which does not involve some distortion" (3FL 34, 28; PAF 34). Moreover, one's "values" "shift" as certain

---

[3] Paris does not want the "intrinsic conscience" implicit in this standard to be associated with the "superego" (3FL 37), perhaps because the latter prohibits more often than animates.

"needs" are "gratified" and their "satisfiers" are "underestimated" or "derogated" (PAF 33). These reservations are fully reasonable, but it is hardly reassuring to contemplate that "the vast majority" are "imperfectly developed people" who "do not constitute the essential nature of man" (PAF 31). In Maslow's estimate in fact, "self-actualizing people comprise no more than one percent of the population and perhaps less" (PAF 36). Again, we sense how wary the optimism of this approach really is.

"Self-actualizing persons" are the most likely to be "objective," that is, their "'thought'" can "'contemplate its object fully and recognize it in relative independence from the thinker's needs and fears'" (Schachtel 1959: 273) (3FL 40). This "allocentric" viewpoint enables "complete openness and receptivity" toward "the object" "perceived in its suchness" and a "clearer perception of what is there," including "seeing other people as they are in and for themselves" (3FL 40f). "Defensive people," in contrast, are "subject-centered" and "autocentric": they do not "focus on the object in its own right" (3FL 40). This opposition prolongs the old subject-object dichotomy too readily (cf. Ch. 1); we might say instead that in processing new experiences, "allocentric" perception seeks evolution, whereas "autocentric" seeks confirmation.

Opposite this brighter prospect of an "allocentric" realization of human potential lies the darker prospect developed by Horney of "the neurotic processes which occur as a result of the frustration of the needs for safety, love, and self-esteem" (PAF 35). She devised a typology of "defenses" with "three main ways" a person can "establish himself safely" "in a threatening world" (PAF 55). A "bargain" is struck with "fate" to act a certain way in exchange for certain advantages.[4] A person can "adopt the compliant or self-effacing solution and move *toward* people" by seeking "affection and approval"; "he can develop the aggressive or expansive solution and move *against* people" by seeking "mastery"; "or he can become detached or resigned and move *away from* people" by "seeking privacy" and "secrecy" (PAF 55, 57, 59, 63). The "expansive" type is further subdivided. The "narcissistic person seeks to master life 'by self-admiration and the exercise of charm'" and is firmly convinced of "'his greatness and uniqueness'" (Horney, 1950: 194) (PAF 60). The "perfectionistic person 'feels superior because of his high standards, moral and intellectual.'" The "aggressive-vindictive person" is "ruthless and cynical" in pursuing "triumphs" over every "rival" (PAF 60f). These three subtypes contrast starkly with the "compliant" person, who strives to be "good, self-effacing, loving and weak," needing to be "part of something larger and more powerful than himself"; and with the "detached" person, who "disdains the pursuit of worldly success and has a profound aversion to effort" (PAF 57, 62).

"In order to gain some sense of wholeness and ability to function," an "indi-

---

[4] "Bargains with Fate" is a phrase from Horney (1950) and figures in the title for Paris's forthcoming book on the characters of Shakespeare.

vidual" "will emphasize one move more than the others," which then "operate unconsciously" and "manifest themselves in devious and disguised ways" (PAF 55f)—thus entering and controlling the domain Freudians call "the uncon-scious." The "neurotic" nature of the three "character types" results from "over-emphasizing" one "element" of "basic anxiety": "helplessness," "hostility," or "isolation," respectively.

All these types and subtypes are seldom found in pure form either "in litera-ture" or "in life" (PAF 56). More common are mixtures situated within "an indeterminate range of intermediate structures" (Horney 1950: 191). We should therefore use terms like "healthy" and "neurotic" not for people, but for ten-dencies and episodes in human life and for the accompanying processes of interpretation. In healthy episodes, experiences are used constructively to im-prove the scope and coherence of one's understanding of life. In neurotic ones, experiences are used destructively to draw lessons about the insensitivity or perversity of "fate."

The neurotic impulse is thus to push one's problems outside oneself, "external-izing" them so as to "not be aware" of them (3FL 58). One "interprets personal problems" as "historical or existential" (3FL 32). Or, one avoids conflicting insights by means of "projection": "choosing those whose personalities and value systems are parallel to one's own" (3FL 35) and avoiding any others. As such impulses suggest, we might subsume all neuroses under the general concept of a refusal of awareness, a denial of occasions for knowing and evolving. Therapy would then be a process of transcending that refusal; and the chance that art might offer one such therapeutic occasion will be the theme of this chapter.

Conceiving the personality to be a spectrum of tendencies, episodes, and mixed types provides a less drastic view of it. Admittedly, defensive persons suffer significant drawbacks: being prone to "distortion"; "accounting for all needs in terms of the ones in focus"; being "alienated from their spontaneous desires"; or tending to "overrate their capacities," make "exaggerated claims," and "equate standards and actualities" (3FL 29, 51, 49). Nonetheless, recognized social vir-tues can be attained and can even become "necessary" to one's "defense system" (3FL 47). The "compliant defense" favors the "values" of "goodness, sympathy, love, generosity, unselfishness," and the "belief in the goodness of human na-ture." The "values" of the "aggressive" person include "success, prestige," "recog-nition," "efficiency," "resourcefulness," and a "zest for living" (3FL 48f). The "narcissistic" person attains "buoyancy," "perennial youthfulness," and "opti-mism," and wants to be "the benefactor of mankind" (3FL 49). The "perfec-tionistic" person "strives for the highest degree of excellence" (PAF 60). The "detached" person is capable of "serenity," "imagination," "ironic humor," and "stoical dignity," and respects "freedom," "individuality," and "self-reliance" (3FL 51f). Only "arrogant-vindictive" persons have scant virtues, beyond being "competitive" and "self-sufficient" (3FL 50).

These descriptions alleviate the pessimistic vision of a society in which self-actualization is extremely rare. Apparently, defensiveness, however alienating its origins, can be productive and positive in its effects—one such effect being attainable through art and literature. We find a related outlook, though for very different rationales, in the theories of Holland and Bloom. Those two scholars propose that psychic defenses determine the specific forms of art works. Paris proposes rather that defensive personality strategies affect the representation of human character in the works, and "the author's interpretations, rhetoric, and fantasies" (letter). The three approaches complement rather than exclude each other.

Third force psychology is "humanistic" in the sense of fostering an understanding of human interests and values and asserting the human capacity for self-realization. Literature supports this message of humanism, this broad horizon wherein "all rubricizing" is "an attempt to freeze the world," to "stop the motion of a moving, changing process world" "in perpetual flux" (Maslow, 1954: 212f) (p. 132). "There can be no closed system of beliefs, no unchanging set of principles" (Rogers, 1961: 27). The "satisfaction of any one need produces no more than a momentary tranquillity" (PAF 37).

Indeed, as Paris argues, literary authors typically represent more of the human situation than they are able to interpret explicitly. They offer us alternative realities to contemplate, without being able to foreclose for us what those realities can mean. Hence, the literary experience moves toward the "enriching" and "vitalizing" "allocentric" mode; and reveals that "the immediate live contact with the ineffable object of reality is dreadful and wonderful at the same time" (Schachtel, 1959: 177, 193). We recognize "existential problems" in "the disparity between our natural wants" and "the unalterable cosmic and historical conditions of our existence" (3FL 31) (a view also held by Fiedler, NT 7). Or, we are beset by the "unmitigable sadness" and "poignancy of the limitations of time, age, and death," and of the "gap between aspiration and opportunity" (3FL 31f). And so on.

A range of literary issues might be addressed within the third force approach, although as Paris concedes, the latter was not intended to support a theory of art. "Maslow includes aesthetic needs" "among our basic requirements, but he does not integrate them into his hierarchy" (3FL 12). Hence, Paris has been obliged to contemplate conventional literary categories and devise his own explications for them. His basic motivation came from a dilemma inherent in the nature of art, which, even more than reality, is a complex interaction of representation and interpretation, of showing things and judging meanings. The artist has special privileges of selection and formation and might thereby seem free to make the two activities correspond exactly. In practice, though, a disparity can appear precisely in the most esteemed works: the artist does better in presenting things than in telling us what they should mean. The drive to "account" for such "disparities" originally stimulated Paris's research (PAF x).

The history of literature shows authors trying to correlate representation and interpretation in various ways. Within what Auerbach (1957) calls "the classical moralistic" perspective, "life" was "represented" "in terms of" "a priori and static" "canons of style" and "ethical categories" (PAF 6).[5] The work could be a pretext for illustrating some moral or lesson the author would usually announce. But the works which survived were those whose experience kept exceeding or escaping the moral. The didactic openings of Gottfried's *Tristan* and Wolfram's *Parzifal* are so woefully inadequate for the import of each epic that I have always suspected them of being camouflages or ritual tributes to a narrow-minded convention no work of epic scale could affirm throughout.

The alternative is what Auerbach calls the "'problematic existential perspective,'" the "'conviction that the meaning of events cannot be grasped in abstract and general forms of cognition'" (PAF 7). Here, we encounter "a stylistically mixed, ethically ambiguous portrayal which probes 'the social forces underlying the facts and conditions'" (PAF 6f). Though this "perspective" may be obvious enough in modern trends—Fiedler, for instance, makes it a central aspect of literature (Ch. 6) —the moralistic one was slow to yield, at least as an official guideline. It was doubtless more congenial to narrow, superficial notions of the social "usefulness" of literature. Also, it could serve the classic aesthetics insisting on a "harmony" the work must clearly display (cf. p. 12). A moral code acted as a unifying device to ensure that the entire work would be understood as ultimately conveying the same idea.

Yet the disadvantages were severe. To the degree it genuinely was one, the moralistic work collapsed into oblivion when morals changed. As Iser demonstrates (p. 148), societies evolved into steadily more complex forms, wherein it became increasingly hard to assert that reality should serve as a moral lesson; hence, realism and mimesis conflicted with moralist canons and eventually undermined them. Authors often resorted to the subterfuge of paying tribute to morality without making it an exclusive or controlling factor. "In many realistic novels," "the classical moralistic perspective continues to exist alongside of, and often in disharmony with, the concrete" "representation of life" (PAF 7).

Criticism too has been reluctant to abandon the moral aspect, again perhaps because the latter helps to justify the social usefulness of literature and to demonstrate harmonious unity. Wayne Booth (1961: 112), for instance, claims that "a story will be 'unintelligible'" "unless the reader is made clearly 'aware of the value system which gives it its meaning'" (PAF 17). "The author, therefore, must not only make his beliefs known; but he must also 'make us willing to accept that value system, at least temporarily.'" If, for Booth, "the rhetoric of fiction" brings about "a concurrence of beliefs of authors and readers," then authors have the responsibility to organize a work explicitly according to a valid, convincing systems of values and beliefs—thus affording an ideal aid to the critic's search for a unifying and valid interpretation.

Karen Horney (1950: 330f) also tends toward this standard. For her, "art may

---

[5] See Auerbach (1957: 391, 27 and 433f) for the original formulations cited here and below (on "'inferior social groups'").

resemble dreams" wherein "'our unconscious imagination can create solutions for an inner conflict'" (PAF 128). Whether these "solutions" are "constructive or neurotic" "has great relevance" "'for the value of an artistic creation'" (PAF 128f). "'If an artist presents only his particular neurotic solution,'" then the work's "'general validity'" may be "'diminished,'" "'despite superb artistic facility and acute psychological understanding'" (PAF 129). "'Artistic presentation can help many wake up'" to the "'existence and significance'" of "'neurotic problems'" and "'clarify'" these. Horney appears to demand a "consistent and healthy" "moral norm" which "identifies neurotic solutions as destructive and suggests constructive alternatives."

Paris goes in a different direction from Booth and Horney. His arguments improve upon theirs by uncoupling the success of the literary process from the author's adherence to a binding moral norm.[6] He thereby pays due homage to the basic insights of third force theorizing that one's "present position" is always "most likely an incomplete one"; and that "there is no one perspective which does not involve some distortion" (3FL 28; PAF 34). He concludes that mimesis resists a representation that can be exhausted by any interpretation delivered along with it. "The mimetic impulse that dominates most novels often works against total integration and thematic adequacy" (PAF 9). "Mimetic characters" who are "truly alive" "tend to subvert the main scheme of the book," "to escape the categories by which the author tries to understand them, and to undermine his evaluations of their life styles" (PAF 11; 3FL 15). This effect is especially likely when (in Auerbach's words) "'more extensive and socially inferior human groups'" become the "'subject matter'" (PAF 6). Readers must then integrate into their experience characters for whom older literary types are less readily available, and can thereby develop a broader and more flexible concept of personhood.

As Fiedler and Iser also stress (Chs. 6, 8) literature allows the appreciation of values society officially rejects. Becky Sharp can be "a monster" and yet "the most fascinating character in the novel," "exciting admiration and sympathy" (PAF 83). Thackeray himself "'unremittingly makes her represent evil'" and yet takes "obvious delight in the pomp and splendor" she attains (PAF 83, 103). Of course, as Paris notes, many of Becky's defeated adversaries are either "powerful enemies" who embody "oppressive social institutions," or else "caricatures and grotesques" (PAF 83f). Yet evidently, we can empathize through literature with values we do not endorse in life, without becoming—as simple-minded moral-

---

6 Fiedler solves this problem by using "moral" in a favored sense for the author, and in a disfavored sense for society as a whole (p. 79). Bleich decries the "moral" but supports the "ethical," which turns out to be centered on "the human body" (SC 26f) (p. 187ff). Iser and Jauss regard moralizing as a mark of trivial literature (pp. 144, 371).

7 Compare Tilford (1959); Leavis (1950). Bleich's students defended Becky even against Thackeray: "Poo on him she is MY heroine" (RF 83).

ists assert—"immoral" persons. This multiplicity of motivations should restrain critics from passing judgment from a single vantage point and charging, for instance, that Heathcliff is "an unsatisfactory composite," or that Becky is an "unremittingly evil monster," or that Maggie Tulliver is "immature" (HEA 101; PAF 83, 165).[7]

Whereas Holland and Bleich focus on readers, Paris concentrates more on "the minds of the implied authors and the minds of the leading characters" (PAF 1). Typically, he gets to authors by projecting from the inferred personalities of those characters. Since, in principle, the latter "are more frequently self-alienated than self-actualizing," "Horney's theory" of "the defensive strategies that arise in the course of self-alienation" is the "most useful" of the third-force theories "for the study of literature" (3FL 12). The "absence" of self-actualizing types in literature could be "accounted for" by the "widespread feeling that health is uninteresting" (3FL 62). But then too, Paris's favored genres, the novel and (more recently) the drama, depend on conflict, and are therefore likely to represent disparate characters, whose attacks and defenses, expansions and self-effacements move the plot along. Narrative and dramatic interest is maintained by the interactions of "aggressive" types with each other or with their "compliant" counterparts, often leading to reversal and revenge (cf. PAF 93ff, 116ff). A world of exclusively self-actualizing characters could scarcely sustain a plot, nor would it seem mimetic to many readers. Such a character, such as Sir Thomas More in *A Man for All Seasons*, soon comes into conflict with a social order that fosters self-alienation (3FL 62ff).

Paris offers to restrict his method to "realistic characterization" (3FL 13). "Not all literary characters are appropriate objects of psychological analysis. Many must be understood primarily in terms of their formal and thematic functions in the artistic whole of which they are a part." If the "characters" of a "realistic novelist" are "subordinated to their aesthetic" "function, they will be lifeless puppets" (PAF 11). Conversely, "a highly realized mimetic character whose human qualities are not compatible with her aesthetic and thematic roles," such as Austen's Fanny Price, may be hard for readers to "identify" with (JA 22).

Paris concludes that we should not "go to novels looking for unified aesthetic systems" (HAR 212). The implication that aesthetic considerations can compete with characterization might seem puzzling: virtually by definition, "character" is a unifying conception for a person's diverse actions and attitudes. However, Paris is contesting the more classical aesthetics of harmony (PAF 2f).[8] He follows the typology of Scholes and Kellogg (1966), who distinguish between "aesthetic,

---

[8] Holland is said to subscribe to this thesis of harmony (PAF 2f), but as remarked (p. 162), his approach is hardly aesthetic at all and makes no provision for beauty. Though Paris seems to identify aesthetics with harmony (compare Note 16), he links "the aesthetic perspective" with "a free, contemplative, non-needing mode of perception" (3FL 66), thus reaching back to Kant's (1790) definition.

illustrative, and mimetic characterization" (PAF 11f; JA 18). "Aesthetic types" "exist mainly to serve technical functions or to create formal patterns and dramatic impact." "Illustrative characters" act as "'concepts in anthropoid shape'" in "works governed by the classical moralistic perspective." "Mimetic characters" are "'highly individualized figures who resist abstraction and generalization'"; their "motivation" can be seen in terms of "the ways in which real people are motivated." If so, only these "individualized" characters—Forster (1927) called them "round" —would be construed to "have an internal motivational system" (3FL 13).

This typology implies that the old aesthetics of harmony would have led critics to neglect characterization as a domain more dominated by conflict. This avoidance could explain why such schools as the New Critics would "'retreat from character'" and devote their attention to "'imagery, symbolism, or structural features'" instead (PAF 2f).[9] Along with Scholes and Kellogg, Paris is uneasy lest a character be conceived merely to even out "formal patterns" (PAF 11) —a principle which, to say the least, is unrealistic compared to the development of human personalities in life.

But the danger is probably not acute if we adopt a more encompassing conception of "aesthetic" standards demanding from the author not so much "harmony" as a balance between authorial freedom and closure. The author is free to invent "facts" for a literary world, but not to supply or foreclose all their meanings. In any work of genuine human interest, formal structures are filled in with characters who function as much more than bits of a pattern. Consider, for instance, the symmetry when the aggressive characters in novels by Dickens or Thackeray pursue their goals unchecked up to a point and then abruptly collide with characters previously portrayed as compliant or detached. The aggressor's goal disintegrates, but for 19th-century authors or readers, the compensation feels integrative: they can now "enjoy" "without guilt or reservation" the "aggressive behavior" of wronged characters rising up in revenge (PAF 95). This "release of tension" helps balance the personality without "violating the taboos" against "aggression." Hence, the characters both fill in a pattern and powerfully involve the reader.

Despite what Paris suggests (PAF 11f), "realistic" or "mimetic" literature is not the only kind wherein readers interpret characters in motivational terms. The inferring of plans and goals is a basic condition for participation in all narrative and dramatic literature: a "protagonist" is a character whose goals readers favor and use as a standpoint for comprehending and evaluating the events of a literary world; an "antagonist" blocks those goals.[10] Nonrealistic characters, even gods, wizards, and heroes, still have motives which real people might share and which

---

[9] This "retreat" was diagnosed by W.J. Harvey, who "intended to halt it" with his *Character and the Novel*. (PAF 2). Holland is named among the retreaters.

[10] For detailed discussion and examples, see Beaugrande and Colby (1979).

are therefore psychologically intelligible. Otherwise, reading would lack involvement. If motives in a work seem flimsy or contrived, I would tend to judge the work not as unrealistic, but as poorly executed or alienating.[11] Yet I should bear in mind that the motives of complicated or unorthodox characters may not be transparent or compelling for everybody, for example, those of Monsieur Teste, Malte, Leopold Bloom, Randle McMurphy, and so on; and this opaqueness can be a realistic trait of interesting, complex personalities.

If "fiction" is a complex mixing of real and unreal to challenge our capacities for integration (Ch. 2, 8), motives can easily seem realer than the characters who harbor them. What nonmimetic literature mainly presents, I think, is not the absence of believable motives, but the pursuit of believable motives with unbelievable means. Magic is an appealing force for attaining goals without the usual effort or conflict. Yet the plans of gods and wizards do not triumph simply, and sometimes not at all, being out of step with those of humans. This tension lends nonrealistic characters their human interest, at least as literature rather than as theology or cosmogony. We can, as Paris does, perform a motivational analysis on a fantastic character like Prospero, who enlists his magic for the fairly ordinary goals of being avenged on his old enemies, getting his daughter properly wed, disciplining his servants, and so forth. Shakespeare himself can solve the "problem" of "how to take revenge and remain innocent" —a wistfully "unrealistic" prospect reserved for "romances" (3FL 84f).[12]

Literary "realism" obliges the author to accept a mimetic orientation as a constitutive artistic principle. Events and characters cannot be so openly used as illustrations for a teleological structure of supernatural provenance. However, the artistic task and intent imposes upon the selected elements a different order of teleology, as when Balzac intends his *Human Comedy* to be a resumé of the human situation at large (cf. PAF 7). In nonrealistic literature, such an artistic teleology is supported with a nonmimetic principle, but with the same intent: the author pursues reality through unreality just as fantastic characters pursue believable goals with unbelievable means.

In realistic literature, the characters' own teleologies encounter conflicts, and unbelievable means of resolution are hard to justify. Here, the tension is less between real goals and unreal powers, as in the fantastic, than between real powers and unreal goals. Characters command no superhuman knowledge that guarantees success, but only their several partial perspectives that leave the outcome uncertain. A "great" realistic work retraces this shifting of perspectives without insisting on any harmonious teleology. The "great realist," says Lukács (1964: 11), "will, without an instant's hesitation, set aside" "his most cherished

---

[11] Compare the "critics" who judge Heathcliff an "unrealistic" character because "his behavior has escaped their comprehension" (HEA 102).

[12] Frye would define "romance" as having a "hero" "superior in degree to other men and to the environment" (AC 33). Paris implies that such a superiority rests on fragile devices for evading guilt.

prejudices or even his most sacred convictions" and "describe what he really sees"; only "the second-raters" "nearly always succeed in bringing their own Weltanschauung into 'harmony' with reality" (PAF 10). The workings of "fate" are inscrutable not only to the characters, but, in some degree, to the author, even though he or she is playing the role of "fate" by inventing the sequence of actions and events, deciding outcomes, and allotting rewards or punishments (cf. 352f). In realism, this role is specifically restricted; causalities cannot be simply abridged or skipped over with miraculous devices. At most, the author can decide whether the linkages will make "fate" seem "just" or "unjust," "tragic" or "comic," and so on.

Playing "fate" always turns out to be less fun and free than expected —it's an old story. In early times, authors could draw fairly directly on myths, whose authority, as Frye and Fiedler note, is unconsciously taken for granted and whose origins seem to reach back to the very beginning of things. Changing the myths or inventing new ones may have once been a sacrilege in some cultures. But myth passed into mythology and became literary (Chs. 5, 6); authors gained freedom but lost authority. They might confront their predicament head-on and treat myth as exactly what is *not* believed. They can then claim their story deserves a hearing because it is extraordinary, incredible—a pervasive refrain in the "Arabian Nights," where even an evil genie or a despotic caliph can't resist a rousing tale. This tradition lived on in the gothic mode and down into science fiction of the present.

But already in the gothic, authors were busily forging sources and justifications to supplant the function of myths. Indeed, the history of the novel is replete with devices pretending to explain how the author came to know the "facts" represented by the work. The author might appear as a character, either as narrator or as a person to whom the narrator told the story. Or, the author might purport to be editing someone else's manuscript or reproducing letters or diaries the characters wrote. Such ritual gestures for delegating responsibility were often patently transparent, the hypothetical narrator displaying knowledge or stylistic skill he or she could not have possessed. The ritual gesture alone was evidently enough, and nobody minded being asked to believe a person could report the lengthiest episodes and conversations in exact detail many years after they had supposedly taken place.

Still, the large middle-class readership that had gathered to consume the novel wanted to be assured in their own terms that they were doing something worthwhile. The "moralistic" perspective mentioned above offered one solution. The author could claim to be instilling exemplary precepts, especially in the young. "Interpretation" would thus tend to "outweigh" and "govern representation" (PAF 7). Yet as I said (p. 213), this tactic also often retained the character of ritual gesture, much like the faking of sources. The author would provide explicit interpretations without really expecting them to cover the story. Quite a few novels claimed to be socially or morally edifying and yet, as Fiedler likes to show, were in fact disturbing and subversive. Novelists must have guessed that too much straight moralizing dooms the work to a speedy obsolescence and to an inadequate grasp of reality.

At all events, representation is in principle less vulnerable than interpretation. Readers might implore an author not to let the pure heroine or the innocent child die, or not to forbid the union of lovers; but once the author has done so anyway, we can't say, "no, that's not what happened." However, we can demur if the same author tells us that the story proves our world is but a vale of tears, or whatever. We don't quarrel with Thackeray if he says that Amelia Sedley preferred the aloof George Osborne over the devoted William Dobbin; but we can dispute his moral that "'it is those who injure women who get the most kindness from them'" (PAF 78). We've agreed to let him make up his plot, but we reserve the right to contest what it demonstrates, particularly if his conclusions seem objectionable, as in this aggressive-vindictive accusation of women drawn from a single example.

What is called "modernism" is in part a tactic of evading this whole dilemma by minimizing authorial interpretation.[13] Or, refuge is sought in "irony," "the means by which the implied author negates what he has affirmed and protects himself from the consequences of commitment" (PAF 87). Our reality no longer seems to illustrate any moral, or at least none we want to go on record for approving (Ch. 8). Moralizings and interpretings now seem obtrusive where they wouldn't have to an earlier reader. We find them incomplete, unsatisfactory, or partisan alongside the literary world represented. Paris's research was prompted from the start by this very uneasiness, as he felt it when confronting a work like *Vanity Fair* (PAF x), which irritated Bleich's students for comparable reasons.[14] Paris turned to third force psychology for a model of authors and characters that would account for his experience without alienating him from the works or their creators.

Paris accordingly resigned his ambition to regard literature as a source of "ethical guidance" (PAF 20). He conceded that "realistic fiction itself" enacts a "conflict of values"; "some of its effects" are naturally "incompatible with others" (PAF 283f). "The writer of realistic fiction is doomed to leave somebody, and perhaps everybody, unsatisfied" (PAF 22). Hence, it becomes less disturbing that in many "novels," "interpretations are not only inappropriate or inadequate to

---

[13] Booth finds "the central problem of modern fiction to be the disappearance of the author," yet asserts that the author "'can never choose to disappear'" (PAF 16f). This contradiction reflects Booth's implicit plan to advocate "prescriptively" that "interpretation" "should always be present" for "moral and aesthetic reasons" (PAF 17). Iser gives a historical explanation for the author's retreat (IR).

[14] The responses of Bleich's students to the novel are reported and analyzed in RF 81-95. He thinks the author's intrusions are typical of "Victorian novels" in general (RF 90). Compare Note 16 to Ch. 10.

the experience dramatized, but they are also inwardly inconsistent" (PAF x). "Inner conflicts" can render "the author's attitudes toward his characters self-contradictory" (3FL 16).

In this outlook, the structure of the authors' personalities influences their control over the creative process. Their "value judgments are bound to be influenced by their own neuroses" (PAF 13). Their works reflect their "recurring preoccupations, the personal element in their fantasies, the kinds of literary characters they habitually create, and their rhetorical stance" (3FL 84). Their "rhetoric will affirm the values, attitudes, and traits of character which are demanded by their dominant solution, while rejecting those which are forbidden by it" (3FL 84; JA 169). "Rhetoric" can also be enlisted to "glorify" or "romanticize" particular "strategies of defense" or "neurotic solutions" (PAF 279; 3FL 16; HAR 234).

Evidently, "wisdom and health are not essential to great art" (PAF 22). Artists are more often than not "self-alienated" —another reason why "Horney's theory" of "defensive strategies" is so "useful for the study of literature" (3FL 12). Only rarely does "the implied author emerge as a deeply integrated and coherent being" (PAF 14). More frequently, "implied authors" are "no wiser or more consistent" than anybody else; and "as interpreters of experience" they "usually do not know what they are talking about" (PAF 20). Paris has to conclude that "great psychological realists have the capacity to see far more than they can understand" (PAF 8; 3FL 15; HAR 215).[15] However, they may be able "to resolve their inner conflicts by showing themselves, as well as others, the good and evil consequences of the various trends that are warring within them" (3FL 84). They may "glorify unhealthy attitudes, while at the same time *showing* their destructiveness" (PAF x).

For such reasons, the variety and divergence of attitudes subverting valid interpretation is no genuine disadvantage, but a crucial aspect of the intent to be realistic and literary at the same time. Whereas the "rhetoric" of the "great realist" "may be a reflection of his conflicts or a justification of his predominant solution," his "mimetic" achievement in "portraying reality" is "a triumph of healthy perception" (HAR 236). "Even if we cannot accept the implied author's values as adequate either to his fictional world or to life outside, we have a marvelously rich portrayal of a particular kind of consciousness making ethical responses to a variety of human situations" (PAF 24). "The implied author, too, enlarges our knowledge of experience." We become "phenomenologically aware of *his* experience of the world. When we see him as another consciousness, sometimes the most fascinating one in the book, it becomes more difficult to regret the technical devices by which it is revealed, even when they produce aesthetic flaws." In third force terminology, we approach allocentric perception by experiencing idiosyncrasies in an author's autocentric orientation.

---

[15] "Conceptual" rather than "intuitive" "understanding" is meant here (cf. HEA 102).

Accordingly, many benefits can be derived from the incongruities of literature. Despite "thematic confusion and a troubling disparity between interpretation and representation" in *Vanity Fair,* "no other technique could have produced the same brilliance in social satire and comedy" (PAF 132). Even so
bizarre a character as Heathcliff can "show us some very real potentialities of our
own personalities" (HEA 116). Jane Austen's "inner conflicts contribute" to "her
remarkable understanding of a wide range of psychological types" (JA 198). She
"is constantly trying to achieve an equilibrium between opposing forces; she has a
need to criticize each solution from the point of view of the others, and a strong
movement in any one direction tends to activate the opposing trends" (JA 199).
She "longs" "for aggressive triumph" despite "her insistence on goodness and her
criticism of expansive values" (JA 181). She has to maintain a freedom of perspective that lends her novels "immediacy" even for readers who find her "morality
quaint and her themes outdated" (JA 21).

Despite these positive aspects, Paris knows his portrayal of the personality
conflicts of authors may be taken as sacrilege against personages our culture
widely reveres. "We are disturbed by a critical perspective which frustrates" the
"craving to see our great authors" as "sages" or "god-like figures" (PAF 280).
When an author's "attitudes, judgments, and world views are seen as expressions" of a "defense system," they may "lose weight as truths about the human
condition and as guides to life" (PAF 286). Paris retorts that the mythologizing of
authors really makes us underestimate their achievement. If we merely "rationalize their inconsistencies," we tend "to remain unaware of the richness of their
personalities" (PAF 280). Moreover, "if we judge them as authorities, we are
likely to make much of the fact that they so often" give "interpretations" we find
"confused, too simple, or just plain wrong"; we then have to "condemn them as
false prophets" (PAF 280, 276), for instance, taking Thackeray's silly generalization about women to be a lapse of understanding.

But no such condemnation is implied if we see in the author a "dramatized
consciousness whose values can be as subjective and confused as those of an
ordinary" person (PAF 25). Even an author as momentous as Shakespeare may
owe "the richness and ambiguity of his greatest art" to his own "inner conflicts"
(3FL 85). Paris's "psychological approach" "suggests" we can "appreciate" authors "best if we lay aside our own value hungers and needs for authority and see
them allocentrically, as utterly fascinating objects of contemplation" (PAF 280).
Their "genius in characterization" appears all the more impressive alongside
their "deficiencies in analysis" (3FL 16).

Paris's critical move whereby psychological analysis uncovers disparities and
then explains them, perhaps as mimetic triumphs, in terms of human motives,
retraces the move whereby third force psychology recovers a guarded optimism
out of pessimism. The author's failure to deliver the "right" interpretation or
evaluation of what is represented holds the work open to the continued participation of diverse readerships. We might feel reminded of de Man's dialectic of

"blindness and insight," a motto Paris in fact borrows (3FL 88) (Ch. 13). For both critics, an author's blindness is not mere error that could be set right once and for all, but a constitutive aspect of a significance no author can conclusively grasp. Yet Paris situates in the conflict-solution structure of the personality a problem that de Man, who de-emphasizes the self, situates in the rhetoricity of language. For de Man, the text's undermining of its own required premises leads to its "unreadability." Paris's critiques rather enhance readability by demonstrating coherence even within that tendency to undermine. In his view, the authorial self is not disseminated, but actualized and consolidated while remaining partly blind to the work's implications and achievements.

However much it affirms of the values of literary fiction, the third force outlook may not be welcomed by criticism in general. The huge investment in adulative biographical criticism seems misplaced when the greatness and insight of the work are systematically uncoupled from the author's image as a sage and interpreter. It no longer seems so urgent to "preserve the glory of the author by demonstrating the perfection of his creation"; or to "attribute" to authors a "higher degree of integration," "greater wisdom, and a more coherent set of values than other people have" (3FL 17).

Calling in question the author's own interpretations undercuts not only Hirsch's plan to lend them the highest authority for "validation" (Ch. 7), but also any critic's intent to give a single, complete interpretation of the motives and meanings in a novel. All exponents of constant or authorized meanings and values will be disturbed by a model wherein "human needs and conflicts" (JA 21) enforce a process of continually projecting diffuse meanings from shifting angles.

Worse yet, third force psychology implies that critics as a group can be studied to see how their literary responses are influenced by their own personality with its conflicts or solutions. This enterprise would advance the epistemology of criticism, but would weaken the critics' traditional claims to accurate judgment based on disinterested discernment and good taste alone. Such judgments might now be found to reflect the critic's "recurring preoccupations," "the personal element in his fantasies," and the preference for "value systems" "parallel to one's own" (cf. 3FL 84, 35). The critic would "tend to glorify" authors or characters whose "strategies are similar to his own and to criticize those who embody his repressed solutions" (cf. 3FL 84; JA 20). A gallery of defensive critical types might emerge: aggressive ones like Fiedler, narcissistic ones like Bloom, perfectionistic ones like Hirsch, detached ones like de Man, and so on. But this gallery would be far too simple, the more so as such terms are better applied to episodes than to persons. "It is a very risky business" "to psychoanalyze one's fellow critics on the basis of their criticism" (3FL 87).

For the time being, Paris has discreetly confined his probes of critics' responses to his own case. In his early criticism, George Eliot's "self-effacing solution" was given a "full, accurate, and sympathetic exposition" (3FL 88). But he failed to see the "destructiveness of the solutions at which her characters arrive" (3FL 89). Only later, when he began "trying to exorcise the self-effacing trends" that "got in the way of his self-actualization," did he notice how he failed to "distinguish between her representation of a character, which is usually complex, accurate, and enduring, and her interpretation, which is often misleading, over-simple, and confused" (3FL 89f, e.d.). His "psychological evolution" impelled him to revise his evaluation of literary works. A similar change occurred when he was first "attracted" to the novels of Thomas Hardy and later "disenchanted" by them (HAR 203). These personal stories have happy endings though,[16] because, thanks to the new insights, the novelists' lack of "coherent moral vision" no longer clouds his appreciation of their "great genius in the observation and portrayal of human experience" (HAR 209, 203).

As far as I know, Paris has not given much consideration to the converse possibility that literary response can alter one's personality rather than reflect it— a prospect also neglected by Holland, but entertained by Bleich (p. 202). If whole cultures alter their personality concepts under the impact of characters like Saint-Preux and Julie, Werther and Lotte, Clarissa and Lovelace, as Jauss and Fiedler demonstrate (EH, LD), the individual obviously can do so too. "Literary figures" can "provide a ready-made formulation of the idealized images toward which their imitators are tending" (letter to me).

Yet this consideration seems to reintroduce the authorial responsibility for cogent and healthy interpretation Paris rejected against Horney and Booth. Few critics, and certainly not Paris, would want to proclaim that literary authors must place their works explicitly in the service of the mental health of society. That degree of control over audience response could not be maintained even if all authors pledged to try. We would merely revert to the old "moralistic" imposition whose drawbacks we examined using Auerbach's critique (pp. 211ff). Literature must protect its freedom of perspective against any one system of criteria for "normality."

Opposition can also be anticipated from the critical schools who believe that the proper "psychology" is the one derived from Freud or Lacan. Due to the rhetoricity of these two analysts, their reputation in literary criticism has outdistanced that in psychology. Freud moves away from language, whereas Lacan moves just as resolutely toward it. But both analysts have inspired methodologies of allegorical rewriting that displace the literary text with another text purporting to be somehow more basic, closer to human nature. Typically, this new text reflects the prevailing fascination with pessimism, regression, deformed sexuality, and bodily dismemberment (cf. Chs. 6, 9, 13-15).

Third force interpretation goes directly against these tendencies. It is not a rhetorical approach with a vocabulary of primal or archetypal symbols and im-

---

[16] Even though for Paris, the "happy ending," however "aesthetically pleasing," "sacrifices" "plausibility and realistic detail" (PAF 277). For Iser and the early Fiedler, the "happy ending" is so affirmative it properly belongs to entertainment fiction.

ages. Striving to be "faithful to the distribution of interests in the work itself" (cf. PAF 4), it contacts the work only at certain points with explanations that leave the imagery and content intact, indeed looking more forthright than ever. Whereas Freudians regularly confirm the author as a "neurotic" (TL 82), Paris attains a more optimistic, though still mixed judgment: the work itself is an occasion of potential health, whatever the state of the author. In place of the autocentric experience of enjoying hidden fantasy content dictated by libidinal phase fixation, Paris's reader moves toward an allocentric release from his or her habitual perspectivism. Finally, third force analysis is not attuned to a dark thematics of pain, violence, and atavism. In fact, the method is too reasonable to bank on the controversy and sensationalism that makes the other psychoanalytic approaches so noticeable. A method with no madness in it is handicapped on the current scene (cf. pp. 444f).

On the other hand, some traditional critics might complain that the third force approach merely supplants literary criteria of validity with psychological ones. But Paris's work does not claim to offer any new system for making "correct" interpretations to replace the author's "wrong" ones. Such an ambition could only repeat the limitations and ultimate failures that plague the author's interpretive intrusions. "The psychologist enables us to grasp certain configurations of experiences analytically, categorically, and (if we accept his conceptions of health and neurosis) normatively" (PAF 26). But the results do not constitute binding standards for the art work. They are drawn from "categories and abstractions" which could never "replace the values of literature," and they "interfere with the immediate response by putting the reader into an analytical frame of mind" (PAF 25; 3FL 21). Unlike such critics as Fiedler and the Yale group, Paris upholds this separation of criticism from literature.

The real grounds for resisting third force criticism would be an unwillingness to place an expansion of techniques onto the agenda of academic criticism, even though the ultimate effect would be to consolidate the literary experience rather than dilute it. Paris's model goes well beyond an account of what critics have always been doing. His hierarchy of values largely abstracts away from the usual bases of critical judgments by refusing to monumentalize the author or to objectify the text. It is not so much the artist or the art work that is self-actualizing as the occasion of encountering art and performing "repeated acts of perception employing a variety of perspectives" within which "one thing" is seen "clearly" and "the others" are "relegated" "to the background" (PAF 284) (cf. p. 138). That experience implies a utopian foreshadowing of what it might be like to escape "the limitations of human perception." Surely this dynamic disparity merits our consideration as much as the conventional critic's formalized unity.

For Paris, the "illumination" that "art supplies" is not "wisdom," but a "phenomenological knowledge of reality," "an immediate knowledge of how the world is experienced by the individual consciousness, and an understanding of the inner life in its own terms" (PAF 23). "Mimetic characters" have "universality and perpetual relevance" and are "endowed with the human interest which real people always have" (PAF 281). Just as the human personality must encompass diverse skills and impulses, "a novel's weaknesses and strengths are often complementary"; it is "impossible to realize all the values of fiction simultaneously" (PAF 132).

In sum, third force criticism expounds the function of literature as a means for experimenting with "allocentric perception" difficult to encounter in ordinary life, but constituting "the healthiest component of literature" and attainable by experiencing major "mimetic achievements" (3FL 66; PAF 286f). The diversity of characters, including many unhealthy or "immoral" ones, encourages us to read with variegated perspectives, freely questioning or revising the author's own judgments and perhaps eventually appreciating that we create "fate," not vice versa. "What third force psychology has to offer" is "a sense of selfhood without magic" (3FL 65).

I therefore thought it worthwhile to juxtapose the method of Bernard Paris with Holland's Freudian one and Bleich's Piagetian one. Paris's approach gives a fresh opportunity to see "highly individualized human beings, with different histories, problems, inner lives, and human qualities" (PAF 285). His method also allows a sense of "empathy and concern for the peculiarities" of an author's "own situation" (3FL 20). Then, since the "values" of any criticism "can be experienced only in the aesthetic encounter," we can "go back to the work" for the "immediate experience" no criticism can "replace," but only "enrich" (PAF 26, 285).

12

Jonathan Culler[1]

Jonathan Culler is best known for mediating literary theories of other scholars, especially Europeans. His major objective is to encourage a general theoretical reflection on the enterprise of literary studies. Certainly, a strong trend in this direction has appeared in America, and Culler's work may have been a material contributor. Whereas *Structuralist Poetics* (completed in 1973) tried to "introduce" "critical and theoretical writings" to "an English and American audience that had little interest in continental criticism," *On Deconstruction* (1982) aspired to "intervene in a lively and continuing debate" already well under way (OD 7). Culler came to devote more attention to American critics, albeit most of those he mentions had been working in theory for some time and he is often skeptical about their efforts.

Culler's own theoretical position is a complex issue. Despite his apparent empathy with particular theorists, he functions less as a disciple or advocate than as a weathervane for the climate in contemporary critical theory. I will therefore concentrate on how his positions have been formulated and modified over the years. Since he does not necessarily endorse what he reports, his own commitments have to be inferred from his selection and evaluation of theories. His seeming inconsistency in moving his focus from one mode of theorizing to another can be read as a consistency on the higher level from which he surveys the "apparently incompatible activities" within "the field of criticism" (OD 17).

As his career reveals, he welcomes in later trends a more consequential treatment of problems he was contemplating all along. The reservations and critiques in his earlier work eventually led to more radical consequences. In poststructuralist theories he saw a means to bring into the theoretical center the problems he had found structuralism marginalizing as dissonant or disruptive. He was thereby able to attentuate his uneasiness regarding his sources. If he had seemed to treat structuralism as if he were preparing a vaccine from an originally pathogenic substance, he now seems to advertise deconstruction as a basically sound or benign medicine some critics mistake for a malady.

---

[1] The key for Culler citations is: OD: *On Deconstruction* (1982); PO: *Structuralist Poetics* (1975); and PS: *The Pursuit of Signs* (1981).

"Structuralism" is a vague general heading for a generation of theories.[2] Although "to call oneself a structuralist" may have been a "polemical gesture," many "disciplines" "have long been concerned with structure"; one might even "describe all theoretically oriented critics as structuralists" (PO 3; OD 19). But this usage would be unduly broad. The "diverse projects of structuralists" are "unified" by their use of "linguistics" as a "methodological model" for the "investigation of a text's relation to particular structures and processes, be they linguistic, psychoanalytic, metaphysical, logical, sociological, or rhetorical" (PO 4; OD 21). "Languages and structures, rather than authorial self or consciousness, become the major source of explanation" (OD 21).

During the ascendancy of descriptive linguistics, researchers developed "procedures of segmentation and classification" and looked for "abstract units of structure" and "functional distinctive features which determine class membership" (PO 206, 10). Great attention was paid to "oppositions" and "differences," under the Saussurian assumption that these alone "make meaning possible"; "in the linguistic system, 'there are only differences with no positive terms'" (PO 10, 245; OD 28).[3] This assumption worked well enough in "phonological analysis," "for many structuralists" "the model of linguistics itself" and "based on a reduction of the sound continuum to distinctive features, each of which 'involves a choice between two terms of an opposition'" (PO 14; cf. PO 93). Similar success was attained in analyzing the sound structure of poetry, notably by Jakobson (cf. PO 65ff). Culler too keeps using word sounds as the star evidence for the centrality of binary oppositions (PO 10-14; PS 28; OD 96, 224).

But both linguistics and poetics had trouble applying the same conception to other levels of structure. The assumption that "elements of a text acquire meaning as a result of oppositions into which the various areas of experience have been organized," raised the prospect of using the methods of linguistics to analyze "culinary, gustatory, olfactory, astronomical, acoustic, zoological, sociological," and "cosmological" "codes" (PO 52).[4] Yet as Culler demurred, "binarism" "permits one to classify anything"; "binary oppositions can be used to order the most heterogeneous elements" and "can be very misleading" when deployed to "present factitious organization" (PO 15f). If all language levels are broken down this

---

[2] Culler's survey has some major gaps, notably his omission of Marxist ideas (Note 17). In exchange, he covers at least briefly some work often classed under other headings, such as "formalism" (Propp, Šklovskij, Eikhenbaum), and, with stronger reservations, "New Criticism" (Empson, Brooks, Crane).

[3] This thesis is routinely invoked (as here) without considering Saussure's immediate qualification: "But the statement that everything in language is negative is true only if the signified and the signifier are considered separately; when we consider the sign in its totality, we have something that is positive" (1966 [1916]: 121). On the residual "logocentrism" of Culler's argument, see Fletcher (1984).

[4] This proliferation of codes was particularly pronounced in the work of Lévi-Strauss and Barthes (cf. PO 32-54, 227).

way, "linguistic categories are so numerous and flexible that one can use them to find evidence for practically any form of organization" (PO 62).

The drift in linguistics from descriptive to generative encouraged a new look at critical theory. Just as "semiotics"[5] should "make explicit the implicit knowledge which enables people within a given society to understand one another's behavior," a "theory of literary discourse" should "make explicit what is implicitly known by all those" "concerned with literature" and "interested in poetics" (PO 32, 118, 258). "Just as the speaker of a language has assimilated a complex grammar which enables him to read a series of sounds or letters as a sentence with a meaning, so the reader of literature" "has semiotic conventions which enable him to read series of sentences as poems or novels endowed with shape and meaning" (PO viii). Culler uses notions from generative theorizing to depict the work of Ruwet, Barthes, Todorov, and Kristeva (cf. PO 25, 118, 215, 218), although they were not following Chomsky's version of "generative grammar" very directly (cf. PO 7).

Culler declines to see an "opposition" between "structural linguistics and generative grammar" (PO 27). "At the level of generality which concerns those looking to linguistics for models," "Chomsky's work can be taken as an explicit statement of the programme implicit in linguistics" "but not hitherto adequately or coherently expressed" (PO 7, 27). For Culler, all "grammars must be generative"; "they have simply not been explicitly" so (PO 24). He quotes Chomsky's (1965: 9) own technical definition of the term "generate" ("assign a structural description to"), but routinely uses it in the everyday sense of "produce." Things that get "generated" include: "episodes," "forms of the text," a "novel," an "interpretation," "metaphors," "writing," and "paradox" (PO 109, 146; PS 63, 193; OD 90, 201). The "generating" agents include: a "system," "formal devices," "formal procedures," a "reordering of codes," an "interpretation," "neatness," "metonymy," and even "nature" (PO 109, 146, 107; PS 63; OD 90, 201; PS 193, 162). Most of these uses, though hardly compatible with the technical definition, are characteristic of much literary theorizing in that period.[6]

All in all, Culler distrusts the importation of linguistic models into the literary theories of structuralism. He decries the naive "assumption" that when an "analysis" or "interpretation" proceeds from the "methods" and "metalanguage" of "linguistics," the results must be "correct" and have "interest and value" (PO 73, 218). Since "the linguists" they "read did not devote much time to discussion of

---

[5] Culler feels "it would not be wrong to suggest that structuralism and semiology are identical," but "such shifts in terminology are of little moment" except for "history" (PO 6). He does stipulate that "semiology" is the more inclusive term.

[6] Especially confused from a technical standpoint is the locution "generate structural descriptions" (i.e., assign them to themselves) (PO 218). To be sure, Culler's sources have the same metaphorizing tendency, as when Barthes (1966: 57) writes of "works" "generating" "variations of meaning" (PO 118).

the conditions which a linguistic analysis must meet," the "structuralists" believed that "if a metalanguage seemed logically coherent" and "if its categories" resulted from "systematic inquiry," "then no further justification was required" (PO 206f; cf. PO 49). The "terms" of "linguistics," being "already linked by a theory," were thought to endow any study with "ready made" "coherence" (PO 102). Culler objects: "the value" of "conclusions and interpretations" is "totally independent of the linguistic model" being applied (PO 109). At worst, a "linguistic argument" may be "pure obfuscation" (PO 108). "Specious arguments," "spurious rigor," "confusion," and "failure" are diagnosed in the projects of Jakobson, Barthes, and Greimas (PO 34f, 37f, 61, 72, 76f, 84f).

The question is then whether such problems might be resolved by some correction or modification, or whether they are intrinsic to the entire research program. Whereas Culler's earlier work favors the former conclusion, his later work favors the latter. In this he parallels several prominent critics who traded their previous "structuralist" positions for "post-structuralist" ones (cf. OD 25).[7] Culler doesn't accentuate this shift, since it reflects his own, but claims that "enterprises now deemed post-structuralist" "were manifestly under way" in "structuralist writings" (OD 25). The "theories" and "arguments" of the *Tel Quel* group "against the notions of a literary system and literary competence" still "presuppose these notions" (PO 243). Lewis (1982: 8) contended that "the structuralist enterprise" had " 'an acute self-critical awareness from the start,' " and Kristeva (1969: 30) called for " 'perpetual self-criticism' "; but such avowals collide with structuralism's "narcissistic relation to its own rhetoric" (OD 25; PO 251; PS 35; OD 21).

Culler also opines that "structuralists generally resemble post-structuralists more closely than many post-structuralists resemble each other" (OD 30). This effect might be predicted, since the later movement depended vitally on the earlier and yet greatly surpassed it in diversification. Culler thought it "extremely difficult to go beyond" "structuralism": "any attack on structuralist poetics" will "fail to provide a coherent alternative" (PO 243, 253). "While structuralism cannot escape from ideology and provide its own foundations," "critiques" of it "cannot do so either and through their strategies of evasion lead to untenable positions" (PO 253). Even though Culler still says "deconstruction has not refuted structuralism" (PS x), he has clearly moved his own point of orientation— first judging post-structuralism by the standards of structuralism, and then doing just the reverse.

Meager results in critical theory had caused general confidence in linguistics

---

[7] Culler compares Harari's (1971) "bibliography of structuralism" with the same editor's (1979) "anthology of post-structuralist criticism" as grounds to include among the transfers Barthes, Deleuze, Donato, Foucault, Genette, Girard, Marin, Riffaterre, and Serres, leaving Lévi-Strauss and Todorov as "the only true structuralists" (OD 25). However, anthologies often pursue famous names rather than theoretically sound groupings.

to decline, and scholars turned their attention to philosophers whose works foreshadow or circumscribe the dilemmas a science of language would encounter: Vico, Rousseau, Nietzsche, Husserl, Heidegger, Cassirer, Merleau-Ponty, and so on. Derrida inherited and reformulated these dilemmas in striking ways. Culler was initially unconvinced, accusing Derrida of ignoring "crucial differences between the conventions of oral communication and those of literature" "in Western culture"; and of "losing the distinction which translates a fact of our culture. Communication does take place. Many instances of language are firmly situated in the circuit of communication" (PO 133). These objections might "arrest the play" of Derrida's "concepts" and rebuke his attempts "to replace a metaphysic of presence by a metaphysic of absence" and "to invert the relation between speech and writing so that writing engulfs speech." Culler also upheld the "distinction between understanding and misunderstanding" without which "there would be little point to discussing and arguing about literary works" (PO 121).

Later, Culler saluted the trend by undertaking a synopsis of "deconstruction," now extolled as "the leading source of energy and innovation in recent theory," and "bearing on" its "most important issues" (OD 12). His earlier objections are expressly countermanded (OD 68, 89-103, 175f, 178). Sobered perhaps by his own prior reaction, Culler cautions that "deconstruction is ambiguously or uncomfortably positioned and particularly open to attack and misunderstanding" (OD 150f). He wrily hopes his "misreading of Derrida may in some contexts pass as sufficient understanding" (OD 178). It certainly suffices to disconfirm the simplistic outcry that Derrida is "playing with words" or "championing a principle or rule that any word in a text has all the meanings ever recorded for it" (OD 146, 219).

"To deconstruct a discourse is to show how it undermines the philosophy it asserts, or the hierarchical oppositions on which it relies, by identifying in the text the rhetorical operations that produce the supposed ground of argument, the key concept or premise" (OD 86). "The logocentrism of metaphysics" is attacked, along with "the orientation of philosophy toward an order of meaning—thought, truth, reason, logic, the Word—conceived as existing in itself, as foundation" (OD 92). "Deconstruction" "reveals" "the inability of any discourse to account for itself and the failure of performative and constative or doing and being to coincide" (OD 201).

"Derrida" "pursues with the greatest possible rigor the structuralist principle that in the linguistic system there are only differences, without positive terms" (OD 28). We can imagine no "first structure" or "originary event" in "language," because "we must assume prior organization" and "differentiation" (OD 96). "If in the linguistic system there are only differences, Derrida notes, every "'sign'" must "'relate to another element which is not simply present,'" and must participate in an "infinite referral in which there are only traces" (OD 99). A discourse is thus replete with "traces of forms that one is not uttering," so that an item "can function as a signifier only insofar as it consists of such traces" (OD 96). This scheme enables endless inversions and displacements by bringing out presupposed "traces" from within the texture of the discourse, or, in Barbara Johnson's (1978: 3) well-known metaphor mixing militarism with hairdressing, by "'teasing out the warring forces of signification within the text'" (PS ix; OD 213; cf. OD 199, 220).

If the identity of any entity depends on its own opposite, then the latter is implicitly included as well as excluded, and the opposition is not stable. Instead of "promoting one term" of the "opposition" "at the expense of the other," "the second term," usually "treated as a negative, marginal, or supplementary version of the first," is now found to be "the condition of possibility of the first" (OD 213). Since, according to Derrida, "'the hierarchy of binary oppositions always reconstitutes itself,'" "'a movement that asserts the primacy of the repressed term is strategically indispensable'" (OD 173).

Yet a certain dualism inhabits such moves. On the one hand, "one demonstrates that the opposition is a metaphysical and ideological imposition" by "bringing out its presuppositions and its role in a system of metaphysical values" and by "showing how it is undone in the texts that enunciate and rely on it" (OD 150). On the other hand, "one simultaneously maintains the opposition" by "employing it in one's argument" and by "restating it with a reversal of status and impact." This technique is demonstrated on a series of key oppositions: "essential" versus "contingent" (or "inessential"), "inside" versus "outside," "central" versus "marginal," "present" versus "absent," "performative" versus "constative" (or "cognitive"), "literal" versus "figural," "literary" versus "philosophical," "signifier" versus "signified," and so on (OD 146, 140, 107, 196, 95, 147, 182, 148, 188).

For Derrida, the "'traditional philosophical opposition'" is "'not a peaceful coexistence'" but "'a violent hierarchy'" in which "'one of the terms dominates the other,'" so that "'to reverse the hierarchy'" might be to undo a "'repression'" (OD 85). Still, to the extent that these oppositions are presupposed in many discussions of language and thought, such an undoing can be mistaken for a willful or aimless act of original violence, rather than a strategically designed response of counter-violence. The "'general displacement of the system'" due to "'intervening in the field of oppositions'" can be misconstrued as "anarchism" (OD 86, 151).

Hence, Culler feels impelled to make the "large claims" of deconstruction seem "more comprehensible" and less "excessive" or "irritating" (OD 107, 204, 133). He solicitously deflates the "rumor" that "treats deconstruction as an attempt to abolish all distinctions, leaving" "only a general undifferentiated textuality" (OD 149). He assures us we have "no reason to stop work on theory" when we realize that "the language of theory always leaves a residue" (OD 133). He rejects the "belief" in the "humanities" that "a theory which asserts the ultimate indeterminacy of meaning makes all effort pointless." This belief is merely a pretext to evade the prospect that "the notions of meaning, value, and authority promoted by our institutions are threatened" (OD 179). "The identification of the normal as a special case of the deviant helps one to question the institutional forces and practices" of "legitimation, validation, or authorization that produce differences among readings and enable one reading to expose another as a misreading." These "forces" are naturally disturbed when we inquire whether "all reading is misreading."

Structuralism had been quite emphatic about its scientific character. "Linguistics can give literature the generative model which is the principle of all science" Barthes (1966: 58) promised (PO 128). "Theories" would be "testable" in terms of "reproducing" "attested facts" about "literary competence" and about "the 'grammar' of literature" whereby people "convert linguistic sequences into literary structures and meanings" (PO 122, 114). Research should best be carried out via some "algorithm," some "mechanical" and "automatic procedure" that would guarantee correct, consistent results and eliminate "the subjective decisions of the analyst" (PO 76, 81f, 94f, 123, 259). In accord with "generative grammar," "rules" "stated" as "formal operations" were judged the proper format "to make the implicit explicit" (PO 122). The powerfully metaphorical nature of this theorizing, a factor Culler stresses (PO 96-109, 255), was not widely acknowledged.

Later on, deconstruction placed scientific ambitions in a very different light. "Theory may well be condemned to a structural inconsistency" (OD 109). "Theories grounded" on "an ideal norm that subsists behind all appearances" —and a grammar has this status—"undo themselves, as the supposed foundation or ground proves to be the product of a differential system, or rather, of difference, differentiation, and deferral." These three terms are needed to render Derrida's "différance," "alluding" to "the undecidable, nonsynthetic alternation between the perspectives of structure and event" (OD 97). "A scrupulous theory" "can never lead to a synthesis," because it "must shift back and forth between these perspectives," each of which "shows the error of the other" (OD 96). For Culler, this reservation undermines the linguists' division between "langue" ("the system of a language") and "parole" ("speech acts") (OD 96; PO 6), though he doesn't draw the corollary that "competence" (a main concept in his early theorizing) gets blurred with "performance." His treatment of "speech acts" points up "the impossibility of controlling effects of signification or the force of discourse by a theory, whether it appeal to intentions of subjects or to codes and contexts" (OD 128). This conclusion is argued via the hardly contestable "boundlessness" of "contextual possibilities."

In exchange for withdrawing as a conventional science, deconstruction might exert significant pressure on science and politics as institutions. Culler concedes that "such effects may be slow to work themselves out," but is optimistic that "the most abstract or recondite problems may have more disturbing consequences than immediate and intense political debates" (OD 157f). "Deconstructive 'analyses'" may "have potentially radical institutional implications" if the "concern" with "the conditions and assumptions of discourse" empowers us to "engage the 'institutional structures governing our practices, competencies, performances'" (OD 159, 156). "Self-reflexivity" and "inversions of hierarchical oppositions" "open possibilities of change" in "assumptions, institutions, and practices" (OD 154, 179).

This outcome would go far beyond the earlier project of merely "making the implicit explicit." Derrida (1982) recommends that "deconstruction" "should seek a new investigation of responsibility" and "question the codes inherited from ethics and politics" (OD 156). He does not advocate "a methodological reform that should reassure the organization in place, nor a flourish of irresponsible" "destruction" sure to "leave everything as it is and to consolidate the most immobile forces within the university." Yet an underground philosophical revolution seems tenuous to the degree that deconstruction "remains implicated in or attached to the system it criticizes and attempts to displace" (OD 151).

Consider in this perspective how deconstruction encouraged a shift in linguistic theorizing. Formerly, structuralism had been beleaguered by its tendency to expound modest if not vacuous ideas as significant findings,[8] and to mistake an ostensibly more formal statement of a problem for a genuine solution. Typically, the only radical aspect was the reductiveness, such as treating the literary work as if it had the same structure as a sentence (cf. PO 82f, 104). Post-structuralism was much more radical in carrying linguistic theorems to the point where their implications become disconcerting and disruptive.

Alarmed by the abruptly radical uses of their staid science, linguists like Searle[9] protest that linguistics is being misunderstood. They fail to appreciate that a conscious and intentional displacement has been deployed to signal that any science of language is potentially deconstructable because of what it excludes and represses, and that even its own fundamental theorems can be rigorously pressed to support this argument. Deconstruction never claimed that pioneer linguists like Saussure or Austin would approve its new readings of their work. Their writings have merely been enlisted as strategic spaces for a discourse driven by a quite different program.

Deconstruction clinches the point by yielding apparent misreadings and paradoxes that *must* be read performatively, because our habituated mentality makes

---

[8] Typical cases are Greimas's (1966) precepts that "first and second person pronouns" "are replaced by 'the speaker' and 'the listener,'" and that "the story of a quest will have a subject and an object" like a "sentence" (PO 82); or Todorov's (1969: 28) proposal to "treat characters as proper names to which certain qualities are attached" in the same way as "'properties'" accrue to "'the grammatical subject'" of a sentence via "'conjunction with a predicate'" (PO 235).

[9] Searle (1977: 203) has to detect Derrida's "penchant for saying things that are obviously false" because conventional linguists delight in rehearsing what is obviously true, for example, that a promise implies one's intent to carry it out. This vacuity is probably due to the habit in linguistics of viewing language as a system independent of contexts (cf. Beaugrande 1987b).

it so hard to read them constatively. The philosophical conditional obverts the objects and concepts customarily discussed in the scientific indicative. This move offers literary theory the chance to initiate a paradigmatic impulse of dissonance and demystification vis-à-vis the sciences, where, despite a similar pressure from philosophical metatheory, the traditional disregard of the performative still serves the interests of professional decorum.

Some illustrative radicalizations may clarify my projection. A binary opposition derived simply by opposing the presence of an entity to its own absence remains vacuous or trivial until we question or invert the privilege of presence and uncover the metaphysical stakes involved. To assert that language is a system containing only differences is a noncommittal abstraction or an expedient dismissal of substance[10] until we regard the activity of differentiating as an endless deferring or cross-referring within a system that is thus either centripetal or without any center and can yield only "ex-centric" meanings; equally disquieting is the consequence that "referentiality" is continually "postponed" (OD 251). To assert that meaning is composed of "semes" and that coherence is a classifying of them (cf. PO 77, 79, 87) merely makes the whole issue less tangible than ever, at least in lack of consistent, effective means for discovering semes; but the issue regains momentum when such units are set in motion to perform uncanny disseme-inations, e.g. via puns and etymologies.[11] The division between constative and performative, or between serious and nonserious speech acts seems tranquilizing until the opposition gets blurry and the supposedly "parasitical" second term begins to absorb the first as its "special case" (cf. OD 112f, 116-125, 134; PS 223). Though these readings of linguistic theorems are "ex-centric" (in the sense just proposed), they are evidently not impossible, and we might gain more insight by being concerned less about their (constative) authorization than about their (performative) impact.

Culler's exposition has to walk a fine line by justifying these radicalized propositions without reducing them to mere reformulations of familiar aporias. Culler incurs such a risk when he adduces the variability of reading according to time, circumstance, and reader (cf. OD 176) as grounds to see in Derrida's transformations of linguistic theorems only reasonable circumscriptions of everyday reading. Or, Derrida's notion of "open" "possibilities" of meaning is explained in terms of the "boundless" room for "other specifications of context"

---

[10] "Identity of substance" is made the hallmark of "traditional studies which treat individual works as 'organic wholes,'" as compared to structuralist criticism that finds a "homology of differences" (PO 97). One might however see substantialism in the objectifying of grammatical concepts by Barthes or Todorov.

[11] Rorty (1978: 146f) finds "'puns'" and "'etymologies'" among "'the most shocking things about Derrida's work'" (OD 144). The "pun" is able to "treat" "an 'accidental' or external relationship between signifiers" "as a conceptual" one (OD 91f; cf. OD 190ff, 240). "Etymology'" can "put in question" the distinction "between the contingent and the essential" (OD 146). Both figures are dear to the Yale group.

(OD 123f, 131)—an account with no more force than the earlier structuralist prospect of "multiplying the codes" when "reading" "any particular stretch of discourse" (PO 52). The concept of the "unreadable," set down especially by de Man to designate "violent ambivalence," "the way" "the system of values in the text both urges choice and prevents that choice" (PO 106; OD 81; cf. OD 257ff, 276f), is occasionally flattened by relating it to "tedious," "modern," or not "intelligible" (OD 259; PO 190). It would be quite contrary to Culler's intent if his "brisk common sense" (cf. OD 27)[12] adjusted the precepts of deconstruction until they lean toward the self-evident and inconsequential. This result would leave the study and use of language and literature exactly as before, except that its customary blind spots would have been remapped with a new cartography, just as Gödel's proof has been absorbed without forcing a genuine realignment of the ambitions of formal logicians (cf. OD 133).

Culler's solution is a precarious one, as "ambiguously" "positioned" and "open to attack and misunderstanding" as the theory he expounds (cf. OD 150f). He combines the disruption of reversals and interventions with the reassurance that they do not have the effects they would in a traditional disputation. Deconstruction is portrayed as perpetually requiring and thus conserving its ideological counterpoints. For instance, the contention that "causality" is "produced" by the "tropological operation" of "metonymy or metalepsis" "does not lead to the conclusion that the principle of causality is illegitimate" (OD 86f). Or, the thesis that " 'every signified is also in the position of a signifier' " "does not mean that the notion of sign" "should be scrapped," nor that "there are no reasons to link a signifier with one signified rather than with another," nor that a "text" is merely "a galaxy of signifiers"; "on the contrary, the distinction between what signifies and what is signified is essential to any thought whatever" (OD 188f). Or again, the sign's "possibility of endless replication" "does not propose indeterminacy of meaning in the usual sense: the impossibility of choosing one meaning over another," but "only the failure of signifieds to produce closure" (OD 189).

What detractors of deconstruction cannot seem to understand is that "an opposition that is deconstructed is not destroyed or abandoned but reinscribed" (OD 133). Trained in traditional binary logic, their minds reject "the double procedure of systematically employing the concepts or premises one is undermining" (OD 87f). They feel cheated because they expect that once a concept is put in question, it should be thrown out in favor of some less questionable counterpart which deconstruction does not provide. And they resentfully construe the stance of such criticism as "skeptical detachment," rather than as the "unwarrantable involvement" it intends to demonstrate (cf. OD 87f). In the course of this chapter, we shall retrace some aspects of this involvement in Culler's own theorizing.

---

[12] The phrase is Miller's (1976: 336). Culler returns the charge by describing as "canny" Miller's presentation of "uncanny" criticism (OD 27). Compare Note 27.

Deconstructive theses seem helpful for literature, a discourse that also subverts oppositions, such as fact versus fiction, reality versus imagination, specific versus general, internal versus external, and so on. It thereby systematically undermines attempts to impose definitive closure or complete interpretation, however much it may invite readers to try. It is a "mode of writing distinguished by its quest for its own identity" (OD 182). "The essence of literature is to have no essence, to be protean, undefinable"; it "transcends any account of it and can include what is opposed to it" (OD 182f). "Deconstruction" may agree with Hirsch in not viewing "literature" as "a privileged, superior mode of discourse" with an "authoritative epistemological status" (VAL 210; OD 183f) and still promote explorations which fit literature better than his (cf. Ch. 7).

Indeed, deconstruction might be too readily absorbed into the established corpus of critical practices in America, leaving them hardly altered. Culler would like to ward off that outcome by clarifying what is at stake. Since "Derrida" "has not dealt directly" with "the task of literary criticism, the methods for analyzing literary language, or the nature of meaning in literature," "the implications of deconstruction for literary study must be inferred" (OD 180). Culler's deliberated, conscientious effort to draw out those implications can be mapped from the development of his stated positions during his apparent "structuralist" and "post-structuralist" phases.

In some measure, Culler's view of the nature of literature has remained constant, as the following mosaic of quotations should prove. He upholds "the centrality of literary structures to the organization of experience" (PS 215). "Literature takes as its subject all human experience," which it "orders, interprets, and articulates," while "commenting on the validity of various ways" to do so (OD 10; PS 35). In addition, it is "a continuous exploration and reflection on signification in all its forms," "an exploration of the creative, revelatory, and deceptive powers of language," and a "powerful, elegant, self-conscious" "manifestation" of "sense-making" (PS 35, 217). Hence, it is "the most complex of sign systems" and "explores" "the limits of intelligibility" (PS 35; OD 11). It offers "the best occasion" to "watch the complexities" of "the signifying processes" of "order and meaning" "work freely" (PO 264; PS 35).

Like many theorists (e.g., Wellek and Warren, Frye, or Bloom) Culler maintains that "poetry lies at the centre of the literary experience" and "most clearly asserts the specificity of literature" (PO 162). "For structuralists," "poetry undermines the function of ordinary language" and, for Kristeva (1969), "includes by definition all possible varieties of signification" (PO 183, 247). Invoking Derrida, Culler says that "in literature," "we have the least cause to arrest the play of differences by calling upon a determinate communicative intention to serve as the truth or origin of the sign," an insight restating the traditional view that "a poem can mean many things" (PO·133).

Reading literature is correspondingly seen as a recovery against odds, a "process" Culler terms both "naturalization" and "recuperation" —"one of the basic activities of the mind," subsuming "the common operations of reading" (PO 137f, 178; cf. PO 178-88, 225). To "interpret something is to bring it" within "a mode of discourse which a culture takes as natural" (PO 137). "Structuralists" "imply that rhetorical figures are instructions about how to naturalize the text by passing from one meaning to another—from the 'deviant' to the integrated," using "rule-governed steps" (PO 179f), though much more may be involved.[13]

Throughout, Culler notes how "literature announces its fictional and rhetorical nature" and shows "awareness of rhetorical structures and forces," and of "textuality" (OD 183; PS 226). Yet a change of emphasis occurs. "Structuralism" followed "rhetoric" in classifying tropes into tidy formal categories (PO 179ff). "Metaphorical interpretation" was viewed as a "coexistence" of "added" "semantic features" with the "old" ones they "contradict" (PO 86). "Metaphor and metonymy" were argued to be cleanly opposed, for instance, via neurological function by Jakobson or via historical sequence by Hayden White with Culler (1976) following suit (PS 60, 192, 63ff, 216).[14] The later Culler finds this outlook, including his own contribution, "a very dubious enterprise" of manufacturing "contrasts," such as the "opposition" having "an ambitious and deluded Romanticism, committed to an organic theory of imagination" and to "a continuity between form and meaning" or between "subject and object," on one side; and "an ironic, self-conscious modernism" that "questions these assumptions" on the other (PS 64, 155).

The post-structuralist tendency is rather to trace displacements from one class of tropes to another (cf. Ch. 13, 14). "The distinction" between "metaphor, based on" an "essential similarity," and "metonymy, based on a merely accidental or contingent connection" is "put in question" as a plan to "assert the responsibility" of "rhetoric" by "privileging" "cognitively respectable" "tropes" (PS 190, 194, 198, 191, 199). De Man for instance is said to "reverse" the "metaphorical privileging of metaphor by assimilating metaphors metonymically to metonymy" (PS 199; cf. ON 243ff). Similarly, the "opposition" is blurred whereby we might "maintain the priority of the literal over the figurative" (PS 206). "The figurative is the name we give to effects that exceed, deform, or deviate from the code," but these "get codified" and "create opportunities for new turns" (PS 209). "In general," "any attempt to ground trope or figure in truth always contains the possibility of

---

[13] A comparable conception can be seen in many models: Fish's reader recovering from wrong hypotheses, Riffaterre's "transcending mimesis," Hirsch's applying "validation" procedures, Iser's "filling in gaps," Holland's reverting to "fantasy content," and so on (cf. OD 37, 64-73; PS 52, 80ff, 219). But in each case, the recuperation is described differently. Compare also Culler's idea that "fantasy" is "the unnatural that the reader accepts as other nature" (PS 61).

[14] White (1973) has the "sequence" arranged as "metaphor, metonymy, synecdoche, and irony" (PS 65). Culler "suspects" this scheme is "not a movement of history" but "a narrative curriculum with its own propulsive forces." Earlier, though, he confidently made his own categorical classifications, e.g.: "in novels most symbolic operations follow the models of metonymy and synecdoche" (PO 226). He becomes steadily more uneasy about the status of "literal" meaning (PS 61, 70, 197).

reducing truth to trope" (PS 204). However, Culler still vows that "the very notion of rhetorical effect" "requires there to be a distinction between literal meaning and metaphoric meaning" (PS 41)—again remaining involved in an opposition while undermining it.

At one time, "semiotics" was a "metalinguistic enterprise" "to describe the evasive, ambiguous, paradoxical language of literature in a sober, unambiguous metalanguage" (PS xi). "In recent years, it has become clear" that, just as in "deconstructive" "analysis" the "discourse is shown to repeat the structures it is analyzing," "critical and theoretical discourse shares many properties with the language it attempts to describe" (OD 139; PS xi). "Deconstruction" has "particularly" illustrated how "theories" have an "uncanny involvement" in their own "domains" and "how critics become engaged in a displaced reenactment of a text's scenario" (PS xi). Moreover, "literary works" "contain" their own "metalinguistic commentary" which determines "to a considerable extent" "the authority of critics' metalinguistic position" (OD 199). Though it "is always at work," "the distinction between language and metalanguage" "evades precise formulation."

Still, unlike Bloom or Hartman,[15] Culler does not envision erasing the boundary between literature and criticism. He can't see why "the critic must deem himself a poet"; "on the contrary," critics should "continue the pursuit of signs, the attempt to grasp, master, formulate, define," to "capture in their prose evasive signifying structures" (PS xi, vii). This "pursuit" leads to no final end, since "a literary analysis is one that does not foreclose possibilities of structure and meaning in the name of the rules of some limited discursive practice" (OD 182). We may not even "accept" a "definitive commentary" inside "the work," "telling us where to stop"; we may go on and finally "stop when we feel we have reached" "the place of maximum force" (PO 229).

Following Derrida's lead, Culler is more inclined to erase the boundary between literature and philosophy (cf. OD 147, 181; PS 223), though, like other deconstructive gestures, this one subverts itself: "the distinctiveness of philosophy is" "maintained within the argument that seemed to obliterate distinctions by treating philosophy as literature" (OD 184). Indeed, "the distinction between literature and philosophy" remains "essential to deconstruction's power of intervention" (OD 149f). So the "unwarrantable involvement" (OD 88) persists again.

For some scholars, deconstruction is an occasion to erase the boundary between literature and criticism in the opposite direction, namely, by making the literature function as its own criticism. For Hillis Miller, "the text already contains the operation of self-deconstruction, in which two contradictory principles

---

[15] Culler is strangely tolerant of Bloom and Hartman, who have clouded the public view of deconstruction more than Miller, whom Culler so insistently rebukes. Bloom's failing is made out to be ours: "we" "take what he says about a poem and its intertextual, tropological genesis as an interpretation" and "are affronted" that it "should be so extravagant" (PS 14). Culler writes me he has "now corrected" his "tolerance of Hartman."

or lines of argument confront one another"; and "this undecidability 'is always thematized in the text itself in the form of metalinguistic statements'" (PS 15). "'Great works of literature,' Miller" (1975: 30f) "insists, 'have anticipated explicitly any deconstruction the critic can achieve.'"

Culler repudiates this "shift" "taking place" "when deconstruction comes to America" and enabling it "to succeed" here whereas "Marxism and structuralism have not" (PS 15f). [16] If "the text" "is *about* self-deconstruction so that a deconstructive reading is an interpretation of the text," then "deconstruction" is "tamed" and "made into a version of interpretation" specialized for "particular" "privileged" "themes, such as "undecidability" and "the relationship between performative and constative." Culler expounds deconstruction so as to deauthorize such an outcome, however much the latter may have enhanced the success of the trend in his country. Evidently, new criteria for success are needed to promote the version of deconstruction Culler favors.

Although he singles out "Paul de Man and Barbara Johnson" as its "best practitioners," Culler does not proclaim only certain versions of "deconstruction" to be legitimate (PS 16; OD 227f). "One is tempted to speak of an original practice of deconstruction in Derrida's writings and to set aside as derivative the imitations of his admirers, but in fact these repetitions, parodies," or "distortions are what bring a method into being" (OD 120). The fact that Culler "would not wish Miller's interpretations to be taken as the very models for deconstructive reading does not mean they are to be excluded from deconstruction" (letter to me).

Culler has been quite consistent in opposing interpretation, a stance that attracted him to both structuralism and deconstruction. Like Iser, he considers "the interpretation of individual texts" to be "an ancillary activity" "only tangentially related to the understanding of literature" (PO 118; PS 5). "The notion that the goal of analysis is to produce enriching elucidations of individual works is a deep presupposition of American criticism" and foments "resistance to the systematic projects of structuralism, Marxism, and psychoanalysis" (ON 221). Though he disclaims the intent to "condemn interpretation," Culler makes it the "atomistic" "enemy of poetics" and the culprit that "subsumes and neutralizes the most forceful and intelligent acts of revolt in American criticism"; its misdeeds include "emasculating" the "promising mode of investigation" in "New Criticism," and "nullifying" the "insights" of the "potentially valuable formalism" in Fish's "theory" (PO 118; PS 9, 11, 7, 130f).

We are exhorted to "loosen the grip" of "interpretation" on "critical discourse" and "consciousness" (PS 5; PO 119). Culler borrowed from structuralism the "generative" idea that "the task of linguistics is not to tell us what sentences mean," but "how they have the meanings" that "speakers give them," as an

---

16 Culler opines that the "shift" was "subtly inaugurated" by de Man and "transformed into a central methodological principle" by Miller (PS 15), both of whom certainly were successful.

argument why literary theory cannot be expected to tell us what individual works mean (PO 74, 31, 97; PS 218; OD 21). Later, he welcomed deconstruction as a model that might resist "assimilation" to "interpretation" by "precluding the possibility of interpretive conclusions" (ON 222). He is dismayed when "American criticism has found in deconstruction reasons to deem interpretation the supreme task of critical inquiry and thus to preserve" "continuity between" "New Criticism" and "the newer criticism" (ON 220). If (in line with Miller's contention) "deconstruction reveals the impossibility of any science of literature and discourse" and thereby "returns criticism to the task of interpretation," problems arise: "deconstructive readings" fail to "respect" the "distinctiveness" and "integrity of individual works," and focus instead on "issues," "structures of language, operations of rhetoric, and convolutions of thought" (OD 220f).

Culler has all along claimed that the proper "task" should be "to construct a theory of literary discourse" so as to "account for the possibilities of interpretation" and the "conditions of signification" (PO 119; OD 20). This approach can make "the proliferation of interpretations" into "an object of knowledge" (PS 48). We might "explain on what basis a range of interpretations" for a work "could be produced: what conventions and interpretive procedures enable critics to draw the inferences and make the statements they do" (PS 76). Although we won't prove what the work "really means," we can uncover the "restrictive conventions of reading" without which "interpretation would be impossible" (PS 76; PO 250).

How far interpretation can be deemphasized in practice is uncertain. A theory that did *not* deliver any interpretations as vital evidence of its own range and necessity might go unnoticed. Barthes and Todorov, for instance, gained prominence because their unconventional studies of Balzac's *Sarrasine* and Boccaccio's *Decameron* opened new interpretive possibilities. Culler performed a similar service on the works of Flaubert. Even within deconstruction, we are told that "hierarchical reversals are likely to be the most convincing when they emerge from critical readings of major texts" (ON 174).

Conversely, the unconvincing nature of structuralist interpretations reinforced Culler's criticism of their theories. When Greimas failed to present his "procedures of extraction at work on an actual text," Culler suspected (as I do) that the "project" "may be impossible, in principle as well as in practice" (PO 84; cf. PO 213, 234). Culler is probably most uneasy about theories whose inadequacies are concealed behind the brilliant interpretations performed by their proponents—a tactic he notices in Fish and, more guardedly, in Riffaterre (cf. PS 127ff, 93ff).

Culler's real argument must therefore be that interpretation should be not so much curtailed as assigned a fundamentally different status and function: "the work" is "interpreted" as "the vehicle of an implicit theory of language" (PO 98; cf. PO 103). "The reordering of codes generates a different sort of interpretation": "the ultimate meaning of episodes and formulations is what they tell us about literary discourse" (PS 63). "The combination of context-bound meaning and boundless context" "urges that we continue to interpret texts" and "elucidate the conditions of signification" (ON 133). Most of the sample critics in my survey would accept this formulation, though for diverse motives.

Culler emphatically called for "an explanation" of "the striking fact" that "a work can have a variety of meanings but not just any meaning" (PO 122). "If each text had a single meaning," then "this meaning" might be "inherent to it and depend on no general system" (PO 243). "The text" can have a "plurality of meanings" "because it does not itself contain a meaning, but involves the reader in the process of producing meaning." Thus, "the fact that a variety of meanings and structures are possible is the strongest evidence we have of the complexity and importance of the practice of reading." "Variations in interpretation are not an obstacle," but "the fact with which one starts" (PS 124). "In general, divergence of readings is more interesting than convergence" (PS 51). An "emphasis on the variability of reading" "makes it easier to raise political and ideological issues" —a gesture whereby Culler grants "Marxism," whose impact on structuralism via such figures as Lévi-Strauss, Goldmann, and Althusser his survey had utterly ignored,[17] to be "not an illegitimate distortion, but one species of production" (OD 38).

Culler deliberates how the variability of readings might be circumscribed. He attributes "intelligibility" in "poetics" to "operative conventions" (PO 123). The "experienced reader of literature" has "assimilated" an "interpersonal" "system" (PO 128). Hence, "certain expectations" and "ways of reading" "impose severe limitations on the set of acceptable, plausible readings" (PO 127). Culler is confident that "an account of literary competence" should emerge when a critic "notes his own interpretations and reactions to literary works" and "formulates a set of explicit rules" for those results (PO 128; cf. PS 78). Such confidence looks odd next to some other judgments: "considering what particular prior readers have achieved, we tend to conclude that they failed to understand what they were doing" and "were influenced by assumptions they did not control"; and "few of the many who write about literature" have "the arguments to defend their activity" (OD 80; PO vii).

Nonetheless, Culler believes the "considered reactions" of published critics to be "more than adequate as a point of departure for a semiotics of reading" (PS 53). "By consulting the interpretations which literary history records for any major work, one discovers a spectrum of interpretive possibilities of greater interest and diversity than a survey of undergraduates could provide." A critic's

---

[17] Apart from asides like this one, the only coverage is a belated mention of Lévi-Strauss's dependence on Marx (PS 25ff). Derrida's "investigation" is compared in passing to "Marxism" as a "systematic expanding analysis of the overt and covert relations between base and superstructure or institutions and thought" (OD 221). Culler apparently shares "American criticism's" "resistance" to "Marxism" (cf. OD 221), although the latter should be prized because it does not "easily become a method of interpretation" (PS 16).

own reading makes a good model because "an explicit formulation of one's own interpretive operations would have considerable general validity." "The processes of writing" about them would "accentuate everything that is public and generalizable in the reading process" (hardly a deconstructive vision of writing!). If "to read is to operate with the hypothesis of a reader" and "to interpret is to posit an experience of reading" (OD 67), then a critic's own activities are already an implicit theory waiting to be made explicit and public. Naive, nonprofessional readers, for whom many authors wrote, can be disregarded.

We should not be surprised that Culler has consistently tended to supplant the reality of reading with an idealization. For him, our proper concern should be "not what actual readers happen to do, but what an ideal reader must know implicitly in order to read and interpret works in ways which we consider acceptable" (PO 123f; cf. OD 34, 41, 79). This "theoretical construct" can be inferred "not" from "the immediate and spontaneous reactions of individual readers," but from "the meanings they are willing to accept as plausible and justifiable when explained," these being precisely "the meaning of a poem within the institution of literature" (PO 124; OD 35). This argument suggests why the "critic" "does not begin by taking surveys to discover the reactions of readers" (PO 50). But it risks delivering a fresh rationale for interpretation, namely to "explain" "meanings" for other "readers" to "accept."

Culler resists evaluating the fact that "texts have meaning for those who know how to read them" (PO 50) as an urgent empirical problem. Throughout his oeuvre runs the self-deconstructive dualism of referring an issue to readers while vigorously arguing against studying them directly. On one side, he avers that "the meaning of the work is what it shows the reader"; "poetics is essentially a theory of reading"; "a literary taxonomy must be grounded on a theory of reading"; "semantic description must provide a representation of the structuring activity of the reader"; "a theory of plot structure ought to provide a representation of readers' abilities to identify plots"; and so forth (PO 130, 128, 120, 92, 205). He counsels that "one might start from data about the effects of poetic language and attempt to formulate hypotheses"; "to test whether the patterns isolated are in fact responsible," one may "alter the patterns to see whether they change the effects" (PO 68f; cf. PO 256). He feels "the conventions of poetry" are "easier to study" "as the operations performed by readers than as the institutional context taken for granted by authors," since "the meanings readers give" and "the effects they experience are much more open to observation" (PO 117) (cf. p. 196). "Though the meaning of poems may not be reducible to the judgments of individuals," such "are the only evidence we have" (PO 50f).

On the other side, he warns against "the dangers of an experimental or sociopsychological approach which would take too seriously the actual and doubtless idiosyncratic performance of individual readers" (PO 258). "Holland's well-intentioned empirical research" is decried as "miscarried" and "irrelevant" (PS 53). The idea from linguistics that "performance may not be a direct reflection of competence" is deemed a reason why it "would serve little purpose" "to take surveys of the behavior of readers" (PO 123). Just as "the competence that the linguist investigates is not behavior," the latter being *always* at some distance" from the "rule," "claims about literary competence are not to be verified by surveys of readers' reactions which the analyst attempts to explain" (PO 10, 8, 125f, e.a.).

We are therefore to take it on faith that "literary competence" "excludes any readings which seem wholly personal and idiosyncratic" (PO 128). Executing the same maneuver he notes in Fish, Culler says "we have little difficulty setting aside the idiosyncratic response whose causes are personal and anecdotal" (PS 125; OD 41). The "we" must be "the competent readers" who have "learned" "a series of techniques and procedures" and can decide which "readings" ought to be "placed outside the normal procedures of reading" (PS 125).[18] This group alone stands to profit by asserting that "the notion" of "critical argument makes sense only if reading is not an idiosyncratic process" (PO 258).

His deconstructive standpoint offers Culler a fresh rationale against empiricism. "Theories of reading" are designated "stories of reading" that may be "dramatic" (Riffaterre's), "sad" (Stephen Booth's), "merry" (Holland's), and so on (OD 69; cf. OD 64-83). But due to "a gap or division within reading," these "stories" typically "argue for a response that no one" "ever had" (OD 67; cf. Reichert, 1977: 87). So Culler need no longer judge their accuracy, as he had tried to before, but merely portray "the problematic situation to which stories of reading" (including his own earlier one) "have led us" (OD 83; cf. OD 79). He seizes the occasion to remark magisterially that "deconstruction" is "the culmination of recent work on reading" "because projects which began with something quite different in mind are brought up against the questions that deconstruction addresses" (OD 83). This conclusion again illustrates how a deficit left by structuralism, this time the lack of an empirical grounding, becomes a plus for poststructuralism.

Though even in his early view Culler did not "believe" "in a single correct reading" "for each work" (PO 122), he did not renounce the mentality that divides right from wrong or "understanding" from "misunderstanding" (PO 121f). "To reject the notion of misunderstanding as a legislative imposition is to leave unexplained the common experience" of "grasping a mistake" and "the tacit knowledge" needed to do so (PO 121, 123). His more recent formulations better fit the thesis that "a semiotics of reading leaves entirely open the question of how much readers agree or disagree in their interpretations" (PS 50). Now, being right is more properly viewed as a performance. "A correct reading" is "imposed" by "cultural authority"; "'truth is but a fantasy of the will to power'" (Johnson, 1980:

---

[18] Culler agrees with Frye (AC 10f) that literary study leads to an "implicit" "'mental process'" just as "'coherent and progressive'" as the "explicit" one in "science" (PO 121). But note the vigorous complaints Frye lodges against many critics (pp. 47ff).

14); "'a single'" "'meaning'" would be "'theological,'" a "'"message"'" of an "'Author-God'" (Barthes, 1977: 146); "the concepts of criticism" "are a displaced theology"; and so on (PS 77; OD 178, 33; PS 160; cf. OD 187).

From a deconstructive perspective, "a gap or division within reading" "always prevents there from being experiences that might simply be grasped and adduced as the truth of the text" (OD 67f). At most, "we have a stake" in "maintaining our belief" in such an "experience" and "seeing misunderstanding" as "an accident" or "deviation" (OD 68, 175). But "in fact the transformation or modification of meaning" in "misunderstanding is also at work" "in understanding" (OD 176). "A formulation more valid than its converse" would be "that understanding is a special case of misunderstanding," one "whose misses do not matter" or "have been missed" (OD 176, 178). "This account of misunderstanding is not, perhaps, a coherent and consistent position," but "it resists metaphysical idealizations and captures the temporal dynamic of our interpretive situation" (OD 178). This argument forms the background against which Hartman, Bloom, and de Man "treat literature and reading as a repeated historical error or deformation" (PS 13).

Again balancing out a disruptive move with a reassuring one, Culler bases his modified "position" upon "the most familiar aspects" of "interpretive practice" (OD 176). The "acts of reading" at different times or by "different readers" are "not identical." Moreover, "every reading" is "partial" because it must "select and organize" when faced with "the complexities of texts, the reversibility of tropes, and the extendibility of context." "Interpreters" "can use the text to show that previous readings" are "misreadings," and the same can later happen to their versions; in this sense, "the history of readings" reveals how some "misreadings" "may have been accepted as readings" (OD 176). "The historical perspective enables one to recognize the transience of any interpretation" (PS 13).

Thus, the temporal variability and the provisional, utopian nature of understanding are deployed to subvert the "hierarchical opposition with institutional implications" wherein "misunderstanding" is a "complication or negation" that "might be eliminated" (OD 175ff). But the danger impends that this reassuring account may seem revisionistic.[19] Or, it may leave the way open for a critic such as Bloom or Hartman to continue traditional projects within a more ornate and dramatized rhetoric, or to reinject theology in a more personalized and devious form.

Problems were again converted to advantages when the status of the text was shifted. Structuralism believed that "in reading poems or novels, one does establish a hierarchy of semantic features" (PO 53). The function of "the text" was to "throw up semantic features and invite one to group and compose them," "bridging the gap between the semantic features of words and the meanings of sen-

---

[19] "Revisionism" is defined by Jameson (MF xv) as "the act of making a theory comfortable and palatable by leaving out whatever calls for praxis or change" and is unfit for "purely contemplative intellectual consumption."

tences or texts" (PO 236, 77). If the text is "assigned" "properties" "only with respect to a particular grammar," we "need not struggle" "to find some objective property of language which distinguishes the literary from the non-literary" (PO 113f, 128f). The decisive factor is "conventions" of "reading," both "general" (e.g., "impersonality, unity, and significance") and "specific" (PO 178, 114). "Genres are not special varieties of language but sets of expectations which allow sentences of language to become signs of different kinds in a second-order literary system" (PO 129).

The issue of what texts do to people and vice versa remained a thorny question. For Riffaterre, "the reader is 'under strict guidance and control'" "'because of the complexity'" of the text's "'structures,'" "'the multiple motivations of its words,'" and its "saturation by the semantic and formal features of its matrix'" (PS 94). For Eco, the "open text outlines a 'closed' project"; "'you cannot use the text as you want but only as the text wants you to'" (OD 70). Fish vacillated between "a reader who actively takes charge" and one "buffeted by fierce sentences" (OD 71).

Deconstruction offered a resolution by making this indecision axiomatic. "Theories of reading demonstrate the impossibility of establishing well-grounded distinctions between what can be read and what is read, between text and reader" (OD 75). Culler will admit "no compromise formulation, with the reader partly in control, and the text partly in control," but only a "juxtaposition of two absolute perspectives" (OD 73).

The tension between text versus context, or intrinsic versus extrinsic, which troubled Wellek and Warren, is equally suspended. Influenced by critics like Barthes and Kristeva, Culler came to view the "text" as a metaphorical "space," which he usually calls "intertextual" (less often "dialogical," "discursive," "ironic," etc.) (PS 105f, 109, 118; PO 107, 184, 261; PS 116, 113; OD 33).[20] "Poetics" could adopt "two limited approaches to intertextuality": "to look at the specific presuppositions of a given text, the way in which it produces" "an intertextual space whose occupants may or may not correspond to other actual texts"; or else at "the conventions which underlie that discursive activity or space" (PS 118).

"Infinite intertextuality" shows that "the autonomy of texts is a misleading notion" (PS 103). "The possibility of endless replication" that "is constitutive" of the "structure" of the "sign" makes the "'text'" a "'multidimensional space in which a variety of writings'" "'blend and clash,'" "'a tissue of quotations drawn from innumerable centers of culture'" (Barthes, 1977: 146) (OD 188f, 32f). The

---

[20] "Spatial fictions" abound in Culler's theorizing, though he diagnoses them in Fish (PS 119; on Eco's "spatial" vision, see PS 201). The term "space" is also applied to "literature" at large, "metaphor," "the individual," and (quoting Barthes) "the reader," plus the more banal "typographic space" of a poem on a page (PS 7, 207; PO 230; OD 33; PO 184). One "discursive space" is said to have "sentences" as "constituents" (PS 117). Elsewhere, a parallel is drawn to a "gap in the mental process" (PO 184; cf. PO 77; OD 67), variously typified by conceptions of Brooks, James, Ingarden, and Iser (OD 36f).

corollary that the "text" is "'a machine with multiple reading heads for other texts,'" "a weaving" "produced only through the transformation of another text" (OD 139, 99) is reflected when Bloom dwells upon combat with a mighty predecessor, and Hartman upon a haunting by alien voices (Chs. 14, 15). If certain "stories of reading" still "reinstate the text as an agent" that "produces stimulating, unsettling, moving, and reflecting experiences," this strategy is just a way to create "more precise and dramatic narratives" and to "celebrate great works" (OD 82).[21]

As we might surmise from Culler's treatment of the text, the question of its "organic unity" (PO 137) has caused him some inconsistencies. Within structuralism, he saw "totality" as "the end which governs" the "teleological process" of "understanding," a view he attributes in "various forms" to Jakobson, Greimas, Todorov, and Barthes (PO 171f). "Unity is produced not so much by the intrinsic features" of texts "as by the intent at totality of the interpretive process" controlled by "the expectations" of "readers" (PO 91). This "intent" "may be seen as the literary version of the Gestaltist law of Prägnanz: that the richest organization compatible with the data is to be preferred" (PO 174) (cf. p. 136). "As Merleau-Ponty" (1964) "says," "it is only in the light of hypotheses about the meaning of the whole that the meaning of parts can be defined" (PO 92). The "expectation" of "totality" is "often" "disappointed," but is still "the source of the effects," as when "modern poetry" "fails to realize, except momentarily, the continuity promised by formal patterns" (PO 172).[22] Culler himself used "unity" and "totality" as central constructs for discussing particular poems (PO 172-74; PS 68-76). He invoked "the importance" and "power of the convention of unity" and averred that "readers of poems" "feel an overwhelming compulsion to transform" their "heterogeneous experiences unto a unified vision" (PS 69ff). Since "we think of a successful literary form as a synthesis," "critical interpretation seeks a unified totality" (OD 252).

On the other hand, Culler wanted to swerve away from "traditional," "organic," or "New" critics by questioning whether "the task of criticism is to reveal thematic unity" (PO 119; cf. PO 67, 116; PS 3ff; OD 202-05). Culler now thinks it a "major point" of "agreement" that "literary works" are "not 'organic wholes,'"

---

[21] Barthes says "the artistic text" "works untiringly, not the artist or consumer" (OD 70). Culler has "sentences" doing such things as "leading us through a garden" and "revealing" "an orchard," or "forming a drama of innocence" (PO 194, 202). He also attributes to Derrida the theses "the sign has a life of its own," and "the written word is an object in its own right" (PO 248, 133).

[22] Such passages indicate that certain theorizing may apply only to special kinds of works, such as "'open works'" that "invite the reader to play a more fundamental role"; or "works" that are "violently explicit in their dealings" and make a "radical contribution to a theory of signs and signifiers," or "modern" "fiction" with its "faceless protagonists" (OD 37; PS 36; PO 231). Such avant-garde critical theories as structuralism and deconstruction typically have affinities for modern art, however much they may generalize their claims for all art. As de Man says, "the affinities between structuralism and the *nouveau roman* are obvious" (BI 61). Robbe-Grillet once told me Derrida "feels close to me" ("se sent proche de moi").

but "intertextual constructs" (PS 38). A "principle of structural semiotic analysis" was that "elements of a text do not have intrinsic meanings" but "derive their significance from oppositions" "related to other oppositions in a process of theoretically infinite semiosis" (PS 29).

Deconstruction further blurs the boundaries between the "inside and outside" of the text, projecting it as "already riven by contradictions and indeterminacies inherent in the exercise of language" (OD 199; PS 43). "Distance, absence, misunderstanding, insincerity, and ambiguity" are postulated to be "features of writing" and of "speech" as well (OD 101, 103). "Derrida suggests" "the meaning of meaning" "is infinite implication," "the unchecked referral from signifier to signifier" (OD 133). We now face "the impossibility of ever mastering and making present the intertextuality of a particular text" (PS 118). Still, we are not left only with "interpretation which applies one text to another in order to produce new readings," as practiced by "Bloom and others." We should also strive to be "acute analysts of intertextuality" and "engage with all the pragmatic presuppositions, the conventions of discourse, and the sedimentation of prior texts."

Unity ultimately gets the usual deconstructive treatment that both undermines and preserves, keeping an unwarrantable involvement. It is "not easy to banish" "notions of organic unity"; even "critical writings" that "celebrate heterogeneity" continue to "rely" on them (OD 200, 220). Though "deconstructive readings show scant respect for wholeness and integrity," "deconstruction leads not to a brave new world in which unity never figures, but to the identification of unity as a problematical figure" (ON 220, 200). "Interpreters are allowed to argue that a work lacks unity, but to ignore the question of unity is to flout the obligations of their task" (OD 220f). "Deconstructive criticism" "engages with the hierarchical oppositions on which the unifying understanding depends" and with the "elements" it "represses"; "the result is not a new unified reading or an alternative unity," but a "limit perpetually transgressed" by "the significations of the text" (ON 256, 260) (cf. Brenkman, 1976).

Culler scrutinizes Brooks' analysis of Donne's *Canonization* poem and focuses on these lines: "Our legend [. . .] will be fit for verse; / And if no peece of Chronicle wee prove, / We'll build in sonnets pretty roomes; / As well a well wrought urn becomes / The greatest ashes, as halfe-acre tombes, / And by the hymnes all shall approve / Us *Canonized* for Love: / And thus invoke us." Culler adds up "the legend describing the lovers, the verse representation of this legend, the celebratory portrayal of the lovers in the response of those who heard the legend," and so on (ON 203). He concludes: "we have not so much a self-contained urn as a chain of discourses," a "series of self-representations, invocations, and readings" "within the poem and outside it," coming to "no end" (OD 203, 205).

This tendency to interpret a work as both self-referential and self-disseminating is standard among deconstructionists and their heirs; de Man, Bloom, and

Hartman all do it with virtuosity (Chs. 13-15). Indeed, this result is attained in so many deconstructive readings that it becomes the new unifying conception within whose purview a critic can discover "the same thing" or a "comparable logic" or "the same structure" in the most diverse pairs of authors, such as Marx and Hugo, Marx and Kant, or Austin and Lacan (OD 260f). The unity within the text is supplanted by a unity between texts —the repressed converse of those procedures, "put in question" by Culler, whereby "a difference within" gets "transformed" "into a difference between" (ON 215; cf. ON 68, 133).

The dissolution of the subject, about which we will hear more (Chs. 13, 15, 18), rearranges the constellation of author, text, and reader. We already noticed the structuralist proclivity for "rejecting" "the notion of subject" and treating "language and structures, rather than authorial self or consciousness," as "the major source of explanation" (PO 28; OD 21). In this spirit, Lévi-Strauss (1964: 20) declaimed that "'myths think in men, unbeknownst to them'"; and Foucault (1966: 15) ordained that "'man is a fold in our knowledge who will disappear in his present form'" (PO 50, 28, 231; PS 32; OD 223), where one has to wonder who "our" can refer to (plainly not to women). Barthes first looked into "the obsessions of the writer as subject," but soon was "no longer willing to make the individual subject the source of the structures he discovers in the works" (PO 98).

Similarly, "deconstruction" "concentrates on conceptual and figural implications rather than on authorial intentions" (OD 110). "A totalizing notion of the self" is "irreparably subverted by aspects of language," such as "citation and allusion, whose interpretation can never be limited by an authorial project" (PS 166). "Intention" is "not something prior to the text that determines its meaning," but "always a textual construct," "an artifice of reading," and "a way of dramatizing" one's own "claim about the subject's relation to language and textuality" (OD 217f). Therefore, "the attempt to reconstruct an author's intentions is only a particular, highly restricted case of rewriting" (OD 38)—a special imitative performance.

"To divert attention from the author as source and the work as object," "the concepts of *écriture*[23] and *lecture*" were "brought to the fore" (PO 131). Just as "'écriture'" must be "'grasped'" via "'the institution (literature)'" rather than "'the idiolect of the author'" (Barthes 1971: 8), "intertextuality comes to take the place" of "intersubjectivity" (PO 135, 139). The thesis that "language" is "the privileged, exemplary case" to be viewed as "a system of rules" "which escape the subject" fits generative linguistics (cf. PO 28f). "The notion of competence does not lead" "to a reinstatement of the individual subject as the source of meaning"; "the subject" here is "an abstract and interpersonal construct" "constituted by a

---

[23] "Écriture" is not well translated as "writing," since it is much broader, subsuming the "set of institutional conventions within which the activity of writing can take place" (PO 134). It is in this broad sense that Derrida includes speech inside writing (cf. OD 90ff).

series of conventions" (PO 258; cf. OD 111). "Emphasis falls on the reader" not as a person," but as "a function," "a place where codes" "are inscribed" (OD 33).

A striking duplicity among structuralists is that their theorizing is countered by their own conspicuous, flamboyant practices as writers. They proclaim the "decentering" of "the subject" (Foucault, 1969: 22) (PO 29) while parading their own subjectivity; they disperse the "self" while self-centeredly forcing their audience not merely to contend with their imperious style, but to grant them license to disdain usual evidential or logical procedures. Even the sympathetic Culler admits their "self-indulgent love of paradox" and "bizarre interpretations" (OD 21). This duplicity passed on into post-structuralism, yet there it was no longer an anomaly, but just one more self-deconstructing technique for undermining on one level what is asserted on another, and for mismatching the performative with the constative.

The thesis that the "self can no longer be identified with consciousness" (PO 28) has a Freudian cast. As befits his nonempirical stance, Culler remarks that "students of theory" might "read Freud without enquiring whether later psychological research may have disputed his formulations" (OD 9). Like Frye, Fiedler, and Holland, Culler is prepared to assume that "the logic of dreams and fantasies proves central to an account of the forces at work in all our experience" (OD 160). Yet unlike those critics, he doesn't want to psychoanalyze the author. Any "comprehensive" "intention" of an author would be "divided" between "conscious and unconscious," and "the line between" them is "highly variable, impossible to identify, and supremely uninteresting" (OD 127; PO 118).

Instead, Culler "claims" that "literature can illuminate and situate the problems addressed" in "psychoanalysis" by sharpening our "awareness of rhetorical structures and forces" (PS 226)—a project of the Yale group for different reasons. He recommends an "investigation of Freud's writings as simultaneously an analysis of tropes and a tropological construct" (PS 217). "Freudian theory makes narrative the preferred mode of explanation" by "reconstructing a story" with a "decisive" "primal event" that is found to be "in fact a trope" (PS 178ff). "The motive turns out to be a motivation of signs" (OD 191). Freud admitted that "the figurative language peculiar to psychoanalysis" is needed before we can "become aware" of, let alone "describe, the processes in question" (OD 266). "The determining event in a neurosis never occurs," but is "constructed afterwards" by a "textual mechanism of the unconscious," like a "reproduction without an original" (OD 163f).[24] For instance, the "Oedipus complex" is "a structure of signification," a "product of discursive forces" (PS 175). Oedipus decides his guilt "on the force of meaning, the interweaving of prophesies, and the demands of

---

[24] The "Wolfman" (in real life, Sergei Konstantinovich Pankejev), who intrigues other critics, e.g., Holland (PIP 157; 5RR 257) and Bleich (SC 80ff), is exhumed here as well (OD 163, 190f; PS 179). Compare Note 6 to Ch. 19. On the whole case see Freud (1973).

narrative coherence" (PS 174). This procedure whereby the cause is seen as an interpretation elicited by the effect is repeatedly adduced by Culler as a Derridean reversal. [25]

Freud's own "texts" have "considerable deconstructive" "force" and provide "an excellent example" of how "an apparently specialized or perverse investigation may transform a whole domain" (OD 159f; cf. OD 169). Freud "deconstructs" the "hierarchical oppositions" privileging the "normal" over the "pathological," the "real" over the "imaginary," the "conscious" over the "unconscious," and "life" over "death," and "shows that in fact each first term" is "a special case of the second" (OD 160). Moreover, "Freud invokes a complex writing apparatus" "to represent the paradoxical situation in which memories become inscribed" "in the unconscious without ever having been perceived." Derrida hails Freud's "'formidable'" "'theme'" that "'the present is not primal but rather reconstituted'" (OD 164).

In the main, Freudian theorizing serves here to construct speculative versions of communicative activity, such as associating "metaphor" with "the father" and "metonymy" with the "maternal" (OD 60). [26] Or, the "parallelisms and repetitions commonly at work in literary compositions" are not accounted for though "unity of meaning," formerly one of Culler's guiding interpretive principles but now seen in the "interest" of "phallogocentrism" (OD 61); instead, the new account invokes the "repetition compulsion," a "powerful mobile psychic force" (OD 261f). This idea ties in with "the transferential structure of reading, as deconstruction has come to analyze it," which "involves a compulsion to repeat independent of the psychology of individual critics, based on a curious complicity of reading and writing" (OD 272). At most, an "interpreter" might "control" and "master the effects of repetition by casting them into a story" (OD 264).

This usage of Freudian theory is contrasted with the practice of a critic like Frederick Crews that "makes psychoanalysis a source of themes" to use for "interpretation" —here too, in Culler's opinion, "restricting the impact of potentially valuable theoretical developments" emerging (as usual) among "French" scholars (PS 9f). Early Holland would presumably be open to the same complaint, and Bleich to a lesser degree. Hillis Miller (1976: 335f), in contrast, does abstract Freud's ideas into a theoretical model by opposing "'canny'" criticism, with its "'promise of a rational ordering of literary study'" through "'solid advances

---

[25] Culler's demonstration with "the phenomenal order, pain . . . pin" "producing the causal sequence, "pin . . . pain" (OD 86) (a "mosquito" does the deed in PS 183) is not well chosen, the causality being far more elementary than most perceptions of the world. Fletcher (1984: 52, 55) suggests that in Culler's syllogism, "philosophical concepts of experience are asserted, and then denied by philosophical concepts of rhetoric," thereby making "rhetoric function as a transcendental signified."

[26] Fiedler breaks literary creation down like this: "the personal element" is "the Son, the conscious-communal the Father, and the unconscious-communal the Mother" (NT 321).

in scientific knowledge about language,'" against "'uncanny'"[27] criticism whose "'deepest penetration into the actual nature'" of "'language'" occurs "'when logic fails'" (OD 23). Culler feels "dubious" about this "division" between the "two camps" (OD 24f), perhaps troubled by the memory of his own progress from the one to the other. And as we saw, he deplores making deconstruction into one more tool for interpretation (p. 240f).

A more disturbing outlook on Freud arises when Culler's exposé of deconstruction turns to feminism as a special hierarchical inversion.[28] Instead of looking "radical," Freud is found here to be "a prisoner of the most traditional philosophical and social assumptions" (Irigaray 1977) (OD 169). As Millett also notes (Ch. 16), Freud's "account shows that the male's own sexual situation gives him an interest in formulating theories" for "validating" "the debasement of women and the authority of the male" (OD 170). His vision of "intellectuality" as a "patriarchal power" is refuted by the impetus of "feminist criticism" as "one of the most powerful forces of renovation in contemporary criticism," with "a greater effect on the literary canon than any other critical movement" (OD 59, 30).[29] "Feminist criticism" owes its "impact" to its timely "emphasis on the reader and her[30] experience" (OD 42). It "analyzes and situates the limited and interested interpretations of male critics"; indeed, "feminist" might be a good designation for "all criticism alert to the critical ramifications of sexual oppression" (OD 55f). The goal would be not just "a woman's reading," but "a comprehensive perspective" whereby "concepts" produced by "male authority are included within a larger textual system" (OD 58, 61).

"The concept of a woman reader" "asserts" a "continuity between women's experience of social and familial structures and their experience as readers" (OD 46). "'Reading'" is said by Kolodny (1980: 588) to be "'inevitably sex-coded and gender-inflected'" (OD 51). According to Showalter (1979: 25), "'the hypothesis of a female reader changes our apprehension of a given text, awakening us to the significance of its sexual codes'" (OD 50).

---

[27] Freud (1919) expounds "'the uncanny'" as the "'class of the frightening that leads back to the familiar'" (OD 24; cf. OD 262ff). Such a definition warns us that "uncanny" criticism, however bizarre its procedures, is apt to produce familiar results. Still, Miller often goes the other way, starting with a familiar theme and pushing it toward the frightening.

[28] Deconstruction is episodically enlisted for feminist purposes, such as postulating "the differential meaning in the single term 'woman,'" or noting that, when "Freud posits for the woman an original bisexuality," he undercuts his own concept of penis envy by making the woman "the general model of sexuality" and enabling a "rhetorical reversibility of masculine and feminine" (OD 64, 171)—a point also made by Millett (SX 270ff). For a far more elaborate merger of deconstruction and feminism, see Irigaray (1974, 1977) and my summary of her proceedings (Beaugrande, 1987c).

[29] Deconstruction is not being bested here, since "Derrida" "is not primarily engaged" in "reforming the canon" (OD 221).

[30] Culler briefly stops using male pronouns for the reader in favor of female ones (e.g. OD 31, 63), but overlooks such male-based locutions as "Man" and "fall guy" (OD 149, 32). His image of interpretation "emasculating" criticism (PS 7) is worthy of a "phallogocentric" theorist.

Ideological "critiques" can be made of "the phallocentric assumptions that govern literary works" and of the corresponding "phallic criticism" traditionally practised (OD 46, 54). In the "usual situation," "the perspective of the male critic is assumed to be sexually neutral, while a feminist reading is seen" as "an attempt to force the text into a predetermined mold" (OD 55). Beyond the general thesis that "objectivity is constituted by excluding the views" of "women" (among others) (OD 153), Culler has several ideas about how criticism offers "male stories of reading" (cf. OD 42). "Patriarchal" "literary criticism" is prone to see "the role of the author" as "paternal"; to manifest "great concern about which meanings were legitimate" or "illegitimate"; and to "control intercourse with texts so as to prevent the proliferation of illegitimate interpretations" (OD 60f)— tactics we might see in Hirsch's approach. The idea of a "woman reader" "seduced, betrayed by devious male texts" (OD 52) seems reminiscent of Fish, who makes no proposal for the "resisting reader" advocated by Fetterly (1978) (cf. OD 53).

Some critics "emphasize male characters, male themes, and male fantasies" (OD 46), which should hold in varying degrees for Frye, Fiedler, Holland, Bleich, de Man, Bloom, Hartman, and Jameson. Fiedler is cited for invoking a "'male'" "'universality'" in "literature," and Hartman for comparing "'reading'" to "'girl-watching'" (OD 51, 44). Bloom is noticed for "making explicit the sexual connotations of authorship and authority" (OD 60), yet Culler forbears to mention the overt machismo of Bloom's belligerent method. Perhaps a feminist viewpoint might revise the new theologies from Yale: Bloom's explicit one in light of Millett's exposé of religion as a tool for male supremacy (e.g., D.H. Lawrence); and Hartman's more concealed one in light of Freud's "apparent suggestion" that "God" is made "invisible" to reinforce "paternal authority" in the face of the "invisible" "paternal relation" (OD 59).[31]

Culler prudently gives no advice about whether "feminists" should "minimize" or "exalt sexual differentiation"; whether they should "neutralize" and "transcend the opposition between male and female," or else "celebrate the feminine, demonstrating its power," "independence," and "superiority"; whether they should "adopt" and "master" "'male' modes of writing" or "develop a specifically feminine mode"; and so on (OD 172). He merely points to "deconstruction" as a model for "working on two fronts at once, even though the result is a contradictory rather than unified movement" (OD 173). Still, feminism will need to go beyond deconstruction in order to escape "unwarrantable involvement" (cf. OD 88).

Although far from exhaustive, my survey has tried to cover a cross-section of the critical issues Culler has expounded in his main theoretical volumes during his mobile career so far. I suggested that his changes of focus need not mark

---

[31] Culler situates Hartman's "resistance to deconstruction" in its intent to "ignore the sacred" (OD 44), which matches my conclusions (Ch. 15).

changes in intent or program. He has been consistent regarding numerous major issues: the complexity and universality of literature; the baleful predominance of interpretation in American criticism; the status of the subject as a product of codes and conventions; the uselessness of empirical studies; and a general skepticism toward the appropriation of linguistic theories and toward the theoretical efforts of other American critics.

He progressed from confronting structuralism with its problems over to using post-structuralism to incorporate them into the theoretical base, so that, in true deconstructive fashion, the marginal was displaced to the center. This tactic entailed some inconsistency respecting the relationship between literature and criticism, the division between right and wrong readings, and the concept of unity. But all these issues are naturally affected by his adaptation to the changing context of critical discussion. Besides, we have seen how the deconstructive mode allows Culler to remain involved in his earlier positions he puts in question. In the future, these might be inverted back to dominance whenever their dispersal is felt to be unstrategic.

The most consistent aspect I find in Culler's work is its balancing tendency. He established that structuralists were achieving less than was commonly supposed and repudiated its unearned praise; he also established that post-structuralism was achieving more and refuted its undeserved censure.[32] In the process, he gives us a lesson in circumspection about judging literary theories too absolutely, taking their claims at face value, or crediting popular rumors about them.

This lesson expediently argues the need for mediation by metatheoretical explicators like Culler. But it may also foreshadow the moment when the integration of the seemingly marginal and disruptive will constitute a new movement toward centralization and stability. At that point, Culler's role may impel him back to the restraining function he vacated for his current energizing function. If deconstruction becomes too reassuring and reasonable, Culler may handle it in a less genteel and more antagonistic manner. Still, even its eventual displacement from the critical scene would bring one more confirmation of its own thesis on the impossibility of "saying the last word, arresting the process of commentary" (OD 90).

---

[32] Culler's diction is a bit waspish at times. Roger Poole's (1970: 21) praise of Barthes's paper on fashion as "'a correct piece of analysis'" reveals "pernicious ignorance" (PO 38). The "rumors that deconstructive criticism denigrates literature" and "celebrates" "free associations" are "comically aberrant" (OD 280).

13

Paul de Man[1]

Until his recent untimely demise, Paul de Man commanded a considerable following who "acknowledged" his "pre-eminence in the field of literary theory" (Godzich, preface to BI, xv). He was hailed by Hartman as a "boa-deconstructor" and by Culler as one of the "best practitioners of deconstruction" (DC ix; PS 16). Like many critics in his "generation," de Man was impelled by "local difficulties of interpretation" to "shift from historical definition to the problematics of reading" (ALG ix). The further he probed, the more he became convinced that the "dialogue between work and interpreter is endless" (BI 32). The "act of reading," for which "criticism is a metaphor," is "inexhaustible" (BI 107).

His vision might appear to be a dualistic or ironic version of the utopia[2] sketched in Chapters 1 and 2. He forever undertook to read texts and master their meanings while categorically asserting the elusiveness or impossibility of the procedures for doing so. With this tactic, he pursued the implications of deconstruction in a more rigorous and consequential way than the other critics I survey, although he tended in this direction even before he read the books of Derrida, and the two writers proceed rather differently.[3]

For De Man, "all true criticism occurs in the mode of crisis," because it "puts the act of writing into question by relating it to its specific intent" (BI 8; cf. BI 62). "The act of criticism" is "defined" by "scrutinizing itself to the point of reflecting upon its own origin" and "necessity" (BI 8). "Recent developments" reveal additional "outward symptoms" of "crisis." One is "the incredible swiftness with which often conflicting tendencies succeed each other, condemning to immediate obsolescence what might have appeared as the extreme point of avant-gardisme briefly before" (BI 3f). "Crisis" is also diagnosed "when a 'separa-

---

[1] The key to de Man citations is: ALG: *Allegories of Reading* (1979a); BI: *Blindness and Insight* (1983); RT: "The Rhetoric of Temporality" (1969); and SD: "Shelley Disfigured" (1979b).

[2] De Man refers to "utopianism" as a "trap of impatient 'pastoral' thought" (BI 241). For him, a utopia in my sense (Ch. 1) might be on the order of speaking with "a single voice that, by the rigor of its negativity, finally coincides with what it asserts" (ALG 172). Compare Note 15 on "rigor."

[3] De Man's convictions about the "infinite plurality of significations" and "the deep division of being" (BI 236f) were declared in a piece written even "before the advent of Structuralism on the literary scene" (BI 229).

tion' takes place, by self-reflection,[4] between what, in literature, is in conformity with the original intent and what has irrevocably fallen away from this source" (BI 8). The "hesitations" of the formalists already indicated a "conception of poetic consciousness" as "essentially divided, sorrowful, and tragic" (BI 241).

One resolution for the crisis could be that the "dizziness of a mind caught in an infinite regression prompts a return to a more rational methodology" (BI 10). The "attempts" to "inaugurate a more scientific study of literature have played an important part in the development of contemporary criticism" (BI 107).[5] I.A. Richards based his "scientific claims" on "the promise" of a "convergence between logical positivism and literary criticism" (BI 241). "Certain structuralist tendencies" are on a "borderline": they "try to apply extrinsic methods to material that remains defined intrinsically and selectively as literary language" (BI 107). "Since it is assumedly scientific, the language of a structuralist poetics would itself be definitely 'outside' literature, extrinsic to its object, but it would prescribe (in deliberate opposition to describe) a generalized and ideal model of a discourse that defines itself without having to refer to anything beyond its own boundaries." "Scientific" "methods" could apply only "if literature rested at ease within its own self-definition" (BI 164).

But "this stability" "assumed" by "the structuralist goal of a science of literary forms" "systematically bypasses the necessary component of literature" and "a constitutive part of its language": "the fluctuating movement of aborted self-definition." "Literature can be represented as a movement and is, in essence, the fictional narration of this movement" (BI 159). "Moving from an actual, particular text to an ideal one" is a tactic to "avoid" "the logical difficulties inherent in the act of interpretation" (BI 107). In de Man's view, "the semantics of interpretation have no epistemological consistency and can therefore not be scientific" (BI 109). "Interpretation" is "like scientific laws" in being a "generalization that expands the range of applicability of a statement to a wider area" (BI 29). But whereas "the natural sciences" pursue "predictability," "measurement," and "determination," "interpretation" "claims" to "understand" the "phenomenon" and its "intent."

"In order to protect the rationality" of "science," "structural anthropologists" envisioned "a myth without an author," and "linguists" "conceived of a metalanguage without a speaker" (BI 11f). De Man warns that a "fundamental discrepancy always prevents the observer from coinciding fully with the consciousness he is observing; the same discrepancy exists in everyday language, in the impossibility of making the actual expression coincide with what has to be expressed, of making the actual sign correspond with what it signifies" (BI 11).

---

[4] De Man's world abounds in entities doing things to themselves, whence the many "self-" compoundings (e.g. BI 18, 113, 134, 208, 212, 215, 220; ALG 131; SD 55).

[5] Frye is included here, along with Jakobson and Barthes (Note 21), but all three remained "between the two camps" of "science" and "immanence" (BI 107).

An alternate resolution for the crisis could be to "propose a radical relativism" on every "level" from "specific" to "general" (BI 10). Here, "there are no longer any standpoints that can a priori be considered privileged, no structure that functions validly for other structures, no postulate of ontological hierarchy that can serve as an organizing principle from which particular structures derive." "All structures are equally fallacious and are therefore called myths." But the "myth" still depends on the "arbitrary act of interpretation that defines it." So again, we are brought back "from anthropology to the field of language, and finally, of literature" (BI 11). And if "conceptual language, the foundation of civil society," is "a lie superimposed upon an error," we "can hardly expect the epistemology of the sciences of man to be straightforward" (ALG 155).[6]

This referring of fundamental issues to language and suspending or dissolving them there is among de Man's most thematic moves and helps make his work both intriguing and unsettling to the language-oriented critical profession. Even "in the most physical of modes," "the abstraction and generality of a linguistic figure" can "manifest itself" (ALG 182). De Man's referral is totally unlike that of the structuralists, who evidently sought reassurance in the clarity of grammatical and logical forms. For de Man, language is precisely the archetypal space of unreliability and opaqueness, rent with complications, fissures, and ambiguities of every sort. We have to take de Man's word for it, because no empirical demonstrations are attempted: "reading" is "an act of understanding that can never be observed, or in any way prescribed or verified" (BI 107).

De Man prefers to view "reading" as an "allegory" that "narrates the impossibility of reading" (ALG 77, 205). "The allegorical representation of Reading" is "the irreducible component of any text" (ALG 77). "The assumption of readability" is "found to be aberrant"; "all readings are in error because they assume their own readability" (ALG 202). In de Man's terminology, a text is "unreadable in that it leads to a set of assertions that radically exclude each other," or to a "confrontation of incompatible meanings" (ALG 245, 76). "If one of the readings is declared true, it will always be possible to undo it by means of the other; if it is decreed false, it will always be possible to demonstrate that it states the truth of its aberration" (ALG 76). "Language" is "necessarily misleading" and "just as necessarily conveys the promise of its own truth" (ALG 277).

This view is supported with the deconstructive thesis, also articulated by Culler (OD 201), of "the aporia between performative and constative language" (ALG 131) (the latter alternately called "cognitive"). "A text is defined by the necessity of considering a statement, at the same time, as performative and constative" (ALG 270). Yet "performative rhetoric and cognitive rhetoric" "fail to converge" (ALG 300). In the "process of reading," "rhetoric is a disruptive intertwining of trope and persuasion or—which is not quite the same thing—of

---

[6] This thesis ostensibly follows Rousseau, but de Man, who often speaks in the name of others, seems to endorse it.

cognitive and performative language" (ALG ix). "Considered as persuasion, rhetoric is performative but when considered as a system of tropes, it deconstructs its own performance" (ALG 131). Again, the issue is dissolved into language: "rhetoric is a *text* in that it allows for two incompatible, mutually self-destructive points of view, and therefore puts an insurmountable argument in the way of any reading or understanding." "The predicament is linguistic rather than ontological or hermeneutic" (ALG 300).

"The critique of metaphysics" can thus be "structured as rhetoric" (ALG 131). De Man is not thinking of the "naively pejorative sense in which the term" "rhetoric" "is commonly used" for "a tool" in "the manipulation of the self and of others,"[7] or a "fraudulent grammar used in oratory" —as "opposed to a literal use of language" (ALG 173, 130). Nor does he put much stock in "establishing a taxonomy of tropes" (ALG 63). He views "tropes" not as "grids," but as "transformational systems" that produce "substitutive reversals" (ALG 63, 113).[8] He wants to probe the "structures and relays" in which "properties are substituted and exchanged," and "resemblance" is "used" "as a way to disguise differences" (ALG 62, 16).

To point up the "figural dimension of language" in general, de Man adduces "the divergence between grammar and referential meaning" (ALG 270). Following generative linguistics, he defines "grammar" as "the system of relationships that generates the text and that functions independently of its referential meaning"; indeed, "grammatical logic can function only if its referential consequences are disregarded" (ALG 268f). "We call *text* any entity that can be considered from such a double perspective: as a generative, open-ended, non-referential grammatical system and as a figural system closed off by a transcendental signification that subverts the grammatical code to which the text owes its existence" (ALG 270). "The logical tension between figure and grammar is repeated in the impossibility of distinguishing between two linguistic functions," "performative and constative," which (as we were just told) "are not necessarily compatible." This contention disrupts the "literary semiology" of "Barthes, Genette,

---

[7] Yet he keeps referring to the rhetoricity of texts as "seduction," performed by Rilke, Proust, Rousseau, Blake, or Blanchot (ALG 21, 69, 93, 181, 184, 190, 200; BI 62), as well as by literature and figural language in general (ALG 115). Compare the notion of "metaphor" "as a language of desire and as a means to recover what is absent" (ALG 47), reminiscent of Bleich's (far more literal) explanation of the rise of language in the infant (pp. 189ff).

[8] De Man finds it "notoriously difficult, logically as well as historically, to keep the various tropes and figures rigorously apart" (BI 284). "Numerical and geometrical models, assuming the specificity of each particular trope, though unavoidable, are in the long run intenable" (ALG 66). As if to prove his point, he likes to play off the tropes against each other. Although "metaphor" based on "analogy" and implying "identity and totality" is made to oppose "metonymy" based on "contiguity" and implying a "purely relational contact," the "superiority of metaphor" has to asserted by "using metonymic structures" (ALG 14f, 70). "Chiasmus" is seen less as a criss-cross scheme for word placement (de Man likes it, as in "text of desire" and "desire for text," ALG 289), than as a "crossing that reverses the attributes of words and things" (ALG 38).

Todorov, Greimas, and their disciples" that "lets grammar and rhetoric function in perfect continuity," "without apparent awareness of a possible discrepancy between them" (ALG 6). In certain passages, though, "grammar" can be "rhetoricized," and "rhetoric" can be "grammatized" (ALG 15).

Like Derrida, de Man is impressed by Nietzsche's "critique of the main concepts underlying Western metaphysics" (ALG 119). "The critique" indicates that "in these innocent-looking didactic exercises, we are in fact playing for very sizeable stakes" —the more so as "the key" is "literature," that is, "the rhetorical model of the trope" (ALG 15). Nietzsche remarked that "'logic'" is "'an imperative, *not* to know the true, but to posit and arrange a world that *should be true for us*'" (ALG 120). "The convincing power of the identity principle" essential to logic and to its demands for "noncontradiction" "is due to an analogical, metaphorical substitution of the sensation of things for the knowledge of entities" (ALG 122, 119).[9] Nietzsche's contentions raise "the possibility of unwarranted substitutions leading to ontological claims based on misinterpreted systems of relationship," such as "substituting identity for signification" (ALG 123). The "postulate of logical adequacy" "might well be based on a similar aberration" that "cannot be proven right or wrong"; but "our ontological confidence has forever been shaken."

Here again, language is made the agent and model. "The unwarranted substitution of knowledge for mere sensation becomes paradigmatic for a wide set of aberrations all linked to the positional power of language in general, and allowing for the radical possibility that all being, as the ground for entities, may be linguistically" posited, "a correlative of speech acts" (ALG 123). "The linguistic model as speech act" is "established" to be "universal" and yet "voided" of "epistemological authority" (ALG 129). "The possibility for language to perform is just as fictional as the possibility for language to assert." "The critique of metaphysics" "deconstructs" "the illusion that the language of truth" "could be replaced by a language of persuasion" (ALG 130). "Thought as action" is an "illusion" resulting from an "illegitimate totalization[10] from part to whole" (ALG 129f).

As we saw, de Man would "account for" "the allegorical mode" by describing "all language as figural" (BI 136). A "text" may "go beyond this, however" and make its "statement" in "an indirect, figural way that knows it will be misunderstood by being taken literally." It can "tell the story, the allegory of its misunderstanding: the necessary degradation" of "metaphor into literal meaning." "The

---

[9] Compare Einstein (1956: 68): "concepts can never be regarded as logical derivatives of sense impression. But didactic and heuristic objectives make such a notion inevitable. Moral: it is impossible to get anywhere without sinning against reason."

[10] De Man routinely doubts the propriety of "totalizations" (cf. ALG 237, 249, 256; BI 32, 34), though he acknowledges "the desire for totality" to be "an inherent need of the human mind" (BI 54) (cf. Note 12). And, as I remark at the end, he replaces the totalizing of the literary work with a totalizing from the work to all literature (p. 277).

only literal statement that says what it means to say is the assertion that there can be no literal statements" (BI 133). Only "a figure of the unreadability of figures" might "no longer" be "a figure" (ALG 61). "As the report of the contradictory interference of truth and error in the process of understanding," "the allegory of reading" "would no longer be subject to the destructive power of this complication" (ALG 72). "The statement of the enigma that gives language its necessarily referential complexity might itself be no longer a representation but a single voice that, by the rigor of its negativity, finally coincides with what it asserts" (ALG 172). These prospects would seem to outline de Man's own utopia (though he wouldn't call it that), in which reconciliation is paradoxically attained in the moments of most radical negation.[11]

Not too surprisingly, the closest approximation of this utopia turns out to be literature (cf. Ch. 2). Thanks to its "necessarily ambivalent nature," "literary language" "can only tell this story" —"the allegory of its misunderstanding" — "as a fiction, knowing full well that the fiction will be taken for fact and the fact for fiction" (BI 136). "Literature does not fulfill a plenitude"; its "imagination takes its flight only after the void" "that separates intent from reality," "the inauthenticity of the existential project has been revealed" (BI 34f).[12] Through "irony and allegory" (concepts we will engage further on), "the relationship between sign and meaning is discontinuous"; "the sign points to something that differs from its literal meaning and has for its function the thematization of this difference" (BI 209).

The whole line of argument leads straight to the point where de Man, like most of our critics, was heading all along. He expounds the dilemmas of language in such radical terms as to seem highly original and controversial. Then, he presents literature as both the essence and the counterpoint of language and founds his authority as the visionary mediator of indispensable, though disruptive insights. "The possibility of reading," an act which is "prior to any generalization about literature," "can never be taken for granted" (BI 107). "The literary text is not a phenomenal event that can be granted any form of positive existence," but "merely solicits an understanding that has to remain immanent because it poses the problem of intelligibility in its own terms" (a reason why "all interpretation has to be immanent") (BI 107f).[13] Reading is thereby dramatized to

---

[11] Officially, "reconciliation" too is opposed, especially one "of the self with the world by means of art," as proposed by Starobinski (BI 218) and Iser (AR 135, 154), and foreshadowed by some Marxists (pp. 392f).

[12] If the world could "become a more complete, more totalized reality than that of everyday experience," "art would be the expression of a completed reality, a kind of over-perception" (BI 34) (cf. Doubrovsky, 1966). De Man rejected this prospect on the authority of Merleau-Ponty, whose work led Iser to envision a reader being "made to ideate a totality" (AR 141).

[13] De Man is more doubtful about how far criticism can be "intrinsic" in the sense of Wellek and Warren. Whereas "form" was previously "considered to be the external trappings of literary meaning or content," "intrinsic, formalist criticism" has made "outer form" "the intrinsic structure" and

a degree that makes de Man's achievements all the more striking—a tactic we reencounter, greatly megaphoned, in Bloom's work (Ch. 14).[14]

In this project, de Man predictably "equates the rhetorical, figural potential of language with literature itself" (ALG 10; cf. ALG 15). In his view, "literary" "language" "takes for granted" that "sign and meaning can never coincide"; the "essence" of "literature" is the "mirror-effect" of "asserting" its "separation from empirical reality, its divergence, as a sign, from a meaning that depends for its existence on the constitutive activity of this sign" (BI 17). A "definition" of "literary" is thus derived: "any text that implicitly or explicitly signifies its own rhetorical mode and prefigures its own misunderstanding as the correlative of its rhetorical nature; that is, of its 'rhetoricity'" (BI 136). "The text" "accounts for" this "'rhetoricity'" by "postulating the necessity of its own misreading."

Yet precisely because the "literary mode" is "a form of language that knows itself to be mere repetition, mere fiction and allegory," it is "the only form of language free from the fallacy of unmediated expression" (BI 161, 17). The "paradox inherent in all literature" is that it "gains a maximum of convincing power at the very moment that it abdicates any claim to truth" (ALG 50). So "literature" is "condemned (or privileged) to be forever the most rigorous,[15] and consequently, the most unreliable language in terms of which man names and transforms himself" (ALG 19).

These contentions restore the special ontological status of literature, though not very reassuringly. The "structuralist literary critics" had thought it "imperative to show that literature constitutes no exception, that its language is in no sense privileged in terms of unity and truth over everyday forms of language" (BI 12).[16] They wanted to "show that the discrepancy between sign and meaning (signifiant and signifié) prevails in literature in the same manner as in everyday language." We thus find "the trend in Continental criticism, whether it" draws on "sociology, psychoanalysis, ethnology, linguistics," or "philosophy," of launching "a methodologically motivated attack on the notion that a literary or poetic consciousness is in any way a privileged consciousness" (BI 9).

"referential meaning" the "extrinsic" (ALG 4). "This reversal" shows that "the polarities of inside and outside" situate "formalism" in "'the prison house of language.'" In "the recurrent debate opposing intrinsic to extrinsic criticism" "the inside/outside metaphor" is "never being seriously questioned" (ALG 5). De Man, however, uses "the couple grammar/rhetoric" to "disrupt and confuse" the "neat antithesis"; and finds a case where "the inside is always already an outside" (ALG 12, 199).

[14] As if to tip us off, de Man opens his volume by comparing his announcement of "crisis" with Mallarmé's "rhetoric of crisis" whose "mock sensationalism" and "ironic slant" "baffled his foreign audience" (BI 3ff).

[15] "Rigor" seems to be a mental awareness of the twists and evasions of language (cf. ALG 19, 131, 172, 207)—just what de Man has. It doesn't guarantee "the epistemological authority of the ensuing results" (BI 289).

[16] I.A. Richards is also said to "refuse to grant aesthetic experience any difference from other human experiences" (BI 234).

This trend was closely allied to the denial of the "privileged subject" (BI 12). "In structuralism the loss of the intentional factor" "is due to the suppression of the constitutive subject" (BI 32f). Similarly, "language" is for Blanchot (1949) a "'consciousness without a subject,'" and for Poulet (1965) "the medium" for "a radical questioning of the actual, given self, extending to the point of annihilation" (BI 69, 98). Blanchot (1955: 202) wanted "'to take the work for what it is and thus to rid it of the presence of the author'" (BI 64). "Language" "speaks and writes by itself"; and "the work has an undeniable ontological priority over the reader" (BI 69, 64). In Poulet's vision, "the critic" also "relinquishes his own self in his encounter with the work" (BI 97). "The subject that speaks" in his "criticism" "is a vulnerable and fragile subject whose voice can never become established as a presence" —"the very voice of literature" (BI 101).

These estimations indicate that de Man too is inclined to deny the privileged subject and disperse it into language. We might, he says, "conceive" the "categories" of "subject" and "object" "as standing in the service of the language that has produced them" (ALG 37).[17] "Language" "divides the subject into an empirical self, immersed in the world, and a self that becomes like a sign in its attempt at differentiation and self-definition" (BI 213). "The reflective disjunction not only occurs *by means of* language as a privileged category, but it transfers the self out of the empirical world into a world constituted out of, and in, language."

Literary "fiction, far from filling the void" "the human self has experienced" "within itself," "asserts itself as pure nothingness, *our* nothingness stated and restated by a subject that is the agent of its own instability" (BI 19). Through "the literary work," the "subjectivities" of "author" and "reader co-operate in making each other forget their distinctive identity and destroy each other as subjects" (BI 64). Correspondingly, the "loss of the representational function in poetry" "goes parallel with a loss of a sense of selfhood" (BI 172).[18] For such reasons, De Man feels "literature can be shown to accomplish in its terms a deconstruction that parallels the psychological deconstruction of selfhood in Freud" —a motive for "the intensity of the interplay between literary and psychoanalytical criticism" (ALG 174).[19]

Nietzsche's "critique of metaphysics" concurs by "showing" "that the idea" of "the human subject as a privileged viewpoint is a mere metaphor by means of which man protects himself from his insignificance by forcing his own inter-

---

[17] A Rilke poem is the occasion for this view, which sounds just like de Man to me. The following quote claims to speak for Baudelaire (BI 213).

[18] These views are aired in regard to Lévi-Strauss, Blanchot, Yeats, and Hugo Friedrich (BI 19, 64, 172). But compare the remark on Mallarmé: "poetry does not give up" "its dependence on the fiction of a self that easily" (BI 182).

[19] Freud's concept of "defense" seems close to de Man's diagnosis that "the blindness of the subject to its own duplicity has psychological roots since the unwillingness to see the mechanism of self-deception is protective" (BI 113). Freudian imagery is certainly prevalent in de Man's vision of language and the self (Note 31).

pretation of the world upon the entire universe, substituting a human-centered set of meanings that is reassuring to his vanity for a set of meanings that reduces him to being a mere transitory accident in the cosmic order" (ALG 111). This "metaphoric substitution is aberrant but no human self could come into being without this error." "Making the language that denies the self into a center rescues the self linguistically at the same time that it asserts its insignificance" (ALG 111f). "The usual scheme which derives truth from the convergence of self and other" (as invoked by Hirsch and Bleich, for instance) is "reversed" "by showing that the fiction of such a convergence is used to allow for the illusion of selfhood to originate."

Still, de Man continues to accord literature a special place—as discourse that, while it doesn't "escape" the "duplicity" in "everyday language" (BI 9), is at least conscious enough of it to draw characteristic consequences. "The claim of literary language to truth and generality" is "based on a duplicity within a self that willfully creates confusion between literal and symbolic action in order to achieve self-transcendence as well as self-preservation" (BI 113). Literature "invents fictional subjects to create the illusion of the reality of others. But the fiction is not myth, for it knows and names itself as fiction. It is not a demystification, it is demystified from the start" (BI 18). "Literary history could in fact be paradigmatic for history in general, since man himself, like literature, can be defined as an entity capable of putting his own mode of being into question" (BI 165).

De Man's portrayal of literature expediently aligns it with deconstruction, a move Culler diagnosed in Miller as well (pp. 239ff). In his magisterial fashion, de Man draws this equation for all language, though adducing a literary text each time, often by Nietzsche or Rousseau. One such "text" "establishes that deconstruction is not something we can decide to do or not to do at will; it is coextensive with any use of language, and this use is compulsive" (ALG 125). "The paradigm for all texts consists of a figure (or a system of figures) and its deconstruction" (ALG 205). "Allegories" of "unreadability" are also "allegories of the deconstruction and the reintroduction of metaphorical models" (ALG 257). "Semantic dissonance" is the "residue of meaning that remains beyond the text's own logic and compels the reader into an apparently endless process of deconstruction" (ALG 99). For de Man, "poetic writing is the most advanced and refined mode of deconstruction" (ALG 17).

The same argument cannily justifies deconstructive "critical writing," from which the "poetic" "may differ" in the economy of its articulation, but not in kind" (ALG 17). If (as Schlegel avowed), "all 'modern' literature" is "characterized" "by the ineluctable presence of a critical dimension," "critics can be granted the full authority of literary authorship" (BI 80). "Poetry is the foreknowledge of criticism," which "merely discloses poetry for what it is" (BI 31). Indeed, "the critical and the poetic components are so closely intertwined that is it impossible to touch the one without coming into contact with the other" (BI 80).

Since (as de Man assured us), "they are not scientific, critical texts have to be read with the same awareness of ambivalence that is brought to the study of non-critical literary texts" (BI 110). Because "the criterion of literary specificity" depends on "the degree of consistent 'rhetoricity' of the language," a "critical" "text" that "signifies its own rhetorical mode" is "not more or less literary than a poetic text," albeit criticism proceeds "by means of statements" and poetry "avoids direct statement" (BI 136f).

De Man's version of the Yale-school power play, whereby critics demand the rank of authors and poets, is restrained and uneasy compared to the versions of Bloom and Hartman. For one thing, de Man's view of literature is not calculated to exalt (despite Culler's idea that it "celebrates" "great writings of the past," OD 276). For instance, "literary" and "critical texts" share the "discrepancy between meaning and assertion" that "is a constitutive part of their logic" (BI 110). The two also share the "immanence" of "posing the problem" of "intelligibility in its own terms" (BI 107). Just as literature "becomes authentic when it discovers that the exalted status it claimed for its language was a myth," the critic can follow the same "intent at demystification that is more or less consciously present in the mind of the author" (BI 14). "Texts engender texts," including criticism no doubt, "as a result of their necessarily aberrant semantic structure" (ALG 162). Such parallels with literature hardly endow criticism with the glory or monumentality Bloom and Hartman sometimes conjure.

Moreover, deconstructive criticism is doomed to remain trapped in the same quandaries of language it purports to explicate (cf. Ch. 12). "Deconstructive readings can point out the unwarranted identifications achieved by substitution, but they are powerless to prevent their recurrence even in their own discourse, and to uncross, so to speak, the aberrant exchanges that have taken place"; "they leave a margin of error, a residue of logical tension that prevents the closure of the deconstructive discourse" (ALG 242). In fact, "deconstructions of figural texts engender lucid narrative which produce, in their turn" a "darkness more redoubtable than the error they dispel" (ALG 217).

In consequence, we face "the discouraging prospect of an infinity of similar future confusions, all of them potentially catastrophic in their consequences" (ALG 10). "Nothing therefore prevents the deconstructive labor" "from starting all over again" (ALG 245). At best, we can proceed with a critical "rigor" which is "fully aware of the misleading power of tropes," and which "pursues its labors regardless of the consequences, the most rigorous gesture of all being that by which the writer severs himself from the intelligibility of his own text" (ALG 131, 207).

De Man's model of the uneasy symbiosis between literature and criticism, or between text and commentary, bears as its label a programmatic oxymoron: "blindness and insight." This concept of "blindness," "implying no value judgment," is "the necessary correlative of the rhetorical nature of literary language" (BI 141). "A penetrating but difficult insight" into that "nature" can "be gained only because the critics" are "in the grip" of their own "peculiar blindness," which may be "inextricably tied up with the act of writing itself" (BI 106). Possibly, some "characteristic of literary language causes blindness in those who come in close contact with it." Indeed, the "most enlightened" "writers" elicit a "particularly rich aberrant tradition" that forms "the basis, in fact, of literary history" (BI 141). "Since interpretation is nothing but the possibility of error, by claiming that a certain degree of blindness is part of the specificity of all literature we also reaffirm the dependency of the interpretation on the text and of the text on the interpretation" —a welcome affirmation for criticism.

De Man is not implying that "what the critic says has no immanent connection with the work, that it is an arbitrary addition or subtraction, or that the gap between his statement and his meaning can be dismissed as mere error. The work can be used repeatedly to show where and how the critic diverged from it, but in the process of showing this our understanding of the work is modified and the faulty vision shown to be productive" (BI 109). "The discrepancy between the original and the critical text" is "given immanent exegetic power as the main source of understanding" (BI 110). The critic's "statement" shows "blindness," whereas his or her "meaning" provides "insight"; such is the "constitutive discrepancy in critical discourse." The "interaction between critical blindness and critical insight" is "a necessity dictated and controlled by the very nature of all critical language" (BI 111). A "double movement of revelation and recoil will always" pervade "a genuine critical discourse" (BI 289). The critic is continually "forced to resort to paradoxical formulations, such as defining the modernity of a literary period as the manner in which it discovers the impossibility of being modern" (BI 144).

Still, de Man allows for several variants of literary blindness according to one's point of view. If the author is "not-blinded" because he or she "accounts at all moments" for the text's "rhetorical mode," then the "blindness is transferred from the writer to his first readers"; the task of the subsequent "critical reader" is to "reverse the tradition and momentarily take us closer to the original insight" (BI 139, 141). But if "the literary text itself has areas of blindness," then "reader and critic coincide in their attempt to make the unseen visible" (BI 141). Or, if the "literary text" is both "critical" and "blinded," then the critic's "reading" "tries to deconstruct this blindness" by "undoing, with some violence," what Derrida calls "the 'orbit of significant misinterpretation'" (BI 141, 116). These various arrangements give de Man substantial flexibility for maneuvering his own function in relation to an author or critic. They also further blur the margin between literature and criticism by consigning both to a ward where visual diseases are abruptly contracted or cured.

"Writing critically about critics thus becomes a way to reflect on the paradoxical effectiveness of a blinded vision that has to be rectified by means of the insights it unwittingly provides" (BI 106). In several of well-known essays, de Man "reflects" in just this fashion. He develops special techniques to preserve the positive achievements of criticism not *in spite of,* but *because of* his rejection of its declared principles and results. His negativity affirms while it denies, and rescues underlying truths from behind published errors. This procedure parallels the deconstruction that conserves its undermined counterpositions (cf. Ch. 12).

De Man examines a range of critics whose "insight seems" "to have been gained from a negative movement that animates the critic's thought, an unstated principle that leads his language away from his asserted stand, perverting and dissolving his stated commitment to the point where it becomes emptied of substance, as if the very possibility of assertion had been put into question" (BI 103). "The critics'" "language could grope toward a certain degree of insight only because their method remained oblivious to the perception of this insight" (BI 106). If the critic is "by definition incompetent to ask" "the question of his own blindness," then "the insight exists only for a reader in the privileged position of being able to observe the blindness as a phenomenon in its own right," and "so being able to distinguish between statement and meaning." This "privilege" is de Man's own claim to authority, now that he has argued away the right to determine a correct or original reading for a text.[20]

A case in point is his treatment of the New Critics, whom he proposed, "before the advent of Structuralism on the literary scene," "to introduce" "to French readers" while warning against "the dead-end of formalist criticism" (BI 229).[21] The New Critics practised "reassuring criticism" by "suggesting" a "balanced and stable moral climate," and "refused to grant aesthetic experience any difference from other human experiences" (BI 234f). But despite their idea of a "perfect continuity between the sign and the thing signified," they collided with the "fundamental ambiguity" "constitutive of all poetry" and with an "infinity of valid readings" —the ultimate cause being "the deep division of Being itself" (BI 232, 236f). The New Critics clung to "a reified notion of a literary text as an objective 'thing'" and succeeded in "describing" "literary language as a language of irony and ambiguity" only by making "the concept of form" "function in a radically ambivalent manner, both as a creator and undoer of organic totalities" (BI 104). Thus, their "final insight" "annihilated the premises that led up to it."

In his critique of critiques, de Man seems to defer to the lord high executioner of western metaphysics, Jacques Derrida. The latter is saluted for applying "the rigor and intellectual integrity of a philosopher whose main concern is not with literary texts to restore the complexities of reading to the dignity of a philosophical question" (BI 110). This accomplishment goes beyond that of "critics like Blanchot and Poulet, who make use of the categories of philosophical reflection"

---

[20] However, he still uses the term "correct" for what matches his own beliefs (ALG 135, 166, 202, 229; BI 181, 288). Views he doesn't hold are "wrong" (BI 112) or in "error" (BI 219, 226). "A mistake" is not the same as the the "blind spot" every writer must have (BI 139).

[21] The piece is also an attack on the early Barthes, whose views are said to match the New Critics' (BI 231f, 234, 240f) and whose proclamations of scientific method must have galled de Man.

but "erase the moment of actual interpretive reading, as if the outcome of this reading could be taken for granted in any literate audience." In Derrida's work, the "interaction between critical blindness and critical insight" appears "no longer in the guise of a semiconscious duplicity, but as a necessity dictated and controlled by the very nature of all critical language" (BI 111). "The discrepancy implicitly present in the other critics here becomes the explicit center of the reflection." Hence, "Derrida's work is one of the places where the future possibility of literary criticism is being decided, although he is not a literary critic in the professional sense."

Yet even Derrida gets diagnosed as blind regarding Rousseau, who plays a central role in *De la Grammatologie* (1967). De Man "claims Rousseau to be" a "non-blinded author" that Derrida, in "blindness," "misreads" as a blinded one "for the sake of his own exposition and rhetoric" (BI 141, 139). The "misreading" was "deliberate": "insights that could have been gained from the 'real' Rousseau" are deployed to "deconstruct a pseudo-Rousseau" fabricated by "the established tradition of Rousseau interpretation" (BI 139f). Derrida does not find in Rousseau an author who "fell back into confusion, bad faith, or withdrawal,"[22] but places him in a "tradition that defines Western thought in its entirety: the conception of all negativity (non-being) as absence and hence the possibility" of a "reappropriation of being (in the form of truth, of authenticity, of nature, etc.) as presence" (BI 112, 114).

De Man retorts that in Rousseau, "a vocabulary of substance and of presence is no longer being used declaratively but rhetorically"; "Derrida misconstrues as blindness what is instead a transposition from the literal to the figural level of discourse" (BI 138f). "Rousseau escapes from the logocentric fallacy" of "favoring voice over writing" "to the extent that his language is *literary*," because "literature" "demystifies" "the priority of oral language over written" (BI 137f). "Derrida" is "unwilling or unable to read Rousseau as literature" and "reproaches" him "for doing exactly what he legitimately does himself" —the "established philosophical procedure" of using "a philosophical terminology with the avowed purpose of discrediting this very terminology" (BI 137ff).

The disputed source-work is Rousseau's disquisition on the origin of language, whose thesis that figural usage precedes the literal is shared by de Man, as we have seen (see also ALG 149-54). Derrida, however, states that Rousseau's "theory of metaphor is founded on the priority of the literal over the metaphorical meaning," so that the text reveals "a moment of blindness in which Rousseau says the opposite of what he means to say" (BI 133). "Rousseau" "'relinquishes'" "'literal meaning'" for "'the designation of objects'" but retains it for an "interiorized" "object," namely "a state of consciousness, a feeling or a passion" (cf. Derrida 1967: 389) (BI 133). This interpretation empowers Derrida to place

---

[22] Even the "sympathetic and penetrating" critic Jean Starobinski (1961) tended to "reduce Rousseau from the status of a philosopher to that of an interesting psychological case" (BI 113).

Rousseau within "Western thought" at "the moment when the postulate of presence is taken out of the external world and transposed within the self-reflexive inwardness of a consciousness" (BI 134). De Man, in .contrast, views Rousseau as already deconstructive, provided we read the philosophical works with the same rhetorical awareness as the literary works (cf. also ALG 159, 220, 247).

Derrida expends "a considerable and original interpretative effort that has to move well beyond and even against the face-value of Rousseau's own statement" in order to "demonstrate the strict orthodoxy of Rousseau's position with regard to the traditional ontology of Western thought" (BI 122f). "Representation is conceived as imitation in the classical sense of eighteenth-century aesthetic theory" and thus "confirms rather than undermines the plenitude of the represented entity" (BI 123). De Man disagrees: "Rousseau's theory of representation is not directed toward meaning as presence and plenitude but toward meaning as void"; "the sign is devoid of substance, not because it has to be a transparent indicator that should not mask a plenitude of meaning, but because the meaning itself is empty" (BI 127).

The whole dispute may not seem terribly vital, since both critics agree on the priority of figurality, whether or not Rousseau is counted an ally. Moreover, de Man is not passing a negative judgment on Derrida, but merely gathering fresh evidence that "blindness" is "the necessary correlative of the rhetorical nature of literary language" (BI 141). Still, the debate intriguingly reveals how the authority of one's own statement must be founded by dismantling that of someone else's (an idea Bloom carries further). Having abandoned, at least in principle, the search for the real meaning of texts, de Man claims instead the right to decide what constitutes "blindness" or "insight," and thus the right to support an argument with a source that either disagrees or agrees with him. Derrida prepares his counterposition by making Rousseau's text say the opposite of what it seems to; de Man counters Derrida's text and restores the statement of Rousseau's. We might have saved a deal of trouble by taking Rousseau's word for it from the start. But the deconstructionist mind needs "a sparring partner," "an antithetical mask or shadow" to "gain its momentum" (cf. BI 140) —even if the partner is just another such mind.

In a similar blend of assertion and negation, de Man envisions a "rhetoric of reading reaching beyond the canonical principles of literary history" but still using them "as the starting point of their own displacement" (ALG ix). De Man heretically vows that "considerations of the actual and historical existence of writers are a waste of time from a critical viewpoint" (BI 35). "What we usually call literary history has little or nothing to do with literature"; "literary interpretation" "is in fact literary history" (BI 165).

Like that of the subject, the author's role is marginalized in de Man's view of "literature," which "originates in the void that separates intent from reality" (BI 34). Rousseau, for instance, attained "efficacy" for his "text" by making it "a version" of a "rhetorical model" of "language over which he had no control" (ALG 277). Or, Proust tried to "celebrate the self-willed and autonomous inventiveness of a subject" and yet produced "images relying" on "semi-automatic grammatical patterns" (ALG 16).

Within such an outlook, the question of whether "the themes" of a work are "the expression" of the author's "own lived experience" may seem "irrelevant" (ALG 50). But de Man does introduce authorial history when it supports a reading, as in: "the situation of the scene" "corresponds to the actual predicament of Rousseau at that time"; or the "extension of meaning" is "consistent with the thematic concerns of Mallarmé's other works of the same period" (ALG 175; BI 179). De Man is inconsistent about the consistency of the author. On the one hand, the fact that "Rilke says just about exactly the opposite in a prose text" "hardly invalidates our reading" of a poem (ALG 42). On the other hand, "the unpublished fragments, contemporaneous with the main text" by Nietzsche "reduce" it to "an extended rhetorical fiction devoid of authority" (ALG 101). We see here more illustrations of my reservation (p. 116) about Hirsch's validation procedure: the critic subjectively decides what to do with authorial evidence.

De Man's thinking rejects the traditional "historiography" based on "an organically determined view of literary history" (ALG 80). "The critical 'deconstruction' of the organic model"[23] "creates radical discontinuities and disrupts the linearity of the temporal process to such extent that no sequence of actual events" "could ever acquire, by itself, full historical meaning" (ALG 81). As we'd expect, de Man avers that "society and government derive from a tension between man and his language" (ALG 156). The "political nature" of "all forms of human language" is to be construed "not in the representational, psychological, or ethical sense," "but rather in terms of the relationship, within the rhetorical model, between the referential and the figural semantic fields" (ALG 156f).

We might surmise that for de Man, history is essentially the history of rhetoric. In "the classical sense of eighteenth-century aesthetic theory," "representation is conceived as imitation" and "functions as a memnotechnic sign that brings back something that happened not to be there at the moment, but whose existence in another place, at another time, or in a different mode of consciousness is not challenged" (BI 123). Accordingly, "classical" "theories" "repeatedly state as the main function of art" "the possibility of making the invisible visible, of giving presence to what can only be imagined," and thereby lending "the ontological stability of perceived objects" to "what lies beyond the senses" (BI 124). "The mimetic imagination is able to convert non-sensory, 'inward' patterns of experience (feelings, emotions, passions) into objects of perception and can therefore represent as actual concrete presences, experiences of consciousness devoid of objective existence" (BI 123f).

In "romantic" "texts," on the other hand, "consciousness does not result from

---

[23] In Nietzsche's "terminology," the "organic" approach is called "monumental" (ALG 81).

the absence of something, but consists of the presence of a nothingness; poetic language names this void with ever-renewed understanding" (BI 18) By asserting that "this persistent naming is what we call literature," de Man binds literature much closer to romanticism than to classicism.

Like Hayden White and the early Culler, de Man explores literary history in terms of the evolution of dominant rhetorical tropes.[24] To propose his own version, he naturally has to devise "a historical scheme that differs entirely from the customary picture" and "demystifies" the established "terms" (BI 208, 211). He accuses prior critics of "associating" "rhetorical terms with value judgments that blur distinctions and hide the real structures" (BI 188). He now calls for "a more systematic treatment of an intentional rhetoric."

"The entire historical and philosophic pattern changes a great deal" if one assumes, against a long tradition,[25] that "the dialectic between subject and object does not designate the main romantic experience, but only one passing moment in a dialectic, and a negative moment at that" (BI 204f cf. BI 208). De Man mistrusts "conceptions of metaphor" as "a dialectic between object and subject, in which the experience of the object takes on the form of a perception or a sensation"; and of the "symbol as a unit of language in which the subject-object synthesis can take place" (BI 193, 199).

De Man's view of language being irremediably divided, he devalues the "symbol," whose "superiority" "over allegory" was "asserted" by Coleridge and Goethe (BI 191, 189). "In the world of the symbol, life and form are identical" for Coleridge; "its structure is that of the synecdoche, for the symbol is always a part of the totality that it represents" (BI 191). "Consequently, in the symbolic imagination, no disjunction of the constitutive faculties takes place, since the material perception and the symbolical imagination are continuous, as the part is continuous with the whole." Eventually, "the supremacy of the symbol, conceived as an expression of unity between the representative and the semantic function of language, becomes a commonplace that underlies literary taste," "criticism," and "history" (BI 189).

De Man traces this outlook to his contemporary, Hans-Georg Gadamer. In *Wahrheit und Methode*, "Gadamer makes the valorization of symbol" "coincide with the growth of an aesthetics that refuses to distinguish between experience

---

[24] De Man vacillates between the terms "modes" and "tropes" in the early paper (e.g. RT, 207, 192). White's scheme of tropes is summarized in Note 14 to Ch. 12. Culler has since repudiated his own scheme (p. 238).

[25] See also BI 208. Failure to achieve a synthesis of "subject and object" may be an advantage, linked to "the most original and profound moments in the works, when an authentic voice becomes audible" (BI 204f). Compare de Man's high esteem for Blanchot (ranked above the entire "nouveau roman") in this regard (BI 64). On the utopian projection of the synthesis in Hegelian and Marxist thought, see Jameson (MF 38, 44, 141, 146) and Iser's more hopeful projection (Note 11). On the unity of "mind and nature" compare Wasserman (1964), Abrams (1965), and Dieckmann (1966) (RT 181f, 184).

and the representation of this experience" (BI 188). "The poetic language of genius is capable of transcending this distinction and can thus transform all individual experience directly into general truth." "The subjectivity of experience is preserved when it is translated into language; the world is then no longer seen as a configuration of entities that designate a plurality of distinct and isolated meanings, but as a configuration of symbols ultimately leading to a total, single, and universal meaning." Hence, "the symbol is founded on an intimate unity between the image that rises up before the senses, and the supersensory totality that the image suggests" (BI 189).

All these conceptions don't suit de Man's temperament. He brushes aside "the asserted superiority of the symbol" as a "tenacious self-mystification" (BI 208). He swears that the "symbolical style will never be allowed to exist in serenity" or "to gain an entirely good poetic conscience." At best, the symbol is "a special case" that "can lay no claim to historical or philosophical priority over other figures" (BI 191). At worst, it is a "mystified form of language" and a "pseudo-synchronic structure" that "misleads one into believing in a stability of meaning that does not exist" (BI 132f).

De Man elects to champion "allegory," a mode at whose expense the symbol had been elevated (cf. BI 188ff, 208). For Coleridge, "the allegorical form appears purely mechanical, an abstraction whose original meaning is even more devoid of substance than its 'phantom proxy,' the allegorical representative" (BI 191f). For Gadamer (1960: 70), "'allegory'" is like "'non-art, in that'" it "'has run its full course'" "'as soon as its meaning is reached'" (BI 188f). Allegory was reduced to "a sign that refers to one specific meaning and thus exhausts its suggestive potentialities once it has been deciphered" (BI 188). It "appears as the product of the age of Enlightenment" and is "reproached" for being "drily rational and dogmatic in its reference to a meaning that it does not itself constitute" (BI 189). Even in "recent French and English studies of the romantic and post-romantic eras," "allegory is frequently considered an anachronism and dismissed as non-poetic" (RT 175).

De Man's counterargument invokes "the rhetoric of temporality." He "locates" "the dialectical relationship between subject and object" "entirely in the temporal relationships that exist within a system of allegorical signs. It becomes a conflict between a conception of the self seen in its authentically temporal predicament and a defensive strategy that tries to hide from this negative self-knowledge" (BI 208). Whereas "nature" can reveal "endurance within a pattern of change" or "a metatemporal stationary state beyond the apparent decay of a mutability" that "leaves the core intact," the "self" is "caught up entirely within mutability" (BI 196f). "The temptation exists, then, for the self to borrow" "the temporal stability that it lacks from nature, and to devise strategies by means of which nature is brought down to a human level" (BI 197). This "borrowing" could maintain the "illusionary priority of a subject" (BI 200).

The "allegory" offers a better resolution for the predicament, because in its "world," "time is the originary constitutive category" (BI 207). "The prevalence of allegory always corresponds to the unveiling of an authentically temporal destiny. This unveiling takes place in a subject that has sought refuge against the impact of time in a natural world to which, in truth, it bears no resemblance" (BI 206). The "relationship between signs necessarily contains a constitutive temporal element": "the allegorical sign" must "refer to another sign that precedes it" (BI 207). The "essence of this previous sign" is to be "pure anteriority," apparently because the sign was nowhere inscribed. "The meaning constituted by the allegorical sign can then consist only in the *repetition.*" Accordingly, "allegory designates primarily a distance in relation to its own origin, and renouncing the nostalgia and the desire to coincide, establishes its language in the void of this temporal difference." " 'Allegory' " is thereby able to "suggest a disjunction between the way in which the world appears in reality and the way it appears in language" (BI 191).

This account is symptomatic for the whole rhetorical movement focusing on intertextuality, the way any text refers to others. This phenomenon could be described as "temporal" in the sense that within the entire language system, the use of any sign other than a utter neologism presupposes its prior uses (in Derridean diction, it bears their "traces"). On the other hand, these uses are also believed to coincide at least enough to guarantee that people know what the sign should mean; and the exact timing of those uses is often neither known nor relevant. Allegory is apparently portrayed by de Man as a text which coincides with some uninscribed prior text it declines to declare, so that—in contrast to the traditional view de Man rebukes—its meaning cannot be exhausted.

On close inspection, criticism also might become an allegory by dissolving the prior text to which it refers. An "allegory of reading" might have "universal significance" if it could be a "report of the contradictory interference of truth and error in the process of understanding" (ALG 72). His own writings might be considered an endless attempt to provide just such a report. He insistently reflects on the "allegorical" discourse that "repeats" a "potential confusion between figural and referential statement" or raises the prospect of "the impossibility of reading" (ALG 116, 205). The whole "blindness and insight" dynamics also rests on the irredeemable fusion of error and truth. The danger is that de Man's general critique of language might allow the allegory to gradually absorb all discourse, or at least all literature. Some such tendency might indeed be detected in his development between the "temporality" essay" (1969) and his *Allegories of Reading* (1979), whose title is instructive in this regard.

Temporality also undergoes a related expansion that threatens to absorb all discourse. Due to "the structural characteristics of language," "the visual perception which creates a false illusion of presence has to be replaced by a succession of discontinuous moments that create the fiction of a repetitive temporality" (BI 131f). "All sequential language is a dramatic, narrative language," because "language is a diachronic system of relationships." Correspondingly, "literature is an entity that exists not as a single moment of self-denial, but as a plurality of moments that can, if one wishes, be represented—but this is a mere representation —as a succession of moments or a duration" (BI 159). "Literature" "is, in essence, the fictional narration of this movement." Hence, "chronology is the structural correlative of the necessarily figural nature of literary language" (BI 133).

If de Man's reasoning tends to make allegory swallow everything, much the same happens with irony. He decides that "literary history" is "the dialectical play" between "allegory" and "irony," as well as "their common interplay with mystified forms of language (such as symbolic or mimetic representation), which it is not in their power to eradicate" (BI 226). "Irony and allegory" have "a shared structure" wherein "the relationship between sign and meaning is discontinuous, involving an extraneous principle," but this "aspect may well be a description of figural language in general" (BI 209). The two are further "linked in their common demystification of an organic world postulated in a symbolic mode of analogical correspondences or in a mimetic mode of representation in which fiction and reality could coincide" (BI 222). "The two modes" are "two faces of the same fundamental experience of time," that is, "determined by an authentic experience of temporality which, seen from the point of view of the self engaged in the world, is a negative one" (BI 226).

Still, the two may differ somewhat in their temporality. Irony is more likely to "appear as an instantaneous process" occurring in "the instant at which the two selves, the empirical as well as the ironic, are simultaneously present" —"two irreconcilable and disjointed beings" (BI 225f).[26] Thus, "irony is a synchronic structure, while allegory" (whose "temporality" I outlined above) "appears as a successive mode capable of engendering duration as the illusion of a continuity that it knows to be illusionary" (BI 226). Irony is "the mode of the present" and "knows neither memory nor prefigurative duration, whereas allegory exists entirely in an ideal time that is never here and now but always a past or an endless future." Its link to the "present" rather than to "an ideal time" makes "irony come closer to the pattern of factual experience and recapture some of the factitiousness of human experience as a succession of isolated moments lived by a divided self."

This referral back to the "divided self" we might well have foreseen. De Man's world is distinctly schizophrenic, with language being both cause and effect, plus model and expression. Hence, we're not surprised when de Man relates "irony" to "a problem that exists within the self" (BI 211; cf. BI 212, 214, 219, 226). The self undergoes "duplication" or "multiplication," so that "irony" is "a relation-

---

26 The "symbol," which de Man devalues, is also given "simultaneity" (BI 207). But this exception from the pervasive temporality of literature is not clear to me.

ship, within consciousness, between two selves" (BI 212).[27] "The writer" "constitutes by his language" an "ironic, two-fold self," but "only at the expense of his empirical self, falling (or rising) from a stage of mystified adjustment into the knowledge of his mystification" (BI 214). Thus, the loss of experienced immediacy is accompanied by a gain in self-awareness. "The ironic language splits the subject into an empirical self that exists in a state of inauthenticity and a self that exists only in the form of a language that asserts the knowledge of this inauthenticity." This account agrees with de Man's notion of literature as language that is at least aware of the "separation from empirical reality" (BI 17).

Once stated in such fundamental terms, "irony possesses an inherent tendency to gather momentum and not to stop until it has run its full course; from the small and apparently innocuous exposure of a small self-deception it soon reaches the dimensions of the absolute" (BI 215). De Man's theorizing correspondingly progressed from a concept of irony as a "trope" (RT 192) to the point where "irony is no longer a trope but the undoing of the deconstructive allegory of all tropological conditions, the systematic undoing, in other words, of understanding" (ALG 301). "Irony" "dissolves in the narrowing spiral of a linguistic sign that becomes more and more remote from its meaning, and it can find no escape" (BI 222). "It can know" "inauthenticity, but can never overcome it; it can only restate and repeat it on an increasingly conscious level" without ever "making its knowledge applicable to the empirical world." "All true irony" "has to engender" "irony to the second power or 'irony of irony,'" which "asserts and maintains its fictional character by stating the continued impossibility of reconciling the world of fiction with the actual world" (BI 218). "The author" "asserts" "the ironic necessity of not becoming the dupe of his own irony and discovers that there is no way back from his fictional self to his actual self" (BI 219).

De Man thereby enters Schlegel's vision: "the dialectic of self-destruction and self-invention" which "characterizes the ironic mind is an endless process that leads to no synthesis" (BI 220). "Irony engenders a temporal sequence of acts of consciousness which is endless"; "irony is not temporary but repetitive, the recurrence of a self-escalating act of consciousness" (RT 202). The author "permanently" intrudes into the work in order to "disrupt the fictional illusion" and "prevent the all too readily mystified reader from confusing fact and fiction and from forgetting the essential negativity of the fiction" —a strategy termed "parabasis" (BI 218f, 228; RT 200, 209; ALG 300f) (after the portion of Greek comedy sung to the audience as a direct message from the author). Besides literature, "all philosophical discourse" has "ironic allegory" for its "rhetorical mode" (ALG 116).

---

[27] However, this division is not "intersubjective," because one self cannot be "superior" to the other, for instance, in wanting to exercise "power" or "violence" over the other, or to "educate and improve" it (BI 212; cf. BI 64). But psychoanalysis, whether of Freud, Horney, and Maslow, agrees that one part of the self is precisely seeking power over another.

Like other aspects of deconstruction, the proliferation of irony is by no means "harmless" or "reassuring" (BI 214f). True, a certain "freedom" is gained from "the unwillingness of the mind to accept any stage in its progression as definitive" (BI 220).[28] But we also approach a "dizziness to the point of madness"; "sanity can exist only because we are willing to function within the conventions of duplicity and dissimulation" (BI 215f). "Once this mask is shown to be a mask, the authentic being underneath appears necessarily as on the verge of madness" (BI 216) Hence, "absolute irony is a consciousness of madness, itself the end of all consciousness; it is a consciousness of a non-consciousness." Using "the double structure of ironic language," "the ironist invents a form of himself that is 'mad' but that does not know its own madness; he then proceeds to reflect on his madness thus objectified." De Man's personal touch is his serene acceptance of this dizzying irony that Bloom and Hartman resolve to combat by restoring the power of the Word (pp. 298, 312f).

When he gives a critical reading of a literary work, de Man's rhetorical moves are rendered consistent and predictable by his theoretical program. "One has the feeling beforehand that one knows what de Man will do, yet one still is awed by the elegance, precision, and economy of his performance" (Godzich, preface to BI, xvf). Wherever he looks, de Man finds his own ideas once more, and duly extracts his conceptions of language, literature, and the self as the eventual consequence of every text. In this way, his "readings" are indeed "allegories" — not of reading in general, as he likes to insist, but of a style of reading so specialized Godzich admits it could not be "duplicated" by anyone else.

For example, de Man's reading of *The Triumph of Life* by Shelley keeps broadening out into "a more general interpretation" (SD 62). The poem "warns us that nothing, whether deed, word, thought, or text, ever happens in relation, positive or negative, to anything that precedes, follows, or exists elsewhere, but only as a random event whose power, like the power of death, is due to the randomness of its occurrence" (SD 69).

As usual, the evasiveness of language gets top billing. The poem indicates that "the latent polarity implied in all classical theories of the sign allows for the relative independence of the signifier and for its free play in relation to its signifying function" (SD 60). "Particularly meaningful movements" can be "generated by random and superficial properties of the signifier rather than by the constraints of meaning." A "figure" of language is "constituted" by "the alignment of a signification with any principle of linguistic articulation whatsoever" (SD 61). A similar process marks "the passage from tropological models such as metaphor, synecdoche, metalepsis, or prosopopoeia (in which a phenomenal

---

[28] Barthes' (1970) "liberating theory of the signifier" in S/Z is said to "imply a complete drying up of thematic possibilities," such as would occur in "pure poetry" wherein the "emblematic object is revealed to be a figure without the need of any discourse" (ALG 48). De Man seems to attack Barthes despite the similarities of their views on "free play" (cf. Note 21).

element, spatial or temporal, is necessarily involved) to tropes such as grammar and syntax (which function on the level of the letter without the intervention of an iconic factor)" (SD 61f).

The tactics are the same when the poet's use of the term "shape" is "identified as the model of figuration in general" and as "a figure for the figurality of all signification" (SD 61f). "The figure is not naturally given or produced," but "posited by an arbitrary act of language"; and "the positing power of language is both entirely arbitrary, in having a strength that cannot be reduced to necessity, and entirely inexorable in that there is no alternative to it" (SD 62f). "Language posits and language means (since it articulates) but language cannot posit meaning; it can only reiterate (or reflect) in its reconfirmed falsehood" (SD 64).

"Figuration" gets revenge by "performing the erasure of the positing power of language" and thus becomes "disfiguration," being "the repetitive erasures by which language performs the erasure of its own position" (SD 64f). The "shape" is then "the figure of thought, but also a figure" of "the element in thought that destroys thought in an attempt to forget its duplicity" (SC 65). "The entire scene of the shape's apparition and subsequent wandering is structured as a near-miraculous suspension between these two different forces whose interaction gives to the figure the hovering motion which may well be the mode of being of all figures" (SD 55). The poem's own shape as a fragment (Shelley never finished it) points to another "disfiguration" "the reader" has to "reinscribe"; yet this "challenge," this "fracture" too is deemed "present in all texts" (SD 67). "To read is to understand, to question, to know, to forget, to erase, to deface, to repeat" (SD 68).

Shelley's recurrent imagery of light is construed to "create conditions of optical confusion that resemble nothing so much as the experience of trying to read *The Triumph of Life,* as its meaning glimmers, hovers, and wavers, but refuses to yield the clarity it keeps announcing" (SD 52f). "Light" is made to stand for "metaphor": it is "the bearer of light which carries over the light of the senses and of cognition from events and entities to their meaning," but it "irrevocably loses the contour of its own face or shape" (SD 66). The "rainbow" "represents the very possibility of cognition, even for processes of articulation so elementary that it would be impossible to conceive of any principle of organization, however primitive, that would not be entirely dependent on its power" (SD 57). "The figure of the rainbow is the figure of the unity of perception and cognition, undisturbed by the possibly disruptive mediation of its own figuration" (SD 58).

Shelley's use of mirror imagery is also interpreted in tune with de Man's standard theses. "The scene is self-reflexive: the closure of the shape's contours is brought about by self-duplication" (SD 55), "The light generates its own shape by means of a mirror, a surface that articulates it without setting up a clear separation that differentiates inside from outside." Thus, "the specular structure of the scene" is "merely an illustration of a plural structure that involves natural entities only as principles of articulation among others" (SD 62). Comparably, "the underlying assumption of a paraphrastic reading" is "of specular understanding in which the text serves as a mirror of our own knowledge and our knowledge mirrors in its turn the text's signification" (SD 58).

These interpretations illustrate the critical moves whereby de Man allegorizes the particulars of the literary work into his own theoretical precepts. In effect, the poem provides a commentary on de Man's interpretive procedures, rather than the other way around—a tactic that hints why he might be anxious to equate criticism with literature. The openness of literature is paradoxically narrowed by de Man's obsession with a small group of consistent, interlocking conceptions about that openness. His entrenched blindness to unifying or stabilizing forces generates an unintended insight into the power of those forces. He looks for "randomness," "free play," and "disfiguration," but finds that "Shelley's imagery, often assumed to be incoherent and erratic, is instead extraordinarily systematic" (SD 69, 60, 57).[29]

We encounter the same self-deconstruction on the more general level of theory. De Man consistently denounces "totalizations from part to whole" as "illegitimate," "aberrant," "fallacious," and the like (ALG 256, 129, 237, 249; BI 32, 34). Yet he can scarcely make a statement about a text without generalizing across the whole of language or literature, witness his insistent use of "all," "always," or "any".[30] He delights in epigrammatic or apodictic pronouncements about "all language," "all readings," "all writing," "all metaphors," "all literature," and so on (ALG 111, 202, 290, 65, 50). These are too broad to be subject to proof, and de Man rarely offers any. He merely proves that he—and perhaps he alone—could make the same point with any text he pleased. Even Culler, who makes de Man the star practitioner for deconstruction, is troubled by the "annoying" "strategy of omitting crucial demonstrations" (PS 16; OD 229).

If deconstruction is something we cannot escape because it is built into language and literature, we might wonder why authors and critics didn't resolve to perform it centuries ago. De Man might say they were doing it without knowing it, blinded by a certain metaphysics; the modern practice of deconstruction then appears as an apocalyptic fulfillment of the history of ideas. We might also wonder why de Man, like Derrida, Miller, Hartman, and Bloom, is so selective about the works he reads, ones that seem ready-made for his project. (Rousseau, for example, seems to have come back into fashion in exactly this manner.) Whatever his selective criteria—style, technique, authorial intention, or choice of topics and images—they limit de Man's absolute avowals of inescap-

---

[29] Examples might be the "consistent system of sun imagery" or the "system of relationships" into which the "river" "enters" (SD 51, 53). Blanchot is described as having an "almost obsessive preoccupation with a few fundamental concerns" (BI 61)—not a bad comment on de Man too.

[30] Compare the uses of "all" (ALG 50, 65, 111, 113, 160, 192, 202, 239, 245, 264, 290), "always" (ALG 152, 199, 205, 265), and "any" (ALG 76, 125f, 141, 182, 187, 226).

able figurality. We return to the problem latent in Holland's work: the skilled critic can read the way he or she says everybody does, but the ingenious and surprising results signal the exceptional nature of the performance.

Both de Man and the recent Culler declare that everything is pretty well controlled by language. Among the subjects who dissolve beneath this control are the author and the reader. Deconstructionists did not intend merely to reanimate the New Critical polemic against the "intentional" and "affective" fallacies (cf. BI 24f). De Man (and Bloom even more) simply takes over from both author and reader all decisions about what should be done with the text. He assures us his proceedings are "immanent" or "intrinsic" (cf. BI 107f, 109f; ALG 4f). But the closeness of his criticism to the literary text is rather like that of anti-matter to matter: precisely reflected, but violently explosive upon contact. "The further the critical text penetrates in its understanding, the more violent the conflict becomes" with "the original text" (BI 109).[31]

Still, if de Man sees the self as divided, he has a right to be an example. Why shouldn't he exemplify his idea that "the category of the self" is so "double-faced that it compels the critic who uses it to retract implicitly what he affirms and to end up by offering the mystery of this paradoxical movement as his main insight" (BI 105)? And if he can diagnose Lukács, Poulet, and Blanchot to be writers whose "critical stance" "is defeated by their own critical results" (BI 106), might we not make a like diagnosis of him? Yet he designed the fail-safe mechanism of building this dualism directly into his theory, so that in the very moment we detect him deconstructing himself we find his theory confirmed. He cannot be wrong on one level without being right on another.

Even after he denied that language can convey truth in the usual sense, de Man apparently could not overcome his nostalgia for some form of truth. His compromise was evidently as uneasy as it was complex: to seek new insights by deconstructing rich sources. Only in this circuitous way could he reconcile his own understanding with his theses about the universality of misunderstanding. The prospect that this procedure might imply his exclusion from the universe may have driven him steadily further into labyrinths of allegory and irony where the illusion of his own selfhood was, if not secured, at least preserved in the way deconstruction reweaves what it unravels. "Curiously," "only in describing a

---

[31] In Rousseau, "all examples" for "the 'natural' language of man are acts of violence" (ALG 140). In Shelley, an image is found for a "violent act of power achieved by the positional power of language" (SD 62; cf. SD 64). Compare the violence of de Man's own imagery with its Freudian overtones: "writing always includes the moment of dispossession in favor of the arbitrary power play of the signifier and from the point of view of the subject, this can only be experienced as a dismember-ment, a beheading or a castration"; or "the representation of copulation or murder are the most effective emblems for the moment of literal significance that is part of any system of tropes" (ALG 296, 182). Bloom and Hartman have a similar tendency (cf. Note 27 to Ch. 14; Note 24 to Ch. 15; Note 21 to Ch. 19).

mode of language which does not mean what it says" can one "actually say what one means" (RT 194).

De Man certainly lived up to his own declaration that "literary criticism, in our century, has contributed to establishing" the "crucial difference between an empirical and an ontological self; in that respect, it participates in some of the most audacious and advanced forms of contemporary thought" (BI 50). His mistrust of metaphysics left him among those whose "ontological confidence has forever been shaken" (cf. ALG 123). If, in Nietzsche's words, "we have to cease to think if we refuse to do it in the prisonhouse of language" (PL i), de Man elected to dwell there steadfastly, not planning an escape, hardly even looking out the windows, but exploring and refining the inner layout as a space for constructing and dismantling a microcosm of the world outside. His tools, so far most rigorously employed (like Derrida's) in "the unmaking of a construct" (BI 140), may be turned to new uses by those who come after him. "However negative it may sound, deconstruction implies the possibility of rebuilding."

14

Harold Bloom[1]

A recipe for making your own Harold Bloom out of our other critics would be no mean culinary challenge. From Frye, take the mania for elaborate, numbered schematics and learned terminology from the classical languages; from de Man, the paradox of blindness and insight; from Hartman, the aggrandizing equation of criticism with literature, and the turn to unconventional theology; from Holland, an awed reverence for the writings of Freud and his closest disciples (Rank, Fenichel, Ferenczi, Anna Freud); from Fiedler, the obsession with the dark, daemonic role of the id, and the cultural unease of the American latecomer; from just about everybody, a distaste for empirical studies of communication and Marxist aesthetics, an embarrassment regarding formalism and moralism (those opposites that criticism is so wondrously apt at combining), plus a masterful conviction of having personally created the method literature truly demands; flavor with concentrated anxiety and sorrow; contract the mixture in a Kabbalistic vessel and apply satanic or promethean fire until the vessel breaks apart; and what falls or is thrown out may be but a weak homunculus that could never thrive as Bloom has.

Once a prime academic critic included by Wellek and Warren among those doing "close reading" (p. 24), Bloom has blossomed into an anti-critic par excellence, an enfant plus-que-terrible, a Childe Harold loathing his own belatedness and re-visioning himself as Childe Roland to do battle with the forces of a darkness he himself has summoned to make his candle look brighter. He aspires to be cast (indeed thrown) not in the image of God, but of Satan, whose Miltonic portrayal reveals the "archetype of the modern poet at his strongest" (ANX 19f; cf. ANX 21f, 32; MAP 37, 40, 63, 113).

Bloom is occasionally misplaced among the deconstructionist critics.[2] Though he may at times share their terminology, rhetorical tactics, and sources

---

[1] The key for Bloom citations is: ANX: *The Anxiety of Influence* (1975 [1973]); BF: "The Breaking of Form" (1979); CCP: "Criticism, Canon Formation, and Prophecy: The Sorrows of Facticity" (1984); and MAP: *A Map of Misreading* (1980 [1975a]). MAP and CCP were the texts Bloom himself recommended, but the more radical formulations of ANX were often helpful.

[2] BF appeared as the opener in a volume whose title *Deconstruction and Criticism* announces counterstatements to deconstruction, not just uses of it.

(Nietzsche, Freud, the Romantics, etc.), he uses their program mainly as a point to swerve away from quite emphatically. His development was doubtless affected by their territorial ascendancy at Yale, where he had to keep looking over the fence into their yard. Instead of revitalizing his career by moving in, as Hillis Miller seems to have done, Bloom promoted his by carving out his own bit of stubbed ground in their very shadow and erecting his dark tower, a dead ringer for Childe Roland's tower, as we shall see (pp. 287, 299).

His proceedings have been brilliantly strategic. Deconstructionist dilemmas —that writing and reading are beset by complex displacements, substitutions, tropings, evasions, defenses, and so on—become a backdrop to dramatize his own valorous forays. He seizes the role of a "strong" partisan to lead us in the "struggle" of "reading well," the "very difficult" and "daunting" "task" of "reading a poem properly," the "endless quest of 'how to read,'" and comparably heroic ventures (BF 5, 16; ANX 69; MAP 105). To call such valor "death-defying" turns out to be almost literally accurate, though in a somber sense we will explore later on (pp. 277, 304).

Bloom advocates an "antithetical" method upon which he claims "all inter-pretation depends" (MAP 76, e.d.). He merely "urges criticism" "farther upon a road already taken" (ANX 65). "The term 'antithetical'" has two main meanings, inspired, like much of Bloom's thought, by Freud and Nietzsche: "the counter-placing of rival ideas in balanced or parallel structures, phrases, words"; and "the anti-natural, or the 'imaginative' opposed to the natural" (MAP 88). Also, Yeats "used the term" for "a quester who seeks his own opposite" (ANX 65).

In Bloom's "manifesto," "antithetical criticism" is depicted as a "series of swerves": "to read a great precursor poet as his greater descendants compelled themselves to read him"; "to read" them "as if we were their disciples" and "learn where we must revise them"; to "measure" the first swerve against the second, and to "apply" "the accent of deviation" as a "corrective to the reading of the first poet" (ANX 93f). "The best critics of our time" are those who, like "Empson and Wilson Knight," "misinterpret" most "antithetically" (ANX 95).

Bloom also names his method "revisionism," but not in the Marxist meaning, invoked by Jameson, of "making a theory comfortable and palatable by leaving out whatever calls for praxis or change, whatever is likely to be painful for" "purely contemplative intellectual consumption" (MF xv)—rather the opposite. "Modern revisionism" descends from "heresy," but practices "creative correc-tion" (ANX 29). "The revisionist strives to *see* again, so as to *esteem* and *estimate* differently, so as then to *aim* 'correctively'" (MAP 4). "Revisionism follows received doctrine along to a certain point, and then deviates, insisting that a wrong direction was taken at just that point" (ANX 29).

In "poetic influence," though, this "creative correction" "is actually and nec-essarily a misinterpretation" (ANX 30). Such "influence" is thus identified with "misprision," "misreading," and "misapprehension," and with "perverse revisionism" (ANX 7, 30, 50).[3] If "to imagine is to misinterpret," then "poetry is misunderstanding, misinterpretation, misalliance" (ANX 93ff). "Every poem is a misinterpretation of a parent poem" (ANX 94). "Strong poets make" "poetic history" "by misreading one another so as to clear imaginative space for themselves" (ANX 5). Thus, poetry is doomed to dwell in the misprision-house of language, where the poet may "raise his Ararat," but never lower his "error" rate (cf. ANX 155; 101; MAP 70, 93).[4] "Error about life is necessary for life, and error about poetry is necessary for poetry" (ANX 120).

In his "larger vision of trope than traditional or modern rhetoric affords," Bloom "re-defines" "a trope" as "a willing error, a turn from literal meaning" (MAP 93). Such "turns" "'occur between the meanings of intention and the significances of linguistic utterances'" (BF 10). In this large sense, "any critic necessarily tropes" in "giving a reading of a specific poem," because "a trope is troped wherever there is a movement from sign to intentionality, whenever the transformation from signification to meaning is made by the test of what aids the continuity of critical discourse" (BF 10f). Moreover, "emotion" is "experienced as trope"; the expression via a poem is "a revisionary further troping"; and the poem "is necessarily still further troped in any strong reading" (BF 16).[5] So much "tropicality" "makes a mockery of most attempts at reading."

If "fictions and poems can be defined, at their best, as works that are bound to be misread, that is to say, troped by the reader," then "reading well" must be the "struggle" Bloom vows it is (BF 5f). Correspondingly, "criticism" explores "unique acts of creative misunderstanding" (ANX 93). If "all poems" are "antithetical to their precursors," "criticism then necessarily becomes antithetical also." "Perhaps there are only more or less creative or interesting mis-readings"; "there are no interpretations but only misinterpretations" (ANX 43, 95). "Most so-called 'accurate' interpretations of poetry are worse than mistakes" (ANX 43). Bloom thus confronts such projects as Hirsch's method for "valid interpretation" with a conception of "misreading" so pervasive that even the sympathetic Hartman finds it "a wrong-headed term, more spirited than helpful" (CW 52).

Nothing daunted, Bloom claims his approach "should help us read more accurately any group of past poets who were contemporary with one another"

---

[3] Though "imagination's gift comes necessarily from the perversity of the spirit," "the strong poet's imagination cannot see itself as perverse" (ANX 85; cf MAP 200). Despite the shock value of such avowals, Bloom allows for "health" in this "perversity," as compared to mere "pathology"; "we cannot assume that poetry is a compulsive neurosis" (ANX 85, 105, 66).

[4] The "Ararat" figure is transposed from Ferenczi's vision of the "'flood'" over to Artaud as an artist flooded by influence (ANX 154f) (keeping in mind the "flow" stem in "influence"). Water imagery pervades Bloom's vision, as I remark toward the end of the Chapter (p. 300).

[5] These three stages of "troping" are surely not the whole story. Further stages of must occur if a critic is to define and expound his reading of the poem; again if (as in my case), one critic discusses another's readings; and so on.

(ANX 11). This approach is "corrective" in being able to "foster a more adequate practical criticism," "a newer and starker way of reading poems" (ANX 5, 58). In place of the "failed enterprise of seeking to 'understand' any single poem as an entity in itself," we can embark on "the quest of learning to read any poem as the poet's deliberate misinterpretation" "of a precursor poem or of poetry in general" (ANX 43). "Whether the theory is correct or not may be irrelevant to its usefulness for practical criticism" (MAP 10). Bloom does, however, periodically express the hope that it is in fact "correct" (ANX 148; MAP 74, 178). Moreover, his "map" is confidently offered as "a single scheme of complete interpretation" suitable to support criticism the way "a paradigm works" in "normal science" (MAP 71; BF 19).

When I asked Bloom if he felt his position had been consistent over the years, he quoted his revered Emerson: "a foolish consistency is the hobgoblin of small minds." Disregarding all the small minds I have known who were foolishly inconsistent, I would revise the Emersonian formula for Bloom, to wit: "a cunning inconsistency is the daemon of strong minds." The claims of a method to engender both "misreading" and a "corrective" or "correct" theory is one striking illustration. Another is the density of scholarly source-namings without the customary footnotes or bibliographies, as if Bloom were both hailing and defying his own precursors, or conjuring on great names without revealing their texts. Bloom's short, feisty *Anxiety*, though bristling with allusions and quotations, ends not with references and indexes, but with a poem (followed by nine blank pages filled in my copy with my scribbled index of his terms and obsessions).

The problematics of language are emphasized. "I only *know* a text, any text, because I know a reading of it, someone else's reading, my own reading, a composite reading"; "words" are "only words, not things or feelings," and "words will not interpret themselves" (BF 8f). The goal here, as for the deconstructionists, is by no means the intersubjective consensus projected by Hirsch or Bleich. The critic instead seeks out the "agon,"[6] a desperate conflict in which "every poem" "begins as an encounter between poems," and "all interpretation depends on the antithetical relation between meanings, and not on the supposed relation between a text and its meanings" (MAP 70, 76). Because "the meanings of an intertextual encounter are as undecidable and unreadable as any single text is," "every poem becomes as unreadable as every other" (BF 9). "A more antithetical criticism" might "persuade the reader" to "take on his share of the poet's own agon" (MAP 80).

Bloom's "practical" outlook sallies into battle against much contemporary critical theory. He castigates the "reduction" performed by "rhetorical, Aristo-

---

[6] Frye uses "agon" in the sense of "conflict," "pathos," or "death struggle" and finds it most characteristic of "romance" (AC 187, 192). Bloom extends the idea of a "quest" to criticism itself (Note 11). Compare Note 30 to Ch. 5.

telian, phenomenological, and structuralist criticisms"; the "impasse of Formalist criticism"; the "barren moralizing that Archetypal criticism has come to be";[7] and the "anti-humanistic[8] plain dreariness of all those developments in European criticism that have yet to demonstrate that they can aid in reading any one poem by any poet whatsoever" (ANX 94, 12f). Against the "formalist view still held in common by archetypalists, structuralists, and phenomenologists" that "criticism teaches" "a language of criticism," Bloom champions "a language in which poetry already is written, the language of influence" (ANX 25).

By such lines of reasoning, Bloom attains the most assertive version of the Yale-school power play that raises criticism to the rank of literature and poetry. "Poets' misinterpretations or poems are more drastic than critics' misinterpretations or criticisms, but this is only a difference in degree and not at all in kind" (ANX 94f). If a "poem" performs an "interpretation of other poems" (MAP 75), the critic merely extends rather than interrupts the process.

The "manifesto" that "all criticism is prose poetry" (ANX 95) should be considered in view of the exalted status Bloom accords to poetry. He invokes Vico's "system of primitive magic" whereby "poetic wisdom" is "founded upon divination" (ANX 59). "What the ephebe" (novice artist) "enters upon, when he begins his life cycle as a poet, is in every sense a process of divination" (ANX 152). "Isaiah" the "prophet" is emblematic of the "preternaturally strong poet" (ANX 73). "In most" of such "strong poets," "there is a context against which the numinous shines forth" (ANX 101).

At times, Bloom even seems to make "gods" out of poets (ANX 21, 107, 117, 152; MAP 116), especially Milton (MAP 87; ANX 79, 152), as if to invite himself into their company, less Prometheus than Tantalus,[9] hands outstretched toward elusive glory. Though fire no longer waits to be discovered or stolen from heaven, "the candle of the Imagination as God" may yet "light the dark" (MAP 66). Bloom's own "imagination" (a faculty identified in the opening words of the "Manifesto" with "misinterpretation," ANX 93) and "eloquence" might support the "self-preservation" that "makes us giants and heroes and magical, primitive formalists again" (MAP 67f). After all, "the imagination can do anything."

Yet another cunning inconsistency meets us here. Bloom readily concedes that "we after all (myself and those for whom I write) are not poets, but readers" (ANX 122). "Poets, or at least the strongest among them, do not read necessarily as even the strongest of critics read" (ANX 19). "The poet in every reader does not

---

[7] Bloom complains because "archetypal interpretation too readily posits a shared generosity of spirit" and "over-spiritualizes" "criticism" (MAP 79), steps he deplores (cf. Note 25).

[8] Bloom is no great champion of humanism himself, since it clashes with his vision of the "perverse," "ungenerous" "savagery" of "the strong imagination" (ANX 85f) (cf. Note 3). "The only human virtue we can hope to teach" "is the social virtue of detachment from one's own imagination" (ANX 86), this too an echo of Frye (AC 348).

[9] To ascribe the "devouring" of an "infant" to "Prometheus" rather than Tantalus (ANX 115) almost gives away the whole show; it would be a very complex Freudian slip.

experience the same disjunction from what he reads that the critic in every reader necessarily feels" (ANX 25, e.d.). "Our sorrows as readers cannot be identical with the embarrassment of poets, and no critic ever makes a just and dignified assertion of priority" (ANX 65). "Critics, in their secret hearts, love continuities, but he who lives with continuity cannot be a poet" (ANX 78).

A closely related inconsistency turns up in Bloom's proposal to "de-idealize" the poetic and critical transactions traditionally displayed among "academics" (BF 6; ANX 5). Though "we have idealized Western poetry almost since its origins," he avows that "humanism" can "never" be "founded upon" any "idealized mirroring" of the "implicit categories of literature" (ANX 120, 86). For "an Idealizing critic, even one of great accomplishment," "poets are concerned" "only with the anxieties of form," not of "influence" (MAP 173). To comprehend "the reader's defense" and "anxiety," "we need to be less idealistic about interpretation than we generally are" (MAP 74). Among his "de-idealizing" precursors, Bloom mentions Schopenhauer, Emerson, Freud, Burckhardt, Curtius, Browning, and "the heirs of Nietzsche" in "the school of Deconstruction," "among whom Derrida, de Man, Hillis Miller are most distinguished" (BF 5; MAP 89, 119, 79).

Yet Bloom doesn't want to push this alliance too far. He complains that "criticism" is "being excessively despiritualized" by the deconstructionists (MAP 79). He wants to "follow Emerson, as against Nietzsche, in declining to make of de-mystification the principal end of dialectical thought in criticism" (MAP 175). Besides, the "de-idealizing" "achievements" of "Deconstruction" "seem to rely both upon too narrow a canon of texts, and upon only parts of texts, where intratextual differences tend to cluster or even protrude" (MAP 79).

Bloom "favors a kind of interpretation that seeks to restore and redress," "rather than to primarily deconstruct meaning" (MAP 175). A "self-deconstructed reader" is "hardly equal" "to the antithetical restoration" of meaning as "burden and function of whatever valid poetry we have left" (MAP 5). In addition, "poetry and fiction share with criticism the mystery that poststructuralist speculation seeks to deny: the spark we call personality or the idiosyncratic, which in metaphysics and theology once was called presence" (CCP 9). "Nietzsche's" "attack" would "deconstruct the thinking subject itself, by dissipating the ego into a 'rendezvous of persons'" (MAP 86).

Bloom's prime tactic for "de-idealizing" is to "call into question" the "myth" of "the innocence of reading" and the "mystique of a somehow detached yet still generous, somehow disinterested yet still energetic, reading-process" (BF 6). "Strong poets" "should always be condemned by a humanist morality" for being "necessarily perverse"; their "imagination comes to its painful birth through savagery and misrepresentation" (ANX 85f). To "idealize" is a trait of "weaker talents" (ANX 5). "Idealism's" belief that "influence" is transmitted via "generosity of the spirit" applies only to "minor or weaker" or "poorer" "poets" (ANX 30). "Literature" is an "antagonistic," "competitive," and "combative" domain, "built upon the ruin of all that is most generous in us" (ANX 85; BF 5). "Nothing is less generous than the poetic self when it wrestles for its own survival" (MAP 18). Vico's "poetic wisdom," "this magic formalism, was cruel and selfish, necessarily" (ANX 59). Depictions of literary creation as "stealing" (ANX 31, 56) suggest a similar judgment.

Yet this judgment is no mere antithesis-Bloom-bah-humbug anti-cheer-leader's scorn of literary creation. Hardly has idealistic humanism been hurled with hideous ruin and combustion down, when the daemonic arises from the fall with a desperate heroism heralding a re-idealizing and re-mythologizing "upward fall"[10] to far loftier (though more precarious) heights than before (cf. ANX 104). For Bloom at least, pride goeth after a fall. "Quickening power comes when the Selfhood," "a sense of one's own divinity," "stands in its own defense" (MAP 64). We already encountered the invocation of Vico's idea that poetic "divination" might allow one to "become a god" by "foretelling" (ANX 59; MAP 19). Shelley, for instance, "compels us to see him in the company of angels, the daemonic partners of his quest for totality" (ANX 104).

"Quests" of every sort are proclaimed,[11] with Bloom himself counted a "quester" (MAP 175, 59, 91) in the august company of poets like Shelley and Browning (ANX 104; MAP 24), characters like Childe Roland and Ulysses (MAP 106, 156), and indeed all "ephebes" and "strong poets" (ANX 10 35, 79, 36, 63). The "impossible heroic" nature of such "quests" (MAP 174; ANX 10) dooms them to "failure" as their "goal and glory," for which the fate of Childe Roland is peculiarly emblematic (cf. ANX 79, 104, 131; MAP 31, 108f, 114, 117). "Roland has triumphed by failing precisely as his precursors failed" (MAP 119). "The Dark Tower is the self-negating element in the activity of art, and Roland is the poetic consciousness at its most dangerous." "The Tower" "stands for the blindness of the influence process, which is the same as the reading-process," and "for the possibilities" and "limitations of metaphor" (MAP 113).

The goal of such heroism is nothing less than the defiance of death. "In our poetry, what is being evaded ultimately is fate, particularly the necessity of dying" (BF 9). "Every poet begins (however 'unconsciously') by rebelling more strongly against death's necessity than all other men and women do" (ANX 10). "The goal of divination is to attain a power that frees one from all influence, but particularly from the influence of an expected death, or necessity for dying" (MAP 13). Accordingly, "poetic anxiety implores the Muse for aid in divination, which means to foretell and put off as long as possible the poet's own death, as poet and (perhaps secondarily) as man" (ANX 61). "Divination, in this sense, is both a rage

---

[10] This term "upward fall" resounds among the Yale group, appearing in Hartman's *Beyond Formalism* (1970: 160) and *Criticism in the Wilderness* (CW 238), and in de Man's rendition of Binswanger (BI 46). See Note 14 to Ch. 15.

[11] Compare the wide range of uses for "quest" from heroic to trivial (as a synonym for try, look for, etc.) (ANX 10, 13, 35f, 54, 63f, 79, 104, 125, 140; MAP 24, 59, 66, 91, 105f, 109, 156f, 174f).

and a program, offering desperate intimations of immortality through a proleptic magic that would evade every danger, including nature itself" (MAP 13).

For such valorous heroism, the great poets must be "strong," a Bloomian term influenced perhaps by Emerson's use of it for the "'great'" "'geniuses'" that "'inspire,'" "'derange, and deject us, and perplex ages with their fame'" (MAP 166). We are assured that "strong poets are infrequent"; "great poets" may have "enormous gifts" and yet "fail of continuous strength" (MAP 9). For "our own century," Bloom lists "only Hardy and Stevens writing in English," though later relents to acknowledge "Ashbery and Ammons" (MAP 9, 161, 199). At least occasional strength is granted to Yeats, Lawrence, and Frost, along with Robinson, Moore, Eliot, Aiken, Ransom, Jeffers, Cummings, Crane, and Warren (MAP 9, 162, 197). For earlier periods, Bloom nominates Browning, Whitman, and Dickinson plus Milton, Shelley, Blake, Wordsworth, Baudelaire, Rilke, and, apparently, Keats and Tennyson (MAP 9, 11, 177; ANX 91; MAP 144f). Pound and Williams are denied "strength" in one listing but awarded it in another; Bloom seems to resent them and their "schools" for "scoffing at the notion of the anxiety of influence" (MAP 9, 162, 199), a privilege he reserves for Milton alone (ANX 34). Shakespeare is disregarded because he "belongs to the giant age before the flood, before the anxiety of influence became central to poetic consciousness" (ANX 11).[12]

With yet another cunning inconsistency, Bloom typically offers his arguments as valid for "all poems" or "every poem" (ANX 93; MAP 19, 69), not just for "strong" ones. For him, any "poem" is "anxiety"; and "influence" is "a figuration for poetry itself," including "the greater relation of latecomer poet to precursor, or of reader to text, or of poem to the imagination, or of the imagination to the totality of our lives" (ANX 94; MAP 71). "Necessarily" is among Bloom's favorite modifiers for making the processes he depicts seem inescapable.[13] "Poems" "are necessarily about other poems"; "poetic influence is necessarily misprision"; "all literary tradition is necessarily elitist"; and so forth (MAP 18, 20, 39). For the formulation "strong poets are necessarily perverse," Bloom explains that "necessarily" "means as if obsessed," (ANX 85), though surely he is in that state as much as they.

To capture Bloom's rhetoric, we might raise "hyperbole" to "superbole," a term for an exaggeration proudly pushes toward ultimate limits. "Shelley" is "the most truly poetic of all true strong poets" (MAP 11). "Whitman is at once the greatest and the most repressed of all American poets" (MAP 178). "Angus

---

[12] Shakespeare had only "Marlowe, a poet very much smaller than his inheritor" (ANX 11). Besides, Shakespeare's form was "dramatic," not "lyric," a reservation suggesting that Bloom's entire method is limited to lyric and epic, though I don't see why it has to be.

[13] In addition to the uses of "necessarily" cited here, see those in MAP 25, 34, 47, 49, 51, 55, 75; ANX 7, 19, 30, 25, 85, 92, 93, 95, 100, 117; BF 10, 16. The term almost gains the force of a prophetic shibboleth.

Fletcher" is "the most daemonic and inventive of modern allegorists" (MAP 129). One poem shows Whitman performing a "more direct" "defense of undoing the poetic self" "than anywhere else in the language"; another poem by Tennyson "achieves itself by one of the most complex misprisions in the language"; and so on (MAP 181, 144).[14] Since the standards for assigning such superlatives have been mainly invented by Bloom, we can't very well dispute him.

If "there is no method other than yourself" (CCP 9, e.d.), then Bloom's values can be as personal as he likes. He is free to declare what is "grand," "immense," "triumphant," "brilliant," "astonishing," "exalted," "glorious," "magnificent," and so on (ANX 124, 133, 143, 153; MAP 182f, 186). I am sometimes puzzled by his preferences, such as the lofty esteem for the gloomy poetry of the aged Thomas Hardy, whose "During Wind and Rain" is called "as good a poem as our century has given us," and "few books of twentieth-century verse in English compare with *Winter Words* in greatness" (MAP 20f). Apparently, the decisive factor is whether Bloom is moved to strong emotions: "intensity" of "anguish," "sorrow," "uneasiness," "enormous nostalgias," and the like (BF 24, 31, 36). "As I Ebb'd" is for him "the most moving of all Whitman's poems"; Stevens' "Auroras of Autumn" contains "the single passage that moves me most in all his work" (MAP 178, 189). Like Dr. Johnson, Bloom presumably "praises" a "passage" in which his "own deepest anxieties are openly expressed" (ANX 149). Like Whitman, Bloom may fear that he " 'too but signifies at the utmost a little wash'd-up drift' " (MAP 181). Like Stevens' persona, Bloom may be a " 'scholar of one candle' " who " 'sees an arctic effulgence flaring on the frame of everything he is,' " and " 'feels afraid' " (MAP 189f).

To accent the originality of his own approach, Bloom trenchantly swerves away from the established scholarly methods of literary history. Against the "absurd myths" and "gossip"[15] of "literary pseudo-history," he expounds "true poetic history: how poets have suffered other poets" (ANX 69, 94). "Poetic history is indistinguishable from poetic influence" —defined exactly to fit Bloom's own critical movements, namely as "a history of anxiety and self-saving caricature, of distortion, of perverse, wilful revisionism" (ANX 5, 30, e.d.). The "historicism" in his "scheme of interpretation" "deliberately reduces to the interplay of personalities" (MAP 71). He allows, however, that "an application of literary history," though "not strictly necessary for the study of misprision," would be "greatly desirable" (MAP 116).

With equal assertiveness, Bloom wants to "distinguish once for all" between his "poetic influence" and "traditional 'source studies,' " whose scholars he goadingly spurns as "carrion-eaters of scholarship" (MAP 116, 17, 21)—a quaint jibe

---

[14] Compare also "the most violent and sustained hyperbole in all of Stevens"; or "Warren's" "transumption without rival in American poetry since 'Auroras of Autumn'" (MAP 189, 197).

[15] Stanislaus Lee's formula, " 'myth is gossip grown old' " (MAP 65), gives "myth" a far lower status than in the work of Fiedler and Frye.

for a critic who ruminates on cannibalism and "wrestling with the dead."[16] Bloom's vision provocatively empties the encounter between poems or poets of its historical factuality. "Source study is wholly irrelevant" in an "antithetical criticism" for which "the meaning of a poem can only be another poem," a "central poem by an indubitable precursor, even if" the later poet "*never read* that poem" (ANX 70). The "precursor" "may well" "be an imaginary, composite figure" (ANX 121).

Bloom issues his greatest challenge of all when he upsets chronology with the prospect that an earlier poet was influenced by one who lived much later. "Examples abound; the hugely idiosyncratic Milton shows the influence, in places, of Wordsworth; Wordsworth and Keats both have a tinge of Stevens; the Shelley of *The Cenci* derives from Browning" (ANX 154). Indeed, "the strongest poets" are those who "achieve a style that captures and oddly retains priority over their precursors, so that the tyranny of time almost is overturned, and one can believe, for startled moments, that they are being *imitated by their ancestors*" (ANX 141).

This "drastic" and "absurd" "phenomenon" is a deconstructive reversal which remains involved in the hierarchy it undermines. Bloom occasionally backslides by offering historical testimony about "influence," perhaps one more cunning inconsistency, designed to conciliate more traditional scholars. For instance, he cites a letter to Schiller in which Hölderlin complains that "'to you, my dependence is insurmountable,'" and "'I sometimes strive to put you out of my mind so as not to be overcome by anxiety'" (BF 17). Or, Dryden is called in to "testify" that "'Milton has acknowledged to me that Spenser was his original,'" and a passage of Milton's own is adduced to the same effect (MAP 127). In this case, though, "the paternity required no acknowledgement"; and we might say as much for the obvious, sometimes stifling, resemblance of Hölderlin's poetry to Schiller's.

On a grand scale, Bloom proposes to equate "the history of fruitful poetic influence" with "the main tradition of Western poetry since the Renaissance" (ANX 30, e.d.). At first, he saw a major historical break in the Enlightenment. "By the 1740's," "the anxiety of style and the comparatively recent anxiety of influence had begun a process of merging that seems to have culminated during our last few decades" (ANX 150). "The great poets of the English Renaissance are not matched by their Enlightened descendants, and the whole tradition of the Post-Enlightenment, which is Romanticism, shows a decline in its Modernist or post-Modernist heirs" (ANX 10). The precursors of the Romantics, Milton and Dr. Johnson, become the "prophets" of "Post-Enlightenment" poetry" and "criticism," respectively (BF 12).

Milton is indeed "the central problem in any theory and history of poetic influence in English" (ANX 33). "No poet compares to Milton in his intensity of

---

16 On cannibalism and wrestling with the dead, compare ANX 78 115f; MAP 17, 26. In the ratio of "apophrades," the poet is nourished by the dead, though more through possession than ingestion.

self-consciousness as an artist and in his ability to overcome all negative consequences of such concern" (MAP 125). Even great successors like Wordsworth,
Keats, and Shelley have to be situated "in the shadow of Milton," the "god" or
"subgod," "the awesome blind ancestral bard" (MAP 144ff; ANX 152, 74; MAP
54). The neglect of Shakespeare, "the greatest poet in our language," who (as we
saw) was "excluded" from the "argument" for not having had major precursors
(ANX 11; MAP 142), is a disturbing one here, since his shadow is at least as vast
as Milton's.

Bloom later "recanted" his "previous emphasis on the anxiety of influence as a
Post-Enlightenment phenomenon"; "the affliction of belatedness" "is a recurrent
malaise of Western consciousness" (MAP 77). Historical variations are mainly
"differences in degree, rather than in kind." Still, "Romantic tradition differs
vitally from earlier forms of tradition" in being "*consciously late,* and Romantic
literary psychology is therefore necessarily a *psychology of belatedness*" (MAP 35).

History enters most forcefully in hindsight via this feeling of "belatedness."
Bloom's *Map* is "a study of creative misreading, or the belatedness of poetic
reading" (MAP 4). "The subsuming" of "literary tradition" "by belatedness" is an
"inescapable phenomenon" (MAP 36). "A full critical awareness" of this "phenomenon and the resultant misprision worked by revisionism might lead to a
kind of criticism we rarely possess" (MAP 79). "We need to begin again in
realizing for how long and how profoundly art has been menaced by greater art,
and how late our own poets have come in the story" (ANX 70). This "our" may
well refer to "Americans," who are especially "latecomers," "and we are better off
for consciously knowing it" (MAP 27). "From the origins of our nation until this
moment," "evidences" of "belatedness" can be sought "most usefully in our
poets" (MAP 27, 52).

Modern times represent "a cultural situation of such belatedness that literary
survival itself seems fairly questionable" (MAP 39). Bloom is "aware that this
must seem a Gospel of Gloom," but he prefers it to "evasions of Necessity" (MAP
39). And whereas Nietzsche considered "the sense of being a latecomer" "pernicious," Bloom "insists" it is "now" "salutary," a means to recognize "the energy
of humanistic performance" (MAP 29, 83).

However, the pervasive "darkness" of Bloom's vision is hard to overlook.[17]
Highly characteristic is his reverent invocation of Milton's fallen Satan as "archetype of the modern poet" (ANX 19). Only through a catastrophic fall can the
creative spirit rise up. Bloom's preoccupation with "daemonization" makes him a
reverse exorcist who, far from casting out a daemon, "summons him" under

---

[17] For instance, "the strong dead" "darken the living"; "anxiety of influence is dark and demonic"
(ANX 139, 25). Freud is called upon for his "darkest wisdom," and his "darker view of instinct" (ANX
63; MAP 89). Bloom in turn expounds "dark truth," "dark sense," "darker relationships," and so on
(MAP 33; BF 11, 15). If it makes his candle look brighter, as I claimed (p. 281), Bloom has reason to
bless the darkness.

"many names," because "the anxiety of influence" is "identical" with "'the daemonic' in poets,'" or is at least a "dark and daemonic ground" (ANX 35, 103, 25, 58). "Daemons" are, however, not merely negative; they are, in Drayton's words, those "'who for greatness of mind come near to Gods'" (ANX 100).

Without doubt, Bloom's dark vision reflects his own keen consciousness of being a latecomer. Instead of seeing in critical theorizing a recent and original trend (as Culler does), he traces "our latest mimic wars of criticism" all the way back to the "Hellenistic" rivalry between the partisans of "analogy," the "equality of ratios," versus the partisans of "anomaly," the "disproportion of ratios" (BF 13f, e.d.). "Whereas the analogists of Alexandria held that the literary text was a unity and had a fixed meaning, the anomalists of Pergamon in effect asserted that the literary text was an interplay of differences and had meanings that rose out of those differences." It would seem that New Critics and post-structuralists are neither "new" nor "post-."

For his own part, Bloom finds a different ancestry in a venerable tradition rarely touched by academic criticism in the West, namely Kabbalism.[18] "The psychology of belatedness" "is the invention of Kabbalah," which "remains the largest single source for material that will help us to study the revisionary impulse and to formulate techniques for the practice of antithetical criticism" (MAP 4f). "All Kabbalistic texts" "interpret" "a central text that perpetually possesses authority, priority, and strength, or that indeed can be regarded as *text itself*" (MAP 4). "In its stance toward the precursor text, its revisionary genius and mastery of the perverse necessities of misprision," "*Zohar*, the most influential of Kabbalistic books, is the true forerunner of Post-Enlightenment strong poetry" (e.d.).

Such a framework refounds the authority of the text against deconstructive dissemination and erasure of origins. Magical and prophetic discourse are models in which words partake of the actual substance of the objects and events they name,[19] and in which statements cause the realities they depict. The text is endowed with a quasi-sacred origin that it revises so as to gain strength. "If the Imagination, in poetry, speaks of itself, it speaks of origins, of the archaic, the primal, and above all of self-preservation" (MAP 67). "Meaning cleaves more closely to origins the more intensely it strives to distance itself from origins" (MAP 62). Hence, "the prestige of origins is a universal phenomenon against which a solitary demystifier like Nietzsche struggled in vain" (MAP 46). "All sacred history, as Nietzsche knew, was against him."

The prestige of origins is invoked by Bloom's etymologizings—a stark contrast

---

[18] The precursor here is Gershom Scholem, who "emphasizes" the "Kabbalah's" "work of interpretation" (MAP 4, 31).

[19] Bloom includes "magic" in his lament that "words refer *only* to other words" (BF 9). For the magician, though, words are real things, real powers. Magic and myth may indeed have begun as devices for grounding the power of words in something besides words. Compare the prominence of naming and commanding in the Biblical account of creation.

to the deconstructionists' use of etymologies to uncover traces and disseminate meanings. Bloom reminds us that "the word 'influence'" had a "root meaning of 'inflow'" and designated "an emanation or force coming in upon mankind from the stars" (ANX 26). "A power—divine and moral" —"exercised itself, in defiance of all that had seemed voluntary in one" (ANX 26f). Small wonder that "influence" may "make poets" "more original," not "less" (ANX 7). Bloom's image (taken from Blake) of a "Covering Cherub" as "the emblem of Poetic Influence" (ANX 38) intimates a similar tie to the sacred, though within a more oppressive tension. A comparable etymology is traced for the "antithetically primal word" *"chesed"* back to a "root" of "'eagerness' or 'sharpness'" that "moves from 'ardent zeal' to 'jealousy,' 'envy,' and 'ambition'"; the outcome is that "Covenant-love is uneasily allied to a competitive element" (MAP 53). This argument supports Bloom's turn to Old Testament sources to depict an aggressive "Covenant-love between two poets" (MAP 115). The same "antithetical element" in this Hebrew word "leads to the ephebe's first accommodation with the precursor" and thereby to the "archaic, ritual sense" in which "the young poet adopts" the *"persona"* like "a mask representing the *daimonic* or tribal father" (MAP 54).

Again etymologically, "the word *Kabbalah* means" "tradition or reception" and was a "version of Oral Tradition" able to "shatter" the "Written Torah" (MAP 44). A bit surprisingly, "much of Derrida," who "seeks to demonstrate that the spoken word is less primal than writing is," is found to be "in the spirit of the great Kabbalist interpreters of Torah," who "create baroque mythologies out of those elements in Scripture that appear least homogeneous in the sacred text" (MAP 43). "Though he nowhere says so," "Derrida may be substituting *davhar,* the "dynamic word" that is "at once an object or a thing and a deed or act," "for *logos,*" the "intellectual concept" of "gathering, arranging, and putting into order" (MAP 42f). If so, "Derrida" is "correcting Plato by a Hebraic equating of the writing-act and the mark-of-articulation with the word itself" (MAP 43).

Freud is placed together with the Kabbalists for also having "developed" "the psychology of belatedness" (MAP 4, 52). This association is logical if Freud is "more in the oral than the written tradition" and thus a "curiously direct continuator of his people's longest tradition" (MAP 50). He is also welcomed for being a "de-idealizer" (MAP 89), as we saw, though he still seems "humane," "amiable," "optimistic," and "not severe enough" to the more sinister Bloom (MAP 107, 109, 119; ANX 8). "Influence" is construed to be the "true subject" of Freud's *"Beyond the Pleasure Principle"* (MAP 12).

Unlike Holland, Bloom is a "deliberate revisionist" of "Freudian emphases" (ANX 8).[20] One major revision is to "transform" "the family romance" "so as to place the emphasis less on phallic fatherhood, and more upon *priority*" (ANX 64). Thus emended, the "family romance" serves among Bloom's favored images

---

[20] Bloom feels that Freud "revised himself" sometimes (ANX 135). But another "revisionist's," "Derrida's interpretation of Freud," is apparently rejected as not "correct" (MAP 50) (see Note 23).

for "the relations between poets" (ANX 8, 27, 56f, 62, 94). Another large revision foreign to Holland is to refocus "sublimation" from "sexual instinct" over to "aggressive instinct" —at least, via a "suggestion" Freud "should have developed," in the process of "poetry" (ANX 64, 115; MAP 101). "Whether sublimation of sexual instincts plays a central part in the genesis of poetry is hardly relevant to the reading of poetry, and has no part in the dialectic of misprision" (ANX 115).

Using these various sources, Bloom offers to "chart how meaning is produced in Post-Enlightenment strong poetry by the substitutive interplay of figures and of images" (MAP 87). He presents four sides of a "scheme of complete interpretation, at once rhetorical, psychological, imagistic, and historical" (MAP 71). Rhetoric and psychology are aligned by "surmising" "that the poets invented all of the defenses, as well as all the tropes"; Bloom can "seek to take back from Freud precisely what he himself took from the poets," and besides, Freud was himself "the strongest of modern poets" (MAP 178, 89f). The imagistic is brought in to accommodate "the common reader," who "cares little to be taught to notice tropes or defenses" (MAP 178). The historical aspect we have already explored.

Bloom's alignment of rhetoric and psychology again swerves from deconstruction by maintaining a balance of the self against language. For Derrida, "'there is no psyche without text'"; for Lacan, "the structure of the unconscious is linguistic"; for de Man, "the linguistic model usurps the psychological" (MAP 48, 76). For Bloom, though, it "trivializes human action" to "conceive textuality so diffusely that all human action is textual" (CCP 1). His concept of "influence" is a "subject-centered relationship, not to be reduced to the problematic of language" (MAP 77). Yet cunningly inconsistent here too, he may envision "a precursor" who is "no less a text than we are"; or insist that "acts, persons, and places, if they are to be handled by poems at all, must themselves be treated first as though they were already poems" (MAP 167, 70). The war of poets implies a war of texts, but texts conceived so broadly as to water down Bloom's proclamation that every poem is "about another poem" (MAP 198).

Bloom's "map" contains "revisionary ratios" that are "not tropes only, but also psychic defenses"; "from the viewpoint of criticism, a trope is just as much a concealed defense, as a defense is a concealed trope" (MAP 71, 77; cf. MAP 89). A number of Freud's central concepts are called "tropes," for example: "the understanding of health through sickness"; "fixation as the basis of repression"; and the "resemblances between sexuality and intellectual activity, including poetry" (MAP 48, 56, 101). The "death instinct" is "a Sublime hyperbole" and an "extraordinary oxymoron" (MAP 91). Certainly, such a description befits Bloom's own "antithetical formula" that "defenses can be said to trope against death, rather in the same sense that tropes can be said to defend against literal meaning" (e.d.). "Death" "is a kind of literal meaning, or from the standpoint of poetry, literal meaning is a kind of death."

"Primal Scenes" figure in a whole range of "tropes": Freud's "Oedipal fantasy" and "the slaying of a father by his rival sons"; Derrida's "Scene of Writing"; and Bloom's "Scene of Instruction," "the most Primal" of all (MAP 47ff, 55). This "Scene of Instruction" "is staged" in "the psychic place of heightened conscious-ness, of intensified demand," "a place cleared by the newcomer in himself." "The metaleptic or transumptive trope of a Scene of Instruction" provides "the origins" of the "hyperbole" that is "the unconscious" itself (MAP 56).

"Repetition compulsion" is allied to "the daemonic" (ANX 77, 87), a force we saw identified with the "anxiety of influence" (ANX 103).[21] Bloom "offers" this "anxiety" "as a variety of the uncanny," the trait of "our inner tendency to yield to obsessive patterns of action" (ANX 77f). To gain "freedom" from the "demon of continuity," that is, "the Covering Cherub," "discontinuity" is "vainly but per-petually" sought as "the strong poets' defense against repetition," especially among "Romantics" (ANX 39, 87; MAP 36). Even while pursuing this "fantasy," they still "perversely" "manifest" "repetition compulsion" and cannot escape the "doom" of "hateful exclusiveness" (MAP 36; ANX 85, 117). "Roland's equivocal triumph is an instance of Kierkegaardian 'repetition'" (MAP 120). But surely so is Bloom's own critical triumph, with his obsessive style and proud fealty to a central group of intertwined, though warring, ideas.

By appropriating Freud's major conceptions as tropes, Bloom escapes the dilemma confronting Holland, namely that contemporary psychoanalysis has amended or rejected a number of those conceptions (p. 181). Whereas Holland's case depends on a fairly literal acceptance of Freud's arguments, Bloom "revises" Freud quite freely, as we have seen, and tropes while he borrows. Like Fiedler, Bloom adheres to the darker side of Freud's thinking, and focuses on the "id." The Freudian formula of "where Id was, ego shall be" is for Fiedler, I think, (p. 86), "where ego and superego were, id shall be"; Bloom's version is "where my poetic father's" ego was, id "shall be, or even better, my" ego "more closely mixed with" id (ANX 110).[22] Accordingly, "Freud, unlike Nietzsche and Der-rida, knows that precursors become absorbed *into the id* and *not into the super-ego*" (MAP 50).[23]

The "revisionary ratios" in Bloom's "map" are "interpretations of influence," "ways of reading/misreading poetic relationships," or "ways of reading a poem" (MAP 71). The etymological root of "ratio" as "thought" is invoked alongside its "mathematical" and "monetary" designations for "relations between unequal terms" (MAP 95). "The ratios of revision work" "against" a "spectral image or

---

[21] But Bloom treats "repetition compulsion" under "kenosis" rather than "daemonization" (ANX 77). He identifies "repetition" with "thrown-ness," an obscure concept from Valentinus and Heideg-ger (ANX 79, 84), reminiscent perhaps of the fall Bloom sees before creativity (pp. 287, 291).

[22] For consistency, I use "Ego" for "I" and "id" for "it." See Note 29 to Ch. 8.

[23] This argument is held to refute "Derrida's interpretation of Freud" that "writing" is "as primal as coitus" (MAP 50). "The inhibition of writing" is not, in Bloom's opinion, due to the "superego," but to the "id." Yet his claim that writing is "more automatic" than speech is simply not true for most people (Beaugrande 1984a).

blocking agent," this too designated a "Covering Cherub." Each ratio "names intertextual differences," and "characterizes a total relationship between two poets, earlier and later" (BF 19).

The Kabbalistic foundations for Bloom's map center on the "sixteenth-century master" "Isaac Luria's" "story of creation": "the best paradigm available for a study of the way poets war against one another in the strife of Eternity that is poetic influence" (MAP 5). The "story" comprises "*Zimzum,*" "the Creator's withdrawal or contraction"; "*Shevirath hakelim,*" "the breaking-apart-of-the-vessels" in a "vision of creation as catastrophe"; and "*Tikkun,*" "restitution or restoration—man's contribution to God's work." Surely a critic should feel flattered to use a map that mimics the divine creator's own dialectic. And this use again portrays the establishment of meaning as a grandiose struggle.

To Bloom, "six" ratios "seem to be minimal and essential to my understanding of how one poet deviates from another" (ANX 11). The number is not crucial: they "could as well be more," though "the three pairs of ratios" handily "form the pattern of what has been the central tradition of the greater modern lyric" (ANX 11; MAP 96). He later decides that "the ratios work in matched or dialectical pairs," "with each pair following the Lurianic pattern of limitation, substitution, representation" (MAP 95f, 4).[24] This three-part design matches the "three main stages" in Luria's "story of creation" (MAP 5, 96f) just described.

The ratios "could take quite different names than those" Bloom "has employed" (ANX 11). The names are variously culled from "Lucretius," "St. Paul," "mystery cults," and the philosophies of "Neo-Platonists" and "pre-Socratics," with a few intermediaries like "Coleridge" and "Lacan" (ANX 14f, 42, 87; MAP 200; ANX 67). Though "the revisionary ratios" are said to be "the invention" of "the High Romantics" (BF 13), and the "Four Master Tropes" of Burke and Vico are "followed" (MAP 94), a repressed precursor for such a multilevel scheme with erudite labels might well be the "terminological buccaneer" Northrop Frye (AC 362), whom Bloom rebukes for "Platonizing," "over-spiritualizing," and "idealism" (MAP 30, 79; ANX 31).[25]

Here is a compressed summary of the ratios (following ANX 14ff, 101; MAP 71ff, 84): (a) "clinamen," whereby a poet "swerves away from," and seems to "correct," a precursor; (b) "tessera," whereby a poet "retains the terms" of the precursor, but "means them in another sense, as though the precursor had failed to go far enough"; (c) "kenosis," whereby the poet "breaks" by "moving toward discontinuity with the precursor," who gets "removed from his context"; (d) "daemonization," whereby the poet creates a "counter-sublime" against the pre-

---

[24] "Substitution" has no special content of its own: no trope, defense, or ratio. It is represented in Bloom's chart only by a bidirectional arrow, as if it is a movement entailed in all transactions.

[25] Bloom's real objection is probably that in Frye's vision, archetypes and myths are a form of influence that doesn't have to be stolen or wrestled away from precursors, since they belong to the whole culture. Bloom must see this as "Platonizing the dialectics of tradition" (MAP 30). See Note 7.

RATIO	TROPE	IMAGE	DEFENSE
a. clinamen	a. irony	a. presence/ absence	a. reaction-formation
b. tessera	b. synecdoche	b. part/whole	b. turning against self reversal
c. kenosis	c. metonymy	c. fullness/ emptiness	c. undoing isolation regression
d. daemoniza-tion	d. hyperbole	d. high/low	d. repression
e. askesis	e. metaphor	e. inside/ outside	e. sublimation
f. apophrades	f. metalepsis	f. early/late	f. introjection projection

Fig. 14.1.   (after Bloom, MAP 84)

cursor's "sublime," and "the Great Original" "loses his originality" to "the world of the numinous, the sphere of daemonic agency"; (e) "askesis," whereby a poet "yields up part of his own imaginative and human endowment," so as to "separate himself from his precursor"; and (f) "apophrades," whereby the poet deliberately "holds his poem open to the precursor" in order to usurp the latter's priority.[26]

Each ratio is assigned a dominant "rhetorical trope," giving us the series: (a) "irony," (b) "synecdoche," (c) "metonymy," (d) "hyperbole," (e) "metaphor," and (f) "metalepsis," respectively. Also, each ratio is assigned a dominant "image in the poem," giving us the series: (a) "dialectic of presence and absence," (b) "part for whole or whole for part," (c) "fullness and emptiness," (d) "high and low," (e) "inside and outside," and (f) "early and late", respectively. Finally, each ratio is assigned a dominant "psychic defense," giving us the series: (a) "reaction-formation," (b) "turning against the self, reversal," (c) "undoing, isolation, regression";

---

[26] This last ratio is the one whereby the "strongest poets" can seem to have been "imitated by their ancestors" (ANX 141). See Note 16.

(d) "repression," (e) "sublimation," and (f) "introjection, projection," respectively. The whole configuration is shown in Figure 14.1 (cf. Bloom's own figure, MAP 84). The bunching of terms in the "defense" series is due to fitting Bloom's "six primary defenses" to Anna Freud's "ten" "basic" "defenses" (MAP 92). He consoles us that "just as tropes blend into one another, so defenses are difficult to keep apart" —which seems to make theoretical difficulty into a virtue at the risk of erasing the differences that delineate the whole scheme.

The meaning of the text undergoes a traumatic career as the ratios get to work. "As tropes of contraction or limitation, irony withdraws meaning through a dialectical interplay of presence and absence; metonymy reduces meaning through an emptying-out that is a kind of reification; metaphor curtails meaning through the endless perspectivizing of dualism, of inside-outside dichotomies. As tropes of restitution or representation, synecdoche enlarges from part to whole; hyperbole heightens; metalepsis overcomes temporality by a substitution of earliness for lateness" (MAP 94f). "Hyperbole and metalepsis I add as progressively more blinded or broken representation, where 'blinding' or 'breaking' is meant to suggest the Lurianic breaking-of-the-vessels or scattering-of-the-light" (MAP 94). The meaning seems to get severely brutalized, which reminds me of Bloom's view of "representation" as "a mutilated part of a whole," a "masochistic impulse" of "strong poems in our tradition, from Wordsworth on" (BF 28).

De Man and Hartman also have a penchant for violent tropes deriving from Freud.[27] But de Man ultimately leaves all tropes in the control of irony, whereas Hartman and Bloom allow for a "restitution" or "restoration" (e.g., CW 42; MAP 5, 175)—slyly associated in the Lurianic "story" with "man's contribution to God's work" (MAP 5), quite in line with the Bloomian mythologizing of the critic. "Antithetical" "restitution" can oppose the nihilism of "Deconstruction's ironies" with "a supermimesis achieved by an art that will not abandon the self to language" (BF 37). As Hartman remarks, both he and Bloom retain a "stake" in the "persistence" and "provenance" of "pathos" (DC ix).

To support the "practical applicability" of his "map," Bloom proudly announces its benefits. "The insight our map of misreading gives us here is precisely how the part/whole image of representation directly restitutes for the absence/presence image of limitation" (MAP 181). "What the map of misprision helps us to see is the desperation of this heroic hyperbole" (MAP 158). And so on.

Bloom's discussions of "a remarkable number of poems" reveal a striking isomorphism between their rhetorical or dialectic structure and his scheme of ratios (MAP 105). He attributes this less to own his ingenuity than to the poem or the poet. "It should be clear how closely Wordsworth's 'Ode' sets or follows the patterns of our map of misreading" (MAP 146). Keats' "one resource" is "further

---

[27] On a similar tendency among the other Yale theorists, see Note 31 to Ch. 13; Note 24 to Ch. 15; and Note 21 to Ch. 19. Only Bloom fully aligns the violence of metaphorics with that of armed combat.

internalization, which condemns him to a fairly strict following of the map of misprision" (MAP 152). "Ashbery" "tends like Stevens to follow rather precisely the crisis-poem paradigm that I have traced in my map of misreading" (MAP 205). Sometimes, however, "only a broad and rough" "application of the map" is feasable (MAP 180). "Variants and displacements of course abound, though generally in clearly discernible schemes of rearrangement," and "the rebellion from the model is frequently equivocal" (MAP 105). One poem by Stevens "calls for its own version of the map of misreading" (MAP 186). Dickinson "often" "passes beyond our revisionary model" because "her originality extends so far" (MAP 184).

Bloom concedes that his own "defensive emotions" play a part in finding the same "sequence of revisionary ratios in so many poems," but he insists that "the sequence is *there* in the sense that image and trope tend to follow over-determined patterns of evasion" (BF 29). "What matters is not the exact order of the ratios, but the principle of substitution, in which representations and limitations perpetually answer each other" (MAP 105).

In any case, the isomorphism looks less surprising if we bear in mind the status of the ratios as sufficiently flexible tropings to be tailored to all sorts of passages or imagery. To maintain his sequence, Bloom interprets "trailing clouds" as an image for "fullness" and "emptiness" in "kenosis," and later the "wind" "disturbing" "clouds" as an image for "presences" and "absences," which should belong to "clinamen" (MAP 146, 149f). If considerable ingenuity is involved in such readings, then Bloom's critical achievement seems all the more valorous and brilliant. His own "antithetical strength" has been demonstrated by the triumph of his map over the poem. Thus, like most of the critical theories I survey, Bloom's casts him in the role of the most indispensable critic. In the manner of Childe Roland, he "rides with us as interpreter" on a quest, but armed only with his map for an "ordeal," a "trial by landscape" (cf. MAP 106); and goes even beyond Borges' royal cartographers in making the map not merely coincide with the dimensions of the landscape, but also fill in t(r)opological contours not previously visible.

In my exploration of Holland's work, I noted the wide flexibility of his "dictionary of fantasies" (p. 166ff). A small repertory of these fantasies—Oedipal, Primal Scene, castration, and the like —was extended to a very wide range of literary instantiations. The total effect is a powerful reduction, however much ingenuity the critic expends. Bloom's map is far richer and more open. It does not make the "defenses" the privileged rock-bottom, but moves continually to tropes and images as elements of equal import. The map often enriches the texts as well as reduces them.

However, a leveling effect appears elsewhere, namely in the role projected onto the poets. Their personalities are rather uniformly painted as defensive and beset by anxiety, sorrow, melancholy, and the fear of death, against all of which they react with aggressive and usurping countermoves. They all look like Bloommeanies, cruel, jealous, and selfish, untouched by generosity or modesty. Whether a given poet was following a precursor by conscious or unconscious intent, or just by accident, makes no difference for the portrayal. Bloom "projects" and "introjects" his own personality into each "strong" poet. "Projection" "attributes outwardly all prohibited instincts" "to others"; "introjection" "is a fantasy transposition of otherness to the self" (MAP 101f).

Bloom's own personality is certainly distinct in his style of writing. His "manifesto" that "all criticism is prose poetry" (ANX 95) offers considerable license for statements few besides Bloom would make. A few examples will suffice. "Each strong poet's Muse, his Sophia, leaps as far out and down as can be, in a solipsistic passion of quest" (ANX 13). "The ephebe's first realm is ocean, or by the side of the ocean," "but the antithetical impulse will" "send him inland, questing for the fire of his own stance" (ANX 79). "The God of poets is not Apollo, who lives in the rhythm of recurrence, but the bald gnome Error, who lives at the back of a cave; and skulks forth only at irregular intervals to feast upon the mighty dead, in the dark of the moon" (ANX 78). I can't imagine a Hirsch, a Culler, or a Jauss writing this way; and if Fiedler did, I'd think he was spoofing.

Such quasipoetic critical statements are strategically hard to challenge in a genuinely substantive dispute. For example, I am not convinced by Bloom's method that "the central American poems are houses founded on the sea," a claim he places at the head of a chapter, just below a motto from Emerson (1850) (MAP 177). But I have no idea what sort of evidence could serve to refute or confirm the claim. The poems he cites in that chapter do not all mention sea or water. Certain of his theses may be relevant, but they are just as apodictic and puzzling, for instance: "the precursors flood us, and our imaginations can die by drowning in them"; or the "revisioning of the inventors of an American Sublime" came from a "new vision that rises up" as an "'unnamed flowing'" (ANX 154; MAP 26). Or, we might look to Ferenczi's "apocalypse" of "'the raising of Mount Ararat out of the waters,'" and to Wordsworth's "metaphoric vision" of "the immortal sea" (ANX 154; MAP 11, 146f). Since such evidence never adds up to an actual demonstration, I can only choose to believe or disbelieve.

Again like the Deconstructionists, Bloom rallies support for his theory by selecting poems that seem to embody it. The appropriation of Browning's "Childe Roland" for this purpose has been noted (p. 287). On another occasion, Bloom finds "the defense of repression" in a Keats poem "so finely obvious as to make commentary redundant" (MAP 154). Or, the "dramatic monologue" of "Tennyson's Ulysses" gets "read as the belated strong poet's act of judgment upon the Romantic tradition" (MAP 156). By equating criticism with poetry, Bloom can slip in and out of the diction of his "strong" poets with as much proximity and sympathy as he likes—the more so if the poems are, as I conjectured, selected because they lend voice to Bloom's own deepest anxieties (p. 287).

One revealing analysis, published somewhat uneasily at the start of an anthology on "Deconstruction and Criticism," uses as its "proof-text" John Ashbery's

"Self-Portrait in a Convex Mirror" (BF 22-37).[28] The point of departure for Ashbery's discursive poem (552 lines) is a self-portrait by Parmigianino (1503-1540), a post-Renaissance manneristic painter struggling with the problem of perspective in a two-dimensional medium. Seeking an illusion of depth and space, he substituted for a canvas a wooden half-sphere on whose convex surface he painted his own image as he saw it in a convex mirror. Ashbery's poem is a similarly radical inquiry into perspective, with the viewer/painter and the painting representing the "soul" and its experienced world. The physical enclosure of the painted image in the sphere becomes the spiritual enclosure of the soul: "The soul establishes itself. / But how far can it swim out through the eyes / And still return safely to its nest? The surface / Of the mirror being convex, the distance increases / Significantly; that is, enough to make the point / That the soul is a captive, treated humanely, kept / In suspension, unable to advance much farther / Than your look as it intercepts the picture" (BF 24). "One would like to stick one's hand / Out of the globe, but its dimension, / What carries it, will not allow it" (BF 26).

With particular virtuosity, Bloom works through his six "ratios" in their original sequence, relating each to one of the six successive divisions of Ashbery's poem. This isomorphism is achieved because the sphere can readily suggest ratios between fullness and emptiness or inside and outside; and Ashbery's imagery also supports such ratios as part for whole, presence and absence, and early and late. He dwells on the portrait as a microcosm, on the loss of the visible and tangible, and on the passage of time.

To demarcate full or empty, inside or outside, Ashbery's globe has a limiting surface. Correspondingly, "The soul has to stay where it is;" "It must move / as little as possible. This is what the portrait says"; "the soul fits its hollow perfectly" (BF 24f). A parallel antithesis between stability versus instability is implied by images and tropes wherein life is beset by forces that transform and disperse. Ashbery prominently enlists "dream," "wave," "wind," and "time." These forces antithetically perpetuate what they render insubstantial and transitory, as in: "The time of day or the density of the light / Adhering to the face keeps it / Lively and intact in a recurring wave of arrival"; "Like a wave breaking on a rock, giving up / Its shape in a gesture which expresses that shape" (BF 30). Or, the "wind's" drift brings an ominous restoration: "A breeze like the turning of a page / Brings back your face: the moment / Takes such a big bite out of the haze / Of pleasant intuition it comes after. / The locking into place is 'death itself'" (cf. BF 33). This turn reminds us of Bloom's contention that "in our poetry, what is being evaded" is "the necessity of dying" (BF 9) (p. 287).

These illustrations suggest how Bloom's map can interweave with the texture of a poem that offers a congenial terrain. The poem is cast as an antithetical

---

[28] The title of the essay, "The Breaking of Form," must refer to Lurianic creation (cf. MAP 5). In some spots, I have added more of Ashbery's poem to clarify Bloom's responses.

structure of tropings in metaleptic interchanges. Paradoxically, this excellent fit between the poet's work and the critic's map exerts a centripetal momentum upon a poem that seems conceived to be rather more centrifugal. Bloom consoles himself and defends against dispersal by drawing the poem together in his tightly locking scheme. De Man, in contrast, heightens dispersal by interweaving the poem with his elusive theory (pp. 275ff).

Still, Bloom's method has a centrifugal aspect too, when his reading turns the poem outward toward other poems. He mimics the evasiveness of Ashbery's poem by hovering on its margins to record associations with such poems as Keat's "Ode on a Grecian Urn" and "Ode to a Nightengale," Whitman's "Song of Myself," plus Stevens' "Poems of Our Climate," "Asides on the Oboe," and "Poem with Rhythms" (BF 22ff). Bloom portrays Ashbery's poem as a "version or revision" of these sources, whose authors "are ancestral presences in 'Self-Portrait'" (BF 22). Some of the associations he constructs are "verbal resemblances," which he had disdained as hallmarks of "traditional 'source studies'" (cf. MAP 19, 116). He compares the "'waking dream'" written by both Ashbery and Keats (BF 35); Ashbery's "'peculiar slant of memory'" with Dickinson's "'certain slant of light'"; or Ashbery's "'the hand looms large'" with Stevens' "'the hand has a will to grow larger'" (BF 35, 28, 26). Even the single word "As" at the beginning of "Self-Portrait" is taken to be "one of Stevens' 'intricate evasions of as'" (BF 23) (from "An Ordinary Evening in New Haven" and the opening motto for *Anxiety*, ANX 4). Also conventional enough are relations based on common themes and emotions. Ashbery's poem is classed with Keats "Ode on a Grecian Urn" and Stevens' "Poems of Our Climate" because all three are "reveries upon aesthetic distance and poetic coldness" that "share a common sorrow, and manifest almost a common glory" (BF 24).

But relations may be postulated quite independently of resemblances, or may be detected "despite appearances," as when Hart Crane is made into an "ancestral presence" on the grounds that "the language of the poem engages, however covertly and evasively, the central Emersonian tradition of our poetry" (BF 22f). If poets are genuinely defensive, influence may well be signaled by what a poem "does not say," or "what is missing in the poem because it had to be excluded" (BF 15; MAP 178). For example, "Whitman" is "as large a hidden form in Stevens as Shelley was in Hardy" (MAP 26). We might recall that Holland's "dictionary" also worked well enough with missing evidence, p. 168).

Hence, Bloom's map does not crucially require a convenient textual surface, though the texts that have it are likely to seem "strong" to him. We could describe Bloom's readings by troping on Ashbery: "the sample one sees is not to be taken as / Merely that, but as everything as it / May be imagined outside time." In this spirit, Bloom moulds Ashbery's text after his own affinities. The poem is claimed to move "towards a lament for the confinements of art and the artist" (BF 25f). Ashbery's tropes are further troped into concerts of art: "the portrait of a ship suggests the perils of poetic art"; "the chamber" is "the suicide" "of a self-regarding art" (BF 32, 37). "The poignance of extreme dualism" that is "almost constant throughout the poem" might be related to the "constant consciousness of dualism" which is "the state of Satan" and the "honest acceptance" of which "unites" Milton, Wordsworth, Keats, and Stevens (BF 25f; ANX 32f).

Whether or not we happen to accept Bloom's interpretations, we gain little by debating their correctness in any traditional philological or historical sense. Yet as we saw, Bloom does not abandon all claims to correctness (p. 284). "The 'will to power'" and "'interpretation'" "'combine in the forceful reading that presents itself as absolutely true but can then, it its turn, be undermined'" (MAP 69f; cf. de Man, ALG 76, 277). "In order for a reading (misreading) to be productive of other texts, such a reading is forced to assert its uniqueness, its totality, its truth. Yet language *is* rhetoric, and intends to communicate opinion rather than truth" (MAP 70). Or, he invokes the authority of de Man, in whose "paradigm" "intratextual encounters" match Bloom's "literary misprisions." "De Man's implicit irony that error cannot be distinguished from imagination" "seems essential to any account of intra-poetic relationships."

Like most of our sample critics, Bloom is in the usual fix of presenting a powerfully original and personal method as the best or true one inherent in the very nature of both literature and criticism. The more extravagant his procedures become, the more acute this dilemma must seem. He has gone through deconstruction and come out the other end, which I suppose makes him (and Hartman) a post-post-structuralist. He prefers to "restore" meaning rather than to leave it deconstructed; he opposes the dissolution of the human self and action into language; he swerves from Derrida's readings of Freud and Nietzsche; he seeks the prestige of origins; and he retains his faith in the Word (though substituting Hebraic *davhar* for Greek *logos*). Against the deconstructive "heirs of Nietzsche," he admonishes that "*belatedness*" "is the true dungeon of the imagination, rather than the prison-house of language" (MAP 68).

Yet however "post-post-," Bloom would be absurdly classed as an ultra-modernist. His method passionately looks back to the archaic and the primal, to some time which was not yet so dismally belated. To him, Plato was already a latecomer; "'Modernism,' a shibboleth many of us think we may have invented," is an "inheritance" of "the first literary scholars wholly distinct from poets," the "Alexandrians" (MAP 34). Kabbalah, Torah, and Bible (Old Testament, of course) are venerable pathways to still older traditions. "In the sorrow of origins," "art rises from shamanistic ecstasy and the squalor of our timeless human fear of mortality" (ANX 58). Bloom professes to "find this return to origins inescapable, though distasteful"; but it promises "splendor," and "shamans" who, like Bloom, "had memory of the beginnings" are held in "continued awe" (ANX 58f; MAP 58, 47).

The "map" itself has some affinities to a magical formula. Its "ratios" enable multifarious manipulations of dimension, shape, and time, as if in some ultimate alchemist's dream. The absent can become present, and vice-versa; emptiness can be fullness, lowness can be highness, lateness can be earliness. If "tropes" "defend against literal meaning" and "literal meaning is a kind of death," would not a map of tropings be a grand defense for "putting off as long as possible" the critic's death (cf. MAP 91; ANX 61), the very anxiety pervading Bloom's morbid rhetoric?

The founding of the map on the "story of creation" (MAP 5f) is no accident or colorful sidelight, but a foretaste of power. Bloom seems to have bested the would-be-robbers in the Monty Python group's movie *Time Bandits*, who snatched God's map of time to guide their plans of thievery, but seldom managed to use it without disaster. Bloom is in undisputed possession of *his* map of "creation," and the model for his "restoration" is, after all, "man's contribution to God's work" (MAP 5). How better to combine "'the will to power'" with "interpretation" (cf. MAP 69f)?

And so the acceptance of Bloom's map and method or of his "theory of poetry" is essentially a matter of faith, and the benefits it heralds for its believers are substantial. "Bloomian" critics hover at least on the doorstep of poetry and if they are "strong" enough, may usurp power from a poet. Their reading can be strikingly creative and complex yet interwoven with the original text at every step. They are buffered by the proclamation of universal "misreading" and "misprision" against being wrong in any traditional sense. They are inured to failure by their glorification of failure as the heroic and death-defying culmination toward which every poem moves (cf. ANX 79, 104f, 107; MAP 31, 186, 206).

All this power has to come from someplace. The biggest losers are of course the "weak" poets and critics who "idealize" and fondly imagine creativity to be carried on in a "generosity of the spirit" (ANX 5, 30). Bloom would apparently just drop them from the canon and ignore them out of existence, except when it's time to show how "entire generations go wrong in their judgments," e.g., by esteeming Cowley, Cleveland, Denham, and Waller to be "great poets" (MAP 28). He "asserts for literary tradition" the "valuable" "pragmatic function" of "stifling the weak" (MAP 28f). A formulation like "the poet Wordsworth was long dead" before "the man Wordsworth" (ANX 140) suggests that even great poets get tossed on the junkpile when they lose their strength.

Some loss is sustained even by "strong poets." Total originality is categorically abolished, as if poetic creation resembled pasting up a collage of echoes and allusions, whether you intend to or not, perhaps of works which you never read or which haven't even been written yet. In this context, "strength" is a very ambivalent grant, since what power you get is probably stolen from the dead or the not-yet-born. Defiance is but an inverse form of compulsion and doomed anyway, pre-cursed, like trying to sweep back the sea. For instance, Bloom's "revisionary patterns" embody the "fixed or all-but-fixed relations between tropes and defense" that "are set by Wordsworth and Whitman" and "reappear in Baudelaire, Mallarmé, and Valéry, in Hölderlin and Rilke, in Yeats and Stevens and Hart Crane" (BF 13). How could lesser talents than these hope to rebel against such fixity?

And the poems may lose something too. With so much focus on personal combat, the poem looks like a ringside report of a wrestling match. Amid the flood of influences, the boundaries of the individual text waver and blur until we get confused: are we reading Shelley or Browning, Stevens or Ashbery? In addition, the criteria for being a "strong poem" are a trifle narrow, a "density of allusiveness" apparently being the top criterion (cf. MAP 125), though it doesn't save Pound. While Bloom claims "the anxiety of influence" to be "the *covert* subject of most poetry for the last three centuries" (ANX 148, e.a.), he isn't taking any chances. He assigns high ratings to poems which can be conveniently read as tropes for that anxiety, and responds strongly to overt moods of pessimism, gloom, and morbidity. Among the odder consequences of such criteria is the offhand treatment of poets, however great, who didn't betray the anxiety Bloom looks for. Shakespeare is shut out from the whole discussion, despite his enormous influence and exuberant borrowings, and Pound and Williams are tersely mauled in in gruff asides (cf. pp. 288, 291). In exchange, the "greatness" of Hardy's morose late poetry is vastly inflated (cf. p. 289).

In addition, an unduly rigid application of the "map" would impose a disquieting family resemblance on all poems and thus affirm the "continuity" that "critics love" but "Ideal or Truly Common readers" do not (cf. ANX 78). The sequence of limitation, substitution, and representation must be dutifully performed not just once for every poem, but three times, one for each "dialectical pair" among the six "ratios" (MAP 95). Though these "ratios" were set up to "name intertextual differences" (BF 19), and though "antithetical criticism" calculates the exact "accent of deviation" in the "swerves" of "descendants" away from "precursors" (ANX 93), the project might become monotonous in the hands of a less erudite critic than Bloom, who never runs out of alludable sources. The old "source-studies" he despises were limited to purportedly real influences detectable in highly specified classes of evidence, and the results indeed became boring and "pedantic" (cf. ANX 7). If Bloom is the irreplaceable energy source—if "there is no method" here "other than himself" (cf. CCP 9) — how "practical" is his map for the critical profession? Can we "renew the study of poetry" (ANX 43) on the idiosyncratic moves of one man without a counterpart in the whole world?

At one point, Bloom defines "critics" as "common readers raised to the highest power," yet avers at another point that "the Ideal or Truly Common Reader still waits to be born" (ANX 31, 78). He himself, though born at least once, is certainly a most uncommon reader. Despite his claims that "if we are human, then we depend upon a Scene of Instruction," and that "poetry is crucially pedagogical in its origins and function" (MAP 38, 32), I can't see much hope that common readers could raised to the power at which Bloom operates. He predictably suggests that "no strong student can fail to be chosen by his teachers" just as a "strong writer" is "chosen by" "his precursors" (MAP 39). But that method doesn't seem very sound for the literary profession practiced in our times.

The prospect of Bloomian criticism gaining the upper hand evidently provokes some real anxiety in those areas of the critical community who fear to find themselves adrift in a perplexing shift of power and decorum. The "academy's social standards of civility" (BF 6) would yield to permanent warfare, the victors enjoying substantial benefits, and the losers cast into an oblivion as empty as Milton's Chaos. Although Bloom implies his map of ratios might "function the way a paradigm works in the problem-solving of normal science" (BF 19), things wouldn't be "normal" in any accustomed sense.

But this anxiety may be misplaced. Bloom remystifies at least as much as he demystifies. The "achieved dearth of meaning" he projects onto "strong" poems (BF 12, e.d.) is richly refilled by his analysis. Moreover, he denounces as "silly" any intent to "liberate" "poetry" "from the academy," and is convinced of the "necessarily elitist" nature of "all literary tradition" (MAP 34, 39). He will not "acknowledge any shade of the recent Marxist critiques of our profession" (MAP 29), and his low esteem for feminism (par for the Freudian course) is made clear enough.[29]

Indeed, Bloom's continuing professional success indicates that however bizarre and disruptive his gestures, they bear a haunting resemblance to those of critical tradition. Bloom's own "family romance" seems to be imagining himself a "changeling" with heroic fathers (cf. ANX 62)—Isaiah, Luria, Valentinus, and Vico, not merely Emerson, Burke, Wilson Knight, de Man, and, yes, William K. Wimsatt, to whom *Anxiety* is antithetically dedicated. Like many critics, Bloom reveres poetry with unbounded commitment and sings paeans to it in a style of "superbole" (p. 288); he makes poetry refer mainly to itself by comparing similar passages or themes and tracing ancestries or descendences;[30] and he treats his own values as self-evident. Like most literary theoreticians, he presents his model as true and valid for all literature of real merit, while implying that he alone had the wit to discover it. The many cunning inconsistencies I described in

---

[29] If the revered Milton does not "appear to leave some room for the female in all creativity" (MAP 78), neither does Bloom's rhetoric of father-son influence. ANX opens with a Valentinus quote in which "strengthless" and "female" are juxtaposed. In MAP (36), Bloom says "it would lead to something more intense than quarrels if I expressed my judgment upon" "the 'literature of Women's Liberation.'" He does however "prophesy" that "the burgeoning religion of Liberated Women" will, if it "dominates the West," "bring about" "the first true break with literary continuity" (MAP 33). So his negative evaluation may mark his place among the "critics" who "in their secret hearts, love continuities," rather than among the "ideal" "readers" who "love discontinuities" (ANX 78).

[30] Possibly in a smack at the New Critics, Bloom remarks: "to say that a poem is about itself is killing, but to say it is about another poem is to go out into the world where we live" (MAP 198). But who is this "we"?

his proceedings are strategic defenses against most charges or attacks except that of inconsistency itself; many of our critics are far more vulnerable because of their overanxious maneuverings to buttress their strong claims on transliterary universals—Hirsch, Holland, and Bleich come to mind. Bloom's borrowings from psychoanalysis, theology, and philosophy are elaborately stitched onto the literary domain until they seem like unobtrusive family members.

I have heard it remarked, even among Bloom's ardent sympathizers, that he writes only for himself. If "criticism is the discourse" "of the solipsist who knows what he means is right, and yet that what he says is wrong," do we have here another "Childe Harold" "grown old and perfect in his solipsism" (ANX 96; MAP 156)? Has Bloom, like Emerson, "carried his individuation to the borders of a sublime solipsism" (MAP 166)?

Something of the sort may be in progress, but with a positive and expansive aspect alongside the more obvious negative and isolative one. As he observes for both "strong poet" and "solipsist," "egocentricity" is "a major training in imagination" (ANX 121). The "Second Birth" wherein a "poet" "first discovers poetry as both external and internal to himself" (ANX 25) finds a counterpart in a "criticism" that "is the art of knowing the hidden roads that go from poem to poem" (ANX 25, 96). The seemingly "autonomous ego" of the "solipsistic" "poet" is in fact "caught up in a dialectical[31] relationship" with many others (ANX 91). Bloom's quest is to show us precisely this "dialectic" before which all solipsism fades, including his own. Like "Satan" perhaps at last, "imposing a discipline despite the visible darkness," Bloom too may persist in "a heroism that is exactly on the border of solipsism" (ANX 22).

---

[31] "Dialectic" is among Bloom's favorite terms (ANX 43, 62, 80, 82f, 88, 91, 99, 109, 112; MAP 4, 28, 35, 42, 58, 75, 104, 122, 145, 149, 163, 175, 180), but—again like Frye—not in its Marxist sense.

15

Geoffrey Hartman[1]

When I approached Geoffrey Hartman about the problems of portraying his work, he suggested I was having trouble because he "never comes clean." Toward the middle of one book, he peers out at us with "Where am I going, you wonder" (CW 119); and I did. "For truth to be dialectical," he says, "I must engage to be I; but here my conflicts and rhetorical complexities betray me," and "the playful or evasive quality of my words" (CW 260). "Hartman is merely artman."

Proceeding on the assumption that Hartman can reliably be said to have a consolidated personal project is a calculated risk. Whether he is endorsing the theoretical positions he invokes or merely playing off or against them is hard to determine. His rhetoric can be fitful and mutable, like the calling of a prodigiously erudite mockingbird in a dense thicket of literature, "philosophy, theology, linguistics, sociology, and psychoanalysis" (CW 240), plus, of course, criticism. More than the other Yale-birds from the prisonhouse of language, he seems to illustrate his vision of being haunted by alien voices and beset by "the 'ghostly' question" of "who is speaking, to whom, from where" (cf. SAV xxi).

The cunning inconsistencies of Hartman's strong mind are even more complexly striated than Bloom's. One of Hartman's is "to insist on the priority of reading over theory even while insisting on the importance of theory" (CW 175).[2] He agrees with Ransom (1938) that "theory" "always determines criticism, and never more than when it is unconscious" (CW 174). Yet he is "skeptical about the possibility of a truly comprehensive literary theory," let alone "a comprehensive theory of verbal artifacts, comprising prose and poetry, ordinary and extraordinary language" (CW 299, 40).[3] "Theory-making" "can only provide finer mental and verbal instruments"; "the act of reading" and of "specific and

---

[1] The key for Hartman citations is: CW: *Criticism in the Wilderness* (1980); DC: "Preface" to *Deconstruction and Criticism* (1979a); SAV: *Saving the Text: Literature, Derrida, Philosophy* (1981); and WOR: "Words, Wish, Worth: Wordsworth" (1979b).

[2] This "insistence" is attributed to "the avant-garde essay" (CW 175), a category which may include Hartman's own writings, though it would be out of character for him to say so.

[3] This statement appears in Hartman's much-favored format of the rhetorical question, a device whereby he can leave us guessing what answer to prefer. We will be encountering many more.

self-reflective interpretation remains essential" (CW 3). Instead of merely "adding to the heap and increasing the burden it was supposed to remove," "theory is (in theory) supposed to do away with itself, and lead to more exact, concrete, focused insight" (CW 238f).

"Since the neo-classical period, criticism has been primarily an 'ordinary language' movement," a "prose of the center," a "middle or conversational style" "developed for" "drawing room or salon" (CW 163, 155, 135). In its adherence to "neoclassical decorum," such "enlightened," "over-accommodated prose" threatens to "reduce literature to formal conversation," and to "reduce art" "to a single principle" or "standard" (CW 137, 85, 155). "New Criticism," for example, "limited the critical essay by reducing its sphere of competence to specific, formal or evaluative, remarks on art" (CW 6).

After the "Arnoldian concordat," "criticism no longer had a standing or creative potential of its own" (CW 6f). The "concept of literature" was "unduly narrowed" by an "anti-self-consciousness principle" fostering an "unfortunate and purely hypothetical separation of thinking and feeling" (CW 174, 20, 44). The "genteel tradition" encouraged a "pseudoclassical reduction of the critical spirit" and an "assignment of criticism to a noncreative and dependent function" (CW 14). "Great talent" gets "reduced to quarreling about what interpretation (evaluation) is or is not correct" (CW 248). "We have caused our own impotence by allowing the concept of practical criticism to reduce to its lowest social or utilitarian value" (CW 291f).

One "recent revival of methodology" is "due to the parascientific disciplines of structuralism and semiotics" (WOR 187). They promote "close reading and formal analysis," and "sensitize the reader to complexities hardly noticed before" (CW 6). Still, the "formalist and structuralist" approach to "style" is "an evasion if it rests with a distinction between the language of description and the language of the object described, and privileges the former as a scientific metalanguage, instructive because rarified"; but not "if it discloses the demand for order and organization in both art and science" (CW 156). "Technical criteria or forms of analysis are useful in a preparatory way," but "their scientific virtue" does not "make of every user an efficient critic" (CW 162)—which, of course, no method can do.

"Science" has had an "obvious success" "in turning its provisional mastery of the world into a real imposition," but "what goes under the name" of "a science of language is more like a methodological miscellany, a pleasingly ordered chaos" (SAV 2). "To compile an inventory of meanings in their structural relations ('structuralism') or of the focusing and orientative acts of consciousness in *their* relations ('phenomenology') seems rather distant from what we do as critics" (CW 270). We should "take back from science what is ours" and not "depend on the physical or human sciences for the model of a *mechanism* that fascinates by its anonymous, compulsive, impersonal character." In this spirit, Hartman "favors moving 'indeterminacy' from the area of grammatical, semiotic, or phenomenological reduction to that of humanistic criticism."

"At present," Hartman sees four "'other worlds' that tempt the interpreter—(1) the midrashic or polysemous world of biblical interpretation, where extremely bold hypotheses and strict rules of exegesis keep company; (2) existential hermeneutics," "in which the authentic text is always strange and requires interpretation"; "(3) transactive or dialogic theories of reading, which stress the importance and complexity of the 'orders' of speech that the literary work encodes, as well as the close link between language, community, and understanding"; and "(4) the conceptual, even noumenal, rhetoric that Parisian movements" "are developing" in order to "motivate the deconstruction of reality (social or mental)" while "providing the only instrument for analyzing, articulating, or criticizing it" (CW 237f). He supplies the names of Hamann and Heidegger for (2), and of Lévi-Strauss, Lacan, Foucault, and Derrida for (4). The names are listed elsewhere for (3), the "'dialogic,' 'dialectic,' or 'transactive' model": Gadamer, Jauss, Iser, Holland, Fish, and Jameson (CW 226). Among the critics I survey, Frye is probably intended for (1) along with Bloom, in whose visionary company Hartman has long lived and whose spirit haunts Hartman's *Wilderness* so pervasively at times that to credit him for every influence might convey the impression of repetition-compulsion.

Hartman is generally more sympathetic toward the scholars in groups (1), (2), and (4) than toward those in (3). He disputes Fish's belief that "indeterminacy" "merely *delays* the determination of meaning" so as "to slow the act of reading till we appreciate" "its complexity" (CW 270). For Hartman, "the delay is intrinsic"; "to keep a poem in mind is to keep it there, not to resolve it into available meanings" (CW 274). Holland is decried for "evangelizing the very difficulty of gaining an interpretation" (CW 269) though Hartman evangelizes the same thing in a different way. The "objective" and "subjective" "criticisms" of Hirsch and Holland both "leave art behind"; they "ignore equally the resistance of art to the meaning it provokes."[4] This complaint too is strange, since that very resistance was their starting point and motivation.

Strangest of all are Hartman's charges that reader-response critics do not attend to "the history of interpretation" and the "great movements in theology or political philosophy"; and do not consider "the reader both intrinsically, or as he is in himself, and historically as someone set concretely in a changeable field of influence" (WOR 186). Jauss, Iser, and Jameson do exactly that (Chs. 17, 8, 18), though again in a different way from Hartman. Though he protests "the resis-

---

[4] For Holland, and for Bleich as well, the resistance is in the mind, not the art, except insofar as art is shaped by "defense." Hirsch, we recall, describes initial reading with Schleiermacher's term as a "divinatory moment" (pp. 109); Hartman and Bloom envision a divination as well, but one that is not to be recontained by validation procedures (p. 285, 322f).

tance to theory in Anglo-American criticism" (CW 297), he deprecates some of the more prestigious and accomplished theorists on the literary scene.

Hartman has a particular affinity for deconstructionism, although he professes himself "barely" a "deconstructionist" and "even writes against it on occasion" (DC ix). The approach he favors "acknowledges the deconstructionist challenge as necessary and timely, if somewhat involved," yet "only occasionally reflective of analogies to its own project" (SAV 121). He offers "not a refutation but a different turn in how to state the matter." Like Bloom, he would be an eccentric post-post-structuralist who is at once modernist and conservative. Both critics use deconstructionist arguments as backdrops for a countermovement toward a bizarre decorum.

One area of deconstructive influence can be seen in Hartman's view of language. "Language appears as a restless medium that both transcends and negates its relation to the phenomenal world" (CW 152).[5] "Words" "are maddeningly complex and equivocal"; their "very existence" "indicates a breach with the phenomenality" and "evidentiality" of "things" (SAV 122, xvi). "Words can only be words by not being things, by aiming referentially at things yet overshooting them" (SAV 3). "The signifier" "cannot attain, touch, transmit"; "words remain words while striving for definitive, transcendent status" (CW 80, 90; compare Bloom, BF 9).

Therefore, "all statements are potentially overdetermined and have a circumference larger than their apparent reference" (CW 265). "The more pressure we put on a text in order to interpret or decode it, the more indeterminacy appears" (CW 202). The "textual surface" is "always in movement, always betraying or exceeding synthesis, as if language had a life of its own" (CW 88). "In any significant act of reading, there must be (1) a text that steals our consent; and (2) a question about the text's value at a very basic level": is this a "forged" or an "authentic experience?" (CW 25). Correspondingly, "writing is a calculus that jealously broods on strange figures, on imaginative otherness"; "no writer who goes through the detour of a text gets himself unmediated" (CW 27, 48).

It is the essential "'hollowness' in language, an abysmal or unsoundable quality in it, which keeps the old quarrel between rhetoric and dialectic alive" (CW 231). "A fresh literature" can "limit that feeling of a hollowness"; but "our finest readers" keep "demonstrating over and over again that everything natural or spontaneous in language is a rhetorical device, and that behind the appearance of originality there is bricolage, or the canny embezzlement of previous art" (CW 230f).

Still, Hartman doesn't seem disposed to adopt the "mode of criticism" "fashioned" by "Derrida and de Man," because it remains "helplessly ironic in its

---

[5] This portrayal is presented during a discussion of the "style" of Hegel, who is treated rather like a practitioner of deconstruction.

emphasis on displacement, on words rather than the Word" (CW 112). Hartman would be more inclined to agree with Burke, for whom "the turn from words to the Word is the very place where artist and critic dwell"; or with Eliot, who is said to "seek to move us from words to the Word" (CW 90, 153). "For Derrida, the rhetoric of representation" "is a sham," and his theory "tries to free rhetoric from representational ends" (SAV 120). Again like Bloom, Hartman prefers to propose "a restored theory of representation"; "criticism deracinates itself when it evades the issue of representation in its many, including theological, aspects" (SAV 121; 113).

"Anti-representational modes of questioning disturb the alliance of signifier with signified by deconstructing a stable 'concept,' or by undoing the 'unique' charm of particular texts: the illusion that they have a direct, even original, relation to what they represent" (SAV 121). "Yet how good an antidote" is "this deconstructionist reversal, which claims" "that when we talk of reality we are dealing with a metonymic charm, the substitution of cause for effect, or with an illusion of depth built up" by "intertextuality?" "The problem" "with anti-representational theories" "is that they are more referential than they know"; "they have secretly declared" "representation itself, the very force and pathos of mimetic desire and envy," to be "the *bad* magic"; yet "they consistently and rigorously doubt that it can be remedied by the *good* word, or any word-cure" (SAV 120). "Whereas for deconstructionist criticism, literature is precisely that use of language which can purge pathos, which can show that it too is figurative, ironic, or aesthetic," Hartman insists that "the ethos of literature is not dissociable from its pathos" (DC ix).

Unlike many of our critics, Hartman can't decide on a label for the approach he favors. The "diversity" of "the post-new critics" or "the latest grouping of critics," sees to it that "no one can agree on what to name" them (CW 239f). "Are they 'revisionists' or 'hermeneuticists' or 'deconstructivists' or 'Yale' rather than Russian 'formalists'? Are they formalists or anti-formalists? Do they really have a common program, or is their unity simply that of achieving a 'critical mass' at Yale?" (CW 240). Elsewhere, he lists de Man, Miller, Bloom, and Derrida as "the new 'revisionist' or 'hermeneutic' critics," but adds at once that the grouping is a "mere polemical convenience" (CW 226). Far from announcing his personal credo in a Bloom-style "manifesto," Hartman is a hard man to pin down, like the speaker in a radio receiving several channels at once, some in foreign languages, along with bursts of static.

Hartman advocates a "hermeneutics" that "tries to understand understanding through the detour of the writing/reading experience" (CW 244). "There is no other way" than a "detour," because "writing is a labyrinth, a topological puzzle, and a textual crossword; the reader" "must lose himself" "in a hermeneutic 'infinitizing' that makes all rules of closure appear arbitrary." "The process of understanding, of hermeneutic revision," is "endless" (CW 299). This factor has been overlooked in "the attempt to establish an objective or scientific hermeneutics" as "an act of defensive mastery" over "an unruly, changeable language" (CW 247).

"Revisionism" is now extolled as an "extraordinary language movement"[6] that "urges readers to take back some of their authority and become creative and thoughtful" (CW 161). This method will not "make art stranger or less strange than it is" (CW 26). The "otherness" of art "demands of understanding an extraordinary, even self-altering effort" (CW 27). We face the "spectacle of a critic's mind disoriented, bewildered, caught in some 'wild surmise' about the text and struggling to adjust" (CW 20).

Performing his own version of a move we found in de Man and Bloom, Hartman "shuttles between" "works of art and works of reading" in order to "suggest that criticism is *within* literature," "not outside it" (CW 5f, 298). "Art" "allows a response as free, imaginative, and self-tasking as its own must have been" (CW 62). Schlegel is called to witness that "the work of criticism is superfluous unless it is itself a work of art as independent of the work it criticizes as that is independent of the materials that went into it" (CW 159). "All criticism entails a rethinking, which is itself creative, of what others hold to be creative: a scrutiny of the presence of the fictive" "in every aspect of learning and life" (CW 14).

"The revisionists" are credited with "challenging the attitude that condemns the writer of criticism or commentary to nonliterary status and a service function" (CW 9). The way to "attack the isolation of the critic" is to "disclose in a radical way" the "variety and indeterminacy" of "the relation of creativity to criticism" (CW 9). Instead of the "subtle idolatry" in "the automatic valuing of works of art over works of commentary," we might attain a (Wordsworthian) "'interchangeable supremacy'" between "criticism and creation" (CW 103, 259). "How criticism is a genre, or primary text," Hartman himself "hopes to show by suspending the a priori valuation of art over criticism and reading even the critical work closely" (CW 6). For instance, "the theory" of "the avant-garde essay" "is a textual entity to be worked through like a poem or prose artifact" (CW 175).

Once equated with literature, criticism no longer has to be "less radical" "than art" (CW 113). "Great art is radical" because it "slanders an established order, good or bad, by not conforming" (CW 98). "Art" "gives the lie to every attempt to impose a truth by state-sponsored power." "No formula may preempt what the effect of its openness will be" (CW 99). "Major art in its very negativity or terrifying respect for exact witness cannot be co-opted" (CW 183). Hence, the

---

6 Elsewhere, an "extraordinary language movement" is said to include writings of Coleridge, Carlyle, Nietzsche, Benjamin, Burke, Bloom, Derrida, and Frye (CW 85, e.d.). Compare the "'ordinary language' movement" Hartman dates from "the neoclassical period" (CW 163).

"reader-critic is deeply involved in not allowing art to be shunted aside or co-opted by the newest ideology" (CW 99). The evasiveness of Hartman's writings might be a reflection of this involvement; for him, "critical thinking respects heterogeneity" and "keeps in mind the peculiarity or strangeness of what is studied" (CW 26; cf. Frye, AC 348; Bloom, ANX 86).

"Each work of art, and each work of reading, is potentially a demonstration of freedom: of the capacity" "for making sense by a mode of expression that is our own" (CW 2). "Visionary poetry" in particular attains "freedom *over* rather than *from* sources" (CW 103).[7] Correspondingly, "criticism is freed from neoclassical decorum" (CW 85). Critics no longer need to be "scared to do anything except convert as quickly as possible the imaginative into a mode of the ordinary" (CW 27). They can abjure the old "historical reflection" with its "fine and fruitless dialectic, calculating the influences, establishing by fiat what is positive and what is negative, and aiming at a doubtful synthesis" (CW 102f). The "hermeneutics of indeterminacy" aimed at by "contemporary criticism" "has renounced the ambition to master or demystify its subject (text, psyche) by technocratic, predictive, or authoritarian formulas" (CW 41). In return, "the quality of reading" might "increase to preserve the great or exceptional work as something still possible" (CW 165).

However, Hartman's confidence in such utopian prospects is uncertain: "can reading be all that watchful now?" (CW 165). "The more conscientious it is, the more besieged and burdened it is." "Criticism as a kind of hermeneutics" "reveals contradictions and equivocations, and so makes fiction interpretable by making it less readable" (CW 32; cf. CW 188). "The strangeness of fiction" cannot be "understood" by a "careful" "explication" (CW 31). "Critical commentary" resembles "fiction" by trying to "contain" the "bewilderment" in "the critic's mind" (CW 20, e.d.). Yet "criticism" also "differs from fiction by making the experience of reading explicit" and "showing how a reader's sympathies, defenses, are now solicited, now compelled" (CW 50).

As history shows, "the critical spirit" "does not automatically place itself on the side of reason, enlightenment, or demystification" (CW 40). "Returning to a larger and darker view of art as mental charm, war, and purgation" may call for a "terrorist style" in which "humanism" is "attacked by name" (CW 101, 151). "Derrida" for one "does not fear the seemingly absurd or anomalous idea a strong theory may bring to birth," and "often values nonsense" in "theories that have tried to make sense of sense" (SAV 46f). Or, Bloom "restores" "complexity" to the "interpretive relation": "the disguised text asks us to woo it in the name of what it is, but appears not to be" (CW 61). "He will not believe that art is consolation, or that poetry can endure as an abiding force unless it can survive a greater degree of

---

[7] Here too, Bloom's outlook is rendered with considerable sympathy, ranging from his early *Visionary Company* (1961) up to "his later and openly gnostic phase" (CW 103f).

probing than the New Critics, even with their criterion of toughness, applied." He "puts poems up against interpretations so different in their verbal decorum that the disjunction becomes alarming."

So we have been warned not to expect the "prose of the center" Hartman diagnosed in conventional criticism (CW 155). "The essays of the more intellectual practitioners of the art of literary or philosophical criticism make greater demands on the reader" than "poems" do; and "make the text a little harder to understand" (CW 197). Because "it does not see itself as subordinated in any simple way to the books on which it comments," "critical commentary" "that challenges the dichotomy of reading and writing" (as do Bloom, Blanchot, Derrida, and Barthes) "puts a demand on the reader that may cause perplexity and resentment" (CW 20). "Whenever a critic fudges the line between commentary and fiction," "the psychological drama of reading" —"centering on" an "aroused merging: a possible loss of boundaries, a fear of absorption, the stimulation of a sympathetic faculty that may take over and produce self-alienation" — "is felt to be too threatening" (CW 50f). When a critic like Bloom "seeks to break the illusions of art by subjecting them to the extremest, the most reductive aspects of Freudian or Nietzschean analysis," "the entire enterprise of criticism becomes unreal: no longer a distinct, well-fenced activity" (CW 61, 58).

Such methods indicate that "if we respect the language of art, it is often because of critics whose language is but a lesser scandal" (CW 157). As Horkheimer remarks, "'it may not be entirely senseless to continue speaking a language that is not easily understood'" (CW 64).[8] In Hartman's own hands, criticism inherits from "English poetry" "a promiscuous intermingling of various linguistic inheritances, a jostling of high and low styles" without much in the "middle" (cf. CW 88, 135). He delights in working expressions like "jazzed up," "junk," "old codgers," "paydirt," "highjinks," "bad vibes," and so on (CW 119, 226, 96, 264), into a polyphonic scholarly discourse bristling with more than enough solecisms, foreignisms, and neologisms to stump the readers his slang feigns to address. And he frantically strews puns about, not merely as if they were going out of style, but as if he wanted to make us wish they would.

Once more like Bloom, Hartman has many sources and yet feels anxious about sources. "Our problem, basically, is that of holding fast to the faculty of understanding as our one genuine source of apodictic knowledge, an understanding always in danger of being alienated by religious or scientific or practical attitudes" (CW 166). He "prefers to remain unsystematic when there is so much exploration still to be done" (SAV 44).[9]

Though Hartman professes to be a "non-philosopher" (CW 166; SAV 1), he

---

[8] An illustration might be the "crowded language" of Walter Benjamin, which is "curiously unprogressive or exitless" (CW 64).

[9] This "preference" is a reason for not attempting a "systematic analysis" "starting with Freud's understanding of the rebus in *The Interpretation of Dreams*" (SAV 44).

insists that the "only program" of "contemporary criticism," namely the "revaluation of criticism itself," should "hold open the possibility that philosophy and the study of art can join forces once more" (CW 41). Both "literary and philosophical inquiry" have "always" been concerned with the "relation of language to thought" (CW 3). Also, "philosophy" has the attraction of making "less of a distinction between primary and secondary literature" (CW 20; cf. CW 211, 298).[10] "Ask a philosopher what he does and he will answer philosophy"; "it could be argued, in the same spirit, that what a literary critic does is literature" (but surely this formula demands "criticism"?). Hartman envisions a "philosophical literature" or a "philosophic work of art," as exemplified by writings of Pater, Coleridge, and Schlegel, and, apparently, Shelley, Kleist, Emerson, and Derrida as well (CW 45, 38, e.d.).[11] "What is required is a work of power in which philosophy recognizes poetry" (CW 38).

Of course, not all of philosophy is amenable to Hartman's project. He is not concerned with its "quest for an absolutely logical, nonpoetic or purified kind of prose" (CW 235). "Neither pure logic nor a cloudy empiricism can get hold of the workings of our language" (SAV 155). At certain times, "philosophy claimed to ground its truth on the right use of language" and "wished to curb the quasi-magical effect of strong figures, and perhaps a religious 'enthusiasm' associated with that effect" (CW 149). Even "Derrida and de Man" see "philosophy" as "a mode of writing that tries to achieve the break with representational values through scrutinizing or purging all figures"; but for Hartman, "philosophy remains a bleached sort of poetry, figurative discourse despite itself" (CW 112). "Some of the difficult critics," including Derrida, may be "frustrated poets" (CW 198)—a common suspicion about critics of all kinds (if you can't do, preach).

Hartman seems to propose a "philosophical criticism" whose "most peculiar feature" is the "difficult alliance" between "speculation and close reading" (CW 174). "Considered as a development in the history of prose, it tends to reject previous rules of expository spareness, pedagogical decorum, and social accommodation." "Yet the critical essay, while recouping its freedom to theorize, continues to bind itself to close reading," and "the post-new-critical critics remain close readers" (CW 175, 248). This way of reading enables the "close-ups" in "the critical essay today" that "show what simplifications, or institutional

---

[10] "Philosophical criticism in the European tradition," "breaking down" "the distinction" "between creative and discursive modes," is attributed to "Sartre, Heidegger, Ortega, Lukács, Derrida" (CW 298; cf. CW 211).

[11] "Few" "intellectual poems" "exist in the sphere of literary or cultural criticism" (CW 196). Those of "Arnold or Pater" survive, despite "dated remarks," as "part of the heaven of English literature." Yeats and Stevens are claimed to "echo Pater's mode of philosophic criticism" (CW 45). Kleist's *Marquise of O_____* could be his contribution to "philosophic art" (CW 38). For Schlegel, the *Athenaeum* fragments" are cited as "synthesizing criticism that would combine art and philosophy" (CW 38; cf. de Man, BI 80, 219ff).

processes, are necessary for achieving any kind of unitary, consensual view of the artifact" (CW 196f).

Hartman does not feel in need of "recourse to a special interpretive system like psychoanalysis" or "speech-act theories," though he is sometimes "prompted" by them and "appreciates" their "areas of concern" (WOR 208). Also, "semiotics" "may produce an unfeeling language of description" and fail to reach "the affective power of voice," or "the relation of particular words to that resonating field of pathos and power" "we call the psyche" (SAV 154, xxii). For Hartman, "the relation of 'text' and 'soul'" (or "psyche") is the true "province of a theory of reading" (WOR 186). Hence, he uses "psychoanalysis" after all as a way to "reduce" things "to something prior and deeper" and to search for "universal" "givens of human nature" (WOR 207f).

In such matters as "the hypothesis of a primal word-wound," he declines to "worry the question of the relation of empirical evidence to theory" and prefers to be "cautionary rather than assertive about the clinical aspects of word-therapy" (SAV 154, 122). "Psychoanalysis" "reveals once more the unresolvable ambivalence of passion as both suffering and ecstasy"; "we are made to realize how easily the psyche is punctured by image, photo, phantasm, or phrase" (SAV 97). The term "wounding" is used for "the expectation that a self can be defined or constituted by words, if they are direct enough," and for "the traumatic consequences of that expectation" (SAV 131). "Because" "life is as ambivalent in this regard as words are equivocal, the psyche may have to live in perpetual tension with its desire to be worded." "Lately," though, "we have been accustomed to" "say" that "the self has its boundaries fixed or unsettled by language" (SAV 2). "The ego is dethroned as the magisterial or controlling center," but "a new illusion surfaces"; "those who put author or ego down are still potentially mastered by the idea of presence" when they "accord" "privilege" "to voice" (SAV 5).

Hartman wonders: "is psychoanalysis" "a form of art, on the basis of the 'universal thing called playing'?" (CW 263). Or, does "art constitute a region" "in which the human desire for omnipotence is still in force, but as a counter-neurosis?"; if so, "psychoanalysis merely defines the place of art in 'the complex structure presented by the compensation for human wishes'" (CW 218). Either conception could suggest parallels between "a literary or historical perspective" and "the psychopathology of everyday life" (SAV 155).

One such parallel compares the "frame" of "writing" to the "voices that enter through dreams and psychotic states" (SAV xxi). "Lacan and Derrida develop" their "indeterminacy principle" "from dream logic and literary language, beginning with the Id" (SAV 98). "Freud's genial analysis of the latent content of dreams" is a "persuasive mode of allegoresis"; his "Eros and Thanatos are drives with the names of gods" (CW 180).

Another parallel compares "wit" to "lust" as "two infinities" that have always plagued the decorum of social existence" (SAV 48). "Neoclassical theories of decorum" "attacked" "wit," fearing that "an infectious or promiscuous variety" might "bring a leprous insubstantiality into language and nature" (SAV 45f). If "Freud showed clearly enough that wit is language-libido," the startlingly witty Hartman could be a lustful or libidinous figure, a devotee of "pornosophy, so at home in France" (SAV 48, 97). His pastiche of styles does at times seem to enjoy "'wild pairings without a priest'" (cf. SAV 48).

And the priest's may indeed be one of his own changeable faces. Certainly, religion and theology seem to be Hartman's center of gravity just as much as wit is his center of levity. More like Frye than Bloom for once, he does not openly profess a personal theology. Of course, he seldom declares himself anyway, but he may also be showing some deference toward the orientation of "contemporary thinkers" for whom "theology remains a junkyard of dark sublimities" "littered with obsolete and crazy, or once powerful now superstitious ideas" (WOR 206). He concedes that "after Marx and Freud, there is a tendency to make religion part of the problem rather than of the solution and to expel it from the enlightened analysis of the human experience" (CW 63). "We fear" "the danger of being suckered by charismatic persons and their miracles of rare device" (CW 83).

And yet behold: "the sacred has so inscribed itself in language that while it must be interpreted, it cannot be removed" (CW 248). "As all poetry, and indeed all writing—not only that of prima facie religious eras—is scrutinized by the critical and secularizing spirit, more evidence of archaic or sacred residues comes to light." "It would be a great relief to break with the idea of the sacred, and especially with the institutions that claim to mediate it"; "yet the institution of language makes every such break appear inauthentic" (CW 249). "So vast is our inheritance of an art immersed in myth and religion, and so steeped is our language in their terms, that any project of secularization becomes invested with the pathos it would expel" (CW 181). Critics might undertake, like Bloom or Burke, "a perplexed return to the personal and oracular vein"; or, like Ricoeur, a "restorative criticism" that "discloses the identity" of "the concepts of immediacy and the sacred" (CW 155, 42).

"The subtle tyranny of secularization" is blamed for "making us forget until recently the analogy between criticism and theological discourse" (CW 180). "The immense energy" that "theology" "expended" upon "sustaining and perpetuating canonical texts" is "focussed" "today" by "criticism" "on a literature that—a crucial difference—cannot be set off as holy and inspired." "Literary-critical discourse," is "like literature itself, a profane 'troping'" (CW 180f). "The consciousness of profanity overshadows at present the critical rather than the creative writer"; "criticism seems unable to achieve an easy conscience about the secularization it is struggling toward" (CW 181). Frye's "theory of formulas (archetypes) is presented as a scientific or structural project of description, but it saves art in a world split between scientific and religious (or ideological) imperatives" (CW 182). It is "the most liberal theology or justification of art the modern professional has managed to devise" (CW 184).

Quite unlike Bloom's thunderous, prophetic embrace of Kabbalistic ancestry, Hartman's own liberal theology is subtly woven into his complicated rhetoric. His writing style seems designed to reflect his view that "religion" is "a mixed matter, a complex phenomenon not easily reduced to ideals of purity, totality, or ascesis" (CW 99). Besides, he needs to respect his own view of "art" that "no formula may preempt what the effect of its openness will be." All in all, though, the tenet that "criticism is a contemporary form of theology" (CW 54) has a decidedly positive import for Hartman.[12]

His stylistic shuttle entwines theology with art in elaborate and particolored patterns. "Art is a radical critique of representation, and as such is bound to compete with theology" (CW 115). "However opposed art may be to religion, hierarchy, or the very idea of the sacred, it exhibits the kind of energy, concentration, and compulsive structure we associate with its despotic opponents" (CW 98). "Arnold" "predicted that only the poetry implicit in religion would remain"; "one is tempted to reverse it": "what remains of poetry is its heterodox theology, or mythmaking" (CW 180, 248).[13] Also, the voice of this shuttle is raised to quote other voices: "'the arts have taken on a prophetic function in society'" (Frye); "'the Religions of all Nations are derived from each Nation's different reception of the Poetic Genius, which is everywhere called the Spirit of Prophecy'" (Blake); and so on (CW 95).

Hartman's (unmediated?) vision perceives "in our own century, countless if less vigorous testaments for the rebirth of the supernatural through intellectual or even technological means" (CW 43). "Technique is a modern and demystified form of magic"; and "technology is theology modernized and made aesthetic" (CW 34, 83). "Investing technology, and perhaps inventing it, is the old desire for mastery and dominance" —the "cultic desire for control of self and others" (CW 82f). In the very midst of "our fascination with technique" we unexpectedly find ourselves looking homeward to angels and adoring a holy "ghost in the machine" (cf. CW 83).

"Religion" and "language" are juxtaposed as the "major battlegrounds" for "purity" (CW 117). "The language of religion especially; but also the religion of language." "Unless you abandon words altogether," "the project of purification accrues strong religious overtones" (CW 181). Poetry is important here to the degree that "good poetic diction is felt to be a language within language that purifies it, restoring original power" (CW 117). Yet "any call for purification is

---

[12] For Bleich and perhaps Culler too, the theological groundings of criticism are manifested in its claims for truth and are a liability (SC 33f; PS 160). Hartman abruptly adopts the same view in his critique of the profession: "the emphasis on correctness in interpretation" "is as close to theology as to science" (CW 297f). Also, "the concept of organic form" is also called a "secular" "equivalent to the check imposed on knowledge by religious faith" (CW 296). That Hartman should make theology both a reproach and a resource is among his most cunning inconsistencies.

[13] "Myths" are associated with "religion" and "sacred patterns" and thus with the "logos" (CW 181; SAV 48f; cf. CW 249; Note 10).

dangerous"; "it is always purity having to come to terms with impurity that drives crazy." Resulting aberrations, at least in Hartman's view, might include "the puritanism" of "critical writing" in "its modest but unconvincing subservience to art"; or its attempt to "gain" "purity" "through a technical 'language of description' clearly separate from the 'object language' of the work of art" (CW 161, 235). He asks: "should we give up the entire idea of purification and illustrate or adorn the language of criticism until it achieves a character of its own?" (CW 235). Like most of his rhetorical questions, this one goes unanswered, except insofar as his whole oeuvre may be one huge affirmative. If "literature" "represents and belies" the "language trajectory" of a "purifying desire" for "absolute diction" (CW 142), so must a criticism that is "within" literature.

The signs for a new bond between criticism and theology, though numerous, are often intricately delineated in Hartman's prose. Criticism may be expounded in terms that are linked to theology in other contexts. We read, for example: "criticism is haunted by an archaic debt, by the eccentric riches of allegorical exegesis in all its curiously learned, enthusiastic, and insubordinate modes" (CW 85). Elsewhere, we read: "allegorical exegesis" makes Freud's approach into "psycho-theology"; "the issue of enthusiasm is not separable from that of religion"; and so on (CW 180, 49). Such subtle procedures again reveal Hartman as a master of weaving, a re-resartor showing that "wit and mystery go together" (cf. CW 47).

If, as Hartman's contends, the separation of art from criticism is unjustified, then critics would be not merely interpreters of a sacred Word, but its dispensers. At one point, he opines that a truly "watchful" "reading would have to become an endless prayer or jeremiad" (CW 165). But his ambitions do not coincide with Bloom's, whose Kabbalistic model, as we saw, sees "restoration" as "man's contribution to God's work" (MAP 5). For Hartman, "it is unrealistic to vest the critic with a religious aura" in a "flamboyant style" which "points to a wildish destiny that cannot be sustained in this manifest way" (CW 11).

Perhaps if we watch Hartman engaging a literary work, we may get some idea of the "aura" his kind of critic radiates. As with most of our critics, his practice serves to advocate his theoretical program. As we saw with de Man and Bloom, this tendency is particularly strategic for a criticism striving to merge with the literary work. The creativity and openness of the interpretive process as expounded by Hartman, and his complex, incorporating rhetoric, readily enable him to appropriate a poem as an instantiation of his own ideology. Even when the end result is surprising (as is the case in his treatment of *Glas*, pp. 324ff), we can scarcely say just where his drift leaves the work behind. Like the original, his critical text itself "steals our assent" and yet leaves a "basic" "question" whether it is "authentic" (cf. CW 25). The chain from allegory to allegory makes his "upward fall" by subtle degrees very hard to gauge.[14] When he remarks about a

---

[14] The term "upward fall" was used in Hartman's "1964 essay on Marvell's sense of temporality" (CW 254, 238; cf. de Man, BI 46; Bloom, ANX 104; Note 10 to Ch. 14).

poem that "no easy, integrating path leads from the absolute or abrupt image to the mediation that preserves it" (WOR 186f), he might be describing the genesis of his own commentary.

His discussion of Wordsworth's poem "A Little Onward Lend Thy Guiding Hand" is a revealing instance. The fact that the poem opens with a genuine quotation (in its title), one coming from Sophocles via Milton, is taken to be a sign that "the effaced or absorbed memory of other great poems motivates its own career" (WOR 179). In that "sense," "perhaps every poem" "begins with a quotation and develops against the shadow of it," though "not as directly as here."

A level of psychoanalytic overtones is duly added. "Poetry" is a "working through of voices, residues as explicit and identifiable as the usurping passage from Milton, or as cryptically mnemonic as rhythm and dream phrase" (WOR 190f).[15] Because Wordsworth knows that "imagination may not be on the side of nature," he "both acknowledges and refuses" the "vehicular, visionary power" of "the voluntary or involuntary utterances that rise in him"; "imagination" yields to "quotation," so that "an unmediated psychic event turns out to be a mediated text: words made of stronger words" (WOR 185f). Such "poetry" might be "echo humanized, a responsive moment represented here in schematic form" (WOR 195). Yet "the 'power in sound' cannot be humanized by a sheer act of will or the arbitrariness of metaphorical speech." We now find out that Hartman's prison-house of language is a haunted one: the poet's "voice" is set against "his ear-experience" of "mutterings, sobbings, yellings, and ghostly blowing echoes" (WOR 195; cf. CW 122, 146).[16]

Still more insistent is the echo of theological overtones. "The doctrine of the Logos" "evokes a parallel enlightenment," but "the Logos dwells with God and when it comes to men is not understood" (WOR 195). Wordsworth "sought to convert a divine or willful imperative into a responsive or timely utterance," but "utterance itself" "blocks or delays the wish or alters it" (WOR 199). Moreover, "the fiat is waylaid on its way to utterance because the poet is anxious lest he speak the opposite of a creating word" (WOR 201). "The creative will, or the wish to respond with timely utterance" "may become willful and turn against what it wishes to bless; and 'thereof comes in the end despondency and madness'" (WOR 203). "The assumption of visionary status by the poet" might "revive" "ancestral, fearful, unenlightened" "voices" (WOR 202).

Wordsworth himself is therefore "evading the divine Word, or a privative imagination" (WOR 185). Such "poetry" is "undecidably" both "a purely reflective, mediated kind of language" and "oracular-visionary speech" (WOR 179f). "The poet's voice is usurped by a visionary reflex" (WOR 180). He "continues to live in this problematic area of divine intimations," though he is "free of guid-

---

[15] Frank Heynick of the Technical University of Eindhoven (Netherlands) has collected many samples of dream speech that disconfirm Freud's conjectures.

[16] Compare the invocation of haunting noises in CW 61, 68, 97, 100, 152, 266.

ance, and the source rather than dupe of oracles." His "psyche" is "preoccupied" by "a recession of experience to a boundary where memory fades into myth, or touches the hypostasis of a supernatural origin" (WOR 183). The "turn from words to the Word" ("the place in which both artist and critic dwell") (CW 90, 153) is perfectly evident in such commentary.

Poetic influence travels through comparably theological channels. "Milton's use of the Classics recalls" to Wordsworth "a more absolute beginning," "a 'heavenly' origin perhaps" (WOR 183). Yet Wordsworth was "defensive" toward the "Classics," which "recall to him a more absolute beginning: a point of origin essentially unmediated, beyond the memory of experience or the certainty of temporal location" (WOR 204, 183). The "voice of Samson-Oedipus" (in the poem's opening quotation) "rising so forcefully from the mind's abyss, could represent the felt though repressed power of pre-Christian literature," which "points to the possibility of unmediated vision."[17]

The same source gets a psychoanalytic twist. "Reintegrating the Classics" is compared to "reintegrating a childhood conceived as the heroic age of the psyche" (WOR 182). "Childhood, or its continuous role in the growth of the mind, is the truth Wordsworth discovers"; "heroic and classicizing themes" "return" "as a yet deeper childhood, capable of reaching through time and renewing itself in the poetic spirit" (WOR 184).

Though I have greatly abridged the detailed richness of Hartman's analysis, some powerful tendencies should be evident. He proceeds on several levels that he allows to flow easily into each other; but the controlling level remains the theological one. He can even detect the "Logos" or "divine Word" by virtue of its absence as something the poet is "evading." The "shift" from "visionary voice to visionary text" via "a vast metaphoric activity identifiable with creative power itself" (WOR 202) is restaged in Hartman's criticism. "Creation and response merge" (WOR 199)—his dictum on Worthsworth might fit his own work. The stakes are not modest: "creativity appears as metaphoricity," which "lodges" "in the formulaic and performative utterance of a sacred voice" (WOR 202). And the "imagination" brings "vertiginous power" (WOR 178), as Bloom also claimed (MAP 67f).

Hartman's bid to raise the authority of the critical text becomes remarkably complex when he "takes" "Derrida's *Glas*," one of the most advanced self-deconstructing texts in wide distribution, to be an "example of literary commentary as literature" and "criticism" "in an extreme contemporary form" (CW 204). Confronted by the deconstructive unravelling of the text, Hartman counters with an ingenious strategy for "saving the text." He reads *Glas* with the same engagement and intensity he would expend on a great literary work. He forwards his project of merging criticism with literature by relentlessly adopting and adapting

---

[17] Both Oedipus and Samson attained some divine status but were blinded for having violated the order of things—a grisly enactment of de Man's formula "blindness and insight."

Derrida's rhetorical ambience, and even has fun doing it. *Saving the Text* could be a "strong misreading" of *Glas* in a Bloomian sense, except that here the precursor had yearned to abdicate the power—had pre-cursed it in fact—that the successor seeks. For the very text that enlisted such striking mannerisms in its will to non-power, in its drive toward self-dissemination, to get unexpectedly, parodistically yet somehow religiously "saved"; surely that would be a miracle for a "restorative method."

Since Hartman had been hovering on the borders of the deconstructionist camp, which had after all been pitched at the same university, his interweaving was not too difficult.[18] In fact, it's no small matter to recognize where Hartman swerves from Derridean argument and where he merely expropriates or extends it. Even close paraphrases of Derrida may have a familiar Hartmanian ring. But I think we may uncover in Hartman's exegesis a very different intention, related, I said, to authority and power.

Derrida is given a title he wouldn't give himself: "the leading philosopher in France" (SAV 6). He has created "a new, nonnarrative art form," which "like art," "begins by confusing and estranging" (SAV 2, xix)—Hartman's idea of philosophy merging with art (cf. CW 41, 204; and Culler, OD 147, 181). "Derrida deconstructs not only others, but also himself: the activity, that is, of philosophizing in general," although "as a philosopher," he ought to "honor" the "totalization of knowledge as an encyclopedic system" (SAV 23, 4).[19]

Derrida "writes 'between styles' and constructs sentences by *bricolage*," that is, by "the canny embezzlement of previous art" (SAV xxiii; CW 231). He "strives for elegant opacity" by "multiplying citations and texts, framing them in unexpected ways" (SAV xxv). "The seriousness with which an intelligence of this order employs devices that may seem to be at best witty and at worst trivial" may help to "foreground language" and to demonstrate a "totally nonmystical professional understanding of style as the personal appropriation of the impersonal medium of language" (SAV 22, xxv). Hartman speculates that "style may be a *continued* solecism," a "habitual transgression," an "apparent deviation from natural speech" (SAV 144, 156)—a view many stylisticians have held, within a different rationale (cf. Ch. 2).

"Derrida knows that philosophy is *in* language, and that its style is radically metaphoric"; and "he doubts that philosophy can get beyond being a form of language" (SAV 46, 23). "Verbal prestidigitation can create an apparently ordinary, yet totally *constructed*, prose that would be hypocritical (since it has nothing ordinary about it) if it did not expose itself continually as resolutely overdeter-

---

[18] In an interview, Hartman said he had been reading, "in a non-professional way," many of the same sources as Derrida before he encountered the latter's work —Hegel, Heidegger, and Freud in particular.

[19] Here Hartman implies that philosophy is more devoted to totalization than he implies by making deconstruction central to philosophy. On De Man's inconsistency, see Ch. 13, Note 10.

mined words that slip the leash of meaning without escaping meaning" (SAV xxiii). "Verbal tricks" "make us aware" of "language" "as the only subject, compared to which ego and author are episodic notions discarded by an interminable demonstration" (SAV 22). "The re-entry into consciousness of contradiction or equivocation through such 'freeplay' appears to be unbounded"; "there is endless material at hand" (SAV 22f). No danger of putting yourself out of business here.

"A desacralizing and levelling effect" ensues from filling "one's prose" with "puns, equivocations, catachreses, and abusive etymologies," "ellipses and purely speculative chains of words and associations" (SAV 22). "The contemporary Anglo-American reader" might wonder if "such licensed puns may not cheapen and weaken an argument of importance" (SAV xxiii). Yet "every pun, in Derrida's style, is philosophically accountable." "Puns" help "raise" "our consciousness of words" "to the point where an embarrassment of riches returns us to a state of reserve and uncertainty, to an appreciation of the *mute* letter" (SAV 46).

The form of an argument pinned together with puns is instructive, especially for "a theory that could deduce texts" "from a 'sacrifice' or 'dissemination' of the identity-feeling encased in one's proper name" (SAV 17). Derrida's "broken phrase 'je m'éc . . .'" (from Genet) becomes the "German word" "*Ecke*," "meaning corner, or French *coin*, and may introduce a bilingual pun via the English *coin*, which is what circulates in an economy"; "but *Ecke* is also the word for angle or German *Winkel*" (SAV 85). "All these meanings" and "some others (e.g., the German word *Stück*, in French *pièce* or *morsure*, *pièce* reintroducing the idea of coin or money) are joined in the Wartburg dictionary to the matricial word *Canthus*, from which also the German word for board or edge, *Kante*, and, by autonomasia, *Kant*, the philosopher, who now emerges as Winkel-mann (Angle-man)." These acrobatics "bring in" "Winkelmann" and make a "commentary on Hegel and Genet" also be "a commentary on Kant" —the more so as "in *Glas*, words are always falling off the page," i.e. over the "*Kante* as edge." Is this morsure-code more cant than Kant, more shtick than *Stück*? Or a inkantation using names for a magical counter-spelling?

Puns allow "images" to "enter philosophical discourse casually" for "illustrating an argument" (SAV 3). The "book of textuality" goes to the German equivalent "*Buch*" and thus to "bush." "Other images" then "suggest themselves: ambush, web, trap, labyrinth." These "instances" "compensate for a felt abstractness or loss of immediacy in philosophical discourse." Moreover, though seemingly "marginal, supplementary, accidental," they "tell us that the essence is missing; the thing instanced" becomes "a disgruntled representative of the absent thing, and paradoxically gains more authority than the argument it was intended to supplement." "Literary studies" does the same when it "seizes on" "images" and "reflects on whether this allowance of dream or icon may not be closer to the real subject."

As such techniques indicate, "the rhetoric that interests Derrida derives solely" "from texts in which language discloses its groundlessness," as contrasted with the "traditional rhetoric" that, "as the art or persuasion, relies on a smooth consensual calculus of means and ends," or on a "correspondence" between "specific verbal devices" and "specific mental or affectional states" (SAV 120). He "wants to liberate language from a doctrinal effectiveness that is honorific rather than authentic." "But can Derrida's analysis justify a massive displacement of interest" "from the conceptualization that transforms signifier into signified" over toward "those unconceptualizable qualities of the signifier that keep it unsettled in form or meaning?" (SAV 119). At times, his "freeplay reaches" a "methodical craziness,"[20] during which "a series of slippery signifiers" "establishes itself on the basis of the problematics of the subject, its construction and subversion" (SAV 62).

"We tend to suppose that every act of speech, spoken or written, has a specifiable frame of reference" that "allows us" to "synthesize or disambiguate" the "words" (SAV xxi). "Should the frame be lost, so that the speaker or the addressee becomes indeterminate, then the meaning also becomes less settled. The 'ghostly' question arises of who is speaking, to whom, from where"; "a basic structure of orientation—everything we subsume under the concept of 'intention'—is put in doubt." This Halloweenish reading of Derrida (as a Jacques-o-lantern?) bears a haunting resemblance to Hartman's own obsession with "ghosts" (CW 56, 58, 59, 61, 83, 104, 138, 152), one we just beheld in his analysis of Wordsworth (cf. p. 322).

Language itself seems menaced by death. "Derrida's commentary" "is so radical" that it "forces on the reader a sense of the mortality of every code, of every covenanted meaning," and "undermines both spatial and temporal perspectives, until we are left with no single unifying theme" (SAV xvi, xix). His "art form" is also the "most acute of impersonality theories": "if predecessors" are "capable of interacting with successors through texts or reliques, then they are, to that extent, contemporaries"; "and the concept of 'person' or 'individual' becomes socialized into a complicated blend of symbolic—and sometimes negative or depersonalizing —properties" (SAV xxv). The "ultimate eschatological desire for presence or embodiment" encounters a equally strong "sense of ghostliness, of 'atrocious exclusion,' depersonalization, of an otherness that is too intimate" (SAV xxvi). The previously mentioned dissolution of the self into language ties in here.

Hartman is happy to notice how deconstruction both dismantles and constructs (cf. de Man, BI 140). "Deconstructive work" "magically conserves the texts it works through" as "fragments with the force often of aphorisms," like

---

[20] Statements like this madden Culler, who hears them repeated by Wayne Booth (OD 132). Culler "alerts" us to Hartman's "remarkable scenario": "chastened and purified, criticism can turn to *Saving the Text*" "from a frivolous, seductive, and 'self-involved' deconstruction that ignores the sacred" (OD 44). Hartman's term "Derridadaism" (SAV 33) serves to "blot out Derridean argument" (OD 28).

"extracts from works now lost" (SAV 28). "Deconstruction may lead to new construction, of which we are here seeing a first installment or prelude." "Derrida's aphoristic energy disseminates given texts as epigrammatic fragments but also reconstitutes them into a seemingly interminable, insatiable web of his own" (SAV 4)—just what Hartman is also doing. "The idea arises" that "the energy or sensuous presence of speech must be restored by some" "magical or restorative" "counterentropic, revolutionary science" (SAV 43)—created by Hartman perhaps, though not "credited" by Derrida?

The argument leads to the "ingenious" "characterization" of Derrida, the writer of "radical" "commentary," as "a conservative thinker" (SAV xvi, 24). "The 'Monuments of unageing intellect' are not pulled down" (SAV 24). "They are, in any case, so strong, or our desire is so engaged with them, that the deconstructive activity becomes part of their structure." Again, the merger of commentary with art work is proudly displayed, though naming Derrida as conservative is an incomplete and premature judgment. The "Monuments" are after all held in place by a correspondingly monumental inertia. Derrida's "subversive devices" at least "trap us into rethinking a great many texts," whereas genuine conservativism lulls away all impulses to rethink.

Also a bit surprising, though prefigured in Bloom (MAP 43), is the comparison of Derrida's text to "the Hebrew liturgy that quotes God against God to plead a covenant in danger" (SAV 19). Derrida "quotes words against words to save the contract between word and thing." His "method" of "'deconstruction'" "reveals" the "wrong turn, at once rhetorical and conceptual," "being taken, not only against the will of the author, since it is preinscribed in language, but because any author who stands in that turn cannot express" the "experience" of "impersonification, except by words that sound, willy-nilly, mystical, like a displaced or negative theology" (SAV 7).

Such arguments are emblematic of the way we are induced to see, through a *Glas* darkly, Hartman's own concentric image, his self-portrait in a complex mirror. Derrida sets about exposing and undermining the theological groundings of voice and speech, and ends up within the purview of a "negative theology," as if deconstructive discourse were intended to un-create via anti-divine fiat, still in the Maker's image, but reversed, like Satan (Bloom's master poet). "Dissemination" is said on the one hand to "substitute the image of a creative self-scattering for the 'collected' imitation of a divine pattern: the 'legein' of the logos"; but is likened on the other hand to Bloom's "quasi-divine creation" (SAV 48, 56). And Bloom is, in a way, a counter-exorcist who casts new spirits in even while he drives old ones out. Is revisionism to be the new restoring Ararat after a deconstructive deluge? Abruptly, Hartman's term "creative criticism" resounds with cosmogonic overtones.

"By calling this book *Saving the Text*," Hartman says he does "not imply a religious effort in the ordinary sense: the allusion is to the well-known concept of 'saving the appearances' *(sozein ta phainomena)*" (SAV xv). But is this reassuring when *Saving the Appearances* is the title of Owen Barfield's book that, together with works of Burke and Bloom, is extolled by Hartman for "indicating a new awareness of how learned or mystical systems of theology sustained and perpetuated canonical texts" (CW 180)? "To call a text literary" is "a way of 'saving the phenomena' of words that are out of the ordinary or bordering on the nonsensical—that have no stabilized reference" (SAV xxi). It is "to *trust* that" the text "will make sense eventually, even though its quality of reference may be complex, disturbed, unclear." "Modern hermeneutics" may be "a negative hermeneutics. On its older function of saving the text, of tying it once again to the life of the mind, is superimposed the new one of doubting, by parodistic or playful movement, master theories that claim to have overcome the past, the dead, the false" (CW 239). Yet "even a negative commentary tends to save the text by continuing it in our consciousness" (CW 268).

Negate and save, curse and bless, disperse and gather—Hartman's vision of criticism is rife with uneasy inconsistencies and polarities. They carry over into his aspirations that criticism can regenerate both itself and art by assuming a different role. He presents a gloomy picture of its traditional function in order to promote the more creative function he advocates. He is obliged to oscillate between a grim, realistic estimate of the current woes of the profession and an inspirational, unrealistic vision of "a new epoch of creativity" that "modern criticism" not merely finds in art, but appropriates for itself (cf. CW 204).

"Arnold's" "prediction" "that our errand in the wilderness would end: that a new and vital literature would arise to redeem the work of the critic" "stands as the epigraph" to Hartman's own book (CW 14f). But a provision is added: "what if this literature is not unlike criticism, and we are forerunners to ourselves?" (CW 15). For Arnold, the "new epoch" was "'the promised land toward which criticism can only beckon'" and which it cannot "'enter, and we shall die in the wilderness'" (CW 204). For Hartman, "perhaps it is better that the wilderness should be the Promised Land, than vice-versa" (CW 15).[21] "The great divide between creation and criticism" is therefore put "in dispute" (CW 204).

Whether or not it happens, the assimilatiion of criticism to literature has interesting implications. If, as several of our critics argue (e.g., Frye, Iser, Jauss, Jameson), literature is free to present alternative realities, then criticism too might attain a greater freedom than it had. One step in that direction is the now prevalent abdication of the search for the "correct" meaning or intention, in which Hartman joins. Yet we have seen his anxiety that the text should somehow be "saved." He has "sometimes thought" "that we have genuine criticism only when interpretation reinforces perception, or does not erode it" (SAV 150). "The ideal act of criticism would circle back, in that case, to the design (the partial or

---

[21] With his typical coquetterie, Hartman says "Ah, Wilderness" (CW 204) and leaves us to recall the rest of the quote that makes "wilderness" into "paradise enow."

complete object) that stimulated it; and this circling would take on a form of its own, closed enough to be recognizable as form, open enough to be extended." "The form of interpretation rather than a positive content would respect the sense of closure associated with art."

Now, he is hesitant about "theologies or theories of reading" that "evolved" "to subordinate art to a regulated principle of imitation" and to impose "closure" in the name of "harmony, identity, and reconciliation" (SAV 50, 149). "Criticism in the past was able to invent new types of closure to stem the drive toward endless interpretation" (SAV 149). "Plain-sense theories counter allegoresis; and concepts of organic form or Classicist distinctions between genres and media prevent limitless experimentation." "Today we retain an interest in the 'aesthetic' dimension of art"; "we also tolerate presentational and often meretricious devices that restore immediacy, though not always beauty, to art." Yet when "interpretive readings" like Burke's "erode forms of closure in art and concepts of beauty," it seems as if "the aesthetic charm" may "gradually disappear from the interpreted work of art, and leave us but an intellectual construct, one with a fascinating, fallacious, teasingly evasive mode of being." "In significant art there is a generalized sensitivity to premature closure, one that delays or multiplies endings and creates limits that prove to be liminal" (SAV 150).

In consequence, "our broadened historical perspective" makes us "more helpless about interpretation as it stretches toward an infinity of statements and contaminates art itself" (SAV 149). "Liberal and thoughtful" "reading" "discloses" "indeterminacy" as a "conflict of interpretations or codes" that "can be rehearsed or reordered but not always resolved" (CW 265). "We have no certainty of controlling implications that may not be apparent or articulable at any one point in time."

Living with such dilemmas has inflicted Hartman with a peculiar condition: "brooding of the eyes" and "brooding of the ears" when "art" "shapes his consciousness" (CW 1). In tribute to his erudite spirit, we might coin learned terms for the condition, such as "ophthalmoepoiasis" and "otoepoiasis," whose "epoiasis" stem ("brooding" in the chickeny sense)[22] could be punned with "poiesis" ("making" in the poetic sense). "That writing is a calculus that jealously broods on strange figures, on imaginative otherness, has been made clear by poets," but not, so far, "by the critics" (CW 27). "The English habit of practical criticism" "does not brood over questions that perhaps cannot be answered" (CW 245). "The circle" of "interpretation" "limits the word as a subject of endless brooding; closure formally seals that brooding" (SAV 150). The "'anti-self-consciousness principle'" (p. 310) recommends "the use of art to limit the brooding, self-exposing, restless emission of speculative ideas" (CW 241). For Hartman,

---

[22] The form is in the fifth-century Attic dialect Plato might have used. I am indebted to D. Gary Miller and Lena Hatzichronoglou for the coinages.

though, "we begin with" "a confusion in thought and language; we brood over that chaos to purify it, or to produce order" (CW 3). "Theory-making is part of this brooding and ordering."

Hartman's brooding has been egged on by Derrida, who "tells literary people only what they have always known and repressed" (SAV 23). What he "tells" them is presumably this: "there is no knowledge except in the form of a text—of écriture—and that is devious and dissolving, very unabsolute, as it leads to other texts and further writing" (SAV 24). "For Derrida," "the conceptual given is always, already, a text," "mediated by other texts, whether past or to come" (SAV 29). "The unity or autonomy of the text becomes uncertain": "using words that have been used already, we trace or cite or echo them in ways that change and perhaps distort" (SAV 8). "Texts stand interminably between us and absolute knowledge" (SAV 30).

Such a viewpoint is likely to be "repressed" by "literary people" who consider it their job to explain what a text "means." They develop "reading techniques" that "exploit" "the text" and make it, in Hartman's view, "too readable" (CW 188). So he is pleased when "the text" "is made" "unreadable again" "by 'decon-struction.'" If "through the work of reading the work of art never comes to rest" (CW 186), then Derrida's "interminable" "analysis" (SAV 22) should keep the text in motion or, using fashionable parlance, "in play." Hartman "raises" "the question": "what connection is there between playing and thinking, playing and interpretive criticism?" (CW 261). "What reality belongs to play, and especially wordplay?" His "conclusion" is that "the notion of play is too radical to fit any totally secular and empirical scheme" (CW 264). But then his scheme is, we have seen, hardly "secular" anyway, and even less "empirical."

Hartman's "restored theory of representation" (SAV 121) does not in any case lead to a criticism that simply reverses or abolishes the deconstructive process.[23] Deconstructed, then restored, the literary work is doubly transformed, first out of itself and then back into a far stranger version of itself than we had perceived — the same pattern of breakage and perverse reassembly found in Bloom's ap-proach.[24] Such criticism is "creative" in the way it produces the work with its specialized vision and thereby grafts itself onto the text's texture. The "Monu-ments" that "are not pulled down" by Derrida (SAV 24) get refurbished in the Yale architectural style. When "the sounding word has reverberations that tran-scend the economy of clarity and form," "contradictions arise that shake the 'temples of wisdom and science'" (SAV xxii); yet when the dust clears, the temples have resettled into even solider shapes.

---

[23] Hartman places the "charges" "against" "deconstruction" in a new light by noting how they were once "uttered" by Van Wyck Brooks "against the New Criticism" (CW 267).

[24] Hartman stresses that "combat and play are interactive," citing Huizinga (CW 262). The Yale critics make us wonder how to keep the two apart. On the violence of Yale styles, see Note 31 to Ch. 13; Note 27 to Ch. 14; and Note 21 to Ch. 19.

Questions about the authority of the critical text scatter and regroup themselves in puzzling ways. To refuse the quest for validated interpretation is, in
Hirsch's eyes, an ethical breakdown (p. 119); could a rejection of Hartman's
mode of interpretation be sacrilegious? Is the famous "suspension of disbelief" for
the art work to be revisioned in a fresh affirmation of belief in criticism? Are
Hartman's readings of Wordsworth on the same plane of credibility as Wordsworth's readings of nature? Is this union generally proposed for all criticism, so
that to quarrel with Dr. Johnson's or T.S. Eliot's portrayals of Milton is as
captious as to quarrel with Milton's portrayal of God and Satan? Are Eliot's
conservative critical works as indisputable as his progressive artistic works?

Rhetorical questions, as you can tell, force themselves upon the exegetist of
Hartman's work. He himself uses them almost compulsively and lauds the device
for an " 'open-endedness' " that "discloses a freedom of thought" (CW 273). Just
as they clustered around his refusal to select a label (p. 313), they dominate his
meditations on how "every developed theory attempts to separate criticism from
sheer nihilism" (CW 268). "The diversity" of ways for doing this "is perhaps not
totally reducible. Can we understand anything without an inner movement of
assent? Is that question best approached through a 'grammar,' " "through existential dialectics or through speech-act theory?" "Should we perhaps be content with
hints derived from fusion or identification theories," or with "debates concerning
the relation of understanding to belief"?[25]

To answer all this, Hartman says: "In terms of systematic thought, I have
nothing to add." But he seizes the moment to remind us how he had already
asserted, in *Beyond Formalism* (1970: 74), that "the problem of meaning cannot
even be faced without considering the necessity or fatality of some primary
affirmation," of which "the founding of a fictional world" and "religious belief"
are two examples. He now reaffirms this "insistence" as part of an argument that
"the destinies of fiction and criticism are joined" (CW 268). Here, "criticism"
fills the slot of "religious belief"; the displacement is no accident. So we might
have foreseen that deconstruction would provide Hartman just one more occasion to perform his characteristic, though devious, turn to theology. The effect is
all the more striking because deconstruction is avowedly anti-theological in
novel, relentless ways. You'd think critics who live in *Glas* houses shouldn't stow
Thrones and Cherubim there.

Hartman's *Wilderness* concludes with a somber estimate of "the literary humanities" (CW 284).[26] The main "preoccupation" is "the lack of interaction
between their profession and the mainstream of society." "This lack," "is, we
think, our own fault: we have not done enough" (CW 286). "We have not been

---

[25] "Vico, Dilthey, Poulet" were "fusion" theorists; "Richards, Eliot, and the New Criticism" were
concerned with "belief" (CW 268).

[26] Hartman feels "unused to this open kind of rhetoric" found in his critique, whose style lacks his
usual arabesques. On his about-face on theology in this piece, see Note 12.

able to persuade ourselves" "that what we are doing is as essential to society's well-being as law or business or the performing arts" (CW 287). "Instead of deepening the idea of interpretation we turn against it" (CW 286). "A new science, whether structuralism or semiotics, is called upon to curb the adventurism or subjectivism of the reader; and it joins with those who denounce multiplying interpretations, seeing them as an economic need of the publishing professor rather than as an authentic literary and intellectual task" (CW 286f).

The origin of the malaise is announced: "We have caused our own impotence by allowing practical criticism to reduce to its lowest social or utilitarian value" (CW 291f). "We claim, for example, that the only function of hermeneutics is to aid close reading in its quest for correct or verifiable meaning" (CW 297). "Practical criticism," which is "more of a pedagogical and propaedeutic than mature activity," "wrongly usurps the whole of literary inquiry" (CW 296). "We live with a false conception of the rift between theory and practice"; and "our antipathy to theory" has "seriously weakened" "English" "at the advanced level" (CW 297, 295; cf. WOR 187). A similar "resistance" fends off "imported ideas from non-English countries or from other fields of inquiry" (CW 297).

"What can be done?" Hartman wonders. (CW 292). "The economic realities seem overwhelming." He proposes that "to encourage contact between the professions, the concept of liberal education should be carried upward into the graduate and professional schools" (CW 294). "Law" and "medical students should be asked to take an advanced course in literary interpretation," while the literary students "would do well to have a seminar with a clinical psychiatrist, or a professor of law dealing with legal interpretation." Moreover, "joint programs" could be "established," as well as "continuing education supplements" and "small research centers encouraging faculty seminars." Funding could come from the "money" "presently being channeled into interdisciplinary or cross-disciplinary programs at the research" and "undergraduate levels" (CW 295).

Notwithstanding his pleas, Hartman's work displays little awareness of how to approach the other disciplines. Having myself lectured or participated in conferences where I was virtually the only academically credentialed "literature person" —the others being mostly psychologists, engineers, linguists, or educational researchers —I can testify that other disciplines are interested in literature or literary study because these domains are, like their own, focused on problems of communication and interpretation.[27] But hermetic styles like those of the Yale critics, wherein the problems are posed, acted out, and played with rather than resolved, is not a very productive idiom for addressing these disciplines. Hartman admits that "forms of critical commentary" "challenging the dichotomy

---

[27] For his interdisciplinary project, Hartman says: "If we give special attention to fiction and poetry, it is because they are insufficiently examined elsewhere, and not because they are privileged" (CW 296). This disclaimer is not merely inconsistent with Hartman's critical practice, but gratuitous, since I find researchers in other fields are typically willing to grant some such privilege.

between reading and writing" "may cause perplexity and resentment"; and that "the new theoretical criticism" may create the impression of "philosophical pretensions," "conceptual armory, and galloping jargon" (CW 20, 287, e.d.).

Quite apart from style, the Yale critics sometimes imply that communication can't be done. Picture lawyers, physicians, and natural scientists thronging into our halls and being told that "understanding is like a frame or context always beyond the horizon" (CW 266). Or that in "hermeneutics," "evidence fails or is disabled, and unusual or ungovernable types of interpretation come into play" (CW 283). Or being reminded of "the artificial nature or purely conventional status of formal arguments or proofs." Will they be edified when thanks to the "appearance of Bloom," "the entire enterprise of criticism becomes unreal" (CW 58)?

At the end of a thick Hartman volume, we are rewarded with the aphorism that "our life remains a feast of mortuary riddles and jokes that must be answered" (CW 301). By then, we aren't surprised. In Hartman's writings, and Bloom's too, the "dead" rise up so often that their collective momentum threatens to accidentally trigger the Last Judgment. Hegel is not the only author whose arguments "raise the specter of an interminable mode of analysis that could make a ghost, or a verbalism, of every phenomenon" (cf. CW 152). Hartman too avers that "every voice with presence" is "already speaking from the realm of the dead" and hence is "a ghostly *effet de realité* produced by words" (SAV 121).

As Hartman concedes, "to ask the literary humanities to take back their own, to reenter an abdicated sphere, is not specific enough and may be mind-bogglingly unrealistic" (CW 292). In my view, the unrealistic part is to expect the discourse favored by critics like him to be adequate for "allowing the humanities to play a full rather than a service role in the university and national affairs" (CW 295). However restorative a Hartmania or a Bloomanism may be vis-a-vis deconstruction, much more integration will be needed before their insights can be effectively communicable in transdisciplinary discourse.

Meanwhile, we would all agree, I think, that "literary studies must rejoin the humanities" (CW 295f). "It must become what it hoped it would be: the training, in the fullest sense, of personal judgment, by passing the student through the fires of interpretation and exposing him not only to literature narrowly conceived, but also to important texts in philosophy, history, religion, anthropology, and so forth."

16

Kate Millett[1]

Kate Millett is a critic who, like Fiedler, reads literature from a cultural perspective and culture from a literary one.[2] Yet instead of accepting culture as the given backdrop for art, she advocates sweeping changes in social coding, and ultimately the creation of a new culture. Literature in turn becomes the backdrop for her program, a documentation of the problems and conflicts we must overcome.

Within this distribution of interests, she advocates "a criticism which takes into account the larger cultural context in which literature is conceived and produced" (SX xiv). "Literary criticism" is "capable of seizing upon the larger insights which literature affords into the life it describes or interprets or even distorts." However, since "literary history is too limited in scope to do this," and "aesthetic" "criticism" such as " 'New Criticism' never wished to do so," Millett's "essay composed of equal parts of literary and cultural criticism, is something of an anomaly, a hybrid," and a "hypothetical," "tentative" enterprise (SX xiiif). Her chief innovations lie in her special perspective and her use of exceptionally comprehensive reading to put in question the dominant ideologies not just of literature, but of psychoanalysis, sociology, anthropology, and political science.

Her initiative focuses on "the role which concepts of power and domination play in some contemporary literary descriptions of sexual activity" (SX xiii). Like our other critics, she emphasizes the centrality of her concern. She concurs with Genet that "sexuality" is "the fundamental human connection" and "the nuclear model of all more elaborated constructs" (SX 27). She holds "coitus" to be "set so deeply within the larger context of human activity that it serves as a charged microcosm of the variety of attitudes and values to which culture subscribes" (SX

---

[1] The only abbreviation for Millett citations is: SX *Sexual Politics* (1978 [1970]).

[2] The parallels between Millett and Fiedler are numerous. Both draw a link between sex and violence, or between love and death. Both portray the sexual division as a war between social classes. Both recognize sentimentality as a pretext for skirting sexual issues and disguising the problems of marriage and family. Both perceive the image of the American male as a boy. And both detect the tactic of white males to project their own sadist fantasies onto dark-skinned races as a pretext for exploitation or warfare.

31). Engels' (1884) conjecture was "probably true" that "the origin of property began in the subjection and ownership of women" (SX 157, 155).

Such views have the pessimistic corollary that "sexuality" acts as "the very prototype of institutionalized inequality" (SX 27). "Sexual caste supersedes all other forms of inegalitarianism: racial, political, or economic." In historical evolution, "sexual dominance became the keystone to the total structure of human injustice" (SX 170). John Stuart Mill (1869) "discovered" "in sexual super- and subordination" "the psychological foundations of other species of oppression" (SX 145f). Indeed, "sex" is "the most pernicious of our systems of oppression" and "the cage in which all others are enclosed" (SX 30).

Millett defines "politics" as "a set of stratagems designed to maintain a system" (SX 31). "Sexual politics obtains consent through the 'socialization' of both sexes to basic patriarchal politics with regard to" "temperament, role, and status" (SX 35). In this configuration, "temperament" is "the psychological" "component," "role" "the sociological," and "status" "the political," although they "form a chain" of "interdependence" (SX 35f). "Temperament" "forms the human personality along stereotyped lines" of "'masculine' and 'feminine'" (SX 35). "Role" "decrees" an "elaborate code of conduct, gesture and attitude for each sex." "Status" solicits "a pervasive assent to the prejudice of male superiority."

"Patriarchy" is the major "institution perpetuated by" "political" "techniques of control" (SX 31). "To recognize its basis in patriarchy," wherein "the relationship between sexes is essentially political," is "the most pertinent and fundamental consideration one can bestow upon our culture"; "no other system has ever exercised such complete control over its subjects" (SX 90, 378, 44). Its "chief institution is the family," which "mediates between the individual and the social structure" and "effects control and conformity where political and other authorities are insufficient" (SX 45) (cf. Goode 1964). "The patriarchal family" has a "feudal character," "granting the father nearly total ownership over wife or wives and children" (SX 46). The "family" is expected to "socialize the young" into "patriarchal ideology's prescribed attitudes" (SX 48). "The patriarchal mind" is distinguished by the way it "equates" "human affection and reproduction with slavish subordination, excessive or accidental progeny, and servile affection," and "cannot separate the liberation of women from racial extinction and the death of love" (SX 249).

Millett's assessment of the status quo is undeniably grim. "Delusions about sex foster delusions of power, and both depend on the reification of woman" (SX 28). In "our society," where "sexism may be more endemic than racism," "the sexual politic" can engender a "hopeless mess," a "sick delirium of power and violence" (SX 54, 28, 30). The "belief that sexuality is incompatible with social effort and dedication" and "antithetical to collective" or "cultural achievement" is not found only in contemporary Western society; it is an "ancient error" persisting in Freud and even in "the revolutionary mentality" of the Soviet Union, where "new liberties" were "gradually eroded" via a "humanistic justification of traditional strictures" (SX 240f, 243). The greatest loser is always the "woman," who is "denied sexual freedom and the biological control over her body through the cult of virginity, the double standard," and "the prescription against abortion" or "contraception" (SX 76). In "America," "young women neglect contraception, unconsciously willing pregnancy" as "punishment" (SX 244).

Sexual politics has fragmented modern culture. "Because of our social circumstances, male and female are really two cultures, and their life experiences are utterly different" (SX 42). "Under the aegis" of "the categories 'masculine' and 'feminine,'" "each personality becomes little more, and often less, than half of its human potential" (SX 44). "In patriarchy, the function of norm is unthinkingly delegated to the male," such that "the female is 'other' or 'alien'" and inspires "fear" (SX 43, 65). "The basic division of temperamental traits" is "along the lines of 'aggression is male' and 'passivity is female,'" while "all other traits" are "aligned to correspond" (SX 43). Typically, "masculine" gets associated with "strength," "intelligence," "force, and efficacy," along with "cruelty, indifference, egotism, and property"; "feminine" gets associated with "weakness," "ignorance, docility, 'virtue,' and ineffectuality," along with "ravished" and "subjugated" (SX 476, 35, 26). "The limited role" "arrests" "the female at the level of biological experience" and "animal activity," where "any display of serious intelligence" is "out of place" (SX 35, 81; cf. SX 283). Through a characteristic "logical inconsistency," "feminine passivity is reasoned from anatomy, but masculine activity is reasoned from history and technology" (SX 304).

Millett clarifies the confusion by distinguishing "sex" from "gender": "sex is biological, gender psychological, and therefore cultural" (SX 41) (cf. Stoller, 1968). "In terms of masculine and feminine, and in contradistinction to male and female," "there is no differentiation between the sexes at birth"; "psychosexual personality is therefore postnatal and learned," and "gender" may appear, according to Money (1965: 13), "'with the establishment of a native language'" (SX 41f) (a contingency neither Holland nor Bleich brings into focus). "Removed from their contexts of social behavior," "the words 'masculine' and 'feminine'" thus "mean nothing at all and might well be replaced with what is biologically or naturally verifiable—male and female" (SX 271).[3] Millett proposes a "reassessment" of which traits are "desirable": "violence" and "passivity" might be cast off as "useless in either sex," while "efficiency, intellectuality," "tenderness, and consideration" might be "recommended" for "both sexes" (SX 86).

The social position of women is in an equally discouraging state. On the one hand, "the female has fewer permanent class associations than does the male"; "economic dependency renders her affiliations with any class" "tangential,

---

[3] Most of the time, Millett is careful to follow this advice. However, "male" and "female" do turn up where "masculine" and "feminine" should go (SX 28f, 51, 59, 122, 264, 402). The reverse displacement is much rarer (SX 262, 402).

vicarious, and temporary" (SX 52). Treated as "unpaid domestics" without "many of the interests and benefits any class may offer its male members," "women" "have less of an investment in the class system" (SX 52f).

On the other hand, some variations among classes deserve notice. "In the lower social strata, the male is more likely to claim authority on the strength of his sex rank alone," the extreme form being "'utmost habitual excesses of bodily violence toward the unhappy wife'" noted by Mill (SX 50, 141; cf. SX 172). Also, "the unpropertied classes make practical use of women, while the propertied convert her into a decorative or aesthetic object with only limited uses," as pointed out by Engels (SX 171).[4] Thorstein Veblen (1899) argues that "the bourgeois class displays its wealth" by granting "idleness and expensive vanities" to "its women" (SX 102). Women were distracted away from "solidarity" and from the "struggle for personal fulfillment or liberation" by a "dream" of "gilded voluptuousness" attainable through "sexual patronization of the male." Genuine "economic independence," in contrast, is "perceived to be a direct threat to male authority" (SX 122).

Following Wirth (1945), Millett defines "minorities" in terms of "status," not "numerical size"; they are "'singled out'" for "'differential and unequal treatment'" (SX 77). She then draws analogies between the status of women and that of other minorities, particularly racial ones.[5] In analyzing a study of sexual roles, she remarks: "Were one to substitute white and black for male and female, one would have a perfect picture" of "a racist society" (SX 326). "Being born female in a masculine-dominated culture" matches "the traumatizing circumstance of being born black in a white racist society" (SX 255). Though women may now "compete" as "labor" with "racial minorities," "feminists once combatted slavery" as "active and dedicated abolitionists," and later "were inspired" by "black protest" during the "Civil Rights" movement (SX 56, 112, 506). This trend was "logical" not merely in view of their "service ethic," but also in view of the "frequent parallels" (detected by Mill and Engels) between the "bondage" of women and "slavery or serfdom" (SX 112, 128, 175). For Engels, "the disguised domestic slavery of women" makes "the man" "the bourgeois," and "the woman" "the proletariat" (SX 177).

The consequences Millett draws from this state of affairs are indeed radical. The programs of action advocated by our other critics mainly concern reshaping the uses of literature. Millett, however, envisions for cultural criticism a vastly

---

[4] Because "inherited property is germane to the foundations of patriarchal monogamy," Millett suggests that "patriarchy is less strongly entrenched economically among the dispossessed" (SX 171f), even though she singles out the "lower classes" as assertively male and more violent (SX 50, 141f, 172). The picture is further complicated if "middle-class women" who take on "employment are falling a step below the class of their birth" (SX 205).

[5] In older legal systems, women were "placed in the same class" with "lunatics or idiots"; or they were minors like "children" (SX 94, 123). Allowing some women to attain the "characteristic virtues of masculinity" is likened to "conceding an exceptional negro or peasant or native" (SX 296).

larger goal: a "sexual revolution" leading to "a system of political, economic, and social equality between the sexes" and "bringing us all a great deal closer to humanity" (SX 103, 507). It is "mandatory that we develop a more relevant psychology and philosophy of power relationships" among "races, castes, classes, and sexes" (SX 32). We must relieve the "continuous" "oppression" of "groups" with "no representation" in "recognized political structures" (SX 32). "Revolutionary theorists" can promote "emancipation" only if they "move beyond agitation to provide an analysis of the past and a new model for the future" (SX 152). "Chernyshevsky, Mill, Engels, Bebel, and Veblen" have achieved this—especially Engels, who cast aside "fatalistic or 'biological' versions of the origin of human institutions" and advanced "equitable and feasible recommendations for the general conduct of sexuality in a revolutionary society" (SX 152, 155, 176).

Major objectives of the "revolution" include: "an end of traditional sexual inhibitions and taboos";[6] "a permissive single standard of sexual freedom" "uncorrupted by the crass and exploitative economic bases of traditional sexual alliances"; "an end" to "patriarchy" and "the ideology of male supremacy"; "an integration of the separated sexual subcultures," plus "an assimilation" of "previously segregated human experience"; and "an end of the present chattel status and denial of rights to minors" (SX 86). Further objectives are to relieve "the problem of overpopulation" and to entrust "the care and education of children" to "the best trained practitioners" (SX 87, 178; cf. SX 223).

Millett stresses that "the arena of sexual revolution is within human consciousness even more" than in "human institutions" (SX 88). The "social change involved" is "a matter of altered consciousness, the exposure and elimination of social and psychological realities underlining political and cultural structures" (SX 506). Though "to be free" should be "the ambition of every conscious young woman in the world," the "consciousness" of the current "majority" must be "raised" before "liberating radical solutions" can be "contemplated" (SX 204, 53). "The emergence of a positive collective identity" must "precede revolutionary awareness" (SX 496).[7]

As "a dependency class who live on surplus," women have so far a "marginal life" that "frequently renders them conservative" (SX 53). Besides, "oppression creates a psychology in the oppressed," who are "corrupted" by "how deeply they envy and admire their masters," and are "polluted by their ideals and values"; "even their attitude toward themselves is dictated by those who own them" (SX 490). Thanks to "the totality of their conditioning," "many women do not recognize themselves as discriminated" (SX 78). Although Millett sees a "way out": "to rebel and be broken, stigmatized, and cured," she owns that "to be a rebel is not

---

[6] Particularly singled out are "taboos" that "threaten patriarchal, monogamous marriage: homosexuality, illegitimacy, adolescent, pre- and extra-marital sexuality" (SX 86).

[7] The same argument is made more elaborately by Jameson, for whom the "achieved Utopian or classless society" brings "the ultimate concrete collective life" (PU 291).

to be a revolutionary"; it may be just "a way of spinning one's wheels deeper in the sand" or of inviting an "even greater reaction" (SX 329, 488, 88).

In Millett's view, "the sexual revolution" failed in the past because it "left the socialization processes of temperament and role differentiation intact" and "insufficiently affected" "patriarchal marriage and the family" (SX 250). "Systems of oppression will continue to function simply by virtue of their logical and emotional mandate in the primary human situation" (SX 29). "Legislative reform" "represents" "superficial change" rather than "sweeping radical changes in society" (SX 119).[8] Moreover, a "counterrevolution" or "reaction" set in, and "the great impetus of the sexual revolution was brought to a halt" (SX 221). Opponents of "feminism" would vilify it as a plot to "end" "home, family, and motherhood" and as an "ally of nihilism, anarchy, anti-Semitism, Communism, racism" (SX 294, 292)—even though anti-feminist outlooks often combine with such ideologies, especially the anti-Semitism and racism fostered by fascism (cf. SX 53f, 213, 235, 237, 389ff, 455f).

Another counterrevolutionary force was the thesis in psychoanalysis and social science that patriarchal society and the oppression of women are natural and fundamental states of human life.[9] Research on social and sexual issues is determined by "the extent to which" "scientific interest" is "so deeply affected by the culture" (SX 313). "Science" often "assumes" "psycho-social distinctions to rest upon biological differences between the sexes, so that culture" merely "cooperates with nature" (SX 36; cf. SX 38, 264, 316). The "formula" "anatomy is destiny" then makes "sexual status, role, and temperament" into "fixed entities" (SX 268, 286, 288, 300). Millett observes that "social scientists" are "often remarkably gullible" toward "physiological evidence" (SX 305) (though hardly "remarkable" in view of her exposé of the vested interests of patriarchal institutions). Insisting that "'the biological factor is really the rock bottom'" (SX 266, 309)[10] allows "biological difference" to "explain and rationalize" the "inferior status" of "an oppressed group" (SX 320).

Millett retorts: "Today," "the best medical research" shows "sexual stereotypes have no bases in biology" (SX 36). "The sexes are inherently alike, save reproductive systems, secondary sexual characteristics, orgasmic capacity, and genetic and morphological structure" (SX 131). In fact, these real differences lend

---

[8] Millett attaches small importance to suffrage for women: it did not "challenge patriarchy at a sufficiently deep and radical level," and women were still denied "candidacy or election to office" (SX 118, 116). However, "franchise" "mobilized the greatest consciousness and effort" in "the sexual revolution" (SX 117).

[9] Literary authors also adapted some version of science amenable to their purposes. Hardy "fancied he was following scientific law in awarding his characters instincts" and "hereditary traits" (SX 185). Lawrence made both explicit and implicit use of Freud (SX 338, 345ff, 349, 353, 407).

[10] The phrase is Freud's, duly echoed by Erik Erikson, who however "pleaded that the preordained historical subordination of women be abridged by a gallant concession to maternal interest" (SX 266, 309, 300).

women a superior rather than inferior status: according to "all the best scientific evidence," "the female possesses" "a far greater capacity for sexuality than the male," as measured by the "frequency of coitus" and "orgasm" (SX 164) (cf. Masters & Johnson,1961). Moreover, the "clitoris" of the female is "the only human organ specific to sexuality and pleasure" (SX 166) (the real reason, I suspect, why Freud prescribed "the elimination of clitoral sexuality," SX 262— the converse of "penis envy"). And "recent embryological research leads to the conclusion that the female is the race type": "all embryos begin as girls" (SX 281).

The "patriarchal myth" about the "greater sexual capacity in the male" was merely a device to "sanction the double standard" whereby "society" "punishes the promiscuity in women it does not think to punish in men" (SX 167, 172).[11] Arguments based on "superior physical strength" are scarcely compelling, if "civilization" "substitutes other methods" of power, such as "technic, weaponry, knowledge"; and "physical exertion" is "generally a class factor," not a biological one (SX 37; cf. SX 153).[12] Similarly, such factors as the "'debilitating' effects of pregnancy in the female" and the "discomfort" of "menstruation" are more "psychosomatic and cultural" than "physiological" and "biological" (SX 153, 65). A "masculine-dominated culture" "invests biological phenomena with symbolic force" (SX 255).

In such ways, sociology uses biology to rationalize current politics. Thus, "conservative social science" "takes patriarchy" to be "the state of nature,"[13] "the first form of human grouping, the origin of all society, and therefore too fundamental to merit discussion" (SX 78, 312). "The leading school of thought," "'functionalism,'" "taking the situation at hand, measuring, stating, and generalizing from it," "neglects" the "causality" of "learned behavior" in "patriarchal society" (SX 311). "Sociology" "pretends to take no stand," "thereby avoiding the necessity to comment on the invidious character of the relationship between the sex groups" (SX 328).

"Yet by slow degrees of converting statistic to fact, function to prescription, bias to biology," research "comes to ratify and rationalize." "Its pose of objec-

---

[11] This definition fits most uses of the term "double standard" in Millett's book (SX 79, 167, 203, 267, 294, 306). A related yet distinct sense—needed to fabricate a group of promiscuous women—splits the woman in the "socio-sexual division" of "wife and whore" (SX 125; cf. SX 52, 99, 211, 236, 360). Some passages don't clarify which is meant (SX 9, 86, 222, 452). On one occasion, the reference is the license of homosexuality for men, but not for women (SX 374).

[12] This argument is dubious in view of Millett's thematic references to violence in both social (J.S. Mill) and psychological (Marie Bonaparte) sources (SX 141, 290). She owns that "control in patriarchal society" would be "inoperable unless it had the rule of force to rely upon"; and that "patriarchal force relies on a form of violence, particularly sexual in character, and realized most completely in the act of rape" (SX 60f). She also thinks "violence" "likely to be the leading counter-revolutionary symptom" (SX 502, cf. SX 29).

[13] "Nature" is deemed "an emotional term" enlisted to "justify class absolutism and feudalism," so that its use is "preeminently a political gesture" (SX 130, 132).

tivity" "gains a special efficacy in reinforcing stereotypes." "Description inevitably becomes prescriptive," and "conformity is strongly urged" (SX 311f). "Any woman who fails to conform" is issued a diagnosis of "maladjustment" expressed in a "mediating terminology," a "polite intervening semantics," and a "turgid cipher of language" intended to seem "disinterested and beyond opinion" (SX 322ff). Millett's analysis attains a deconstructive insight: a "study" whose results embody "the unconscious sexual-political impressions of the social scientists" "is a study of itself" (SX 327), reproducing what it claims to put in question.

Freud's account of the psyche fit the pattern in "the emerging social sciences of psychology, sociology, and anthropology" (SX 251). He too sought a "connection with the more readily validated sciences of biology, mathematics, and medicine." His "fallacious interpretations of feminine character" were in fact "based upon clinical observations of great validity" (SX 252f). Yet he took "his patients' symptoms" "as evidence" not "of a justified dissatisfaction" with a "limiting" "society," but of "an independent and universal feminine tendency" (SX 253). He "appears to have made a major and rather foolish confusion between biology and culture, anatomy and status" (SX 265; cf. SX 268).

He "based his theory of the psychology of women" on "the idea of penis envy" (SX 254). "The child's discovery of the anatomical differentiation between the sexes" was depicted as a "cataclysm," a "catastrophe" that "haunts a woman all through life" (SX 254f, 259). In consequence, "Freud believed," "women" "accept the idea that to be born female is to be born 'castrated'" (SX 254; cf. SX 66; cf. Holland, DY 48). He had "no objective proof," and followed the "subjectivity" of his own "masculine" or "male supremacist bias" (SX 257f). His "etiology of childhood experience" enabled him to "bypass the more likely social hypothesis" on the origins of inequality (SX 255). "As it would appear absurd to charge adult women" with "literal jealousy of the organ," he derived "personality" from "childhood biography" (SX 259, 288). As a further step, "the female is bested even at reproduction" when "childbirth" is depicted as "a hunt for a male organ," a "surrogate penis" (SX 262).

With such theses, "Freud's work" served to "rationalize the invidious relationship between the sexes, to ratify traditional roles, and to validate temperamental differences" (SX 252). His "redaction of durable patriarchal assumptions" was carried to greater lengths by his "popularizers" (SX 477, 252). "Although the most unfortunate effects of vulgar Freudianism far exceeded the intentions of Freud himself, its antifeminism was not without foundation in Freud's own work" (SX 252). Despite his reputation as "a prototype of the liberal urge toward sexual freedom," he became nothing less than "the strongest individual counterrevolutionary force in the ideology of sexual politics" (SX 251f). His "doctrine of penis envy" "came at the peak of the sexual revolution" as a "withering," "destructive weapon against feminist insurgence," "enabling masculine sentiment to take the offensive again" (SX 267).

Thanks to Freudian theory, it could henceforth "be said scientifically" that "the woman" is "constitutionally unfitted for civilized life"; "she enjoys her oppression and deserves it" (SX 285, 287). Her "'intellectual inferiority'" was attributed to "'the inhibition of thought necessitated by sexual suppression'" (SX 280). Her "'physical vanity'" and "'charms'" were a "late compensation" for "'original sexual inferiority'" (SX 279). Her "'demand for justice was a modification of envy'" (SX 264). Her "'vaginal sensitivity'" was an "'acceptation'" of "'immense masochistic beating fantasies'" and a "'love'" of "'violence'" (SX 290) (cf. Bonaparte 1953). "Psychoanalysis" "forced woman to 'adjust' to her position" and "accept her fate" by seeking "fulfillment in passivity and masochism" (SX 277, 287). "Summarizing these effects of long subordination," "Freud" and "his followers" "concluded they were inevitable" and "prescribed them as health, realism, and maturity" (SX 279).

Millett's analysis again assumes a deconstructive tendency when she uncovers psychoanalytic presuppositions that undermine each other (cf. p. 252). Such conflicts are to be expected in a framework which rationalizes contradictory social practices, as when "patriarchy" "converts woman to a sexual object," but does not "encourage" her "to enjoy" "sexuality" (SX 168). Freud called upon women to "sublimate" their sexuality and renounce such activities as "clitoral" stimulation and "masturbation," yet insisted that the woman "has less sexual drive than the male," and thus should have very "little sexual instinct to sublimate" (SX 283, 262, 285). Or, Freud's "prescription" of strong role differentiation "ignores" his own notion of "bisexuality" as the common state of young children, the more so if women who fail to conform are denounced for "backsliding" into bisexuality (SX 277; cf. SX 270, 272, 290). Related ambivalences figure in literary treatments of male-female relations, as will be seen below.

"Myths" is Millett's designation for the commonplaces of sexual politics underlying Western civilization, a "system" whose "coercive agents" are both "actual" and "mythical" (SX 28). Thus, the concept of "myth," highly valued by critics like Wellek and Warren, Frye, and Fiedler, gets a decidedly negative rating here. Millett views "the myths of a political system" as "the psychic basis of racial-sexual beliefs" (SX 404). According to her historical scheme, the "taboo and mana" that "primitive society" utilizes to "practice its misogyny" "evolve into explanatory myth," which later takes on "ethical" and "literary" forms (SX 71). In "the two leading myths of Western culture," namely "the classical tale of Pandora's box and the Biblical story of the Fall," "earlier mana concepts of feminine evil have passed through a final literary phase to become highly influential ethical justifications for things as they are." In this sense, "myth" is simply "a felicitous advance" in "propaganda," "basing its arguments on ethics or theories of origins." "Sexual fallacy" engendered the "old myths" of "sin and virtue," "guilt and innocence," "cowardice" and "heroism" (SX 30). Correspondingly, the invention of new "myth" is a symptom of the "counterrevolution" (SX 29,

219, 251), such as Lawrence's "fraudulent myth" of "the penis as deity" (SX 403; cf. SX 394f, 409). Millett bleakly concludes that "elements of myth" "have enslaved consciousness in a coil of self-imposed absurdity" (SX 30).

More precisely, the oppression of women is mythologized from two diverse standpoints. The one sparked by "the myth of religion" with its "fallacy of sin" holds that "the female is sexuality itself and therefore an evil" (SX 27f; cf. SX 72, 187). This "connection of women, sex, and sin constitutes the fundamental pattern of western patriarchal thought" (SX 75). Such "archetypes" "condemn the female through her sexuality and explain her position as her well-deserved punishment for the primal sin" (SX 72). Even when our "rationalist era" has "given up literal belief" in "the myth of the Fall, it maintains its emotional assent intact" (SX 73). "This mythic version of the female as the cause of human suffering" is "still the foundation of sexual attitudes." Women themselves participate when their "personal insecurities" reflect "the gnawing suspicion" that the "myth" "might be true" (SX 79).

The other standpoint mythologizes in the opposite direction, claiming to exalt the woman as a superior being and as the conscience of the human race. The "general tendency to attribute impossible virtues to women" helps to "obscure the patriarchal character of Western culture" and "confines" women within a "conscribing sphere of behavior" (SX 51). "Chivalry" is both a "palliative to the injustice of woman's social position" and "a technique for disguising it" (SX 50). "Courtly and romantic" "love are 'grants'" "the male concedes out of his total powers" in order to practice "emotional manipulation" and to "obscure" the "burden of economic dependency" (SX 51). The Victorian view, typified by Ruskin (1865), that "the salvation of the world" "should come from women" was "a concoction of nostalgic mirage, regressive, infantile, or narcissistic sexuality, religious ambition, and simplistic social panacea" (SX 151). A "perfect ethic" was created "for a harsh business society": the "female" was to "serve as the male's conscience and live the life of goodness he found tedious"; "the male" can "exploit other human beings" while his wife "replenishes his vanishing humanity" (SX 132, 51; cf. SX 147).

The "doctrine of the separate spheres," also enunciated by Ruskin, included "war, money, politics, and learning" under "male 'duties,'" leaving "philanthropy" as a "female 'duty'" (SX 127, 146). Whatever "education" the woman received "should prepare her" to "exercise some vague and remote good influence" and "dispense a bit of charity" that is in reality "humiliating to the poor" in "presupposing a benevolent master and grateful serf mentality" —a brand of "neo-feudalism" (SX 135, 148). All such "chivalrous blandishment" merely assisted "expediency, even duplicity": as Mill observed, "'we are perpetually told that women are better than men by those who are totally opposed to treating them as if they were as good'" (SX 149).

Though she assumes the role of a literary critic (and formerly taught as an English professor), Millett harbors complex misgivings about both literature and criticism. She detaches herself from conventional critics, with their "tricks of the trade" and their "dutiful round of adulation" (SX xiv). She suspects "literature" and "scholarship" of contributing to the "intellectual origins" of "the counter-revolutionary era" via "the wholesale defection of literary and critical minds from rationality into the caverns of myth," abetted for instance by "T.S. Eliot's piety" and "the neo-orthodoxy" in "New Criticism" (SX 251). She likes to point out how "critics are often misled"; how they "fudge the meaning" by "mumbling vaguely that it is all allegorical, symbolic"; how they "mask disagreement" by tendering "sympathetic readings" or evasive suggestions that the artist is "a 'poor technician'" (SX 342, 402, xiv).

To be sure, she does employ some standard critical methods. She pays skilled attention to language and usage, detecting "the pretense that 'man' and 'humanity' are terms" for "both sexes," or comparing the custom of "referring to" "women workers as 'girls'" with that of "addressing" "black men as 'boy' right through senility" (SX 76, 352). She delivers close readings of texts, showing for example how "Lawrence's images of genital topography" signify "the supernatural origin of the penis," "the miracle of an erection," and "the negation of the womb"; or how Henry Miller's thematics "link" "sex" "with money" and present "sex as a war of attrition waged upon economic grounds" (SX 409, 417, 419). Or, she demonstrates how the "'deep unfathomable free submission'" Lawrence preaches for women is unmasked by his own metaphors and imagery as a "plunge" into "sleep, even death" (SX 392, 341, 372; cf. SX 400, 406, 416).

Yet these familiar methods fulfill a special function in Millett's criticism. They provide subsidiary tactics for her leading objective of uncovering the sexual politics of authors and their works. Sometimes, the message can be readily extracted from the more overt thematics of the work. Like Jameson,[14] she is prone to discover "object lessons," such as "how monstrous the new woman can be"; or how "the lot of the independent woman" is "repellent"; and so on (SX 368, 366; cf. SX 370, 400, 435). But such straightforward lessons are likely to be rare if, as Millett emphasizes, attitudes about sexuality are typically kept outside conscious awareness (cf. SX 88, 182, 208, 251). Indeed, Millett appears to mistrust literary techniques and products precisely to the extent that they may be made into vehicles for covert sexual politics.

Her sketch of literary history is conceived accordingly. She senses in very early literature the traces of a repressive period in which patriarchy was superseding a still earlier, prehistoric matriarchy (cf. SX 71, 154f, 158). She takes "the Furies" in "Aeschylus" to be "the deposed powers of a matriarchate, reduced already to

---

[14] This habit is strongest in Jameson's *Political Unconscious* (PU 164, 168f, 173f, 198, 217, 259). Millett's connection to Marx is mainly through the latter's impact on Engels' ideas about the family (SX 171, 175). She complains that "Marxism" "has often neglected" "to notice how thoroughly the oppressed are corrupted by their situation" (SX 490). Jameson's book agrees with "radical feminism" that "to annul the patriarchal is the most *radical* political act—insofar as it includes" "more partial demands, such as the liberation from the commodity form" (PU 100).

the level of harridans," but, as the play's ending suggests, originally "fertility goddesses" (SX 159, 161). Their outcry against Orestes "has something of the sound of matriarchy's last stand in the ancient world" (SX 159). They confront "patriarchal justice" when "Apollo" rules that "'the mother is not the parent,'" but merely the "'nurse'"; to prove that "'father without mother may beget,'" "Athena, born full-grown from the head of her father," comes to witness and advocate "'male supremacy in all things'" (SX 160f).

Suggesting that "this triumph went nearly uncontested" until Ibsen's *Doll's House* (SX 162), Millett leaps all the way to the time of the industrial revolution. She notes in passing that "Ancient, Medieval, and Renaissance literature in the West each had a large element of misogyny" (SX 63; cf. Rogers, 1966). The middle ages are briefly featured for their literature of "courtly love," which however "had no effect upon the legal or economic standing of women, and very little on their social status" (SX 50f) (cf. Valency, 1958);[15] besides, "the new idealization of woman" subsisted alongside "the old diatribes" (SX 63). The "Renaissance" is commended for its interest in "liberal education," including "for women," and for its possible "glint" of the "sexual revolution" (SX 90, 103, 91), but specific works of literature are not analyzed in any detail. The "Enlightenment" is treated in much the same way (cf. SX 90, 104).

The Victorian period is central to Millett's literary analysis. Though "only at the extreme of each" "were unmixed attitudes to be found," she distinguishes "three different responses to the sexual revolution" (SX 182, 179). First, "the realistic or revolutionary" school (e.g., Engels, Mill, Ibsen, Shaw, Dickens, and Meredith) included "radicals," "reformers," and "moderates," who expressed "a critical attitude toward the sexual politics of patriarchy" (SX 179). It produced mainly "theory," "polemic," "theater," and "novels." Second, the "sentimental or chivalrous school" (e.g., Ruskin) made an "appeal to propriety" and a "protestation of its good intentions," hoping to "forestall change of any kind by proclaiming the status quo both good and natural." It "sentimentalized the monogamous family, which it refused to see as an economic unit." It produced mainly "escapist" "poetry" and more realistic "novels" (SX 180).

Third, the "fantasy" school expressed the "unconscious emotions of male response to what it perceives as feminine evil, namely sexuality" —being "actually" "the sexuality the male has perceived in himself, and despising it, casts upon the woman" (SX 180f). The dominant genre is "poetry." This school made a "considerable contribution" "to the sexual revolution": "through its tactics of refuge in the unconscious[16] and in fantasy, it released more sexual energy and

---

15 The problem with the literature of courtly love affirming the status quo also troubles Jauss and Iser, who were originally medievalists. They propose opposite views: this art "fortified the existing system against the challenge of social change" (AR 77f); or it "contributed" to the "emancipation" of "communication between the sexes" (AL 18). Compare Note 22 to Ch. 8 and Note 15 to Ch. 17.

16 On the same page, she insists that the "old myth of feminine evil" had now become "deeply self-conscious." Several critics, such as Wellek/Warren, Frye, Fiedler, Iser, Holland, and de Man, picture authorship as an interaction between conscious and unconscious.

expressed more tenuous and deeply buried sexual attitudes," including "sexual 'deviance,'" "than did its rivals" (SX 182). "It was able to explore sexual politics at a more inchoate primary level." In return, though, "the fantasists" were "often so incoherent as to be liable to subversion."

As we might infer from this brief history, Millett is concerned lest the creative powers of literature be harnessed to cloak objectionable ideologies. It can "endorse what it appears" "to parody," or "vindicate" "virility" "while seeming to caricature" it, conveying for example a "'secret admiration'" for "'violent people'" (SX 450f, 443; cf. SX 456, 461).[17] It can "pander to pornographic dream": "the liberal, the humanistic, and the well-meaning are satisfied with the fable at its surface level, while the aggressive, the malign, and the sadistic are provided with greater sustenance below the surface" (SX 403). Literary style is also suspect. In Tennyson, she notes the strategic use of "the hyperbole of chivalrous stereotype," and the intent to "render inherent biological differences into pretty phrases" (SX 109f). Or, Ruskin's "history of women is based on the gossamer of literary idealization" (SX 142). Or, Lawrence "veils the sanctities of sex in vague phrases about cosmic flight" (SX 334).

A similar concern is reflected in Millett's criteria for rating genres. Her ideal would seem to be the nonliterary genre of the ideological essay. Next to that, the novel is of greatest interest; it may be more "tepid" and "less objective" than the "theoretical and rational" work of "Mill and Engels," but it can (as in Brontë's case) ingest "the informative addition of the conflicts" "the sexual revolution" "involved" and "the emotions" it "awakened" (SX 125, 208). Millett is less at home with "poetry," which "often" works on an "unconscious level" and uses "the accommodating vehicle of myth," notably "the myth of feminine evil," whereas "prose fiction" "demands" a "more honest explanation" in "social and economic" terms (SX 208, 181). Moreover, "poetry" is claimed to have "nearly always been identified with the ruling class, its views, values, and interests,"[18] as in the "escapist" maneuver of "resolutely shunning the contemporary world" (SX 180). Such evaluations resemble Millett's commendation that Dante Gabriel Rossetti's "finest poem" is one written "in the best analytical and rational vein of the novelists"; or her complaint that it suited Ruskin's "purpose" "to ennoble a system of subordination through hopeful rhetoric" when he "trusted to poetry" as an "accurate picture of the condition of women," or when he "eked out" an "educational program" from certain "poems of William Wordsworth" (SX 212, 138, 142f, 136f).

This perspective would treat literary genres according to their adaptability for

---

[17] The phrase is Mailer's own from a retrospect on his work. Elsewhere, Millett diagnoses a split within Mailer's "oeuvre": "ideas one is convinced are being satirized" in his "fiction" "are sure to appear with straightforward personal endorsement" in his "other prose writings" (SX 460).

[18] The same suspicion seems to involve prose when she implies that the "working-class ideal of brute virility" became "middle class" when it became "literary" (SX 52). To be consistent, she might have to make this provision for the ideals of Genet, her model revolutionary arisen from the lowest possible class.

ideological programs. However much literature as a whole resists ideological control, the specific author is prone to assimilate operative ideologies during the concrete task of representing human relations (cf. Ch. 18). Some position is necessarily implied between regressive and progressive politics, between reaction and revolution; and Millett's useful exposé brings this frequently neglected factor of choice into sharp perspective. Her special concern is with cases where authors, whether consciously or not, deploy literature as a defense against troubling aspects of sexuality.

This conception of "defense" gives a more comprehensive picture than Bloom's vision of poetry "defending" against primeval anxieties or overpowering precursors through an overt politics of masculine aggressiveness (which would probably remind Millett of the typical "fascist tone": "jealous of prerogative" and "spoiling for a war," SX 395f); or Holland's vision of literature as both carrier of and defense against infantile bodily fantasies. Neither vision materially clarifies the social and political engagement of literature, since they situate the transaction more in the individual personality than in the process of patriarchal socialization and manipulation. Both critics seem to think the defensive function normal, if not inevitable—healthy for Holland and morbid for Bloom, but not an issue of ideological choice. Their theories could thus be special cases of Millett's, cases where for motives of defense, a certain class of responses is judged natural or universal. The two critics can thereby remain more complacent than Millett with the institution of literature as it stands. She might, in fact, include their ideologies within the whole spectrum she wants to see transcended by a revolutionary break with prevailing critical tactics.

Due to this ambition, Millett frequently contradicts traditional critical estimations of authors. She shows supposed sexual liberators to be still dependent on the "puritan" values they were thought to write against (SX 6, 355, 376, 397, 408, 414, 429, 433, 452f), notably the drive to "separate sexuality from sex" (SX 408, 420). She contravenes the "critics" imagining that Lawrence "recommends both sexes cease to be hard struggling little wills and egoists"; he really felt that "only women must desist to be selves" (SX 342). She demonstrates that Miller was by no means "the liberated man" "representing 'sexual freedom,'" but "actually" "a compendium of American sexual neuroses," obsessed with a "sense of defilement in sexuality"; "under the brash American novelty" lie "guilt, fear, a reverence for 'purity,'" and "a deep moral outrage whenever the 'lascivious bitch' in women is exposed" (SX 412f, 433f). "Mailer once put himself forward as a hero of the sexual revolution," but later embraced the "attitudes" of a "parish priest" —"lyric about 'chastity,' ferocious about abortion," "opposed to birth control," and preaching that "guilt" is "'the existential edge of sex,' without which the act is 'meaningless'" (SX 451ff).

Conversely, she upholds the reputations of other authors. She repudiates the criticism that would "convert" the Brontë sisters "into case histories" and "label" their "bitterness and anger" "neurotic" before "attacking every truth the novels contain" (SX 208).[19] Her vision of "anxious pedants who fear that Charlotte might 'castrate' them or Emily 'unman' them with her passion" raises the prospect of probing the sexual politics of literary criticism itself, an implication in Holland's work (p. 169). But this task is not the main goal of her book, though it did inspire much work of this kind. She is content to refer us to the pioneering work of Mary Ellman on "phallic criticism," exemplified by Mailer, that "measures intelligence as 'masculinity of mind'" and "praises good writers for setting a 'virile example'" (SX 461f).

Nor is Millett mainly concerned with furnishing a new set of standards for evaluating literary works—a totally separate enterprise from exploring their sexual politics.[20] She takes pains to reassure us that "counterrevolutionary sexual politicians" (SX 329) can be great writers. Her "radical investigation" may "demonstrate why Lawrence's analysis of a situation is inadequate or biased, or his influence pernicious, without ever needing to imply that he is less than a great and original artist" with "distinguished moral and intellectual integrity" (SX xiv). He attained a "superb naturalism" in his "most convincing and poignant prose" —"probably" the "greatest novel of proletarian life in English" (SX 346f). "Lawrence is remarkable in having felt" "so keenly and recorded so memorably" "events" in "the ordinary progress of masculine experience in our culture" (SX 394).

Miller is redeemed as "avant-garde and a highly inventive artist" whose "most original contribution" was to give "the first full expression" to "sentiment which masculine culture had long experienced, but always rather carefully suppressed" (SX 434, 439). He "articulated" "the disgust, the contempt, the hostility, the violence, and the sense of filth" with which "masculine sensibility" "in our culture" "surrounds sexuality" and "women" (SX 413). He "gave voice" to "the yearning to effect a complete depersonalization of woman into cunt, a game sexuality of cheap exploitation," and "a childish fantasy of power untroubled by the reality or persons or the complexity of dealing with fellow human beings" (SX 439). And Mailer is lauded for having best "described" "the practical 'working-day American schizophrenia'"; his "powerful intellectual comprehension of what is most dangerous in the masculine sensibility is exceeded only by his attachment to the malaise" (SX 440).

---

[19] Her thesis that "to label it neurotic is to mistake symptom for cause in hope of protecting oneself from what could be upsetting" (SX 208) might apply to her own judgment of Miller, whose "attachment to Mara" is termed "a case history of neurotic dependence" (SX 436), were she less careful to show how Miller's outlook represents masculine sensibility at large.

[20] She apologizes for not "paying tribute to Henry Miller's considerable achievement as an essayist, autobiographer, and generalist," since she is "restricted to an examination" of his "sexual ethos" (SX 412). Mailer's writings get broader coverage, probably because his fiction is too evasive by itself (see Note 17).

Such estimations suggest that authorial honesty commands respect, even (or especially) when reporting disturbing aspects of human existence.[21] "A great novel" gets valued "because it has the ring of something written from deeply felt experience" (SX 345)—just the criterion Wellek and Warren soundly rejected (TL 80). Lawrence's "great" work "conveys more" of his "own knowledge of life than anything else he wrote" (SX 345). Charlotte Brontë is commended for "justice" of "analysis," "fairness" of "observations," and a "generous degree of self-criticism" (SX 208). "Genet's feudal system" is "more honest than that of our other authors in its open recognition of power" (SX 472). Even Miller's "virulent sexism" is at least "an honest contribution to social and psychological understanding"; "there is never reason to question the sincerity" of his "emotion": its "exploitative character" and "air of juvenile egotism" (SX 439, 414).

To the extent that these estimations address the merit of the works involved, Millett holds a broad conception of authorial responsibility for ideological implications, whether or not these are conscious during the act of composition. The "counterrevolutionary politicians" in Millett's gallery were widely misread as liberators when they took advantage of the "abatement of censorship" to "express what was once forbidden" "outside pornography"; yet their "explicit" portrayals were consistently "anti-social," not "revolutionary," voicing the "masculine hostility" that "outdistanced romance in interest" when women's "gains in this century" "provoked" "jealous patriarchal sentiment" (SX 63f, 444, 470). Millett delineates how Lawrence and Miller exploited the modern freedom of expression to "deplore" or "stave off" the "sexual revolution" —the one by "renovating and romanticizing masculine dominance" and "feminine" "subservience"; the other by "converting the female to commodity" and by "isolating sex" within the "utter impersonality" of a "biological event between organisms" (SX 383, 437, 386, 417, 420; cf. SX 365, 415f).

"Sentimentality" is regarded by Millett as yet another literary means to "hide" "sexual politics" (SX 111). It helps to idealize patriarchal institutions, such as the "family," and "beautify the traditional confinement of women," while "deploring" their "prostitution and poverty" (SX 179f, 111; cf. SX 341, 425). More ominous is the "masculine sentimentality" in depicting "relationships with other men"; the "tone" is "boastfully masculine, jealous of prerogative, stupidly patriotic, and spoiling for a war" (SX 70, 396).[22] Evidently, "in the experience of the American manchild, sex and violence, exploitation and sentimentality, are strangely, even wonderfully, intermingled" (SX 435)—most dramatically revealed when literary imagery combines intercourse with murder (cf. SX 29, 410f,

---

[21] Presumably, the use of "movie script," "Hollywood," and "cinema" as the epitome of bad quality (SX 443, 405, 445) reflects the lack of honestly Millett attributes to that medium. Holland makes no difference between film and literature for his analysis (p. 174f).

[22] Millett follows Riesman (1967) in confirming that "sport and warfare are consistently the chief cement" of male "camaraderie," as attested by the "men's house of Melanesia" (SX 68).

421, 429, 442ff, 446ff, 503).[23] Even Henry Miller, when "in love, reverts to" a "narcissistic" "sentimentalism" and a "sludgey 'idealism'" (SX 436). Only Genet eventually manages to "present" a "revolt" with "explicitness devoid of romantic sentimentality" (SX 492) (p. 354f).

In exploring how far the author "took his sexual politics with him" in his work (SX 395), Millett's analyses reveal a wide spectrum of results and admissable evidence. Sometimes, she uses fairly commonplace biographical materials: Meredith's "wife" and "father-in-law," Charlotte Brontë's "half-mad sisters" and "domestic tyrant" of a "father," Ruskin's "mother" and "child-mistress," Swineburne's "sexual peculiarities," Miller's "ménage à trois," and so on (SX 190, 207, 136, 151, 213, 426). Meredith is said to have taken over members of his family directly into a novel, though without "the revenge one would inevitably expect," whereas Ruskin, Lawrence, and Miller are taxed with having written to air their resentment against lovers or wives (SX 191, 136, 396, 426). Also, "all of the romances" of Lawrence's "later fiction" are interpreted as "reworkings of his parents' marriage" (SX 349; cf. SX 343, 348). But such tendencies, even if we accept them literally, account for general attitudes more than for the specific development of characters and plots.[24]

A related tactic is to read literary characters as projections of the author's own self. This identification is practised above all on D.H. Lawrence, who is claimed to be his own protagonists Oliver Mellors, Paul Morel, Rupert Birkin, Aaron Sisson, Rawdon Lily, and Richard Sommers (SX 343, 346, 369, 379, 393). In only one case is this identification documented, by citing Lawrence's preface: "'The novel pretends only to be a record of the writers's own desires, aspirations, struggles'" (SX 369). Miller is duly equated with his protagonists (e.g., SX 4), and seems to have desired such a reading; yet Millett finds "the major flaw in his oeuvre" precisely in "too close an identification with the persona, 'Henry Miller,'" "operating insidiously" against the thesis that "Miller the man is any wiser than Miller the character" (SX 414) (cf. Hassan, 1967).

Still, Millett acknowledges these equations to be problematic, because the resemblances between author and character are typically tenuous. Lawrence for instance had the habit of bestowing "adulation" and "admiration" on his protagonists, for example, as "'an utterly desirable man'"—which, as Millett drily injects, "is rather a lot to say of oneself" (SX 346, 369). It is also hardly credible that Miller would expect to be taken seriously if he "calls himself" "the 'undisputed monarch' of the 'Land of Fuck'" (SX 424).

---

[23] These images do fit the "primal scene" imagery that Holland wants to see in every instance of watching a performance (compare SX 47 with DY 110f). The parallel to Fiedler's "love and death" was cited in Note 2.

[24] Millett relies too heavily on biographical parallels when she cannot comprehend the "waspishness" of Lawrence's "portrait" of a "new woman" because Lawrence was on amicable terms with the real person presumed to have been the model (SX 369).

Millett routinely explains these discrepancies between character and author by interpreting the former as the author's "surrogate,"[25] a vehicle for "idealized self-portraiture" and "wish-fulfillment" (SX 379, 397, 352f, 381, 395, 485). "Lawrence novels" are seen as "a compensatory dream to offset the author's failures at home," where he was unable to "establish seignory" (SX 395f). Lawrence might indulge in "pretentious fantasies," such as "extra-marital" episodes that "fall just short of consummation," yet "satisfy" a "whole pack of vanities" (SX 393, 397). Or, he might permit a "talented" working-class male to "escape and rise above his class" and be adored by the higher classes, just as Lawrence "wished to be better than the working class" as well as "the middle and upper class" (SX 379; cf. SX 343, 349, 352f, 379f).[26] Or, he would assign his protagonists "the adoration" of "males" and imagine "a desirable homosexual lover" he did not seem to meet in life (SX 379, 343; cf. SX 373ff, 381f, 400). Contrarily, he would exact "spiteful revenge" on characters who reject his protagonists, for instance, by "heaping insult upon insult"; or would launch a "savage personal attack" on some figure of "the new woman as intellectual" (SX 376).

We might attempt a more elaborated account for this problem. Millett declares her intent to "take an author's ideas seriously when they wish to be taken seriously or not at all" (SX xiv). But a broad or literalized conception of authorial responsibility may be far too demanding and restricting. Identifying authors so closely with their characters means holding the former unduly accountable for the sayings and actions of the latter. Lawrence might have a character calling for a return to "'slavery'" and slandering "'Asiatics'" as "'vermin,'" "'niggers'" as "'wallowers,'" and "'Jews'" as "'despicable'" (SX 390f), and yet not intend to make a solemn public declaration of his own personal opinions. If, as Millett contends, authors are busily borrowing characters from the world around them, surely they can borrow opinions with the same alacrity. Moreover, Millett explicitly demonstrates that biased authors are formed by genuine pressure from patriarchal culture, such that even the ideology they openly endorse is not of their own fabrication; and that escaping it is hardly a step to be taken for granted—which is why we need feminist criticism.

Consider this problem from the standpoint of constructing a fictional world. Millett's synopses of literary plots often paint the authors as potent creators making something happen. They "cause" one character "to fail her exams" and another "to become a catamite"; they "condemn" yet another "to a lifelong

---

[25] A woman can serve for a male author, as when one heroine is a "female impersonator" and Salome is "Oscar Wilde" in "drag" (SX 399, 217, 220; cf. SX 400, 405).

[26] The desire to overreach this snobbery of class with a snobbery of sexual prowess no doubt contributed to the "aristocracy of sexual dynamism" imagined by Lawrence, and to Miller's frantic need to compensate for his "seedy" "jobless" "existence" in "commerce" "by shining in a parallel system of pointless avarice": "if he can't make money, he can make women" (SX 343, 417f).

sentence"; or they actually "murder" and "execute" characters for various motives (SX 368, 479, 485, 185, 405, 368, 375, 422). This way of putting matters lends the author an aura of superhuman power. Yet her authors are often found running against limitations or creating characters and events they would be expected to dislike or devalue. Even the authors Millett considers devoted to "wish-fulfillment" or "fantasy" keep portraying incidents in which their male protagonists' desires for social and sexual mastery are not met (SX 358, 364f, 375ff, 386ff, 423, 454f). Thus, we need to inquire which factors in Millett's analysis might be identified as limitations on the authorial license she places in the foreground.

One factor might be that diversity is essential to the complexity of art and the dynamics of narrative. A novel in which all characters shared the same set of attitudes, however warmly approved by the author, would be dull and stagnant. Of course, the author can portray different attitudes and yet control the action to ensure the triumph of the favored party; and Millett detects this option on several occasions. Lawrence can devise powerful intelligent women as long as they "spend each book learning their part as females"; these "realistic" exemplars of the time when "the female has actually escaped the primitive condition" get put in a story wherein they "relinquish" their "self, ego, will, individuality" (SX 402, 342; cf. SX 359, 406). Miller can portray "'good girls'" who make "tough lays," or "women who have a soul and a conscience" and want to be "recognized" "as a person," because their "resistance" dramatizes "the enterprise of conquest" and "the exhiliration of the chase"; "the more difficult the assault, the greater the glory" (SX 423ff, 421, 419, 439). Mailer can "render homage to the enemy as a worthy opponent" and imagine "the desirable woman" to be a "tough fighting spirit" in order to satisfy "his combative urges" (SX 457). He is "concerned" that "the male struggle to retain hegemony will have the spice of adventure."

Another restraining factor would be the author's "ambivalence" or "ambiguity" regarding social and sexual policies (SX 181ff, 357, 365, 440, 196, 405, 443, 450; cf. SX 107, 204, 209ff, 456, 461). "A male supremacist society" would tend to affect "the psyche of a woman" so as to produce not only a female character (Lucy Snow) who was "full of conflict" and "self-doubt," but also an author (Virginia Woolf) who was "argumentative yet somehow unsuccessful, perhaps because unconvinced, in conveying the frustrations of the woman artist" (SX 197) (cf. Showalter, 1977). C. Brontë "retorted" to "a division in the culture" by "splitting her people in half" and representing a "dichotomy" between "revolutionary spirit" versus the "old ways which infect" the "soul" (SX 204). "Deep in Lawrence's own nature" were "perverse needs," leading to an oscillation between "the masochistic" and "the sadistic" (SX 405). Mailer got trapped in a "conflict between his perception and his allegiance": his "attitude toward" the "posturing of heroes" "vacillates between mild irony and gratified participation" (SX 461, 456).

Ambivalence and conflict can affect the quality of the work. In Tennyson, "mixed feelings" constitute "a virtue" that "creates tension and interest" (SX 211). The "fantasists," in contrast, were "so ambivalent they could hardly be relied upon for more than" "cultural information" (SX 182). And Lawrence can be "so ambivalent" "that he is far from being clear, or perhaps even honest," and he "begins to lose rapport with his characters" (SX 357, 365).

Similarly, the work may suffer when authors hesitate or fail to carry out their projects to the full extent. Meredith recognized "the feudal character of patriarchal marriage and the egotism of male assumptions," but was "incapable of transcending them and consequently mistook the liberating turmoil of the sexual revolution" (SX 196). Hardy offered a "savage criticism" of "marriage and sexual ownership," yet was "troubled and confused" about "the sexual revolution," and "far too timid" to "be identified" with "notorious feminists"; he "abdicated to period opinion" (SX 188f, 184).[27] Lawrence "was too puritanical or too timid to risk the accusation" of "unmanliness" or to portray "sodomy" (SX 397, 376).

This explanation is once more reminiscent of the Freudian concept of "defense," whereby literature defends on one level against what it fantasizes on another (Ch. 9). Even authors consciously disposed to transcend prevailing sexual politics can be impeded by unconscious inhibitions. Still, an author may succeed, for instance, in creating a "truly feminine sensibility" (Brontë), or "transcending the sexual myths of our era" (Genet) (SX 196, 299). Even these exceptions had no easy victory: Brontë had to "deal with" both a "private" and a "public censor" by deploying "devious fictional devices"; and Genet had to heal a "dichotomy" between his "irony" and his "romantic myth" in his "earlier works" (SX 206, 489). Thus, Millett's outlook might be compared to Paris's: in their works, authors express inner conflicts they may not overcome or even notice, or only with much effort. We should therefore not demand a consistent policy or unlimited wish-fulfillment in plots or characterizations.

Genet, in fact, becomes a star achiever because of his exceptional accomplishment in the face of huge odds. He alone took the "step from rebellion to revolution" and moved "toward the creation of new alternative values" (SX 489; cf. SX 495). He "alone" "took thought of women as an oppressed group and revolutionary force, and chose to identify with them" (SX 498). Moreover, he "achieved the lowest status in the world," the "perfection of opprobrium in being criminal, queer, and female," yet he found in "the utterly abject" a "condition" close to "saintliness" (SX 24). "Through the miracle of Genet's prose," "art" "can effect" the "transformation to nobility"; the "masochism" of "slaves is converted to the aura of sainthood" (SX 481). He also "rebelled" from "social judgment" "by embracing crime and converting it by 'certain laws of fictional aesthetic' into his own version of evil as good" (SX 486). And his "aesthetics of bad taste" exalted "the accoutrements of the poor" (SX 495; cf. SX 481f, 484).

---

[27] According to Culler, "the possibility of quarreling with Millett," for example, by interpreting "Hardy's 'confusion'" as "'careful nonalignment'" (Jacobus, 1975: 305), "should not obscure the main point": her "feminist response" remains the "point of departure" (OD 48).

In Genet's "painstaking exegesis of the barbarian vassalage of the sexual orders," the power structure of 'masculine' and 'feminine'" is "revealed by a homosexual criminal world that mimics with brutal frankness bourgeois heterosexual society" (SX 25). "In the hierocratic homosexual society" of his "novels," "sexual role is not a matter of biological identity but of class or caste" (SX 22). Paradoxically, therefore, his "homosexual characters represent the best contemporary insight" into the "constitution and beliefs" of "heterosexual society." "His critique of the heterosexual politic points the way toward a true sexual revolution" needed for "any radical social change" (SX 29). Because "both his groups are male," his "use of the terms" "masculine and feminine" "reveals" them as poles of an "odious" "social code" and "terms of praise and blame, authority and servitude, high and low, master and slave" (SX 480).

Genet thereby illustrates how "role" is "arbitrary," a "function of a nakedly oppressive system" (SX 480, 26). He has deconstructed and "negated" the opposition of "gender"; he does the same with the opposition of right and wrong by unmasking "how crime and law are but each other's shadow" (SX 480, 483).[28] Also deconstructive is his involvement with themes he is at the same time denouncing. Lawrence, for example, quite seriously presents the "common fantasy of the white world" wherein "the white woman is captured," "raped, beaten, tortured," and "murdered" by "'savages'"; this "tittilates the white male," "intimidates 'his woman,'" and slanders the persons upon whom the white male has shifted the burden of his own prurient sadism" (SX 402f). Genet, "whose perceptions are more acute," recognizes this "self-seeking white fantasy" as a "maniacal myth" serving to "excuse atrocities"; he caustically has a group of "clowns" costumed as "blacks" "replay" this "murder" as "entertainment" (SX 404, 494).

Millett's reading of Genet provides a hopeful conclusion to her preponderantly pessimistic treatise on sexual politics. In retrospect, her "postscripted" promise, penned in the late 1960s, of "a growing radical coalition" between "the new women's movement" and "blacks and students" (SX 507) seems a bit wistful now, when everyone is avidly scrambling into the establishment and the family is being resentimentalized by TV preachers and their doting audiences. Yet precisely now, her exploration of the conditions and motives of sexual politics urges a pressing claim upon our consideration. What has been widely imagined a "sexual revolution" in our lifetimes emerges from her analysis as yet another of those "revolutions" bringing little benefit for "one half of humanity" (cf. SX 90); only males enjoyed a genuine expansion of privilege.

Millett's point that "human consciousness" is the major "arena" for any real "revolution" —a point made by numerous contemporary Marxists as well— attains conviction through her probing of literature, a cultural vehicle whose

---

[28] Another deconstructive move might be seen in Genet's subverting black and white by having "black actors" dress up as "the White Court who judge the ritual murder of whiteness as performed by another group of blacks" (SX 494). The affinities between feminism and deconstruction are especially developed by Irigaray (1974, 1977) (Beaugrande, 1987c).

ideological implications had seldom been so keenly scrutinized from a sexual standpoint. As a forum for alternativity, literature engages with ideologies that seem invisible because they are ingrained in the very activity of reading. When they are foregrounded, they turn suddenly, oddly, opaque, far from indisputable or inherent in the nature of things. Moreover, Millett compels the author, a participant whose presence in the literary transaction has been de-emphasized in recent critical theory (p. 19f), to leap back into focus as a shaper and partisan of cultural policy. Certainly, Millett's book has vitalized the upswing of feminist criticism. She has contributed, in the words of Carolyn Heilbrun (1971: 390), "an unexpected, even startling point of view," "not the last word on any writer, but a wholly new word, little heard before and strange"; "her aim is to wrench the reader from the vantage point" "long occupied, and force" us "to look at life and letters from a new coign."

17

Hans Robert Jauss[1]

Hans Robert Jauss has drafted an ambitious new program for literary history. That discipline has been in "a steady decline" during "the last one hundred and fifty years" and is "now drained of all exemplary scholarly character" (TAR 3, 49). Historians would "arrange" the "materials unilinearly according to the chronology of great authors" or situate "the individual work in a chronological series" formed by some "general tendency" or "genre" (TAR 4). "The authors' biography and the evaluation of their oeuvre pop up in some accidental spot." The weaknesses are plain: "the development of genres" gets "dismembered"; "the presentation" of "closed periods" in a "closed past" stays "one to two generations behind" the "standpoint of the present time"; "the research into tradition neutralizes the lived praxis of history"; and so on (TAR 4f, 7, 9). Indeed, "the form of literary history sanctioned by the historian is conceivably the worst medium" to "display the historicity of literature" (TAR 51).

"At first sight, history in the realm of the arts presents two contradictory views" (TAR 46). "With the first, it would appear that the history" of art "is more consistent and coherent than that of society," because "the chronological sequence of works of art is more closely connected than a chain of political events, and the transformations of style are easier to follow than the transformations of social history" (TAR 46). Thus, "the history of art" might serve as "a paradigm of historical knowledge" (TAR 48). "Pragmatic histories are of monotonous uniformity; only through the perfection of the arts can the human spirit rise to its own particular greatness" (cf. Voltaire, 1751) (TAR 49). "'Political and war history'" only tells us how a "'people'" "'let itself be governed and killed,'" but not how they "'thought,'" or what they "'hoped and wished for'" (Herder, 1796) (TAR 50). "The history of the arts" can be "a medium through which the historical indi-

---

[1] The key for Jauss citations is: AL: *Aesthetic Experience and Literary Hermeneutics* (1982a); EH: *Ästhetische Erfahrung und literarische Hermeneutik* (1982b); and TAR: *Toward an Aesthetic of Reception* (1982c). Though due to the processes of compilation and translation, these works were all published in the same year, there were originally of very diverse date. EH is a much revised and expanded German version of AL, the original of which appeared in 1977. All quotes from EH are my translation. I occasionally amended the translations in the English books. Inconsistencies between AL and TAR (e.g., "aesthesis" vs. "aisthesis") were resolved.

viduation of the human spirit is presented throughout the course of times and nations."

"With the second view, the paradigm of art historiography" "shows that this greater consistency of detail is purchased at the price of an overall inconsistency as regards the links between art genres as well as their relation to the general historical and social process" (TAR 46). "The sequential link between one work and the next is lost in a historical vacuum" (TAR 47). One might wonder "whether art history" must "borrow its overall coherence from pragmatic history" —typically seen as the "factual ruler-and-state type of history" (TAR 47f). Whereas "historicism," "positivism," and "orthodox Marxism" focused on pragmatic history (TAR 47, 51, 10f), Jauss focuses on a mode of art history for which he outlines a program.

Past approaches to literary history were guided by several main ideas. "Before it turned to tracing the history of style, art history had always taken the form of artists' biographies" organized according to "chronological order," "categories of authors," and "patterns of 'parallels'" (TAR 46). Due to a fascination with "'golden ages,'" the "appearance of art split up into a variety of different elemental courses," each "directed toward its own 'point of perfection'" (TAR 47). Later, research pursued "the idea of a national individuality" as "'the one basic idea that permeates'" an entire "'series of events'" (cf. Gervinus, 1962 [1883]) (TAR 8, 6). "To represent" that idea "in the history of literary works" was the "highest goal" (TAR 3). "National unification" or "national classicism" was considered the "peak" and "fulfillment" of the whole enterprise (TAR 7, 51).

But gradually, "the teleological model of idealist philosophy of history," seeking to "comprehend the course of events from an 'end, an ideal high point'" fell into "disrepute" as "unhistorical" (TAR 7). The eventual successor was "positivism": "the application of the principle of pure causal explanation to the history of literature" (TAR 8). "Objectivity" demanded that "the historian should disappear before his object," namely, the "series of events in an isolated past" (TAR 7, 21). "Representing the 'objective facts' of literary history are data of works, authors, trends, and periods" (TAR 51f). A "blind empiricism" stressed "externally determining factors" (TAR 8f). "Source study" "dissolved the specific character of the literary work into a collection of 'influences'" (TAR 8f) (a practice also disdained by Bloom, ANX 70; MAP 116).

"The protest" against "positivism" "was not long in coming" (TAR 8). The history of ideas ("Geistesgeschichte") "set an aesthetics of irrational creation in opposition to the causal explanation of history and sought the coherence of literature in the recurrence of atemporal ideas and motifs." This trend "allowed itself to be drawn into" the "literary studies of National Socialism" and was therefore replaced in Germany "after the war" with "new methods" (TAR 8).

In contrast to these past approaches, "the modern theory of literary studies" "lays emphasis on stylistic, formalist, and structural methods" (TAR 51). New attention is given to "literary sociology," notably in Marxism, and to "the work-immanent method,"[2] notably in Formalism (TAR 9). These two directions tried to "solve the problem of how the isolated literary fact or the seemingly autonomous literary work could be brought back into the historical coherence of literature" (TAR 10). Jauss accordingly treats the Marxist and Formalist schools as plausible groundwork to be revised and synthesized within a general hermeneutics or aesthetics.

By relating "artistic production" to "the material production and social praxis of human beings" in "the appropriation of nature," "Marxist literary theory" tends to "deny" "art" its "own history" (TAR 10; cf. TAR 75). "The orthodox theory of reflection" favors the "reduction of cultural phenomena to economic, social or class equivalents that, as the given reality, are to determine the origin of art and literature and explain them as a merely reproduced reality" (TAR 11). "The concrete multiplicity of works and genres always had to be traced back to the same factors or conceptual hypostases, such as feudalism, the rise of the bourgeois society," and "early, high, or late capitalistic modes of production" (TAR 12). Curiously, "Marxist theory" extended the "classical aesthetics" of the "'imitation of nature'" by "putting 'reality' in the place of 'nature'" (TAR 11). "Bourgeois realism" functioned as "the mimetic ideal." Conversely, the "modern development of art and literature" was deemed "decadent" because "'true reality' was missing."

This outlook led to the "striking contradictions" diagnosed in Lukács (TAR 13). He upheld "the normative value of classical art" and attempted the "canonization of Balzac for modern literature." But "if one denies" "any independence to the artistic form," "how can the art of the distant past survive the annihilation of the socioeconomic basis" (or infrastructure) and "'still provide us aesthetic pleasure'"? Lukács "helps himself along" with the "concept of the 'classical'" that "transcends history" and makes art live on despite being "a mere reflex of a long-overcome form of social development." Here, "determinations of a timeless ideality" contravene the "dialectical materialist mediation" whereby reality determines art. The same problem arises when Lukács says that "'each superstructure not only reflects reality, but actively takes a position for or against the old or the new basis'"; again, "economic necessity" seems weaker than was assumed in orthodox Marxism, for instance by Engels (TAR 13f).

Jauss opposes the "reduction of the work of art to a merely copying function" (TAR 11). For him, "literature, in the fullness of its forms, allows itself to be referred back only in part and not in any exact manner to concrete conditions of the economic process." "Literary works" absorb "historical reality" in various ways, according to their "genre" or "period" (TAR 12). "An interpretation of the conditions of the economic infrastructure is seldom to be had" "without" a

---

[2] The "work-immanent method" was something of a German counterpart to American "New Criticism" after World War II, but with the added impetus of disowning the cultural chauvenism of the Hitler period.

"method of allegoresis" (TAR 172; cf. Jameson, PU 32f; MF 215). Such a method is "thoroughly legitimate hermeneutically when it recognizes its subjective heuristics and therefore its partiality," instead of claiming to "achieve the true" and "'objective' reading" (TAR 173).

"The more rapidly changing" rate of "literary production," as compared to "the economic structure," collides with the outlook, attributed to Lucien Goldmann[3] as well as to Lukács, that "literary production remains confined to a secondary function of only allowing an already known" "reality to be once again recognized" (TAR 12, 14). Jauss observes that art can also be "formative of reality," as more recent Marxist theorizing has acknowledged: "'art both expresses and forms reality that exists not next to the work nor before the work, but precisely only in the work'" (Kosík, 1967: 123) (TAR 14). The account of a "dialectical relationship between the production of the new and the reproduction of the old" prevents the "revolutionary character of art" from being "foreclosed" (TAR 12, 14). For Jauss, "the specific achievement of artistic form" is not just "mimetic," but "dialectic as a medium capable of forming and altering perception" (TAR 16). One such alteration was brought about by Baudelaire's "style of decadence" designed to "bring to light" "hitherto unacknowledged suffering under the unnatural conditions of the contemporary society" (TAR 171).

In contrast to Marxism, "Formalism" insisted on "a rigorous foregrounding of the artistic character of literature" (TAR 16). Yet when the "result" of a work is "defined" as "'the sum total of all the stylistic devices employed in it'" (Šklovskij),[4] the "work" is "detached" "from all historical conditions." The centrality of the "opposition between poetic and practical language" seems to "sever the link between literature" and the "praxis" of life. We risk losing sight of that "functional relationship to the nonliterary" whereby "art" is "a means of disrupting the automatization of everyday perception" (cf. pp. 133, 398).

Whereas Formalism at first "made art criticism into a rational method in conscious renunciation of historical knowledge," "history" was later comprehended as "the 'dialectical self-production of new forms'" (Eikhenbaum, 1965 [1927]: 47) (TAR 17). Perception can be renewed by departing not just from everyday language, but also from "the givens of the genre and the preceding form of the literary series." Yet Formalism did not go on to "place the 'literary series' and the 'nonliterary series' into a relation" revealing the parallel between "literature and history" (TAR 18).

Jauss complains that in both "Marxist and Formalist methods," "the reader" "plays an extremely limited role." They "conceived the literary fact within the closed circle of an aesthetics of production and representation" and neglected "the dimension of its reception and influence." "Orthodox Marxist aesthetics

---

[3] Goldmann is said to "postulate a series of 'world-views' that are class-specific, then degraded by late capitalism" and "finally reified" (TAR 14).

[4] Šklovskij's "formula" —cited after Erlich (1955: 90) —was soon "improved upon with the concept of an aesthetic 'system' in which each artistic device had a definite function" (TAR 195).

treats the reader" "no differently from the author" with respect to "social position" in "the structure of a represented society," and "candidly equates the spontaneous experience of the reader with the scholarly interest of historical materialism" examining "relationships between superstructure and infrastructure in the literary work" (TAR 18f). "The Formalist school needs the reader only as a perceiving subject who follows the directions in the text" by applying "the theoretical understanding of the philologist who can reflect on the artistic devices, already knowing them." Hence, both methods used their own procedures as a model for the act of reading. They "lack the reader in his genuine role" "as the addressee for whom the literary work is primarily destined"; even "writer," "critic," and "literary historian" are "at first simply readers" (TAR 19).

Jauss also scrutinizes "structuralism" in two of its more developed approaches. In the Prague school, Vodička (1969 [1941-42]) proposed to "reconstruct" the "literary norm" and "the hierarchy of literary values of a given period"; and to "ascertain" "literary structure through the 'concretization' of literary works" (TAR 72).[5] Here, "literary history" "arises out of the dynamic tension between work and norm." This "polarity" is to be "materialized and historically described according to the manner of its perception."

In the Paris school, the "elitist idea of culture and art" was displaced by a "new interest in primitive art, folklore, and sub-literature" (TAR 66).[6] Lévi-Strauss (1968) searched "behind the myths" to find "the closed synchronic system of a functional logic." "Every work of art" should be "completely explicable through its function within the secondary system of reference of society; every act of speech is reduced to a combinatory element in a primary system of signs" (TAR 67). Jauss demurs that such a view opens a "gulf between structure and event, between" "system and history," by "merging" "all meaning and individuation" "into an anonymous, subjectless system." He also echoes Starobinski's (1968) complaint that "structuralism in its strict form is applicable only to literatures that represent a 'regulated play in a regulated society'" where literature does not "question the given order of institutions and traditions" (TAR 71), such as the rituals in primitive cultures. "Cultic participation" is quite different from "aesthetic reflection" (AL 154).

Jauss offers his own program to meet the "challenge"[7] of "literary history."

---

[5] "By concretization, Vodička means the picture of the work in the consciousness of those 'for whom the work is an aesthetic object'" (TAR 73). Iser uses the same term in a comparably phenomenological sense (p. 140).

[6] Jauss suggests that Northrop Frye similarly wanted to see "literature as a complication of a relatively restricted and simple group of formulas that can be studied in primitive culture" (TAR 66). But Frye is more preoccupied with the archaic than the primitive.

[7] "Provocation" is the more polemical term in the title, appearing within the text only for "Marxist literary theory's" denial of a separate art history (TAR 10). The bulk of Jauss' "challenge" is grouped around "seven theses" about "how literary history can today be methodologically grounded and written anew" (TAR 20). I do not follow this seven-part format exactly, though I cover the main points.

Here, "history" is viewed in terms of "the triangle of author, work, and public," and of the "dialogical" and "processlike relationship between work, audience, and new work" (TAR 19). "The methodology of literary studies" must be "opened to an aesthetics of reception and influence if the problem of comprehending the historical sequence of literary works is to find a new solution." Due to "the dialogical character of the literary work," "philological understanding can exist only in a perpetual confrontation with the text" and in the ensuing "reflection" and "description" as a "moment of new understanding" (TAR 21). "The history of literature is a process of aesthetic reception and production that takes place in the realization of literary texts on the part of the receptive reader, the reflective critic, and the author in his continuing productivity."

"The retrospectively established, 'actual' connection of literary 'facts' captures neither the continuity in which a past work arose nor that in which the contemporary reader or historian recognizes its meaning and importance" (TAR 52). The same holds for attempts of "historicism" to "explain a work of art by the sum of its historical conditions" and to make "literary history" "a mere imitation of the external linking of events" (TAR 51, 47). Instead, "the historical coherence of works among themselves must be seen in the interrelations of production and reception" (TAR 15).

In such a program, "a literary work" "is not a monument that monologically reveals its timeless essence" (TAR 21). Nor is it "an object that stands by itself and offers the same view to each reader in each period," as "the prejudices of historical objectivism" imagine (TAR 20f). The "'facts' that wind up in conventional literary histories" are "merely left over from this process" —just a "pseudo-history" (TAR 21). The work is "not a fact that could be explained as caused by a series of situational preconditions and motives." "In contrast to a political event, a literary event has no unavoidable consequences subsisting on their own that no succeeding generation can ever escape" (TAR 22). "Readers" must "again appropriate it," or "authors" must "want to imitate, outdo, or refute it."

In view of the "discrepancies of the various 'histories' of the arts, law, economics, politics, and so forth," "any historical period must" "be imagined as a mixture of events which emerge at different moments of their own time" (TAR 36f). This idea fits Siegfried Kracauer's (1963, 1969) rebuttal of the notion that "everything that happens contemporaneously is equally informed by the significance of this moment" (TAR 36). Actually, "literature that appears contemporaneously breaks down into a heterogeneous multiplicity of the noncontemporaneous," which "coalesces again for the audience" within "the unity of a common horizon of literary expectations, memories, and anticipations that establishes their significance" (TAR 37f).

If this process could be clearly defined, "the history of art, through the manner of its progression in time, and the study of art, through its continuous · mediation of past and present art, would become a paradigm" for any "history that is to show 'the development of this present'" (TAR 62). "But art history can take on this function only if it overcomes the organon-principle of style, and thus liberates itself from traditionalism and its metaphysics of supratemporal beauty." "Literary production" must be "seen as a 'special history' in its own unique relationship to 'general history'" (TAR 39). Hence, as noted before, Jauss favors a centrifugal focus proceeding outward from art history to history at large.

"The diachronic perspective," which Jauss says is "previously the only one practiced in literary history," should be complemented by "arranging" "synchronic cross-sections" of "contemporaneous works in equivalent, opposing, and hierarchical structures," "so as to articulate historically the change" "in its epochmaking moments" (TAR 36). "Horizonal change in the historical process of 'literary evolution'" should be "established" not just through "the web of all the diachronic facts and filiations," but also through "the altered remains of the synchronic literary system" revealed in "the literary horizon of a specific historical moment" (TAR 38f). Such a "system" contains "a limited number of recurrent functions" (TAR 83). The "relatively fixed relations" of "literature" can be viewed as "a kind of grammar or syntax": "the traditional and the uncanonized genres; modes of expression; kinds of style, and rhetorical figures"; plus "the more variable realm of semantics: literary subjects, archetypes, symbols, and metaphors" (TAR 38).

The selection of "points of intersection between diachrony and synchrony" should not be "arbitrary," but should single out the "works that articulate the processlike character of 'literary evolution'" in its "formative" "moments" (TAR 39). This task can rely neither on "statistics[8] nor the subjective willfulness of the literary historian," but only on "the history of influence." Appropriate "structural analysis, still lacking for many literary genres, could gradually lead to a synchronic cross-section in which the organization" of "genres appears not as a logical classification" (an "organon"), "but rather as the literary system of a definite historical situation" (TAR 87). This "historical systematics" "demands further cross-sections of literary production in the before and after of diachrony." However, in his study of "identification with the hero," Jauss first "works out" the "levels" "diachronically" and "only then" "describes their functional connection synchronically" (AL 162).

For so large an enterprise, the "interpreter" needs sufficient "experience" to survey "the past horizon of old and new forms, problems, and solutions" "recognizable" "within the present horizon of the received work" (TAR 34f). "Founding 'literary evolution' on the aesthetics of reception" "opens to view the temporal depths of literary experience" as well as "the distance between the actual and the virtual significance of a literary work." "The artistic character of a work" might not be "immediately perceptible" at "its first appearance," but only after "a long process of reception to gather in that which was unexpected and unusable within

---

[8] However, "the statistical curves of bestsellers" can "provide historical knowledge" if studied with respect to "horizonal change" (TAR 27).

the first horizon" (TAR 34f; cf. TAR 26). Such cases can "reopen access to forgotten literature," as when "the obscure lyrics of Mallarmé and his school prepared the ground for a return to baroque poetry" (TAR 35).

The "literary history of readers" is formed by the way their "horizon" "changes" over time (TAR 27). "Change" can come about "through negation of familiar experiences or through raising newly articulated experiences to the level of consciousness" (TAR 25). Some "works" "at the historical moment of their appearance are not yet directed at any specific audience, but break through the familiar horizon of literary expectations so completely that an audience can only gradually develop for them" (TAR 26). Contrarily, "aesthetic distance" can disappear for later readers when "the original negativity of the work has become self-evident" —just one more "expectation" for "the horizon of future aesthetic experience" (TAR 25). "The classical character of the so-called masterworks" is due to "this second horizon change"; "it requires a special effort" to recover "their artistic character" (TAR 25f).

Quite against the grain of commonplace cultural adulation, the "classic" functions here as the negation of a negation and hence—in a model that prizes negativity—as an object of diminished functional value. Jauss opposes theoreticians who make the classical a standard for value, in his view Lukács, Gadamer, Hegel, and adherents of Lévi-Strauss (TAR 13, 30, 31, 40).[9] The "classical" all too readily stands for "probability," "simplicity, harmony of part and whole" or of "form and content," and so on (cf. TAR 29, 41, e.d.). For Jauss, "art" is "in no way bound to the classical function of recognition" as prescribed by the "aesthetics of mimesis" that dominated "the humanist period" though not the "medieval" or "modern" periods (TAR 31). Moreover, that "function" is only a later imposition, since "classical art at the time of its production did not yet appear 'classical'" (cf. p. 12).

"The reconstruction of the horizon of expectations" "enables one" "to pose questions that the text gave an answer to," and "to discover how the contemporary reader could have viewed and understood the work" (TAR 28). The dialectic of "question and answer" is accordingly a thematic concept in Jauss's work (e.g., TAR 5, 19, 29, 32, 38, 41, 44, 65, 68, 113, 117ff, 142, 185)—matching Gadamer's (1960: 355) dictum, following Collingwood, that "'to understand a text means to understand a question'" (TAR 65). "The answering character of the text" is "a modality of its structure," not an "invariable value within the work itself" (TAR 69). The "author" may not have "formulated an explicit answer in

---

[9] The classicism in Lukács was already discussed (p. 359). Gadamer is thought to have "taken over from Hegel" the "concept of the classic that interprets itself"; and to "elevate the concept of the classical to the status of a prototype for all historical mediation of past with present" (TAR 30f). Goldmann's "ideal of 'coherent expression' is claimed to "betray" his "classicism," as in the "unity of content and form" (TAR 14). The "literary structuralism" "which appeals, often with dubious justification," to Lévi-Strauss, "still remains quite dependent on the basically classical aesthetics of representation" (TAR 39f).

his work"; "the answer" may remain "indeterminate" so as to preserve the "aesthetic effectiveness" and "artistic character of the work," as "Iser has shown" (TAR 69). During the "act of interpretive understanding,"[10] the "interpreter" has to "uncover or reformulate the question," "proceeding from the answer that the text" "appears to contain" (TAR 142, 65, e.d.). "A past work survives not through eternal questions, nor through permanent answers, but through" the "dynamic interrelationship between question and answer, between problem and solution, which can stimulate new understanding and allow a resumption of the dialogue between present and past" (TAR 70).

This dialectic of a reader "posing a question" that the "work can answer" escapes the "platonizing dogma" that the text's "objective meaning" is "determined for once and for all" and "is at all times immediately accessible to the interpreter" (TAR 28, 32). "The coherence of question and answer in the history of an interpretation is primarily determined by categories of the enrichment of understanding," and "only secondarily by the logic of falsifiability" (TAR 185). All the same, "the historical communication of question and answer limits the mere arbitrariness of interpretation," and "can be falsified" less by "historical errors or objective mistakes" than by "falsely posed or illegitimate questions on the part of the interpreter" (TAR 69, 185). A "question" counts as "legitimate" "when it is shown that the text" is "consistently interpretable as the meaning of this response" (TAR 185). Moreover, the "question" must not "completely abolish the answer" that a previous interpreter "found in the text to his questions." "Different responses" need not "falsify one another"; they may only "testify to the historically progressive concretization of meaning in the struggle of interpretation."

Accordingly, "literary hermeneutics" is "no longer interested today in interpreting the text as the revelation of a single truth" (TAR 147). "The understanding within the act of aesthetic perception may not be assigned to an interpretation" that "reduces the surplus of meaning of the poetic text to one of its possible utterances" (TAR 142). "A reader may" "hypostasize one among other possible significations of the poem, the relevance of which for him does not exclude the worth of others for discussion" (TAR 145). "In the horizon of aesthetic experience," "different interpretations need not contradict one another, because literary communication opens a dialogue in which true and false can only be measured by whether a further interpretation contributes to the development of the inexhaustible meaning of the work of art" (EH 703) (cf. Jauss, 1979).

Still, control is exerted by "textual signals" "within their syntagmatic coherence as the givens of the course of reception that establish consistency"; and by "the pregiven elements of the reception" which "limit the arbitrariness of readings that are supposedly merely subjective" (TAR 144, 141). Jauss suggests

---

[10] This "act" is in the second stage of Jauss's three-stage scheme for an experimental self-study I report later.

that "as a regulative principle," "the aesthetic character of the text" "allows for there being a series of interpretations" "capable of being reintegrated with respect to the meaning made concrete" (TAR 148). This account is far more moderate than Barthes' (1973b) "theory of the 'plural text,'" with its "interminable play of a free-floating intertextuality" and its "limitless arbitrary production of possibilities of meaning" (TAR 147).[11]

In this way, Jauss joins Iser in maintaining that "the psychic process in the reception of a text is, in the primary horizon of aesthetic experience, by no means only an arbitrary series of merely subjective impressions, but rather the carrying out of specific instructions in a process of directed perception, which can be comprehended according to its constitutive motivations and triggering signals, and which also can be described by text linguistics" (TAR 23). The "work" will be found to "predispose its audience to a very specific kind of reception by announcements, overt and covert signals, familiar characteristics, or implicit allusions."

Within this framework, Jauss hopes to "avoid" the "pitfalls of psychologism" by "describing the reception and the influence of a work within the objectifiable system of expectations that arises for each work in the historical moment of its appearance, from a pre-understanding of the genre, from the form and themes of already familiar works, and from the opposition between poetic and practical language" (TAR 22). Whereas Wellek (1936: 179) argued that "the individual state of consciousness," being "momentary and only personal," cannot "be determined by empirical means," Jauss salutes new "empirical means that had never been thought of before —literary data that allow one to ascertain a specific disposition of the audience for each work, a disposition that precedes the psychological reaction" and "the subjective understanding of the individual reader" (TAR 22f). If the reader's "horizon of expectations can be objectified," we might then "comprehend and represent the history of literature in its unique historicity" (TAR 22). Again like Iser, Jauss conceded however that he himself does "not yet suffer from not having become an empiricist" and "has yet to provide the model for the overdue empirical research into reception" (TAR 144). Later on, he did a study of himself performing a reading, the results of which I summarize below (pp. 375-79).

Jauss is adamant that the experiences provided though literature are the only objects literary history has. "Aesthetic distance can be objectified historically along the spectrum of the audience's reactions and criticism's judgment" (TAR 25). He will admit "no objective link between work and work that is not brought

---

[11] Jauss commends Barthes for "showing what the structuralist analysis of a literary work could really achieve"; and for "rehabilitating aesthetic pleasure" (TAR 67; AL 29) (compare Note 16). Yet Barthes' method is attacked for its "yawning gap of subjective arbitrariness" within "the open relation between meaning, question, and answer" and for its "naive fusing of horizons" (TAR 68, 147). In the TAR-introduction, de Man laments "Jauss's lack of interest, bordering on outright dismissal" of "the 'play' of the signifier" (TAR xix).

about by the creating and receiving subjects of literature" (TAR 52). "Intersubjective communication separates the historicity of literature from the factual objectivity of pragmatic history." A work's "historically concrete appearance" "has its basis in the form and meaning created by the author" and "realized by his readers" "over and over."

"The analogy" "between art history and pragmatic history" can now be defined: it "lies in the character of both the work of art and of the historical fact as an event" (TAR 53). "This difference narrows" when we "accept that diffuse events are only 'understood and combined'" through their "'interpretation as a coherent process'"; and that they "can also be interpreted differently from the later standpoint of the observer" (TAR 52). We thus arrive at a thesis latent in the theories of other critics, especially Iser: that the "classic form of historiography" is derived from "unacknowledged fictional narrative forms" and "made possible" by "the aesthetic categories of the history of style" (TAR 53) (cf. Ch. 3).

Johann Gustav Droysen (1967 [1857-63]) already worked to "expose the illusions that accompany the apparently objective narration of the traditional facts." "The historical narrative uses the law of fiction, that even disparate elements of a story come closer and closer together for the reader, and ultimately combine in a picture of the whole" (TAR 54). "The illusion of the completed process" projects a "finished chain of events, motives, and purposes" (TAR 53). "The illusion of the first beginning and the definitive end" derives from "the Aristotelian definition of the poetic fiction, which must have "a beginning" "that does not originate out of something else," "a middle, and an end" "followed by nothing" (TAR 54). "The illusion" of the "objective picture of the past" refuses to realize that "'the facts'" "'would be dumb without the narrator who makes them speak.'" The "judgment, selection, motivation, or linking of events presupposes the hindsight of the historian," and cannot be "inherent in the original event" (TAR 55f). "The flourishing historiography of the nineteenth century, which sought to disavow the artistic character of historical writing in order to gain recognition as a science, devolved upon the fictionalization" that "history" can "tell its own story" (TAR 55).[12]

The "positivist" and "objectivist" demand that "the historian should disappear before his object" was thus doomed (cf. TAR 7f). When science was less narrowly conceived, the concept of the "horizon of expectations" could "play a role in the social sciences since Karl Mannheim" (TAR 40).[13] The concept is also taken up by Karl R. Popper (1964), "who would anchor the scientific formation of theory in the prescientific experience of a lived praxis." Yet the arguments

---

[12] In the "historical novel," Sir Walter Scott developed the "narrative" with "the narrator" "completely in the background" and created "the illusion" that "the reader" is "present at the drama" and "can make his own judgments" (TAR 55). Iser's analysis of Scott contains the remark that "history can best be captured by aesthetic means" (IR 96).

[13] Bleich salutes Mannheim for similar reasons (SC 25). Wellek and Warren decry Mannheimian "sociology of knowledge" for "its excessive historicism" (TL 108).

marshalled not only by Jauss and Iser, but by Holland, Bleich, Culler, de Man, Bloom, and Hartman, reveal that objectivism lives on, a polemical adversary and target in our own times.

The "relapse into objectivism" implied for instance in Wellek's (1936) plea for "'isolating the object'" (TAR 30) may have been triggered by the acute dilemma of disparate times. "The actual standards of a past could be so narrow that their use would only make poorer a work that in the history of its influence had unfolded a rich semantic potential." The "judgment of the present would favor a canon of works that correspond to modern taste." For Jauss, the solution is to treat the "original horizon" in "'fusion'" with "the horizon of the present" (TAR 29f) (cf. Gadamer, 1960: 289). "The 'verdict of the ages'" must be viewed as "the successive unfolding of the potential for meaning that is embedded in a work and actualized in the stages of its historical reception as it discloses itself to understanding judgment, so long as this faculty achieves in a controlled fashion the 'fusion of horizons' in the encounter with the tradition" (TAR 30).

We might thereby "correct the mostly unrecognized norms of a classicist or modernizing understanding of art" among "interpreters who, supposedly bracketing themselves, nonetheless raise their own aesthetic preconceptions to an unacknowledged norm" (TAR 28f). "Whoever believes that the 'timelessly true' meaning of a literary work must immediately, and simply through one's mere absorption in the text, disclose itself to the interpreter as if he had a standpoint outside history and beyond all 'errors' of his predecessors," merely "'conceals the involvement of the historical consciousness itself in the history of influence'" (TAR 29) (cf. Gadamer, 1960: 283). "He denies 'those presuppositions'" "'that govern his own understanding,' and can only feign an objectivity 'that in truth depends on the legitimacy of the questions asked.'"

This "denial" is still prevalent enough to make Jauss emphasize the dynamic processes involved. "A historical fact as event—just like a work of art—is constituted by the range of its possible meanings and can therefore be made concrete only through the interpretation of later observers or performers" (TAR 60). A historiographer like Leopold von Ranke (1852-61), who "believed" "that the historian need only disregard his own partiality and cause his present to be forgotten in order to capture an undistorted past" has no better "guarantee" of "truth" than do "poets and novelists" (TAR 54). "Precision" gets sacrificed to "harmonious flow," and "the contingency of events" gets converted into a "continuity of significant moments" (TAR 58). The "presentation" "brushes aside the heterogeneity" of "historical processes" and moves toward the "culminating point" at which "all heterogeneous trends are homogenized" (TAR 57f). "The concept of tradition" "harmonizes history" and "suppresses the contrary, the revolutionary, the unsuccessful" (TAR 63) (cf. Adorno, 1966).

To resolve such dilemmas, "the closed horizon of the classical narrative form must be surmounted," so that "historical explanation" can "keep open the possibility of further narrative statements about the same event" (TAR 60f) (cf. Danto, 1965). "Paradoxically, the poetics of modern literature offers paradigms" for an " 'anti-literary' form of presentation—with a limited perspective, aware of its own location, and a horizon that is left open" (TAR 60). If the "aesthetic effect is to be avoided and the imagination prevented from closing the gaps" to get a "picture of the whole," "special preventive measures are required" that are "common to modern artistic prose" (TAR 54). Jauss points to "the modern novel," which, "since Flaubert, has systematically dismantled the teleology of the epic story and developed new techniques in order to incorporate the open horizon of the future into the story of the past, to replace the omniscient narrator by localized perspectives, and to destroy the illusion of completeness through unexpected and unexplained details" (TAR 61).

Though Jauss does not borrow avant-garde literary techniques for his own treatises, he does seem to follow Droysen's proposals for making the "narrative" "include and reflect 'our interpretation of important events,' " and for introducing such "non-narrative forms" as "the 'examining,' the 'didactic,' the 'discursive' " (TAR 59). Yet if "narrative" is already a "basic category of historical perception," then the "narrative link" is hard to eliminate (TAR 60). Moreover, aesthetic harmonizing and closing of gaps might occur in Jauss's own projects of "discovering an overarching system of relationships in the literature of a historical moment" and of making the "heterogeneous multiplicity" of "literature" "coalesce again" within "the unity of a common horizon of literary expectations" (cf. TAR 36ff).

Jauss's enterprise is thus still implicated in a literary approach to historiography—which may raise its appeal among literary scholars nostalgic for "a coherent whole" (cf. TAR 50). Yet he is far removed from the principles of traditional art history. He does not rely on the "exemplary character" of "classical art" (TAR 46f): He denounces any referrals to a "normative element of perfection" (TAR 50). He castigates the "substantialist misconception" that "in the history of genres the multiplicity of historical events is countered by an invariable form which, as 'historical law,' subsumes every possible historical form of a genre" (TAR 61). And he follows Droysen in rejecting "the false doctrine" of the "organic development in history" implicit for instance in Herder's (1796) "natural history of art" with its "imagery of growth and old age, the cyclic completion of every culture" (TAR 54, 50).

Jauss accepts "the hermeneutic principle of partiality," whereby the "meaningful whole can be found only through a selective taking of perspectives" (TAR 145f). He also assents to the "hermeneutic" "hypothesis" that "the concretization of the meaning of literary works progresses historically and follows a certain 'logic' that precipitates in the formation and transformation of the aesthetic canon" (TAR 147). By studying "the change of horizons," we might even be able to "distinguish absolutely between arbitrary interpretations and those available to a consensus, between those that are merely original and those that are formative of a norm" (TAR 147f).

Ideally, "the process of reception becomes describable in the expansion of a semiotic system" operating "between the specification and the correction of a system" (TAR 23) (cf. Jauss, 1959; Stempel, 1971). The "corresponding process of the continuous establishing and altering of horizons also determines the relationship of the individual text to the succession of texts that forms the genre." "Variation and correction determine the scope, whereas alteration and reproduction determine the borders of a genre-structure." Readers rely on such "factors" as the "familiar norms of the immanent poetics of the genre"; "the implicit relationships to familiar works of the literary-historical surroundings"; and the "opposition between fiction and reality, between the poetic and practical function of language, which is always available to the reflective reader during the reading as a possibility of comparison" (TAR 24).

The "act of distancing" "demanded" in "all aesthetic experience" registers the "disparity between the given horizon of expectations and the appearance of a new work" (AL 160). "The new is thus not only an *aesthetic* category," concerned with "innovation, surprise, surpassing, rearrangement, or alienation," but also a *historical* category," helping to decide "which historical moments are really the ones" that make something "new in a literary phenomenon" (TAR 35). We can probe "to what degree this new element is already perceptible in the historical instant of its emergence; which distance, path or detour of understanding were required for its realization in content; and whether the moment of its full actualization was so influential that it could alter the perspective on the old, and thereby the canonization of the literary past."

Though Jauss allows that every "response links up with an expectation or supposed meaning" either by "fulfillment or nonfulfillment" (TAR 69), he usually follows the Formalists (and Adorno and Iser) in attaching a higher value to nonfulfillment (cf. EH 695). "The Formalist method would relate the series to one another and discover the evolutionary alternating relationship of functions and forms" (TAR 33, e.d.) (cf. Tynjanov, 1929). "The new work arises against the background of preceding or competing works," so that "the dialectical production of forms" "requires no teleology," but only "innovation" (TAR 32f).

Jauss objects here that "mere opposition or aesthetic variation does not suffice to explain the growth of literature" because "innovation" "does not alone make up artistic character" (TAR 33f). We cannot "reduce the historical character of literature to the one-dimensional actuality of its changes," nor "limit historical understanding to their perception" (TAR 34). We must also consider the "mediation" within "the step from the old to the new form in the interaction of work and recipient (audience, critic, new producer)" and examine "the formal and substantive problem 'that each work of art, as the horizon of the "solutions" which are possible after it, poses and leaves behind.'" "The next work can solve formal and moral problems left behind by the last work and present new problems in turn" (TAR 32).[14]

Jauss would base the "determination" of "aesthetic value" on the more general "criterion" of how "the literary work" "satisfies, surpasses, disappoints, or even refutes the expectations of its first audience," or how an "audience experiences formerly successful works as outmoded and withdraws its appreciation" (TAR 25ff). "Innovation" is balanced against the "return" of the "forgotten," as developed in the aesthetics of Baudelaire and Proust (cf. AL 33f, 87ff, 160f, 251f). In the "modern period" at least, "the totalizing power of memory" can be "the ultimate authority of aesthetic production" (AL 12) (cf. Gombrich, 1960).

Nonetheless, Jauss was disposed to believe that "for progress" "in the experience of life, the most important moment is the 'disappointment of expectations'": then, "'we actually make contact with reality'" (Popper, 1964: 102) (TAR 41). This emphasis on "the productive meaning of negative experience" extends a thesis also implied by Marxism and Formalism: that literature can be a means of human emancipation via an aesthetic renewal and alteration of perception. "The experience of reading can liberate one from adaptations, prejudices, and predicaments" in life by "compelling a new perception of things" and "broadening the limited space of social behavior for new desires, claims, and goals."

Conversely, commercialized "entertainment art" "fulfills expectations prescribed by a ruling standard of taste": it "satisfies the desire for the reproduction of the familiarly beautiful"; "confirms familiar sentiments"; "sanctions wishful notions"; "makes unusual experiences enjoyable as 'sensations'"; and "raises moral problems, but only to 'solve' them in an edifying manner as predecided questions" (TAR 25; cf. Iser, IR 284; AR 46, 174, 219).

Such remarks indicate that the violation of expectations acted as a transhistorical value standard in Jauss's theorizing. He may have been motivated by his search for predispositions, which become most visible when violated. He once suggested that "the ideal cases" of "literary-historical frames of reference are works that evoke the reader's horizon of expectations, formed by a convention of genre, style, or form, only in order to destroy it step by step" (TAR 23f). He later realized he had "almost exclusively foregrounded" "the norm-breaking function" because of his "dominant interest in the emancipatory function of art" (EH 751). He had been overanxious to separate "constitutive negativity" from the "affirmative character of mere entertainment literature" (EH 695). For a theory like Adorno's, "affirmative works of art remain a vexation," the more so since we have

---

[14] One demonstration is Jauss's comparison of Valéry's *Mon Faust* with Goethe's *Faust* (TAR 110-38). "No overarching significance can be determined from shared and distinguishing features alone"; the works "only enter into dialogical relationship" if we "recognize the questions that, in Valéry's view, Goethe left behind" (TAR 113). A comparison of Rousseau and Goethe is summarized below (pp. 387ff).

"an incomparably larger number" of them (AL 15f). "The history of art cannot be reduced to the common denominator of negativity" (AL 16). As was already argued, "classical" works "tend to lose their original negativity" as they undergo "incorporation in institutions that confer cultural sanction" and "reaffirm authoritative traditions" (AL 16). Yet "the halo of the classical, positive, and eternally ideal" "need by no means have merely affirmed" "the state of a given society when it appeared."

Consequently, Jauss revised his earlier polarity by situating in between the two extremes of negating or "norm-breaking" and affirming or "norm-imposing," a region he called "motivating or norm-forming" (EH 751). In this new middle ground, "a whole spectrum of practical achievements" ranges from "heroic" to "didactic" art (EH 752). "The literature of courtly love" supported "a developing social norm or life-style" when it enacted an "affirmative transformation" in the name of a new "love ethic" and "contributed" to the "emancipation" of "communication between the sexes" (AL 18).[15] Even art that is "devalued" by "aestheticism" and "engaged literature" can have an "exemplary" role in "the formation of identity" (EH 752). Jauss's new tolerance, like Fiedler's, reflects a concern for the "question of whether and how art today can recover its almost lost communicative function."

The emancipatory function of literature must be estimated in view of "the fundamental ambivalence of aesthetic experience" (AL 96; cf. AL 158, 161). Art "may break the hold of the real world but in so doing, it can either bring the spectator to a free, moral identification with an exemplary action or let him remain in a state of pure curiosity" or "in manipulated collective behavior" (AL 96). "The exemplary" further "includes two possibilities of imitation: the free, learning comprehension by example" versus "the unfree, mechanical following of a rule" (AL 110).[16]

The tradition has been to stress the positive aspects. For Goethe, the "beautiful appearance" "has the function of conveying the illusion of a higher reality along with what is true to nature" (AL 59). For Hegel, "man satisfies his general need to be at home in the world by producing art" and "makes" the "world" "into his own product" (AL 34). In "Baudelaire's theory of aesthetics," anticipating "Freud's and Proust's," a "sharpened perception of the new" "requires" a "concurrent" "rediscovery of buried experience" (AL 12). For Valéry, "the artist experiences his work as a blissful seizing of the possibilities of his own, finite world" (AL 11).

The formalists and structuralists also stressed the brighter side. For Muka-

---

[15] Iser also allows medieval courtly-love literature to be both affirmative and high in quality (AR 77), but Millett rejects it on comparable grounds (SX 50f). See Note 22 to Ch. 8 and Note 15 to Ch. 16.

[16] Compare Barthes' "double canon" of "affirmative pleasure" ("plaisir") versus the "subversive" "negative" enjoyment he called "jouissance" (TAR 29).

řovský (1970 [1936]: 95), "the aesthetic function" is a "dynamic principle" of "potentially unlimited" scope: "'it can accompany every human act, and every object can manifest it'" (AL 115). "Because the aesthetic function" "lacks unequivocal content," it "can take hold of the contents of other functions and give their expression the most effective form" (AL 116). "Aesthetic experience can illuminate the structure of a historical life world, its official and implied interaction patterns and legitimations, and even its latent ideology" (AL 121). Thus, "art" can be "a specific shaping" and a "humanization of reality" (AL 116) (cf. Kalivoda, 1970).

Though hoping that "art could serve as a paradigm of non-alienated labor" (AL 55), Marxist theorizing was less uniformly optimistic. For Marcuse (1968), "all aesthetic experience falls under the suspicion of being idealistically corrupted" (AL 45). The "more ideal world" of "culture detached" from "civilization" via "the rule of the commodity form" becomes a mere "escape route from an increasingly reified world." For Adorno (1970), "taking pleasure in art" is "the precondition for the culture industry" that "serves hidden ruling interests in a cycle of manipulated need and aesthetic substitute gratification" (AL 27). On the other hand, Adorno believes art can become "the agency of a social truth before which the false appearance of the factual, the untrue and the unreconciled in society's actual condition must reveal itself'; hence, art "makes clear that 'the world itself must change'" (AL 15). "Bloch saw the disclosing quality of aesthetic experience as a utopian harbinger" able to "give linguistic expression to something hoped for" (AL 9). Adorno concurred by relating the "negativity" of such an "experience" to "the utopian figure of art" and to the "'measuring'" of "'the gulf between praxis and happiness'" (AL 15).

This guarded optimism is found in Jauss's method as well. He strives to maintain a view of the "entire range" of "possibilities for the social effectiveness of art" in between "the extremes of the norm-breaking and the norm-fulfilling functions" (AL 154). On the reader's side, "aesthetic experience" "offers through the function of discovery the pleasure of a fulfilled present" (AL 10). "It perfects the imperfect world not merely by projecting future experience but also by preserving past experience which would continue unrecovered" if it were not "transfigured and monumentalized" by "the luminosity" of "poetry and art." Hence, the "experience is effective both in utopian foreshadowing and in retrospective recognition." On the author's side, artistic "production" can "give perfect expression to all the things that the demands and conventions of daily existence would otherwise cause to remain mute, suppressed, or unrecognized." "The poet who transforms his experience into literature also finds a liberation of his mind which his addressee can share." Moreover, "a revelatory power" is attained for "showing the reader in exemplary fashion that human passion is a distinctive characteristic of individuality" —a power beyond "biology," "empirical psychology," or "psychoanalysis" (cf. Plessner, 1971) (AL 8).

In recent times, "the growing alienation of social existence" imposed another "task" upon "aesthetic experience" "which had never previously been set for it in the history of the arts" (AL 92). A need arose "to counter the shrunk experience and subservient language of the culture industry by the language-critical and creative function of aesthetic perception." "In view of the pluralism of social roles and scientific perspectives, such perception was also to preserve the experience of the world others have and thus to safeguard a common horizon which, the cosmological whole being gone, art can most readily sustain."

This task re-emphasizes "the social formative function that belongs to literature as it competes with other arts and social forces in the emancipation of mankind from its natural, religious, and social bonds" (TAR 45, e.d.). This "function" is "a genuine possibility only where the literary experience of the reader enters into the horizon of expectations of his lived praxis, preforms his understanding of the world," and "has an effect on his social behavior" (TAR 39). Indeed, the sociological concept of role" has itself "been shaped by the history of aesthetics" (AL 134; cf. AL 137, 165; Plessner, 1960). "The doubleness of the public and the private individual" is an "aesthetic paradigm" (AL 137). "The threshold between social and aesthetic role behavior would always be crossed when the implicitly adopted role distance" "is made explicit" in "the aesthetic attitude" that "frees" a person from "the seriousness and motivational pressures of daily roles" (AL 138). Perhaps "the latitude of interpretation that becomes available to man through the self-estrangement of role enactment" might "make up for the inevitability of predetermined behavior" (AL 138).

Jauss feels that the pleasure or enjoyment in aesthetic experience has received insufficient consideration. Adorno mistrusted "pleasure" as a "bourgeois reaction" to "the intellectualization of art" and believed art could be "'autonomous only where it rids itself of taste and its pleasures'" (AL 27, 21). So he favored an "ascetic experience of art" such as befits the works of Samuel Beckett or Philippe Sollers (AL 27f, 87).

Jauss replies that "in all its uses, literary communication retains the character of an aesthetic experience" only if "enjoyment" is not "sacrificed" (AL 36). He stipulates, however, that "neither mere absorption in an emotion nor the wholly detached reflection about it, but only the to-and-fro movement, the ever renewed disengagement of the self from a fictional experience" "makes up the distinctive pleasure" in "aesthetic identification" (AL 160). "All aesthetic experience, including such primary levels as admiration or pity, demands an act of distancing" "which never breaks its connection with the offer of emotional identification." "The avant-gardism of modern *écriture*" (e.g., Sollers), which engages in "continual reflection about narrative functions," "can expect no more from the mocked reader than a theoretical and philological interest in a reference-less language game" (AL 87). It "surrenders the cognitive and communicative efficacy of aesthesis along with the aesthetic pleasure it denies" (cf. Wellershoff, 1976). As we see, modernism is accepted here only as far as basic artistic functions are preserved.

Jauss identifies "three" "fundamental categories of the attitude of aesthetic enjoyment" corresponding to "three concepts of aesthetic tradition" since Aristotle (AL 34). "Three functions" are listed: "for the producing consciousness, in the production of world as its own work (poiesis); for the receiving consciousness, in the seizing of the possibility of renewing one's perception of outer and inner reality (aesthesis)"; and "in the assent to a judgment demanded by the work, or in the identification" with "norms of action" ("catharsis") (AL 35). These three form "a nexus of independent functions" in a "reciprocal relation of results." "Catharsis" is not merely the "release" of "aroused passions" (Aristotelian sense), but "the fundamental communicative aesthetic experience," and "corresponds" both to "the practical enjoyment of the arts" whose "social functions" include "conveying, inaugurating, and justifying norms of action"; and to "the ideal object of all autonomous art[17] which is to free the viewer from the practical interest and entanglements of his everyday reality" (AL 23, 35). Hence, catharsis is also the function in which "subjective opens up toward intersubjective experience" (AL 35).

Jauss also has a scheme for describing "identification" on five "levels" of response to the "hero." This response may be: "associative" when the audience "assumes a role in the closed, imaginary world of a play action"; "admiring" when the "model" has a "perfection" beyond "tragic or comic"; "sympathetic," when the audience "projects itself into an alien self" and "eliminates" "distance" in favor of "solidarity with the suffering hero"; "cathartic," when the audience is "freed" "from the real interests and entanglements of its world" and finds "liberation through tragic emotion or comic relief"; and "ironic" when the "identification" is offered to the audience "only to be subsequently refused" by "the destruction of illusion" (AL 164, 167, 172, 177, 181f).[18]

Frye too used the ratio between audience and hero for a framework of classification (p. 67). There, the hero is simply superior, equal, or inferior to other people, including the audience. In Jauss's scheme of responses, the audience need not perform such comparisons. We might feel admiration, association or sympathy with characters who seem far above or below ourselves. Moreover, Jauss's responses differ from Frye's in not purporting to separate "tragic" from "comic." Hence, Jauss's scheme is more flexible and detailed than Frye's and seems better adapted to the mixing of genre and to the variability of individual response.

Jauss conducted an "experiment" on himself to explore how "the three moments of understanding," "interpretation," and "application" might be "described

---

[17] The "autonomy" of art broadly designates not just freedom from "everyday reality," but the "break with the imitation of nature" and the "detachment from social functions" (AL 52, 179).

[18] Note the different sense of "cathartic" here. Apparently, the rule that "all aesthetic experience" "demands an act of distancing" is amended; "pity," "sympathetic identification," and the "comic of the grotesque" are said to "eliminate" or "annul" "distance" (AL 160, 157, 172, 163).

phenomenologically as three successive readings" of the same text (TAR 139f)—though these three are not systematically related to his the triad of poiesis, aesthesis, and catharsis.[19] "Poiesis" would be less in focus here, being associated with "the producing consciousness" (AL 35). If "aesthesis" is "perception" "able to rejuvenate cognitive vision or visual recognition" (TAR 142), it should go mainly in the first stage ("understanding"). The broad relation of "catharsis" to "social functions" and "norms of action" (AL 35) would best fit the third stage ("application") that can "disclose a possible significance for the contemporary situation" (TAR 143).

This three-stage model—Jauss considers it "one of the most exact applications of his theory" (interview, August 1984)—indicates how "the poetic text can be disclosed in its aesthetic function" "when the poetic structures that are read out of the finished aesthetic object as its characteristics, are retranslated out of the objectification of the description, back into the process of the experience of the text" (TAR 140f). This "processlike effect" cannot be "directly deduced from a description" of the "final structure" of the text as "artifact" along the lines of "traditional stylistics," "linguistic poetics, and 'text analysis'" (TAR 140).

However, Jauss's account of how "the reader" "takes part in the genesis of the aesthetic object" (TAR 141) is still a scholarly reconstruction presupposing a fairly advanced stage of appreciation. The moment when the text is only "the point of departure for its aesthetic effect" (TAR 141) is necessarily revised by the scholar's attempt to articulate it in retrospect. Jauss produces a miniature history (Culler would say a "story of reading") which, like history in general, devolves upon the conventions of fictional narrative. Introspection is his only channel for relating his narrative to some empirical record of his actual activities of processing when he read the poem.

Jauss "goes further and in another direction than Riffaterre" (TAR 141). The latter's "model for the reception of a poem presupposes the ideal reader ('super-reader')" who commands all "literary historical knowledge available" and can "consciously register every aesthetic impression and refer it back to the text's structure of effect" (TAR 144). Jauss "escapes this dilemma" by dividing himself into different people. In the first stage, he assumes the role of "a reader with the educational horizon of our contemporary present" —someone "experienced" with "lyrics" but able to "initially suspend" "literary historical or linguistic competence." "Beside this" "reader" Jauss "places a commentator with scholarly competence, who deepens aesthetic impressions" of the "reader" engaged in "pleasure, and who refers back to the text's structure of effect as much as possible." In the second stage, we are back to just one "reader," and in the third, Jauss personally steps into the foreground.

---

[19] Jauss says this "triad" is "the precondition for the hermeneutic" one (letter to me, October 1984). He "situates all five identification patterns in the domain of catharsis," which seems odd if one pattern is called "cathartic."

Jauss grants that his "three stages" are not "normally" "distinguished" in "philological commentary" and "textual analysis," and that the "distinction between" them "must be fabricated to a certain degree" (TAR 139f). But they follow the traditional "triadic unity of the hermeneutic process" envisioned for theology and jurisprudence and recently "brought back to light" by Jauss's teacher Gadamer. Jauss also sees a correspondence to "the three horizons of relevance": "thematic, interpretive, and motivational," which, "according to Alfred Schütz" (1971), "determine the constitution of the subjective experience of the life-world" (TAR 143)—a further link between aesthetics and sociology.

From a more practical standpoint, "repeated readings" are "often" needed to make "the horizon of expectations of the first reading" become "visible in its shaped coherence and its fullness of detail," especially when dealing "with historically distant texts," "hermetic lyrics," or "modern poems" (TAR 141f, 148). This argument doesn't say why we need exactly three readings; the number was probably picked because of the older "triadic unity" just cited. In at least some particulars, the materials Jauss includes must reflect a larger number, since he "already knew and valued the poem for a long time," although he claims "an unknown poem would not have materially changed the experiment" (letter to me).

Jauss implies that the three readings occur in an operational sequence, whether or not any real-time boundaries can be demarcated. In the first stage, the process of "understanding the text as an answer to an implicit question" (cf. p. 364f) "can for the time being remain suspended," so that "the reader" can "experience language in its power, and thereby, the world in its fullness of significance" (TAR 142). Here, the reader "performs the score[20] of the text" "verse after verse" and moves "toward the ending in a perceptual act of anticipation" (TAR 145). He or she "becomes aware of the fulfilled form of the poem, but not yet of its fulfilled significance."

In the "second reading," "the reader will seek to establish the still unfulfilled significance retrospectively" in "a return from the end to the beginning, from the whole to the particular." "What the reader received in the progressive horizon of aesthetic perception can be articulated as a theme in the retrospective horizon of interpretation" (TAR 143). Here, "'understanding'" the text "'as an answer'" can "only concretize significances that appeared or could have appeared possible to the interpreter within the horizon of his preceding reading" (TAR 142). This proviso helps limit the range of meanings; and any initial misunderstandings are disregarded.

Finally, "the third" "reading" concerns "the historical horizon" that "conditioned the genesis and effect of the work and that once again delimits the present reader's interpretation" (TAR 146). "This third step" "is the one most familiar to

---

[20] German "Partitur" is a musical score, equated here with the literary text to stress the performative aspect of reading. Holland's "promptuary" is even more emphatic (Note 17 to Ch. 9).

historical-philological hermeneutics" seeking to "privilege historical understanding" over "aesthetic appreciation." But for Jauss, "the aesthetic character of texts" is what "makes possible the historical understanding of art across the distance in time in the first place." In exchange, "the historicist-reconstructive reading" "prevents the text from being naively assimilated to the prejudices and expectations of meaning of the present", and "allows the poetic text to be seen in its alterity," its "'otherness.'" One can "use literary communication with the past to measure and to broaden the horizon of one's own experience" (TAR 147).

Jauss's treatment of the poem is explicated in three stages, each purporting to cover one "reading" of the text (TAR 149-85). The first reading is presented with two typographical styles, one for the "'historical reader of the present,'" and one for the "scholarly" "commentator" looking over his shoulder (TAR 144, 150, 156). In this stage, Jauss does not report any responses in the first person, but only those which "the reader" or "one" experiences (e.g., TAR 152ff, 156, 158). The "author" is conspicuously absent too. Throughout the first and second readings, "Baudelaire" enters as the author of the poem only twice (TAR 164, 167), though some mention is made of his career and his other works (TAR 157, 162, 166, 168). More often, Jauss infers a "lyric I"[21] from the text (notably from first person pronouns), e.g., as the one who "describes his state of mind" and tries "to rebuild the collapsed world within the imaginary" (TAR 156, 165). The text also appears as agent, e.g., when "the poem" "announces itself," "the title" "discloses the horizon," or "the lyric structure confirms" (TAR 152, 163).

The hypothetical reader is often puzzled by the poem when his "expectations" are "not fulfilled" (TAR 156, 157, 159). He is "burdened" with an "enigma" or has to "step across a threshold into the unreal and the uncanny" (TAR 160, 156). He "expresses" his "wonder" in "questions": "will this movement come to an end?"; "will the 'I' perhaps arrive at itself?"; "who can speak in such a manner, and with what authority?" (TAR 155, 159). He is able to notice style, both generally in terms of "high lyrical tones" or a "tone of definitional formality," and specifically in terms of formal features, such as a "repeating vowel," the "rhythm" of a "line," or a "typographical signal" like a "dash" (TAR 158, 151, 155, 159).

Meanwhile, "the scholarly analyst adds that" our reader is aware of such subtle effects as "parallel line openings" and a "distant but still audible internal rhyme" (TAR 156f). The analyst further comments in his own right on a variety of "phonetic," "morphological," "syntactic," and "semantic" issues, including "subtle word meanings" and such "technical details of prosody" as "onomatopoeia" and the "Alexandrine" (TAR 150ff, 154f, 159ff). He also appreciates the "lyric consistency" in which "everything works together," and reminds how "in the medium of poetry the everyday and the occasional can take on a new and deeper significance, or recover an older, forgotten meaning" (TAR 151f). And he

---

[21] In view of the psychoanalytic reading we'll get to in a moment, the coincidence of "I" and "ego" in German "Ich" may be of interest. I use "ego" here where I feel it's appropriate.

decides what is "beautiful," be it "disorder," "regularity," "monotony," or "withered roses" (TAR 154, 158f). [22]

The second reading is managed by just one "reader," still in a dialogue with "the lyric I" (e.g. TAR 162ff). "The conjectures and questions left open by the first reading" now "allow themselves to be brought formally and thematically into a certain common denominator" (TAR 161). "An overarching motivation" and a "latent principle of unity" offset "lyric movement," which appears "manifestly fragmentary" or occurs in "an asymmetrical unfolding and retraction" (TAR 161f). A classic Formalist or New Critical move is performed when "the formal discovery coincides with the thematic one": "the asymmetrical development of the rhythmic movement" "being cut off" "coincides with the fragmented continuity of an experience of self become ceaseless" (TAR 165).

The "psychiatry of anxiety-psychoses" is brought in to interpret the "anxiety" "described" in the "poem": "the collapse of the primordial situation, that is, the construction of the world from out of the 'ego'-body center" (TAR 166). Baudelaire's general use of the "personifying allegory" is said to "make visible the overpowering of the self through the alien," or "the ego through the id" (TAR 168). However, we are reassured that "the poem transcends its psychopathological substratum," just as "aesthetic sublimation" "always" succeeds in "mastering" "anxiety" "in its literary representation" (TAR 167). This concession reminds us of the approach propounded by Holland, who is however "oriented more toward the psychic disposition of the reader and the forms of his fantasies" than toward "the communicative achievement and the interaction patterns of aesthetic experience" (AL 158; cf. AL 163).

In the third reading, Jauss finally steps forward with "my opinion" and "my interpretation" (TAR 179, 184). The author also comes to the fore: Baudelaire is mentioned by name on every page (TAR 170-184), and the question is raised, "how might the author himself have understood his poem?" (TAR 170). Jauss now explores "which expectations on the part of its contemporary readers," including ones related to some "literary tradition" or some "historical and social situation," the poem can "have fulfilled or denied." He sorts out "the meaning given to it by the first reception" versus those "made concrete" in "later history." This "brings into view the temporal distance that was leaped over in the first and second" "readings" and makes an "explicit separation of past and present."

Jauss adduces Théophile Gautier's "famous forward to the 1868 edition of *Fleurs du mal*" as a "first appreciation of the work" (TAR 170f). This "eyewitness" "recognized more clearly than other contemporaries just what kind of horizonal

---

[22] "Beauty" is detected in the scene where the Sphinx sings at sunset (TAR 169). But we should recall Gautier's premonition that "the beautiful may no longer owe anything to nature"; and "Baudelaire's definition of beauty via an indeterminacy that leaves free play to 'conjecture'" (TAR 173, 161). Jauss's Freudian reading (below) brings to mind the fact that "the communicative function of aesthetic experience" is "missing in Freud's theory," though Jauss thinks (and I don't) that it "can easily be supplemented on the intersubjective side" (AL 34). See Note 16 to Ch. 8.

change had unexpectedly been introduced" (TAR 171). Gautier's "avant-garde" status (TAR 174), though it empowered him to see a norm-creating event, also made him a nonrepresentative reader. We might feel uneasy when his "interpretation" is said to "already specify everything that the ideological research of our time might know how to investigate," including "social expectations and illusions" and "material conditions of the life-world" (TAR 172). From this perspective, "Baudelaire's intention" was that his "cycle of poems" be "understood" as "a critique of the present age, of the ideology and the morality of appearances of the society of the Second Empire." Yet a method concerned with first responses should keep in mind that the "thoroughly offended" "contemporary reader" who raised a "public uproar" (TAR 172, 174) can hardly have grasped this intent.

Whereas Jauss seems to trust Gautier's judgment by virtue of its progressive anticipation of later norms, skepticism greets several other witnesses to the poem's reception, ranging from "a trend-setting *Figaro* critic" of 1857 though Walter Benjamin down to the "most recent" scholar Laurent Jenny (1976) (TAR 171, 179f, 183ff). Jauss disagrees with their interpretations in part, even when, as with Benjamin, he shows an overall sympathy.[23] We get the impression that these witnesses may be unreliable, as when Jauss "must doubt whether" a critic's "initial grasp of the poem," "presupposing" "the classicist harmony of form and content," "could withstand a historical critique" (TAR 182). Of course, Jauss owes it to his own historical hindsight that he can doubt his "predecessors" and pose "questions left unposed" by them (cf. TAR 185).

To some degree, historical understanding offers the benefit of both including and transcending one's predecessors. When Jauss prefers the untypical Gautier over more typical critics of the same period, simple hindsight helps decide whose opinion to accept. But Jauss is also applying his own innovative theoretical program that set certain priorities as he developed it. "The Formalist and Marxist schools" were his "first point of orientation"; "later, it was Adorno and Gadamer" (letter to me; cf. EH 26ff). He therefore began with a strong commitment to innovation and emancipation, as we have seen, and subsequently attenuated it, though without granting fully equal merit to affirmative literature.

"The verdict of the ages" about particular works of art is thus only one guideline within his restrospective summation, alongside the insights made available by theories which past sources couldn't have consulted. "Petrarch did not yet have at his command aesthetic perception as a world-appropriating understanding" (AL 77). Gautier made a "groping attempt to describe something for which the theory of the unconscious was not yet available" (TAR 174). Even a recent critic like Judd Hubert (1953) "did not yet have the hermeneutic key of the

---

[23] Benjamin is praised for "recognizing the 'modern allegorist' in Baudelaire," but elsewhere blamed for his "violent attempt to bring dialectical materialism to bear on the *Fleurs du mal*" (TAR 179f; AL 82f).

allegorical method at his disposal" and tried to apply "a universal code of symbolic meanings" (TAR 180f). Or, an adherent of "linguistic poetics" like Karl Blüher (1975) produced an "interpretation" in which "the singular meaning and individual shape of the poem" got "lost" (TAR 181).

The problem here is that past theories or concepts Jauss does not share — timeless truth, organic growth, harmony of form and content, art for art sake, and so on—were historically real enough to influence the development of art for a time. The "classicism" Jauss sees as a potential impediment to progress, individuality, and perceptual renewal, dominated various periods in European literature and artistic theory. Just as we may now fail to experience the original impact of the "classicalized" work, we may discount the vitalizing effect of classicism in the past, as when the French stage had to move beyond the confines of commedia dell'arte (cf. AL 16, 180).

Like critics, authors may not seem to us properly aware of what the issues were. Jauss's method, seeking more leeway for the reader, does not bind the text to authorial data as much as most historical approaches. For him, "the validity of texts does not derive from the author's authority" (AL 36). "The author cannot tie the reception to the intention with which he produced the work"; the latter "unfolds a plenitude of meaning which far transcends the horizon of its creation" (AL 35). "In all aesthetic experience, there is a gap between genesis and effect which even the creative artist cannot bridge" (AL 115). "The activity of the observer who concretizes the significance of the finished work neither directly continues nor presupposes the experience that the artist gained in the course of his work."

Authors are, of course, also readers of other authors, and Jauss's question-answer model capitalizes on this factor. In one study he commended to my attention, he traces the function of Goethe's *Werther* as an "answer" to Rousseau's *Nouvelle Héloïse* (EH 627). In this act of "productive reception," as "often happens under the pressure of the 'anxiety of influence,'"[24] "imitation and continuation, renewal and revision of the basic pattern" occur all at once.

Rousseau had "diagnosed a division between natural and bourgeois existence" and "reversed the traditional relation between fiction and reality" (EH 619, 600). "The horizon of expectations" he "left behind" was "transcended" when Goethe's work presented "an altered relation to nature" and "retreated into the interiority of the feeling self" (EH 626, 621, 638). Yet Goethe also "fulfilled Rousseau's postulate that the task of literature" should be "to unmask the illusions of prevailing society and to prepare the way for authentic experience and realization of the self" (EH 630). Goethe "actually" "performed the reversal of the traditional

---

[24] The English phrase "anxiety of influence" appears in the German text to signal the association with Bloom, whose categories are deemed "better" than "'organic' metaphors" (AL 133). "Tessera" is Jauss's favorite ratio (TAR 114, 122; EH 514). But he suggests that "the intuitive results of antithetical criticism" need to be "subject to hermeneutic control" (TAR 136).

relation of fiction and self-realization," an act Rousseau only "announced." But neither novel managed a "dialectic resolution of the antinomies of natural and social existence, of sentiment and reason, self-sufficiency and morality" (EH 638)—a tall order for any work.

"For both Rousseau's and Goethe's novels, very rich materials have already been collected and published, but not interpreted in terms of the horizonal change between French Enlightenment and German Idealism," one that affected both "literary and social experience" (EH 588, 629). Being unable to cover everything, Jauss proceeds by a "selective expansion of context" (EH 589, 614). He brings in a number of literary sources, both for Rousseau's text (Petrarch, Plutarch, La Fayette, Richardson, pastoral novel) and Goethe's (Homer, Goldsmith, Klopstock, Lessing) (EH 590-95, 615-18). Most of these are fairly plainly alluded to by the novels themselves, though a "secret model" may exert its influence, as in the relation between these same two novels (EH 623, 625, 627). "All direct testimony" on Goethe's part about his use of Rousseau "conceals more than it reveals" (EH 623).

A variety of readers' reactions are also documented, but the picture is again complicated by the extent to which the novels were not received as Jauss thinks they should have been.[25] The responses of the "men of letters" to Rousseau's book "demonstrate a scandalous misunderstanding" (EH 587). Undaunted by the "applause of general public," "official criticism" "rejected" the book and "completely missed" its "dual utopian and critical function" (EH 622 601). Goethe's book was "trivialized" "into a sentimental love story" by the public, and assailed by critics who demanded "moral edification" for having "omitted any moral comment" (EH 602, 630f).[26] "Only a small group of readers met the expectation" of a "self-reliant reader" freed from the "tutelage of the Enlightenment" (EH 632). I feel uneasy about a history that casts naive readers mainly as perpetrators of inadequate readings.

In hindsight, Jauss finds a theme few eighteenth-century readers could have imagined. Rousseau's thesis that "the state of society" is a human "product" that makes them "misconstrue their true nature," implies a "concept" he didn't define as such, namely "alienation" (EH 607). Goethe went "far beyond Rousseau's critique of civilization" and "to an astonishingly farsighted degree beyond the horizon of expectations of his contemporaries" (EH 638). He "saw in the division of labor the basic principle of the nascent bourgeois economy and denounced it as the true evil of alienated existence." Jauss was perhaps aided in finding this idea by Ulrich Plenzdorf's recent critical adaptation of *Werther* for the East German stage (cf. EH 642, 806-11).

---

[25] Even Rousseau is judged mistaken about his own source, the myth of Abelard and Heloisa (EH 590).

[26] The scandal aroused by *Madame Bovary* was similarly stirred because its "impersonal narration" created an "alienating uncertainty of judgment" that could "turn a predecided question of public morals back into an open problem" (TAR 42ff).

Evidently, the "historical reception" Jauss judges "indispensable for the understanding of literature from the distant past" (TAR 28) is prodigiously dynamic. Not only must the critics continually rewrite history as time passes; their own intervention becomes part of that history and calls for a fresh estimate. The "open horizon of meaning" of "the work of art" "becomes apparent in the never-ending process of interpretation" (TAR 63). In this sense (a different one from the Yale-school's method), literature and criticism merge and blend within a complex totality of production and reception. Intertextuality asserts itself and erases the borders of the text—not as a "historical-sequential" "event," but as the "fact" to which it had been "reduced" by "positivistic literary theory" (TAR 32).

The wealth of material Jauss adduces in his historical readings indicates the ambitious size of the tasks he envisions for literary history. Problems of selectivity and scope become much more acute here than in critical theories which make no promise of historical depth or dialectical synthesis. In principle, expectations are likely to be less specific and more diffuse than textual occurrences, so that the "horizon" would always be far wider than the text itself.

"For a cross-sectional analysis of the literary horizon of expectations in 1857," for instance, "700 lyric pieces" were "collected, classified, and interpreted as representations of communicative patterns" (AL 270), though no one piece could be read as thoroughly as in the three-stage Baudelaire explication. Moreover, "sociological theory" (e.g. Schütz & Luckmann, 1975) was consulted to expound "the social history of the family" (AL 287, 284). This combined mass of evidence showed how the "interaction pattern" within this "subuniverse" "idealizes norms and values of bourgeois life" as "naturally given," while "the reality of working for a livelihood" is "ignored" (AL 289f). The various poems range from "legitimation" over to "denunciation of social conditions" (AL 280f).

This range matches the "fundamental ambivalence" we found Jauss admitting for aesthetic experience in general (AL 96). In this set of materials, "detemporalization and idealization" "increase" the "suggestiveness" of the "patterns" of such "experience" and "poetically legitimate their norm-creating or norm-sustaining function" (AL 283). "But the semblance of timeless validity" also allow them "to serve as means of ideological obfuscation." The Rousseau-Goethe demonstration suggests that the latter result is quite common, so that criticism needs to counteract it.

Criticism also has to contend with "those in authority," who are "interested in making" art's "powers of seduction and transformation serve their ends" (AL 13). "Aesthetic experience is always and necessarily suspected of refractoriness" (AL 4). "The uncontrollable effects of art" "become the target of polemics carried on in the name of religious authority, social morality, or practical reason" (AL 97). "The claim of the arts to autonomy" "provoked the opposition of Christian and social authorities, and even of an enlightened morality" (AL 39). Still, as Jurij Lotman (1972) remarks, "art" can "always rise again and outlive its oppressors" (AL 13).

Despite the flood of materials, certain kinds of historical evidence may be unobtainable. Jauss concedes that "the forms" of "aesthetic experience" are "less amply documented in historical sources" than "other functions of everyday life" (AL 3). Similarly, "documents detailing the specific sensory perception of past periods" are "usually lacking" (AL 64). In the social sphere, a prominent theme such as "paternal authority" might "normally go unmentioned" or be "tacitly passed over" (AL 272, 285). De Man's introduction to TAR even claims that "the historical consciousness of a given period can never exist as a set of openly stated or recorded propositions"; and that the "horizon of expectations brought to a work of art is never available in objective or even objectifiable form, neither to its author nor to its contemporaries or later recipients" (TAR xif). However, de Man is plainly speaking for himself, not for Jauss, whose efforts to "objectify" the background we examined above.

Much remains to be done.[27] Jauss "regards as necessary the destruction of literary history in its old monographic or 'epic' tradition, in order to arouse a new interest in the history and historicity of literature" (TAR 71). Until recently, "no theory of understanding has been developed for texts of aesthetic character" (TAR 140). "Aesthetic appreciation," "identification," and "role concept" have "hardly been considered" (TAR 146; AL 158, 138). "Analysis of the dialectic of question and answer" that forms literary tradition "has scarcely even begun" (TAR 70). "Cross-sectional analyses" have "not yet been attempted" (TAR 38). "For centuries no attempt has been undertaken to bring the totality of literary genres of a period into a system of contemporary phenomena" (TAR 95). "The social function of literary genres" has been "ignored in medieval scholarship" (TAR 99). And so forth.

Thus it is that Jauss' project of looking back to history looks still more emphatically forward. Properly "reconstructed," "the horizon of expectations of a work allows one to determine its artistic character by the kind and degree of its influence on a presupposed audience" (TAR 25). But this reconstruction waits on the enormous research it requires. The effort will be rewarded to the degree that "the past belongs" "to our suffering present" (letter to me). Paradoxically, the old can be itself again only when it becomes new for us.

---

[27] Jauss points out to me in a letter that this gallery of failings was "addressed to traditional philology in Germany," which is "interested neither in hermeneutics nor aesthetics." He says "the New Critics" created a better situation in the United States.

18

Fredric Jameson[1]

Whereas our other critics typically disregard Marxism (e.g., Culler, Bloom) or else stake out their own position against it (e.g., Fiedler, Jauss), Fredric Jameson makes Marxism the center for critiquing or reformulating all other positions. He continually sets literature and criticism into motions that illustrate the movements he defines for the Marxist modeling of thought. In the process, familiar issues and theories are recontextualized in fresh ways that might regenerate their critical potential and their relevance for an analysis of society at large.

Jameson rates Marxism above any "philosophy which does not include within itself a theory of its own particular situation," an "essential self-consciousness along with the consciousness" of its "object" (PL 207). Although he doesn't "defend Marxism as the most suitable and all-embracing orthodoxy" for "literary critics," he "thinks such a defense might well be made" (MF 321). "Marxism" can "claim to be an interdisciplinary and universal science" by accessing "textual and interpretive problems" not only in "cultural studies," but also in "philosophy," "political science, anthropology, legal studies," and "economics" (PU 37f).

"Marxism subsumes other interpretive modes or systems"; "the limits of the latter can always be overcome, and their more positive findings retained, by a radical historicizing of their mental operations" so as to include "the content of the analysis," "the method," and "the analyst" within "the 'text' or phenomenon to be explained" (PU 47). "Only Marxism offers a philosophically coherent and ideologically compelling resolution to the dilemma of historicism": the "double bind between antiquarianism and modernizing 'relevance'" (PU 18f). "Marxism" "retells" history "within the unity of a single great collective story" based on "a single fundamental theme": "the collective struggle to wrest a realm of Freedom from a realm of Necessity" (PU 19).

Jameson is anxious to deflect commonplace, old-fashioned, or rigid conceptions of Marxism. He strongly repudiates "vulgar Marxism," alternately called "economism" or "orthodox" or "classical" "Marxism,"[2] namely the doctrine of

---

[1] The key for Jameson citations is: IT: "The Ideology of the Text" (1975-76); MF: *Marxism and Form* (1971); PL: *The Prisonhouse of Language* (1972); and PU: *The Political Unconscious* (1982).

[2] The equation between these terms is made by the indexing under "Marxism," "economism" (MF 429); compare also MF 221f, 292f. Still, Jameson uses the "economic" in many ways, such as a means to "approach the concrete" (MF 322).

the "'ultimately determining instance' of the economic" (PU 32). In that "theory of levels," the "base or infrastructure" (alternate translations for Marx's German word "Basis") is constituted by "the economic" or the "mode of production," and the "superstructure" (Marx's "Überbau") by "culture" and "ideology," along with the "legal" and "political" systems. "The conception of class interest supplies the functional link between a superstructural symptom or category and its 'ultimately determining' reality in the base" (PU 33).

This model is suspected of "allegorical" or "idealistic" overtones: it "translates" the "concrete" into the "abstract" and takes "the cultural text" as "an essentially allegorical model of society as a whole" (PU 32f; MF 215; cf. PL 181; MF 375; cf. Jauss, TAR 172). It "stresses the imaginary status of the symbolic act so completely as to reify its social ground" into an "inert given that the text passively or fantasmatically 'reflects'" (PU 82). It "reduces characters to mere allegories of social forces" and "symbols of class," thereby "presupposing immutable forms, eternal Platonic ideas" that "leave out" "the unique historical situation," as "Sartre has pointed out" (MF 193; cf. PU 33; Frye, AC 113, 346).

For Jameson, genuine "Marxism" is "a *form* of understanding," "a mental operation" "characterized as a kind of inner 'permanent revolution'"; "every systematic presentation of it falsifies it in the moment in which it freezes over into a system" (MF 378, 362). In this sense, "system" is associated with "metaphysical content" "resulting from a hypostasis of the mental processes, an attempt to hold something aside from the concrete operation of the mind" in order to "treat" it "in absolute fashion, as the universally valid" (MF 361f).

Hence, "Marxism takes as its object something utterly distinct from the object of the more academic philosophical systems" (MF 208). It "may be seen as the 'end' of philosophy, in that in its very structure it refuses system"; and "philosophy" "abolishes itself as thought grows increasingly concrete" (MF 361, 331). Still, "Marxism" "does not seem to exclude the adherence to some other kind of philosophy," such as "existentialist, phenomenologist," "realist," or "empiricist" (MF 207).[3] Moreover, "the attempt to dispense with the baggage of system or metaphysical content," as undertaken by the "formalism of all the great schools of modern philosophy," "veers about" into the "'absolute formalism' of Marxism" (MF 373).

Jameson centers his powerful claims for Marxism on its special "mental operation" of "dialectical thinking," which he likes to call "thought to the second

---

[3] This tolerance is limited, though. At one point, "realism" is termed a "philosophical enemy" of "the materialist dialectic," though as a literary style, it is "central" to "Marxist aesthetics" (MF 366, PU 104). "Empiricism" is even more severely denounced (MF x, 54, 367; PL 23f). "Existentialism," thought to be a "conceptual containment strategy," is condoned, provided it is not a "metaphysic" or "ideology," but a "properly existential analytic" of the kind developed by Sartre (PU 216, 259). Lukács' Marxist critique of existentialism is decried as a "crude effort" based on "clumsy mediations" (PU 259f).

power" (MF 372f, 45, 53, 153, 307).[4] It is a "self-conscious" "attempt to think about a given object on one level, and at the same time to observe our own thought processes," thereby "reckoning the position of observer into the experiment" (MF 340). Via a "conscious transcending of an older, more naive position," "the mind reckons itself into the problem" and "deals with itself just as much as the material it works on" (MF 308, 45). If "the potentialities for development of a given mode of thought lie predetermined" "within the very structure of the initial terms," "genuinely dialectical criticism" must always "question the sources of its own instruments" and evade "preestablished categories of analysis" (MF 9, 399, 333). "Such thought" "recites its own inevitable falsifications at every moment"; its "thoroughgoing critique of forms" "destroys" "every possible hypostasis of the various moments of thinking" (MF 56).

Appreciating that the "whole" "thought process" is "implicit in any given object" "dramatizes the irresistible link between a formal concept and the historical reality in which it originated" (MF 338, 335). "The mind" thereby "restores and regrounds its earlier notions in a new glimpse of reality," and is "reminded" that "the self-evident draws its force from hosts of buried presuppositions" (MF 372, 308).[5] The "dialectical process" was thus "designed to dispel" that "substantiality of thought" whereby a "theory about the world" "tends to become an object for the mind" with the "permanency of a real thing," as in the "academic thinking which mistakes its own conceptual categories for solid parts" of "the real world" (MF 56f). "There is a profound incompatibility between a 'scientific' method, which seeks to restrict its work to pure positivities, and a dialectical one," which, pursuing the "paradoxical element of the negative, is alone capable of doing justice to 'mixed' phenomena like ideology" (IT 211).

Hence, "dialectical thinking was designed to overcome" the "positivistic and empirical illusion" that "emphasizes" the "individual fact or item at the expense of the network of relations" and pursues "the overt presentation of content in its own right" (MF 54, x). "Anglo-American empiricism" has a "preference for segments," "isolated objects," and "free-standing elements" in order to "avoid observation of those larger wholes and totalities which if they had to be seen would force the mind" "into uncomfortable social and political conclusions" (PL 23f; cf. MF 183).

"Marxism," in contrast, implies an "imperative to totalize," that is, to "put"

---

[4] Jameson finds "the non-dialectical character of much of what passes for Marxist criticism" even in such major figures as Christopher Caudwell, who is barely mentioned, and Lucien Goldman, who is so marginalized (e.g., for being "not properly Structuralist," whatever that means) that Jameson devotes a footnote to a "reminder" of Goldmann's "incomparable role" "in the reawakening of Marxist theory" (MF 375; PL 128, 213, ix; PU 44).

[5] This process is divided into two stages; first, the "Hegelian" "consciousness of the way in which our conceptual instruments" "determine the shape and limit of the results"; and second, the "specifically Marxist consciousness" of "the profoundly historical character of our socio-economic situation" (MF 372f).

"details" "in perspective as parts or functions of some larger totality" (PU 53; MF 183). This "totalization" is a not merely a harmonizing or levelling, but a "dialectical" "project" "involving" "negation" (MF 231). The "profoundly comparative character" of "dialectical work" depends on the "differential perception" that "allows us to see what something is through the awareness of what it is not" (MF 311; cf. PL 119, 168). In "dialectical thinking," "phenomena are defined *against* each other" (MF 95f). "Ideas are best located and defined with respect to their opposites" (MF 287).

In "a genuine dialectical opposition," one term is "positive" and the other is "negative" (PL 119). "The dialectical reversal" "turns" a "phenomenon into its opposite," "transforming from negative to positive, and from positive to negative" (MF 309). Such a "changing of valences" (as "used by Bloch") "suggests" "that every negative" "implies a positive which is ontologically prior to it" (MF 132f)— a converse of deconstruction's privileging of absence over presence.[6] In an "abundant society," "the philosopher" must attempt the "revival of negation" as the "process," according to Marcuse (1955), whereby "a genuinely human existence can only be achieved" (MF 110, 108). Marcuse fears that "the consumer's society, the society of abundance, has lost the experience of the negative" because "the system" wields "the power" "to transform even its adversaries into its own mirror image" (MF 108, 111). "The Utopian idea, on the contrary," "takes the form of a stubborn negation of all that is" (MF 111). "Happiness" can be "a measure and an enlargement of human possibilities" only "as a symbolic refusal of everything" the "consumer's society" "has to offer" (MF 112). "Negation" is thus essential to "the revival of the Utopian impulse" (MF 110), as will be noted further on (p. 401).

A mental movement related to the dialetical reversal is the polarizing of "contradiction," a "notion" "central to any Marxist cultural analysis" (PU 80). "The practice of negative dialectics" moves "away from the official content of an idea" toward the "contradictory forms" "such ideas have taken" within "the concrete social situation" (MF 55). The "antinomy, a dilemma for the human mind" "on the level of pure thought," "'reflects' some more basic contradiction in social life" (PL 213, 161; cf. PU 117, 166).[7] "The imaginary resolution" of "an

---

[6] Jameson suggests that "Derrida's" "entire work may be read" as a "demystification of a host of unconscious or naturalized binary oppositions in contemporary and traditional thought" (PU 111). But seeing "the ultimate origin of the binary opposition in the older 'centered' master code of theocentric power societies" leads from "metaphysics" to "ethics" as "the ideological vehicle and legitimation of concrete structures of power and domination" and therefore advocates a move "from Derrida to Nietzsche."

[7] Elsewhere, Jameson distinguishes between the "dialectical" "contradiction" and the "semiotic" "antinomy" (PU 166). He suggests that since the "contradiction" is not "immediately conceptualized by the text," it finds "symptomatic expression" in "a system of antinomies," whose "privileged form" is the "binary opposition" "articulated" in the research of "semiotics" (PU 82f). However, "Soviet semiology" "explicitly assimilates the binary opposition to a dialectic of presence and absence" (PL 120). See p. 403.

objective contradiction" is termed an "ideologeme," constituting "the smallest intelligible unit of the essentially antagonistic collective discourses of social class" (PU 118, 76, 87).[8] "Class discourse" is "essentially *dialogical*," and "normally" "*antagonistic*": "two opposing discourses fight it out within the general unity of a shared code" (PU 84) (cf. Bakhtin, 1973a, 1973b). All this fits the tenet of "Marxism" that "the constitutive form of class relationships is always dichotomous" "between a dominant and a laboring class," with the corollary that "capitalism," unable to "understand" the "historical existence of the environment," "is the primal contradiction upon which all later, more specialized and abstract dilemmas are founded" (PU 83; MF 186).

Because "for dialectical thinking," the "ultimate system of systems" is "history," Jameson's "imperative" is "always historicize!" (PL 93; PU 9). But like Jauss,[9] he warns against "naive historicism" that records "only individual changes, isolated facts" in a "scientific but meaningless" fashion (PL 97, 5) (cf. Eikhenbaum, 1936). "Marxism" is a "concrete movement of reflection" "in a consciousness of ourselves as at once the product and the producer of history" (MF 372f). The "historical situation" does not operate in a direct "causal" fashion, but "shuts down" some "possibilities" and "opens up" "new ones" (PU 148; cf. MF 345). That is, "history" "pre-selects a certain number of structural possibilities for actualization" from among "the total number of permutations and combinations inherently possible in the model in question" (PL 128).

"For Marxist historiography," "permanence and continuity" "are the illusion, and change and struggle the reality" —"a constant working out of hidden contradictions, a perpetual but concealed violence which comes to the surface from time to time" (MF 259; cf. MF 219, 288, 325). However, "Marxism" offers "two alternate languages" "in which any given phenomenon can be described": "history can be written either subjectively, as the history of class struggle, or objectively, as the development of the economic modes of production and their evolution from their own internal contradictions" (MF 297).

"Marxists" "hold" that "the forms of human consciousness and the mechanisms of human psychology are not timeless and everywhere essentially the same, but rather situation-specific and historically produced" (PU 152). "Not

---

[8] The "-eme" ending marks the word as a calque from descriptive linguistics with its "phonemes," "morphemes," and so on. Yet whereas those "minimal units" could be almost mechanically isolated and identified by the analyst, the "inventorying" of "ideologemes" is an "immense" "task" "scarcely even begun" (PU 88). Jameson makes them all "essentially narrative," presumably to link them to "history"; one example is "ressentiment" (PU 88, 201).

[9] Although Jauss and Jameson don't notice each other in their books, they agree on many points: the paradigm character of art for history, politics, or sociology; the question-answer character of the art work; the situating of each art work in its historical series; the interface of synchronic with diachronic; the historical variability but non-arbitrariness of interpretation; the allegorizing tendency of orthodox Marxism; the construal of Freud's work as a theory of human relations to the past; and so on.

only the theories, but the very problems and categories of thought" are "in constant historical change and have no fixed and objective reality" (MF 343). Hence, "the problem of the concept of history is essentially a question of models and not of realities" (PL 188). "All conscious thought takes place within the limits of a given model" and "is determined by it" (PL 101). So "the history of thought is the history of its models," which, "for the Structuralists" at least, would "replace" the "history of objects" (PL v, 129).

Each "model" has a "lifetime" during which it first "permits hosts of new perceptions and discoveries" and "enlarges or refocuses corners of reality which the older terminology had left obscured or had taken for granted"; it then "declines" as it demands frequent "readjusting," and is finally "exchanged for a new one" (PL v, 132). Jameson feels "certain" that "such a replacement marks an absolute break" and "the beginning of something hitherto unprecedented" (PL vi). "The new" cannot be "consciously prepared" or "devised" "out of whole cloth." This rather Kuhnian[10] emphasis on discontinuity matches Jameson's "dialectical" determination to "define" "phenomena" "against each other" (MF 95f). We may also appreciate his focus on the "originality" of a person or source.[11]

This interest in mental models does not, however, lead toward idealization. "Genuine dialectical thinking" must avoid "the idealizing tendency inherent in abstract thought" by attaining a "more vivid apprehension of reality" (MF 371f). "Abstraction" is "a reduction" whereby we "substitute" "simplified models, schematic abstract ideas," and thereby "do violence to reality" (MF 222). "Alienation" may set in, and "the abstract mind" may be "powerless" to "analyze genuine three-dimensional action" (MF 164, 211).[12]

"The dialectical method," in contrast, "can be acquired only by a concrete working through of detail, by a sympathetic internal experience of the gradual construction of a system according to its inner necessity" (MF xi). "Concrete reality" enters "knowledge" as "concrete thought" (PL 107; cf. Althusser, 1965). "The hermeneutic dimension of dialectical thinking" can "restore to the abstract cultural fact" "its concrete context" (MF 348). Since "the ultimate object" is "the concrete," "the method" maintains "preference for the concrete totality over the separate abstract parts" (MF 309, 45). This "totalizing, wholistic character"

---

[10] Kuhn is said to have "independently" illustrated the "Structuralist theory of models" (PL 136). I find Kuhn's metascience hardly dialectical in a Jamesonian sense, but rather more in the fragmenting Anglo-American tradition Marxism repudiates. The history of science is treated as a matter of facts about scientists and discoveries.

[11] MF 12, 31, 66, 87, 106, 163, 184, 317; PL 4, 26, 39, 58, 82, 105f, 111, 136, 157, 177; PU 29, 57, 93, 126, 133, 156, 191, 257.

[12] The concept of "alienation" diverges from the "Hegelian opposition" of "the concrete and the abstract" by "quietly eliminating" "the Utopian moment" (MF 163f). The "powerlessness" alluded to here is "demonstrated" in Sartre's "earlier plays" (MF 211f).

creates "the peculiar difficulty of dialectical writing" —"as though with each new idea you were bound to recapitulate the entire system" (MF 306).

"Totalizing thought" might "lead to a vision of social life as a whole" (MF 368; cf. MF 232). Within this project, "the concrete" allows us to "mediate between one level and another of reality, and translate technical analysis of the idea into its truth in the lived reality of social history" (MF 354). "Mediation" is here "characterized" as "the invention of an analytic terminology or code which can be applied equally to two or more structurally distinct objects or sectors of being" (PU 225). Against the notions of "homology (or isomorphism, or structural parallelism),"[13] Jameson argues that "it is not necessary" that "each of the objects" "be seen" as "having the same structure or emitting the same message" (PU 43, 225f). "Mediation" is rather a "dialectical mechanism" for applying "the same language" to "quite distinct objects or levels of an object," for "moving or modulating from one level or feature of the whole to another," and for "adapting analyses and findings from one level to another" (PU 28, 226, 39).

We may thereby "restore, at least methodologically, the lost unity of social life" beset by "fragmentation" in "late capitalism," and "demonstrate that widely distant elements of the social totality are ultimately part of the same global historical process" in their "underlying reality" (PU 226, 39f). "Mediation" "establishes" the "background" of "general identity" against which "local identification or differentiation can be registered" (PU 42). We can for instance "unify a whole social field around a theme or idea"; or "demonstrate" that "the same essence is at work in the specific languages of culture as in the organization of the relations of production" (PU 28, 39f).

We see here a Marxism that reassembles as it dismantles. Such proceedings have "Utopian" overtones, above all in Ernst Bloch's (1959) "hermeneutic" whereby "everything" becomes "a manifestation of that primordial movement" "toward ultimate identity with a transfigured world" (MF 120). "All class consciousness" is "Utopian, insofar as it expresses the unity of a collectivity" as a "*figure* for the ultimate concrete collective life" of a "classless society" (PU 290f). "Utopian thought", though it diverted "revolutionary energy into idle wish-fulfillment" in "older society," now "keeps alive the possibility of a world qualitatively distinct from this one"; "practical thinking" is "a capitulation to the system" (MF 110f). As Marcuse (1955: 144) insists, "the Utopian concept" is "'the attempt to draft a theoretical construct beyond the performance principle'" (MF 111).

---

[13] A negative opinion is given on the "'homologies'" developed by Lucien Goldman (1964, 1973) (PU 43f; MF 375) (cf. Note 4). Such a conception is said to be the true target of Althusser's attack on "mediation" as "the establishment of symbolic identities between the various levels" which "thereby lose" their "constitutive autonomy" that Althusser insists must be "respected" (PU 39, 44). Against the "Hegelian" "expressive causality" of classical "mediation," he argues for "structural causality," wherein "mediation" must "pass through the structure" of the "totality" (PU 39, 41).

"Utopia" is definable as "a world in which meaning and life," "man and the world" "inside" and "outside," are "at one"; or as a "moment" of "adequation of subject to object" (MF 173, 143, 146). "The transfigured time of Utopia offers a perpetual present" with a "total ontological satisfaction of every instant"; even "death cannot damage" such "a life fully realized" (MF 143).[14] The nature of "the Utopian impulse" to "point to something other" and to "speak in figures" might explain why the "allegorical structure of being" is given "symbolic and allegorical expression"[15] by "art and religion" (MF 142f). "In art, consciousness prepares itself for a change in the world"; "the experience of the imaginary offers" "that total satisfaction of the personality and of Being" whereby "the Utopian ideal, the revolutionary blueprint, may be conceived" (MF 90).

"The proving ground for all Utopian activity" is "concrete narration" (MF 173). "Narrative modes" lend a "Utopian significance" to "concrete experiences of time," and "presuppose" a "mutual reconciliation" of "subject" and "object" (MF 149, 190) (cf. Lukács, 1917-18, 1962; and Iser, AR 135, 154). "The movement of the world in time toward the future's ultimate moment" parallels the "formal" "sense in which all plot may be seen as a movement toward Utopia" (MF 146). Jameson characteristically prefers a "formal" "notion of Utopia" enacted in the "novelists'" "formal organization of their styles" rather than in the "use" of "Utopian material as content" (MF 145f, 174).

This high regard for narration comes into sharper perspective when Jameson avows that "history" "is *not* a text, for it is fundamentally non-narrative and nonrepresentational"; yet adds at once that it "is inaccessible to us except in textual form" (PU 82, 35). Hence, he proposes to "restructure the problematics of ideology," "of history, and of cultural production, around the all-informing process of *narrative*" as "the central function or *instance* of the human mind" (PU 13).[16] He agrees here with Lukács that "narration is our basic way of coming to terms with time itself and with concrete history" (PL 62).

"Historicism" (or "expressive causality") as envisioned by Althusser would be "an interpretive allegory in which a sequence of historical events or texts and artifacts is rewritten in terms of some deeper, underlying, and more 'fundamen-

---

[14] "This deathless promise" is a "symbol of hope" that gets "distorted" in "otherworldly religious forms" (MF 114). But Frye managed to "assimilate the salvational perspective of romance to a reexpression of Utopian longings" (PU 104f).

[15] "Symbolic" and "allegorical" are opposed, following Bloch (1959), as tendencies toward "unity" and "difference," respectively (MF 146) (compare de Man's "temporal" account, pp. 270f). Sometimes, Jameson uses "allegorical" as a pejorative term, as in the reproaches he brings against "orthodox Marxism" (PU 32f). Elsewhere, though, the "allegorical" is simply an aspect of "interpretation," for example, to "open up of the text to multiple meanings, to successive rewritings and overwritings" (PU 10, 29) (cf. p. 398).

[16] Compare Arthur Danto's (1965) demonstration (also cited by Jauss, TAR 60f) that "even so-called scientific historiography may be said to have an essentially narrative structure" (MF 205). However, Danto's "definition of historical narration as any form of causal explanation" (PL 66f) is so broad it would be hard to get outside it.

tal'" "hidden master narrative," such as the "providential history" of "Hegel or Marx" (PU 28). "Such master narratives have inscribed themselves" in "texts as well as in our thinking about them" and "reflect a fundamental dimension of our collective thinking" and "fantasies about history and reality" (PU 34). Jameson correspondingly prizes "the novel" as "a way of coming to terms with a temporal experience that cannot" be "dealt with any other way"; and as "a symbolic act that must reunite or harmonize heterogeneous narrative paradigms," each with a "specific and contradictory ideological meaning" (PL 73; PU 144). The "novel" is "problematic in its very structure," "a reflection on the very possibility of story-telling" (MF 172).

The "Utopianism" of a "reconciliation between the subject and objectivity, between existence and world," "would be possible only in a society" where "the individual was already reconciled" with "the organization of things and people" (MF 38, 49). In "the modern experience of the world," however, "the primacy of the subject," required "in Hegel" as the "foundation" of "the dialectic," is an "illusion"; "subject and outside world can never find such ultimate identity" (MF 55f). So "a negative dialectic" must "affirm the notion and value of an ultimate synthesis, while negating it" "in every concrete case" (MF 56).

"The dialectic" also "provides a way for decentering the subject concretely, and for transcending the 'ethical' in the direction of the political and the collective" (PU 60). The "'decentering' of the consciousness of the individual subject" becomes a "painful" step in "the dialectical reversal" between "individual and class" (PU 283). For "structuralism," "the subject is a function of a more impersonal system or language structure" (PL 134; cf. Culler, PO 28, 258). But for "a Marxist point of view, this experience of the decentering" and "the theories" "devised to map it are to be seen as the signs of the dissolution of an essentially bourgeois ideology of the subject and of psychic unity or identity" (PU 125). "The disintegration of the autonomous subject" "marks" "the gradual alienation of social relations" and their "transformation" into "self-regulating mechanisms" that "reduce" the "independent personality" to a "component part," a "receiving apparatus for injunctions from all levels of the system" (MF 27f). When "the entire business system" "depends" on "the automatic sale of products" unrelated to any "biological or social need," "marketing psychology" "reaches down into the last private zones of individual life" to "awaken artificial needs" (MF 35f). "Thus the total organization of the economy" uses new "techniques of mystification" to "dispel the last remnant of the older autonomous subject or ego" (MF 36). "What remains of the subjective" can "no longer" "distinguish between external suggestion and internal desire," or between "the private and the institutionalized." This "death of the subject" in "post-industrial monopoly capitalism" is oddly parallel to "the collective structure of some future socialist world" (PL 140f).

"The disintegration of the autonomous subject" in "Western middle-class society" is reflected in "psychoanalytic theories" and especially in "the Freudian topology of mental functions" (MF 27; PU 125 cf. Iser, AR 159). Hence, Jameson envisions a reconciliation between Marx and Freud, the two "great negative diagnosticians of contemporary culture" who devised "two codes or languages into which behavior may be alternately translated" (PU 281; MF 214). "Freudianism and Marxism" shared the "conviction 'that understanding consists in the *reduction* of one type of reality to another; that true reality is never what is manifest on the surface; and that the nature of truth may be measured by the degree to which it tries to elude you'" (PL 142; Lévi-Strauss, 1955: 49f).[17] The "confrontation between Marx and Freud dramatizes" the "fundamental contradiction" "between the outside and the inside, between public and private, work and leisure, the sociological and the psychological," "between the political and the poetic, objectivity and subjectivity, the collective and the solitary—between society and the monad" (MF 85; cf. IT 219).

Like Holland,[18] Jameson eulogizes psychoanalysis. It is "the most elaborate interpretive system of recent times," and "the only really new and original hermeneutic" since the "medieval system" of "four levels" (PU 61, 31).[19] Its "prestige and influence" "as a method and a model" have "never been so immense" (PU 65). Also, "Freud's topology is the most striking model of time oriented toward the past" (MF 128; cf. Jauss, AL 12).

Like Bloom (ANX 115), Jameson has less "interest" in the Freudian "sexual symbolism" (PU 65) foregrounded by Holland, Bleich, and Millett. He merely remarks that the "symbolic possibilities" of "sexuality" "are dependent on its preliminary exclusion from the social field" (PU 64). Only its "isolation" made it "develop into an independent sign system" for decoding "overtly nonsexual behavior." The "priority" of "sexual oppression over that of social class" is deemed a "false problem"; "sexism and patriarchy" are "forms of alienation" arising from "the oldest mode of production" "with its division of labor between men and women" —a thesis that makes "radical feminism" calling to "annul the patriarchal" "perfectly consistent with an expanded Marxian framework" (PU 99f).

---

[17] "Structuralism" was naturally prone to "read Freud and Marx" as "twin versions of the gap between signifier and signified"; and "either to ignore the specific content of the two systems, or else to interpret it allegorically" (PL 195; cf. PL 169).

[18] Holland's work is mentioned occasionally, e.g., his "powerful critique of myth criticism" (PU 67) (cf. Note 31), but not prominently used, perhaps because Holland focuses on individual identities, not social collectives. Jameson's conjecture that "the surface" of a "work" may be "but a pretext, serving both to divert the mind from its deepest operations and fantasies and to motivate those fantasies" sounds like Holland, except that a "fantasy" of "collective life" is at once appended (MF 406).

[19] Jameson in fact sees "analogies" between the "Freudian" "repressive simplification" and the "reduction" that "the medieval system of the four levels" creates in aligning the "collective history" of "the people of Israel" with the "individual" "life of Christ" (PU 30). Jameson regards the two levels of the "moral" and the "anagogical" as "interpretations" whereby "the textual apparatus is transformed into a 'libidinal apparatus,' a machinery for ideological investment." The "moral" yields a "psychological reading," while the "anagogical" yields a "political reading" (PU 31). Compare Note 23.

Jameson prefers to focus on "the more burning question of interpretation" and the "contribution" of "such fundamental hermeneutic manuals as *The Interpretation of Dreams* and *Jokes and the Unconscious*" (PU 65), the works preferred by critics in general (e.g., Holland, DY 54). Like Freud, Jameson is attuned to "the essentially figurative quality of unconscious or regressive thought," whereby "all drives are mediated through their object language" of "images or fantasies" (MF 99). "Freudian theory" envisions "two stories at work in the topology of the psyche": the "surface story" as a "disguise," and the "repressed, unconscious desire" or "fantasy-satisfaction" (MF 98). Freud first "supposed the unconscious fantasy to have actually taken place in reality"; but he later "abandoned" this idea and retained the "fantasy" for "its dramatic and narrative value as a *scene*" (cf. Fiedler, NT 308; Bleich, SC 30f; Culler, PS 180).

Jameson acknowledges Deleuze and Guattari's (1977) "recent attack" on "Freudian interpretation" for being "a reduction and a rewriting of the whole rich and random multiple realities of concrete everyday experience into the contained, strategically pre-limited terms of the family narrative" (PU 21f). They "denounced" a "system of allegorical interpretation in which the data of one narrative line are radically impoverished" by "rewriting" them "according to the paradigm of another narrative" "taken as" "the master code" and "proposed as the ultimate hidden or unconscious *meaning*" (PU 22). Jameson approves their intent to "reassert the specificity of the political content of everyday life and to reclaim it" from the "reduction to the merely subjective." Indeed, his own proposal to integrate Freudianism with Marxism has much the same goal.

A "substantial and reflective shift" of the "Freudian hermeneutic" occurred in "the Lacanian rewriting": "consciousness" and its "illusions (feeling of personal identity, the myth of the ego or self, and so forth) become rigorous and self-imposed limitations" on "individual wish-fulfillment" (PU 66). Though still "couched in terms of the individual biological subject," "Lacan's work" moves its concern from "unconscious processes or blockages" over to "the formation of the subject and its constitutive illusions" in a manner "not incompatible with a broader historical framework" (PU 153). He is credited with "underscoring the relationship between emerging psychoanalysis and its historical raw material" (PU 62).

"Lacan's doctrine" resembles Structuralism by its "translation of the Freudian topology into linguistic terms" (PL 169). When children "acquire language," he asserted, they enter "the Symbolic Order" that is "impersonal or superpersonal," yet enables the "sense of identity" (PL 130; cf. PU 175f). The "structure of language" would then "determine" the "secondary phenomena" of "consciousness, personality," and "the subject"; and "the unconscious" could be grasped as "language which escapes the subject in its structure and effects" or as "discourse of the other" (PL 130, 138, 171). For example, Lacan's opined that "the dream has the structure of a sentence" beset by "syntactic displacements" and "semantic condensations" (PL 120f). "Neurosis" would be "a movement of repression" which "attempts to stem the flight from one signifier to another by fixating on a single one, by choosing for itself a transcendental signified"; "psychosis" would be "a writing out of all the possible variations of a given paradigm" (PL 138f). Though Jameson is also preoccupied with language and appropriates "Lacanian terminology and thematics," a model is still needed to "transcend individualistic categories and modes of interpretation" (PU 152f, 68).

Accordingly, Jameson advances his "doctrine of the political unconscious" (PU 152f, 68).[20] "Our approach" to "history" "as an absent cause" and "to the Real itself necessarily passes through its prior textualization, its narrativization in the political unconscious" (PU 35).[21] "All literature" must therefore "be informed" by the "political unconscious" in the sense of being "read as a symbolic meditation on the destiny of community" (PU 70). Having "elaborate hermeneutic geiger counters," "the political unconscious" can "raise, in symbolic form, issues of social change and counterrevolution"; reveal the "permanencies" of "material production" "underneath" the "formal structures" of a "text"; "restore to the surface of the text the repressed and buried reality" of "fundamental history," that is, the "uninterrupted narrative" of "'class struggle'"; and so on (PU 173, 215, 20).

Seen from this perspective, "the archaic fantasy material psychoanalytic criticism feels able to detect must always pass through a determinate social and historical situation" (PU 142). "The fantasy level of a text would then be something like the primal motor force" "diverted to the service of other, ideological functions, and reinvested" by the "political unconscious." Jameson's dialectical thought reappears in the idea that "the unconscious master narrative" —whose "initial unworked form" is "the Imaginary" in "fantasy" and "wish-fulfillment" — is a "contradictory structure," whose "functions" and "events" "demand repetition, permutation, and the ceaseless generation of various structural 'resolutions' which are never satisfactory" (PU 180).

This merger of social, cultural, and psychological critique, as I have tried to outline it, yields Jameson's foundation for a "theory" such as "literary-critical practice" "presupposes" (cf. PU 58). "The verbal construction of literature" "allows it" to "serve as a paradigm for other, more properly sociological, sign systems" (PL 146; cf. Jauss, TAR 62). "Cultural studies" can hence be a strategic "place for Marxism to reassert its claim" as a "universal science," because "textual

---

[20] This solution recalls Jung's expansion of the "unconscious" into a collective dimension. But Jameson regards the Jungian "system" in *Psychological Types* as "historical thinking arrested halfway, a thought which, on the road to concrete history, takes fright and attempts to convert its insights into eternal essences, into attributes between which the human spirit oscillates" (MF 93f). Frye's approach is another target of this accusation.

[21] The "Real" is capitalized to signal its derivation from Lacan, for whom it is a "notion" of "that which 'resists symbolization absolutely'"; Jameson twice mentions it in close proximity to Althusser's "history as a absent cause" (PU 35, 82). For Lacan, the "Real" is an order opposed to the "Imaginary" and the "Symbolic," but is nonetheless inaccessible (Ragland-Sullivan 1986: 130f, 90; Lemaire 1977: 40f, 51f, 115f).

and interpretive problems are in them more immediately visible and available for study and reflection than in the more apparently empirical sciences" (PU 38).

Jameson "argues the perspectives" and "critical insights" of "Marxism as necessary preconditions for adequate literary comprehension" (PU 75). Just as "Marxism" insists that "pure thought functions as a disguised mode of social behavior," our "analysis" can "explore the multiple paths that lead to the unmasking of cultural artifacts as socially symbolic acts" (MF 161; PU 20). "Literature plays a central role in the dialectical process" as a "privileged microcosm in which to observe dialectical thinking at work" (MF xi). "Literary criticism" becomes "dialectical" too when it "reconciles the inner and the outer, the intrinsic and the extrinsic, the existential and the historical" (MF 330, 348, 416). We can reveal how the "world of daily life" is "the determinate situation, dilemma, contradiction, or subtext" for which "the practice of language in a literary work" "comes as a symbolic resolution" (PU 42; cf. MF 43, 348, 383; PL 24, 161, 197, 212; PU 79f, 83, 85; Lévi-Strauss, 1958; Adorno, 1969-70). The "concreteness" of "art" "permits life and experience to be felt as a totality" (MF 169).

Jameson also "argues" the "priority" and "semantic richness" of "a Marxist interpretive framework" as compared to "ethical," "psychoanalytic," "myth-critical," "semiotic," "structural," and "theological" "methods" (PU 10, 17). Since "the political perspective" is "the absolute horizon of all reading and all literature," he presents "Marxism" as "the 'untranscendable horizon' that subsumes such apparently antagonistic or incommensurable critical operations, assigning them an undoubted sectoral validity within itself," "at once cancelling and preserving them" (PU 10). The "juxtaposition" of these other "methods" "with a dialectical or totalizing, properly Marxist ideal of understanding" should "demonstrate" their "structural limitations," "the 'local' ways in which they construct their objects of study," and "the strategies of containment" for "projecting the illusion that their readings are somehow complete and self-sufficient." The "contemporary American 'pluralism'" fosters "the coexistence of methods" in "the intellectual and academic marketplace" (PU 31). There, Jameson suspects a "negative" "program": "to forestall the systematic articulation and totalization of interpretive results which can only lead to embarrassing questions" about "the relationship between them," "the place of history, and the ultimate ground of narrative and textual production" (MF 32).

Dialectical as usual, Jameson maintains that "literariness, the distinguishing element of literature," "depends" on an "awareness of what the element is not, of what has been omitted from the work," as well as "what the element is" (PL 43). "One of the terms of the dialectical opposition is always outside the work; it is the work's other side," "its otherness in the face of history" (PL 120). It would be "undialectical" to seek "some ultimate and changeless element beneath the multiplicity of literary appearance" (PL 45). He therefore elects not to "study" "the 'objective' structures" of the "text, the historicity of its forms and content," its "linguistic possibilities," or "the function of its aesthetic" (PU 9).

Instead, he adopts the "organizational fiction" that "we never really confront a text immediately" as a "thing in itself," but only "as the always-already-read" (PU 9).[22] "We apprehend" texts "through sedimented layers of previous interpretations, or —if the text is brand-new—through sedimented reading habits and categories" of "inherited interpretive traditions." In Jameson's "method" of "metacommentary," "the object of study is less the text itself than the interpretations through which we attempt to confront and appropriate it," where "interpretation" is "construed as an essentially allegorical act" of "rewriting a given text in terms of" a "master code" (PU 9f). "Interpretation proper" is a "strong rewriting" and "presupposes" "some mechanism of mystification or repression," some "censored dimension," so that we need to "seek a latent meaning behind a manifest one, or to rewrite the surface categories of a text in the stronger language of a more fundamental interpretive code" (PU 60; MF 413). "Dialectical self-consciousness" supports this search by impelling "a sudden distancing which permits the most familiar elements of the reading experience to be seen again strangely, as though for the first time, making visible the unexpected articulation of the work into parts" (MF 52) (cf. Adorno, 1958-65).

Jameson contemplates criticism as a "semantic enrichment and enlargement of the inert givens and materials of a particular text" (PU 75). This process is to occur "within three concentric frameworks": "political history" as "a chroniclike sequence of happenings in time"; "society" as "a constitutive tension and struggle between social classes"; and "history" as "the sequence of modes of production and the succession and destiny of the various human social formations." "These distinct semantic horizons" correspond to "distinct moments of the process of interpretation";[23] "each phase" "governs a distinct reconstruction of its object," "'the text'" (PU 75f). The project Jameson outlines might further Hegel's initiative to "subsume intrinsic and extrinsic criticism" by treating "the work of art on its own terms" and yet "replacing it" in its "larger external context" (MF 330). Yet the project is hugely ambitious and arduous, and Jameson concedes he has only made a modest start (cf. PU 88; MF xi, 339f).

"Within" the "first" "horizon," "the object of study" is "the 'text'" "coinciding with the individual literary work," although "grasped" "as a *symbolic act*" (PU 76). This "act" "generates" its "own context" for purposes of "transformation," and "brings into being that very situation" "to which it is also" "a reaction" (PU

---

[22] The formula "always already" is traced to Althusser ("toujours-déjà-donné"), (PL 184), whence it passed through Derrida to the (un-Marxist) Yale group, who use it like a nervous tic, perhaps to elide causes and origins. "Capitalism" is an example of "just such an always-already-begun dynamic" (PU 279f).

[23] This division is likened to Frye's "successive 'phases' in our interpretation" (PU 75), but no precise mapping between the two schemes is offered. Jameson's first "horizon" appears to subsume Frye's first three, leaving the second and third to match Frye's "archetypal" and "anagogical," respectively. But Frye's levels are designated in ways that I find scarcely historical, and not at all political, focused more on the "eternal essences" Jameson in fact sees there (MF 93f).

81f). The act thereby "encourages" "the illusion" that "there was never any extra- or non-textual reality before the text" (PU 82). Jameson proposes a corresponding "type of interpretation": "rewriting" the literary text in such a way that the latter may itself be seen as the rewriting or restructuration of a prior historical or ideological *subtext*" "(re)constructed after the fact" of "external reality" (PU 81). "The literary or aesthetic act therefore always entertains some active relationship with the Real" by "drawing" it "into its own texture." The "ideological" aspect of "the aesthetic act" also inheres in its (already cited) "function of inventing imag- inary or formal 'solutions' to unresolvable social contradictions" (PU 79). Dis- covering these "contradictions" reveals the "text's symbolic efficacy" and "con- strues purely formal patterns as a symbolic enactment of the social within the formal and the aesthetic" (PU 77).

Within the "second" "horizon," "the object" is "the great collective and class discourses" composed of "ideologemes," the latter being, as noted (p. 389), mini- mal units representing "the imaginary resolution" of "an objective contradiction" (PU 76, 118, 87). The "illusion" of "autonomy which a printed text projects must now be systematically undermined" (PU 85). "Individual phenomena are re- vealed as social facts and institutions" when "the organizing categories of analysis become those of social class" (PU 83; cf. MF 376-382). In "dialogical" or "antag- onistic" "class discourse," the "ruling class" will "explore" "legitimation," while "an oppositional culture" will try to "undermine the dominant 'value system'" (PU 84). Here, the "text is grasped as a symbolic move" in an "ideological confrontation between the classes" (PU 85). The "contradiction," which in the first "horizon" had been "limited to the situation of the individual text," now "appears" "dialogical as the irreconcilable demands and positions of antagonistic classes." The critic attempts an "artificial reconstruction of the voice" to which "cultural monuments" "were initially opposed," especially the "voice" of "popu- lar cultures" (PU 85; cf. MF 377). Jameson grasps "hegemonic forms" "as a process" of "the cultural universalization of forms which originally expressed the situation of 'popular,' subordinate, or dominated groups" (PU 86; cf. Wellek and Warren, TL 46).

Within the third and "ultimate horizon," that of "human history as a whole," "both the individual text and its ideologemes" are "read in terms of" "the *ideology of form*, that is, the symbolic messages transmitted to us by the coexistence of various sign systems which are themselves traces or anticipations of modes of production" (PU 76; cf. PU 33). Here, "history itself becomes the untranscend- able ground" and "limit" of our "textual interpretations" (PU 100). The "object of study" is nothing less than "*cultural revolution*, that moment when the coexis- tence of various modes of production becomes visibly antagonistic, their contra- dictions moving to the very center of political, social, and historical life" (PU 95). This "concept" can "project a whole new framework for the humanities, in which the study of culture in the widest sense could be placed on a materialist basis" (PU 96). The "task" of "analysis" will be "the rewriting of its materials" such that "this perpetual cultural revolution" can be "read as the deeper and more permanent constitutive structure in which the empirical textual objects know intelligibility" (PU 97). Through "technical and formalistic analysis," the "text" is "restructured as a field of force in which the dynamics of sign systems of several distinct modes of production can be registered" and aligned with "a number of discontinuous and heterogeneous formal processes" "within the text" (PU 98f). Marxism and Formalism emphatically unite in this stage.

Despite Jameson's avowed intent to absorb other critical methods into his encompassing project just outlined, he harbors distinct reservations about some. "Ethical criticism" —"still" "predominant" "despite repudiation by every succes-sive generation of literary theorists" —offers only "weak rewriting" and mistakes "historical and institutional specifics" of "class cohesion" for "permanent features of human experience" (PU 59f). "Immanent criticism," from "New Criticism" to "post-structuralism," is "argued" to be "a mirage" (PU 57). The "New Critics" "fetishized language and made it the source" of "ahistorical plenitude"; they remained "within purely ethical limits" and did not "translate those ethical categories" "into social and historical terms" (MF 332). "Post-structuralism" is termed "anti-Marxist," "repudiating" "totalization in the name of difference, flux, dissemination, and heterogeneity," yet "reconfirming the status of the con-cept of totality" by the "very reaction against it" (PU 60, 53) (my own remark on de Man, p. 277).

Since "the appropriate object of study emerges only when the appearance of formal unification is unmasked as a failure or an ideological mirage," Jameson's version of a "properly structural interpretation" aims for an "explosion of the seemingly unified text into a host of clashing and contradictory elements" (PU 56). Yet the "post-structural celebration of discontinuity" should be followed by a stage where "the fragments, the incommensurable levels" and "impulses of the text" are "once again related, but in the mode of structural difference and determinate contradiction" (PU 56).[24] Jameson has thus "found it possible" both to "respect" "totalization" and to attend to "discontinuities, rifts"; "the apparently unified cultural text" can also be viewed as "a synchronic unity of structurally contradictory or heterogeneous elements, generic patterns, and discourses" (PU 56f, 141).

Somewhat surprisingly in a Marxist context, "the only philosophically coherent alternative" to an "interpretation out of the social substance" is asserted to be "one organized on a religious or theological basis, of which Northrop Frye's system is only the most recent example" (MF 402). "The greatness of Frye" "lies in his willingness to raise the issue of community" and to "draw basic, essentially

---

[24] "In Althusserian literary criticism," "the authentic function of the cultural text" is "staged" as "a subversion of one level by another" (PU 56). "Althusser and Pierre Macherey" believe "the work of aesthetic production" to be "the objectification of the ideological" as "the privileged form of this disunity."

social interpretive consequences from the nature of religion as collective representation" (PU 69). "For any contemporary reevaluation of the problem of interpretation, the most vital exchange of energies inevitably takes place between" "the psychoanalytic and the theological, between the rich and concrete practice of interpretation contained in the Freudian texts," and "the millenary theoretical reflection on the problems and dynamics of interpretation, commentary, allegory, and multiple meanings" "preserved in the religious tradition." Jameson also resembles Frye in "using the word myth not in the negative sense of that which calls for demystification, but rather in the positive meaning" of an "ordering of experience" (MF 258).[25]

Yet Frye is reproved for having propounded a "'positive' hermeneutic, which tends to filter out historical difference and the radical discontinuity of modes of production and of their cultural expressions" (PU 130). "Political and collective imagery is transformed into a mere relay in some ultimately privatizing celebration of the category of individual experience" (PU 74). A "negative hermeneutic," in contrast, would "sharpen our sense of historical difference"; "a social hermeneutic" would "restore a perspective in which the imagery of libidinal revolution and of bodily transformation" "becomes a figure for the perfected community." (PU 130, 74). Eventually, Jameson "argues" for a "Marxist" "hermeneutic" that is both "negative" as "ideological analysis" and "positive" as a "decipherment" of "Utopian impulses" (PU 296) (though we recall the negation of current society by Utopian thought, pp. 388, 412).

In a particularly thorough and sympathetic engagement with alternative approaches, Jameson presents a "survey" and "critique of the basic methodology" "Formalism" and Structuralism," whose "most tangible achievements" were in "literary analysis" (PL x).[26] He proposes to "lay bare" as "intellectual totalities" their "absolute presuppositions," which "are too fundamental to be either accepted or rejected."

Though "the Formalists" thought of "Marxism, in its Soviet form," as "an ideological adversary," they were "far more" "dialectical" than the "New Critics" (PL 102, 47). Hence, Jameson does "not regard Formalism" as "at all irreconcilable with Marxism"; its "aesthetic concept" of "'making-strange'" is a "manifestation" "on the aesthetic level" of "the movement of dialectical consciousness" (MF 409, 373f). Such a reconciliation seems to be on the agenda of *Marxism and Form*, with its vision of the "'absolute formalism' of Marxism," its "essen-

---

[25] The illustration is the "myth of revolution" as a "notion" "best understood not so much in direct political and theoretical terms" as "in terms of time and of narration, in what are ultimately literary categories" (MF 257f). This prospect would make "revolution" a matter of "form" via "the new temporal order of experience it permits" (MF 258).

[26] Culler's survey of *Structuralist Poetics* makes no reference to Jameson's earlier one, which may not have appeared in time; and Culler was anxious to leave Marxism out in any case. Jameson critiques Culler's work on Flaubert (IT 225-32) fairly genially, though it does "not really supply" the "framework" of "history" (IT 231).

tially" "Formalist" "analyses," and its insistence that all sorts of things—"sociology of culture," "Marxist literary criticism," "historical evolution" and "revolution," plus "all visible matter," including "commodities" —are "forms" (MF 373, 409, 4, 378, 58, 39, 96; cf. MF 196, PU 99).

"Structuralism," being "one of the first consistent and self-conscious attempts to work out a philosophy of models," also merits a "genuine critique" so that we can "integrate present-day linguistic discoveries into our philosophical systems" (PL vii, 101). The "point of departure of Structuralism" was "the primacy of the linguistic model," with "language" being the "master code" and holding an "incomparable ontological priority" among "all the elements of consciousness and of social life" (PL vii; PU 61; cf. PL 112, 193; cf. Culler, PO 4). The "signifier" "seems able to exist as a kind of free-floating autonomous organization," while the "signified" is "never visible directly" unless "the analyst" "organizes it into a new sign-system" (PL 145, 149). Hence, the "arbitrary and absolute decision" was made to treat "reality in terms of linguistic systems" (PL 185). "Reality" emerged as "a series of various interlocking systems" of "signs" —an "essentially cryptographic" entity (PL 33, 142). "Truth" would then be a matter of "translating from one code to another" —an "exact formal definition" whereby "the Structuralist procedure" might become "a genuine *hermeneutics*" (PL 216; cf. PL 133).

Jameson would concur that "all perceptual systems are already languages in their own right" (PL 152). But he would not simply "displace the problem of the referent" by having the latter "constantly reabsorbed into language" (PL 212). He wants to "determine" "the precise nature of the relationship of such systems to those more overtly verbal ones which Marxism sees as forming the superstructure" (PL 212). Moreover, his "dialectical thinking" makes "history," not "language," the "ultimate system of systems" and rejects the "metaphysical presupposition as to the priority of the signifier" (PL 93, 131). Still, he can engage with a model despite such disagreements, because his own thinking is well adapted to "hold together in the mind" "distinct and even antithetical methods," albeit his "terms are not what the Structuralists themselves would have chosen to describe their work" (PL 74f, 101).

Whereas the "organic model" from "Romantic philosophy and nineteenth century scientific thinking" took "the organism as a prototype" and favored "substantialism" by treating "objects of study" as "autonomous" and "stable entities," Saussurian linguistics moved to a "relational type of perception" wherein "no object is given at any time as existing in itself" (PL vi, 36, 33, 13f). When "atomistic empirical perception of an isolated thing-in-itself" had been "abandoned," "language" was recognized as a "peculiar entity" that "nowhere takes the form of an object or substance" and has "'no immediate recognizable concrete units,'" but "only values and relationships" (PL 33, 24, 15; cf. Saussure 1966 [1916]: 149). "The category of the class" rested on "opposition or difference" rather than on "the resemblance or identity" among "elements" (PL 116). Moving in the reverse direction as Structuralism, that is, from language to society, we might detect here a parallel to Jameson's "differential concept" of social "class" with "each class" "defining itself against the other" (MF 380, 301); and, as we'll see in a moment, he has a similar idea.

By "reckoning in the position of the observer" (cf. MF 340), Jameson can see the "binary opposition" "both as underlying structure and as a method of revealing that structure" (PL 115). It functions as a "basic mechanism of thought" and a "technique for stimulating perception" or for "generating order out of random data" (PL 113, 117). If any "concept or term" "structurally presupposes" a "binary opposition" as the "basis for its intelligibility," Jameson can call "Saussure's opposition" "dialectical": "every linguistic perception holds in its mind at the same time an awareness of its own opposite" and of "the interplay of the same and the other" (PL 164, 24, 35, 168) (cf. Trier, 1931; Trubetzkoi, 1939). The "most profoundly dialectical" "opposition" is the "tension between presence and absence, positive and negative," in accord with "the Hegelian law that determination is negation" (PL 34f; cf. PU 49).

Yet Jameson acknowledges that "semiotics" saw "the binary opposition" as a "static antithesis," an "insoluble" "antinomy," or at best an "arrested" version of the truly "dialectical" "contradiction" (PL 36; PU 166f; PL 119; PU 50, 83, 117). This "model of ideological closure" "can be reappropriated" for "dialectical thinking" if we make "the concept of the signifier" not just "a series of binary oppositions," but "an attempt to *resolve* such oppositions, now thought of as contradictions" (PU 47, 83; PL 161; see p. 388). In a "dialectical reevaluation of the findings of semiotics," "this entire system is taken as a projection" of "a social contradiction" not "directly or immediately conceptualized by the text," but finding "symptomatic expression" in "a system of antinomies" (PU 82f). "Narrative" attempts to "address and 'resolve'" this; the "antinomy" "cannot be unknotted" by "pure thought" and must "generate a whole more properly narrative apparatus—the text" —to "dispel" "its intolerable closure."

This tactic of moving to a higher and broader dialectical plane might also mediate "between the synchronic methods of Saussurian linguistics and the realities of time and history" by "resolving" into a "synthesis" Saussure's "a-historical and undialectical" "distinction between synchronic and diachronic" (PL 18, x, 22).[27] In the Formalism of Tynjanov (1924), "the synchronic structure of the work includes diachrony in that it carries within itself as a negated or cancelled element" those "modes" against which it "innovates" (PL 92f). Conversely, a "genuine law of the story" demands "transposing" the "diachronic sequence of narrative events" into "a synchronic structure"; the same occurs in "periodization" (PL 69; cf. PL 96; PU 218). Moreover, Jameson's vision of "time" inherent in "the form of the sentence" and his linking "syntax" with "history" and "change" (MF xiii; PL 39) suggest a diachronic dimension even in grammatical patterns, though linguistics seldom saw it (cf. Morgan, 1975).

Still, Jameson shares the "suspicions of a dialectical tradition" about the "distortions," "problems," and "dangers" of "synchronic thought" —seeing "change and development" as "contingent" or "nonmeaningful"; fostering a "model of the 'total system'" devoid of "the negative"; and so on (PL x; PU 95, 91f). His comment on "ontological foundations," with the "synchronic" based on "the immediate lived experience of the native speaker" and "the diachronic" based on a "construction" "substituting a purely intellectual continuity for a lived one" (PL 6), discounts the way academic linguistics used synchronic models to suppress the "lived experience" of language. Symptomatic tendencies emerge when Saussure's "system of signs" "is deflected from the whole question" of "referents" or of the relation of "word to thing"; or when "structuralism" "isolated the signifier" "from what it signified" (PL 32, 111; cf. PL 83, 105f, 131, 198, 212).

A different but equally familiar dichotomy, namely "form and content," is mastered by Jameson's "dialectical notion" wherein "either term can be translated into the other" (MF 403). For him, "Saussure's concept of the 'system' implies that" "content is form" (PL 14; cf. PL viii). Correspondingly, "Formalist" "analysis" "refuses content and transposes" it "back into projections of the form" (PL 88). "The implication is that a work only seems" to "intend a determinate content; in reality it speaks only of its own conditions of coming into being, its own construction" in respect to "formal problems in the context" (PL 88f). Thus, a Formalist like Šklovskij "leaned toward" an "art which takes itself for its own subject matter" and "presents its own techniques as its own content" (PL 76).

This "optical illusion projected by the Formalist procedures" in analogy to "Saussure's disconnection of the referential" (PL 89, 83) has consequences a Marxist might regard with dismay: that "ideological content" is "only the result of the form"; that "social critique" is "merely a pretext" for "concrete technical effects"; that "'art is beyond emotion'"; that "psychological" "insights" are "mirages" "of 'truths' given off by the operation of the artistic process"; and so on (PL 78, 57, 83f). But Jameson hopes to rescue "the social basis of Formalism" by making "literature" a "double-functioning substance": "all literary works" both "speak the language of reference" and "emit" a "lateral message about their own process of formation" (PL 154, 89).

Along similar lines, the "most characteristic feature of Structuralist criticism lies" in a "transformation of form into content" (PL 198f). Here too, "literary works are about language" and are "a construction to a higher power"; "the ordinary signifier/signified relationship is complicated by yet another type of signification which bears on the nature of the code itself" (PL 199, 155). The

---

[27] Jameson's uses of "synchronic" and "diachronic" are hardly Saussurian. "Synchronic linguistics" concerns "the logical and psychological relations that bind together coexisting terms and form a system in the collective mind of speakers"; "diachronic linguistics" concerns "relations that bind together successive terms not perceived by the collective mind, but substituted for each other without forming a system" (Saussure, 1966 [1916]: 99f). Jameson goes in different directions, such as "the diachrony or sequentiality of narrative discourse" and of "the novel's form" up to the "synchrony" of its "ending" (IT 219; PL 74f).

"formal distortion inherent in the model" made "Structuralists read the content of a given work as Language itself" (PL 200f). "Poetry" in particular would be "a total linguistic system" designed for "renewed perception of the very material quality of language" (PL 49f). Again, Jameson refers us back to the "double-functionality" that got "simplified" (PL 198).

In any case, such formulations are not too uncongenial for Jameson's own interpretive program, which "construes purely formal patterns as a symbolic enactment of the social within the formal and the aesthetic" (PU 77). "Dialectical thought" is a "reversal of the form-dominated, artisanally-derived model" of "Aristotle"; "form is regarded not as the initial pattern or mold," "but the final articulation of the deeper logic of the content" (MF 328f; cf. MF 402f). [28] "Content, through its own inner logic, generates those categories in terms of which it organizes itself in a formal structure"; and "favors or impedes the development of the literary form which makes use of it" (MF 335; PL 96). "Form" is "the working out of content in the realm of the superstructure," and hence a kind of "conceptual operation" or "process of thought" (MF 329, 4; PL 132). In "the ideology of form," " 'form' is apprehended as content"; via a "dialectical reversal," "formal processes" are "grasped" as "sedimented content" "carrying ideological messages of their own, distinct from the manifest content of the works" (PU 99). The "diachronic sequence" can also be "expressed as a contradiction between form and content"; in "Marx's model of revolutionary change," "latent content works its way to the surface to displace a form henceforth obsolete" (MF 327f).

If "for Marxism the adequation" of "form to content" is "an imaginative possibility only where" "it has been concretely realized in social life," "so that formal realizations" are "signs of some deeper corresponding social and historical configurations" for "criticism to explore," then "our judgments on the individual work of art are social and historical" ones (MF 331, 329). "Content does not need to be" "interpreted," because it is "immediately meaningful" and "already concrete," being "essentially social and historical experience" (MF 403f; cf. MF 169). "Criticism" is less "an interpretation of content than a revealing of it, a restoration of the original message" "beneath" the "censorship" —a claim "implying" that "the surface of the work is a kind of mystification" (MF 404, 413).

If "form" is "the final articulation," then "content" could be described as "raw material" (PL 95f; MF 11, 27, 153, 196, 328, 402f; PU 147; cf. Wellek and Warren, TL 140f). This domain is said to possess a "logic" and a range of "possibilities" or "potentialities" (MF 328, 348; PU 147; MF 315, 39). The variety of "raw materials" mentioned in Jameson's books is extensive: "life," "society," or

---

[28] Hjelmslev's (1953) concept of "the 'content of form'" is cited and "adapted" (PU 99, 147). A more energizing source is "Marx's economic research," being "the most striking model" of how "content" "generates those categories" whereby it organizes itself in a formal structure" —his insight that "change" arises from this process has "an explosive and liberating effect" (MF 335, 328).

"social life"; "contemporary reality"; the "moment of history" and "historical sensibility"; "language"; "ideologemes"; "the human elements of the work, the characters"; "sedimented types of generic discourse"; "inherited narrative paradigms"; "associative clusters of mythology"; the "musical realm"; and so on (PU 238; MF 164f, 169, 153, 328, 403; PU 147; MF 278, 52; PU 147, 185; MF 196; PU 144, 151; PL 115; MF 30, 39). The "raw materials" from "the system of 'everyday life'" with its "sub-systems of verbal expression" are the "closest to the literary system" (PL 94). Of course, "the development of the work of art is seen to be influenced by the availability of the proper raw material" (PL 95). And Jameson escapes "the windless closure of the formalisms" (PU 42) by pointedly discovering "object lessons" that bring up "social," "historical," "political," "didactic," and "existential" aspects of both literature and criticism (MF 7; PU 173, 198; MF 17, 338; PU 168; MF 159; PU 164, 174, 217, 259).

For Jameson, a "shift from considerations of form" to those of "content" "coincides" with a "shift of consideration" from "the writer" to "his public" (MF 384f). Authorial intention is marginalized when the critic "sees the individual writer as the locus or working out of a certain set of techniques, as the development and exhaustion of a certain limited set of possibilities inherent in the available raw material" (MF 315). "The profound impersonality of the logic of content" renders "the artist" "merely an instrument" and "uses the accidents of his personal life" "according to its own intrinsic laws" (MF 329; cf. PU 246). Contemplating "the death of the subject," Jameson comments: "Our possession by language, which writes us even as we imagine ourselves to be writing it," is "a limiting situation against which we must struggle at every instant" (PL 140).

In a "dialectical reversal," "our model readjusts from an *active* to a *passive* conception of the way in which art reflects its social ground" (MF 384). "Our judgments" of "great novelists," for instance, "fall not on them, but on the moment of history they reflect" —as befits the "insignificance of the individual actor" facing "the impersonality of history" (MF 42, 225). Yet an author can be reprimanded for the "inadequacy" of a "work to its raw material," or for the failure to give a "genuine model" of an "objective" "situation," as when Marx and Engels rebuked a play by Lasalle (MF 193).

The author's relation to society may vary considerably: at one end, "'art for art's sake'" signals a "'hopeless disaccord with the social environment'"; at the other end, "'utilitarian art'" that "'participates in social struggles'" signals a "'mutual sympathy'" between artists and "'some considerable part of society'" (Plekhanov 1936) (MF 386). The "dialectical critic" naturally "plots" the "change" in an "artist's development" as "a series of moments which generate each other out of their own internal contradictions" (MF 51).

The loss of "attention to the artistic process" is offset by the "greater precision with which" "the class uses of artistic form are described." In Sartre's view (1964a), "the public" as "a group possessing certain social characteristics" and

"certain types of knowledge" "is implicit in the writer himself and follows logically from the choices of material and the stylistic formations which are the acts
of his own solitude" (PL 28). "The monographic study of an individual writer"
"imposes an inevitable falsification," an "artificial isolation" for the sake of an
"illusion of totality" (MF 315). When Jameson does "violate" the "taboo against
biographical criticism," he typically brings in the social and political affiliations
of an author or of the author's family, as adduced by Sartre for Flaubert and by
Jameson for Sartre (PU 179; MF 382ff, 218f).

Social criticism strikingly merges with Formalism when Jamesonian analysis
proposes to show how society and language join forces to control an author. We
are told that "the shape of the sentences determines the choice of the raw
material" (MF 53). "Hemingway," for example, "wished to write a certain kind of
sentence" because "the experience of sentence-production" would be "nonalienated work"; yet since "American social reality is clearly inaccessible to the
careful and selective type of sentence he practices," the repatriated Hemingway
was driven to "stylistic impotence and suicide" (MF 409, 411ff).

All in all, Jameson remains confident that "each literary work," "beyond its
own determinate content, also signifies literature in general" (PL 155). This
claim is universalized still further: "there is a sense in which *every* enunciation
involves" a "lateral statement about language" and "includes" an "autodesigna-
tion within its very structure, signifies itself as an act of speech and as the
reinvention of speech in general" (PL 202, e.a.; cf. Jakobson, 1960). Yet Jameson
is not totally clear about whether "ultimately, all literary structures may be
understood as taking themselves for their own object, as being about literature
itself"; or whether such occurs only in a specific historical situation, such as
"literary modernism" (PL 89). It is similarly uncertain whether the technique
called "'baring of the device'" is "characteristic of all literature" or only Šklovskij's hypostasis of "his own unique personal and historical situation" (PL 89f).

And "modernism" is itself a slippery notion, especially if thought to be the
converse of "realism." "From a historical point of view," "this opposition is an
unsatisfactory one" (IT 233). "Realism" is only "a 'ground' or blurred periphery"
that "permitted the phenomenon of modernism to come into focus." If we
scrutinize the realists, we "discover that, as though by magic, they also have
every one of them been transformed if not into modernists, at least into precursors of the modern—symbolists, stylists, psychopathologists, and formalists."

Historical conditions naturally determine how we see modernism. For
Jameson, it is not a "mere reflection of the reification of late nineteenth-century
social life," but a "revolt against" that process—a "Utopian compensation for
increasing dehumanization on the level of daily life" (PU 42). The "overexposure
to language" "in the commercial universe of late capitalism" "obliges" "the
serious writer" "to reawaken the reader's numbed sense of the concrete through
the administration of linguistic shocks, by restructuring the overfamiliar" (MF

20f). "Modern literature has developed special techniques, elaborate methods of symbolism, in the express hope of giving meaning" to "stubbornly resistant things" (MF 168).

Even so, "the framework of the work of art is individual lived experience," in which "the outside world remains stubbornly alienated" and "we are incapable of living directly" "what we can understand as abstract minds" (MF 169). The "collective dimension" where "human institutions" "become transparent" is the "realm of disembodied abstract thought," and not of "the work of art." Here, modernism figures as an evasive hope, a promise forestalled by that same alienation in modern society that it sought to subvert. A pessimistic conclusion, adverse to the Utopian perspective of recent Marxism, impends: "it is irreconcilable with the very form and structure of literature" for "the modern work of art" to cause "the illusion of inhumanity" to "disappear" by "making enough connections between" "disparate phenomena and facts" until "the content of the work would be completely comprehensible in human terms" "on a far vaster scale than before" (MF 168f).

Still, "modernism" is an effective force in all eras to the degree that "aesthetics" entails some "renewal of perception," even if not always the total "primacy of the new" which Jameson associates with "modern aesthetics" (PL 54). Šklovskij's "psychological law" of "defamiliarization" ("ostranenie"), serving to "distinguish literature" from "other verbal modes," "describes a process valid for all literature" without "implying the primacy of one particular literary element" or "genre" (PL 51f). "Defamiliarization" is "always" "polemic" and "depends on the negation of existing habits of thought," "perception," and "presentation"; it is a "transitional, self-abolishing" "concept" comparable to an "artistic permanent revolution" which might justify "a new concept of literary history" as a "series of abrupt discontinuities" (PL 90, 75, 52).

Here, we can "turn our attention from the history of works to the history of perception" by "trying to account for" the "mystification" or "perceptual numbness" that art "attempts to dispel" (PL 59; cf. MF 374; cf. Iser, Ch. 8).[29] In Tynjanov's (1924, 1929) "dialectical" "model," "dominant techniques are perceived in a tension with the secondary" ones; "one group of factors" is "promoted" "at the expense of others" (PL 92). This account, later termed "foregrounding" by the "Prague Circle," "has the advantages of including the norm within the work of art" as "the older elements relegated to the background"; and of "grounding" "innovation" in "the very structure of the literary object" (PL 92, 128).[30] The "analysis" of "the structural approach" concerning "the play of

---

[29] Such passages appear ambivalent alongside the claim that "the surface of the work *is* a kind of mystification" (MF 413, e.a.). The ambivalence of art is discussed later (p. 412).

[30] However, it "undermines any general historical awareness" to treat "literary change as a uniform mechanism" (PL 59). This complaint should disparage Eikhenbaum (1936), for whom "'history'" is "'scientific only to the degree that it succeeds in transforming real movement into

structural norm and textual deviation" can then be taken as "a three-term process," with "history" as the "nonrepresentable" "third variable" (PU 145f). "The deviation of the individual text from some deeper narrative structure" is traced to "those determinate changes in the historical situation that block a full manifestation" "on the discursive level" (PU 146).

A Marxist should hardly relish the "advantage" that the Formalists' "model" did "not spill outside the work" into "social problems"; nor their "denouncing as eclecticism" the "explicit attempts to connect literature with the systems farthest away from it, such as the economic" (PL 92, 94). Jameson continually probes "the relationship" of "the literary system" to "neighboring and more distant ones in the totality of experience" (PL 96). He finds in Tynjanov's work "two possible movements of relationship from one system to another" (PL 93). The "autonomous evolution" of "literature" is upheld when "the literary system" "absorbs elements of other systems into itself and uses them according to its own laws," but is "suspended or even altered" when "literature is absorbed into some other system."

Whether some such absorption might occur between literature and criticism is uncertain. Unlike the Yale group, Jameson finds it "not" "becoming in critics to exalt their activity to the level of literary creation"; —claims he notes in "France" (MF 415). But the opposite extreme is also castigated: it is "fatuous" "to glamorize" the "critique of ideology" by likening it "to real work on the assembly line" and "genuine manual labor" (PU 45). Still, he argues that "theory is a kind of production: it works with tangible objects and transforms them" "as in the production of the material world" (PL 107).

In structuralist research, criticism could be a "metalanguage" that "abstracts the structure of another more primary language" and becomes the "signifier," making the other its "signified" (PL 159; cf. Culler, PS xi). "Metalanguage" is "the form that self-consciousness takes in the realm of language," and "a set of signs whose signified is itself a sign-system" (PL 207). Whereas "older literary history" was "metonymic" in linking the work to "the influences and the historical period which surrounded the absent moment of creation," "literary criticism" can now be a "metaphorical" practice that "seeks to replace the work with a description of its structures, with a new 'metalanguage' that resembles it" (PL 123). The newer method performs "interpretation" by "unfolding successive layers of the signified, each of which" is then "transformed into a new signifier" —an "infinite" "process" (PL 176). In a related vein, Derrida's display of "the distance from itself that all language bears within itself" "means" "that "inter-

---

patterns and models'"; and Propp (1928), who "reduced the individual events to various manifestations of some basic idea" and hence to "a single timeless concept" (PL 97, 69f). Yet Propp is also blamed because his "'functions'" "fail to attain an adequate level of abstraction," not being "sufficiently distanced methodologically from the surface logic of the storytelling text" (PU 120f) (cf. Lévi-Strauss, 1960).

pretations are generated out of an ontological lack within the text" and "that the text can have no ultimate meaning."

This line of argument should dissolve the struggle over right or wrong interpretations. Jameson does confess "devoting" "little attention" to "interpretive validity and to the criteria by which a given interpretation may be faulted or accredited" (PU 13). He "feels that no interpretation can be effectively disqualified on its own terms by a simple enumeration of inaccuracies or omissions." Without mentioning him, he follows the totally un-Marxist Bloom (cf. MAP 29) in declaring that "interpretation" "takes place on a Homeric battlefield" as a "conflict" of "a host of interpretive options." "If the positivistic conception of philological accuracy be the only alternative," Jameson prefers to "celebrate" "strong misreadings over weak ones."

We are reassured, however, that "the interpretation of a work can never be an arbitrary process" (MF 403). Against "the infinity of possible meanings and their ultimate equivalence" maintained by "pluralism," Jameson argues that "there are only a finite number of interpretive possibilities in any given textual situation" (PU 31f). "As a matter of practical criticism," "the mind is not content until it" "invents a hierarchical relationship among its various interpretations" (PU 31f). All the same, the Derridean implication that "the process of interpretation is infinite" (PL 176) might attract a critical profession in search of inexhaustible challenges.

Philological accuracy could hardly be decisive for a critical method which constantly expands the work's horizon outward toward the totality of society. A "genuine literary sociology" can adduce only "mediated and indirect relationships" (PL 95). Jameson continually points to "absent causes," which are "nonrepresentable," "cannot be directly or immediately conceptualized by the text," and are "nowhere empirically present as an element": "social contradiction," "history," "mode of production," "the synchronic system of social relations," and so on (PU 146, 82, 35f). The critic must deal not only with "the manifest text" and "the deep structure tangibly mapped out before us in a spatial hieroglyph" (and how this can be "tangible" is a bit mysterious), but with a "third term" which is "always absent," namely, "history itself" (PU 146) (for Althusser the "absent cause," PU 35, 82).

Somewhat like Ingarden (1931), Jameson envisions a "layering" of the text, except that here, "sedimentation" designates "the persistence" of "repressed content" beneath the "formalized surface" (PU 213f; cf. Jameson 1976). For example, to "grasp the text as a socially symbolic act, as the ideological" "response to a historical dilemma," he places one work (Eichendorff's novella *Aus dem Leben eines Taugenichts*) in its "generic series" to expose "a marked or signifying absence"; a "comedy of errors" is "grasped as a displacement that performs an indispensable diversionary function" of "drawing off the power" of a "taboo" against "miscegenation" between "peasant" and "aristocrat" (PU 138f). "The aristocratic main plot has been structurally repressed" because it would "serve as an unavoidable reminder, for a new post-revolutionary readership, of the survival in Germany of a quasi-feudal power structure" (PU 138).

More elaborately contextualizing is Jameson's reading of a Balzac novel *(La Vielle Fille)* as "a political object lesson" that attempts to "'manage'"[31] "the irrevocable brute facts of empirical history" by "transforming" them "into an optional trial run against which the strategies of the various social classes can be tested" (PU 164). This attempt is submitted to a complex psychoanalytic probe. "At some wish-fulfilling or fantasy level," Balzac imagined himself "a strong man who combines aristocratic values with Napoleonic energy," and gave an "object lesson" to prove such a man was needed (PU 168f). In this "libidinal investment," "the working distinction between biographical subject, Implied Author, reader, and characters is virtually effaced" (PU 155). Correspondingly, Jameson situates "the historical originality of the Balzacian object" at a time before "the subject" became "a closed monad" (PU 156, 160; cf. PU 124, 179). In the novel's "evocation of a provincial townhouse," "the desire for" this "particular object" is "allegorical of all desire"; its "pretext or theme" has "not yet been relativized and privatized by the ego-barriers that jealously confirm the personal and purely subjective experience of the monadized subjects they thus separate" (PU 155f).

Such explications exert a rather untraditional claim to validity. For Jameson, "historical truth" can only "be formulated" via a "determinate negation" that proceeds both by "specifying" "historical events" and by "replacing them in larger contexts" (MF 360). If every "work of art" "reflects" "class conflict," then "the truth" of "Marxist analysis" is "measured" by "the completeness with which the cultural fact has been reexpressed" in the "code of the life and death struggle of groups" (MF 381). The critic must "prolong interpretation to the point" where the "contradiction" between "antagonistic classes" "begins to appear" (PU 85).

Being congenial for such a program, "realism" is "traditionally" "the central model of Marxist aesthetics" and the ambience for "the renewal of the sources of artistic production in collective life" (PU 104; MF 386). "Realism" depends on "access to society as a totality" and "to the forces of change in a given moment of history" (MF 204f). But "Marxism" can also maintain an "association" with "romance," which "offers the possibility of sensing other historical rhythms," plus "a renewed meditation on the Utopian community" (PU 104f) (the ultimate classless collective, as we recall, p. 391).

Marxism is also able to foreground the "dark underside" of the ambivalence of art (cf. PU 299). "Marxism" "devalues" "cultural activity," "lays bare the class privileges and the leisure it presupposes," and registers "the guilt inherent in the

---

[31] The term "manage" is attributed to Holland (DY 289-301), who hardly treats the "historical and social, deeply political impulses" Jameson examines (PU 49, 266).

practice of literature" (MF 161; PL 158).[32] "Benjamin's identification of culture and barbarism" reminds that even "the greatest cultural monuments" have "had a vested interest in and a functional relationship to social formations based on violence and exploitation" (PU 299). "Within the symbolic power of art and culture, the will to domination perseveres intact."

Still, Jameson does not mistrust art, but certain uses of it. Among these is the "planification of the work of art" to abet a "new totalitarian organization of things, people, and colonies into a single market-system" (MF 36). In *Beyond Culture*, Lionel Trilling (1965) contrasts "the institutionalization" of "modern classics" with the "negation" that engenders "the profoundly subversive spirit of the works themselves" (MF 22). According to Marcuse, "society" "attempts" to "neutralize" the "increasingly antisocial character of the greatest works." Hence, when a modern artistic trend attains "popularity" in "the dominant world of fashion and the mass media," the "revolutionary" "point of view" "suspects" it of making itself "useful" for "the existing socio-economic structure" (MF 414).

The need increases for a "dialectical" criticism to "readjust" "the point of view we take on our own situation" (MF 389). This dialectic would distinguish between a trend that is "progressive" "because of what it is against," and one that is "reactionary" "because of what it is for."[33] Indeed, the "Marxist hermeneutic," as demonstrated by Bloch, Marcuse, and Benjamin, can "read" the "content and formal impulse of the texts" of "our culture" as "figures" of "the drive toward Utopian transfiguration —of the irrepressible revolutionary wish" (MF 159). As in his treatment of Frye (p. 401), Jameson ultimately pleads for a "Marxist hermeneutic" that combines the "negative," "instrumental" "practice of ideological analysis" with a "positive," "communal reading" of "the Utopian impulses of these same still ideological cultural texts" (PU 296). "The privilege of aesthetic experience is to furnish" "an immediate channel" for "experiencing" "implicit judgments" "on the uniquely reified world in which we ourselves live," and for "attaining a fleeting glimpse of other modes of life" (IT 235).

Despite claims that "all events carry their own logic, their own 'interpretations' within themselves" (MF 345), the hermeneutic demonstrated here is indispensable for its results. The problem is how it can avoid becoming that "hypostasis" of its own "moments of thinking" which a "negative dialectic" vows to destroy (cf. MF 56). Apparently, Jameson's dynamic movements in respect to contradiction, antinomy, reversal, decentering, displacement, resolution, and so on,

---

[32] The "folktale" should be a valid counter-example, since there, "the individual" is "the least essential characteristic," and the "essence" is "collective" (PL 29). But this aspect may fade when "literary evolution" "lifts" "popular forms" up to "literary dignity" (PL 53). Later, Jameson pictures "high literature" and "mass culture" as "generally incompatible spaces," though he situates this "contradiction" after the time of Balzac (PU 207f).

[33] The diagram on the same page (MF 389) must be be drawn backwards, making the "negative" "reactionary" and the "positive" "progressive," unless there is a mix-up in terms ("negative" meaning "having a bad value").

should subvert any commitment to doctrine. Equally agile is his dialectic movement between the poles of traditional pairings or oppositions: presence and absence, inner and outer, content and form, abstract and concrete, familiar and strange, synchronic and diachronic, active and passive reflection, and so on.

Yet a certain tension between theory and practice remains, a negating circularity wherein each disowns the other. Jameson acts out the "struggle for priority between models and history, between theoretical speculation and textual analysis, in which the former seeks to transform the latter" into "mere examples" for "abstract propositions, while the latter continues to imply" that "theory" was just "methodological scaffolding which can readily be dismantled once the serious business of practical criticism is under way" (PU 13f; cf. PU 145; Hartman, CW 174).

"Marxism" is offered as a "third position that transcends" these two, and "affirms the primacy" of both "theory" and "History" (PU 14). "Marxism" seeks the "coordination of immanent formal analysis of the individual text with the twin diachronic perspective of the history of forms and the evolution of social life" (PU 105). It would derive from "Structuralism" "a genuine hermeneutics" to "disclose the presence of persisting codes and models and, by reemphasizing the place of the analyst," "reopen text analytic processes to all the winds of history" —a "development" that can "reconcile" the "apparently incommensurable demands of synchronic analysis and historical awareness, of structure and self-consciousness, language and history" (PL 216, e.d.).

As a critic with such an ambitious program, Jameson cannot quite heal the "ambiguity in Marxist revolutionary theory" between "personal choice" versus the "fate sealed by the logic" of one's "moment of history" (MF 198). "The revolution cannot come into being until all the objective conditions are ripe"; yet "Lenin can apparently force this condition by sheer willpower." Jameson may be in a similar fix of trying to exert such a force, since "we do not even find ourselves in a prerevolutionary, let alone a revolutionary, situation" (MF 115). He exerts all his own will to define and engender the requisite consciousness.

As if to struggle against his awareness that he cannot produce historical or social politics, but only more language grappling with a barely manageable superstructure of diversifying ideologies, he places great store in the practice of critical writing. He even proclaims that "thinking dialectically means nothing more or less than the writing of dialectical sentences" (MF 53, xii). However, the appropriate sentence form would not be the traditional seamless synthesis of subject and object, but a complex, disruptive field modeled on the rhetorical figure of chiasmus or crossover (interview, April 1986).

The strenuous styles of Structuralists —"the classical pastiche of Lévi-Strauss," "the bristling neologisms of Barthes," "the self-conscious and over-elaborate preparatory coquetterie of Lacan, or the grim and terroristic hectoring of Althusser" —can be read as symptoms of an "unhappy consciousness" unable to "signify some ultimate object-language forever out of reach of the language of the commentary" (PL 209). Jameson is prodigiously engaged with his own multi-functional style, as if his whole enterprise depended upon his formulative energy. For instance, he constantly modifies an abstract noun with "very" and/or "itself" or (much less often) capitalizes it,[34] as if such writing might make it concrete right there on the page.

Eventually, he "expects" "the specific problems addressed" by the "social science" of "literary and cultural analysis" "today" "to present suggestive analogies with the methodological problems of the other social sciences" (PU 297). The "concepts" of "totality" and "structure" were "originally adapted" in "aesthetics and linguistics" and "prepared for their later, more immediately figural uses" in "social theory" (PU 55; cf. Jauss, AL 134-42). Now, Jameson wants to practice social analysis without sacrificing his formalist credo that "any concrete description of a literary or philosophical phenomenon" must "come to terms with the shape of the individual sentences" (MF xii; cf. MF 53). To handle "reality as a logos," he can "resort to" a "decipherment of experience" modeled on the "hermeneutical exegesis of a text" (MF xii), a method Fiedler announced long before (p. 78f).

This approach is strategic if the thesis that "change is essentially a function of content seeking its adequate expression in form," is "transparent and demonstrable in the cultural realm," but "unclear in the reified world of political, social, and economic realities" (MF 328). "Understanding" "revolution" "not so much in terms of content as in terms of form" works better in the "ultimately literary categories of time and of narration" than in "political" "terms" (MF 258, e.d.). But the "danger" of such expediency is clearly recognized: though "in practice," "it is much easier to extract linguistic structures" from texts "than from the economic realm," this method can "encourage intellectuals in the belief that with a little ingenuity their analysis of historical reality can be manufactured inside their own heads" (PL 214).

Hence, Jameson's own form of "unhappy consciousness" might be that the expanding and encompassing structure his work performs is a massive attempt to reverse the customary marginalization of Marxism and dialectical method in Anglo-American criticism, the latter being itself at one remove from the marginalization of literary communication in the fabric of Anglo-American society (Ch. 2). His own strenuous virtuoso performance, sustained by immense personal talent and conviction, involuntarily calls to mind a soloistic heroism that appears nostalgic, perhaps even mythicizing, in view of his urgent call for the

---

[34] Examples with "very" or "itself" can be found on almost every page. The two are often combined, as in: "the very feeling of temporality itself"; "the very element of individuality itself"; "the very method itself"; and so on (PL 72; MF 334; PU 46). I often can't see what would be lost by leaving these specifiers out. Capitalizing is rare in the earlier books, but common in *The Political Unconscious*; the favorite is of course "History" (PU 14, 28, 30, 35, 55, 100ff, 235, 261, 264, 277-80, 299), or "History itself" (PU 14, 28, 100, 299).

formation of a true collective. That goal may be both advanced and postponed by the engagement of individual charismatic voices in the struggle for a new communal identity, since the theory of a cultural revolution cannot aspire to dispense nonalienated class consciousness from a thought laboratory out to the classes themselves.

Nonetheless, Jameson continues to hope he can contribute to "creating a Marxist culture" (interview). Marxism has at least established and maintained its presence in the academic scene, despite the consolidation and high visibility of right-wing factions in the America of the 1980s, who have failed to produce a genuine ideology of their own. Jameson can make available critical positions and dimensions in anticipation of a historical situation wherein they can take hold upon the course of events only if they have been so prepared.

This projection might indicate why perspectives of Utopia are thematic in Jameson's work. Utopia foretells the ultimate resolution of the most urgent and recalcitrant contradiction of art: that our faculties of understanding, which art shows to be inadequate and complacent, are our only resource for undertaking their own revision during the experience of art. "Ideological distortion" "persists even within the restored Utopian meaning of cultural artifacts" (PU 299). Only through "a simultaneous recognition of the ideological and Utopian function of the artistic text" can "a Marxist cultural study hope to play its part in political praxis, which remains, of course, what Marxism is all about."

19

Literary Theory Past and Future[1]

We have now surveyed how sixteen major critical theorists of our time essay to think through the literary transaction from their respective standpoints and to situate criticism appropriately. Despite the condensed, compressed quality of my survey, the variety and complexity of theoretical issues must be obvious. Although no one theorist can pretend to have covered the whole range of issues, a cross-section of critical discourse might enable a reasonably encompassing assessment. A concerted synthesis of diverse theories and proposals, however intractable to attain, deserves a central place on our future agenda—utopian perhaps, but in the productive sense of unconstrainable advancement (Ch. 1).

Recent developments have undercut any prospect that explicit reflections upon the nature of literature and its relation to criticism would put everything neatly in place inside an exclusive authoritative account. On the contrary, even the most trusted precepts have undergone such a violent shaking that none of them seems secure enough to provide an absolute foundation for the literary enterprise. The quest for the site of literature and criticism has generated a bewilderment of cartographics locating them everywhere and nowhere from one moment to the next, now close together, now far apart, now containing or engendering each other like an impossible optical illusion created by M.C. Escher.

The traditional critic sought to master the still-hidden complexity by sheer energetics, as a vibrant factotum aspiring to play every part with the hearty, if improvised, alacrity of Bottom the Weaver. Borrowing the voice of the author, the reader, or the work itself, the critic would address the world in the name of art and its instances, or of taste, culture, history, or timeless truth. A vertiginous act, no doubt, but for that very reason uncannily appealing. Recently, though, the whole arena has suffered tremors and shocks that enforce a ceremonious

---

[1] My statements and references in this chapter cover only the works I reviewed, not the entire opus of the critics. Where I could not repeat the passages cited for issues such as "objectivity" or the "unconscious," the Index of Terms can be consulted to locate the original citations.

debate upon what remains or will become of the ancestral performance called "criticism"; the very name becomes a captious irritant to the longing for identity.

On close inspection, the old division of labor is seen to be paradoxical. On the one hand, criticism has been clearly derivative upon literature and subsisted as the secondary agency in a tightly attuned symbiosis of action and reaction, of production and judgment. That criticism would be illegitimate without art seemed a mere truism. On the other hand, criticism has projected the semblance of having always already known the goals which art envisions but does not always attain. An influential critic or school could decide the success of authors or works, affect the production of future art, or bring neglected art back into favor. The prerogatives of judgment and explication implied that the critic's taste and expertise were above, or at least not subjected to, those of the authors being judged—as if art might be illegitimate without criticism.

When literary and critical theory came to the fore, the guiding intent may have been to simply define this delicate balance without overturning it. We might have revealed the status of criticism much as we would explore and map the bedrock upon which a monument or temple reposes. This foundation might have regrounded the authority of criticism, past and future, with a minimum of change or damage to the superstructure. Instead, we unearthed a perverse jigsaw of perplexing fragments that disperse or regather as we chart them, denied even the stony repose of dismemberment allotted to Ozymandias, whose passion yet survives by being stamped on lifeless things. Our supposedly well-fenced activities now seem irreducibly problematic; and the discourse to formulate and expatiate a rationale for them ventriloquizes rather than ventilates the labyrinth of our habitation and habituation.

As criticism faces itself and finds its wonted complacency unjustified, de Man's motto gains an unruly momentum: "all true criticism occurs in the mode of crisis" (BI 8). The great works of art we were once content to celebrate and monumentalize become disquieting, subversive, disrupting our solemn ministrations and withholding their approbation from our struggle to explain their meaning. The very acts of writing and reading, formerly treated as facts of life, come to look diffuse, evasive, exitless, utopian. Every step has to be laboriously worked through under the agonizing suspicion that nothing may prevent us from starting all over. Our agony is a paradigm for the general crisis of modern epistemology, and our bootstraps are barely broken in yet, supposing we gain some ground to stand on and some feet to carry us.

Meanwhile, the critical performance adds more frames around frames, more fictitious sources and narrators, more asides to the audience. Disputes among the personnel, the stage managers or actors, get incorporated into the show; rehearsals are opened to the public and stage-machinery left crudely in view; the script is rewritten or misremembered; signatures and credits are pirated or effaced. Yet somehow the old perquisites persist, ceaselessly reinscribed and reentitled, forever arising to bow at the end, even after the most somber death-scenes.

All in all, literary theorizing is a process of rarefaction constantly battling not to lose essences. The theorist has to be more explicit than either society or customary criticism about what art has to offer. In the process, the prospect of diverging from social or critical experience and praxis remains painfully acute. The utopian imperative of literature combines with the critical drive for discovery and elaboration to impel our theorizing further and further beyond the bounds of what can be visibly demonstrated. The generalizing perspective of theory foments a natural discontent with any one set of standards or practices, however time-honored and well-anchored. The ambition to gather and focus the forces of literature becomes more assertive as the public grows more estranged from art. Perhaps, theory offers a rugged terrain for criticism to bury its own past with a suitably monumental inscription, in a prelude to bidding for a different mode of authority.

But what can be realized in the current scheme, when our theorists seem so agonizingly, or agonistically, divided about what we're up to? Might the society that marginalizes art and rejects modernism do the same to modern critical theory? It might indeed, unless we can adduce good reasons to the contrary; this fate is among our more reliable certainties. So far our case rests uneasily upon the babel of critical discourse, a towering multitude of idioms, styles, terminologies, sources, and models, basking in attention, prestige, and funding, but showing a sense of direction far below what its momentum promises. So we must again set out in search of a rationale, sobered this time by the recent vision of our own wildness, wilderment, and wilderness.

Our possible futures point out in many directions. The grandest project is a full-scale cultural revolution (Jameson, Millett), unrealistic at this moment, but all the more urgent to design. More immediately, we face a new methodology that might engage wider sectors of society in artistic interaction than has been feasible in the past (Frye, Fiedler, Hartman, Iser, Bleich). One major benefit might be the increased fulfillment of the reader's personality and identity (Holland, Paris). More gradual or intangible influences are also foreseeable, directed to conditions of perception (Iser), intellectual and cultural breadth (Frye), creative power (Bloom), rhetorical self-consciousness (de Man), historical awareness (Jauss), and redefinition of institutions (Culler). Our prospects are certainly not meager; but they just as certainly overreach our ordinary practice.

We can no longer deny that the customary functions of criticism, roughly labeled as historicizing, classifying, evaluating, and interpreting, are far less straightforward than business as usual lulls us into believing (Ch. 3). The upheaval of critical theory has at least made us restively self-conscious about exercising these functions, and their fate hangs in many balances. At present, they are activities criticism must disown even as it must perform them—repetition compulsion, the Freudians might say? We may abjure our innocence about history by opening our inquiry to all the winds of culture, society, and power, as Jameson, Jauss, and Millett have done; we may renounce the search for bigger and finer taxonomies of genres or tropes, as post-structuralism has; we may call for an end to evaluation or interpretation, as Frye, Iser, and Culler have variously done. But we can hardly take a step without surprising ourselves in the acts we have disclaimed. Our options reduce to stealth or self-revelation, and we shuttle between them.

Turned loose, the critical functions spiral around themselves in proliferating recursions. Classifying gets classified, interpretation interpreted, evaluation evaluated; and historicizing is revisioned as a historically determined praxis. And they carom with each other in multifarious trajectories, as when interpretation is summarily classified into a multitude of incompatible types in deconstruction; or when history is imperiously overtaken by the problematics of interpretation in the heterodox hermeneutics of Jauss or the remarshalled Marxism of Jameson.

The assumption that literature itself can be classified should make a reasonable starting point. Surely such a prominent phenomenon as literary communication must be if not well-defined, at least definable. But this first step already proves refractory, plunging us into the disheartening perplexities invoked in Culler's motto: "It is the essence of literature to have no essence, to be protean, undefinable" (OD 182). Such paradoxes buy time while we meditate on how to face our major, if hidden, task of explaining and motivating the use of literature in a society inclining to marginalize it. Eventually, we must demonstrate this simultaneous avowal and evasion of essence, this protean motivity, and its purposes, rewards, and repercussions.

Taken together, the definitions and descriptions of literature propounded by our theorists compose a multiplex picture: "a system" or "structure of signs, serving an aesthetic purpose" (TL 141); a "verbal structure" in which "the final direction of meaning is inward" (AC 74); "texts" that "relate to" "models or concepts of reality, in which contingencies and complexities are reduced to a meaningful structure" (AR 70); "the most complex of sign systems," "commenting on the validity of various ways of interpreting experience" and "exploring" "the creative, revelatory, and deceptive powers of language" (PS 35); "any text that implicitly or explicitly signifies its own rhetorical mode and prefigures its own misunderstanding" (BI 136); a mode for "transforming" an "unconscious fantasy" into "conscious meanings" (DY 28); and so on.

Some critics prefer to address "poetry": the "mediator between mythos and logos," "the Marvelous as Credible" (NT 300, 303); "works" that "begin as an encounter between poems" and that "are bound to be misread" (MAP 70; BF 6); and so on. This limitation is not necessarily severe, since poetry is frequently made to stand for all of literature or to be its central instance (TL 142, 24; AC 17; PO 162; ALG 17; compare the Formalist view, PL 50). In some cases, however, prose forms, especially the novel, are chosen because they reward a different kind of attention (Fiedler, Iser, Paris, Millett, Jameson).

The teaching that literature is essentially about itself has weathered better than other parts of the heritage of New Critics, those bad fathers against whom our theorists rebel, often with implacable nostalgia. In Fiedler's opinion, "a work of art is on one level about its own composition" (NT 48). In de Man's, we just saw, the "literary" "text" "signifies its own rhetorical mode" (BI 136). In Frye's, "fact and truth are subordinated to the primary literary aim of producing a structure of words for its own sake" (AC 74). Even Jameson seems to "believe that there is a certain sense" in which "ultimately, all literary structures may be understood as taking themselves for their own object, as being 'about' literature itself" (PL 89). Bloom varies the formula, preferring not "to say that a poem is about itself," but that "it is about another poem" (MAP 198), albeit his method most radically encloses poetry in a space of its own.

However, these meditations making literature into its own exponent are again more dilatory than resultful, a bid to buy time. We bend the problem of classifying literature back upon it, as if asking it to declare itself and release us from the job. Our act is not unjust: the classifier comes to suspect that literature is itself a mode of classification, running far ahead of us and upstaging our efforts. But a profession that can't explain what its concern is supposed to be will continue to intimate an aura of crisis that draws the baleful gaze of accountability-minded authorities and a skeptical public.

The project of classifying literature as a special brand of language has not been markedly successful. Hardly had Wellek and Warren declared this approach "the simplest way of solving the question" when they found their own proposed "distinctions" "between the literary, the everyday, and the scientific uses of language" "by no means simple in practice" (TL 22). "Many mixed forms and subtle transitions undoubtedly exist"; literature can "approximate" "the scientific use" or deploy "resources" "pre-formed" by the "anonymous workings" of "everyday language" (TL 22ff). The quandary was eventually defused through a shift of emphasis enunciated by Culler: when we "stress literature's dependence on particular modes of reading," we "need not struggle" "to find some objective property of language which distinguishes the literary from the non-literary, but may simply start from the fact that we can read texts as literature and then inquire what operations that involves" (PO 128f). Here too, "simply" sounds discordant with our actual results; but the shift has opened new terrains to explore.

In a parallel drift, the special ontological or linguistic status of literature, once accepted as a matter of course, is placed in debate. That status is upheld by Wellek and Warren, Frye, Iser, Paris, and Bloom, yet denied by Hirsch, Holland, and officially by deconstruction.[2] Several theorists hedged their positions. Fiedler at first accepted, then repudiated, the idea of a special canon. Frye suggested that the myths and metaphors of literature pervade all texts, yet he

---

[2] Culler warns against "inferring" "that for deconstruction literature is a privileged or superior mode of discourse" (OD 183). Still, the "claim for superiority" based on "explicitly announcing its fictional and rhetorical nature" is not refuted, though shown to be unprovable; and de Man seems to accept it (OD 183; BI 136).

sought to circumscribe a host of specialized literary forms. Culler, de Man, and Hartman widen their critique to the point where literature becomes a more radical or self-conscious vehicle for aporias inherent in all language, a more deliberate engagement with rhetoricity and with the odd fit between signifier and signified.[3]

The total consensus would have to be a synthetic position: that literature is a distinctive, yet inescapably dialogical phenomenon. It draws back from other domains, but only a prelude for a movement toward renewed interaction. Indeed, the friction between literature and general discourse, we now find, constitutes its major contribution to culture. Being both similar and different, reflective and transformative, is a vital precondition for literature to exert its peculiar relevance as a mode of human understanding. When other domains come in contact with literature, they become more special rather than making it less so.

Criticism in effect retraces this movement as it oscillates between confining and expanding its fields of concern. Formalism and New Criticism foregrounded the otherness of literature, especially poetry. Structuralist and psychoanalytic schools revoked that otherness in the name of top-heavy generalizations about language and mind. The archetypal and mythical schools genially looked both ways, since their prize examples for what they judged universal came from literary representations. All these schools take their place within a grand dialectic of closing and opening, dividing and fusing, that literature prefigures, ahead of us here too.

The transactive, bidirectional capabilities of literature are echoed in many theoretical formulations. We find many passages stating or implying that literature enables a rise in consciousness (e.g., AR 159, 212; IR 175; AC 88; BI 222; TAR 73, 144; DY 50; PIP 98). Criticism could be a mode for encouraging that process (cf. WL 131; CW 268; SX 88, 506; PL 207; MF 52). However, our critics often suggest that literature makes a special appeal to the unconscious (TL 88, 148; AC 88; NT 325; WL 137f; DY 28, 52, 310; RF 5; PAF 128; SX 182; TAR 174; PU 180). How the increasingly self-conscious activities of criticism could be made compatible with that appeal is by no means established. The danger of disturbing the channels of communication with our exploratory surgery is not easy to ban.

The impact of literature on human life is relevant here. Iser sees in "the production and subsequent negation of fictions" "the condition for establishing an open situation as regards life in general" (IR 268). Jauss maintains that "the experience of reading can liberate one from adaptations, prejudices, and predicaments of a lived praxis in that it compels one to a new perception of things" (TAR

---

[3] In his plea for interdisciplinarity, Hartman says: "If we give special attention to fiction and poetry, it is because they are insufficiently examined elsewhere, not because they are privileged" (CW 296). His own proceedings indicate a difference more in degree than in kind, especially where philosophical texts are the point of comparison.

41). Fiedler argues that "art" enables people to "achieve" a "coherence, a unity, a balance, a satisfaction of conflicting impulses which they cannot (but which they desperately long to) achieve in love, family relations, politics"; these "activities are represented in a perfectly articulated form" and thus "revealed in all their intolerable inadequacy" (NT 7). Jameson believes that "in art, consciousness prepares itself for a change in the world" and "learns to make demands on the real world which hasten that change" (MF 90). And so forth.[4]

Hence, literature is the most conducive mode of communication for demonstrating that "'reality, when it includes human beings, is no longer just that which is, but also everything that is missing in it, everything that it must still become'" (Garaudy, 1969: 214) (TAR 15). "The distinguishing element of literature" "depends" on an "awareness of what the element is not" (PL 43). "Literature" can "encompass whatever might be situated outside it" and "include what is opposed to it" (OD 182f). "Reality" "pales to insignificance beside the vast number of unseen and unfulfilled possibilities" (IR 206).

These visions are best honored if literature is conceived in a sphere of interchangeable influence with reality, rather than in the dependent role of imitation or reflection assumed by older mimetic theories or by orthodox Marxism (TAR 11; PU 33). Our theorists sometimes suggest that literature moves us out of or away from reality (TL 25; WL 139; DY 70; BI 17, 191; AL 35). They direct their appeals not to "objective reality" (PIP 2; SC 15f; MF 343), but to the literary processes of creating "models" or "illusions of reality" (AR 70; PL 188; BI 18; IR 92, 198). We can view "literary experience as a part of the continuum of life," and explore how "literature" "contains life and reality in a system of verbal relationships" or how it "relates to life" "after first relating to other figurations" (AC 115; 122; MAP 75; cf. AIM 109). Moreover, readers can heighten their "phenomenological knowledge of reality," or direct their "attention to the interaction between perception and reality," or recover a "repressed and buried reality" (PAF 23; IR 210; PU 20). And they can encounter "the 'disappointment of expectations'" whereby "'we actually make contact with reality'" (Popper 1964: 102; TAR 41).

The Yale group, however, makes criticism an occasion to foreground the failure of reference to reach beyond language, for instance: "a work of fiction asserts, by its very existence, its separation from empirical reality" (BI 17); or "language appears as a restless medium that both transcends and negates its relation to the phenomenal world" (CW 152). In both structuralism and deconstruction, the signified is annexed as a further layer or system of signifiers (PL 149, 185; OD 188; cf. LD 29). These positions affirm the leeway proper to the modality. Literature necessarily implies that language always gets there first and stays there last, no matter where or whither we take flight from it.

As we might expect, theorists agree that "the reality of a work of fiction" is not

---

[4] A critical awareness of "ideology" is recommended as well (WL 129; AR 202; CW 99; PU 296).

"primarily a reality of circumstance" (TL 213). "Literary texts take on their reality by being read" (AR 34). "The reader, in striving to produce the asthetic object, actually produces the very conditions under which reality is perceived and comprehended" (AR 103). The "concreteness" of art and of its representations is also invoked (e.g., TL 129; AC 281; TAR 52, 148). The term "concretization" for the reader's realization of the work is emblematic here (e.g., TL 155; AR 149; IR 173; TAR 73).

In accord with this trend, "truth" in the everyday sense is rarely considered central to literature or criticism.[5] "A work of literature" "does not finally depend for its force and conviction on 'truth' of action, character, or detail" (NT 147). A work's "'truth to reality'" is "deeper": its "view of life" (TL 213, 34), though some critics deny this (PAF 286; BI 12). "Questions of fact or truth are subordinated to the primary literary aim of producing a structure of words" (AC 74). A negative accent may appear: "it is the function of art" "to disturb by telling a truth which is always unwelcome" (LD 432, e.d.).

Abstentions become central to recent theories. In the subjective paradigm, "truth is not a viable goal" "in literary response and judgment" (RF 48). "Literary hermeneutics" is also "no longer interested today in interpreting the text as a revelation of a single truth" (TAR 147). In structuralism, "if the process of thought bears not so much on adequation to a real object or referent, but rather on the adjustment of the signified to the signifier," "the traditional notion of 'truth' becomes outmoded" and yields to one of "translation from one code to another" (PL 133, 216). In post-structuralism, truth forms one pole of an irreconcilable tension. "Language" is "necessarily misleading," and "just as necessarily conveys the promise of its own truth" (ALG 277). "The process of understanding" involves the "interference of truth and error" (ALG 72). "A reading" that is "productive of other texts" must "assert" "its truth," which "can then, in its turn, be undermined" (MAP 69f). "A gap" "within reading" "always prevents" "experiences" being "grasped" as "the truth of the text"; "any attempt to ground trope or figure in truth always contains the possibility of reducing truth to trope" (OD 67f; PS 204). Only Hirsch is left defending the outpost where "the theoretical aim" is "the attainment of truth" (VAL viiif).

"To believe that the timelessly true meaning" must "disclose itself" is to "conceal the involvement of the historical consciousness" in order to "feign objectivity" (TAR 29). In general, our theorists, like Fiedler, do not claim to "speak" "objectively," for instance, when dealing with "values," "classifications," "the 'horizon of expectation,'" or reader "tests" (NT xiv; TL 249, 59f; TAR xii; 5RR 42). "Objectivity" is chiefly regarded as a species of performance, perhaps one with a "fictional," "religious," "authoritarian," or "solipsistic" nature (PIP 130; SC 123, 34, 151, 295). The prestige of "objectivity" as a "scientific ideal"

---

[5] Compare the wariness about looking for "facts" (TL 104, 239; AC 74; LD 486; WL 119; BI 219; TAR 32, 52; IT 211; MF x).

fails to recommend it (TL 16; CW 162; TAR 7; SX 328). Nor is "literature" itself expected to be "objective" (TL 104; WL 167; SX 208), though it might help to reconcile "subject" and "object" (AR 135, 154; MF 44, 38, 141, 146; cf. PS 155; PIP 99, 125). However, probably from force of habit, the text is occasionally designated an "objective" entity (DY 108; SC 129; PU 9). And Frye and Hirsch hold out, vowing to achieve objectivity either by excluding values or by marshaling evidence (AC 18; AIM 33).

Nonetheless, "subjectivity" (or "subjectivism") is still treated with misgiving, even among the more flexible theorists (TL 18, 42, 44, 152, 156, 162, 168, 173, 249; AC 18, 28; VAL 37; AR 23; PIP 1; PO 81; TAR 39, 68, 141; SX 258). Only Iser, Bleich, and Jameson fully accept subjectivity as a natural aspect (AR 19, 21; IR 134; SC 15f, 151; MF 297), though the "decentering" of the "subject" in modern thought may have affected it (AR 159; PU 60, 283; PL 140f; PO 29; BI 32f). The notion of "intersubjectivity" has been a popular synthesis (TL 156; AR 123, 151, 230; SC 28; TAR 52; AL 35). After all, most of our theorists started out as regular critics and have not lost their ambition to generalize their own responses and beliefs (cf. AR 18f). Though subjectivity can no longer be simply denied, it might be viewed as the foundation for whatever objectivity we can still have (cf. AC 20; AIM 99; AR 24f; 5RR 231; TAR 173).

As we would predict, Hirsch's campaign for establishing the "valid" meaning and "increasing the probability" "that our interpretive guesses are correct" (VAL 207) is rather isolated. Jameson devotes "little attention" to "interpretive validity" (PU 13). Hartman laments the spectacle of "great talent" "reduced to quarreling about what interpretation" is "correct" (CW 248). Iser's notion of "aesthetic fecundity of meaning" denies any "frame of reference to offer criteria of right or wrong" (AR 230). The Yale group, and recently Culler, clinch the point by making "misreading," "misunderstanding," or "misinterpretation" the general case, not the deviation (ALG 277; ANX 30; CW 52; OD 179). They cover all bases with the tactic whereby a critic like Bloom is found, as de Man says, "to be wrong in precisely the way that his own theory of error anticipates" (BI 275). Also, de Man's vision of the "unreadable" text "leading to a set of assertions that radically exclude each other" (ALG 245) has stirred a wide interest.

Two motives for these trends seem plausible. First, the fixing of meanings is inimical to the alternativity that makes literature worthwhile; the authority of correctness too readily glides into the authoritarianism of exclusion. Second, the possibility of correctness is properly an issue for theory to put in question, not merely to accept at face value. Hence, we need not be surprised when our theorists converge on the divergence of meanings. Culler advocates "a semiotics of reading" that "leaves entirely open the question of how much readers agree or disagree in their interpretations"; "in general, a divergence of readings is more interesting than a convergence" (PS 50f). Jauss repudiates an "understanding" that "reduces the surplus of meaning of the poetic text to just one" (TAR 142). Iser warns that "to impose one meaning as the right, or at least the best, interpretation" is "a fatal trap" that obscures "the *potential* of the text" (AR 18). Bleich is willing to find "a truth value in any seriously given reading"; "to find complexity and value in a variety of readings" "is more relevant to literary study than the use of standards of interpretive accuracy" (SC 112, 104). Holland sees no "need" for "one central meaning": "almost any coherent thought about the work will open up paths of gratification" (DY 185).

However, critics do not so easily relinquish control over meaning. They caution that the attainment of meaning cannot (or should not) be "arbitrary" (TL 42, 152; AR 85; PIP 148; BI 109; TAR 23, 69, 141, 147; MF 403). Hartman's vision of a "hermeneutic 'infinitizing' that makes all rules of closure appear arbitrary" (CW 244) is evidently unsettling. Again, most theorists retain the critic's gesture of proceeding in the name of consensus. But even projects for strengthening that consensus—such as "criticizing a part of our knowledge in light of the higher standard set by another part" (TL 154), or obeying "the principles which underlie the drawing of objective probability judgments in all domains of thought" (VAL 207) —suggest how fragile it may be.

As we see, the intent to classify literature cannot be pursued very far without immersing us deep in the issues of interpretation and communication, along with cognition and representation of life, reality, and certainty. Such a fate may await all relentless clarifying initiatives directed toward literature. The most hazardous "fallacy" now is the exact converse of those assembled for censure by Frye (p. 47f): truncating the issue at the moment when it becomes unwieldy but peculiarly vital. Being "right" about literature is a far less relevant aspiration than being flexible and radical, that is, etymologically, ready to dig down to the roots.

Instead of classifying literature, we might hope to classify the actions and actors within the literary transaction. This recourse looks attractive at first: the author produces the text, the reader reads it. But as we come to terms with literary versions of this interchange, all straightforwardness and boundedness evaporate once again. The identities of author and reader seem unstable—part historical, part symbolic, part irrelevant. The text sometimes appears to get free and lead a life of its own, or to get the upper hand over its makers and users; other times, it goes mute and inert, utterly helpless by itself, like a stone graven with an inscription in a lost language.

Traditional "literary criticism" was not plagued by doubt about who should be classified in the leading role: "the author's point of view" was the "main concern" (IR 57). The displacement of this view is unmistakable, though the motives involved are not well analyzed. The close interaction between authors and critics has declined, in part because institutionalized criticism felt uncomfortable dealing with contemporary works (TL 8, 44), and in part because authors had to strive with rising anguish to satisfy a reading public with tastes quite divorced from those of criticism (EI 200). Perhaps too, the fate of criticism in our time depends on forces only indirectly related to authorship, such as the rediscovery of reading.

The once-hallowed devotion to authors' biographies barely rates a nod these days. For Fiedler, to be sure, "the poet's life is the focusing glass through which pass the determinants of the shape of his work" (NT 315); and for Bleich, "biographical understanding becomes the starting point for response, interpretation, and literary pedagogy" (SC 160); but neither of them pursues these priorities throughout his practice. For other theorists, the "taboo against biographical criticism" seems to be the order of the day (cf. PU 179). "Considerations of the actual historical existence of writers are a waste of time from a critical viewpoint" (BI 35). "The monographic study of an individual writer" "imposes an inevitable falsification" (MF 315). Nor can a work be used to "draw any valid inference as to the biography of a writer" (TL 76). Even Hirsch, who reveres authorship, keeps verbal meaning distinct from "autobiographical meaning" (VAL 16).

The psychonanalytic theorists, as might be expected, do take some interest in the author's implied personality. Usually, the main source here is the author's works (e.g., DY 241f; RF 4; 3FL 4); conventional biographical materials are chiefly annexed to support a reading.[6] The direct formula of construing literary characters as fantasy projections of the author's self is used by Fiedler and Millett (e.g., LD 115, 252, 498; SX 352, 379, 397). But the strain is noticeable, since as we remarked, literature is no longer seen in a reliable relation to reality.

The author's intention also carries little weight in our times. Wellek and Warren sounded the keynote: "The whole idea that the intention of the author is the proper subject of literary history seems" "quite mistaken"; "the meaning of the work is not exhausted by, or even equivalent to, its intention" (TL 42). Other theorists have followed suit. "The author cannot tie the reception to the intention with which he produced the work" (AL 35). "The interpretation of an aesthetic object is not motivated by a wish to know the author's intention" (SC 93). "In literature, we have the least cause to arrest the play of differences by calling on a determinate communicative intention" (PO 133). "Intention" is "not something prior to the text that determines its meaning," but "always a textual construct" (OD 216). "The attempt to reconstruct an author's intention is only a particular, highly restricted case of rewriting" (OD 38). As usual, Hirsch alone mans the deserted front, fervently ordaining that "the only proper foundation of criticism" is "the philological effort to find out what the author meant" (VAL 57).

The burgeoning skepticism probably pays tribute to a merely practical difficulty: the author's intention is frequently less accessible to scrutiny than the work, which may be the only clue (TL 148; SC 263; OD 216). This circularity, Hirsch hopes, can be broken by gathering "all clues" about "the cultural and

---

[6] To be fair, we must remember that biographical data are traditionally seldom of the kind personality analysis considers most revealing, e.g., about early childhood and psychic traumas. Compare Holland's use of H.D.'s recorded therapy with Freud (PIP 13-59). The Wolfman's rich case history turns up so often (PIP 59, 157, 170; SC 80ff; PS 179; OD 163, 191, 227) that it seems a great pity or else a great blessing that he didn't write literature.

personal attitudes the author might be expected to bring to bear" (VAL 240); but the decision regarding what counts as a clue is likely to be even more circular. Hirsch moves from interpretation to "evaluation" to sidestep the prospect that an "intention" might be quite unlike the "accomplishment" (VAL 12; cf. TL 149).

The author's prerogative to decide who the reader shall be is equally back-grounded in recent theorizing. Iser contemplates a "transformation" whereby we might "become" "the author's image of his reader," but doubts whether a "read-er" can "have an identical code to that of the author," a case that would make "communication" "superfluous" anyway (IR 30; AR 28f). "Writers" may "imag-ine a reader," Holland says, but only to "assuage" their "inner needs"; they do "not predict the ways of real readers" (5RR 219). Conversely, "the reader symbol-izes the author," often into a version "based entirely on his reading" (Bleich, SC 159). The balance is further relaxed and complicated by repudiating "the idea that an author might be his own ideal reader" (TL 148; AC 6; AR 29). To reenter the spotlight, the author takes the role of a reader, as in the question-answer dialectic adapted by Iser, Jauss, and Jameson, or the threads of influence traced by Bloom. But the Yale group chips away at even this dignity by making the author a "misreader," no more accurate anyone else, though maybe "stronger."

And so all power goes to the reader, that modest participant so indispensable, yet barely visible during centuries of criticism. The gold rush of critics into theory and the grubstakes of funding have made reader and reading into a landscape dotted with innumerable camps hotly contesting bits of territory. So far, the reader is largely an abstraction and thus holds a status differently weight-ed from that of the author, whose historical existence is brought into play at strategic moments. What is being classified is not so much participants as modes of reading, that is to say, types of interpretation or response. The number of types keeps growing as more critics scramble to carve out a personal chunk of the reader.

The fact that reading is going on all the time and might be recorded or observed hardly interests our average theorist so far. Wellek and Warren remark that although we might "reconstruct" "concretizations" "from the reports of critics and readers," "the psychology of the reader" "will always remain outside the object of literary study" (TL 155, 147). Decades later, Culler performs the same advance and retreat: "poetics is essentially a theory of reading," but "claims about literary competence are not to be verified by surveys of reader's reactions" (PO 128, 125).

Rather than concretely studying general readers, our theorists develop strat-egies of containment more congenial to their wonted proceedings and commit-ments. Culler holds "the considered reactions" of published critics to be "more than adequate as a point of departure for a semiotics of reading; a "survey of undergraduates" would be of scant "interest" (PS 53). The tradition whereby "the critic does not begin by taking surveys to discover the reactions of readers" (PO 50) can be expediently perpetuated: the critic merely "notes his own interpretations and reactions to literary works" and "formulates a set of explicit rules" (PO 128). This advice in effect transforms the new reader back into the familiar critic. But the apparent convenience brings severe drawbacks. The chance to motivate nonprofessional readers is insouciantly undercut.[7] The margin between how critics read and how literature might be read is suppressed before it can be theoretically gauged. Besides, the prospect of finding "explicit rules" may be little more than wishful thinking that ultimately leads to Hirsch's desiccated hermeneutics.

Some of our theorists openly present themselves as readers with peculiar predispositions and personalities (Fiedler, Holland, Bleich, Paris, Jauss). Others invoke or act out a reader prominently abstracted from their own theoretical interests (Iser, de Man, Bloom, Hartman, Millett, Jameson). Neither group pursues the full implications of generalizing themselves in this way. Instead, personal elements are routinely treated as instantiations of tendencies most readers would enact in comparable terms. Only Holland and Bleich tried to confirm their exemplarity by interviewing more ordinary readers, and even there a certain pressure was exerted to fit one's style to the theorist's. All the same, the "actual and doubtless idiosyncratic performance of individual readers" that Culler thought "dangerous" to "take too seriously" (PO 258) was treated with respect and interest.

The problem of representing the reader is most often handled with a mixed strategy of containment, namely, to enrich the theorist's own idea of how to read with various idealized suppositions about general or desirable conditions and results. Early Fiedler drily remarked that "the mature writer must write" for "the ideal understander," a "nonexistent perfect reader" "represented imperfectly but hopefully by a self-perpetuating body of critics" (EI 209). Culler's line of argument, inspired by "linguistics," has a similar tenor, minus the sarcasm: "The question is not what actual readers happen to do but what an ideal reader must know implicitly" (PO 123f). "The meaning of a poem within the institution of literature is not" "the immediate and spontaneous reactions of individual readers but the meanings which they are willing to accept when explained" (PO 124). Here, the "ideal reader" is responding not to literature, but to criticism!

An idealizing strategy, though not always named as such, also influences the procedures of Frye, Hirsch, Jauss,[8] Jameson, Bloom, and Iser. Each theorist idealizes in a peculiar way. Frye's reader surveys at a glance mighty expanses of human culture. Hirsch's is devoted to strict discipline and logical method. Jauss's is finely skilled in hermeneutics, Jameson's in dialectics. Bloom envisions a

---

[7] Throughout his ruminations on why the "reader" now has "'a starring role'" (OD 32ff), Culler never names the intent to motivate ordinary readers with a more challenging view of their role. But of course, his position is mainly anti-empirical and elitist.

[8] We saw Jauss finally trying to make the reader concrete by using himself (pp. 375-79), but his results still seem idealized in scope, order, and detail.

superreader ("Überleser")," "a new mythic being" who "negatively fulfills and yet exuberantly transcends self" (MAP 5). De Man seems to be an example: an executor of "reading" as an "allegory" that "narrates the impossibility of reading" (MAP 5; ALG 77, 205). Iser's strategy is particularly emblematic when he rejects both the "ideal reader" as a figment from "the brain" of "the critic himself" or a "structural impossibility," and "the 'real' reader" "reconstructed from documents," in favor of "the implied reader," construed in terms of "a network of response-inviting structures which may impel the reader to grasp the text" (AR 27ff, 34). As we noticed (pp. 145ff), this "reader" is still ideal, willing to "adapt" and "modify himself" to "an unfamiliar experience" or to "a creative examination" of both text and self (AR 153, 85; IR 290). But more importantly, the reader is essentially deduced from the text, which thereby becomes a full third agent in the transaction.

The "polite fiction" "that books do things to people" (PIP 3) had enjoyed a long career in criticism, presumably as a handy means for hiding both critic and reader behind the text, along with ideology, taste, and much else besides. Most of our theorists officially disavow the fiction but, as I kept pointing out, persist in having texts and sentences perform actions. Iser prefers to reshape the fiction by expanding the text from a linguistic artifact to a phenomenal patterning, entraining blanks or gaps which may be filled in more or less appropriate ways, and implying counterparts or negations of available experiences.[9] Though his model is still problematic and difficult to document in detail, he does make a spirited attempt to align text and reader in an interaction during which both of them undergo changes. Fiedler has a darker, but still transformative conception: "popular literature makes us more at home with" the "more perilous aspects of our own psyches" (WL 50). Holland's position is intermediate: "the words on the page and the character patterns a reader brings to them" are "fixed," though the "transaction is highly fluid" (PIP 127). "The reader tries, as he proceeds through the work, to compose from it a literary experience in his particular lifestyle" (PIP 77). Iser protests here: "literature would be superfluous" if it "merely" "demonstrated the functioning or non-functioning of our psychological dispositions" (AR 40). For him, genuine "experiences" demand that "our preconceptions have been modified or transformed" (IR 262). "The reader" "can "bring to light a layer of his personality that he had previously been unable to formulate in his conscious mind" (AR 50). Probably, Holland's model is closer to Iser's than the polemics suggest; the Freudian framework just happens to be far more deterministic than the phenomenological one. Whether readers become different people or just get a better view of themselves as they are is not a burning issue as

---

[9] The "negative" potential of art is deemed essential by many theorists (NT 6f, 13, 20; BI 219; CW 183; TAR 41; EH 695; PL 90). That aspect might be a reason for applying the "negative" methods of dialectics (IT 211; PU 296) or Derridean deconstruction (SAV 7).

long as the relation between real and imaginary personalities remains loosely defined.[10]

Deconstruction has furthered a conception of the text being not merely a third agent, but a strenuously disruptive one. The structuralist notion of "the subject" as "an abstract and interpersonal construct" "constituted by a series of conventions" easily leads to the vision of "the reader as a function rather than as a person" —"a place where codes" "are inscribed" (PO 25; OD 33). With de Man and Hartman, language mushrooms into an inappeasable agent of dispersal, a force field whose oscillations no reader can neutralize very long. Literature figures as an unending self-involved rehearsal of the problematics of reading. Paradoxically, however, these critics, far from evaporating in the process, remain starkly conspicuous in their relentless obsession with using every text to make this point and with abjuring mastery in the most masterful style.

A long distance has clearly been traversed since the New Critics banned the "affective fallacy" of failing to maintain a theoretical distinction between the text and a reading of it. The conception of "the work existing only when read," once dismissed as an invitation to "complete skepticism and anarchy," heralding "the definite end of all teaching of literature" (TL 146), is now serenely voiced by such mutual antagonists as Hirsch and Bleich (VAL 13; SC 109; cf. Iser, AR 20). The related idea that each rereading is a different experience, formerly harnessed as an argument against "psychological method" (TL 147) or "psychologism" (VAL 32ff), is welcomed by Iser: "the structure-determined unrepeatability of meaning" enables "innovative reading" "on repeated viewings" (AR 150; IR 281).

Descriptions of text and reader are complicated by the theorists' subsidiary projects of appreciating texts and of motivating reading. Whatever their proclaimed stance, critics by nature can scarcely pass up an occasion to make text and reader appear ever more special. Interpretation gets evaluated, not merely classified and interpreted. Hence, a fair share of contemporary theory is concerned, though frequently beneath the surface, with expounding the benefits of reading in certain ways. Yet this concern impels theorists toward distasteful compromises. Literary roles should be pictured as interesting and challenging, but still feasible and accessible. The transactive, utopian qualities of literary communication are hard to present to the current pragmatic and practical mentality of Western culture. That audience expects the very simplifying and stabilizing that minimize creative participation in literature. Perhaps some of the solecisms of our theorists—the stylistic obscurities, the peremptory arguments, the omission of crucial demonstrations, the strivings for bizarre revelations and paradoxes—are a defense against a leveling utilitarian appropriation of literary

---

[10] Jauss is among the few critics attempting to give some historical concreteness to the reader's acts of identifying with fictional "heroes" (AL 152-188). He blames the general neglect of this issue on Freud for having equated such acts with "daydreaming" (AL 160).

theory into the culture industry. Unfortunately, this defense may also be putting a severe strain on many people sincerely pledged to let literature be itself, if they just could learn what that means.

Adolph Tomars' slogan, approved by Wellek and Warren, that "aesthetic institutions" are "social institutions" (p. 38) must have had a shock value in 1941 for a critical profession wherein "art for art's sake" was still a fully respectable doctrine rather than an admission of social resignation (cf. TL 101; MF 386). But the promise behind the slogan has been slow in its fulfillment. Little is gained by merely asserting that "such traditional literary devices as symbolism or metre are social in their very nature" because they "could have arisen only in society" (TL 94). More interesting is the prospect that "the aesthetic" is not "the final resting place," because "the work of art" "participates in the vision of the goal of social effort" (AC 348f, 95), but Frye too is sketchy with details. Moreover, certain theses imply a contrary drift, notably that "literature" is "'pure' of practical intent" (TL 239) and invokes "depragmatized norms" or "conventions" (AR 184, 61). "These conventions are taken out of their social contexts" "and so become objects of scrutiny in themselves" (AR 61). Even supposing this process has occurred, the reader is still challenged to bring the results of that "scrutiny" back to bear upon "social contexts"; and Iser too is not entirely clear about how that move might be guaranteed for readers who lack his own virtuosity.

In the context of society, literature is uncomfortably positioned between description and change. Our theorists often indicate that reading it helps loosen readers from social roles and strictures (e.g. AC 233, 348; AR 6, 212; IR xiii; PIP 46; SC 150; PAF 6f; TAR 41, 45; AL 154; PU 79). Yet an explicit interaction with "sociology" or "social science" is recommended by some (LD 10; WL 115; 5RR 270; SC 25f; CW 240; TAR 9, 40; AL 287; PU 297) and mistrusted by others (TL 16, 95, 130; PO 258; SX 312). Perhaps we don't relish being told how society is marginalizing the arts. Or we are nervous about the prospect of art being judged solely for its usefulness to current social systems. But some contact with social science is needed for probing how "literature" "tends to influence 'real life'" without being its "mirror" (LD 31; TL 103). Moreover, the notion that art and aesthetics have contributed to the concepts of sociology deserves attention (TL 102; PU 55; 5RR 261f; AL 134; PU 55, 297).

Wellek and Warren's view that "it will be the task of literary sociology to trace" the "exact social status" of the "intelligentsia" (TL 98) has intriguing implications for literary scholars and theorists. Frye proclaims "the social task of the 'intellectual'": "to defend the autonomy of culture" (AC 127). Our theorists are themselves undeniably intellectuals (cf. EI xii; DY 222; CW 197), and they affirm the value of "intellectual respectability" (VAL 164; DY 184) or "integrity" (BI 110; SX xiv). Yet current discussions signal an uneasiness that "intellectual" persons and activities can limit or distort experiences, including literary ones (e.g. TL 192; IE 7; RF 69; PL 6, 214). For Millett, "intellectuality" has traditionally been a "masculine" monopoly (SX 86, 280). For Paris, it marks "the 'perfectionistic' person" (PAF 60). For Holland, "academics and intellectuals often present the appearance" of "'cold fish,'" because they "put up a barrier between sensuous emotional experience and the intellectual problems with which they concern themselves" (DY 171). For Jameson, they are devoted to "purely contemplative" "consumption" (MF xv). Hence, the social role of the intellectual might be to surround the arts with strategies of containment that serve ruling interests. Perhaps our theorists disparage traditional ideals in an attempt to escape suspicions leveled at the very establishment they work in for being "set apart from the general public" and "speaking a different language" (EI 6; cf. CW 284).

While interpretation gets evaluated, evaluation clamors to be interpreted. Values have usually been incorporated or presupposed in the discussion as if they were self-evident. Later, theorists like the structuralists (and Frye) proposed to disregard values. The recent consensus is that values cannot be eliminated, but their use can be subjected to concentrated scrutiny. To keep the merit of literature or its works as an unexamined initial premise is to miss a cultural opportunity. The elitism, abjured by Wellek and Warren and espoused by Bloom (TL 21f; MAP 39), of refusing to contemplate anything but "great" works, is too costly for theory, especially when, as in Bloom's case, the standards of greatness are obscure. We not only overlook popular literature, which sheds light on central literary concerns, such as the transmission of myths and archetypes or the formation of expectations (cf. TL 46; AC 17, 108; WL 36, 129; PIP 128; AL 270f; PU 85f; MF 377). We also narrow our vision of potential criteria that encourage or discourage people to value literature.

No doubt, values seem intractable for theory on multiple grounds. They are nominally absent from scientific methods. They vary among different individuals, cultures, or times. They pervade virtually all experience, with no special demarcations for art or literature. Their relation to other aspects of a literary work is often submerged and problematic. But although "value-judgments," as Frye says, are "not statements of fact" (AC 20), the activity of making them is a fact of human response—a crucial one for any argument in favor of reading.

Within the contexts of theory, value criteria have multiple functions. In a personal context, they motivate and guide the procedures of each theorist moving between a general theory and a specific work. In a social context, they account for the motives any group of real readers might have for working through literature. In a research context, they set future goals for theoretical explication. Few social activities today reflect values as diffuse and disputatious as our uses of art, and so far, our theorists have largely evaded the problems by idealizing reading and proclaiming values in very abstract terms: complexity, coherence, allusiveness, negativity, reflexivity, insight, pleasure, and so forth.

Since the social context is by far the most urgent at present, it deserves our primary focus. The privilege of trying out forms of experience without having to confront the material consequences of real life is claimed for literary reading by Fiedler, Iser, Holland, Bleich, Paris, Jauss, and Jameson. Readers can escape their normal limitations without surmounting practical difficulties or setting off irreversible chains of events. Yet the ambivalence of this freedom is acknowledged by Iser, Jauss, Jameson, and Millett: readers may refuse the occasion for insight. Just as no author, critic, or teacher can directly enforce a single literary response, no theorist can guarantee that literature as a whole will be used according to its more productive imperatives. At most, we can work to create favorable conditions for the uses we advocate; and the rise to power of critical theory gives reason to hope that this project has a chance.

Potential obstacles abound, as even the most hopeful theorists admit. Art may be severed from its alternativity and negative potential, and enlisted in an affirmation of the world as it is, or in a fantasy of pure escapism (Fiedler, Iser, Jauss). Or, art may be made to carry reactionary programs encouraging society to return to outworn ideologies or to ignore social change (Millett, Jameson). In the view of Freudians like Fiedler, Holland, and Bloom, literature activates darker instincts, deflecting perhaps some more dangerous release, but not effectively lifting a reader above libido or savagery. Millett, on the contrary, proposes an enlightened counter-reading to transcend the power of instinct. She repudiates the Freudian orthodoxy that people irresistibly flee from all experiences which are perceived, however unrealistically, as threats, and tolerate literature only to the degree that it abets rather than dispels self-mystification.

Theorists who posit a genuine increase in understanding as a benefit of literature, such as Frye, Iser, Bleich, Paris, Jauss, and Jameson, often propound a multistage model of reading expanding from narrower out to larger concerns: from text to context, from private to public, from personal to social, from the present to history, and so on. Bleich and Jauss have traced in considerable detail how this sequence might be navigated for a specific work. Frye's and Jameson's progressions are less fine-tuned, their end-stages being hugely amplified—at the point where "literature" "imitates the thought of a human mind" "at the circumference" of "reality," or at "the ultimate horizon of human history as a whole" (AC 119; PU 76).

Another benefit of literature is typically designated "freedom" or "emancipation" (AC 348; AR 177; TAR 45; AL 110; EH 751; CW 2; MF 86, 101). On occasion, a "revolutionary" act of consciousness may be performed (AC 344; SX 29, 489; PL 90; PU 97). Yet because of "the emancipatory chance," "those in authority are interested in making" art "serve their ends" (AL 13). Besides, "cultural activity" "presupposes" "class privileges" and "leisure" (MF 161). A special way of reading is thus required to offset these dangers, such as a Marxist "hermeneutic" that can "read the very content and formal impulse of the texts themselves as figures" of the "revolutionary wish," of "psychic wholeness, or freedom, or of the drive toward Utopian transfiguration" (MF 159).

Aesthetic experience is generally regarded as a further benefit, an emancipation of a particular sort (e.g., TAR 41, 45). However, theorists are much sketchier about the nature and operation of this experience than about its rewards. The contemplation of beauty at the center of classicist aesthetics is regarded with distrust, mainly because it underrates the active, dynamic aspect of response. As Iser says, "the aesthetic quality" properly "lies in" the "structure" of "performances of meaning" (AR 27). Attempts are made to reinterpret the concept of a "renewal of perception" inherited from critics since Aristotle down to the Formalists (AL 12; PL 54). For Jauss, the "aesthetic" "makes possible a mode of perception at once more complex and more meaningful" than "everyday perception" (TAR 142). For Jameson, "the *ostranenie* or 'making-strange' of Russian Formalism" and "indeed the profound drive everywhere in modern art toward a renewal of our perception of the world, are but manifestations, in aesthetic form and on the aesthetic level, of the movement of dialectical consciousness as an assault on our conventionalized life patterns," "an implicit critique and restructuration of our habitual consciousness" (MF 373f).

The unity of the work, another mainstay of classicist aesthetics, is still assumed at times (TL 27, 78; AC 77, 80, 82, 246; NT 7),[11] but more often put in question. Wellek and Warren remark on the ensuing "rigid" quality of "tone" (TL 234). Holland moves "unity" from the "text" over to the reader's "identity" (PIP 112; 5RR 111, 259f). Paris suspects that demands for unity of viewpoint cloud readers' appreciation for the mimetic value of disparities between representation and interpretation, or between diverse perspectives of characters (PAF 11; HAR 212). Iser's ideas that "aesthetic" "designates a gap in the defining qualities of language," and that its "experience" reveals "the gulf between illusion and reality" (AR 22; IR 111) find a counterpart in the deconstructionist pursuit of incurable "gaps within reading," between sign-systems, between constative and performative, and so on, whereby "the unity of the text becomes uncertain" (SAV 8; cf. OD 256, 260; ALG 40, 44, 99, 249).[12] But this trend is sometimes restrained: Culler abandoned his confidence that "unity is produced" by "the intent at totality of the interpretive process," but retained "unity as a problematic figure" "not easy to banish" and as a "question" "interpreters" cannot "ignore" (PO 91; OD 200, 220).

The problems of aesthetics reveal critical theory again caught between describing and reestimating. The attempt to tell us how aesthetic experience works can lead to a protest that both society and previous aestheticians have been significantly misled; instead of merely documenting widespread expectations, theorists now try to disavow them. Evidently, traditional aesthetics is considered

---

[11] A typical instance would be Cassirer's (1953: 182) position, called in question by Paris, that "'in every artistic creation, we find a definite teleological structure,'" wherein "'every facet of the work is part of a coherent structural whole'" (PAF 71). The notion of "'materials' of a literary work" being "pulled into polyphonic relations by the dynamics of aesthetic purpose," as propounded by Wellek and Warren after Ingarden (TL 241), reconciles diversity and unity, but is perhaps still too strong for recent theorists.

[12] De Man disfavors the "symbol" for being "founded on an intimate unity" between "image" and "totality" (BI 189), but it's hard to see how his general view of language could allow such a unity.

sufficiently inadequate for the literary transaction as to call for an energetic revision, even at the risk of discrediting a common argument in favor of art. One motive might be to tip the balance away from passivizing consumption toward creative participation (Iser, Jauss, Bleich, de Man, Hartman): beauty, harmony, and unity are not achieved by the work for everyone and forever, but, optionally and perhaps optimally, by the experience. Another motive might be to animate society into reducing the lag between its classicist orientation and the praxis of modernist art, and thereby making the reception of art more vital and immediate.

However, our theorists are not necessarily anxious to replace classicism with modernism. Modernist art and literature are occasionally decried as "a dead end," a striving for "extreme incoherence," or an "impoverishing" "disruption" of "old long-felt self-coherent ways of life" (WL 93, 90; TL 192). "The widely intelligible symbolism" of the past yields to "'private symbolism'" (TL 189). "The avant-gardism of modern *écriture*" arouses only "a theoretical and philological interest in a reference-less language game" (AL 87). Now that "the aesthetics of mimesis has lost its obligatory character," "the modern development of art" was "put down" by "doctrinaire" "Marxism" as "decadent because 'true reality' is missing" (TAR 31, 11). Also, a decline in the power of "myths" is diagnosed (TL 192; IR xiii, 200), though Frye finds instead a "reappearance of myth" (AC 42, 48f).

Apparently, our theorists are worried lest modernism "produce novels intended not for the marketplace of their own time, but for the libraries" "of the future"; or "surrender the cognitive and communicative efficacy of aisthesis" (WL 64; AL 87). Iser, however, recognizes the "esotericism," the "increased" "indeterminacy," and the "reaction against the norms of prevailing aesthetic theory" as appropriate for "the modern world," wherein "we are denied direct insight into the meaning of events (AR 208, 206 ll; IR 180). Also, "the modern novel thematizes" "blanks" "in order to confront the reader with his own projections" (AR 194). Accordingly, modern criticism should surrender "the traditional form of interpretation," the quest for "a single 'hidden' meaning" (AR 10). "Modern hermeneutics" becomes "negative" and "doubts" "master theories" (CW 239).

So, having pursued literature through classification, interpretation, and evaluation in various combinations, we come back to historicizing. Our theorists agree the conventional study of literary history has lost much of its credibility and cries out for change (TL 254; AC 62, 315; AR 77, 130; DY xvii; PIP 134; ALG ix; BI 165; ANX 69; CW 102f; SX xiv; TAR 3, 49, 51; PL 5, 97). But little consensus obtains about where to go now. The most urgent project would seem to be situating literature and literary theory in their contemporary historical setting. Yet attempts to do so are tremendously complicated by the range of variations among current programs and projects. The traditional reverence for author, work, and art have all been unsettled. The renewed devotion to the reader still lacks effective unity and is managed with complex strategies of containment.

In whose name then does the contemporary theorist speak, and with whose voice? With a borrowed voice, entering partly by stealthy expropriation, partly by ancestral haunting, said the Yale critics, and did their best to stage it that way. But that reply could be only the darker side of the story. The whole is not just one more "story of reading," as Culler is pleased to say, but a communal story of storytelling about reading, and a drama as well, one which tells us as we tell it, and interchanges roles in the very midst of its episodes. The theme of this story is vision, the possibilities and perils of seeing into and through texts and textuality. The narrative line seems to herald some turn of events, if not a declamatory denouement, at least an upward fall, the start of a more animate life.

Could we at least classify the story? According to Frye's scheme of "modes," when a protagonist is superior to us in kind, the story is a "myth"; when superior in degree, the story is a "romance" (cf. AC 33). We have had many "myths" about authors in the past, and Bloom now invents one more, proffering it for the critic to usurp; but the age of myths seems unrecallable. Even "romance" is impractical to sustain, though the heroics of Bloom and early Fiedler flitter stirringly between metempsychosis and meta-psychosis. So we are left to tell of author, reader, and critic in the "high mimetic mode" of tragedy, the "low mimetic mode" of comedy and realism, or the "ironic mode" Frye feels is most appropriate to our age. The composite story of reading blends these modes, depending on who is cast in the leading role: tragedy (the real Bloom and early Fiedler), comedy (Holland, late Fiedler), realism (Paris, Bleich), and irony (de Man, Culler), plus the learned satire or "anatomy" (with Frye as best actor and Hartman in a close supporting role).

But this classification is itself a satire, another wave of rhetoric washing across the mosaic detritus of criticism. Still, we may profit from the allegory of modes to recall how far the theorist-critic is both acting the reader and casting the dramatis personae for the story of the reader. Differences in vision and action begin to protrude; what is visible to theorist, critic, and reader, so often rolled into one, might be unpacked, situated, historicized.

In the most abstract scenario, the theorist reads a work and responds first as reader, then as critic; this response is thereafter read as a further text to generate another mode of response that foregrounds what is general, permanent, essential, or desirable. This higher response leads to yet another text, being the theory (or model, or method, or approach, or whatever one calls it). Yet real-life performances complicate this scenario at every turn. The critic cannot start as the typical reader, but at most try to compel a momentary reduction or regression into that role. The line between the individual and the general won't hold still, being elasticized by the literary process itself. As a result, the various responses and texts spill over into each other, and the slippage and seepage forms a new scenario, untidy but revealing.

Here, the key moves to watch are the motion whereby the theorist-critics end up treating their own reading (both the act and the report) as the proper one; and their gesture of observing themselves in that motion and explaining the why and the how. When students' interpretations are critiqued or rejected (e.g. VAL 73f, 194f; SC 103f; RF 28f; PS 53), nothing more than the traditional criteria of credentials and expertise may be implicated. But refutations of other critics and theorists imply some claim that the theorist's own model affords a special vision which demands and rewards our consideration.

Our curiosity should be piqued when a theorist introduces subsidiary materials a determined skeptic might refuse to find in the immediately perceived text: "gaps," "blanks," or "minus functions" (Iser), "horizons of expectations" (Jauss), "archetypes" (Frye, Fiedler), "unwitting" "insights" (de Man), "inner conflicts" (Paris), "libidinal fantasies" (Holland), "revisionary ratios" (Bloom), "alien presences" (Hartman), "history as an absent cause" (Jameson), and so on. The theorist's own vision endows such constructs with an assertive presence. But each theorist has difficulty seeing what the others see. To insist that "blanks, "ratios," or whatever, are "present" or "there" "in the text" (AR 216; BF 29) is an anachronistic reflex, a reversion to traditional authorization, understandable but, in this belated era, merely diversionary.

The theorist is thus obliged to enrich the story with a subplot expatiating on differences in vision. Deconstructionists stage a scene of recognition in which other critics are displayed stumbling blindly upon unwanted insights while undermining what is expressly asserted (e.g., BI 28; OD 203ff); since the argument makes this quandary universal, one's own understanding must always be purchased with somebody else's misprision. Jauss surpasses critics who lacked "the hermeneutic key of the allegorical method" (TAR 180); Iser those who "scrutinize a work of art for its hidden meaning" (AR 12); Jameson those who "sort out" "literary history into the classic periodization" in a "nondialectical" fashion (MF 375); and so on.

So far, the favorite protagonist for this kind of subplot is the "unconscious": the agent-space where all manner of processes occur that authors and readers wouldn't know about. As we have observed, some appeal to the "unconscious" is made in the theorizing of all our sample critics, constituting an astonishing unison within the discord of voices. Some of the enthusiasm may be due to a simple lack of knowledge about writing and reading and to the related difficulties of observing what's going on, even for the people involved in the actions. The unconscious has a comfortably intangible quality that makes it a congenial preserve for correspondingly intangible entities. However, unanimity quickly vanishes when our theorists declare what the unconscious contributes. The orthodox Freudian admits only libidinal fantasies; the Jungian revisionist derives collective myths and archetypes; the Horneyan points to inner needs deferred by one's dominant solution (e.g., DY 28; AC 17, 100; NT 319; 3FL 37). Feminists and Marxists interpret the unconscious as political. Post-structuralists hold it to be rhetorical. It even makes guest appearances in the phenomenological and historical methods of Iser and Jauss as a supplier of "symbols" (e.g. AR 158; TAR

169).[13] Hirsch brings up "unconscious meanings" only to filter them out of the author's intention for not involving "the element of will" (VAL 51f).

The borderline between the unconscious and the conscious is also in dispute. For Wellek and Warren, "the relative parts played" by each side are essential for "any modern treatment of the creative process" (TL 88). For Culler, "the line between" the two is "highly variable, impossible to verify, and supremely uninteresting" (PO 118), a view Hirsch too adopts for "many cases" (VAL 51). Still, however the line may be drawn, criticism inevitably reshapes it by "helping to make conscious those aspects of the text which would otherwise remain concealed in the subconscious" (IR 260). For the Freud-Jung group, the result is a loss of power; for phenomenologists, a rise in self-realization; for feminists and Marxists, a gain in social awareness. Whether loss or gain, the status of the revealed materials may be altered so drastically that their original function is hard to estimate. Fiedler is most profoundly troubled by this recycling (EI 146; NT 49; WL 130f): criticism might uproot the power of literature with too much digging.

The story of different visions is strategically dramatized through the Freudian view of the unconscious (or "id" or "libido") waging implacable warfare with the conscious (or "ego" or "superego"). Gaps in vision are created by the "censorship" of messages passing between combatants (e.g., DY 114; SX 393, 402). The cast of characters is a natural hit, with lurid overtones of the battle of darkness and light, evil and good, close at hand. And a stark way to score points is to cast one's lot with the dark side (Bloom, Fiedler, Holland). But more temperate positions proliferate. The theorist may stress the division or decentering of the "self" or "subject" without loading the values (Iser, de Man, Hartman, Culler, Jameson). Or, prospects of a movement toward unity and equilibrium may be raised: the identity theme (Holland), the balancing of needs and conflicts (Paris), a free, nonproprietary sexuality (Millett), or a reconciliation of subject and object (Iser, Jameson). These movements are utopian, but the narrative of literature keeping them ready is poignant—less somber than the rebellion of the underself, and more compelling as a justification for art. Even the stern Freudians even the score by portraying literature as a refined mode of "defense" against fear and inner recidivism.[14]

Another popular story of different visions sets literature in the realm of processes similar to dreaming (Wellek, Warren, Frye, Fiedler, Holland, Bleich, Hartman). This move entails some vague parallels between rhetoric and dreamwork, such as that between "metaphor" and "sublimation" (MAP 100), or be-

---

[13] "Symbolic" qualities of literature are sometimes foregrounded (TL 94; NT 318; LD 28f; AR 158; PIP 151; LEE 125; MF 143; PU 20). But some concern is expressed about the possible deviousness of "symbolic" interpretation (PIP 29; 5RR 218; SX 402; TAR 181; PU 65), and de Man would strip the "symbol" of all its privileges (BI 189, 208). See Note 12.

[14] But Hartman thinks that language itself is partly the agent whereby the "self" is "bypassed" and "unsettled" (SAV 2).

tween "condensation" and "linguistic effects" like "ambiguity" and "wit" (DY 58f). The dream is the classic window into the unconscious, and in the Freudian vision, has the attraction of lending the unreal a peculiarly tyrannical unseen presence. Nonetheless, Freud's theory of dreams makes a shaky foundation after severe setbacks from empirical evidence indicating that a repressed wish is by no means always the origin; that much of the material may be generated via nonsensical signals from the brain stem, which the forebrain does its best to interpret; and that the search for underlying meanings may therefore be otiose.[15] Until now, however, contemporary theorists are unperturbed by the weakening of the dream-process as a *literal* model for the literary experience. As a *figural* model, the exemplary interpretations performed by Freud, Jung, or Lacan continue to spearhead the drive for a more radical hermeneutics, an expanded mode of troping and rewriting.[16] The move to convert defenses and syndromes into rhetorical figurations is highly symptomatic (Culler, de Man, Bloom, Hartman, occasionally Jauss and Frye). The marginalizing of sexuality in Freudian argument is another powerful signal of revision (ANX 115; PU 64f; MF xv).

The story of vision may have helped to set criticism free from the author. The theorist can see what is hidden not only to the ordinary reader or mundane colleague, but to the work's own creator. The putative intention of the author reduces to one proposal among others, possibly, but not necessarily, in contact with privileged information. The author may equally well have been constrained or misled by an inner conflict, a repression of libidinal fantasies, an anxiety about influences, a blindness inherent in the practice of language, and so forth. Theories that expound such constraints empower us to surpass or reshape authorial intentions, even explicitly declared ones. This step in effect brings criticism closer to literary creativity—a prospective grounding for the Yale group's move toward assimilation (but that is another story I'll save for a bit).

The revision of psychoanalysis to suit the purposes of critical theory is only the most developed and widespread example to date of a general modus vivendi, in which claims for special vision are anchored in domains beyond literature. Bleich brings tidings from developmental biology, Hartman from philosophy and theology, Jameson from Marxism, and Millett from feminism. In each case, what results is by no means the routine vision those domains practice. Bleich pleads for the experience of negotiated subjectivity in defiance of the actual evolution of human development. Hartman's appropriation of philosophy and theology pointedly breaks with their hallowed decorum and tradition. Jameson strenuously detaches himself from Marxist orthodoxies. And Millett's expose creates the feminist outlook as much as demonstrates it, and in the process,

---

[15] Compare the references in Note 34 to Ch. 9 and in Beaugrande (1984b).

[16] Jameson's estimation of Freud's *Interpretation of Dreams* as a "fundamental hermeneutic manual" is widely shared, e.g., by Fiedler (WL 138f), Bleich (SC 69, 79), Hartman (CW 290), Culler (OD 160), and of course Holland (5RR 16, 207).

shakes the foundations of social science and psychoanalysis. Within these respective domains, our theorists would be marginal heretics, easily neutralized. But here in critical theory, their stories have the added dramatic momentum of a double heresy whose vision falls on uncharted and unchartered lands in between the two realms they span.[17]

We may thus appreciate why our theorists do not call for a direct importation of scientific method (TL 16; NT 300; WL 115, 131; 5RR 42; SC 14, 33f; BI 109; CW 156; SX 313; TAR 55; PU 38; PL vi). True, they cannot quite quell their nostalgia for discipline and solidarity. Frye claims for literary study a "precisely similar training of mind" to that in "the study of science" (AC 10f). Culler finds the "mental process" in "literary education" just as "coherent and progressive" (PO 121). Hirsch sees "the same" "cognitive element in both" (AIM 149). Fiedler would propose "poetry" as the "conscience" of "science" (NT 300). Even Bloom, who panegyrically ululates that "there is no method other than yourself," likens his byzantine "map" to a "paradigm" in "normal science" (CCP 9, e.d.; BF 19). Still, the project of using "linguistics" to make literary studies into a science is generally disavowed (PO 4, 7, 27, 73; TL 176, 178; AR 31f, 34; SC 100; BI 12; TAR 140, 181; PU 9).[18]

Critical theory prefers to pursue its own modes of vision while offering them to the sciences as a complement rather than a derivate, and stands ready to "reforge the broken links" between "art and science" (AC 354). The key precondition is plain: the relation between the sciences and criticism must be dialogical rather than imitative or imperialistic. Critical theory should interact with philosophy, psychology, psychoanalysis, sociology, anthropology, and so on (AC 350; LD 10; PIP 135; 5RR 270; OD 182; CW 240; PU 37f); but it should not abandon its own methods in favor of theirs—or absurdly command them to give up theirs for its own. Literature can "illuminate and situate the problems addressed by these disciplines by offering a perspective that consists primarily" of the "awareness of textuality" (PS 226). A beneficial expansion of scope is promised, since, as I said, "literary theorists" "are able to welcome theories that challenge the assumptions of orthodox" science (OD 11).

Some of our theorists are already busily unveiling the extent to which literary categories and methods are entailed in psychoanalysis and therapy, in the sociology of roles and identities, or in the representational strategies of historiography, philosophy, and theology. The transactive, dialogical qualities of literature en-

---

[17] Should general systems theory and cybernetics become points of reference, as suggested by Iser and Holland (AR 67, 194, 200f; 5RR 288; DGF 2), a similar revision will be in the offing, since aesthetic systems have none of the classical properties like linearity, closed-loop feedback, or invariant reference standards. Compare Beaugrande (1987a).

[18] Jauss does however foresee a role for "text linguistics" in studying "the psychic process in the reception of a text" (TAR 23). For a survey of the field with many literary examples, see Beaugrande and Dressler (1981).

sure that its theoretical explorations will spill over into the concerns of these domains. It estranges by summarily putting a particular philosophy or theology into a quasi-experiential practice; reanimates history by making us impossible spectators of a past rendered too alive to resist; rewrites human existence by recasting personalities and societies into patterns we see as both fiction and essence; and so forth. In such imaginative spaces, science can realize how far reality includes all that happens to be missing (cf. p. 423).

At the other end of the spectrum from scientific interchanges comes a strange story indeed, simple, old, and yet new enough to awaken the antique surprise of a pre-socratic sophism or a Zen parable. Some theorists carried their search for the realms of literature and criticism to the conclusion that the two are one and the same. This genial stroke sweetens the labors of the search and monumental-izes the practice of critical writing. De Man seems to have been among the first[19] to revivify the aesthetics of Friedrich Schlegel—who succeeded as a critic and failed as an author—in order to decree that "critics can be granted the full authority of literary authorship" (BI 80), but his colleagues at Yale followed suit heartily, startlingly (ANX 25, 94f; CW 6, 9, 152). De Man's view of authors circling in quiet desperation in or around the prisonhouse of language would seem to place criticism beyond any pleasure principle. Hartman's authors, how-ever, hear sacred voices, and Bloom's are prophets, daemons, or gods; the critics stand to inherit a glory of utmost sublimity (cf. pp. 285, 322f).

Notes toward a supreme fiction, a rousing story to enliven an ordinary eve-ning in New Haven? Pursued to its limits, the story unravels, too much like some despotic fantasy woven from the annunciation, the Promised Land, the frog-prince, Narcissus, and Horatio Alger, and staged by Monty Python. The climax is still missing, and most of the possible denouements are dubious. In the most proximate scenario, future anthologies of literature for our times would be filled with Yale-school criticism.[20] Further criticism of those works would be required, but that too should become literature through the same equation, and the cycle might reverberate indefinitely, even into a wholly unliterary study like mine. If made retroactive, the equation would violently inflate the corpus of past litera-ture. Such proliferating might seem desirable if one assumes that new literature will decline while criticism expands to fill the void. This hybrid "art" would dwell entirely in the universities, where writers-in-residence are already estab-lished; but now authorship would be granted along with a degree in criticism. Meanwhile, the study of works traditionally considered "literature" would have

---

[19] The paper on Poulet wherein the claim is made in these words (BI 80) dates from 1969. De Man's austere, sparse work is filled with such hints and flashes that appear in more drastic formula-tions of Hartman and Bloom.

[20] Tom Wolfe (1975: 118f) similarly (and facetiously) suggests that in "the great retrospective exhibition of American Art 1945-75, the three artists who will be featured" will be not painters, but the art critics Clement Greenberg, Harold Rosenberg, and Leo Steinberg.

to compete with the burgeoning self-preoccupation of the new literature-criticism.

A grandiose dream, perhaps, to refound the valence of criticism by swift expropriation rather than by the long trek across the turbulent expanse of closely argued methodologies. The whole equation would be better seen as the figure for a wish that the critic's progress through the work could somehow finally merge into the text it traverses; and as a further move to clear a space for more creative discourse, and to problematize the function of criticism by adding some more extravagant positions to the spectrum. Moreover, the power of literature to prefigure its own criticism becomes thematic as the inversion of the critic's scramble to postfigure literature.

One unmistakable impact of "creative" criticism has been a marked change in verbal decorum in the erstwhile homeland of the dapper New Critics. From the "sober exposition" still practised by Hirsch (VAL 33) to the bombastic manifesto of Bloom or the wrenching word-wit of Hartman stretches a territory made broader and freeer by the annexation of intemperate zones. Complaints are lodged from time to time against a new violence of language, styles, and tropes. But what is at stake may be rather a counteraction answering a presumed original violence of language and representation that academic criticism had solicitously declined to see in our texts.[21] Jameson, Millett, Fiedler, and Holland contemplate from different coigns the troubling undercurrent of physical and social violence in cultural monuments, sometimes explicit, but often carefully repressed, transformed, and displaced, with the compliance of customary criticism. The language of post-structuralism cuts closer to the bone by injecting violence into the very medium of criticism and saluting, rather than masking, the dark denied underside of discourse (cf. BI 109). The "'organized violence' committed on everyday language," discovered in poetry by the Formalists (TL 171), and the "violent dislocations" of "customary logic," seen by Frye in the "satire" (AC 310), drift into criticism for a new purpose.

Viewed as an episode within the full story of critical theory, even the most radical, specialized, or arcane project assumes an incisive valence, as if the fate of reading and criticism are always at stake. Our theorists seem to sense the urgency; their engagement with a text, and be it the briefest fragment, becomes a microcosm, an epigram for the most general drifts and quandaries the use of language can raise. Since some form of practice must match any theory,[22] why not enlist the text as performer and practitioner? That the practice of "écriture" —reading, writing, and the whole institutional nexus they entail—should re-

---

[21] "An eloquent passage in the *Grammatology* argues that the 'originary violence of language' is that of inscribing in a classifying and differentiating system" (SAV 92). The "instance of violent inscription" Hartman provides is contemplated as "the sign of an internal discourse that has become lacunary, because censored or mutilated" (SAV 92, 58). Compare Note 31 to Ch. 13; Note 27 to Ch. 14; and Note 24 to Ch. 15.

main the test of critical theories is only just, forty years after Wellek and Warren inaugurated the "theory of literature" squarely within the purview of the "actual works of art" (TL 139). "Typical" for a whole "generation," de Man "found himself unable to progress beyond local difficulties of interpretation" and "had to shift" to "the problematics of reading" (ALG ix). Since then, "the difficult alliance" "between speculation and close reading" has animated critical practice "to reject previous rules of expository spareness, pedagogical decorum, and social accommodation" (CW 174). Yet still today, "the avant-garde essay insists on the priority of reading over theory even while insisting on the importance of theory" (CW 175). And the "theory it engages" is "a textual entity to be worked through like a poem or prose artifact. Theory is (as yet) part of our textual environment and not an independent or premature agency to unify that environment." Theory thus compounds the task of reading it was supposed to master, assigning us the additional labor of reading ourselves reading, writing ourselves writing; and nothing but inertia or exhaustion can halt the regress into further layers in the onion of our self-consciousness.

In true poetic justice, contemporary theory is left hovering between show and tell, between acting out and analyzing the roles in literary transactions. Our critics want to prove upon themselves how theory can be practiced. They invest enough zeal in the proof to nearly bankrupt their successors with performances of unreachable virtuosity. The anxiety of influence casts a growing shadow upon the future of criticism. The belief in one's own specialness will never rest quietly beside the drive to be a model for the general reader. The very sincerity of the theorist enforces some exercise of duplicity whereby the most intensely personal moment of insight is hinted to be eternal, universal. "That every literary theory is based on the experience of a limited canon or generalizes strongly from a particular text-milieu" (CW 299) is a part of the dilemma and cannot be excised.

Perhaps a theory that extends no further than the talents and powers of its own proponent exerts a weak claim on our concern. As many stars in the theoretical firmament approach the age of retirement, the discipline honors them assiduously with symposia, salaries, and academic distinctions of unprecedented resplendence, as if to congratulate all of us, yet wondering if their performance even allows, let alone guarantees, a future. A sense of common direction can hardly be expected to crystallize by itself out of private charisma in public action. Attempting to follow, say, the act of a de Man, a Bloom, or a Jameson— to say nothing of a Derrida or a Lacan—with echo or imitation is to risk irredeemable parody that most damages what it would preserve. A method with

---

22 Hartman denounces a "false conception of a rift between theory and practice" that "keeps growing" (CW 297). "Even when we engage theory, we often do so to delimit it." Therefore, "the initiative passed so completely to Europe that practice there bears too small a proportion to theory."

no madness in it may seem paltry just now; but contagion is no substitute for generation.

My own impression is that some fundamental policy-making is in order. Not that we should narrow down our options, but that we should enumerate and circumscribe them as points in a sharable space of discourse. We need to see more clearly where they split and converge, cross and uncross, and circle back around certain landmarks familiar and strange at once, as in allegory or dream. We have a set of ways of reading which theorists may not openly prescribe, recalling the rebuke of our older prescriptivism by the scientist; but which are recommended by their very example and the attention they call to their every move. We thus have a range of imperatives to read in particular ways; but their totality is the imperative that we must not read in only one way, ever again, no matter what the partisans of the day proclaim.

I have essayed to push my own reading of a gallery of critics to the threshold where I might try out their respective modes of vision like E.T.A. Hoffmann's wondrous spectacles, perhaps at the risk of being smitten by a marvelously crafted automaton, or of stuffing a new ghost into the machine. Until recently, we might have indeed beheld many mechanical methods in the making. Structuralism certainly, under the tutelage of linguistics, aspired to become automatic, to churn out pure formalisms for attested facts voided of messy contexts and with all content converted to form. And in their own ways, the earlier efforts of Formalism, New Criticism, close reading, and explication de texte had extended some promise of a rationality and efficiency fully independent of user and material, or of subject and object. Today, however, we behold no smooth-running critical machines or factories. Even the ambition to see "schools" in recent theory is swiftly defeated, or maintained only through sly decantings and denaturings. The mass exodus now from Yale of all the "Yale critics" looks only too fitting to someone who has burrowed in search of their commonalities; Bloom may have de Man as a daemon, and Hartman as an apostle-apologist-apostate, but the three super-egos defy seamless subsumption as resolutely as if they had never met each other.

So whatever critical theory may be, it cannot exhaust itself in normalizing reading by making standard intuitions explicit, as Culler once hoped. Instead, we set in motion a problematics that rapidly loses all semblance of regularity or self-evidence upon contact between theory and text, or theorist and reader. The theorist may struggle to contain, delimit, define (Hirsch, Wellek and Warren); or may welcome the tumult (de Man, Bloom); or may start with containment and end in tumult (Frye, Culler); or propose a different mode of order behind apparent disarray (Jameson, Bleich, Paris), previously obscured by an evasion of what is unwelcome to face (Holland, Fiedler, Millett). But none get themselves and their enterprise back unmediated.

In an age of dauntless explorers, individual performances are both inspiring and intimidating. The great master makes the art look unimaginably effortless and effortful at once; that the mastery of reading should be of the same order is surprising only as far as we had been lulled by our slick literacy into routines safely guarded from all extremities. We thought we knew how to read literature. Now we are told, whether noisily by Bloom, or quietly by de Man, or scandalously by Holland and Fiedler, or revolutionarily by Jameson and Millett, or unintentionally by Hirsch, that we do not; yet we cannot help reading, even about the impracticability of reading. Or, we find that when we read we have stepped into contexts so overwhelmingly vast we seem to have no business there, nothing within our poor power to fulfill; and yet we urgently belong there, and we must keep tackling the job. The once-transparent act of reading grows opaque or presents itself as an inscribed pane behind which the shapes of signs blur and waver. Meanwhile, we wonder: is criticism being vivified or vivisected?

This reward is hardly a reassuring return for decades of strenuous exertion. We would have liked to present an armory of proven techniques, or at least an account of implied functions each new generation of readers can reliably exercise and make concrete. We discover instead that the dynamics of the literary transaction keep those functions in perpetual motion; they may be exercised not with greater certainty, but only with greater self-awareness—witness the evasive, self-preoccupied styles and the restless coexistence of contradictory positions within theoretical discourse recorded here. *This* medium at least *is* the message, or story as I called it, though not all of it. We must yet summon new ranks of readers to the challenge and perform without blocking, prefigure without disfiguring, so that we may bring the audience to the center of our stage.

What has been established then? The need for a new departure, surely; and a farewell to authoritarian ambitions for correctness, and to fond hopes for immanent or imminent closure. And the urgency of steering between the dictatorship of a single method and the deceptive freedom of fragmentation: of a pluralism that merrily multiplies positions with no vision of their context, consonance, confluence, contiguity, coterminousness. A determination, then, not to be distracted (though sometimes enchanted) by flashes of brilliance, celebrations of uniqueness, cults of personality, gestures of ritual, or quiddities of taste. My own hope to serve such causes has led me to offer my own consolidated meditations as a moment in an open dialectic—of contraction and expansion, of proposal and counterproposal, of interchangeable supremacy among multiplex negotiable centers—that literature itself most essentially enacts and holds ready.

REFERENCES

As far as I could discern or reconstruct them, I have listed the critical and philosophical sources (as distinct from the literary ones) referred to by the critics as well as by myself. Where relevant, a coded abbreviation (see list on p. x), an original publication date, or an author's alternate name is given in square brackets.

Abraham, Karl. The influence of oral eroticism on character formation. In *Selected Papers*. London: Hogarth, 1927, 383-406.

Abrams, Meyer. Structure and style in the greater Romantic lyric. In Frederick Hilles and Harold Bloom (Eds.), *From Sensibility to Romanticism*. New York: Oxford University Press, 1965, 527-560.

Adorno, Theodor W. *Philosophie der neuen Musik*. Frankfurt: Europäische Verlagsanstalt, 1958.

Adorno, Theodor W. *Noten zur Literatur*. Frankfurt: Suhrkamp, 1958-65.

Adorno, Theodor W. *Negative Dialektik*. Frankfurt: Suhrkamp, 1966.

Adorno, Theodor W. Society. *Salmagundi* 10-11, 1969-70, 144-153.

Adorno, Theodor W. *Ästhetische Theorie*. Frankfurt: Suhrkamp, 1970.

Alexander, Franz. *Fundamentals of Psychoanalysis*. New York: Norton, 1963.

Althusser, Louis. *Pour Marx*. Paris: F. Masparo, 1965.

Althusser, Louis. *Reading Capital*. London: New Left Books, 1970.

Arnold, Matthew. *On Translating Homer*. London: Longman, Green, Longman, & Roberts, 1861.

Arnold, Matthew. *The Function of Criticism at the Present Time*. London: Macmillan, 1895.

Arnold, Matthew. *The Study of Poetry*. London: G.P. Putnam's Sons, 1893.

Auerbach, Erich. *Mimesis: The Representation of Reality in Western Literature*. New York: Anchor, 1957.

Austin, John. *How to Do Things with Words*. Cambridge: Harvard, 1962.

Bakhtin, Mikhail. *Problems of Dostoyevsky's Poetics*. Ann Arbor: Ardis, 1973. (a)

Bakhtin, Mikhail. [V.N. Voloshinov]. *Marxism and the Philosophy of Language*. New York: Seminar Press, 1973. (b)

Bakhtin, Mikhail. *Esthétique et théorie du roman*. Paris: Gallimard, 1978.

Barfield, Owen. *Saving the Appearances: A Study in Idolatry*. London: Faber & Faber, 1957.

Barthes, Roland. *Le Degré zéro de la littérature*. Paris: Seuil, 1953.

Barthes, Roland. *Michelet par lui-même*. Paris: Seuil, 1954.

Barthes, Roland. *Sur Racine*. Paris: Seuil, 1963.
Barthes, Roland. *Critique et vérité*. Paris: Seuil, 1966.
Barthes, Roland. *Système de la mode*. Paris: Seuil, 1967.
Barthes, Roland. *S/Z*. Paris: Seuil, 1970.
Barthes, Roland. Style and its image. In Seymour Chatman (Ed.), *Literary Style: A Symposium*. New York: Oxford University Press, 1971, 3-10.
Barthes, Roland. *Le Plaisir du texte*. Paris: Seuil, 1973. (a)
Barthes, Roland. Analyse textuelle d'un conte d'Edgar Poe. In Claude Chabrol (Ed.), *Sémiotique narrative et textuelle*. Paris: Larousse, 1973, 29-54. (b)
Barthes, Roland. *Image, Music, Text*. New York: Hill & Wang, 1977.
Bazell, Charles. *Linguistic Form*. Istanbul: Istanbul Press, 1953.
Bazell, Charles. The correspondence fallacy in structural linguistics. In E. Hamp (Ed.), *Readings in Linguistics*. Chicago: University of Chicago Press, 1966, 271-298.
Beaugrande, Robert de. *Factors in a Theory of Poetic Translating*. Amsterdam: Rodopi, 1978.
Beaugrande, Robert de. A rhetorical theory of audience response. In Martin Steinmann (Ed.), *Rhetoric 1978: An Interdisciplinary Conference*. Minneapolis: University of Minnesota Center for Advanced Research, 1979, 9-20. (a)
Beaugrande, Robert de. Toward a general theory of creativity. *Poetics* 8, 1979, 269-306. (b)
Beaugrande, Robert de. *Text, Discourse, and Process*. Norwood, N. J.: Ablex, 1980.
Beaugrande, Robert de. Design criteria for process models of reading. *Reading Research Quarterly* 16, 1980-81, 261-315.
Beaugrande, Robert de. The story of grammars and the grammar of stories. *Journal of Pragmatics* 6, 1982, 383-422. (a)
Beaugrande, Robert de. General constraints on process models of language. In Jean-François le Ny and Walter Kintsch (Eds.), *Language and Comprehension*. Amsterdam: North Holland, 1982, 179-192. (b)
Beaugrande, Robert de. Surprised by syncretism: Cognition and literary criticism. *Poetics* 11, 1983, 83-137.
Beaugrande, Robert de. *Text Production*. Norwood, N. J.: Ablex, 1984. (a)
Beaugrande, Robert de. Freudian psychoanalysis and information processing: Notes on a future synthesis. *Psychoanalysis and Contemporary Thought* 7/2, 1984, 147- 194. (b)
Beaugrande, Robert de. Schemas for literary communication. In László Halász (Ed.), *Literary Discourse*. New York: de Gruyter, 1986, 34-68.
Beaugrande, Robert de. Determinacy distribution in complex systems: Science, language, linguistics, life. *Zeitschrift fur Phonetik, Sprachwissenschaft und Kommunikationsforschung*, 1987. (a)
Beaugrande, Robert de. Semantics and text meaning. *Journal of Semantics*, 1987. (b)
Beaugrande, Robert de. Achieving feminist discourse: The difficult case of Luce Irigaray. *College English* 49, 1987. (c)
Beaugrande, Robert de. *Linguistic Theory: Retrospects and Prospects*. In preparation.
Beaugrande, Robert de, and Colby, Benjamin. Narrative models of action and interaction. *Cognitive Science* 3, 1979, 43-66.
Beaugrande, Robert de, and Dressler Wolfgang. *Introduction to Text Linguistics*. London: Longmans, 1981.
Bebel, August. *Women and Socialism*. New York: Socialist Literature Co., 1910.

Benjamin, Walter. *Ursprung des deutschen Trauerspiels*. Berlin: Rowohlt, 1928.
Benjamin, Walter. Über einige Motive bei Baudelaire. In *Gesammelte Schriften I*. Frankfurt: Suhrkamp, 1974, 605-653.
Benjamin, Walter. Zentralpark. In *Gesammelte Schriften I*. Frankfurt: Suhrkamp, 1974 [1938-39], 655-690.
Benjamin, Walter. *Illuminations*. New York: Schocken, 1969.
Bergler, Edmund. *The Writer and Psychoanalysis*. New York: Doubleday, 1950.
Betti, Emiliano. *Teoria generale della interpretazione*. Milan: Giuffré, 1955.
Birkhoff, George David. *Aesthetic Measure*. Cambridge, MA: Harvard University Press, 1933.
Blackmur, Richard. *Language as Gesture*. New York: Harcourt Brace, 1952.
Blanchot, Maurice. *La Part du feu*. Paris: Gallimard, 1949.
Blanchot, Maurice. *L'Espace littéraire*. Paris: Gallimard, 1955.
Bleich, David. Psychological bases of learning from literature. *College English* 33, 1971, 32-45.
Bleich, David. *Readings and Feelings* [RF]. Urbana, NCTE, 1976.
Bleich, David. *Subjective Criticism* [SC]. Baltimore: Johns Hopkins University Press, 1978.
Bleich, David. Literary evaluation and the epistemology of symbolic objects [LEE]. In Karl Menges and Daniel Rancour-Laferrière (Eds.), *Axia: Davis Symposium on Literary Evaluation*. Stuttgart: Akademischer Verlag, 1981, 100-128.
Bloch, Ernst. *Das Prinzip Hoffnung*. Frankfurt: Suhrkamp, 1959.
Bloch, Ernst. *Geist der Utopie*. Frankfurt: Suhrkamp, 1964.
Bloom, Harold. *The Visionary Company*. New York: Doubleday, 1961.
Bloom, Harold. *Anxiety and Influence: A Theory of Poetry* [ANX]. New York: Oxford University Press, 1973.
Bloom, Harold. *A Map of Misreading* [MAP]. New York: Oxford University Press, 1975. (a)
Bloom, Harold. *Kabbalah and Criticism*. New York: Seabury, 1975. (b)
Bloom, Harold. The breaking of form [BF]. In Bloom et al., 1979, 1-37.
Bloom, Harold. Criticism, canon formation, and prophecy: The sorrows of facticity [CCP]. *Raritan* 3/3, 1984, 1-20.
Bloom, Harold, et al. *Deconstruction and Criticism*. New York: Seabury, 1979.
Bloomfield, Leonard. *Language*. New York: Holt, 1933.
Blüher, Karl. Die poetische Funktion der Sprache in der symbolistischen und surrealistischen Lyrik. In Erich Koehler (Ed.), *Sprachen der Lyrik*. Frankfurt: Vittorio Klostermann, 1975, 22-45.
Blumenberg, Hans. Wirklichkeitsbegriff und Möglichkeiten des Romans. In Hans Robert Jauss (Ed.), *Nachahmung und Illusion*. Munich: Fink, 1969, 9-27.
Boas, George. *Philosophy and Poetry*. Norton, MA: Wheaton College, 1932.
Bohr, Niels. *Atomic Theory and the Description of Nature*. New York: Macmillan, 1934.
Bonaparte, Marie. *Female Sexuality*. New York: International University Presses, 1953.
Booth, Stephen. *An Essay on Shakespeare's Sonnets*. New Haven: Yale University Press, 1969.
Booth, Wayne. *The Rhetoric of Fiction*. Chicago: University of Chicago Press, 1961.
Bosanquet, Bernard. *Three Lectures on Aesthetic*. London: Macmillan, 1915.
Brenkman, John. Narcissus in the text. *Georgia Review* 30, 1976, 293-327.
Bridgman, Percy Williams. *Reflections of a Physicist*. New York: Philosophical Library, 1955.

Brooks, Cleanth. *The Well-Wrought Urn*. New York: Harcourt Brace, 1947.

Brunetière, Ferdinand. *L'Évolution des genres dans l'histoire de la littérature*. Paris: Hachette, 1890.

Burke, Kenneth. *Counter-Statement*. Berkeley: University of California Press, 1931.

Burke, Kenneth. *The Philosophy of Literary Form*. Berkeley: University of California Press, 1941.

Burke, Kenneth. *A Grammar of Motives*. Engelwood Cliffs: Prentice-Hall, 1945.

Burke, Kenneth. *The Rhetoric of Religion*. Boston: Beacon, 1961.

Burton, Robert. *Anatomy of Melancholy*. Oxford: Cripps, 1628.

Cassirer, Ernst. *An Essay on Man*. New York: Anchor, 1953.

Cassirer, Ernst. *Philosophy of Symbolic Forms*. New Haven: Yale University Press, 1953-57 [1923-29].

Cavell, Stanley. *Must We Mean What We Say?* New York: Scribner, 1969.

Chase, Richard. The sense of the present. *Kenyon Review* 7, 1945, 218-231.

Chernyshevsky, Nikolai G. *What Is to Be Done?* New York: Humboldt, 1863.

Chomsky, Noam. *Aspects of the Theory of Syntax*. Cambridge: MIT, 1965.

Coleridge, Samuel Taylor. *The Statesman's Manual*. London: Gale & Fenner, 1816.

Collingwood, Robin George. *The Idea of History*. Oxford: Clarendon, 1946.

Coomaraswamy, Amanda. Intention. *American Bookman* 1, 1944, 41-48.

Crane, Ronald S. Interpretation of texts and the history of ideas. *College English* 11, 1941, 755-765.

Crews, Frederick. *The Sins of the Fathers*. Oxford: Oxford University Press, 1966.

Crews, Frederick. Reductionism and its discontents. *Critical Inquiry* 1/2, 1975, 543-558.

Croce, Benedetto. *Aesthetic as a Science of Expression and General Linguistic*. London: Macmillan, 1909.

Croce, Benedetto. *Problemi di estetica*. Bari: G. Laterza & figli, 1910.

Culler, Jonathan. *Flaubert: The Uses of Uncertainty*. London: Elek, 1974.

Culler, Jonathan. *Structuralist Poetics* [PO]. Ithaca: Cornell University Press, 1975.

Culler, Jonathan. Literary history, allegory, and semiology. *New Literary History* 7, 1976, 259-270.

Culler, Jonathan. *The Pursuit of Signs* [PS]. Ithaca: Cornell University Press, 1981.

Culler, Jonathan. *On Deconstruction* [OD]. Ithaca: Cornell University Press, 1982.

Danto, Arthur C. *The Analytical Philosophy of History*. Cambridge, England: Cambridge University Press, 1965.

Darwin, Charles. *The Origin of the Species by Means of Natural Selection*. London: J. Murray, 1859.

Deleuze, Gilles, and Guattari, Félix. *Anti-Oedipus*. New York: Viking, 1977.

De Man, Paul. The rhetoric of temporality [RT]. In Charles Singleton (Ed.), *Interpretation: Theory and practice*. Baltimore: Johns Hopkins University Press, 1969, 173-209. Also in BI, 187-228.

De Man, Paul. *Allegories of Reading* [ALG]. New Haven: Yale University Press, 1979. (a)

De Man, Paul. Shelley disfigured [SD]. In Bloom et al., 1979, 39-73. (b)

De Man, Paul. *Blindness and Insight* [BI]. Minneapolis: University of Minnesota Press, 1983.

Derrida, Jacques. *De la Grammatologie*. Paris: Minuit, 1967. (a)

Derrida, Jacques. *L'Écriture et la différance*. Paris: Seuil, 1967. (b).

Derrida, Jacques. *Marges de la Philosophie*. Paris: Minuit, 1972. (a).

Derrida, Jacques. *Positions*. Paris: Minuit, 1972. (b).

Derrida, Jacques. *La Dissémination.* Paris: Minuit, 1972. (c).

Derrida, Jacques. The conflict of faculties. In Michael Riffaterre (Ed.), *Languages of Knowledge and of Inquiry.* New York: Columbia University Press, 1982.

Derrida, Jacques. *Glas.* Paris: Galilee, 1974.

Dieckmann, Herbert. Zur Theorie der Lyrik im 18. Jahrhundert in Frankreich. In: Wolfgang Iser (Ed.), *Poetik und Hermeneutik.* Munich: Fink, 1966.

Diesing, Paul. *Patterns of Discovery in the Social Sciences.* Chicago: Aldine-Atherton, 1971.

Dillon, George. *Language Processing and the Reading of Literature.* Bloomington: Indiana University Press, 1978.

Dilthey, Wilhelm. Die drei Grundformen der Systeme in der ersten Hälfte des 19. Jahrhunderts. *Archiv fur Geschichte der Philosophie* 9, 1898, 557-586.

Dilthey, Wilhelm. Das Wesen der Philosophie. In Paul Hinneberg (Ed.), *Die Kultur der Gegenwart.* Berlin: Reichl & Co., 1907, 1-72.

Dilthey, Wilhelm. Die Typen der Weltanschauung und ihre Ausbildung in philosophischen Systemen. In Max Frischeisen-Koehler (Ed.), *Weltanschauung, Philosophie, Religion.* Berlin: Reichl & Co., 1911, 3-54.

Doubrovsky, Serge. *Pourquoi la nouvelle critique?* Paris: Mercure de France, 1966.

Droysen, Johann Gustav. *Historik: Vorlesung über Enzyklopädie und Methodologie der Geschichte.* Munich: Oldenbourg, 1967 [1857-63].

Eco, Umberto. *L'opera aperta.* Milan: Bompiani, 1968.

Eco, Umberto. *A Theory of Semiotics.* Bloomington: Indiana University Press, 1979. (a)

Eco, Umberto. *The Role of the Reader.* Bloomington: Indiana University Press, 1979. (b)

Eddington, Arthur. *Space, Time, and Gravitation.* Cambridge: Cambridge University Press, 1920.

Edel, Leon. *The Psychological Novel 1900-1950.* New York: Hart-Davis, 1955.

Edel, Leon. *Literary Biography.* Bloomington: Indiana University Press, 1959.

Edel, Leon. *Henry James: The Treacherous Years 1895-1901.* Philadelphia: Lippincott, 1969.

Eikhenbaum, Boris. *Literatura: Teoria, Kritika, Polemika.* Leningrad: Priboi, 1927.

Eikhenbaum, Boris. *M. Yu. Lermontov.* Moscow: Izd'vo Detskoi Lit'ry, 1936.

Eikhenbaum, Boris. *Aufsätze zur Theorie und Geschichte der Literatur.* Frankfurt: Suhrkamp, 1965.

Einstein, Albert. *Lettres à Maurice Solvine.* Paris: Gauthier-Villars, 1956.

Eliot, Thomas Stearns. *The Use of Poetry and the Use of Criticism.* London: Faber & Faber, 1933.

Eliot, Thomas Stearns. *On Poetry and Poets.* New York: Farrar, Straus, & Cudahy, 1957.

Ellman, Mary. *Thinking about Women.* New York: Harcourt Brace, 1968.

Emerson, Ralph Waldo. *The Journals of Ralph Waldo Emerson.* New York: Houghton-Mifflin, 1909-14.

Emerson, Ralph Waldo. Montaigne, or the Skeptic. In *Representative Men.* Boston: Phillips, Sanson, & Co., 1850.

Empson, William. *Seven Types of Ambiguity.* London: Chatto & Windus, 1930.

Engels, Friedrich. *The Origin of the Family, Private Property, and the State.* Chicago: Charles Kerr, 1884.

Engels, Friedrich. Letter to Margaret Harkness. In Berel Lang and Forrest Williams (Eds.), *Marxism and Art.* New York: McKay, 1972, 51-54.

Enzensberger, Christian. *Literatur und Interesse.* Munich: Hanser, 1977.

Erikson, Erik. *Childhood and Society*. New York: Norton, 1950.

Erlich, Viktor. *Russian Formalism*. The Hague: Mouton, 1955.

Fechner, Gustav. *Vorschule der Ästhetik*. Leipzig: Breitkopf and Härtel, 1876.

Fenichel, Otto. *The Psychoanalytic Theory of Neurosis*. New York: Norton, 1945.

Fenichel, Otto. The scoptophilic instinct and identification. In *Collected Papers of Otto Fenichel*. New York: Norton, 1953, 373-397.

Ferenczi, Sandor. *Thalassa: A Theory of Genitality*. Albany: The Psychoanalytic Quarterly, 1938.

Fetterly, Judith. *The Resisting Reader: A Feminist Approach to American Fiction*. Bloomington: Indiana University Press, 1978.

Fiedler, Leslie Aaron. *John Donne's "Songs and Sonnets": A Reinterpretation in Light of Their Traditional Backgrounds*. Madison: University of Wisconsin dissertation, 1941.

Fiedler, Leslie Aaron. *An End to Innocence* [EI]. New York: Stein and Day, 1971 [1948-55].

Fiedler, Leslie Aaron. *No! in Thunder* [NT]. New York: Stein and Day, 1960.

Fiedler, Leslie Aaron. *Love and Death in the American Novel* [LD]. New York: Penguin, 1984 [1960, 1966].

Fiedler, Leslie Aaron. *What Was Literature?* [WL]. New York: Simon and Schuster, 1982.

Fingarette, Herbert. *The Self in Transformation*. New York: Basic Books, 1963.

Fish, Stanley Eugene. *Surprised by Sin: The Reader in Paradise Lost*. Berkeley: University of California Press, 1967.

Fish, Stanley Eugene. Literature in the reader: Affective stylistics. *New Literary History* 1, 1970, 123-162.

Fish, Stanley Eugene. *Self-Consuming Artifacts*. Berkeley: University of California Press, 1972.

Fish, Stanley Eugene. How ordinary is ordinary language? *New Literary History* 5, 1973, 41-54.

Fish, Stanley Eugene. Interpreting the Variorum. *Critical Inquiry* 2, 1976, 465-485.

Fish, Stanley Eugene. Normal circumstances [. . .] and other special cases. *Critical Inquiry* 5, 1978, 625-644.

Fish, Stanley Eugene. *Is There a Text in This Class?* Cambridge: Harvard University Press, 1980.

Fisher, Seymour, and Greenberg, Roger. *The Scientific Credibility of Freud's Theories and Therapy*. New York: Basic Books, 1977

Fletcher, Angus. *Allegory: The Theory of a Symbolic Mode*. Ithaca: Cornell University Press, 1964.

Fletcher, Barbara. *Reflections on Derrida*. Gainesville: University of Florida dissertation, 1984.

Forster, Edward Morgan. *Aspects of the Novel*. London: E. Arnold, 1927.

Foucault, Michel. *Les Mots et les choses*. Paris: Gallimard, 1966.

Foucault, Michel. *L'Archéologie du savoir*. Paris: Gallimard, 1969.

French, Thomas, and Fromm, Erika. *Dream Interpretation: A New Approach*. New York: Basic Books, 1964.

Freud, Anna. *The Ego and the Mechanism of Defense*. London: Hogarth, 1937.

Freud, Sigmund. *The Standard Edition of the Complete Psychological Works of Sigmund Freud*. London: Hogarth Press, 1953-64.

Freud, Sigmund. The interpretation of dreams. *Standard Edition* 4 and 5 [1900].

Freud, Sigmund. Jokes and their relation to the unconscious. *Standard Edition* 7 [1905].

Freud, Sigmund. Character and anal eroticism. *Standard Edition* 9: 169-175 [1908].

Freud, Sigmund. Creative writing and day-dreaming. *Standard Edition* 9: 143-153 [1908].

Freud, Sigmund. On the sexual theories of children. *Standard Edition* 9: 205-226 [1908].

Freud, Sigmund. The future of an illusion. *Standard Edition* 21: 3-56 [1927].

Freud, Sigmund. Totem and taboo. *Standard Edition* 13: 1-161 [1913].

Freud, Sigmund. The uncanny. *Standard Edition* 17: 219-252 [1919].

Freud, Sigmund. Beyond the pleasure principle. *Standard Edition* 18: 3-64 [1920].

Freud, Sigmund. Note upon the "mystic writing pad." *Standard Edition* 19: 227-232 [1924].

Freud, Sigmund. *The Wolfman and Sigmund Freud.* Harmondsworth: Penguin, 1973.

Frye, Northrop. *Anatomy of Criticism* [AC]. Princeton: Princeton University Press, 1973 [1957].

Frye, Northrop. Myth, fiction, and displacement. In , *Fables of Identity.* New York: Harcourt Brace and World, 1963, 21-38.

Gadamer, Hans-Georg. *Wahrheit und Methode.* Tübingen: Mohr, 1960.

Garaudy, Roger. Statt eines Nachwortes zu'D'un Réalisme sans rivages'. In Fritz J. Raddatz (Ed.), *Marxismus und Literatur.* Reinbek: Rowohlt, 1969, Vol. 3, 210-214.

Genette, Gerard. *Figures.* Paris: Seuil, 1966.

Gervinus, Georg Gottfried. *Schriften zur Literatur.* Berlin: Aufbau Verlag, 1962 [1883].

Gödel, Kurt. Über formal unentscheidbare Sätze der Principia Mathematica. *Monatshefte für Mathematik und Physik* 1934, 38, 173-198.

Godzich, Wlad. Caution! Reader at work! Introduction to de Man 1983 [BI], xv-xxx.

Goldmann, Lucien. *Le Dieu caché.* Paris: Gallimard, 1959.

Goldmann, Lucien. *Pour une sociologie du roman.* Paris: Gallimard, 1964.

Gombrich, Ernst. *Art and Illusion.* London: Phaidon, 1960.

Gombrich, Ernst. *Norm and Form.* London: Phaidon, 1966.

Goode, William J. *The Family.* Englewood Cliffs: Prentice-Hall, 1964.

Greenson, Ralph. Empathy and its vicissitudes. *International Journal of Psychoanalysis* 41, 1960, 418-424.

Greimas, Algirdas. *Sémantique structurale: Recherches de methode.* Paris: Larousse, 1966.

Groeben, Norbert. Empirical methods for the study of literature. *Discourse Processes* 3, 1980, 345-367. (a)

Groeben, Norbert. *Rezeptionsforschung als empirische Literaturwissenschaft.* Tübingen: Narr, 1980. (b)

Groeben, Norbert. *Leserpsychologie.* Munster: Aschendorff, 1982.

Gunzenhäuser, Rul. *Ästhetisches Mass und ästhetische Information.* Quickborn: Schnelle, 1962.

Habermas, Jurgen. *Knowledge and Human Interests.* Boston: Beacon, 1971.

Hamann, Johann Georg. *Zwo Recensionen nebst einer Beylage, betreffend den Ursprung der Sprache.* London: Dodsley & Compagnie, 1772.

Harari, Josué (Ed.). *Structuralists and Structuralism.* Ithaca: Diacritics, 1971.

Harari, Josué. (Ed.). *Textual Strategies: Perspectives in Post-Structuralist Criticism.* Ithaca: Cornell University Press, 1979.

Hartman, Geoffrey. *The Unmediated Vision.* New Haven: Yale University Press, 1954.

Hartman, Geoffrey. *Beyond Formalism*. New Haven: Yale University Press, 1970.

Hartman, Geoffrey. *The Fate of Reading*. Chicago: University of Chicago Press, 1975.

Hartman, Geoffrey. Preface [DC]. In Bloom et al., 1979, vii-ix. (a)

Hartman, Geoffrey. Words, wish, worth: Wordsworth [WOR]. In Bloom et al., 1979, 177-216. (b)

Hartman, Geoffrey. *Criticism in the Wilderness* [CW]. New Haven: Yale University Press, 1980.

Hartman, Geoffrey. *Saving the Text: Literature, Derrida, Philosophy* [SAV]. Baltimore: Johns Hopkins University Press, 1981.

Harvey, William John. *Character and the Novel*. Ithaca: Cornell University Press, 1965.

Hassan, Ihab. *The Literature of Silence*. New York: Knopf, 1967.

Hegel, Georg Friedrich Wilhelm. *Phänomenologie des Geistes*. Bamberg: Goebhardt, 1807.

Hegel, Georg Friedrich Wilhelm. *Ästhetik*. Berlin: Duncker and Humblot, 1835.

Hegel, Georg Friedrich Wilhelm. *Vorlesungen über die Philosophie der Geschichte*. Berlin: Duncker and Humblot, 1848.

Heilbrun, Carolyn. Millett's *Sexual Politics:* A year later. *Aphra* 2, 1971, 38-47.

Heisenberg, Werner. *The Physicist's Conception of Nature*. London: Hutchinson, 1958.

Herder, Johann Gottfried. *Humanitätsbriefe*. Jena: Diedrichs, 1919 [1796].

Hirsch, Eric Donald. *Innocence and Experience: An Introduction to Blake* [IE]. New Haven: Yale University Press, 1964.

Hirsch, Eric Donald. *Validity in Interpretation* [VAL]. New Haven: Yale University Press, 1967.

Hirsch, Eric Donald. Privileged criteria in literature [PC]. In Joseph Strelka (Ed.), *Problems in Literary Evaluation*. University Park: University of Pennsylvania Press, 1969, 22-34.

Hirsch, Eric Donald. *The Aims of Interpretation* [AIM]. Chicago: University of Chicago Press, 1976.

Hjelmslev, Louis. *Prolegomena to a Theory of Language*. Baltimore: Waverly, 1953 [1943].

Hofstadter, Douglas. *Gödel, Escher, Bach*. New York: Basic Books, 1979.

Holland, Norman Norwood. *The Dynamics of Literary Response* [DY]. New York: Norton, 1975 [1968].

Holland, Norman Norwood. *Poems in Persons* [PIP]. New York: Norton, 1973.

Holland, Norman Norwood. *5 Readers Reading* [5RR]. New Haven: Yale University Press, 1975. (a)

Holland, Norman Norwood. Unity, identity, text, self [UITS]. *PMLA* 90/5, 1975, 813-22. (b).

Holland, Norman Norwood. *Laughing: A Psychology of Humor*. Ithaca: Cornell University Press, 1982.

Holland, Norman Norwood. The brain of Robert Frost [BRF]. *New Literary History* 15, 1983-84, 365-385.

Holland, Norman Norwood. Driving in Gainesville, Florida: The shared and the individual in literary response. [DGF]. *University of Hartford Studies in Literature* 16, 1984, 1-15.

Holland, Norman Norwood. *The I* [I]. New Haven: Yale University Press, 1985.

Holland, Norman Norwood, and Kintgen, Eugene. Carlos reads a poem [CRAP]. *College English* 46/5, 1984, 478-491.

Hömberg, Walter, and Rossbacher, Karlheinz. *Lesen auf dem Lande, Literarische Rezeption und Mediennutzung im ländlichen Siedlungsgebiet Salzburgs*. Munich: Fotodruck Frank, 1977.

Horney, Karen. *Our Inner Conflicts*. New York: Norton, 1945.

Horney, Karen. *Neurosis and Human Growth*. New York: Norton, 1950.

Hubert, Judd. *L'Esthétique des Fleurs du mal*. Geneva: P. Callier, 1953.

Husserl, Edmund. *Vorlesungen zur Phänomenologie des inneren Zeitbewusstseins*. Halle: Niemeyer, 1928.

Husserl, Edmund. *The Crisis of European Science and Transcendental Phenomenology*. Evanston: Northwestern University Press, 1970 [1936].

Ingarden, Roman. *Das literarische Kunstwerk*. Halle: Niemeyer, 1931.

Irigaray, Luce. *Le Spéculum de l'autre femme*. Paris: Editions de Minuit, 1974.

Irigaray, Luce. *Ce Sexe que n'est pas un*. Paris: Editions de Minuit, 1977.

Iser, Wolfgang. *Die Appellstruktur der Texte*. Konstanz: University of Konstanz Press, 1970.

Iser, Wolfgang. *The Implied Reader* [IR]. Baltimore: Johns Hopkins University Press, 1975 [1972].

Iser, Wolfgang. *The Act of Reading* [AR]. Baltimore: Johns Hopkins University Press, 1978 [1976].

Jacobus, Mary. Sue the Obscure. *Essays in Criticism* 25, 1975, 304-328.

Jaensch, Erich. *Eidetic Imagery and Typological Methods of Investigation*. London: K. Paul, Trench, Trubner, & Co, 1930.

Jakobson, Roman. Linguistics and poetics. In Thomas Sebeok (Ed.), *Style in Language*. Cambridge, MA: MIT Press, 1960, 350-377.

Jakobson, Roman. Une Microscope du dernier *Spleen* dans les *Fleurs du mal*. *Tel Quel* 29, 1967, 12-24.

Jameson, Fredric. *Marxism and Form* [MF]. Princeton: Princeton University Press, 1971.

Jameson, Fredric. *The Prisonhouse of Language* [PL]. Princeton: Princeton University Press, 1972.

Jameson, Fredric. The ideology of the text [IT]. *Salmagundi* 31/32, 1975-76, 204-246.

Jameson, Fredric. Modernism and its repressed: Robbe-Grillet as anti-colonialist. *Diacritics* 7/2, 1976, 7-14.

Jameson, Fredric. Imaginary and symbolic in Lacan. *Yale French Studies* 55-56, 1977, 338-395.

Jameson, Fredric. *The Political Unconscious* [PU]. Ithaca: Cornell University Press, 1981.

Jauss, Hans Robert. *Untersuchungen zur mittelalterlichen Tierdichtung*. Tübingen: Niemeyer, 1959.

Jauss, Hans Robert. Group interpretation of Apollinaire's 'L'Arbre'. In Richard Amacher and Viktor Lange (Eds.), *New Perspectives in German Literary History*. Princeton: Princeton University Press, 1979, 182-207.

Jauss, Hans Robert. *Toward an Aesthetic of Reception* [TAR]. Minneapolis: University of Minnesota Press, 1982. (a)

Jauss, Hans Robert. *Aesthetic Experience and Literary Hermeneutics* [AL]. Minneapolis: University of Minnesota Press, 1982. (b)

Jauss, Hans Robert. *Ästhetische Erfahrung und literarische Hermeneutik* [EH]. Frankfurt: Suhrkamp, 1982 (c).

Jenny, Laurent. Le poétique et le narratif. *Poétique* 28, 1976, 440-449.

Johnson, Barbara. The critical difference. *Diacritics* 8/2, 1978, 2-9.

Johnson, Barbara. *The Critical Difference*. Baltimore: Johns Hopkins University Press, 1980.

Jung, Carl Gustav. *Psychologische Typen*. Zürich: Raschen, 1921.

Jung, Carl Gustav. On the relation of analytical psychology to poetic art. In , *Contributions to Analytical Philosophy*. London: Kegan Paul, Trench, & Trubner, 1928, 225-249.

Kalivoda, Robert. *Der Marxismus und die moderne geistige Wirklichkeit*. Frankfurt: Suhrkamp, 1970.

Kant, Immanuel. *Critik der Urtheilskraft*. Berlin: Lagarde & Friederich, 1790.

Kardiner, Abraham, et. al. *The Psychological Frontiers of Society*. New York: Norton, 1945.

Kermode, Frank. *The Sense of an Ending: Studies in the Theory of Fiction*. New York: Oxford, 1967.

Kintgen, Eugene. Reader response and stylistics. *Style* 11/1, 1977, 1-18.

Knight, George Wilson. *Chariots of Wrath*. London: Faber & Faber, 1942.

Kolodny, Annette. Reply to commentaries: Women writers, literary historians, and Martian readers. *New Literary History* 11, 1980, 587-592.

Korff, Hermann August. *Geist der Goethezeit: Versuch einer ideellen Entwicklung der klassisch-romantischen Literaturgeschichte*. Leipzig: Koehler & Amelang, 1923-53.

Kosík, Karel. *Die Dialektik des Konkreten*. Frankfurt: Suhrkamp, 1967.

Kott, Jan. *Shakespeare Our Contemporary*. Garden City, NY: Doubleday, 1964.

Kracauer, Siegfried. Time and history. In Max Horkheimer (Ed.), *Zeugnisse: Theodor W. Adorno zum 60. Geburtstag*. Frankfurt: Europäische Verlagsanstalt, 1963, 50-64.

Kracauer, Siegfried. *History: The Last Things before the Last*. New York: Oxford University Press, 1969.

Kris, Ernst. Approaches to art. In Sandor Lorand (Ed.), *Psychoanalysis Today*. New York: International University Press, 1944, 354-370.

Kris, Ernst. *Psychoanalytic Explorations in Art*. New York: International Universities Press, 1952.

Kristeva, Julia. *Semiotiké*. Paris: Seuil, 1969.

Kuhn, Thomas. *The Structure of Scientific Revolutions*. Chicago: University of Chicago Press, 1970.

Lacan, Jacques. *Écrits*. Paris: Seuil, 1970-71.

Lane, Robert. *The Liberties of Wit: Humanism, Criticism, and the Civic Mind*. New Haven: Yale University Press, 1961.

Lawrence, David H. *Studies in Classic American Fiction*. New York: Seltzer, 1923.

Leavis, Frank R. *The Great Tradition*. Garden City, NY: Doubleday, 1950.

Lee, Sidney. *The Place of English Literature in the Modern University*. London: Smith, Elder, & Co., 1913.

Leibnitz, Gottfried. *Lehrsatze uber die Monadologie*. Jena: Meyers, 1720.

Lemaire, Anika. *Jacques Lacan*. London: Routledge & Kegan Paul, 1977 [1970].

Lentricchia, Frank. *After the New Criticism*. Chicago: University of Chicago Press, 1980.

Lesser, Simon. *Fiction and the Unconscious*. Boston: Beacon, 1957.

Lévi-Strauss, Claude. *Tristes tropiques*. Paris: Plon, 1955.

Lévi-Strauss, Claude. *Anthropologie structurale*. Paris: Plon, 1958.

Lévi-Strauss, Claude. La Structure et la forme. *Cahiers de l'Institut de Science Économique Appliquée* 99, 1960, 3-36.

Lévi-Strauss, Claude. *Le Cru et le cuit*. Paris: Plon, 1964.

Lévi-Strauss, Claude. *L'Origine des manières de table*. Paris: Plon, 1968.

Lewis, Philip E. The post-structuralist condition. *Diacritics* 12, 1982, 1-24.

Lichtenstein, Heinz. Toward a metapsychoanalytic definition of the concept of self. *International Journal of Psychoanalysis* 46, 1965, 117-128.

Lipton, S. D. Freud's position on problem solving in dreams. *British Journal of Medical Psychology* 40, 1967, 147-149.

Liu, James J.-Y. *Chinese Theories of Literature*. Chicago: University of Chicago Press, 1975.

Lotman, Jurij. *Die Struktur literarischer Texte*. Munich: Fink, 1972.

Lotman, Jurij. *The Analysis of the Poetic Text*. Ann Arbor: University of Michigan Press, 1976.

Lukács, Georg. Subject-object relationship in art. *Logos* 7, 1917-18, 1-39.

Lukács, Georg. *Ästhetik*. Neuwied: Luchterhand, 1962.

Lukács, Georg. *Balzac und der französische Realismus*. Berlin: Aufbau Verlag, 1953.

Lukács, Georg. *Probleme des Realismus*. Berlin: Aufbau Verlag, 1955. (a)

Lukács, Georg. *Der historische Roman*. Berlin: Aufbau Verlag, 1955. (b)

Lukács, Georg. *Studies in European Realism*. New York: Grosset & Dunlap, 1964 [1950].

Mannheim, Karl. *Ideology and Utopia*. London: K. Paul, Trench, Trubner, & Co., 1936 [1929].

Mannheim, Karl. *Mensch und Gesellschaft im Zeitalter des Umbaus*. Leiden: Sijthoff. 1935.

Marcuse, Herbert. *Eros and Civilization*. New York: Random House, 1955.

Marcuse, Herbert. *Reason and Revolution*. Boston: Beacon, 1960.

Marcuse, Herbert. *One-Dimensional Man*. Boston: Beacon, 1964.

Marcuse, Herbert. *Kultur und Gesellschaft*. Frankfurt: Suhrkamp, 1965.

Marcuse, Herbert. *Negations*. Boston: Beacon, 1968.

Marcuse, Herbert. *Counterrevolution and Revolt*. Boston: Beacon, 1972.

Marx, Karl. Einführung zur Kritik der politischen Ökonomie. In Karl Marx and Friedrich Engels, *Über Kunst und Literatur*. Basel: Behrendt, 1937 [1857].

Marx, Karl. *Economic and Philosophical Manuscripts of 1844*. New York: International Publishers, 1964.

Maslow, Abraham. *Motivation and Personality*. New York: Harper & Row, 1954.

Masters, William H., and Johnson, Virginia. Orgasm, anatomy of the female. In Albert Ellis and Albert Abarbanel (Eds.), *Encyclopedia of Sexual Behavior*. New York: Hawthorne, 1961, Vol. 2.

Matthiessen, Francis Otto. *American Renaissance*. New York: Oxford University Press, 1941.

Mauser, Wolfgang, et al. *Text und Rezeption*. Frankfurt: Athenäum, 1972.

Mauzi, Robert. *L'idée du bonheur dans la littérature et la pensée française du XVIIIe siècle*. Paris: Arthaud, 1960.

Melenchuk, T. The dream machine. *Psychology Today* 17/11, 1983, 22-34.

Merleau-Ponty, Maurice. *Phenomenology of Perception*. New York: Humanities Press, 1962.

Merleau-Ponty, Maurice. *Le Visible et l'invisible*. Paris: Gallimard, 1964.

Merleau-Ponty, Maurice. *Das Auge und der Geist*. Reinbek: Rowohlt, 1967.
Meutsch, Dietrich. *Literatur verstehen: Eine empirische Studie*. Braunschweig: Vieweg, 1986.
Mill, John Stuart. *The Subjection of Women*. London: Longmans, Green, Reader, & Dyer, 1869.
Miller, Joseph Hillis. Deconstructing the deconstructors. *Diacritics* 5/2, 1975, 24-31.
Miller, Joseph Hillis. Stevens' Rock and criticism as cure. *Georgia Review* 30, 1976, 5-31.
Miller, Joseph Hillis. Ariachne's broken woof. *Georgia Review* 31, 1977, 44-60.
Miller, Joseph Hillis. The critic as host. In Bloom et al., 1979, 217-253.
Millett, Kate. *Sexual Politics* [SX]. New York: Ballantine, 1978 [1970].
Money, John. Psychosexual differences. In *Sex Research: New Developments*. New York: Holt, 1965, 3-25.
Morgan, Jerry. Some remarks on the nature of sentences. In Robin Grossman et al. (Eds.), *Papers from the Parasession on Functionalism*. Chicago: Chicago Linguistic Society, 1975, 433-449.
Mukařovský, Jan. *Kapitolý z česke poetiký*. Prague: Melantrich, 1941-48.
Mukařovský, Jan. Standard language and poetic language. In Paul Garvin (Ed.), *A Prague School Reader on Esthetics, Literary Structure, and Style*. Washington, D.C.: Georgetown University Press, 1964, 17-30 [1932].
Mukařovský, Jan. *Kapitel aus der Poetik*. Frankfurt: Suhrkamp, 1969. [translation of 1941-48]
Mukařovský, Jan. *Aesthetic Function, Norm, and Value as Social Facts*. Ann Arbor: University of Michigan Press, 1970 [1936].
Mukařovský, Jan. *Structure, Sign, and Function*. New Haven: Yale University Press, 1978 [1936].
Muller, Herbert J. *Science and Criticism*. New Haven: Yale University Press, 1943.
Nietzsche, Friedrich. *Die Geburt der Tragödie*. Leipzig: E.W. Fritzsch, 1871.
Nietzsche, Friedrich. *Der Wille zur Macht*. Leipzig: Naumann, 1900.
Nietzsche, Friedrich. Fragment on logic. In *Werke: Kritische Gesamtausgabe*. Berlin: de Gruyter, 1970, 8, 53-58 [1887].
Paris, Bernard. *A Psychological Approach to Fiction* [PAF]. Bloomington: Indiana University Press, 1974.
Paris, Bernard. Experience of Thomas Hardy [HAR]. In Richard Levine (Ed.), *The Victorian Experience*. Athens: Ohio University Press, 1976, 203-237.
Paris, Bernard. *Character and Conflict in Jane Austen's Novels* [JA]. Detroit: Wayne State University Press, 1978.
Paris, Bernard. "Hush, hush! He's a human being": A psychological approach to Heathcliff [HEA]. *Women and Literature* 2, 1982, 101-117.
Paris, Bernard (Ed.). *Third Force Psychology and the Study of Literature* [3FL]. London: Associated University Presses, 1986.
Paris, Bernard. *Bargains with fate: A Psychological Approach to Shakespeare*. In press.
Pepper, Stephen Coburn. *The Basis of Criticism*. Cambridge, MA: Harvard, 1945.
Piaget, Jean. *The Origins of Intelligence in Children*. New York: International Universities Press, 1952.
Piaget, Jean. *Biology and Knowledge*. Chicago: University of Chicago Press, 1967.
Plekhanov, Georgi Valentinovich. *Art and Society*. London: Critics Group, 1936.
Plessner, Helmut. Soziale Rolle und menschliche Natur. In *Diesseits der Utopie*. Cologne: Diederichs, 1966 [1960].

Plessner, Helmut. Trieb und Leidenschaft. *Merkur* 25, 1971, 307-315.

Poe, Edgar Allen. *The Poetic Principle.* Philadelphia: John Sartrain, 1850.

Polanyi, Michael. *Personal Knowledge.* Chicago: University of Chicago Press, 1958.

Poole, Roger. Structures and materials. *Twentieth Century Studies* 3, 1970, 6-30.

Poole, Roger. *Toward Deep Subjectivity.* London: Penguin, 1972.

Popper, Karl. *Theorie und Realität.* Tübingen: Mohr, 1964.

Popper, Karl. *Objective Knowledge.* Oxford: Clarendon, 1972.

Poulet, Georges. *Le Point de départ.* Paris: Plon, 1964.

Poulet, Georges. La pensée critique de Charles du Bos. *Critique* 217, 1965, 491-516.

Poulet, Georges. Phenomenology of reading. *New Literary History* 1, 1969, 53-68.

Propp, Vladimir. *Morfologia skazki.* Leningrad: Akademia, 1928.

Ragland-Sullivan, Ellie. *Jacques Lacan and the Philosophy of Psychoanalysis.* Urbana: University of Illinois Press, 1986.

Ranke, Leopold von. *Französische Geschichte.* Stuttgart: Cotta, 1852-61.

Ransom, John Crowe. *The World's Body.* New York: Scribner's, 1938.

Reichert, John. *Making Sense of Literature.* Chicago: University of Chicago Press, 1977.

Reid, Louis Arnaud. *A Study in Aesthetics.* London: G. Allen & Unwin, 1931.

Rhodes, Geri. *The Paterson Metaphor in William Carlos Williams' Paterson.* Medford, MA: Tufts University thesis, 1965.

Richards, Ivor Armstrong. *Principles of Literary Criticism.* London: Kegan, Paul, Trench, & Trubner, 1924.

Richards, Ivor Armstrong. *Practical Criticism.* London: Kegan, Paul, Trench, & Trubner, 1929.

Ricoeur, Paul. *Hermeneutik und Strukturalismus.* Munich: Kaiser, 1973.

Ricoeur, Paul. *The Symbolism of Evil.* Boston: Beacon, 1969 [1960].

Riesman, David. Two generations. In Robert Lifton (Ed.), *The Woman in America.* Boston: Beacon, 1967, 72-97.

Riffaterre, Michael. *Semiotics of Poetry.* Bloomington: Indiana University Press, 1978.

Rogers, Carl. *On Becoming a Person.* Boston: Houghton Mifflin, 1961.

Rogers, Katherine. *The Troublesome Helpmate: A History of Misogyny in Literature.* Seattle: University of Washington Press, 1966.

Rorty, Richard. Philosophy as a kind of writing. *New Literary History* 10, 1978, 141-160.

Rosch, Eleanor. Human categorization. In Neil Warren (Ed.), *Advances in Cross-Cultural Psychology.* London: Academic, 1977, 3-49.

Rosch, Eleanor, and Mervis, Carolyn. Family resemblances: Studies in the internal structure of categories. *Cognitive Psychology* 7, 1975, 573-605.

Rosenberg, Harold. Myth and poem. *Symposium* 11, 1931, 179-191.

Rosenblatt, Louise. *The Reader, the Text, the Poem.* Carbondale: Southern Illinois University Press, 1978.

Rousseau, Jean-Jacques. *Essai sur l'origine des langues.* Bordeaux: Ducros, 1970 [1781].

Ruskin, John. *Modern Painters.* London: Smith, Elder, & Co., 1856.

Ruskin, John. Of Queen's Gardens. In *Sesame and Lilies.* London: Everett & Co., 1865.

Ruwet, Nicolas. *Langage, musique, poésie.* Paris: Seuil, 1972.

Rycroft, Charles. *The Innocence of Dreams.* New York: Pantheon, 1979.

Saintsbury, George. *Collected Essays and Papers.* London: J.M. Dent & Sons, 1923.

Sartre, Jean-Paul. *Critique de la raison dialectique.* Paris, Gallimard, 1960.

Sartre, Jean-Paul. *Qu'est-ce que la littérature?* Paris, Gallimard, 1964 [1948]. (a)

Sartre, Jean-Paul. *Words.* New York: Braziller, 1964. (b)

Sartre, Jean-Paul. Flaubert: du poète à l'artiste. *Temps modernes* 243-45, 1966, 197-253, 423-481, and 598-674.

Sartre, Jean-Paul. *Search for a Method*. New York: Random House, 1968.

Sartre, Jean-Paul. *Das Imaginäre*. Reinbek: Rowohlt, 1971.

Saussure, Ferdinand de. *Course in General Linguistics*. New York: McGraw-Hill, 1966 [1916].

Schachtel, Ernst. *Metamorphosis*. New York: Basic Books, 1959.

Schlegel, Friedrich. Athenäum Fragments. In Peter Firchow (Ed.), *Lucinde and the Fragments*. Minneapolis: University of Minnesota Press, 1967, 161-241 [1796-1801].

Schlegel, Friedrich. *Dialogue on Poetry and Literary Aphorisms*. University Park: University of Pennsylvania Press, 1968.

Schleiermacher, Friedrich Ernst Daniel. *Hermeneutik*. Heidelberg: C. Winter, 1959 [1838].

Schmidt, Siegfried J. *Ästhetizität*. Munich: Bayrischer Schulbuchverlag, 1971.

Schmidt, Siegfried J. *Texttheorie*. Munich: Fink, 1973.

Schmidt, Siegfried J. *Foundations for the Empirical Study of Literature*. Hamburg: Buske, 1982.

Scholem, Gershom. *Major Trends in Jewish Mysticism*. Jerusalem: Schocken, 1941.

Scholem, Gershom. *Tradition und Neuschopfung im Ritus der Kabbalisten*. Zurich: Rhein, 1951.

Scholes, Robert, and Kellogg, Robert. *The Nature of Narrative*. New York: Oxford, 1966.

Schütz, Alfred. *Das Problem der Relevanz*. Frankfurt: Suhrkamp, 1971.

Schütz, Alfred, and Luckmann, Thomas. *Strukturen der Lebenswelt*. Neuwied: Luchterhand, 1975.

Searle, John. *Speech Acts*. London: Cambridge University Press, 1969.

Searle, John. Reiterating the differences: A reply to Derrida. *Glyph* 1, 1977, 198-208.

Showalter, Elaine. *A Literature of Their Own*. Princeton: Princeton University Press, 1977.

Showalter, Elaine. Toward a feminist poetics. In Mary Jacobus (Ed.), *Women Writing and Writing about Women*. London: Croon Helm, 1979, 22-41.

Skinner, Burrhus Frederick. *The Behavior of Organisms*. New York: Appleton-Century-Crofts, 1938.

Skinner, Burrhus Frederick. *Verbal Behavior*. New York: Appleton-Century-Crofts, 1957.

Šklovskij, Viktor Borisovich. *O Teorija Prozy*. Moscow: Federatsija, 1929.

Smith, Frank. *Understanding Reading*. New York: Holt, Rinehart, & Winston, 1971.

Spitzer, Leo. *Linguistics and Literary History*. Princeton: Princeton University Press, 1930. (a)

Spitzer, Leo. Zur sprachlichen Interpretation von Wortkunstwerken. *Jahrbücher für Wissenschaft und Jugendbildung* 6, 1930, 632-651. (b)

Spitzer, Leo. Review of *Style in the French Novel*, by Stephen Ullmann. *Comparative Literature* 10, 1958, 368-371.

Starobinski, Jean. Jean-Jacques Rousseau et le péril de la réflexion. In *L'Oeil vivant*. Paris: Gallimard, 1961.

Starobinski, Jean. La relation critique. Paris: Gallimard, 1968.

Starobinski, Jean. *Psychoanalyse und Literatur*. Frankfurt: Suhrkamp, 1973.

Stempel, Wolf-Dieter. Möglichkeiten einer Darstellung der Diachronie in narrativen Texten. In *Beiträge zur Textlinguistik*. Munich: Fink, 1971, 53-78.

Stoller, Robert J. *Sex and Gender*. New York: Science House, 1968.

Sidney, Philip. *The Defence of Poesie*. London: William Ponsonby, 1595.

Symonds, John Addington. On the application of evolutionary principles to art and literature. In *Essays Speculative and Suggestive*. London: Chapman & Hall, 1890, Vol. 1, 42-84.

Tsugawa, Sadayuki, Yatabe, Teruo, Hirose, Takeshi, and Matsumoto, Shuntetsu. An automobile with artificial intelligence. *Proceedings of the Sixth International Joint Conference on Artificial Intelligence*, 1979, Vol. 2, 893-895.

Tilford, John E. The degradation of Becky Sharp. *South Atlantic Quarterly* 8, 1959, 603-608.

Todorov, Tzvetan. *Grammaire du Décameron*. The Hague: Mouton, 1969.

Tolstoi, Leo. *What Is Art?* London: Brotherhood, 1898.

Tomars, Adolph. *Introduction to the Sociology of Art*. New York: Columbia University dissertation, 1941.

Trier, Jost. *Der deutsche Wortschatz im Sinnbezirk des Verstandes*. Heidelberg: C. Winter, 1931.

Trilling, Lionel. *Beyond Culture*. New York: Viking, 1965.

Trubetzkoy, Nikolai S. *Grundzüge der Phonologie*. Prag: Czechoslovakian Ministry of Instruction, 1939.

Tynjanov, Jurij. *Problema stikhofvornogo yazyka*. Leningrad: Izd'vo pisatelei v Leningrade, 1924.

Tynjanov, Jurij. *Arkhaisty i novatory*. Leningrad: Priboi, 1929.

Tynjanov, Jurij. *Die literarischen Kunstmittel und die Evolution in der Literatur*. Frankfurt: Suhrkamp, 1967 [translation of 1929].

Valency, Maurice. *In Praise of Love*. New York: Macmillan, 1958.

Veblen, Thorstein. *The Theory of the Leisure Class*. London: Macmillan, 1899.

Vico, Giovanni Battista. *Scienza nuova*. Torino: Tipografica economica, 1852 [1730].

Vodička, Felix V. *Počátky krásne prózy novočeské*. Prague: Melantrich, 1948.

Vodička, Felix V. *Struktura vývoje*. Prague: Odeon, 1969.

Vodička, Felix V. *Struktur der Entwicklung*. Munich: Fink, 1975 [translation of 1969].

Voltaire [François Marie Arouet]. *Le Siécle de Louis XIV*. Berlin: C.F. Henning, 1751.

Waddington, Conrad Hal. *Behind Appearances*. Cambridge: MIT Press, 1969.

Waelder, Robert. The principle of multiple function. *Psychoanalytic Quarterly* 5, 1936, 45-62 [1930].

Walcutt, Charles Child. Critic's taste and artist's intention. *The University of Kansas Review* 12, 1946, 278-283.

Walzel, Oskar. Künstlerische Absicht. *Germanisch-romanische Monatshefte* 8, 1920, 321-331.

Wasserman, Earl. *The Finer Tone*. Baltimore: Johns Hopkins University Press, 1953.

Wasserman, Earl. The English Romantics, the grounds of knowledge. *Essays in Romanticism* 4, Autumn 1964, 17-34.

Weber, Max. *Basic Concepts in Sociology*. New York: Philosophical Library, 1962.

Wellek, René. *The History of Modern Criticism 1750-1950*. Cambridge: Cambridge University Press, 1981-83.

Wellek, René. The theory of literary history. In *Études dédiés au quatrième Congrés de Linguistes. Travaux Linguistiques de Prague* 1936, 173-191.

Wellek, René, and Warren, Austin. *Theory of Literature* [TL]. New York: Harcourt, Brace, and World, 1956.

Wellershoff, Dieter. *Die Auflösung des Kunstbegriffs*. Frankfurt: Suhrkamp, 1976.

Wells, Henry Willis. *New Poets from Old: A Study in Literary Genetics*. New York: Columbia University Press, 1940.

Werth, Paul. Roman Jakobson's verbal analysis of poetry. *Journal of Linguistics* 12, 1976, 21-73.

Wheelwright, Philip. *The Burning Fountain*. Bloomington: Indiana University Press, 1954.

White, Hayden. *Metahistory: The Historical Imagination in Nineteenth-Century Europe*. Baltimore: Johns Hopkins University Press, 1973.

White, Hayden. *Tropics of Discourse*. Baltimore: Johns Hopkins University Press, 1978.

Whitehead, Alfred North. *Science and the Modern World*. New York: Macmillan, 1925.

Wimsatt, William K. [and Beardsley, Monroe]. *The Verbal Icon*. Lexington: University of Kentucky Press, 1954.

Wimsatt, William K. The structure of romantic nature imagery. In Wimsatt [and Beardsley] 1954, 103-116.

Wimsatt, William K, and Beardsley, Monroe. The intentional fallacy. In Wimsatt [and Beardsley] 1954, 3-18 [1946].

Wimsatt, William K, and Beardsley, Monroe. The affective fallacy. In Wimsatt [and Beardsley] 1954, 21-39 [1949].

Wirth, Louis. Problems of minority groups. In Ralph Linton (Ed.), *The Science of Man in the World of Crisis*. New York: Appleton, 1945, 347-372.

Wittgenstein, Ludwig. *Lectures and Conversations*. Berkeley: University of California Press, 1967 [1938].

Wolfe, Tom. *The Painted Word*. New York: Bantam, 1975.

AUTHOR INDEX

SUBJECT INDEX